SWINGING THE PACKS OF THE NORTH AUSTRALIAN EXPEDITION OVER A BRANCH OF JASPER CREEK, VICTORIA RIVER, 1856.

SHIFTS AND EXPEDIENTS OF CAMP LIFE
TRAVEL & EXPLORATION
BY W. B. LORD ROYAL ARTILLERY & T. BAINES F.R.G.S.

Rediscovery Books

Reproduced by kind permission of the
Royal Geographical Society

Published by

Rediscovery Books Ltd

Unit 10, Ridgewood Industrial Park,

Uckfield, East Sussex,

TN22 5QE England

Tel: +44 (0) 1825 749494

Fax: +44 (0) 1825 765701

This edition © Rediscovery Books Ltd 2006

To find out more about Rediscovery Books

and its range of titles visit

www.rediscoverybooks.com

Published in association with

**Royal
Geographical
Society**

with IBG

Advancing geography
and geographical learning

The **Royal Geographical Society with IBG** was founded in 1830 to advance geographical science. Today it supports geographical research, promotes geography in schools and through outdoor learning, in society and to policy makers. Geography connects us to the world's people, places and environments.
The **Rediscovery Books** series allow us to see how previous geographers and travellers understood and recorded the world.

In reprinting in facsimile from the original, any imperfections are inevitably reproduced and the quality may fall short of modern type and cartographic standards.

Printed and bound by Lightning Source

CONTENTS.

	PAGE
INTRODUCTION	1

CHAPTER I.
OUTFIT TO TAKE ABROAD 3

CHAPTER II.
BOATS, RAFTS, AND MAKESHIFT FLOATS 80

CHAPTER III.
WORKING IN METAL 168

CHAPTER IV.
HUTS AND HOUSES 236

CHAPTER V.
EXTEMPORE BRIDGES AND MAKESHIFTS FOR CROSSING RIVERS AND RAVINES 280

CHAPTER VI.
TIMBER AND ITS UTILISATION 315

CHAPTER VII.
SLEDGES AND SLEDGE TRAVELLING 351

CHAPTER VIII.
BOOTS, SHOES, AND SANDALS 368

CHAPTER IX.
WAGGONS AND OTHER WHEELED VEHICLES 385

CHAPTER X.
HARNESS AND PACK ANIMALS 408

CHAPTER XI.
CAMELS 425

PAGE

CHAPTER XII.
CATTLE MARKING 433

CHAPTER XIII.
WATER, AND THE SAP OF PLANTS 437

CHAPTER XIV.
CAMP COOKERY 475

CHAPTER XV.
FISH AND AMPHIBIOUS ANIMALS 518

CHAPTER XVI.
POISONED WEAPONS, ARROWS, SPEARS, &c. 548

CHAPTER XVII.
TRACKING, HUNTING, AND TRAPPING 555

CHAPTER XVIII.
PALANQUINS, STRETCHERS, AMBULANCES, &c. 601

CHAPTER XIX.
ON SKETCHING AND PAINTING UNDER THE ORDINARY DIFFICULTIES OF
    TRAVEL 627

CHAPTER XX.
THE ESTIMATION OF DISTANCES AND HINTS ON FIELD OBSERVING . 635

CHAPTER XXI.
HINTS TO EXPLORERS ON COLLECTING AND PRESERVING OBJECTS OF
    NATURAL HISTORY 666

CHAPTER XXII.
ROPES AND TWINES 690

CHAPTER XXIII.
BUSH VETERINARY SURGERY AND MEDICINE 699

APPENDIX 708

INDEX 717

DIRECTIONS TO THE BINDER.

Swinging the Packs of the North Australian Expedition over a Branch of Jasper Creek, Victoria River, 1856 } *Frontispiece.*

Camp Scene in Africa . . . . . . *To face page* 48

Boat Building on the Logier River . . , . . . 110

Sending Line from Wreck to Lee Shore by means of a Kite . 162

Lead Smelting in the Forest . . . . . , . 199

Searching for Gold 220

Indian Lodges 273

The Treatment of Timber by Steam and Saw 333

Sledging over Rough Ice 358

The Wilson Mule Waggon (United States of America) . . 396

Group of Harness 415

Indian Well 451

Hippopotamus Traps 543

Traps for Small Game 593

Various Modes of Carrying the Sick or Wounded . . . 606

Shifts and Expedients

CAMP LIFE, TRAVEL, AND EXPLORATION.

INTRODUCTION.

LIKE two voyagers returned from a long cruise in far-off seas, we throw together our joint gleanings in many lands. These do not consist of jewels, gems, gold, or furs; no piles of costly merchandise do we lay at the reader's feet as offerings from distant climes, but simply the experiences of two roving Englishmen who have roughed it. By those who have to pass through a campaign, travel wild countries, or explore little known regions, shifts must be made, and expedients of many kinds had recourse to, of which the inexperienced in such matters would but little dream.

As necessity is the mother of invention, so is self-reliance the father of its practical application, and it is with a strong desire (by explaining how constantly recurring wants may be overcome, and apparently hopeless difficulties surmounted) to strengthen that quality in those who roam that we write this volume. In our travels and adventures we have not been associated, the paths trodden by us being widely separated. Whilst one was exploring in the wilds of North Australia, the other was dwelling in a canvas-covered hole in the earth before Sebastopol. The scenes change; Southern and Tropical Africa is visited by the late Australian traveller, whilst the

B

Crimea, with its rugged hills and wild ravines, is exchanged for the jungles of Central India by the other. So the two barques have drifted here and there on the world's tide, but are anchored side by side, and have compared logs at last; and if amongst the heterogeneous odds and ends therein contained the reader can find the aid he seeks, our shifts and expedients will not have been made in vain.

CHAPTER I.

OUTFIT TO TAKE ABROAD.

In dealing with this portion of our subject we can but generalise, as the destination of the traveller and the objects he has in view will materially modify the nature and extent of his equipment. The military officer who is bound on a long march, through a comparatively wild country, needs a very different outfit from that which a hunter or trader of experience would procure for himself before starting for the home of the elephant and the savage. The man who, with his wife and family, seeks a new home beyond the border line which divides the unreclaimed wilderness from civilised society, needs an infinitely more voluminous store of requisites—not to say comforts—than the small band of hardy explorers or hunter naturalists, who, with horse, mule, pack and rifle, wend their way over prairies and mountains without path, and thread the forests and thickets where no traveller has penetrated. There are other members of the human family who prefer prosecuting their wanderings alone, carry all their worldly possessions with them, and whose equipment is usually of a particularly simple and practical character. The sea, the inland lake, and the rivers flowing through little known regions, each have their explorers, for whose use a variety of contrivances are needed. Some of these are best made at home; others it will be found most convenient to prepare in the localities in which their aid are required; whilst at times adverse circumstances will render it necessary to improvise rough and ready appliances to save life and prolong its duration when saved. We shall therefore endeavour to give such hints and directions as will enable our readers who intend visiting far-off countries to select such matters as may be best purchased before quitting England, and to avoid encumbering themselves with useless impedimenta. As we have first made mention of the military officer about to depart on service, we will suppose that he is in London, or any other large town, gathering together his traps for a start. We will then accompany him on his shopping expeditions, and give him a few hints as to what will prove

Equipment to be purchased in England.

most useful. On matters of uniform we can have nothing to say further than to advise, as we do in every case of purchase, that it be obtained from some tradesman of well-established reputation. The raiment calculated to meet the requirements of refined society, when the uniform is for the time cast aside, must also be left to the dictates of the prevailing mode and the good taste of the wearer.

Where fashion and the dress regulations of the army end there do we begin, and as flannel is, perhaps, the most important as an article of under clothing, we will first make a few remarks on shirts of that material, of which plenty should be taken. First, then, have them made to measure from flannel which has been previously well shrunk, of thoroughly good quality, of medium substance, and unobtrusive pattern or colour. It well be well to order them of extra length, both of sleeve and body, so as to allow for the shrinkage which is certain to take place after a few washings, in spite of all precautions. Two breast pockets should be made in each. These are very convenient for holding a variety of small matters when no waistcoat is worn. For outer clothing nothing can surpass good heather-coloured tweed, or Waterford frieze, for ordinary wear; jackets of shooting-coat pattern, made with plenty of pockets, formed from much stronger materials than are usually made use of by tailors for that purpose, will be found most useful for knocking about in. One or two pairs of trousers may be strapped up the inside and bottoms of the legs with leather, after the cavalry rough-rider pattern. A pair or two of Oxford cord hunting breeches will also be found useful to wear with long boots, with ankle jacks and gaiters. The waistcoat should be cut rather long, made with four pockets, two breast and two bottom. All these should have flaps or " salt-box " covers to them. Each half of the waistcoat, from about the level of the bottom button and button-hole to where the back is joined in, should be lined with a strip of leather. A long loose gaberdine of woollen stuff, made to button up the front, and secured round the waist by a long narrow scarf or " cummerbund," is an immense comfort in camp or quarters, let the climate be hot or cold. A good supply of reddish-brown woollen socks should be laid in ; a moderate number of long stockings, of the same material, to wear with the breeches ; and a few dozen pairs of the " heelless cotton " socks. For use on board ship, or when the weather is hot, nothing can be more agreeable to wear, except silk, and the cost is a mere trifle when compared to that of other hosiery. White cotton pocket handkerchiefs, as a rule, last their owners very much longer than silk, being less tempting to native servants or followers. Braces should be

Shirt making and clothing.

always ordered of the saddler, and made from the material used for the surcingles of racehorses. One pair of these lasts longer than half-a-dozen of the flimsy affairs usually sold ready made. There are those who dispense with braces, find great relief by the practice, and wear an ordinary waist-belt instead; but to some persons much discomfort is caused by so doing. A soft felt hat, with a moderately wide brim, is a convenient head dress in most temperate climates. Of the head gear used in the tropics and the far north we shall have to speak hereafter. The best gloves for general and moderately rough usage are those sold under the name of driving gloves. They should be obtained of the regular glover, and have buckskin let in between the fingers. A pair of common hedging gloves well repays the trouble of taking, when the brush of the thicket has to be handled and firewood arranged.

Take a blue cloth pilot coat, cut long enough to reach just below the knees; have it lined throughout with woollen material; let the pockets be made extra strong, and order the buttons to be large, of black horn, and sewn on with double-waxed thread. The left hand breast pocket should be deep and lined with leather, as it not unfrequently becomes a resting-place for the revolver when you do not wish to make an ostentatious display of it. Get a couple of real Scotch caps, such as the Highland shepherds wear; nothing can equal them for sleeping in when camping out, and they form a most convenient head-covering for camp use, or when the sun is not too powerful. Get from some sailors' outfitter a regular seagoing sou'-wester hat, with ear and neck flaps, and a pair of oiled canvas overalls to match. Procure also from some first-class maker a thoroughly good india-rubber coat, long enough to come well below the tops of the butcher boots. Buttons should be sewn in at the back and sides of the collar, in order to admit of a hood of the same material being put on when needed. An arrangement of this kind we have found most useful for boat work and in heavy tropical rains. Order also a piece of the best Russia duck, 9ft. by 8ft.; have this subjected to the waterproofing process; have the edges turned in to form a 2in. hem; and at every two feet, at both sides and ends, have good sized wide flanged brass eyelets punched in. Then in the centre of the piece have a longitudinal slit made 16in. in length, have the raw edge bound with a broad strong tape, and at every 3in. on each side have an eyelet of less size than those at the edges put in. This arrangement admits of the slit being laced close when it is not required. A waterproof square of this kind is useful for an almost endless number of

Hats, ground sheets, and india-rubber garments.

purposes. In the first place it can be used as a ground sheet to sleep on; it can, by thrusting the head through the unlaced opening, be converted into an excellent cloak: it can by fastening springs and pegs to the sides, and cutting a ridge pole, be converted into a very fair substitute for a small tent; it forms an excellent carpet to lay by the side of the tent bed, when you are fortunate enough to be able to use one, keeping down insects, and protecting the feet from sharp grass, stumps, and twigs. If during rain the tent should admit water, as it sometimes will (especially if heedlessly touched when saturated with moisture), this universal square of duck can by the aid of some upright sticks or canes, one at the head and another at the foot of the bed, and a bit of rope stretched like a clothes line from one to the other, be at once made use of as a roof to the bed, the sides being made to slope and stand out by attaching pieces of twine to a few of the side poles. Clothes and other matters can be securely carried when rolled up in this, even in the heaviest rain. On a pinch, even a river might be crossed with its assistance, but the method adopted for constructing extempore rafts, boats, canoes, and floats, will be fully treated on when that subject comes under consideration.

Boots and shoes for real work are in no part of the world equal to those made at home, and a thoroughly good stock should be laid in before quitting England. Take "butcher boots," so made as to fit

Boots and shoes. the leg compactly just below the bend of the knee, with low heels, and broad heel seats; also several pairs of shooting boots of the regular ankle-jack gamekeeper's pattern, tipped at toe and heel. A pair or two of high shoes made from soft undressed russet leather will be found very useful to wear instead of slippers, or for camp use when the ground is dry. A pair of Cording's wading boots will be found invaluable. They occupy little space, are comparatively light, and keep the legs and feet dry and warm when nothing else will. The late Mr. Wheelwright— better known in the sporting and scientific world as the "Old Bush- man"—thus speaks of them in a communication to the *Field :* " I can add the testimony of five years' experience to all you can say in their favour. For wading, flight shooting, boat fishing or punting, and all winter water work, they are invaluable. They are a little too heavy for a hard day's walking, and soon cut through in the leg or foot among stakes or bushes; but use them carefully, and they will be found by far the best water boots ever made. They are very warm, stand a long while, are perfectly water-tight to the last, and they have this advan- tage over a leather boot—they want no dressing. Only never keep them near a fire. I lost three or four pairs in the bush by neglecting to draw them off before I lay down for the night before a camp fire. And what is worth all the rest, they never get hard, but are always as easy to draw off and on as a glove." It will be well also to provide two or three pairs of brown leather shooting boots without heels and with single soles, free from nails, and flexible enough to admit of the wearer walking softly and with perfect freedom.

Foot gear, adapted to the nature of most countries to which the traveller is likely to proceed, will be fully described when bush shoe-making is under consideration.

It will be well also to procure from a saddler a good supply of boot-laces. These should be cut straight and in the way of the grain of the hide. The white leather used by carters for mending their harness is by far the best for the purpose. Strips of this cut to about the eighth of an inch square, and well greased with mutton suet, are next to indestructible, and are available for all sorts of purposes apart from that of lacing boots or shoes. Slightly burning or roasting the ends in the candle or fire hardens them sufficiently to pass freely through the lace holes without a tag.

TRUNKS AND BOXES.

For ordinary travel the solid leather bullock trunks, of regulation size, will be found both convenient and durable. All strap guides,

TWO BOXES ON ENDS OF POLE.

loops, and handles must be riveted as well as sewn to the body of the trunk. Spare keys should also be fitted to the locks. In countries where it is customary for baggage to be carried by porters through narrow bush paths, and where destructive insects are numerous, we recommend the use of sheet copper boxes, 16in. long, 12in. wide, and 12in. deep, made with copper wire strengthening rods, worked in the edges of the plates or sheets. Ring handles, also of copper, should be fitted to both sides and ends, as iron when wet would corrode the cop-

RESTING POLE FOR BURDENS ON THE ZAMBESI.

per. These serve to pass straps, cords, or lashings through. In making these boxes great care should be taken to fit the joints and cover so as to render them rainproof. The insides should be tinned just as coppersmiths tin cooking pots. The illustration on page 7 will serve to show the manner in which one porter carries two of these cases, which, to be transported in this way, should not, with their contents, weigh over 20lb. each. If one box is carried, as shown in the annexed engraving, from 35lb. to 40lb. weight may be placed in it. Boxes for Cape waggon travelling should be about 3ft. long by 16in. wide and deep. They are best made of well-seasoned Memel deal, 1in. thick, dovetailed and angle plated. Such packing cases as are taken will require lining; thin sheet lead is convenient for this purpose, as it serves for bullet-making when the boxes are taken on shore.

Shooting Gear.

To the traveller whose means of transport confine him to the possession of one gun, we say, without hesitation, purchase a plain, strong, muzzle-loading, double-barrelled smooth bore of 11 or 12 gauge. Length of barrel, 2ft. 6in., weight $8\frac{1}{2}$lb. without the ramrod. Front action, bar-side locks, and ramrod pipes large enough to carry a rod of extra large size and power. Two pairs of spare nipples, and one pair of fitted main springs, in addition to those in the locks. A bell-metal

Bullets.   or iron spherical bullet mould must be selected with the greatest care, as it by no means follows that because the figure 12 or 11 is stamped on it, that, like a wadding punch, it is calculated for a gun of the same gauge. Our plan, when about to purchase a new mould, is to form, with beeswax, heated in warm water or before the fire, a ball, and to trim, mould, and finally to roll it on a polished table under the hand, until, when placed on a piece of thin, soft, greased kid, and gently pressed down, it fits the bore accurately; then, with this ball as a guide, we search the moulds until one is found just the size to contain it without undue pressure being used in entering the hardened wax ball. This mould we secure, caring nothing for the conventional numbers placed on it. The spherical leaden ball, when encased in kid, should fit the bore just tight enough to require one steady downward thrust of the rod to force it home. If it travels on without pressure, it is too loose; if, on the other hand, tapping with the rod is needed, it is too tight, and liable to welt or disfigure the barrel. We have seen many much injured, and rendered very unsafe, from this cause. If several guns can be taken, then it will be well to purchase one or more breech-loaders of No. 12 gauge.

POWDER CHAMBERS FOR CENTRAL-FIRE BREECH-LOADERS.

At least one pair of these contrivances should accompany every central-fire breech-loader, whether smooth-bore or rifle, intended for use in wild countries, as in the absence of cartridges they convert the arm at once to a muzzle-loader. When first introduced these chambers were made of thin brass and other metals, and were of a very objectionable form of construction. We have had ours turned in the lathe from solid blocks of mild steel, and made so stout that expansion is impossible. The annexed illustration represents a section of one of them on a reduced scale; $3\frac{1}{4}$ drs. of powder exactly fills the interior, just allowing the thick wad to rest on the top and slightly enter. Before placing the steel chamber in the gun the extractor should be removed. Load with a loading rod just as an ordinary muzzle-loader is charged, only that to cap, the gun must be opened. Never cap before loading, or considerable danger will be incurred. Since the publication of the first edition of this work we have devised a double central-fire breech-loader expressly for wild shooting and rough travel. All the forgings of the actions are of extra strength, and the barrels are constructed to throw ball or shot. The weight is about $8\frac{1}{2}$ lb., length of barrel 2ft. 6in., and the bore 12. A gun of this kind, with a pair of the steel chambers fitted to it, can be used most efficiently with either the ordinary cartridge, ball and patch, or loose charge of small shot, slugs or buckshot. It shoots both accurately and hard. These weapons may be obtained at Messrs S. W. Silver and Co.

RIFLES AND MUSKETS.

In the choice of rifles, our readers must be mainly guided by the character and size of the game they intend pursuing. A poly-groove muzzle-loader, No. 12 bore, 2ft. 4in. in the barrels, and of about 10lb. weight, will be found a generally useful and reliable gun. There are, without doubt, many advantages attendant on the use of breech-loading guns and rifles. There are also drawbacks, which, except under peculiar circumstances, more than outweigh them. That the breech-loading form of construction, varied as it is, is of less strength and durability than that of an equally well made muzzle-loader, few will be disposed to dispute. The hinge joints, levers, and slides, should they chance to become bent, loose, or, worse still, broken, would require repair by an experienced gunsmith; whilst, as will be seen as the work proceeds, nearly all the common accidents to which even the strongest and best made muzzle-loaders are liable in the bush, can, by the exercise of a little ingenuity, be readily remedied by their unskilled owners. Gunpowder, lead, and percussion caps, such as they are, can, when your own store is expended, destroyed, or lost, be readily procured even in very out of the way corners of the earth; whilst the cartridges calculated for breech-loaders can only be procured in towns or trading posts of importance, where the cost will, as a matter of necessity, be great, and their efficiency questionable. Strong flint muskets (old army regulation) will be found best calculated for the use of native servants. A bit of agate, common quartz, or iron pyrites, answers the purpose of a flint, should one be lost. Nevertheless, some breech-loaders so perfectly combine the qualities of simplicity of construction, excellence of shooting, and facility of re-loading, that we forbear to put too general a veto upon them, especially when, by inserting the chamber already described, they can be converted into a good substitute for a muzzle-loader. Westley Richards, and others, are favourites in the Cape colony; and we carried for four years in tropical South Africa one by T. Wilson, of Birmingham: it was compact and simple in action, devoid of hinges and levers. The cartridge was easily made with wads of the proper size and a bit of tissue paper saturated with common fat; each shot ejected the greased wad of the previous charge,

Rifles and guns.

cleaning the barrel as it went. It could, if necessary, have been used as a muzzle-loader, and is now, after 1600 rounds have been fired from it, in as good condition as could be desired. The long sword bayonet we never used, but, instead, cut down a smaller sword to the proportion of a bush knife, and, by a little smith's craft and patience, fitted it to be used as a bayonet if needed. A breech-loader has this advantage, that with a small bayonet a man, even in a sharp skirmish, is not defenceless while loading, for he has his point always before him ready for use should his enemy close. We have since had a spring locker let into the stock, to hold half a dozen cartridges and caps; so that, even when snatched up without the belt, the gun should not become useless after the first discharge.

Before quitting the subject, it may not be amiss to give a few hints on the purchase of second-hand guns; these are often to be obtained for considerably less than their original cost, and just as good as when perfectly new. There are many establishments in London, where second-hand fire-arms in considerable numbers are regularly kept to select from ; amongst these may be mentioned Whistler in the Strand, Vaughan in the Strand, Hewett of Blackman-street, Borough, and Watson of 313, Holborn. After deciding on the description of gun you require, and ascertaining the cost, see that the maker's name is a good one, take the number of the gun, and either call, write, or telegraph as to identity and original price, which matters of information the manufacturer will immediately furnish. This is not an unnecessary caution, as, unless the would-be purchaser is experienced in style of finish, and quality of workmanship, he may possibly invest in an article sailing under false colours. That there are guns in the market with names on them which are forgeries few will deny, and it requires both the experience of the dealer, and the caution of the buyer, to guard against being taken in by them. Do not rashly reject a sound useful gun because it is made by a provincial Irish or Scotch maker, as there are many gunsmiths out of London who turn out guns equal in quality and shooting powers to any in the world. When examining a gun you are about to buy, try the locks by cocking and uncocking, see that the pitch suits your mode of shooting, draw the ramrod, lift the hammers to half-cock, drift out the bolt and reverse the barrels, when on looking underneath near the breech you will probably see the proof marks and the number of gauge at which the gun was proved ; place the gun gauge in the muzzles and see that the two numbers correspond, as it occasionally happens that guns are proved at one number and bored out until they represent another—a most reprehensible practice, which militates greatly against the safety of the owner of the gun which has been thus tampered with. Do not, however, hastily cast aside a well-made Irish gun with a known maker's name engraved on it because there are no proof marks, as, for some strange reason or another, the law of proof does not appear to extend to Ireland; and we have seen many guns of surpassing excellence made in both Dublin and Cork unstamped.

Before removing the locks, see that they are neatly and compactly fitted into the wood of the stock; see also that the timber of the stock in the bed of the barrels immediately in front of the false breech is sound; some makers lay in plates of metal at this joint, which is an excellent plan. On removing the bolt and taking off the locks, see that all the cavities into which the projections and springs fit have been cleanly and evenly cut out with the tool. See also that the triggers work freely and have back springs to them. See that the interiors of the locks are well fitted together, and if you can find the name of "Joseph Brazier, Ashes," engraved on the inside of the plate, you may discontinue your scrutiny so far as the lock department is concerned, as it is a guarantee for excellence of quality which we have always found beyond question. Have the breeches and nipples removed; see that both male and female screws are perfect; look carefully through the barrels, and see that the inner surfaces are clear, bright, and free from rust or honeycombing. Cast a general glance over the gun furniture to see that all is firm and sound. See that there are no shakes or cracks in the stock, and if there is no varnish on it so much the better. Whether the barrels are to be of Damascus laminated steel, or twisted stubs, we must leave in great measure to the taste of the purchaser. Each kind has its advocates. We do not advise having guns without ramrods, as we have seen much inconvenience arise in wild countries from having the loading rod to carry and depend on only. It is well to have a ramrod with a large powerful worm inside the driving top or end, but it should be regarded rather in the light of an auxiliary than an instrument to be depended on. It will also be

Testing firearms. advisable, before concluding your purchase, to test the shooting powers of the weapon selected. If a smooth bore, experiment on it first for accuracy of shooting with shot, in order to ascertain if the barrels are accurately fitted together, This is very easily done by trying a few shots from both barrels, at two or three different ranges, at a small object such as a visiting card. By fastening this to the centre of the target, and shooting steadily at it, you will at once ascertain if both the barrels perform their work satisfactorily, and do not shoot to the right or left. With such a gun as we have recommended, 3drs. of powder and 1¼oz. of

No. 5 or 6 shot will be found a fair average charge. Equal quantities by measure of powder and shot form a charge almost universal in its usefulness. The next test should be for pattern or regularity of distribution, at different distances, which may begin at twenty paces and extend to sixty, using the same charge. A large piece of sheet iron, painted over with a mixture of pipeclay or whitening and water, should, in the absence of one of Government pattern, be made use of. Form a round black space in the middle, and, as in the case of the former experiment, shoot steadily at it, at the different ranges indicated. It will then be seen whether the shot are equally and evenly distributed over a moderately large space of the metal. There are two modes of testing penetration usually had recourse to. The most common is to fire the gun, at different ranges, at a number of sheets of paper. Old books, with the covers removed, answer the purpose as well as anything. These, when firmly secured against the target, a door, or tree, are fired at with a fair average charge, in order to ascertain the number of leaves the shot has penetrated. To carry an experiment of this kind out satisfactorily, it will be well to test the intended purchase against some gun of known excellence, as no arbitrary rule can be laid down as to the number of sheets which should be penetrated, no two samples of paper being exactly alike in quality, substance, and mode of arrangement. Tin powder canisters are also used as a test of penetrating power. Some guns will riddle them from side to side, whilst others, with the same charge, and at the same distance, merely throw the shot through one thickness of the tin plate. Powder canisters are not always of the same substance; therefore, we recommend a competitive trial with them.

A rifle, before purchase, should also be carefully tested as to accuracy of shooting; this can be best done on some rifle range. For sporting purposes, accuracy of delivery and power of penetration at moderate distances are much more valuable qualities than length of range. Accuracy of shooting is best ascertained by firing steadily from increasing distances at an ordinary target centre, up to 200yds. A generally useful charge for spherical balls consists of the bullet-mouldful of the very best powder. Use a greased kid patch for the ball; see that it has no defects or faults in it; and never strike it with the driving end of the rod when it has once reached the surface of the powder in the barrel. Send the ball well home with a steady pressure from above, and then withdraw the rod. Should it be found that the balls are sent to the right of the object, Rifle sights. in all probability it will be found on examination that either the hind sight is placed too far towards the right, or the fore sight too far in the opposite direction. So with rifles which shoot to the left. If the hind sight has been shifted in its slot, and driven too far to the left of the exact line, or the front sight in a direction towards the right, the balls will be found to assume an untrue flight; and the greater the distance they have to travel, the more marked will the error become. The handle of an old tooth brush, fashioned with a file into the form of an elongated wedge, will, with the aid of a mallet or hammer, serve to drift the slides into their proper position. This, when once found, should be noted by making a small but deep cut with the point of a penknife across both slide and barrel rib, so that if moved the two ends of the cut will not correspond. Gunmakers usually either cut a notch or punch in a piece of platinum, with the same view. Rifles will not unfrequently need re-sighting from accidents in wild countries, but this subject will be treated of at length hereafter. The penetration of rifle balls is best ascertained by firing them at a number of thin elm boards, placed one on the other like a pack of cards. The number of layers or boards penetrated is at once ascertained by taking off the planks one by one until the ball is reached.

We are not unfrequently asked to advise as to the quantity of ammunition a single sportsman should take abroad in order to

Ammunition. enjoy a fair amount of shooting. The duration of the proposed excursion, nature of game about to be followed, and the proclivities of the intending traveller, will all influence the bulk of the store he should provide himself with. Still, a hint or two may at any rate serve for a basis for him to regulate his purchase by. Supposing, then, that a No. 12 or 11 muzzle-loader, an 11 or 12 bore muzzle-loading rifle, and either a brace of double pistols or a revolver, are taken; take 4lb. of best sporting powder, 2lb. of rifle ditto, 2000 best caps for guns, which *should have nipples alike*, and 250 pistol caps; two 28lb. bags of No. 6 shot, one bag No. 4, and one bag BB. Have sail-canvas bags made to go outside the ordinary shot bags, as these are sure to burst with rough travelling. Take six bags of ordinary mercurial gun wads, and six of extra thick felt ditto as powder wads. These can be split in two if you run short. Wads of this kind are invaluable, as they keep the gun clean, improve its power of shooting considerably, and are less liable to rise in the barrel than those of thin material. Get a stout elm box made; have it lined with sheet lead; have a division of stout plank made in the middle, so that the shot may rest at one end and the powder, wads, and caps at the other. Pack in every crevice with tow, as that will come handy for cleaning purposes, solder down your lead cover, and then screw on your elm box-lid. A stout pair of elm cleets or bars should be secured to both bottom and top of the box. They not only strengthen it, but prevent the planking from coming in contact with the earth or wet decks. They also serve to prevent ropes used in slinging or fastening the case in its various haulings up and lowerings down from slipping. Cleets of this kind are useful appendages to all wooden boxes used by travellers.

The most efficient and powerful pistol we have used is the holster revolver of Colonel Colt, but its weight (4lb. 2oz.) is far too great to admit of its being generally carried except on horseback. There are not so many objections to the use of breech-loading Pistols. revolvers and pistols as there are to guns and rifles made on that plan. In the first place, they are less liable to breakage or derangement; and in the next, from the very limited number of cartridges which would be actually fired, a sufficient number may be very easily taken to last through a long campaign or expedition. It is an immense advantage being able to instantly load or unload the chamber without discharging it. Notwithstanding all the ingenuity which has of late been devoted to the production of breech-loading revolvers, we have not seen one which we can recommend without reservation—the great fault in every case being smallness of bore. Long range is, as a rule, not required in a pistol, but that which is required is the power of inflicting a severe shock to the system at comparatively close quarters. Numerous cases might be cited when, after lodging two or even three of the tiny pellets fired from small revolvers in the body of an enemy, the enemy has had decidedly the best of it, and coolly finishes off the owner of the mechanical popgun with some old-world weapon of greater power. Until a large-bored and handy breech-loading revolver is produced, we recommend for use on horseback, either double-barrelled smooth-bore Lefaucheux-pattern pistols with 7½in. barrels and 14 bore, or muzzle-loaders of the same size and gauge, with bar side locks and swivel ramrods. The over and under double pistol is an excellent weapon, and is carried by many soldiers and travellers of great experience; but for our part, we prefer the barrels mounted side by side, precisely as they are in a double gun. To carry in the belt for use on foot, the Tranter breech-loader is perhaps as good as any, although as a rule the trigger pull is too heavy; but this is an evil which admits of correction. Considerable improvements in the construction of revolvers have taken place since the issue of the first edition of this work. That made by Webley for the Irish Constabulary is as good as any for the use of travellers; the bore is 442, and the barrel short enough to make the weapon very handy. It is a breech-loader, takes a central-fire copper cartridge, and shoots hard.

Powder flasks, barrel rods, &c.

Take three Sykes' powder flasks, one to hold a pound and the others of medium size; have them of tinned copper stitched over with saddle pig-skin. We prefer for carrying shot a double shot-belt with patent side springs to any of the lever cut-off contrivances; it is a very old-fashioned plan we know, but a very effective and useful one for all that. Two sizes of shot can be carried in it; it can be worn much more comfortably than a pouch, which is always getting in the way, and there is no loss of shot from chance blows on the lever: a still greater advantage lays in your being able to *see* that which goes into your gun. If only one size shot can be taken, select No. 6 for general use; but No. 8, No. 4, and Bristol B. should be added if practicable. Gunpowder of excellent quality is now to be obtained of all the first-class makers. For percussion caps, thick felt gun-wads, and ordinary mercurial ditto, go to either Joyce or Ely. The wire cartridges of the latter maker are invaluable if they can be carried: we have done wonders with them. When having your shooting gear put in order, have two well seasoned deal rods made, so that they may fit tightly into the barrels of the gun when covered with two layers of flannel, which must be firmly stitched on; the sticks are cut exactly the length of the barrels, and connected at the muzzle ends by a short piece of strong tape; this serves to draw them out by. Before placing the sticks in the barrels for final packing up, rub them over with mercurial ointment, as should be done to both the outsides of the barrels and the gun furniture; there is little fear of rust attacking your firearms when treated in this way.

A brass mould for casting buck shot will be found very useful. One we have found of infinite service is thus made: Two long narrow cheeks of brass are fitted at one end with a hinge, each cheek has the halves of fifteen shot sockets at each edge, making, when the two halves are closed, thirty perfect spherical moulds for shot. A groove and row of inlets run along each edge, and two movable steel plates cut off the necks of the shot when cool. There are two handles, and the whole affair is not unlike a long narrow pair of nutcrackers. The shot thus cast are about the size of garden peas, and an ounce of them, with 3½ drs. of powder behind it from a No. 11 gun forms a charge which will be found most formidable if used at moderately close quarters. When defending a camp or waggon fort against the attacks of savages nothing is equal to it.

STATIONERY AND ARTISTS' MATERIALS.

It is to be supposed that most persons visiting little-known regions will at least keep a diary for private gratification, if not for public use; and now that drawing from nature is so essential a branch of education, they will most likely also wish to sketch such objects or scenes as may be most interesting. Some who aspire to more exactitude of detail than an artist can hope for in a hasty sketch may wish to practise photography; and in this beautiful art the greatest possible facilities are offered to those who practise it. We have lately seen in London many most beautiful pictures taken by Dr. Kirk on the Zambesi with a small and inexpensive camera, carried as a mere supplement to his private equipment; but unless the traveller possesses, as Kirk did, chemical knowledge enough to enable him to contend sucessfully against the various contingencies of changing climate, impurity or scarcity of water, and innumerable other new and unexpected difficulties, we are inclined to think that the pencil, guided with what artistic skill the individual may be able to command, will afford, if not the best, at least the most certainly available results; and without undervaluing photography, we may in this preliminary chapter notice principally the appliances which will enable a man to keep his journal and illustrate it with sketches of interesting events or objects.

First, then, as to the journal. Of course for purposes of correspondence, a traveller will take care to supply himself with some one of the substantial and economical portable desks in which pens, ink, note paper, and envelopes are The journal. always at hand to enable him to write a creditable letter from almost any part of the world. But the journal or diary is another matter; its value consists chiefly in its being what its name indicates—a diary or diurnal record. It must be written while the events described are fresh on the memory, or there is neither life nor spirit in it. If the journal of to-day is put off, the events of to-morrow will confuse and dim the impressions that ought in all their pristine vigour to have been committed to paper; procrastination is the thief of time, and we may well say that it will rob the journal of the traveller of all that freshness and vivacity which alone can make it interesting.

The traveller will, perhaps, wish to send home one or more copies of his diary as correspondence, and it is absolutely necessary that he himself should retain a perfect copy. Ink he cannot at all times carry, nor could he use it, for the drying up of the fluid,

c

the clogging and corroding of his pens, would be insuperable difficulties; and besides this, as his time is not sufficient for him to

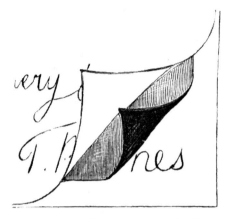

write in detail, even for the first
time, all that he wishes, how
shall he obtain a copy? In
answer we will simply state
the plan we have sucessfully
adopted. Pen and ink we dis-
carded altogether, and trusted
simply to the powers of a good
HH. pencil and a supply of thin
white foolscap interleaved with
semi-carbonic paper, as shown
in the illustration here given.
By this arrangement we were
able at any time to record all needful remarks or observations in
duplicate, and could have extended this if necessary to five copies,
while all the labour of re-writing was saved and all chance of error
obviated by this simple process.

With regard to artist's materials, until we have an opportunity of
going farther into detail, perhaps all that need be said is that
Artist's materials. the traveller, knowing his own capabilities and
requirements, should supply himself with material
from some respectable colourman—Reeves, Winsor and Newton,
or others—with such materials as he requires. To one who has
real facility in sketching, the black-lead pencil and a few quires of
sketching cartridge paper will be the means of affording illustrations
which, compared with the simple means employed, may be accounted
marvellous; but if he has skill in colouring and will add to this a
water-colour box, with tubes, or moist colours in porcelain pans, in
assortments (always kept by the best colourmen), with a few sable
or other pencils, and brushes of the best quality (for there is really no
saving in buying cheap goods), he may obtain results that will in
after years more than repay the cost and labour he has expended upon
them.

Details of our own outfit and expenditure will hereafter be given;
and we may now briefly mention that, for pure and careful painting,
white paper—say Whatman's—is indispensable; but where strict
accuracy of tint is not essential, it is very soothing to the eye,
especially under the fervid rays of an almost vertical sun, to have
the paper slightly tinted with pearl, warm grey, light drab, or
neutral colours, which, if well chosen, will enable the artist to

make very effective drawings in sepia, or colours heightened with Chinese white.

For persons wishing to employ their leisure in pleasing momentoes of the scenes they visit, perhaps the following brief list—amplified should they desire it—will afford sufficient guidance; and they will also do well to choose one or more of the shilling handbooks published by Rowney and Co., or Winsor and Newton.

A sketching portfolio, with folding tin frame to confine the paper while in use, and pocket for spare paper—quarto size. Do not take sketching blocks where they have to stand rough usage.

One of folio size, if desired.

A good strong havresac of canvas, with leather slings for each folio. Stout canvas is almost waterproof. This should have pockets for colour box, water bottle, pencils, and penknife.

Half quire Whatman's drawing paper (white). Some of it should be cut to the size of the folio.

Half quire sketching cartridge for less finished work.

Half quire tinted drawing paper (pearl, light drab, cool and warm greys).

A proportion of all these papers should be cut to the size of the sketch book when purchased; but a few sheets should be kept whole, as a larger drawing may be required.

Two dozen drawing pencils—8 HH., 12 H., and 4 HB. In practice, it will be found HB. is black enough, and it should be used sparingly, as, unless a drawing is fixed immediately, the deep shades are very apt to smear when the backs of other sketches are packed against them.

Two single bladed penknives.

Very compact sketching boxes with assorted colours in cakes, in porcelain pans, or in collapsible tubes, are provided; and the amateur can hardly do better than select one of these with any number of colours from two to twenty-four.

We prefer to use the collapsible tubes, as from them any amount of colour may be placed upon the palette ready for use, without the trouble of grinding from the cake or washing up from the moist pan. Another advantage is that the colour remaining in the tube cannot be spoiled by the admixture of any other—the tubes might be carried loose in the pocket of a white waistcoat without fear of spoiling it. There are, however, a few which do not keep well, as, from their weight, they separate from the medium they are mixed with and become hard. Some of these are seldom used; but, where they are necessary, we should advise that they be taken in cakes.

On tinted paper very nice effective sketches may be made with one tube of sepia and a cake of Chinese white. With these we should advise three brown sable pencils in flat German silver ferrules—Nos. 1, 3, and 6. With the addition to these of the three primitive colours—red, blue, and yellow—a considerable range of subjects may be painted; indeed could we obtain these in perfect purity, we should require no other. But, as this is impossible, we subjoin a list of colours, placing first in order those that we have found most useful (Chinese white and sepia have been already mentioned) :—

Indian yellow,	Rose madder (per-	Mars orange,	Purple lake,
Carmine,	haps in cake),	Payne's grey,	Cadmium yellow
French blue,	Cobalt,	Vermilion (cake),	(cake),
Yellow ochre,	Raw sienna (cake),	Vandyke brown,	Brown madder
Light red,	Burnt sienna,	Emerald green,	(cake),
Prussian blue,	Indigo,	Scarlet lake (cake),	Purple madder
Gamboge,	Yellow lake,	Crimson lake,	(cake).

With these, the whole set from 1 to 6 of the sables in flat albata will be needed, and we advise two each of 1, 2, and 3, as well as one or two larger swans' quills for washing in the sky or flat tints. A tripod sketching stool folding to the size of a special's staff would be useful, but the rivet should be strong and well clinched. Let the watercolour box have divisions on the edge of the palette for every colour it contains. If you take an easel, do not trust an india-rubber collar joint; it will not stand tropical heat; let the joint be brass. The tripod easel, folding up like a single rod, is most portable. We have in this said nothing of oil colours; amateurs will hardly need them in a wild country; but when we treat more at length on this subject our own equipment will be given.

Scientific Instruments.

If the traveller aims at exploring and approximately mapping the country he passes through, astronomical instruments are indispensable, Instruments for and of these none are more useful than the mapping the route. compass; the sextant, with artificial horizon; the note book, conveniently ruled, for recording observations; and the protractor, the scale, and the dividers, for laying them down upon the map. If merely a pleasure excursion in a sufficiently known country is contemplated, a pocket compass will be all that is needed; and even that is dispensed with by hunters and traders, who push further every year into the wilderness without fear of either mistaking their way or being unable to return upon their own tracks.

A great amount of detail may be filled in with the following simple outfit :—A pocket compass, not only showing the points as in common use, but graduated on the outer circle with degrees, reading uninterruptedly from zero all round to 360 : this will give the direction of the road, the bearings of any two objects, and the angle between them. A waistcoat-pocket ivory 6in. folding rule : this will serve the purpose both of scale and protractor; the eighths of an inch may be conveniently taken to represent miles, and by laying the rule upon the compass, so that its joint coincides with the centre on which the needle turns, and opening the legs to the degrees marked upon the circumference, the required angle may be approximately transferred to the note book. For observing latitudes a sextant is indispensable. If great accuracy is not required, a pocket or box sextant of from three to four inches diameter, and reading to half miles, will answer; but for more precision one of at least 8in. radius should be taken, framed entirely of metal, as wood will shrink and warp ; it should read to 15 or even to 10 seconds, or sixtieths of a mile. There are many forms of artificial horizon, but of these the mercurial is the best, and, in fact, the only one we can confidently recommend. The trough should not be less than five inches long by three broad, and we prefer an oval form, with a convenient spout for pouring off the quicksilver when done with. A glass roof is used to protect the surface of the mercury, should there be any wind, and this may be made to fold into a very small compass, if desired. Six, or at least four, pounds of mercury should be provided; and this should be kept in an iron bottle, with screwed stopper and cover, serving as a funnel, which should be further protected by a piece of washleather tied over it. We have used as a substitute a common stoneware ink bottle, with leather securely tied over the cork, but wooden bottles are sure to split and leak when taken to hot countries.

With this equipment, a superior compass, for the more accurate determination of bearings, will be required. A prismatic compass is very useful, but we have used, with great convenience and accuracy, a flat one with a card of three inches diameter, divested of everything but the slit and hair line sights, which are used just as those of a rifle are, and protected only by a stout glass, which saved the trouble of removing and replacing the cover. A small pouch on the waist belt was appropriated exclusively to this. The note book may be of good non-metallic writing-paper, such as is in common use. This may be written on very conveniently with a H. or HH. drawing pencil, which is practically indelible. It would be convenient to have lines ruled along the side of the page for the courses and time or estimated distance ;

£. *s. d.* columns will do very well for this. For mapping, paper may be purchased ruled with squares, of almost any desired size; the inches are marked with strong lines, and the subdivisions, eights or tenths, with fainter. This should be cut to fit one of the quarto sketching folios, with folding frame to confine the sheet in use, and pocket for spare paper as commonly used by artists. The instruments absolutely necessary for plotting the result are a semicircular, or, still better, a circular protractor, marked like the compass with degrees from 0 to 360, and made of brass, or preferably of some transparent material. A 6in. scale, with the usual divisions, and a good pair of compasses or dividers, with points as fine as possible, but somewhat obtuse, to prevent the possibility of their piercing the paper and breaking off in it. For heights of mountains, the simplest and most reliable instrument is the hypsometrical or boiling-point apparatus, which, though not so accurate as the mountain barometer, is sufficiently so for ordinary purposes, and has this great merit—it cannot easily be put out of order. The rainfall, should the country be blessed with any, may be measured by a Casella rain gauge, which we have also used very successfully on a pinch as a funnel for drawing off rum from a barrel. Thermometers reading up to boiling point ought to be carried, and in addition to these the traveller may provide himself with a self-registered maximum and minimum, and a wet and dry bulb thermometer.

THERMOMETERS.

As three different kinds of thermometers are in use, it will be well to fully understand how they are graduated, and the manner in which the results of their action may be compared. We shall first notice, " Fahrenheit's "—the description most commonly made use of in England, North America, and Holland. Its freezing point is marked 32°, and the point at which water boils at ordinary sea levels 212°. " Réaumur's " arrangement is most in use in Spain, Portugal, &c. In it the freezing point or zero, is 0°, and boiling point 80°. A far more common thermometer than this is known as the " Centigrade " or " Celsius," and is the favourite indicator of heat and cold throughout France and northern Europe. Its zero or freezing point is 0°, and boiling point 100°. Much confusion is apt to be caused in the reading and translation of reports and records of travel and exploration if some plain and simple method of comparing and assimilating the results arrived at by the use of all three of these thermometers is not had recourse to. To reduce Centigrade results and those of Réaumur to Fahrenheit's scale, and conversely, multiply the Centigrade degrees by

T. Baines.

9 and divide the product by 5, or multiply the degrees of Réaumur by 9 and divide the result by 4, adding 32 to the quotient in either case, and the result will give the degrees in Fahrenheit's scale. Another method is as follows: From the number of degrees indicated in

Fahrenheit's instrument subtract 32, multiply the remainder by 5 to find Centigrade degrees, or by 4 to find those of Réaumur. The result in either case must be divided by 9 to give the temperature required.

One of the greatest difficulties that an observer working on shore with the artificial horizon can meet with is—that the actual angle to be observed is doubled by reflection in the quicksilver. Few sextants read higher than 120° or 130°, consequently, when the sun is 70° high, it is beyond the reach of ordinary instruments. To meet this, Captain C. George, R.N., of the Royal Geographical Society, has invented a very beautiful little instrument, in the form of a double-box sextant, and the object of which is either to take two angles at one observation, by referring two distant objects to a common centre, and completing at once a perfect triangle, or, by the increased power of the instrument, to take any required angle that may be too great for those in ordinary use. The instrument is best described as being a special arrangement of two sextants placed one over the other. Each sextant is complete in all its essential details, and, if so required, can be detached and separately used.

The "Improved Double Sextant" is capable of being applied to the following uses :—

(1.) To the measurement of angles of nearly double the arc which can be measured by the ordinary sextant.

(2.) To the simultaneous measurement of two angles.

(3.) To laying out a direct line between any two objects, thus acting as a substitute for a Raper's instrument.

(4.) To laying out curves for railways, harbour works, &c., &c.

(5.) It can be used as an optical square.

(6.) It can be used as a dip-sector.

(7.) It can be used on shipboard to measure the supplement of the meridian altitude, in cases were the land intervenes between the observer and the direct meridional horizon.

(8.) It can be used on shore with the artificial horizon in obtaining altitudes of objects near the zenith.

(9.) It is also available as two distinct sextants, one of which can be used in case of the other being damaged, or one can be used by an assistant, and the other retained by the observer.

A pocket compass is now made in which the northern half is black with white points, and the southern white with black points ; the advantage of which by night or twilight is obvious. We prefer that the card should travel with the magnet, as all the points then come naturally into position, and the excessive liveliness of the needle which renders a rapid observation so difficult is obviated. We have carried a pocket compass with a swivel ring, so that it could be worn on the left thumb, while we held the note book and kept the right hand free for writing or guiding the horse. It is easier to make pencil notes on horseback than in a waggon. For the proper registration of the time and distance travelled, a good well-going hunting watch is necessary; and if it has a black dial and white figures so much the better. This will serve sufficiently well for taking time in the observation of lunar distances. Unless under very exceptional circumstances it would be useless for an explorer to trouble himself with a chronometer. A good binocular field glass for day and night will be found useful.

We give a sketch of a very convenient arrangement made for us by Mr. Casella, in which the roof of the artificial horizon, slung with its point downward in a leather case, with pieces of tin let in to protect the glass   Portable observatory. from injury, was filled up with a block of light cedar, with hollows

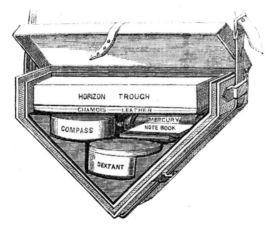

PORTABLE OBSERVATORY.

cut in it for the reception of the pocket sextant, iron-stoppered bottle of mercury and funnel cap, prismatic compass, note book with tables of declination cut from Hannay and Dietrichsen's Almanac pasted in it, pencil, skin of chamois leather, and over all the horizon trough. Lieutenant Skead, R.N., who accompanied the expedition to the Zambesi, frequently used it, and called it "a portable observatory." If the traveller intends to be long absent, he should supply himself with the Nautical Almanac for three years in advance, as well as with Norie's or Raper's Epitome, or Kerigan's Navigation. In addition to the instruments we have described, triangular compasses are very useful for taking the exact relative position of three points, and sliding beam compasses for long distances. Proportional compasses are also very

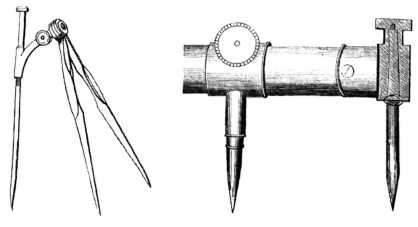

TRIANGULAR COMPASSES.   SLIDING BEAM COMPASSES.

useful in plotting the results of observations ; we were accustomed to pin down half a dozen sheets over each other on the drawing

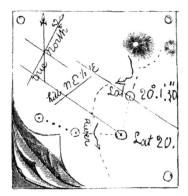

board, and with a fine needle point prick the course through the whole of them ; then by underlaying them with semi-carbonic paper, and writing the names on the upper sheet with a HHH. pencil, three or even more copies at a time might be obtained, the number, of course, depending much on the thinness of the paper we worked on. (See accompanying illustration.) Bear in mind that what an explorer wants is the means of approximately laying down his course and distance travelled, and his latitude precisely ; the sextant and

Measurement of distances.

artificial horizon will do the last within a mile. The compass will give the course very nearly if the traveller walks or rides ; no instrument can be perfectly depended on. A pedometer will do for short distances, but when the wearer becomes weary it counts his feeble steps just as it did his vigorous strides at the beginning, and thus shows more than the truth. If wheel carriages can be used, take a trochiameter, and contrive if possible to have the wheel on which it is fixed exactly *five yards in circumference* ; it saves no end of trouble if there are no odd half inches to calculate. For mapping, do not take a case of instruments unless they are really good; have rather a few good ones wrapped in a chamois skin, a small ivory rule on which the eighths of an inch serve for miles, a pair of good dividing compasses, a good circular protractor, transparent, marked from 0 to 360, a small parallel rule, H.H.H. pencils, a cake of blue for rivers, and carmine for roads, with a couple of sable pencils and a fine incorrodible metallic pen, will enable you to make a very complete and reliable map.

In the map room of the Royal Geographical Society a small selection of practical works is kept, a list of which, by the courtesy of Captain C. George, we are enabled to insert here. It is as follows :—

The Traveller's Library.

Astronomy.

Outlines of Astronomy. Sir J. Herschel, Bart. (Longman and Co. 1858.) 11s.
Astronomy and General Physics, W. Whewell. (W. Pickering. 1857.) 4s.
Illustrated London Astronomy. J. R. Hind. (Ingram and Co. 1853.) 1s. 6d.
Handbook—Descriptive and Practical Astronomy. G. F. Chambers. (J. Murray. 1861.) 10s.
Elements of Plane Astronomy. J. Brinkley, D.D. (Hodges and Smith. 1845.) 6s.
Orbs of Heaven; Planetary and Stellar Worlds. O. M. Mitchell. (N. Cooke. 1856.) 2s. 3d.

Navigation.

Navigation and Nautical Astronomy. Rev. J. Inman. (Rivingtons. 1862.) 6s. 3d.
Complete Epitome of Practical Navigation. (J. W. Norie. 1864.) 14s. [N.B. The latest edition should be asked for.]
Lunar Time Tables. J. Gordon. (Imray. 1853.) 7s.
Handbook for the Stars. H. W. Jeans. (Levey, Robson, and Co. 1848.) 3s. 6d.

Mathematics, Trigonometry, and Spherics.

Manual of Mathematical Tables. Galbraith and Houghton. (Longman and Co. 1860.) 2s.
Mathematical Tracts. G. B. Airy. (J. W. Parker. 1842.) 9s. 6d.
Treatise on Practical Mensuration. A. Nesbit. (Longman and Co.1864.) 5s. 4d.
Practical Introduction to Spherics and Nautical Astronomy. P. Kelly, LL.D. (Baldwin and Co. 1822.) 7s.
Treatise on Trigonometry. G. B. Airy. (Griffin and Co. 1855.) 2s. 3d.

For Travellers.

What to Observe; or, Travelling Remembrancer. Col. Jackson. Revised by Dr. Norton Shaw. (Houlston and Wright, 1861.) 9s. 6d.

Geodesy and Surveying, Military, Nautical, and Land Surveying.

Treatise on Military Surveying. Lieut. Col. Jackson. (Allen and Co. 1860.) 12s.
Outline of Method of conducting a Trigonometrical Survey. Col. Frome. (Weale. 1862.) 10s. 6d.
Practical Geodesy. J. W. Williams. (Parker and Son. 1835.) 7s. 6d.
Trigonometrical Surveying, Levelling, and Engineering. W. Galbraith. (Blackwood and Son. 1842.) 6s. 9d.

Engineering Field Notes on Parish and Railway Surveying and Levelling. H. J. Castle. (Simpkin and Co. 1847.) 8s.

Practice of Engineering Field Work. W. D. Haskoll. (Atchley and Co. 1858.) 17s. 6d.

Treatise on Nautical Surveyings. Com. Belcher. (Richardson. 1835.) 12s.

Weights and Measures.

Weights and Measures of All Nations. W. Woolhouse. (Virtue Bros. 1863.) 1s. 6d.

Foreign Measures and their English Values. R. C. Carrington. (Potter. 1864.)

Construction of Maps.

Manual of Map-making. A. Jamieson. (Fullarton. 1846.) 2s.

Manual of Topographical Drawing. Lieut. R. Smith. (J. Wiley. 1854.) 5s.

Projection of the Sphere.

Projection and Calculation of the Sphere. S. M. Saxby. (Longman and Co. 1861.) 4s. 3d.

Use of Instruments.

Treatise on Principal Mathematical and Drawing Instruments. F. Williams. (Weale. 1857.) 3s. 2d.

The Sextant and its Applications. Simms. (Troughton and Simms. 1858.) 4s. 6d.

Treatise on Mathematical Instruments. J. Heather. (Virtue Bros. 1863.) 1s.

Geography.

Geography Generalised. R. Sullivan. (Longman and Co. 1863.) 2s.

In addition to these, every one ought to possess the Admiralty Manual of Scientific Enquiry, which is a series of papers written for the direction of explorers by men of the highest standing in various sciences; and no better general work can be recomended.

HORSE EQUIPMENT.

A good roomy hunting saddle, turned out as only an experienced English maker can, or, at any rate, so far as our experience has gone, ever does, we look on as the very perfection of that on which a horseman should sit; and we strongly advise every one leaving England for any country in which he has to ride to provide himself with at least one. The various saddles used abroad will be described farther on. It will be requisite to have a number of " Ds " fastened on in the most convenient situations for attaching by straps the various matters which it is at times requisite to carry. Two soft leather holsters should be fitted to the front, and a wallet (see engraving), made to rest behind the off saddle flap and thigh of the rider, suspended by straps from Ds sewn firmly on for that purpose. At the rear of the saddle should also be attached a double row of Ds for the purpose of securing a sort of leather cover or envelope (see

Saddles.

engraving), within which, when on the march, the head and heel ropes, with their pins, are secured. The mode of using these, as well as "knee halters," &c., will be described when treating on that subject. Two "numdahs," or saddle cloths, should accompany the saddle. The best we have seen of late are composed of a thick species of felt; but, during the most rapid and fatiguing forced marches through Central India, at the time of the mutiny, we used

two of quilted cotton of native manufacture, which were put on alternately, one getting dry whilst the other was becoming saturated with perspiration from the horse, and so, by a constant change of these, avoiding one of the worst misfortunes that can befall the horse of the traveller through a wild country, viz., "a sore back." The skin of the klip springer, prepared with the hair on, forms an admirable numdah. Saddles are greatly protected during rough travel, and their durability much increased by having cases made for them of soft "russet" leather, or that which is infinitely better, when it can be obtained, "saumber skin." The stirrup-iron should be of large size, so as to admit of the free passage in and out of a thick boot with some mud or clay about it. Two or three

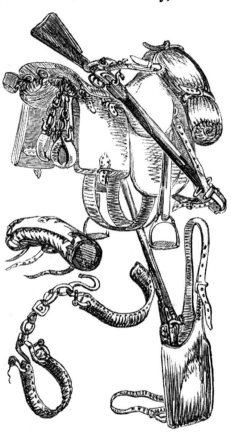

NORTH AUSTRALIAN EXPEDITION SADDLE EQUIPMENT.
NAMAQUA GUN BUCKET.

pairs of substantial hunting spurs, with wide straps, will be found the most reliable kind of "persuader." The most useful bridle we ever had was of the "shifting bead collar pattern" so constructed that, by unbuckling a pair of side straps, both bits, Bridle.
with the reins attached, came off, leaving a strong head collar, with a chin strap, on which was an iron ring for a coil of rope to be suspended from, as shewn in the illustration on page 32.

Numerous opinions exist touching "bits," and much diversity of opinion must remain after all the arguments which have from time to time been expended on the subject; as the temperaments of horses and men vary, and as the peculiar purposes to which the horse, in the number of phases or conditions in which he is called on to minister to the wants and pleasures of his master, are changed, so will some modification of the means used for his control and direction be required. Pall-mall is one place and the forest another; and it by no means follows, because the equipment one has used with English hunters in an English hunting-field has been found all that could be desired, that native bred or colonial horses, ridden in pursuit of game, require no other. We do not think it would be profitable to the reader to enter here on a description of the bits used by various nations and tribes. We advise as nearly as possible adhering in this, as well as in many other customs, to the mode adopted by the particular race or nation amongst whom the traveller may chance to sojourn. Still, we recommend him to take out from England (besides the bit fitted on the head collar bridle, which may be a plain strong snaffle) two " segundras" of medium power. Have no more buckles in either heads or reins than are absolutely needed. Nothing tends to weaken a bridle so much, during the exposure consequent on an outdoor life, as the rusting out of buckles and the breaking or pulling through of their tongues— both sources of endless trouble and annoyance.

For simple and efficient equipment both for pack and saddle horses we do not know a better model than that adopted by Augustus C. Gregory, Commander of the North Australian Expedition, and now Gold Medallist of the Royal Geographical Society, with whom we had the honour of serving from 1855 to 1857.

The pack saddle, made under the direction of Mr. Gregory, consisted simply of two boards of Australian cedar, about twenty inches long by
Pack Saddles. seven broad, inclined at such an angle as to sit fairly on the horse's ribs, and at such a distance from each other that the spine should remain uninjured between them. These were connected by two stout bows of iron, 1½in. broad by ⅜in. thick, arching well clear of the horse's back, and having on each side hooks firmly riveted into them for the suspension of the bags in which our provisions, &c., were stowed. The crupper was buckled round the aftermost bow, and the straps for the attachment of the breasting, breeching, and girths were screwed on the outside of the cedar planks. We hope the illustration on the next page is sufficiently clear to indicate the position of these without further description; it will be seen that the girths cross each other as they pass under the belly.

A pair of pads, sufficiently large to prevent not only the saddle but also the packs chafing the horse, were attached to the boards by thongs passing through holes bored in either end, so that upon occasion we could easily remove them to re-arrange the stuffing, and tie them again in their places. A thick felted saddle cloth was invaluable as an additional protection. The form of the bags will also be readily understood by a glance at the frontis-piece. They were of stout canvas, as wide as one breadth of the material, and the ends were formed by a pear-shaped piece let in, and strongly roped round the seams; the loops at the upper part were bound with leather, and iron cringles or grummets were let in, by which to hang them on the hooks. No other fastening was used, so that if a horse fell in the rugged mountain paths, or

NORTH AUSTRALIAN EXPEDITION PACKHORSE EQUIPMENT.

in fording a rough and swollen torrent, it was an advantage to him to shake off his bags at once, while we were generally able to fish them up again before even such perishable stores as sugar could be reached by water, through the pack and double bags of canvas in which we kept them. Nothing whatever was allowed to be fastened to the bows above the suspension hooks; indeed there was a general order that the horse should carry nothing that was not contained in the side bags. The smaller bags for flour, sugar, and other stores, were also the length of one breadth of canvas. One end was formed by a circular piece of canvas about eight inches in diameter, and the other was left to be closed when they were filled. The inner bag was of plain canvas, and this was covered by another that had been well saturated with boiled linseed oil; these held about fifty pounds of flour, &c., and in each flour bag two ½lb. tins of gunpowder were kept *perfectly secure from fire or water;* we generally ate the flour as fast as we wanted the powder. Each pair of side bags was numbered, and carefully balanced one

against the other, the stowage of each being from seventy to seventy-five pounds, so that the total load of the horse should not much exceed 160lb.

All the horses were furnished with a stout headstall and halter, which may be readily understood from the annexed engraving, and to which, when requisite, the bit and bridle could be buckled by short straps attached to the ring for that purpose.

Our riding saddles were provided with stout Ds, the straps of which were not stitched to the leather, but either firmly screwed into the wood, or passed round the frame of the saddle. Three of these in front served to receive the straps for buckling on "the swag," or a couple of stout red or blue blankets, which, with the extra shirt and trowsers serving as a pillow, formed our sole bedding. This was formed into a roll a little more than 3ft. long, and 6in. diameter, and carefully adjusted so as to arch well clear of the horse's withers. In front of the saddle bar, on the off side, was a stout ring, through which passed the slings of the gun bucket, which was made quite roomy enough to allow a double barrel to be withdrawn or again inserted without trouble, and was kept from collapsing by a ring of iron stitched into its upper edge; and the tedious process of unbuckling the strap usually passed round and round the grip of the gun stock was obviated by the very simple spring and swivel catch shown in the sketch.

It may be mentioned that we found the spring bar a very convenient arrangement, and only once we lost a stirrup leather when a rider had dimsounted to allow his horse to descend more easily a difficult hill; but for such contingencies spare stirrups, &c., had been provided by the commander. Two Ds on either side supported such saddle pouches as were required; we preferred the nearly square form shown in the sketch of saddle on page 36, as being more roomy, containing in one the quarto sketch book actually in use, and in the other, a store of paper, &c., for further supply. Small loops, the attachment of which is just indicated on the inside of one of these bags, led forward for the girth to pass through and keep the pouches from flapping.

Some of us carried a valise, such as is separately represented, and others would make a roll of spare clothing; but it was imperative on all that nothing whatever should be allowed to rest on the horse's spine, but should be padded or otherwise arranged so as to pass clear over it. The hobbles were formed of a band of stout leather, double the required width, turned up and stitched so as to form a flat edge and a round one. In use, the sewn edge was always uppermost, so that the fetlock might not be chafed. They were connected by a short chain, having a swivel in the centre, and a double hook at each end, the hooks having holes pierced in their extremities for the reception of thongs, by which one end of each hobble was moused or secured from falling off. The hobbles were carried on the off side of the saddle, behind the pouches; and were not unfrequently balanced by the pannikin and tin quart, so essential to an Australian. Bells were hung to the headstalls of the horses most apt to stray, but thongs were fastened to the clappers, that they might be tied up during the day's march.

Our personal equipment consisted of a brown leather waist-belt, with snake fastening, carrying a small ammunition pouch, a revolver, and a compass; the naturalist, geologist, botanist, or artist adding to this such instruments as they required. Some few of us favoured braces, but with the majority they were at a discount. A cabbage-tree hat, or one of soft felt, a striped cotton shirt for fine weather, serge for wet, moleskin trousers, light woollen socks, and ankle boots, completing our general costume.

Some hundred fathoms of small rope formed an essential portion of our equipment, the use of which will be best understood on reference to the frontispiece (which illustrates an expedient strictly within the range of actual travel, and is here introduced chiefly to show the form of pack-saddle bag which we found convenient, and can, therefore, recommend to intending explorers). This shift will hereafter be more fully described when we have to treat of those which must be improvised by every traveller on such emergencies.

An excellent method of carrying the gun on horse or ox back we have seen in common use among the semi-civilised Hottentots of Namaqua land; it consists simply of a bag or bucket of tolerably stout leather, large enough to contain the stock of the gun butt downward, nearly as far as the lock; Gun slings.

it can be fastened to the saddle in exactly the same manner as that
in use among us, or it can be fastened to the saddle bar on the
near side and thrown over to the off. It is generally made of the
softened but untanned leather of the country, and fastened by
a thong and noose where we should, for more convenience and

NAMAQUA, WITH GUN, ON RIDING OX.

neatness, use a buckle. Its merits are that the gun lies easily
before the thigh, pointing upward behind the right arm, so that an
accidental discharge, if such a thing were possible, could hurt no
one; it is easily removed by shifting the arm within and lifting it from

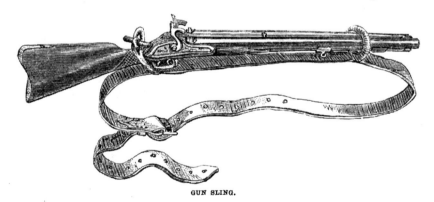

GUN SLING.

the bag without the trouble of casting off any secondary fastening; and
above all, it is impossible that even in the roughest riding the charge
could be jerked forward in the barrel to the imminent danger of
bursting it, as we ourselves have witnessed at the first discharge, where
the gun has been carried muzzle downwards. The illustration below

shows another very convenient form of gun sling, which we have found to answer admirably. When in use, the muzzles of the gun are above the left shoulder, and the stock behind the right thigh. By bringing the right hand back the toggle securing the loop round the grip is instantly released, when the gun drops into the right hand, releasing itself from the ring by its own weight, and is ready for instant use.

CUTLERY.

Do not be induced to encumber yourself with one of those ornamented, highly polished, useless abominations popularly known as hunting knives; they are worse than useless, and only serve to exasperate the owner. For general rough and ready work, nothing is *Knives.* better than a strong well-made butcher's knife. The blade should be continued through the handle, which is formed by pinning two cheeks of hard wood or horn together. The hand grip should be long, and the steel sufficiently soft to be cut by a common hand saw file; and we strongly recommend our readers to apply the file test to every cutting tool they provide themselves with, as the hard woods of tropical countries cause endless breakages and notchings when highly-tempered instruments are made use of. In the purchase of a pocket knife, choose one that is small enough to be a constant companion;

one, or at most two blades will be found sufficient for one handle. A very convenient description of knife is to be met with in most hardware shops. The handle is straight and flat. A stout stick-cutting blade is at one end of the haft, and a strong scalpel-shaped pen blade at the other. The miniature tool chests sold under the name of pocket knives to emigrants are jacks of all trades in their way, having all sorts of supposed capabilities, associated with a general tendency to uselessness. A pair of stout large bowed scissors will be found very useful, as well as a small piece of Turkey or Washita oilstone. This should have a little wooden box with a slide cover made for it, in order to preserve it from breakage. A few *Tools.* tools, well selected, can scarcely be dispensed with. The following list we can recommend, but our readers must of course be

D 2

guided as to the number they will take by the purposes of their proposed journey :—

Small hand axe, felling axe (American pattern).

Belt tomahawk.

Hand saw (medium size).

Three chisels ($\frac{3}{4}$in., $\frac{1}{2}$in., and $\frac{1}{4}$in.), and one cold chisel.

Three gouges (of the same sizes as the chisels).

Three gimblets (from ten-penny nail size downwards).

Six bradawls (assorted), to fit in one boxwood handle.

Six saddler's awls, to fit in one boxwood handle.

Six shoemaker's awls, to fit in one boxwood handle.

One $\frac{1}{2}$in. shell auger (without handles).

One screw driver ($\frac{1}{2}$in).

One engineer's riveting hammer ($\frac{1}{2}$lb).

One pair of carpenter's pincers.

One pair of strong pliers (bell-hanger's pattern).

Three hand-saw files (one rat tail; one flat; one half round).

One rasp, one soldering bolt, one pair of tin snips, ingot of solder, a lump of resin, and small ladle for lead melting.

A few nails, screws, pump tacks, and coils of copper and iron wire will be found useful.

Billhook, as in illustration.

One or more billhooks will be found of great value when traversing the tangled thickets, for dividing vines, lianas, briars, and entangled branches. We have found the following form of hook extremely powerful, and capable of cutting through most formidable impediments. The illustration represents the two sides of

Billhooks.

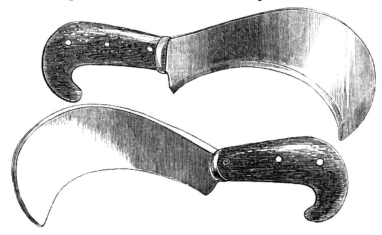

the hook, which, as will be seen on examination, are not alike. The near side of the blade, or that which would, when the instrument is used by a right-handed man, lie towards the left, is slightly hollowed, and the edge, instead of being bevelled, remains perfectly flush with it, like the front of a very large gouge. The off-side edge is bevelled, and exactly like that of a chisel. The plate of the blade should be 10in. long, and stouter at the back than most ordinary English billhooks. Instead of terminating in a tang or spill, the metal should be continued throughout the handle as far as the point at which the curved knob at its end is carved out. Handles for these hooks are best made from natural-grown sticks of suitable bend. The wood must be tough, strong, durable, and well seasoned. When nearly finished, a saw cut must be made the exact length of the continuation of metal from the blade, and this must be opened and widened with a flat file until the plate fits exactly in it. A strong wide ring must now be driven on at the upper end, and three stout soft iron pins passed through both the wood and iron of the handle, riveting the ends securely in countersunk holes prepared for their reception. The handle may now be finished, and made to fit the grip of the hand by the use of the rasp, and some pieces of broken glass as scrapers. The temper of these tools must be regulated by the file test. Leather sheaths should be made for them, with guide straps for the belt to go through.

All the small tools can be conveniently packed and carried in a leather or canvas hold-all. This is merely a long strip of either canvas or leather, with longitudinal bands sewn Tool hold-all on the inside. The tools are arranged side by side under these, and then rolled up and tied carefully together with a wide tape string. All

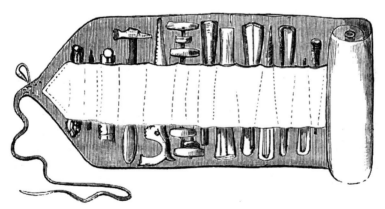

the edge tools should be tempered or let down to meet the file test, ground and set, before being finally packed. The axe handle should be of well seasoned hickory, and so made as to admit of being knocked forward through the eye of the blade, and so removed from it, as shown in the illustration of the group of tools on the next page. A grooved strip of wood should be fitted to the edge of the saw, in order to preserve the teeth and keep the blade straight. A leather bag may be also made for it with advantage. To those who do not require such tools as we have described, and yet wish to provide themselves with a very few, of small size, we can confidently recommend the following arrangement.   Order from a tin-plate worker a stout, wire-edged tin

Portable tool chest.

box, with wire hinges. Let it be 7in. long, 3in. wide, and 2½in. deep. In this, several small files, one or two small chisels, a number of both straight and

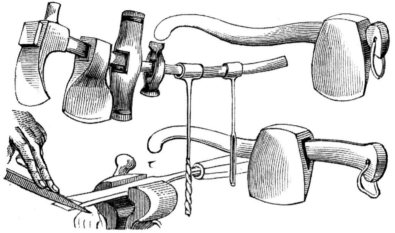

curved awl blades, a screw driver, hammer head, pliers, a few sail needles, a small hand vice, a watchmaker's drill and bits, a jointed blowpipe, some bits of solder, a little lump of resin, bits of brass and copper wire, some pieces of watchspring for cutting metal, a narrow cold chisel, and several other odds and ends, may be conveniently stowed away. A watch-spring saw needs no teeth; it is only requisite to occasionally run the face of a file from end to end, flat on the edge, as if in the act of blunting it, to renew its cutting power. A gun barrel, or a bar of iron the thickness of a walking-stick, can be cut through in an inconceivably short time with one of these little instruments, aided by a little sweet oil.

CAMP FURNITURE.

The best camp bed we ever possessed was made on the stretcher principle. The side bars were of birch wood, and ferruled in

Beds.

the centre, so as to admit of their being taken into four lengths. The legs, also of birchwood, shut and opened like two pairs of scissors. The centre piece of the bed was of stout canvas, sewn into pipes at the sides, through which the side bars passed. The head of the bed was formed by fixing two uprights in holes made for them, and then fixing a cross bar on their ends to keep them in place. A very thin cocoa-fibre mattress, cocoa-fibre pillow, and three thoroughly good brown blankets, are conveniently packed in a painted canvas bag, with the framework of the bed. Camp beds of endless variety are sold by all outfitters; but we describe that mentioned above as having stood the test of no ordinary wear and tear most satisfactorily. The various modes by which beds, hammocks, and litters are extemporised by travellers will be fully dealt with when that subject comes under consideration. In this section of our work we merely point out that which is best purchased at home, leaving the multiplication of the various objects, in some measure, to the judgment of the intending traveller.

A hammock is a very luxurious sort of bed, but most people are

alarmed by the very elaborate system of clews and rings by which it is suspended, and in very deed, even with the most scrupulous cleanliness, these are apt, in places where

Hammock.

vermin abound, to harbour a great many; but this might be avoided by having the canvas 10ft. or 12ft. long, and gathering it at the ends so as to dispense with clews altogether. It would then have the advantage that, when it could not be suspended, it might be folded as a double sheet upon the ground to lay the rest of the bedding on. A hammock can be slung in very unpromising places. We were accustomed to keep two (washed, clews and all, every fortnight), stretched to a bamboo pole, which we slung from the beams overhead. One end may be fastened to a tree or to the waggon wheel, and the rope attached to the other may pass over forked sticks set up as shears, and lead to a tent peg driven firmly into the ground. A sheet may be thrown over the pole or ridge rope to serve as a tent or curtain.

It is a very favourite plan in South Africa to have the blanket covered on both sides with chintz or printed cotton, quilted to it. This keeps it clean for a long time, and makes it much more efficient as a coverlet.

Wrapper.

Most countries have some peculiar wrapper of their own, as the buffalo robe of North America, the opossum rug of Australia, or the Vel Komboars or sheepskin blanket of the Cape colony. We have used as a pillow an inflated swimming belt, but in all cases when india-rubber goods are used, they must be kept from much exposure to the sun, and, above all, from contact with grease. We have had a waterproof overcoat so heated when folded away that we could not again open it; but one of these lined with calico, and covered with thin non-adhesive stuff, we should think would be useful. Thus writes Stanley of the form of bed used in Africa by Doctor Livingstone : " Each night he has it made under his own supervision. First he has two straight poles cut three or four inches in diameter, which are laid parallel one with another at the distance of two feet; across these poles are laid short sticks—saplings three feet long— and over these is laid a thick pile of grass; then comes a piece of waterproof canvas and blankets. Thus a bed has been improvised fit for a king."

STORE LIST.

The following statement will serve to show approximately the nature and quantity of stores, &c., required for an expedition such as that to which we were attached in Australia :—

The Party.—Commander, A. C. Gregory ; Assistant, H. C. Gregory; Geologist, J. G. Wilson ; Artist and Storekeeper, T. Baines ; Surgeon and Naturalist, J. R. Elsey ; Botanist, F. Müller; Collector, Natural History, &c., — Flood; Overseer, J. Phibbs; Farrier and Smith; Harness-maker; Stockmen, European (9) ; Shepherds, Native (2)— Total, 21.

Provisions, &c., for 18 months.—17,000lb. of flour, 5000lb. salt pork, 2000lb. bacon, 2000lb. preserved fresh meat in 6lb. tins, 2800lb. rice, 2500lb. sugar, 400lb. tea, 350lb. tobacco, 350lb. soap, 50lb. pepper, 500lb. salt, 100 galls. vinegar, 300 sheep, 200lb. sago, 640 pints peas, 2 cwt. coffee, 500lb. lime juice, 6 galls. lamp oil, 1lb. cotton wick, 3 cwt. preserved potatoes.

Land Conveyance.—50 horses, 35 pack saddles, 15 riding saddles, 50 horses' blankets, 800 fathoms tether rope 1½in. and 2in., 20 horse bells with straps, 100 pair hobbles, 3 light horse drays; 3 sets harness, 3 horses each; 50 spare girths, 50yds. strong girth web, 50 bridles, 10 pair holster bags, 10 pair stirrup leathers, 5 pair stirrup irons, 40 pair canvas pack-saddle bags, 100 straps, 200 buckles, 4 leather water bags, 20 pair spurs, 150lb. leather for repairs, 600 horseshoes and nails, 240 provision bags, 300yds. canvas, 20lb. sewing twine, 100 needles, 6 palms, 24 saddler's awls, 48 balls hemp, ½lb. bristles, 6lb. resin, 6lb. beeswax, 12 hanks small cord, 6 currycombs and brushes, 25 tether swivels.

Arms and Ammunition.—16 double guns, 4 rifles, 10 revolvers, 10 pistols, 200lb. gunpowder, 1000lb. shot and lead, 30,000 percussion caps, 20 belts and pouches, 15 gun buckets, straps, locks, spare nipples, moulds, punches, 4 ladles, powder flasks, shot pouches, &c., for each gun.

Camp Furniture.—5 tents 8ft. square calico, 150yds. calico, 12 camp kettles (½ to 3 galls.), 6 doz. pannikins, 4 doz. tin dishes (small), 1 doz. large, 4 doz. knives and forks, 4 doz. iron spoons, 6 frying pans, 6 leather buckets, 6 water kegs (6, 4, and 2 galls.), 6 spades, 4 socket shovels, 4 pickaxes, 2 spring balances (25lb. and 50lb.), 1 steelyard (150lb.), 1 sheep net (150yds.).

Instruments.—2 sextants (5in. and 6in.), 2 box do., 2 artificial horizons, 10lb. mercury in 2 iron bottles, 4 prismatic compasses, 11 pocket compasses, spare cards and glasses for compasses, 3 aneroid barometers, 4 thermometers to 180°, 2 telescopes, 1 duplex watch, 1 lever watch, 1 case drawing instruments, ; 2 pocket cases, pillar compass, and protractor; surveying chain and arrows, 2 measuring tapes, 1 drawing board (30 × 40 inches), 2 pocket lenses.

Stationery and Nautical Tables.

Tools.—1 portable forge, 1 anvil (½cwt.), 2 hammers and set of tongs, 10lb. cast steel, 11lb. blister steel, 100lb. bar and rod iron, 3 smith's files, 3 large axes (American), 6 small do.; 1 large tool chest.

Clothing.—120 pair moleskin trousers, 120 serge shirts, 120 cotton shirts, 60 pair boots, 40 oiled calico capes, 40 hats (Manilla), 40 blankets.

Artists' Materials.

Miscellaneous.—5yds. mosquito net, green; 500 fish-hooks, 25 fishing lines, 2 gross matches, 1 gross tobacco-pipes; 2 strong cases of ·instruments, stationery, &c.; 8 doz. pocket-kneivs, 8 doz. pocket-combs, 20 yds. red serge, for presents to blacks, 20lb. iron wire, 5lb. brass ditto, grindstone and spindle, coffee-mill, 3 iron saucepans, 2 iron kettles,

6 galls. linseed oil, 6 pints olive oil, 2lb. red lead, 23lb. alum, 1lb. borax.

Forage for Horses and Sheep from Moreton Bay to Victoria River, 2200 miles, at 14lb. per diem.—13 tons pressed hay, 9 tons bran, 200 bushels maize or barley, 500 bushels corn for horses after landing.

Medical Chest for 2 years and 20 men.

Naturalists' Stores.

We took, for conveyance across rivers, or navigation of any inland waters, a portable canoe of inflated canvas, in four sections, each of which, when inflated and laced to a frame, formed half a boat; the whole forming a double canoe, on which could be laid a platform of 15ft. by 7ft.

Boats.

The boat was made by Messrs Edgington from a model which we had previously constructed and tested as to its buoyancy and sailing

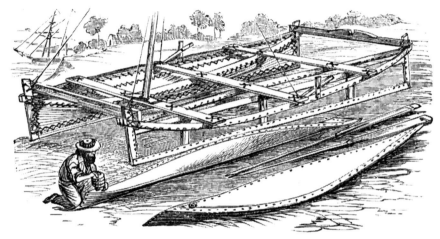

NORTH AUSTRALIAN EXPEDITION INFLATABLE DOUBLE BOAT.

qualities. The framework was of ash battens, 3in. wide and ¾in. thick. The uprights at stem and stern were mortised into the keel, as well as into the corresponding fore-and-aft batten above; they were secured by cross lashings passing through holes properly bored for the purpose. The gunwales were lashed on; and then the thwart pieces, 6in. wide, were secured in the same manner. The four canvas bags, each cut so as to form half a whale boat, 15ft. long and 18in. in the half breadth, were then laced in and inflated. Each rowlock was formed of two pieces of ash screwed to the gunwale, as seen in the preceding engraving; and two oars and a lug sail completed the equipment. The whole might be used either as a double canoe or as two separate boats, and Mr. Gregory was

Inflated canvas boat.

much pleased with them when put together; but, in consequence of a technical difficulty at home, they were not so efficient as they ought to have been. We had agreed with Messrs. Edgington as to the quality of canvas and of the sewing to be used in every part, but on applying to the Waterproofing Company he found they would not waterproof his work, nor allow him to do it. He had therefore to give over the whole of the work to the company. When finished, we found that the seams were not stitched at all, but cemented together; and, though warranted to stand 170° of heat, we found that with the strain of actual use upon them they softened and gave way. If the sections in their proper form were made of stout canvas, with the india-rubber bags, so large that they should bear no strain, inclosed within them, this would be a serviceable boat—for the india-rubber did not actually melt with the heat, but just softened, so that it was unable to resist the strain upon it. We had taken them up the river, about thirty miles, in the schooner's gig, to fill with fresh water, and instead of standing a heat of 170° they burst at 120°.

Although, as we have stated, our double inflatable boat partially failed in Australia, from the inability of the waterproof cement to bear the intense heat to which it was subjected, we believe that, had Messrs. Edgington been allowed to waterproof their own work, or had the company consented to waterproof the sections, properly seamed by practical tentmakers, according to the directions we gave, the finished boat would have been as successful in every respect as was the model.

When required for an exploring trip up the river, we decided to use them not as a double boat, but as two single ones, and we spent some days in securely stitching round every seam that should have been so treated by the original maker. Every one will understand how the fibre of the waterproof cloth would no longer close up round the threads, as would that of the new canvas, so that, notwithstanding all our care, there was always a little air leakage; however, spare bellows had been provided, and one was apportioned to each boat.

Four or five 6lb. tins of preserved beef were thrust in between the sections in each boat, so as to rest along the keel, our lighter stores were laid as might be said "on deck," and with two small oars in each we started, pulling up wherever there was sufficient water, and when we came to the dry intervals, slinging the boats one at a time under two oars, and carrying them easily with all their cargo to the next water. The voyage lasted some days, and the boats, therefore, occasionally required re-inflating.

If the traveller only wishes for the means of ferrying himself over rivers, he might take a couple of waterproof tubes, not less than 7ft. Canoe for long and 8in. in diameter, inclosed in unprepared covers one man. of canvas so tight as to relieve them from any strain, and connected by one breadth of canvas for him to sit upon. A small frame should keep these parallel to each other, and about 20in. or 2ft. apart; and the frame should be kept just above the water, so as not to impede the motion. It is a great thing to be independent of native help. If a man has his own canoe, however small, the people will come to offer theirs; but if he has none, they will make a hard bargain with him.

Perhaps as good a material as any for a boat, if the explorer is able to carry it, is pure sheet copper, of about 1lb. to the square foot. It Metal boats. is flexible, easily worked, will turn and bend in any form and at any angle; it may be folded down to a sharp edge like a sheet of paper, and opened again, a test which no iron ordinarily procurable could stand; it is nearly indestructible, and retains a proportionate value as old copper however much it may be worn.

We have heard of an officer who had the two ends of a yawl or whale-boat built of copper, and, though the stem would frequently be doubled up by touching the ground in crossing the bar of some African river, no leakage took place, and half an hour's skilful hammering brought it into shape again. We believe that the boats, or at least one of them, on the expedition of Mr. Lynch to the Dead Sea and the Jordan, were of copper. If we remember rightly a copper boat was carried in sections upon camels to Lake Chad.

Captain Burton took to Zanzibar a boat of corrugated iron, which was so speedy that the Arabs called her the Runner-away; it would be interesting to know the details of her construction. We at one time experimented with galvanised iron, but did not find it sufficiently flexible to bend so sharply as we required. In consequence of this—when preparing, in conjunction with Mr. Chapman, for a journey across Africa, from Walvisch Bay, on the west coast, to the Victoria Falls, from which we hoped to navigate the Zambesi to the Eastern Sea—we decided on building one of copper; and many reasons induced us to make this on the principle of a double canoe or twin steamer: in the first place, it would be difficult to carry a boat of more than three feet in breadth or depth, in an ox waggon, and these dimensions would afford room only for the closest possible stowage of our own persons, and a very scanty equipment. It was also, probable, that the boats would have, at rapids like Chicova or Kebrabasi, to be taken out of the water and carried over rugged and intricate country, where their length would render it impossible to manage them.

It was necessary, therefore, to build each boat in six watertight compartments, of 4ft. in length, of one sheet of copper, each of which overlapped the one behind it, just as the scales of a lobster are arranged, making the actual length of the boat 22ft. The "skin" of each section was made of three sheets of copper, 2ft. wide, laid side by side with their edges doubled over each other, so as to make a perfectly turned joint that required no riveting, and was only soldered to render it more certainly watertight. The ends of each section were marked to the curve required, but cut three inches larger, the extra circumference being cut with snips directed towards the centre, so that they might be turned outward to fit the curve of the skin, thus leaving a flange of 3in. at each end of the section; a strip of copper 6in. wide was doubled and slipped over both parts, riveted and soldered, the necessary surfaces having been previously tinned.

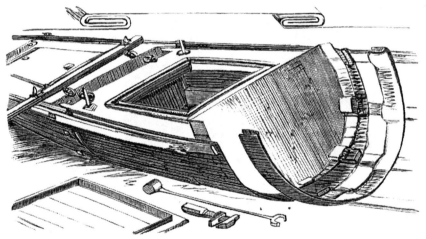

METHOD OF BUILDING AND CONNECTING SECTIONS OF COPPER BOAT.

We hope the accompanying engraving will make this plan tolerably plain. The end to the right is left unfinished, with the separate pieces a little apart ready to be put together; the farther shows the manner in which the flange of the foremost section overlaps the after, and is bolted to it with copper screws and nuts, leaving a space between into which the hand and arm could be thrust if it were needful to reach the bottom; the water would flow in or out of this narrow space freely, the compartments only being guarded against leakage; the nuts were all on the inside, and the iron key shown in the sketch was for the purpose of turning them on or off, while the heads were held outside

by the screw wrench. The copper was kept in shape by an inner
frame of wood, and strengthened externally by seven ribbands or
stringers of good straight grained red deal, running the entire length,
of which two served for gunwales and one for the keel, the ends of
this being let into sockets formed in the pieces of copper which were
doubled over the stem and stern post. One of the connecting beams
is shown in this sketch, and also the rings by which the sections were
to be carried when separated for overland conveyance.

For the purpose of keeping the cargo dry and secure from pilfering,
it was necessary that each section should have its own deck, and this,
to bear the weight of people standing on it, had to be made of ¾in.
plank, covered like the other parts with copper. Around each hatch-

COPPER BOATS ADJUSTED SIDE BY SIDE.

way were two mouldings, ¾in. high, the hollow between which, in heavy
rains, we intended to fill with wax or grease, so that when the corresponding moulding of the hatch fitted into it it might be watertight.
The connecting beams were 12ft. long, and made each of two pieces of
¾in. red deal, 2in. wide, so as to afford us, with the platform laid on
them, an available deck space of 12ft. by 20ft., on which, when the river
was broad and open, we might live or work with comfort; while, if it
narrowed, as we expected it would at Kansalo, Chicova, or Kebrabasi,
we could separate the boats and take each through singly, towing the
deck-raft, or even, if necessary, casting it adrift and trusting to pick it
up as the current brought it down. Two ¾in. planks, 9in. deep and 4ft.
long, so as to catch the bolts at either end of the section, served to
support the rowlocks. Each boat was provided with her own rudder,

and we purposed if necessary, to connect the tillers by a light rod, although we believed she would have steered by one alone. The masts were shipped in a wooden case, between the foremost and the next section, and the mode of setting the lug sails and awning will, we trust, be made sufficiently plain by the engraving. Care had to be taken that no iron or other metal capable of exerting a corrosive action came in contact with any part of the copper that was likely to be wetted.

The difficulties of the road, and deficiency of carriage, which compelled us to leave behind eight out of the twelve sections, and our expedients to replace them, will be more fully described hereafter: we, therefore, append only an abstract of the materials employed in building :—

			£	s.	d.
76 sheets of copper, 4ft. by 2ft. 16oz. to the foot, at 1s. 6d. per foot (but, as the supply was limited, we had to take some heavier, and consequently more expensive), one sheet same size 16lb. for stem, and stern post and rudder fittings			51	12	0
100 ¼in. copper, screwed bolts and nuts 3in., at 1s. 1d. ...			5	8	4
80 ditto ditto ditto 5in., at 1s. 5d. ...			5	13	4
5 ditto ditto ditto 7in., at 1s. 9d. ...			0	8	9
300 leather washers			1	5	0
174½lb. solder, at 1s. 6d. 13 4 4					
5lb. fine tin, at 2s. 3d. 0 11 3			17	10	8½
Extra quantity not specified 3 15 1½					
Men's time for soldering			17	17	6
Coke			1	2	6
2 nut wrenches			0	11	3
4lb. of sal ammoniac, at 1s. 6d.			0	6	0
4lb. of resin, at 4½d.			0	1	6
1 bottle of spirit of salts			0	1	4
6lb. of lead, at 4½d.			0	2	3
3lb. of copper boat nails, at 3s. 6d.			0	10	6
2lb. of nails and 2lb. of rivets, at 3s.			0	12	0
3 steel punches, at 1s.			0	3	0
2 pair of rowlocks, with sockets and screws			0	7	6
Total			£103	13	5½

It is impossible, at this distance of time, to recollect every item used, nor is it necessary to do more than to give an approximate idea of the cost and proportion used of the principal materials. Perhaps the wood, with a lad to assist in working it, cost about 10*l.*; paint, oil, sails, and other extras, about 10*l.* more; and 10*l.* freight from Cape Town to Walvisch Bay. We think 6d. per lb. was allowed on such old copper as was brought back.

Tents, Canvas Buckets and Articles made of Canvas generally.

In an army where men are plentiful and tents very few, the eighteen or twenty fortunate fellows to whom a bell tent may be allotted, can pitch it easily and rapidly enough; one, standing inside, will hold up the central pole, while the others, driving pegs all round, draw out and affix the cords to them. We found, however, when accompanying the division in Kafirland under General Somerset, that we could set up our own tent, shared by Mr. Hoole, the interpreter, almost as quickly alone, leaving our friend's servant at liberty to prepare our meal. Our plan was to make two knots on the cord used for lashing up

Tent-pitching. the tent, one marking the radius of the inner line of pegs and the other that of the outer, setting a central peg into the ground and looping over it the end of the line; we held another at the knots, and with it drew the two concentric circles. Twenty pegs are necessary for each. We, therefore,

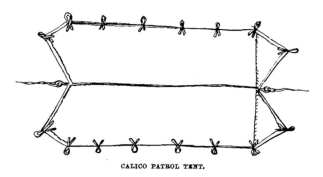

CALICO PATROL TENT.

threw four on the quarters of each circle, and distributing four between each drove them all into the ground; then spreading the tent in the space, we looped on all the lines, and inserting the pole, raised it up, its division into two pieces much facilitating this, and tightened the cords at leisure. (See illustration, " Camp Scene in Africa.")

Our patrol tent was just three yards of double width calico; a small cord was stitched along the middle and loops of tape along the sides. The diagonal pieces cut out of one end were stitched on

Patrol tent. to form the flaps of the other, and a couple of small sticks for the supports, the size of ramrods, were easily secured with the straps of our gun-bucket on the right side of the saddle.

Our little tent weighed next to nothing; it was seven feet in length, thirty inches high, and nearly thirty inches wide. We rolled our blankets in it, and so kept them clean. The package was carried

CAMP SCENE IN AFRICA.

strapped across the front of the saddle, and the latter, when set in one end of the tent, formed an additional protection to the head, and no rain ever penetrated our little dwelling, unless when a violent side wind would force through the interstices of the calico a slight sprinkling of minute drops, which would lie like dew outside the blanket in the morning. Waterproof material is not required for a tent; oiling the canvas or calico would only rot it; stout well-woven canvas is nearly waterproof in itself, and no matter how porous or open the material, the power of a tent to keep out rain depends more on the "pitch" of its sides or roof than anything else. Let a plate of glass lie in a sloping position, and let a drop of water be touched upon its under surface, if that surface makes an angle of less than 45° with the horizon the water will drop off it, but if the angle be above 45° it will run from top to bottom along the lower side; in like manner if the sides of the tent are pitched at a higher angle than 45° with the horizon, the heaviest shower will run down them instead of penetrating. A piece of waterproof is, however, very convenient to lay upon the ground to spread the blankets on.

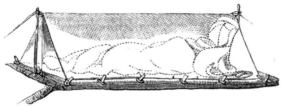

CALICO PATROL TENT.

Most of our readers who have visited the by-lanes and breezy downs of England, will be familiar with, at least, the exterior of the gipsy's tent. Its mode of arrangement is both ingenious and thoroughly practical. We know of no plan by which a comparatively comfortable resting-place can be extemporised equal to *Gipsy tent.* it. Blankets, skins, mats, canvas, or old rugs, serve to form a covering. The thicket furnishes the hazel wands or "benders," of which there are usually eight of 7ft. long, and almost any description of tough wood the "hole piece," and farmers' gate shivers are not unfrequently purloined by the Romany Rye to be thus utilised. A red hot poker serves to bore the holes. A few pieces of odd cord keep the framework in place, and a set of pegs is readily cut from the nearest hedge. The ends of the benders intended for insertion in the earth are usually fire-hardened, and one set will, with care, last a whole season. The above illustration will better explain the mode by which the contrivance is arranged than would any further description.

E

The *tente d' abri*, as used by the French army, is an extremely useful arrangement for a small band of travellers or explorers to provide

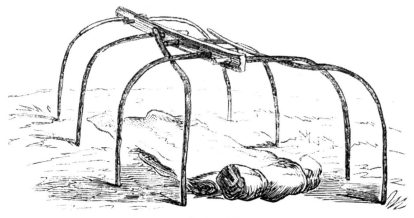

GIPSY TENT FRAME.

themselves with. It is composed of a number of sheets or pieces of
canvas. Each of these has a row of buttons and button-
holes sewn along the sides and upper edges, in order that
they may be joined to each other, much on the principle of a double-breasted waistcoat, as shown in the engraving below. The corners of the sheets are provided with strong short loops of rope, through which the heads of the tent pegs pass when the tent is pitched. The sheets are 5ft. 8in. by 5ft. 3in. Each member of a party of four or six

Tente d'abri.

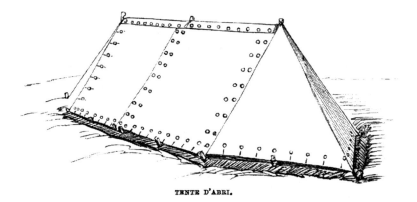

TENTE D'ABRI.

is supposed to carry his share of the tent, which consists of one sheet, three tent pegs, and the half of a round wooden staff ferruled in the centre like a fishing-rod. This, when put together, measures 4ft. 4in. in length, and is 1½in. in diameter. The total weight of each share is 3½lb. Tents of this description can be arranged by either buttoning four or six sheets together, one sheet being considered as representing the accommodation of one man; but when it is considered necessary to close the two ends of the tent, four sheets only are used as a covering, the other two being used as doors. A centre tent pole is also set up so that a tent for six men has, when pitched, three poles, ten pegs, and six sheets of canvas. When both ends are suffered to remain unclosed, as they would be when shade alone is sought, four tent poles or sticks and fourteen tent pegs are required; there would, then, be two spare poles and four pegs. By digging out a cavity in the earth as described at page 62, the comfort and internal capacity of the *tente d'abri* is much increased, and it forms a very convenient and portable shelter.

The Lancers, in Kafirland, used to form very commodious tents by sticking upright in the ground one lance and two swords; a second lance was passed as a ridge pole through the becket or loop of the first and the hilts of the two swords, as seen in illustration, "Camp Scene in Africa." One blanket was stretched over it as a tent, and another, with the saddle cloths, &c., formed a comfortable bed for two soldiers.

Lancers' tent.

A simpler form of tent may be made at a moment's notice. If rain comes on, sit upright, joining the hands above the head as if you were about to dive, supporting the blanket on them, and allowing it to hang down on all sides that the rain may run off. If you have no blanket, you may still keep your gun, ammunition, or sketch-book dry by sitting on them.

TENT EXTEMPORISED FROM A BLANKET.

The tents we used on the North Australian expedition were very light, convenient, and easily set up. They were simply foursided pyramids of calico, eight feet square in the base, and from 9ft. to 10ft. in height (see p. 57). They were lightly roped at the angles, and would set up with four principal pegs, though there were loops for intermediate ones along the sides. Poles could not conveniently be carried on the pack-horses, but there were few places in Australia where we could not cut them if needed; and in fine weather, we mostly dispensed altogether with the tents, except as mere sunshades, and slept only in our blankets. Their weight, dry, was trifling, but, on account of their bulk, they formed the greater part of the load

Australian tent.

E 2

of one horse, and when we had to travel—after a rainy night, without drying them—we found that two wet tents, with the farrier's tools and a few horse shoes, were quite heavy enough as a load for one animal.

A very favourite form of tent in the Cape colony is made like the longitudinal half section of a ridge pole tent. This is fastened to the Cape-waggon tent. roof of the travelling waggon and stretched beside it. When the traveller has two of these, one on each side his vehicle, he will find it of the greatest possible convenience. The waggon, with its own aristocratic kap tent, or humble but more durable wattled roof, serves as the sleeping chamber; while the half tent on one side may serve as a dining or general reception room, and the other as a working or retiring apartment. These may either be raised or lowered according to the position of the sun or wind, or may be com-

THE CAPE-WAGGON TENT.

pletely closed in at night; or, if required, the two halves can be taken away from the waggon altogether, laced together, and, with poles cut upon the spot, set up at once as a double-pole tent, as shown on p. 57.

We have found in Australia and Africa, that the possession of a large square of duck or canvas, eylet-holed at the corners and Extemporary tents. sides, or a couple of good sized sheets, of stout unbleached calico, with loops of tape or cord stitched at the sides and angles, have enabled us to construct extemporary screens from sun or wind, or even rain, and when not so required have served admirably the basis for our bedding. In boat parties the sails or awnings of the boat may be stretched upon the mast or oars, two oars at each end may be lashed crosswise, and set up as shear legs, while the mast is used as a ridge pole, and the sail drawn across them; there is, however, the objection that the blades of the oars if projecting upward will hold wind, and they should therefore be "feathered" toward the quarter whence it may be expected to blow; but never forget that the making of a tent is only a secondary and exceptional use for a boat's gear; if the sail is chafed or cut, its proper usefulness will be much deteriorated; and if the oars are allowed to sag or bend, by undue strain, they become worse than useless. You can no more pull effectively with a warped or twisted oar than you can shoot well with a crooked gun. In a boat voyage on a river, or where you can make fast and shelter your boat at night, if you set up two stanchions three or four feet higher than the gunwale, one at the after and another at the bow thwart, and then make fast a line to the ringbolt in the stern post, and lead it over the stanchions to the other ring in the stem, it will form a ridge rope on which the boat's awning with the yards or stretchers removed may be laid, and the sides sloped down tent fashion to the gunwales, and made fast either to the rowlocks or, still better, to a stout line passed tightly all round the boat outside of and just below the gunwale streak.

If you build a hut, and have not time or material to make it weather proof, the tent may with great advantage be pitched as a lining to it, and it is wonderful what effective shelter may be obtained from very imperfect hutting done in this manner.

We have frequently heard of officers and men setting up their tents or marquees, then building the framework of their hut over them, covering it roughly, and finishing at their leisure, so that, by the time the tents have been worn out, very efficient thatched houses have taken their places.

We should think that a bell tent (such as may be purchased at any town where military stores are kept), cut in half, and supplemented with a couple of squares of canvas, eylet-holed at two inches or more from the edge, so as to lace between the two halves of the bell tent, and used as a double-pole tent, either with a ridge pole or with a rope extended at either end as a stay, would form a very commodious habitation, and would be specially useful where the number of occupants is subject to changes.

When a tent is to be occupied for any length of time, it will be advisable to dig a hole in the earth to pitch it over, doing so not only adds materially to the space inside the tent, but makes it much more comfortable to reside in, from the shelter afforded by the sides of the excavation. Many of the huts built by the Russian soldiers in the neighbourhood of Sebastopol were sunk to a very great depth, being in fact merely large holes in the earth with roofs to them.

Fitting up of tent.

The roofs were of poles thickly laid over with brushwood, and then covered with earth; light was admitted through holes in the low framework of the sides, oiled paper being used as a substitute for glass. About 2ft. 6in. will be found a good depth for the excavation for an ordinary military tent to stand over. In digging it see that the sides are cut down evenly, and that the bottom is level. If planks can be procured to floor and line it so much the better. Some persons leave a round bank of earth in the middle for the pole to rest on, but we much prefer fixing a log of wood, cut from a tree trunk, in the centre of the floor. The habitation we formed for ourselves in the Crimea, when encamped before Sebastopol, was thus arranged. We first made a hole

SECTION OF CRIMEAN TENT.

in the earth a little less than the diameter of the bottom of the tent, and of the depth before referred to; we then made a pit in the centre about 18in. in depth. In this we sank the lower end of a piece of old tree trunk, 4ft. long and 7in. in diameter. In its upper surface we cut with a gouge a cup-like cavity. We then nailed a spiral strapping of forage hoop round a boat mast we were fortunate enough to hunt out at Balaklava; we then rounded the lower end so as to make it loosely fit into the cup on the head of the block. The bell or upper portion of an old tent was then raised on our mast tent pole, and over it our own new and complete tent, forming, so to speak, a double roof, having about a couple of inches of space between the two surfaces of canvas. This, by holding a certain portion of air, added in an extraordinary degree to its sheltering properties. We next dug a deep drain completely round the tent, and placed a quantity of broken stones in its bottom. An old wooden packing case was then let in, by digging into one of the sides of the excavation immediately under the doorway. This not only answered the purpose of a step to enter by, but formed an excellent storehole for all sorts of stray matters. The pipe from a small Maltese stove was carried out through the earth, and discharged its smoke outside a low wall of rough stones which encircled the tent. We drove two strong posts deeply into the earth beside the door ; across their tops we nailed a strong bar, which served to hitch

THE UTILISATION OF WHEELS.

horses to, rest gun against, &c. ; whilst across their lower portions we stretched a piece of forage hoop, edge upwards, to perform the part of a bootscraper. Towards the end of the war we were enabled to procure plank enough to both floor and line the tent throughout, thereby adding much to our comfort. The lining is carried out by placing boards the height of the side banks on their ends, all round the tent, like the staves of a barrel, and then nailing the flooring boards here and there fast to them. The upper ends are kept in their places by nailing short battens of wood across the joints.

The illustration on page 54 is a section of the tent referred to, and shows the manner in which many of the arrangements described are made. Many tents we have seen have been dug out to a sufficient depth to admit of a sort of cellar or lower room being formed; this can only be done at the expense of much trouble and labour. The arrangement of the interior of a tent admits of the exercise of a considerable amount of ingenuity. Cart, waggon, or gun wheels are extremely useful, both for forming a secure base for the pole to rest on, and for a table and gun rack. The tent pole, as shown in the engraving on the preceding page, rests on one wheel, whilst it passes through the centre of the nave of another. The hooks for hanging various objects from are formed by the natural branches of the tree from which the pole has been made. We seldom make use of the ferruled pole furnished with the tent when we have young forest trees at hand; in the absence of these, the conventional deal stick serves to fall back on.

Much of the efficiency of a tent depends on the way in which it is pitched. An experienced hand will so adjust his pegs and lines, that the gale of wind which prostrates the canvas houses of the inex-
perienced, passes his harmlessly by. Much has been said and written in praise of iron tent pegs, and, under some circumstances, they may be found highly useful, but there are very serious objections to their use in wild countries. If of sufficient size and length to be efficient, their weight becomes a matter of considerable importance.

Tent peg.

Their value to natives is so great that to prevent loss by theft is next to impossible; added to which, it is almost certain that one or two will be left in the ground, every now and then, on striking camp. We therefore prefer wooden pegs, made from some tough sound wood. Burn the points in the fire in order to harden them, and keep a good stock always on hand. The timber of the oriental plane makes excellent tent pegs. A strong and useful form of peg is shown in the annexed illustration. The mallet used for driving the pegs should be made of some heavy and hard wood, such as mimosa or baubul thorn. The handle should be made larger at one end than the other, so that it may be removed from the head of the mallet, just as the axe handles before described are separated from the blades. It not unfrequently happens, during tropical rains, or in sandy soil, that pegs driven in the ordinary way will not hold. It then becomes necessary to dig a moderately deep pit at the point at which the peg should stand. Bind together a small faggot of brushwood, reeds, or weed stalks; fasten a loop of rope or thong to it long enough to come 3in. or 4in. above the level of the pit where the faggot is buried. Place

TENT PEG.

Modes of securing tent ropes, &c.

your prepared faggot in the bottom of the pit crosswise, and then well stamp in the earth over it. A bag of sand, a stone, or a bundle of old hide answers the same purpose. In rough stormy weather, it is some-times necessary to *back* your pegs; this is done by driving in an additional one in a line with the first, and then forming a couple of half hitches with the tent rope over its head. It was a common practice in the Crimea to employ an old Russian bayonet in this way, driving it into the earth until the curved neck alone remained above the surface for the hitch to pass round. All tent ropes should be relaxed on the approach of rain, or the tightened cord will, in all probability, draw the pegs, and thus allow the wet canvas to come flapping down about your ears, causing no end of discomfort and confusion. A tent may be securely pitched, even on the sands of the desert, by laying a waggon wheel flat on the ground, fixing the pole over the hole through which

MODE OF SECURING TENT-POLE AND ROPES IN LOOSE GROUND.

the axle passes on the head of a plug driven far enough into it to pre-vent the pole from passing through; secure your ropes to bags of sand buried in the manner before described, and no ordinary weather will blow down a tent thus arranged.

This description of tent is in general use throughout Central Asia, and is preferred by all the nomad tribes inhabiting that vast region. Light, portable, strong, and commodious, the "Karaoy," The Turkoman or black tent, is perhaps the best that could be devised Tent. for the use of wandering tribes enduring the vicissitudes of heat, cold, and storm. The framework is composed of light tough well-seasoned sticks arranged as shown in diagram A (see next page), and lashed at their points of intersection and contact by thongs or cord. B shows the tent pitched and covered with the felt commonly sold in all Eastern bazaars. The height from eaves to ground is usually about six feet, and the diameter is in the proportion shown by the illustration. Two strong lines or ropes are used to give stability to

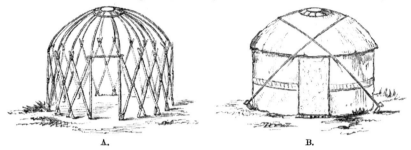

A.   B.

the structure, and are secured to ordinary tent pegs. No tent pole is made use of, and the smoke given off by the fire usually lighted in the centre of the floor passes up through the orifice at the crown of the dome.

SELECTION OF GROUND FOR TENT PITCHING.

In selecting a spot on which to pitch your tent much will depend on the period of time you are likely to spend in the locality. The nature of the country through which you are passing will also influence the choice. When travelling onwards, and merely resting for one or two days at a time, a dry, raised, level spot, in the vicinity of wood, grass, and water, may safely be selected. Do not, however, encamp too *close to water* in countries where venomous snakes are met with, as they generally congregate where it is to be found most abundantly. It is not wise, either in Australia or Texas, to encamp beneath certain trees, as the branches at times drop suddenly off and fall with a crash to the earth. In India or Africa we have always sought the friendly shade afforded by some wide-spreading forest giant, as we have never known an instance of "branch-fall" in those countries. In clearing the ground of stray stones, tufts of weeds, &c., look well about for holes in the earth, and, when any are discovered, stamp suitable stones or pieces of broken wood well into them. Reptiles of many kinds are not unfrequently found in these underground burrows. We have found a large square of tarpauling invaluable as a tent carpet. When about to set up your tent for a long sojourn additional precautions are requisite. See well to the lay of the land as regards the flood level of the nearest river or lake ; the stray bits of driftwood and weeds washed into the branches of waterside trees will be a useful guide. See that no flags or rushes are growing near your proposed resting-place, as they are certain indications of a boggy soil, unfit for camping on. Choose, if possible, an elevated position, well above the influence of the miasma and night mists of the low grounds and rivers. We have often seen a slightly raised hill standing bare and island-like in a sea of humid vapour. See also that no dry grass is allowed to stand in the vicinity of the camp, lest it should be ignited by a stray spark or a hostile native.

A stout carriage umbrella, with a curtain of 3ft. 6in. buttoned or laced round the edge, would make a very convenient shelter for one person. If the curtains were gored so as to give more room below, two persons might sleep under it comfortably. An extra joint would be required to give sufficient length to the handle. A similar frame made proportionately strong, and with a curtain or wall of six or seven feet, might be found useful in cases where the height of the bell-tent or marquee is objectionable. Malacca cane would be a good material for such a frame.

Umbrella tent.

Stout canvas buckets answer very well to carry water in for almost any distance, and if stiffly roped will retain their form when filled, and collapse when empty ; if a little flour is rubbed into the canvas, it will render them somewhat tighter, and will not materially affect the taste of the water, but we prefer to take the stoutest canvas. Keep it perfectly clean, and trust solely to the natural construction of the threads when wet, to thicken up and tighten the material so as to render it for all practical purposes nearly waterproof. India-rubber bags, especially if carried into a hot sun, and not quite full, always make the water taste badly. When we served on the North Australian expedition, we always had a canvas bucket hanging in the door-way of the hut, just shaded and exposed to a free current of air. The partial evaporation through its sides kept the water deliciously cool.

Canvas buckets.

CANVAS BUCKETS.

If the traveller can afford such a luxury, and is likely to have plenty of tent room, and a sufficient train of well ordered and obedient servitors, we should advise him by all means to take plenty of mosquito net, gauze or tarlatan, green or blue. This should be suspended around his bed so as to form an inner tent, pervious in every direction to the cooling breeze, but having no

Mosquito nets.

aperture whatever by which a single insect could gain admission. If the nights are cool, so that he can bear plenty of bedclothing, the face alone may be protected by the net; but if they are likely to be warm, so that he lies with the thinnest possible coverlet, and frequently throws off even that, it must be large enough to inclose the whole bed, and be tucked in or otherwise secured all round; in all cases it must be capacious enough to give him plenty of room to sleep, without touching its sides, for if an unfortunate limb should by any accident touch the gauze, the infinitesimal tormenters would assuredly not neglect to improve their opportunity.

The net may be simply a large square, a portion of the centre may be gathered in the hand, and a cord knotted to it by which to suspend it from above, while the edges are brought round and tucked under the mattrass. If two points of suspension, one near the head and the other at the feet, can be obtained, with a light rod or ridge pole between them, the material may be used to more advantage, and it may, if convenient, be distended by a hoop, square or oblong frame of light canes or twigs, lashed together with a bit of cord.

We had one when in India, cut, and stitched into a cone, or crinoline shape, suspended from above, and tucked around under our bedding, and found it exceedingly serviceable—of course, when the real hard work comes on, all these luxuries go to the rear; but it is wise to enjoy them when you can.

In many parts of the world, we might say in all, where flies are found, dense swarms are sure to seek the shelter of the traveller's tent, causing endless annoyance to the inmates by settling on, or buzzing about, their faces, hands, or the work they may be doing—drinking up every drop of moisture from the angles of the eyes, inserting their probosces into any cut or open sore on the hands for the same purpose.

Odds and Ends.

There are a number of articles which, although not strictly found under either of the heads we have before dealt with, will be found of very considerable service in wild countries. A "*ditty bag*" should be made of some tough strong material, such as fustian, velveteen, or canvas. It should contain a large assortment of needles, especially of the larger and stouter sizes; half-a-dozen medium-sized sail needles, three roping needles, two packing needles, half-a-dozen duck needles, sailmaker's thimble and palm, sail hook, rubber and piercer; roping, sail, and duck twine. (Learn how to use the palm from a sailor on the voyage.)

The ditty bag.

A dozen skeins of black thread, ditto brown; one dozen skeins of carpet thread, brown; six slips of black silk, six white ditto; six hanks of worsted, the colour of the socks and shirts. All these skeins should be wound off on cards, as endless entanglements follow the attempts made by the inexperienced to use thread from the uncut skein. We advise winding on cards, because cut thread is not so well adapted, from the number of short lengths in it, for splicing broken fishing-rod joints, &c. A few reels of strong white sewing cotton, a little bag of buttons of *all sorts*, a lump of beeswax, six pieces of strong tape, a packet of pins, a bodkin, and a pair of strong large bowed scissors. A little ingenuity will enable the traveller to perform an endless number of repairs with the contents of a bag thus furnished. The more needles you can take the better, as they are at all times eagerly sought after by natives.

A small pair of common bellows can be bought for about a shilling. Do not fail to provide at least one of these useful contrivances. It is perfectly surprising to note the number of valuable ends they serve to answer. Stubborn fires, formed of saturated brushwood and damp moss, are, by their aid, forced into a blaze, when ordinary coaxing and fanning only produce suffocating smoke and grievous loss of temper. The fine sand and almost impalpable dust which, in certain regions, finds its way in some strange manner into your very gun locks is best removed by the aid of your bellows. Laid flat on the knees a capital board for writing, drawing, or the examination of minute objects, is formed. When cutting out leather thongs with the knife, or fashioning raw hide covers for various things, they may be used for a cutting-board. When snatching a hasty meal at the camp fire at early dawn, before starting on the march or hunt, we do not sit on the damp earth, but usually place our bellows on the ground and sit on that. Most of our small job work, such as fileing, soldering, fish-hook tying, and tackle making, is performed on the ever-ready surface of the bellows; and when small objects of iron or steel require heating, either to be worked, tempered, or case-hardened, a hole in the ground, a little charcoal and dry cow dung, by the aid of the bellows, enables us to extemporise a small forge. Larger forges will be described when smith's work comes under consideration.

Bellows.

Do not on any account be induced to encumber yourself with what is called a "canteen," a contrivance which is in our opinion much like the many-bladed knife we have before referred to. A few months since, when the expedition in search of Dr. Livingstone was about being sent to Lake Nyassa, two contrivances

Canteens.

for cooking were brought to the Royal Geographical Society for approval, and of these, were they to be used by a man who would take proper care of them, we could only speak in terms of unqualified praise. But they were declined simply because it would be impossible to teach a native cook how to use them, and it would be easier to give him a fathom of calico to buy half-a-dozen earthen pots, and to buy more when these were broken. It is, no doubt, vastly ingenious to make a pepper dredge fit into a tea-canister so contrived as to go into the teapot, which in turn should go into the saucepan; only unfortunately the class of persons to whom utensils of this kind are usually entrusted in wild countries are slow to appreciate mechanical puzzles, and usually throw the whole lot into the first bag they can get, when the spout of the teapot gets knocked off, and the pepper becomes hopelessly amalgamated with the tea, to the decided detriment of both. Rather provide yourself with a few plain useful

Table necessaries.

articles for table use. In giving a list of these, we will suppose that one person has to be catered for : a well-made strong quart tin pot, with both hook and handle, is better for making tea in than the conventional teapot; it is also useful for an endless number of other cooking purposes. A knife, fork, and spoon, should be packed in a leather *hold-all*, like that filled with small tools, which we have already represented on page 37. The knife and fork should have the steel of their blades carried through the handles in a flat plate, to which the cheeks of the haft are riveted; those made with tangs are always shifting round or coming out from being washed in hot water or placed in the sun; the spoon should be of iron, tablespoon size. We have, on more than one occasion, had to melt lead in ours for bullet making, which could not be done if it had been made of any other metal. Get two small wooden bowls, such as bankers keep gold in, take them to a tin-plate worker's, and have narrow copper hoops *let into* the wood just below the edges, this prevents splitting. Nothing is equal to these for drinking hot tea out of; metal cups of all sorts scald the lips if the tea is moderately heated, and earthenware vessels are too liable to be broken. A half-pint horn cup will be found very useful, and is next to indestructible. We have one which we extemporised from an old Russian powder horn we picked up in the Redan. This has travelled many thousands of miles with us since its conversion, and is just as capable of containing good

Pots and pans.

liquor as ever. A frying-pan is worth anything to a campaigner; fish, flesh, or fowl are all equally well cooked in it. Coffee can be roasted, pancakes made, stews prepared, and a whole host of useful offices performed. Do not forget your frying-pan. It is a good plan to have a "parasol joint" as it is called, made in the handle close to the pan, this will, by bending the handle a little admit of its being folded across the pan, and thus more. easily stowed away. It may be well to observe, perhaps, that the "parasol joint" is formed by cutting two slots in the divided ends, fitting in a short plate, running two rivet-pins through them, and then sliding a ferrule over the joint, which keeps it stiff. Take two dinner plates of enamelled iron; these are best kept with the hold-all, in a flat leather pouch with partitions. A leather loop, or D, at each corner enables you to attach the plate pouch to either your own or the pack saddle. Have a tin canister made; it should be of cylindrical form, and should have a division in the middle, a cover at each end, and be capable of holding 2oz. of ground pepper and 4oz. of fine salt.

The most useful kind of cooking pot we know is the common cast-iron crock of Meg Merrilies pattern. Use it with moderate care, and it will last a lifetime. A wooden cover is easily fitted to it in event of the iron pot lid being lost; and should by any misfortune one of the legs get broken off, and a hole made in the bottom of the crock, a good thick pledget of cotton cloth drawn through it will stop the leak, and remain unconsumed during the boiling process. Bread, meat, birds, fish, vegetables, or fruit can be baked readily in or under the crock, as will be seen when bush cookery is treated on. It is also useful for a variety of other purposes, as will be seen as the work proceeds— take a crock therefore, by all means. An all-blaze pan is another most useful utensil. It is thus made : Have two deep copper bowls made of a size sufficient to hold about three pints each. These should each have two lugs or handles riveted to them, and a flange raised round the edges should admit of the mouths of the two bowls fitting closely into each other like a box and its cover. The insides must be tinned in the usual manner, and the handles so adjusted that when the two bowls are joined they are opposite to each other and near enough together to be lashed fast with twine. The formula for preparing food by the use of these pans will be given under the head " Camp Cookery."

A leather bucket, such as firemen use, will also be found of great service for an endless number of purposes. We invariably carried, when

Leather buckets. in Central India, a miniature bucket composed of leather, attached to the pack-saddle; it held a quart, and by the use of twenty yards of ordinary sea-fishing line, which was always coiled away in it, we have often been enabled to obtain water from deep native wells when other travellers not so provided have been destitute of this priceless treasure. In some portions of the East, the wells are very deep and narrow, so that, without some such contrivance as the above, it is impossible to reach their contents. When collecting specimens of natural history in Turkey, we were on one occasion in much distress for want of water, and after a long search discovered one of these tantalising excavations. There lay the longed-for fluid, glittering like silver down below, but far too deep to reach without some shift or expedient, so we betook ourselves to the sea beach which was not far off, to see what good fortune would cast in our way. An empty univalve shell, not unlike that of an overgrown whelk, soon rewarded our search! we fixed a stick across its mouth, dragged forth the trailing vines and creepers from a neighbouring thicket, knotted them together, fastened on our shell in company with a goodly stone to give it weight, lowered away briskly, drew up cautiously, and thus treated the parched palate and dry tongue to that which they so much needed. Again and again did our good sea shell travel up and down, until, having satisfied the cravings of nature, we resumed our journey; and to the sea shell and vine are we indebted for the design of our miniature bucket and cord which now invariably accompany us on our wanderings. We advise, therefore, that one *common* fire bucket of *leather*, and one to contain a quart be provided. Guttapercha buckets are very neat and pleasant to look at, but the sun of the tropics has an awkward habit of causing their bottoms to fall out; we, on one occasion, saw six rendered perfectly unserviceable in one day from this cause. Get a good stock of leather straps and buckles of different sizes from a saddler, these are useful for a variety of purposes. It will be well also to provide a goodly number of padlocks, of two sizes; let the largest be "iron rim," say three inches in diameter, and the smaller size of brass, such as are sold at *one shilling* each—sixpenny ones are useless; keep one key for each size attached to your watch-guard, and carefully lock away all the rest. A butcher's steel, of good quality, is well worth taking. A selection of fishing gear, too, is of the greatest value; of this subject we shall treat at length under the head "Fishing." A corkscrew should be provided, the best pattern we know is that in which the worm fits by a screw into the hollow tube. When Other odds and ends. required for use, the tube is passed through a flat ring in the end of the shank, and forms a cross handle; screws of this kind are conveniently carried in the waistcoat pocket. Tin boxes of wax vesta matches are exceedingly useful; take a good number of these; get also a tube and cap "strike-a-light" with a chain, striker, bit of agate, and spare cotton cord slow match.

MEDICINE AND DRESSINGS FOR WOUNDS.

On one of Nelson's boat expeditions up a tropical river, the medical chest was unanimously voted a piece of lumber; but, before the arduous voyage had been completed, the only regret   Medical was that sufficient medicine had not been taken. An   stores. unmanly fear of fever, or other sickness, would probably aid in bringing it on, but reasonable precaution ought never to be neglected.

Many countries have an unenviable notoriety for the prevalence of peculiar and local diseases : some are perfect hotbeds of fever in various forms; and wounds from gunshot, sharp-edged tools or weapons, bruised and fractured bones, are casualties that may befall the traveller in any country, and therefore a few articles for the dressing of these should certainly find a place among his stores.

In case of wounds, cleanliness and repeated washing in cold or tepid water as may be best for the particular case, is the most generally successful treatment, and for this purpose plenty of sponge or flannel should be provided; the sponges should be of moderate size, perfectly clean from grit or bits of shell, close grained, and soft. Flannel is a good substitute; but if a piece of either is used for washing an unhealthy wound on one person, it should never again be used upon another, as it might convey infection, and, indeed, it would be much safer to destroy it utterly.

Lint is, of course, well known to be one of the best coverings for an injured part, and a good supply ought to be taken, as, although the underclothing, or sometimes even the bedding, of the party, may supply bandages, very few travellers going on a serious exploration in a wild country would think of taking linen shirts, while sheets would be equally scarce among their bedding.

Cambric or *lawn* handkerchiefs would be good substitutes.

Calico, for bandages or rollers, would be more likely to be at hand in some parts of Africa, such as the Portuguese stations on the Zambesi, or at Great Fish Bay, where a wrapper of six feet square forms the dress of the native who borders on the possessions of the white man ; while in Kafirland or Damaraland, where soft untanned leather is the prevailing dress, it would be less certain to form any considerable part of the equipment.

Adhesive plaisters.—Of these perhaps common diachylon is the best ;

F

but in a hot country, like Africa, we have seen a roll of it soften during the journey, and, in exemplification of its name, sticking so fast together that it looked more like a field marshal's baton than anything else, and the spreading out of it again into a sheet was a hopeless task. It would therefore be better to carry the diachylon in a gallipot, and spread it when required on thin cotton. Isinglass and court plaister are useful for keeping clean small hurts—the fluid obtained by boiling tendons in water spread on silk makes a very useful plaister—though, in trifling cases, we are in favour of letting the coagulated blood form the natural covering while the cut heals up beneath it.

Cerate, which may, on occasion, be made of beeswax and pure fat or oil, in such proportions as the temperature of the country may require, is very useful, spread on lint or linen, as a cooling ointment for sores that require to be kept soft.

Spongio pilene, a material composed of small fragments of sponge, attached to a backing of india-rubber sheeting, will be found valuable in applying hot or cold water to injured surfaces. It can be cut with readiness to any required size or shape.

During the Zambesi expedition, Dr. Kirk was provided with a good store of gutta-percha tissue, in sheets, for the purpose of covering poultices, moist applications, &c. The tissue should be cut much larger than the lint or other material, the moisture of which is to be confined. Other sheets were of various thicknesses, from that of writing paper up to cardboard or millboard, so as to give support, if necessary, as well as covering. He also carried gutta-percha splints for the leg or arm, properly fitted, for inside or outside, right or left; and cases might occur in which the possession of one of these, at the moment it was required, would be invaluable. They packed very easily one within the other, occupying little more room than so many flat sheets.

Millboard in strips, 18in. long and 6in. wide, for leg splints, or 15in. by 4in. for the arm, would stow easily, and by moistening would be easily moulded on the limb of a healthy person to the shape required. A few bandages, 3in. wide and 6ft. or 8ft. long, should be kept rolled up in the medicine chest; but if a store of calico is carried, there is no need to tear off more till they are wanted. (N.B. They should *always* be torn—not cut.) It is not to be expected that every traveller should carry or be able to use the formidable array of deadly looking keen-edged knives, of saws, and other instruments of torture; nevertheless, it would be prudent that a small selection should be taken, and we extract

from a clever little work, " First Help in Accidents," the following
list :—

Lint,	Silk,	Scissors,	Lancet,
Compressors,	Small sponge,	Tenaculum,	Dressing forceps,
Rollers,	Tourniquet,	Suture needles.	Scalpel.
Sticking plaister,			

Small pocket cases containing all the requisite instruments are to
be obtained of any surgical instrument maker. Among medicines
quinine stands pre-eminent as an effectual, though perhaps not
always an infallible, febrifuge ; it is, however, so excellent a tonic
that its moderate and occasional use may safely be recommended, and
we do not know of a better remedy in case of fever. It is best
dissolved in wine, if the traveller should be fortunate enough to be able
to carry any. It may be given in rum or other spirit, which is more
portable and likely to be at hand, and which is also useful for preserving
insects ; but if a man wants any peace while passing through most wild
countries, or is doubtful of his own powers of self-denial, we should
recommend him to convert all his wine into a strong solution
of quinine before starting, and to do the same with half his rum
or spirit of wine, having the rest strongly methylated for use,
either in a spirit lamp or preservation of specimens. Let both these
be labelled with a death's head and cross bones, such as is used
by chemists in the Cape and other countries, where many of the
native population cannot read, or do not understand, English, to
signify poison.

A proportion of wine or spirit may, of course, be reserved for prudent
and moderate use, as a glass, or even a bottle judiciously given may go
very far to gain the good will of a native chief, or to induce either the
proper servants or occasional assistants of the traveller to work heartily
in helping him out of some difficulty. We have generally found a good
pannikin of hot coffee accepted readily enough by the people after a
long night journey ; but there are times when a fire could not be made,
and a drop of spirit, imparting a momentary sensation of warmth, even
if it produces no other good effect, has, at least, that of showing that
their employer cares for them, and does what he can to cheer them
after their labour.

In most tropical rivers there are extensive deltas, intersected with
netlike labyrinths of shallow impracticable channels, alternated with
shoals, which the advanced guard of mangroves is just reclaiming from
the sea, and where tangled, dank, and unwholesome wildernesses and
swamps are formed, there fever, in its most deadly forms, is sure to
prevail.

The delta of the Zambesi is also a place of danger from this cause; and persons of a full stout habit are said, and we believe with some reason, to be more liable to fever than others of a spare and meagre build; indeed, the Portuguese, when they see a well-framed athletic man, in prime condition, enter the river, prophetically mark him as one of the first victims.   We have ourselves suffered severely and continuously from this malady, which generally came on with a cold shivering or ague, and was succeeded by the fever, accompanied by intense perspiration, prostration of strength, nausea and inability to eat, or even to retain the necessary medicine or cooling drink; an immoderately exaggerated idea of the length of time; short uneasy slumbers, disturbed by incongruous dreams—generally of some difficulty previously experienced—or total want of sleep, total failure of memory, and in bad cases delirium while awake.

When the "Pearl" first entered the Zambesi Dr. Kirk ordered that a glass of spirit with quinine in it should be served to the men every morning; and we would frequently, as the large doses administered were intensely bitter, make up the quinine into pills with chocolate or cocoa paste, or sometimes place the quinine powder dry on the tongue, and then swallow a copious draught of water to wash it down.

We give, first, Dr. Livingstone's remedy for fever : but, useful and effective as it really is, we cannot say, from experience, that it is infallible; and the fatality among the gentlemen of the mission proves that we do not, as yet, possess a remedy for the fever that will supply the place of a sufficient and generous diet, total cessation of exposure to the malaria, and removal to a more elevated and healthy country, even though it be but a few hours' journey from the infected district. The doctor's recipe is as follows :—

"Linyante, 12th of September, 1855.

"A pill composed of three or four grains of resin of jalap, three or four of calomel, and an equal number of quinine; a drop or two of tincture of cardamoms to dissolve the resin to form the bolus.

"I have had a great many cases in hand, and never met with a single case of failure; it ought not to purge; the quantity of resin must be regulated to produce only a gentle movement, which, when felt, is accompanied by perspiration and a sound sleep. A check to this perspiration has, in my own experience, given rise to vomiting large quantities of pure blood."

In another letter :—

"We make a pill of equal parts of resin of jalap, calomel, rhubarb, and quinine; say for a powerful man eight grains of resin of jalap, eight grains of calomel, four or six grains of rhubarb, and four or six grains of quinine; make the whole into pills with tincture of cardamoms. This relieves the very worst cases in a few hours.

" We then give quinine till the system is affected with cinchonism,* the calomel is removed at once from the system, and, curiously enough, decreasing doses serve. In some of us half a grain of the mass produces as much effect as twenty-four grains did at first."

Thus writes Stanley, on fever and ague in Africa :—

" The remedy applied for three mornings in succession after the attack, was such as my experience in Arkansas had taught me was the most powerful corrective, viz : a quantum of fifteen grains of quinine taken in three doses of five grains each every other hour from dawn to meridian; the first dose to be taken immediately after the first effect of the purging medicine taken at bed time the night previous. I may add that this treatment was perfectly successful in my case, and in all others which occurred in my camp."

A friend in Capetown, who had travelled in the Brazils, gave us the following recipe, used, we believe, by an Italian doctor; there he tells us it was efficacious, but we have had no opportunity of putting it to the test :—

" To one bottle of water add 36grs. of sulphate of quinine, 2 teaspoonfuls of Epsom salts, 34 drops of sulphuric acid, and 40 drops of ether; this mixture is called antiperiodic water; a wine-glassful three times a day as soon as the first symptoms are perceived, and continued for three or four days after recovery. If delirious, an injection of 1 tablespoonful of vinegar to 10 of this water."

Warburg's fever drops are well spoken of. Very large doses of quinine are given in India and Africa, sixteen or twenty grains at a time; and we have frequently taken in powder as much as would lie upon a shilling.

Sometimes violent exertion, producing perspiration and exhaustion, if practised in time, may avert an attack. We have heard of a doctor visiting a man when the shivering fit was about to come on, who locked the door, mixed two glasses of stiff hot grog, put on the gloves, and engaged his patient in a boxing match, which, at least, for that time averted the fever.

We do not give our unqualified recommendation of this treatment; but we have often found that, during a period of severe and long

---

* Singing in the ears.

sustained labour, we have remained in health, but that an attack of fever has accompanied the reaction induced by an intermission of the work.

Simple aperients should be taken; we have used Cockle's antibilious pills, salts, senna, or jalap; and their opposites in case of diarrhœa. With a little opium and a bit of carpenter's chalk, we have been able to give almost marvellous relief to a poor coloured woman in excruciating agony.

Take a good supply of Collis Browne's *Chlorodyne*. Opium both in gum and tincture. A few drops of the latter, placed within the eyelids of those suffering from snow blindness, often prove of the greatest advantage; chloroform must be used with caution; still, in cases of great suffering, it is worth while to try it. We have known one exceedingly severe case of illness in which messengers had to be sent to every white man within 240 miles for medicines, and letters were written on the chance that some passing vessel might take them to a port whence by some other agency a supply of drugs might be forwarded.

Emetics, which are commonly sold in doses, white and grey, and of different degrees of strength.

Sudorifics—among which we have used Dover's powders as a convenient form.

Eyewashes.—Weak solutions, sulphate of zinc and diacetate of lead, or weak brandy and water, may be used.

It may be needful to carry a small quantity of blistering plaister— or rather the materials of which to make it—soft wash-leather, ointment of Spanish fly, &c., or mustard.

Tincture of arnica, used in the proportion of one part tincture to eight parts water, is a valuable application for strains or contusions.

Glycerine, or cold cream, may be used as cooling applications to irritated surfaces.

Effervescing powders.—The blue paper contains carbonate of soda, 30grs.; the white, tartaric acid, 25grs. 1lb. of carbonate of soda, and 13½oz. of tartaric acid, make 256 powders of each sort; or 1½oz. of carbonate of soda, and 3oz. of tartarised soda, packed in blue, and 7drs. of tartaric acid, in white, will make twelve sets.

All salts must be kept in bottles closely stoppered, and only put in paper for immediate use.

Antiscorbutics.—Almost any vegetable; plenty of sugar; fresh fruit; dried tamarinds; good lime juice, vinegar, or citric acid; raw potatoes, with the strong earthy taste as fresh as possible; the pulp of the cream of tartar tree or Baobab in Africa, or of the Gouty-stem (*Adansonia*

Gregorii) in Australia. Dr. Kane, in his Arctic voyages, found fresh raw meat a remedy.

It will be well for the traveller to limit his equipment to a few simple and really useful medicines, of which a sufficient supply for the maladies to be expected in the country he is bound for should be taken. A complicated assortment would serve only to confuse him, and it is better even to trust solely to nature than to tamper unskilfully with dangerous remedies.

Poisoning, whether from accident or otherwise, should always be provided for, and it will be well to be supplied with a few antidotes. Some poisons are best ejected by vomiting— Poisons and draughts of salt or mustard and warm water, half a wine- antidotes. glassful of ipecacuanha wine, or a glassful of warm water with twenty or thirty grains of sulphate of zinc. Antimonial preparations, as tartar emetic, are too depressing, and not controllable. .

In others, the action on the stomach may be diminished by mucilaginous or oily drinks, as milk, barley water, white of egg, and salad oil.

For *poisonous acids* use no emetics ; alkaline remedies are proper. Soda or potash in water, given plentifully ; carbonate of magnesia, Dinneford's solution, common whitening, or chalk in water, followed by some mucilaginous fluid, as milk or barley water.

Against *alkalies*, as potash, soda, &c., acids must be used— diluted vinegar, citric or tartaric acid, lemon juice or sour beer ; soothing drinks as before, after the poison has been neutralised.

For *metallic poisons* an emetic may generally be tried.

For *arsenic*, avoid emetics. Take a mixture of milk and lime water, or soda water in equal quantities. Light magnesia diffused in water may be taken. Common animal charcoal may be tried.

For *corrosive sublimate* give white of egg and plenty of milk if eggs are not at hand, use flour mixed with water.

Vegetable irritants.—Give an early emetic and demulcent drinks.

Narcotic poisons—Opium.—Give an emetic ; pour cold water on the head and neck and shoulders ; place mustard poultices on the calves of the legs or feet ; give hot strong coffee and free air ; keep the patient moving till drowsiness passes off.

Prussic acid in small doses.—Give ammonia or strong coffee ; pour cold water on head and chest, rubbing dry with warm towels, and give free air ; in large doses no treatment will avail.

Strychnine.—In Australia, South Africa, and some other countries strychnine is extensively used ; and a correspondent thus writes in the *Field* concerning it :—" It sometimes happens that dogs are poisoned, accidentally or otherwise, by nux-vomica, or its alkaloid. It may not, therefore, be useless to inform the reader what treatment should be adopted in such a case. The poison acts very rapidly, tetanus comes on, and the dog soon dies, exhausted by the violence of the fits. If the poison have only been just taken, and no fits have occurred, the best remedy is tannin, in the form of pounded galls, or the areca-nut powder so much used in kennels. But if the dog be already seized with teta-nus, the only remedy is the permanganate of potash. I have found, in several experiments on animals, that, when once the tetanic spasm has set in, permanganate of potash is the only remedy giving any chance of recovery; if administered in time it is most successful. Condy's fluid, now so much used in the stable and kennel, is the most convenient form for its administration. A wineglassful of Condy's fluid, slightly diluted, may be given. During the treatment the dog must be kept quiet, and touched as little as possible. This treatment, which has never yet been suggested (to my knowledge), I beg to offer to those readers who may be in need of it; but I cannot speak of its effects on the human subject."

Alcohol in excess.—Evacuation of the stomach, followed by hot coffee, external stimulants and friction.

Suffocation by gases, &c.—Removal to pure air, cold water on face and chest, artificial inducement of respiration, friction of surface, followed by hot coffee or brandy and water.

Animal poisons—stings of insects, snake-bites, &c.—If a sting remains in the wounds, extract it, and apply a strong wash of ammonia in spirit or water, or, in its absence, warm oil; if faintness follows, some stimulant, as brandy and water, may be given freely for snake-bites; in addition to this cauterise the wound with nitric acid or a white-hot iron.

The trappers of America place great dependance on strong whisky; if great exertion can be maintained, so as to produce excessive fatigue and perspiration, the system may throw off the poison.

In the Cape colony an antidote for snake-bites is sold under the name of Croft's Tincture of Life. This was analysed, when we were in Grahamstown, by the faculty, and the ingredients they found were pronounced good; but there were others which the maker would not reveal. We have seen several testimonials as to its efficacy. The medical men, however, arranged a case somewhat larger than a fifty-likeness *carte-de-visite* album, containing lancet, ligature, cupping-glass, a bottle of ammonia, lint, and a piece of lunar caustic; but it was much too large to be carried about by any traveller in expectation of being bitten by a snake. We therefore took a small tin vesta match box, put a lancet, small bottle of ammonia, lunar caustic, in a stoppered bottle, lint, and ligature in it, and kept it in the waggon. We are happy to say we never had to put it to the test, for we were never bitten by a serpent. Sometimes a little judicious humouring of the patient does as much good as medicine.

In the Bushman country around Lake Ngami, where the entrails of the Ngwa or poisonous grub are used to give such fatal effect to the insignificant-looking arrows, a small plant with a yellow star-like flower, called the *Kala-haetlwe,* is used as an antidote. Fat is also rubbed into the wound and also given internally till the effect of the poison is neutralised.

The snake-stone of India, if it has any good qualities, seems to owe them entirely to its absorbent properties, and these would be more efficiently performed by scarification and the cupping glass.

Ipecacuanha, applied as a poultice, has been by some considered a most valuable antidote to snake-bites. This antidote is equally effective in the stings of scorpions and other venomous reptiles.

The fiction of the cup of rhinoceros horn, which caused all poisonous drink to effervesce and bubble over, is so firmly believed, that we have known a Cape trader offer to drink any poison we could give him out of such a cup; but we declined the experiment.

A preparation of the guaco plant is highly esteemed on the Spanish main as an antidote against bites of snakes of all kinds.

Acetic acid rubbed on the wound caused by the bite of scorpions or centipedes is very efficacious. In the absence of this, chewed tobacco is often made use of; but the natives are of opinion that the scorpion inflicting the wound crushed between two stones and laid on the injured part is a certain remedy, and, from what we have been enabled to learn from them on the subject, there seems to be some foundation for the belief.

The imaginary ailments of natives are neither few nor far between; but it is not at all times wise to disregard them. We have known our followers come, night after night, Ailments of with small sicknesses, when we had but - a few doses natives. of fever mixture left, and, by some chance or other, a little currie powder. Now, had we sent away a man with his " little sickness," he would have been really ill next morning. We therefore looked as wise as possible, felt his pulse, looked at his tongue, read a paragraph or two, and sent him to boil some water and bring it to us; we then carefully measured out a spoonful of currie powder, mixed it, saw him drink it off, and sent him to make himself as warm as he could till next morning.

Horse Medicines and Farrier's Stores.

If an expedition is about to be undertaken where the services of many horses or mules are required, a list of medicine stores should be furnished for them, which may be approximately as follows, the quantities being arranged for twenty animals for six months :—

Raw linseed oil, 4 galls.	Tincture of opium, 4lb.	Calomel, 1oz.
Olive oil, 2 galls.	Spirits of ammonia, 4lb.	Nitrate of silver, ½oz.
Spirits of nitre, ether, 4lb.	Spirits of turpentine, 1	Sulphate of copper, 2lb.
Nitrate of potash, 6lb.	gall.	Alum, 2lb.
Barbadoes aloes, 2lb.	Cantharides, in powder,	Sugar of lead, 1lb.
Potassio tartrate of anti-	1lb.	Sulphate of iron, 2lb.
mony, 1lb.	Lard, 6lb.	Powdered gentian, 4lb.
Camphor, 1lb.	Linseed meal, 8lb.	Prepared chalk, 6lb.
Ginger, in powder, 6lb.	Compound tincture of	Stockholm tar, 10lb.
Palm oil, 6lb.	myrrh and aloes, 2lb.	Tow, 6lb.

Old flannel and sheeting for bandages, two or three sponges, a packet of pins, a hank of fine twine, six pieces of coarse tape, a pestle and mortar, set of scales and weights, palate knife, graduated measure, a quire of whitey-brown paper, two pairs of scissors, one straight and the other curved; a drenching-horn, phleam, lancet, (horse size), glyster syringe (quart size), and blood can. Hoof picker, searcher, drawing-knife, buffer, pincers, shoeing hammer, hoof rasp, and set of hobbles. The use of these matters will be treated on under the head of "Veterinary Surgery."

Lamps, Lights, and Lanterns.

About the most simple and effective lamp we have ever seen is that used by the Portuguese at Tette, in their illuminations; it
Lamps. consists of a shallow pan of clay, as large as the palm of the hand, slightly baked, or, perhaps, merely sun-dried—to contain the oil—a spoonful of salt is tied up in a piece of rag, the ends being left just long enough for a wick, and this cheap and simple arrangement serves all the purposes of out-door illumination. Sticks about three feet high, with their upper ends cleft into three parts, which are kept open by the insertion of a wedge, are planted in lines along the streets, and the lamps supported on these, or ranged along the porticoes or fences of the various houses, burn brightly and steadily for many hours, defying even a tolerably stiff breeze to blow them out. The oil used is that of the ground nut, which, beside being cheap and plentiful, is so pure that it may be used

for almost any purpose, scarcely an article of food in Tette being prepared without it; in fact, the nut itself, which may be eaten plain, roasted, treated as a "confect" in various ways, or infused as a substitute for coffee, contains so much essential oil that it will burn for more than a minute with as bright a flame as a good candle; when arranged one over the other on a stick or wire they give a good permanent light.

It is often necessary, however, for the traveller to supply himself with light when the grease at his command is neither liquid enough to rise through the fibres of a wick, nor hard enough to be moulded into a candle. In this case, the wick should be allowed to rest on and overhang a little the sides of the vessel used as a lamp —a cup of earthenware, a common tin cap box, or even a bit of tin or sheet iron bent up will answer well enough; the flame soon heats the side sufficiently to melt a portion of the fat, and a constant supply is thus kept up as the wick requires it.

MAKE-SHIFT LAMPS.

Almost anything will serve as a wick—a bit of old rag, or the flax-like fibres of the various plants used as cordage by the natives; strips of bark beaten to separate the fibres, or even small twigs may be used; rushes with enough of the outer covering removed to expose the pith, while on one side a strip of bark is left sufficiently strong to support it, are also worth looking to in case of need; but it is best to be provided with a sufficiency of cotton, which is cheap, easily carried, and useful for many other purposes. If possible, a good supply of the best sperm candles, or others of material not likely to be affected by changes of climate, should be carried. On the Australian expedition, we used Price's vegetable wax candles; and some of these—after having twice crossed the line, gone round Australia and part of the Indian archipelago, and made the circuit of the globe—are now in Kew Museum in as good condition as when they were issued from the factory.

The common bull's-eye or police lamp is very useful if only required by one person for a specific purpose, such as reading off a sextant after observation of a star, but it does not diffuse light enough for general purposes. In fact, if wood is plentiful, a roaring fire will give greater facility for reading, writing, or such other occupations as are likely to employ a traveller's evening than anything else. If you want warmth, let your fire be on the ground and sit round it ; if you want light to work by, make it on a slight elevation, say from eighteen inches to two feet high. If you want wood, and your native attendants, when called on, make excuses, or Jem tells Sambo and Sambo tells the old woman to fetch wood for the master, do not put yourself to the trouble of scolding them, but take the wood off their fire and put it on your own, and let them settle whose duty it is to bring more. *Experto crede.*

A horn lantern is good " to keep the light from going out ;" but then, perhaps, the operator may desire that the light should not be so literally " kept in ;" and it is said that a piece of rag dipped in salt and water, and wrapped round a candle, will answer the purpose of preserving it from extinction in windy weather without lessening its illuminating powers. This, however, requires continuous attention, in order that it may be cut down as the candle burns low. The Esquimaux lamp is a piece of soft stone with a slight groove along the front edge ; in this is laid a wick of moss or other material, and the heat imparted to the stone being quite sufficient to melt the fat laid on it, it is fed with very little trouble. One who has made a turnip lantern in his youth will seldom be at a loss to extemporise a shelter for his bit of candle. A calabash gourd, with perforations to allow the passage of the light, covered or not with oiled calico or paper ; a worn out pannikin or preserved meat tin ; the body of a quart bottle, the more transparent the better ; or, what is best of all, one of the oblong tins in which fancy biscuits are generally sold, will answer admirably ; the polished surface of the latter serving also as a powerful reflector. We had one of these slung from the roof of the waggon, the bowl of a broken ladle was secured in the bottom of it, and with a bit of cotton wick and a few pieces of hard fat, a light steady enough to work by was secured for the evening; the common forecastle lamp used on board our merchant-men is a useful form, and the shadowless railway lamp we found very serviceable, as long as the glass could be preserved.

We have constructed a very powerful reflecting lamp from a large sheet of tin, nearly two feet in height, curved round so as to form half a cylinder, six or eight inches in diameter ; about eight inches from its base, we made a shelf to sustain the oil lamp, and a socket to contain the candle if we should be fortunate enough to have one, and behind this we arranged a couple of sixpenny trade looking-glasses at an angle of 90° with each other, and by the light thus thrown forward we were able to write or sketch with facility during many hours of the weary night. (See p. 75)

A lamp commonly used in India is a tumbler half full of water with oil on the top, and a wick wrapped round a stone or bit of lead, with its end projecting above the oil; but it has this disadvantage, that rats may upset the glass while drinking the oil, carry off the burning wick, and so expose the house to great danger. A float may easily be made of bottle wire and three bits of cork, in which half an inch of wick is enough to last all night.

It is often desirable to make candles, and for this purpose the hard fat and tallow of any animal that may be killed should be preserved, that is, if it can be spared from the no less important purpose of greasing the axles; or beeswax, if it can be Candles. obtained, may be used either in combination with it or separately. If you wish to make dip candles, take a sufficient number of strands twice the length you require, twist them slightly and double them, and let the parts twist together; pass a small rod through the "bights" of as many of these wicks as you find convenient, say half a dozen; take a bucket-ful of hot water, throw the fat or wax in, and it will soon melt and float upon the surface; let the wicks absorb as much as they will, straighten and let them harden; then, holding the rod by the end left for that purpose, dip them quickly to their full length, withdraw and allow them to cool, and repeat the operation till your candles attain the desired size. If you have fat enough you may have half a dozen or more sets of wicks, and can keep on dipping in rotation, thus allowing each plenty of time to cool before its turn comes round again. If you aspire to mould candles, nothing is better for your purpose than a piece off the end of a gun-barrel—and very few African hunters make a journey without shortening some lengthy weapon by eight or ten inches. In this case, pass a small stick an inch or two in length through the bight of the wick, bring the end out through the " mould " and make it fast to another, or pass it through a gun wad or section of a cork, so as to stretch it fairly and evenly in the centre, and stop the lower end; then pour in the tallow or wax, and, when cool, warm the mould slightly and the candle will draw out. In some countries wood may be found sufficiently resinous to be used as candles, but a supply of sticks cut to a convenient size must be prepared and a rest of some sort contrived so that they may be easily placed in it or withdrawn when nearly burnt out; the angle they ought to make with the horizon varies with the quality of the wood; if very combustible they may be set nearly upright, if less so they must be more nearly horizontal.

All candles, however, waste rapidly unless screened from the wind; if the traveller can carry a spring burner, this inconvenience is in a great measure obviated; but often this is impossible, and he must make the best shelter he can with a bit of bent tin, a joint of bamboo, or whatever material may be at hand. If the candles have to be packed in bags where stowage is of importance, and cases must be thrown away, it is best to cut them in two, as the risk of breakage is much reduced by the diminution of their length; in cutting them the knife should be warmed slightly, as it divides them without chipping off fragments. In lighting the lower half, if you have wax vestas, and stick one of them in alongside the wick that has been cut, you avoid the necessity of cutting down the wax to expose the end, and so may save three quarters of an inch of candle.

We have seen the Malays, in the Island of Timor, take a soft porous stick, or the pith of a peculiar rush, and then wrap round

Torches. it a coating of beeswax, to serve as a torch or candle. The natives of the shores of British Columbia and Vancouver Island use a fish known as the Eulachon, or North-West Capelin, as a source of light. The leaf of the cocoa-nut palm possesses strong illuminating power. The pine knot and birch bark of North America and Canada are extensively used for giving light in deer-hunting, fish-spearing, and on other occasions. The bog deal of Ireland is also used. The Damaras, who have a custom of obtaining their fire only from that kept burning at the hut of their chief, carry with them dry flakes of "Kraal mist" or cattle droppings, ignited and held between the forks of a cleft stick; and the Indian matchlock men carry fire in the same way. The mussalchees or torch-bearers of Central India, who commonly accompany troops during night marches, use long sausage-shaped rolls of cotton cloth; the ends of these they from time to time moisten with oil poured from a vessel carried for the purpose. The hill guides usually employ large splinters cut from the Deodar cedar. In Mexico, the brilliant fire-flies are sometimes caught and used for giving a temporary light; the direction of a letter, or the points of a compass, may be read by them.

The sparks from a flint and steel, a bit of quartz, sulphuret of iron or agate, and a pocket knife, will give light enough to read the compass, or to form a night signal.

There are many very nice arrangements for the purpose of light giving and cooking, which may be obtained from any military outfitter;

but their chief defect is, that they will only answer their purpose under tolerably convenient circumstances, and become useless when the real hard work of travel begins.

Travellers, both on sea and land, often require to cook a small allowance of coffee or tea when, from severity of weather, scarcity of fuel, or the impossibility of halting long enough, it is impossible to kindle a fire in any of the ordinary methods, and frequently when, from the pitching of a small vessel or the jolting of a waggon, it would be dangerous to use a spirit lamp, an Etna, or an uncovered fire of any kind. Under these circumstances we should think the principle of internal heat, as applied in Samovar. the Russian *samovar* or tea urn, might be successfully adopted. This, with various modifications in outward form, may be described as a small furnace for burning wood or charcoal in that part which serves as the base of the urn, with a funnel or stove pipe, wide at the bottom, but tapering rather sharply upward, leading straight

up through the water, and having at top a telescope joint, by which the funnel can be lengthened and the draught increased when requisite.

Our own idea is to have an upright cylinder of copper tinned inside, and from about a couple of inches above the lower part of this an internal cone, like an inverted funnel, exactly fitting the cylinder at its lower edge, and tapering up to a small aperture at top. A double floor would be let into the cylinder about an inch from its base, so that it might be set upon a plank without danger from the fire. The cover would have a central hole for the funnel or smoke pipe to rise through; a small lip spout would serve to pour off the

SAMOVAR.

water, and ring handles, with chains long enough to obviate all danger, would serve to suspend it from the waggon roof, or from the beams of a small vessel, while others on either side would help to stay and steady it. A broad cap or roof of copper hooked on to links of the chains an inch or two above the ends of the smoke pipe would prevent any possible risk from fire reaching any woodwork from which the samovar might be suspended.

CHAPTER II.

BOATS, RAFTS, AND MAKE-SHIFT FLOATS.

In traversing wild countries, or examining their coasts, lakes, or rivers, boats of some kind are indispensably necessary. The traveller may, perhaps, be fortunate enough to possess one or more sound and sea-worthy. More frequently, however, it will be his lot to have either some sun-dried leaky craft, crank canoe, or unstable raft, on which to entrust his life and equipment, when his ingenuity and powers of resource must be exercised in order to successfully contend with the various shortcomings and failings he will certainly discover. If a boat be very leaky, and is so rotten as not to be reparable by ordinary means, cover the whole bottom with canvas to above the water line, and paint it, she will then be perfectly tight, and also very much strengthened and protected against external injury. Should the canvas even be left unpainted, it will be found to reduce the leakage very considerably.

Stopping leaky boats. Turn the boat bottom upwards, take a breadth of canvas for each side, or, if one breadth be not wide enough, increase it as much as necessary by stitching on another. Lay one edge of this against the keel, just below the garboard streak; fasten it with copper tacks, or if with iron pump tacks, dip them previously in thick white paint, varnish or boiled oil, to prevent them rusting the canvas. Wet the canvas, and stretch it tightly, tacking it on the stem and stern post, so as just to cover the insertion of the planking : then stretch the upper edge to the mould-ing, just below the wash-streak, and nail it on there. It might, if necessary, be carried right up to the gunwale; but, in this case, it must be defended by a moulding or ribbon of plank from chafing against the side of a vessel or pier. In the case of a gig, or long sharp boat, the canvas will give or stretch sufficiently to adapt it to the required form; but in one with a short bluff bow and stern, it must be fitted either by neatly folding the parts necessary to be reduced, or by cutting and stitching it to the shape required.

The Norwegians make use of a very ingenious contrivance for stopping leaks in ships' bottoms. It is thus made :—First a large square canvas bag is prepared, and in each corner is placed a small block of wood or some other convenient substance in order that four holding necks may be formed. The bag is then closed by sewing up every side; a rope is knotted Norwegian Leak Stoppers. firmly to each corner neck as shown in the annexed illustration. A slit is cut in one face or side of the bag, and as much sawdust as it will conveniently hold is then thrust in.

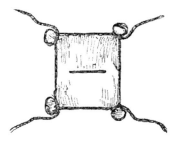

When charged, the bag, slit inwards, is drawn under the ship's bottom at the spot the leak is supposed to be by aid of the ropes, which are then secured. The influx of water carries the sawdust rapidly into the leak, which soon becomes filled with it, and as the dust swells from moisture, so the leak de-creases, and not unfrequently completely stops. A leaking ship was not long since navigated from Plymouth to Norway after one of these bags had been made use of—to render her comparatively sea-worthy.

If a small boat crowded with passengers has to leave a wreck in a heavy sea, she may be preserved from sinking or overturning

BOATS WITH BREAKERS OR SMALL CASKS AS OUTRIGGERS.

by lashing across the gunwales a couple of oars (cut, if there is time for it, to a suitable length), and fastening to them, outside the boat, four small water-casks or breakers; these would somewhat impede her progress, but buoyancy and safety, and not swift sailing, are the chief requisites in leaving a wreck. Breakers lashed under the thwarts, or bow and stern sheets, are sometimes used; Make-shift outrigger.

but, though they impart buoyancy to a water logged boat, they take up room, and do not give the additional stability which is afforded when they are placed outside.

The cumbrous mass of spars, water casks, and other stores, which want of stowage under hatches often forces small vessels to carry upon deck, may easily be converted into a perfectly safe and buoyant raft, ready for instant use on an emergency, by the following arrangement of the lashings. The spars, amongst which will generally be found one fit to make a topmast, another for a lower yard, and, perhaps, one or two more of equal length, are usually laid fore and aft on either side the main hatch; the water-casks, perhaps half a dozen on each side, are lashed to them; while the space between is occupied by the long boat, and, perhaps, one or two casks of meat or other stores, the whole being secured to the deck; but all this floating power is neither connected in itself, nor easily detachable from the sinking vessel. It would not be much more difficult, when securing the row of casks and spars on either side the hatch, to connect all these by short spars lashed across the ends, as shown in the engraving, with a couple more crossing near the bow and stern of the long boat, and bearing others passing fore and aft beneath her bilge, to which she might be secured by lashings perfectly independent of the gripes by which she is fastened to the deck. Indeed, the chief requisite is to keep all the lashings that connect the parts perfectly clear of those which hold the raft to the vessel, so that, in case of need, it could at once be cut clear, and allowed to float bodily off from the sinking hull.

Rafts.

We have stated the absolutely necessary points as simply as possible; but many improvements might easily be suggested, such as the four casks, at the ends, being pointed like conical buoys, so as to offer less resistance to progress through the water; or that in two or more of the aftermost casks a quantity of salt or preserved meat, biscuit, or groceries should be kept in store for any emergency.

The smaller spars, of which there are generally plenty on board, might be crossed upon this framework, so as to make a platform, and a studding-sail spread over would prevent small things dropping through, or help to support the crew or passengers.

The boat, however leaky or battered, would always be a place of security and comparative comfort for the ladies or children, as the power of floatation would be in the spars and casks. We believe the Spaniards always endeavour to secure a boat on any raft they are obliged to make, using her, no matter how much she may be stove or broken, as a place of rest or refuge for the helpless or the weary.

It would be superfluous to give directions for the rigging of a mast or steering apparatus. Seamen in emergencies would improvise these according to the means at hand. Two or three small spars set up as a triangle would carry sail, where, perhaps, a mast could not be stepped; and the oars of the long boat, assisted by the trimming of such sail as could be set, would be most likely the readiest appliances for steering. Sometimes the "bridge" of a paddle steamer is made like a caisson, and shipped in grooves, so as to float off should the vessel sink. Small craft trading in the Indian islands, which carry a quantity of bamboo as small spars, are thus provided with a natural substitute for life-buoys, and a material for constructing rafts, or rendering boats, though leaky as so many sieves, perfectly unsinkable. Rafts of the large hollow stems of the bamboo are frequently used by fishermen in the Indian archipelago.

THE SPARS AND WATER-CASKS CARRIED ON DECK WITH THE LONG BOAT, USED AS A RAFT.

It may, perhaps, be of little use to suggest that before a vessel leaves port attention should be given to the means of saving life should she go down at sea. The possible foundering of a seaworthy vessel is about the last thing a sailor thinks of; he trusts more to his presence of mind and ready application of the means at hand. Nevertheless, provision against danger would cast no imputation on their manliness. The law compels a proportionate number of boats to the complement of crew or passengers. Some owners provide cork belts Life-belts. or jackets for the men, with mattrasses, pillows, or cushions of cork, for the berths or sofas in the cabin; and it would be well if every passenger making a sea voyage were to provide himself, and each of those depending on him, with a life-belt, either of cork or of inflatable material, and likewise see that these were not stowed away in chests below the hatches, but kept at hand in the berths so as to be available when wanted : and also that their use was perfectly understood by those for whom they were provided.

We have seen a waistcoat with inflatable lining carried far into the interior by one of the boldest elephant hunters in South Africa; and it is stated that, after the sinking of the ill-fated steamer " Arctic," some of the passengers provided with belts floated on the surface of the Atlantic for some days, giving, with a kind of desperate humour, the names of different hotels to the piece of floating wreck at which they had "put up last night," or intended to for the next.

A very efficient form of life-belt can be easily made by stringing together, end to end, a goodly number of old bottle corks, and then arranging the rows of "cork beads" in tubes formed lengthways in the body of a double canvas waistcoat, just as the whalebones are arranged in a pair of stays.

It is a pity that none of the waterproof materials at present in use are comfortable in ordinary wear, so that some common article of dress, as a necktie, a belt, or sash, might be made so as to be inflatable when an accident occurs.

Since writing the above we have been shewn an inflatable silk cravat, which can be worn in the usual way when not required as a float; when charged with air through a small mouthpiece and stop it takes the form of a large sausage, which, surrounding the neck and resting under the chin, serves to keep the head above water, and renders sinking next to impossible. These contrivances are to be obtained at the " Explorer's Room," Cornhill.

Of all that we know at present, we should say the most effective, simple, and secure from damage, is the ordinary cork jacket, of the pattern supplied by the Life-boat Institution ; it is sufficiently buoyant, does not impede the exertions of the wearer, and cannot be damaged by collision with rocks or other hard objects.

Perhaps the circular life-buoy now in common use is as good as any, but it requires some address and strength on the part of the swimmer to get it over his head to its proper place beneath his arms ; Life-buoys. it also lies low on the water when thrown overboard, and if at any distance is not easily seen by the swimmer or by the boat's crew who eventually go to his assistance.

In the navy a breaker or small cask is used, with a staff six or eight feet long passed through it, the lower end projects say three feet, and is loaded with lead ; the upper will stand from four to six feet above the water, carrying a small red flag by day, or a port-fire by night.

The slings of the buoy are brought up to the taffrail and looped over a small pin, which is withdrawn by pulling the trigger of a gun lock, and a quick match led to this at night serves at the same time to ignite the port-fire, so that the swimmer, the boat's crew, and the commander of the vessel, have a conspicuous object to make for and are so prevented from losing each other.

In larger vessels, we believe, two breakers are used, connected by saddle-shaped iron bars; these enable one, or perhaps two men to sit, with their shoulders considerably above the surface; while beckets of rope all round would enable a greater number, say the crew of a capsized boat, to support themselves with a fair chance of safety. The size, however, of a life-buoy must always be limited. It is mostly required to save one person who has fallen overboard; and, though perhaps sufficient to support more, it should never be so large as to be dangerous or inconvenient when taken into the boat put out in a heavy and dangerous gale to the rescue.

Several fathoms of small line should be and often are attached to the buoy, so that if is let go in time the swimmer may catch it, and be saved without the necessity of lowering a boat. We have seen a "life line" of coir or cocoa-nut fibre, which is very buoyant, success-fully veered away to an overladen and endangered boat at a considerable distance, when a hempen rope, which sinks by its own weight, would have been of no service.

THE CALABASH FLOAT, MAKORO OR MAKARA, OF CENTRAL AFRICA.

Nearly similar in principle to this last-named life-buoy is the calabash float, described by Dr. Barth as being used by the natives of Central Africa; it is simply a bar or plank of light wood, so laced to the bottom of two large calabashes, Calabash float.
that a man sitting on the bar, as he would upon a saddle, will sink

about waist deep, and may use his hands to paddle himself across the stream.

Our illustration shows how any buoyant article in the traveller's possession might be used in this manner. The boxes shown on pp. 8 and 9 are designed expressly for such emergencies. Small water

REED BOAT.

" vatjies," barrels, or tin cans, wooden boxes, even though somewhat leaky, wrapped in canvas or two or three thicknesses of calico, which need not be cut, would become sufficiently tight for a short voyage.

Reed boat. To make a reed boat, take reeds of any length you wish, a foot or two more than half the length of your boat, lay them lengthwise on level ground, with their small ends toward the ends of your intended boat, and their butts overlapping each other by a foot or two ; take cord or other material for lashing, and interweave it with the reeds till the part in the centre resembles a flat cheese-mat, then bend it round the hoop which you intend for the midship frame. Insert smaller frames toward each end, and finally gather up the ends of the reeds into a point, cover this with some waterproof· material, oiled calico or canvas, &c., or canvas simply pasted with flour and water, and you will have a boat buoyant and more or less durable according to the strength of the material.

About 1844 we made such a boat in Cape Town, using what are there called Spanish reeds, which run between 10ft. and 15ft. in length, three quarters or an inch in their greatest diameter, tolerably strong and very buoyant ; these were lashed on wooden barrel hoops with a ight deal keel and gunwale, and covered with two thicknesses of oiled calico. There was no leakage, and our little skiff was so light that with the assistance of a friend we easily carried her to and from the house in which she was built. We often ventured beyond the shipping anchored in Table Bay, our guns being secured by lanyards to the boat in case of accident.

On parts of the Nile where reeds abound, the natives make them up into bundles of perhaps 8in. or 10in. in diameter at the larger end, and tapering almost to nothing at the smaller; three or four of these are fastened side by side, Reed raft. their points are made to curve up a little, and they form a portable and convenient vessel for crossing the river or conveying small cargoes of grain or other produce to market. The stoutest part of the fan-shaped leaf of the doum palm is used as a paddle. The float is not a heavy load for one man, when carried overland, and one supported by a forked stick, or three or four with their larger ends set on the ground and the smaller resting against each other, form very good sun-shades, or huts to protect the inmates against more inclement weather.

REED RAFT AS USED ON THE NILE.

We have seen very useful and commodious rafts made by cutting very large quantities of marsh reeds, fastening them up roughly in bundles, laying these side by side, and then arranging another layer of bundles across the lower tier. A few vines, or twisted reed bands, serve to keep the bundles in their places, whilst a thick layer of loose reeds on the top makes a level surface for the traveller and his baggage to rest on. As the lower reeds become saturated with water others can be cut, and added to the top. Long river voyages, floating with the stream, have been accomplished on rafts of this description. Bamboo canes, when they can be obtained in sufficient number, form excellent rafts. They are also extremely valuable as outriggers, and outrigger beams for canoes, adding greatly to their stability.

In other parts, where reeds are not so common, floats of wood are used as an assistance to swimmers.

When swimming our horses over many of the wide and rapid rivers of Central India, the natives who were employed in guiding the animals, first swam some across with them without any artificial assistance, and then returned for others with billets of a peculiarly light wood held between their left arms and sides, under the shoulders; with these appliances, they floated with extraordinary buoyancy, and made rapid progress across the stream.

Floats.

The inflated skins or intestines of animals, hollow gourds, earthen pots, bladders, or bundles of bark, may be used as aids in crossing rivers where canoes or rafts cannot be constructed.

On some of the great Indian rivers, large dish-shaped boats are used for the conveyance of horses or cattle. A boat of this description is very quickly made by first forming a basket-shaped framework of bamboo, here and there interwoven; this is securely lashed together with strips of raw hide, twisted cane, or common cord. When completed, the basket, or frame, is turned upside down, on the ground, pegged fast with hooked pegs cut from the branches of the nearest tree, and then covered with raw bullock hides, which are sewn fast to the frame and to each other, grease being well rubbed into the seams. When complete, the boat is not unlike a common tea-saucer—measures between fourteen and fifteen feet in diameter, and is about two feet eight inches deep; made to these dimensions, the hide boat will safely carry from three to four tons of cargo. There is no possibility of upsetting it. When horses or bullocks have to be conveyed in contrivances of this kind, it will be necessary to lay branches of trees and a good layer of reeds, or sedge grass, on the bottoms, in order to prevent the animals from thrusting their hoofs through the hides. The water-draught of hide boats is surprisingly light, from five to eight inches being sufficient to float one with a full load on board. Long-handled shovel-shaped paddles are used to propel them with and a store of raw hide, and some tallow, and an eyed awl, or large needle, for patching, enables the boat voyager to execute with expedition all the repairs his leather craft may need. All hide-covered boats, or floats, should be occasionally placed bottom upwards, on shore, to dry, in order to render the skins more durable.

Cattle boat.

The coracle, so much used by Welsh fishermen, is made much after the same fashion. A smooth level piece of turf being chosen, the frame-sticks, just such as coopers use for making into hoops, are bent and interwoven until the requisite form of the frame has been arrived at, the bottom being upwards. The edge, which afterwards becomes the gunwale, is formed by making a border of hazel-wand basket-work, the ends of the frame-sticks are trimmed off even with this, and a covering of Russia duck, or light canvas, is neatly sewn over all. The coracle is then paid over with tar, or some other water-proofing material; one thwart, or seat, is secured from each end to the framework, holes are made in this for a leather strap to pass through, which enables the fisherman to carry his coracle on his back. A single-bladed paddle, like a baker's *oven pile*, is used to paddle with. Some considerable practice is needed to enable a new hand to conduct, or, as it is called, *drive* a coracle—not a little caution is required in both getting in or out. It is best, if possible, to depart from some shallow sand-pit or gravel bed, where the coracle may be shoved off into deeper water, after the tyro has taken his seat, and established the proper balance. In landing, it will be well to observe the same caution until practice and experience give the confidence and dexterity which they alone can confer. There is a peculiar stroke of the paddle much used in coracle driving, to which the canoe man seldom has recourse. This is gained by turning the left arm round the handle of the paddle, until the hand is a short distance above the blade, and the shaft rest against the shoulder. The paddle blade is then worked in a figure-of-eight direction.

Coracle.

The size of skin or canvas-covered boats will usually be determined by the available amount of skin or covering material. Any waggon ox requires 8ft. of room to work in, and his skin would give a square of leather of very little over 6ft.; the African buffalo would be about the same, the eland somewhat larger, the black or brindled gnoo, the koodoo, and some of the larger antelopes, rather less. Suppose you have two ox skins; cut them straight across where the neck is at its widest, and let the natives or waggon-drivers stitch them together with strong sinews or thongs of hide, using a round awl or piercer, to make a round hole that will close again, and not a sharp-edged one that will cut the hide and so leave holes that will afterwards become leaks. The sheet should be kept damp, not wet, by spreading ox-dung or damp earth upon it till the frame is ready. Suppose it now to be 12ft. long and 6ft. wide; you may make your boat of from 3ft. to 4ft. in width, and 10ft. in length and 2ft. deep. If you care to have definite stem and stern posts, it is very likely that poles may be found with branches projecting at the required angle, but practically it is best to let them curve more or less gradually into the line of the keel, and for this purpose to choose

Skin boat.

two long straight poles ; bend their thick ends round a tree to rather
more than the requisite curve, as they will always straighten again ;
then, having chosen a flat piece of stiff ground, make two holes 10ft.
apart, for the thick ends of your poles to rest in, bend down their thin
ends, let them overlap, the farther the better, and lash them together ;
then take another of about 8ft. (or a foot longer on each side than the
width of the skin), and having curved this, stick the ends into the
ground, about 3½ft. or 4ft. apart, and lash it where its centre passes under
the keel ; do the same with two others, 18in. on either side, and you
will have the three midship frames ; take two poles for each gunwale,
join them by overlapping their thin ends as before, lash them to these
central frames, so far from the keel that the edge of the skin will
just cover them, bend them till they come together at the bow and

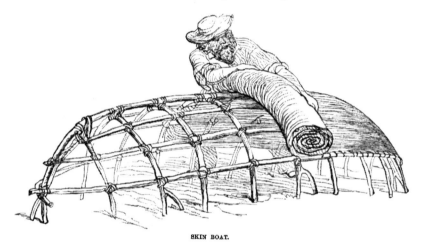

SKIN BOAT.

stern, let them cross each other by a few inches, lash them tightly, and
do not be in a hurry to cut their ends too closely ; the curve they take
will guide you in the insertion of the other frames. As you come
nearer to the bow and stern, forked branches of the proper angle may
be advantageously used, and along the sides, where the rowlocks come,
forks may be left on the extremities of the ribs to serve for them ;
a fork may also be lashed in at either end for steering or sculling.
Lay two or more ribbands or bilge pieces along each side ; fasten in
such boards or poles as you have for thwarts, and, when the whole is
firmly lashed together, spread over it the prepared hide and stitch it
all round to the pole that serves for gunwale, the hair, if you have not
already scraped it off, being inwards ; grease plentifully while it is still
wet, and then let it dry ; look carefully to the seaming ; give this as

much grease as it will absorb, or you can afford ; and when it is quite stiff, saw off the superflous timber ends, not too close ; turn it up, and it is ready for use : never let your boat lie in the water longer than is absolutely necessary, and turn it bottom upwards whenever you haul it ashore. The quagga hide is proverbially rigid ; and we should think that if taken off by merely making one slit along the belly, distending with dry sand and letting it harden in the sun, it would make a tolerably safe boat in smooth water for one person, without any other fitting.

RUSSIAN AND ESQUIMAUX SKIN BOATS.

We have heard of mules or transport animals being killed when water carriage became available ; their flesh jerked for future provision, and even their ribs pressed into service to do duty without even a change of name in the canoes for which their hides served as coverings.

In the United Service Museum is a very carefully-constructed model of a Russian cargo boat from the Aleutian Islands, Russian cargo Commander Pike, R.N., the donor, states that it carries boat. 3½ tons of fur sealskins. No metal is used in it, the wooden frame is pegged or lashed together, and covered with walrus hide. No dimensions are given ; but, as very nearly three feet are required for one oarsman, it is probable that the boat would be 25ft. long and 8ft. wide near the stern ; it will be noticed that there are but single thole pins, and therefore grummets of rope or iron must be fastened on the oars.

The other boat is the *oomiak*, or woman's canoe, of the Esquimaux. The frame is made of drift wood and bone, often in very small pieces, Esquimaux boats. but so tightly pegged and lashed together with hide thongs, that the compound seems fully as strong as a single piece; it is very neatly covered with sealskin.

The method of constructing the frames of both these varies but little from that we have just described, and we think will be made sufficiently plain by the drawings copied by permission from the models in the Museum.

The *kayak*, or man's canoe, is longer, sharper, and narrower, and is completely covered with sealskin, with the exception of a circular aperture in the centre, and from the edges of this a skin comes up so as to tie tightly round the waist of the daring walrus or seal hunter, so that not a drop of water can enter his little vessel; while even if by any accident she should capsize, a vigorous stroke of the double-bladed paddle will suffice to right her; the harpoons or other weapons cannot possibly be lost, for bladders are attached to the lines of those prepared for use; while the reserves are not cast adrift till they are wanted. Marvellously ingenious as these fur-clad boat-builders are, their frail craft are so difficult to handle that no ordinary explorer can, without long practice, hope to use them with much success. Still there are many points connected with their construction well worthy of imitation.

The small sledge in the background has a screen of skins suspended across it, in which a hole is made for the seal-hunter to fire through.

Canoes, hewn and dug from the solid tree trunk, are general and valuable; and there are few portions of the earth where forest Dug-out canoes. trees grow to the requisite size that dug-out boats of some kind are not in use. The natives of British Columbia construct very large and powerful boats from the trunks of the huge cedar trees found in that country. To the fortunate possessor of the axe, the adze, the gouge, and the mallet, the formation of a dug-out canoe is a matter of comparative ease; but to the Indian, unprovided with efficient tools, it is a task of no ordinary magnitude, still he undertakes it boldly, falling back on shifts and expedients to aid him in his toil. With such rude implements as he may chance to be possessed of, he fashions the exterior, flattens the surface of the log, and hews out the bow and stern; the fire, kept within due bounds by the assistance of clay, is brought to bear on the mass of timber, and as the wood ashes form, and the wood becomes charred, a sharpened stone or thick sea-shell is used to remove the mass and expose a fresh surface. By dint of labour, patience, care, and perseverance, the shell of the boat is at length formed, but lacking the curves and contour needed to render it stable and seaworthy. Indian ingenuity again steps in to meet the difficulty. The boat is filled to the brim with water, a huge fire is lighted, and a number of stones heated to redness. These are one by one dropped into the unfinished canoe, until the water is raised almost to the boiling point; then when the wood is under the full and softening influences of the heated water and steam, transverse bars of wood are driven in one after the other, until the requisite breadth of beam and bilge are gained. The water is then removed and the canoe allowed to dry with the bars in it, when the shape thus given remains as long as the boat lasts. The removal of the bars and a little polishing up renders the canoe fit for sea. It is not uncommon for craft of this description, manned by crews amounting sometimes to as many as thirty, to brave the turbulent and formidable seas of the Pacific Ocean, in pursuit of the sea-otter, fish, &c.

We have seen many canoes of this description on the large rivers of Central India, Australia, and on the Zambesi. The aborigines of Australia are also in the habit of using bark canoes of the most primitive form of construction. A sheet of bark of suitable size is stripped from the nearest tree, the ends are guarded by little walls of clay, and with a rude stick for a paddle, and a lump of moistened clay for a fireplace, Corry, armed with his unerring spear, starts on a fish-hunting expedition on the pond or river.

During the years 1863 and 1864, while enjoying the hospitality of our late friend Charles John Andersson, the chief, as he may be called, of the persevering explorers of South-West Africa, we Models of devoted considerable attention to the construction of platform boat. models of boats for the purposes of discovery and river navigation, and of substitutes for them. The first essential in the case before us was that of portability of the boat or of the materials to make it; the second, facility of construction when it reached the water, equal facility of separation into its original parts at any interruption of the river course, and also of reconstruction after it had been carried to a point where navigation could be resumed. Another, and not less important condition, was, that the materials should be such as were obtainable either in Damaraland, or, at farthest, from some of the vessels that occasionally called at its bays or harbours from Cape Town. The conversion of the usual waggon gear into a float will be presently treated on; and we will now describe the model we constructed for our

DOUBLE BOAT OF IRON OR COPPER CONVERTIBLE INTO A SINGLE BOAT WHEN NEEDED.

boat, suggesting to explorers that when they find themselves under the necessity of building, they will save much time, trouble, and anxiety as to the result of their labour, by proceeding nearly in the same way.

In the first place, we had decided on the use of sheet metal, plain or galvanised iron in sheets of 6ft. by 2ft., or copper of 4ft. by 2ft., with screwed bolts and nuts in either case of exactly the same metal as the sheets, so that any galvanic action should be impossible. Next, the framework must be of wood; and as to form, it was absolutely necessary that the boat should have beam and buoyancy enough to launch, without fear of submersion through any rapid that had water enough to bear her clear of rocks, and was not steep enough to be considered as a waterfall. We purposed to put the materials together on the spot; and, therefore, their weight only, and not the dimensions of the boat, were taken into consideration with regard to waggon carriage.

For the mere purpose of passing from the head of the river navigation to the sea, and thus proving that such navigation was possible, nothing more than a single boat would be required. But for observing, mapping, sketching, or otherwise improving to some useful result the various opportunities of the journey, sufficient room must be provided for the voyager to work comfortably on deck instead of sitting cramped up in the stern-sheets, and we, therefore, decided on making ours capable of being used as a double boat when the breadth of the river permitted it.

The advantage of being able to use each part when separate, as an independent boat, so that the sharers in the voyage might trace separate branches of the river, had to be balanced against the disadvantage of having to take each of these singly through rapids, which their dimensions might not insure their passing in safety, and also against the fact that if the "double" is formed of perfect boats, they cannot attain great speed either in sailing or rowing, from the fact that the volume of water admitted between the stems, which may be, for example, 8ft. apart, must be compressed as it passes the midship section, to 4ft. or 5ft., according to the breadth of beam of the boats, and will again have to expand as it passes the gradually increasing space between their "run," or after section. And the loss of power thus expended in "heaping up water," although imperceptible at a low speed, would become enormous if a higher rate were attempted. Therefore we made our model so that when not required as a double, she should become one single yawl or whale boat of 30ft. in length, and 6ft. beam, with 2½ft. internal depth in midships, rising to nearly 4ft. at either end to enable her to shoot a tolerably strong rapid without shipping water; the two sections were therefore each made like half a whale boat, the outer sides having their proper curve and the inner being perfectly flat, so that when used doubly the water might pass without resistance between them, and when singly they might be clamped together as one boat by screwed bolts through the keel, stem, stern posts, and the inner gunwales.

Our first care was to seek out a block of soft, fair grained wood, 30in. long and 3in. wide, and to shape this truly to the form required for one half section of our boat. We next provided a sufficiency of planking, ribands, &c., also on a scale of 1in. to the foot, and then cut out from the thinnest tin case linings, forty pieces of 6in. by 2in., to represent our sheets of iron.

The dimensions of our boat had been previously so arranged that in the midship section the depth of nearly 2ft. on the flat side should leave rather more than 4ft. of the iron available to form the curve on the outer, necessary to give a half beam of 3ft.

In building our model we adopted slightly different plans with each of the two sections. In that intended for the starboard side we laid along the flat or inner side of our block or wooden mould a batten, $\frac{1}{4}$in. square (representing one of 3in.) and 24in. long (each inch being understood to represent 1ft.); to this we fitted the stem and stern post, each 6in. in length, both exactly alike, curving and raking forward and aft like those of a whale boat, so as to have an actual height, before the keel was added, of $3\frac{3}{4}$in. We then laid along the top of the flat side the inner gunwale 1in. deep, but as this would be an impediment to the rowers when the sections were clamped together to form a single boat, we cut out a piece (marked A, p. 106) $\frac{3}{4}$in. deep and 18in. long, so as to be removable at pleasure, the remaining quarter then forming the stringer on which the thwarts would afterwards be laid, the bottom of the three-quarter piece (A) having checks cut in it to allow it to fit over them. We then took the piece of tin representing the midship sheet, and drawing a line across it, $1\frac{1}{2}$in. from its edge, bent it over the keelson, bolting the short end to the thwart stringer, and bringing the longer one of $4\frac{1}{2}$in. round the curve to the outer gunwale; nine sheets were required aft and nine forward of this, and the only difference in laying them was that, as we proceeded forward, the edge of each sheet overlapped by nearly $\frac{1}{4}$in. the one behind it, while in working aft, the edge of each had to be inserted beneath that which lay before it. When the curves of the stem and stern were reached, the sheets had to be cut to the required form instead of being bent, and were bolted in their proper places. The outer gunwale, $\frac{1}{8}$in. thick and $\frac{3}{4}$in. deep, was now laid on and bolted to the metal sheets; another batten, ½in. wide, was laid from stem to stern along the bilge, and the keel, ¼in. thick and deep, was fitted in its proper place and bolted through the metal to the keelson.

Our half boat was now sufficiently firm to be taken off the mould. A short stringer of 18in. was laid internally upon the floor, and another the whole length along the inside on which to lay the outer end of the thwarts; and timbers, ¼in. thick, were bolted in with their heads projecting 1in. above the gunwale, so as to receive cross-beams of ½in. in thickness and 15in. long, by which the sections were kept apart when used as a double boat. We consider it better to secure the beams by cross-lashings than by bolts, which, if the boats worked much in troubled water, would probably rend the parts they served to connect. Along the gunwales, at short intervals, we intended to use lighter cross-

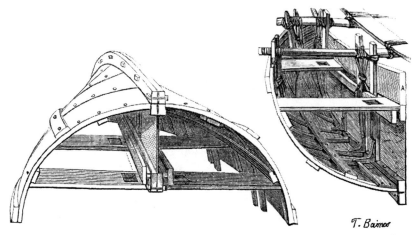

T. Baines

THE SECTIONS CLAMPED TOGETHER AS A SINGLE BOAT, OR USED WITH CONNECTING BEAMS AS A DOUBLE.

beams, probably of bamboo, that is if it were procurable; but having carried out our model sufficiently to establish the general efficiency of our principle, we did not think it needful to spend time in completing every little detail, and this called forth the free but friendly criticism of Mr. Charles Bell, the Surveyor-General of the Cape colony, whose valuable and practical advice we take the liberty of giving (see p. 101).

The only difference of plan adopted in building the other or port section was that we built the whole of the inner or flat side of plank ¼in. thick, by which we were enabled to cut 1½in. off each sheet, and this method in building a full-sized boat would have enabled us to use copper sheets of 2ft. by 4ft. instead of iron of 2ft. by 6ft.

In building a full-sized boat on this model, our plan would be to make the flat side all of ¾in. plank, with the stem, stern post, and keelson all fast in their proper positions, and the keel left slightly apart, so as to allow the sheets of metal, whether iron or copper, to be inserted between it and the keelson. Then, laying the whole flat on its side, we would cross cut with a fine tenon saw our wooden model into eight pieces of equal length, and, carefully enlarging the section of each length, would make as many temporary frames, and set them upon the flat side, cutting checks in them to let in the stringers, which when bent down to the flat at either end would very effectually give the form of the boat. We would then fit the ribs, keeping them as light as possible with due regard to strength, cutting them, if requisite, out of wood selected with the proper natural curve; or, preferably, using flexible wood, such as ash, in pieces 2in. broad, and ½in. in thickness, and placing them not quite 2ft. apart, so that the overlapping edges of the sheets might coincide with the ribs, and the bolts might pass through them and also through the inner stringers, and the outer ribands and gunwales at all their points of intersection. The ends of seven of these ribs, at nearly equal distances (as at sheets 2, 5, 8, 10, 13 and 16, on p. 94), we would leave standing six or eight inches above the gunwale, and about four inches from each we would set up another of equal height, so that the cross-beams might lie between them when required, and be secured by lashings passing down to the first stringer (p. 97), or so that when the two parts were connected as a single boat they might serve as rowlocks. Short struts from the foremost pair of these would give great additional stability to the masts.

Full-sized platform boat.

In laying the deck, we should by all means endeavour to avoid injuring the planks by boring needless holes in them, as they might on an emergency be required for building a smaller boat. We should, therefore, lash them with raw hide to the foremost and aftermost cross-beams, and then laying lighter beams across near two or more of the intermediate ones, fasten them down where requisite by strips of the same material (p. 97).

For connecting the two sections, so as to form a single boat, we should use screwed bolts ½in. thick, and 7in. long, passing at intervals of about 16in. through both keels, stems, stern posts, and inner gunwales, thus firmly clamping both the flat sides together. The two removable portions of the inner gunwale (marked A) previously mentioned would, in this case, be unshipped to allow the oars free play, as in illustration on page 97, and on page 94.

Copper is the only metal we should wish to use or recommend

to others, and all fastenings used with it must be of the same metal. We recommend in this case, screwed bolts and nuts, presuming that the boat would be built for a journey, the exigencies of which might oblige the traveller frequently to take her to pieces and rebuild her; but as our own means were at that time inconveniently limited, we made a calculation of the comparative cost of plain and galvanised iron and of wood.

The mode of setting the sails, spreading the awning, &c., will be sufficiently clear from the engraving (p. 94).

Our little model, when tried upon the flooded flats at Walvisch Bay sailed "like the wind," but had a tendency to bury the lee-bow, which was easily remedied by ballasting the weather quarter; an oar was the readiest and most convenient means of steering.

Estimate of material if the boat be built of copper, the flats or inner sides being of plank :—

<table>
<tr><td></td><td>£</td><td>s.</td><td>d.</td></tr>
<tr><td>40 sheets copper, 2ft. by 4ft., 1lb. to the foot at 1s. 6d. per lb. or 12s. each   ...   .</td><td>24</td><td>0</td><td>0</td></tr>
<tr><td>200 square-headed bolts, ¼in. thick (with nuts), ½in. grip for the skin and ribs,
180   ditto   ditto ½in. thick, 1¼in. grip for skin, ribs, and stringers,
180   ditto   ditto 3in. grip, for ribs, stringers, and timber heads,
90   ditto   ditto 6in. grip, for keel and keelson and for clamping the two sections together when used as a single boat,
Equal to 650 bolts, averaging perhaps 10d. each   ...   .</td><td>27</td><td>10</td><td>0</td></tr>
<tr><td>4lb. copper rivets, assorted sizes, for repairs   ...   .</td><td>0</td><td>12</td><td>0</td></tr>
<tr><td>6lb. copper nails, from 1in. to 3in.   ...   .</td><td>0</td><td>18</td><td>0</td></tr>
<tr><td>1lb. rooves, for clinching nails   ...   .</td><td>0</td><td>3</td><td>0</td></tr>
<tr><td>2 red deals, straight and clean, 21ft. long, 9in. by 3in., cut into six pieces of 3in. square, of which five will suffice, to make the two keels and keelsons; the remaining piece would cut four stringers ¾in. thick. (If these deals could be procured 24ft. long, four pieces would do this, and there would be no necessity for scarfing.)
3 deals of 21ft. each, cut into four ¾in. planks; and 1 deal, cut into one 1½in. and two ¾in. planks, would give fourteen ¾in. planks, of which nine would suffice for the two flat sides, two for the gunwales, 4½in. wide, and three with the spare piece mentioned above for the stringers and ribbands, while the 1½in. plank, by careful adaptation of the requisite curves, would cut for the four stems and stern posts,
Or equal to six deals, say   ...   .</td><td>4</td><td>0</td><td>0</td></tr>
<tr><td>2 galls. boiled linseed oil, in tin cans of 1 gall. each   ...   .</td><td>0</td><td>12</td><td>0</td></tr>
<tr><td>4 galls. raw linseed oil, in tin cans of 1 gall. each   ...   .</td><td>0</td><td>16</td><td>0</td></tr>
<tr><td>28lb. white lead, in iron kegs of 7lb. each   ...   .</td><td>0</td><td>14</td><td>0</td></tr>
<tr><td>14lb. red ditto   ditto   ditto   ...   .</td><td>0</td><td>7</td><td>0</td></tr>
</table>

(The cans and kegs will be useful as cooking or water vessels when emptied.)

	£	s.	d.
30lb. resin	0	10	0
6 paint-brushes and tools assorted	0	6	0
Tinsmith's small shears or snips	0	4	6
Engineer's hammer	0	4	6
6 punches, from $\frac{1}{8}$in. to $\frac{1}{2}$in.	0	9	0
2 screw-drivers, large and small	0	3	6
2 screw-wrenches	0	9	0
1 $\frac{1}{2}$in. auger	0	1	6
1 brace, and set of bits, including rymers, countersinks, and bits for metal	1	4	6
3lb. brass screws, assorted, up to 3in.	0	9	0
3 pieces unbleached calico, double width, for lug sails, awning, &c. ...			
12 copper or composition cringles, small sizes for sails and various purposes			
Manilla rope, 10 fathoms, 3in., for mooring			
Ditto 50 fathoms, 1$\frac{1}{2}$in.	2	0	0
Ditto 50 fathoms, 1in., for running gear, &c., ...			
If the boat be built of iron the same size—			
Forty sheets of plain iron, 2ft. by 6ft. at 4s. 6d.	9	0	0

All the bolts, screws, nails, and other fastenings, must be of plain iron, and none of them must be galvanised.

Galvanised iron would not be much cheaper than copper, and would be very intractable in working. We should not recommend it to a traveller who intends to build his own boats in the wilderness and expects to have to take them to pieces and rebuild them two or three times.

Tinned charcoal iron would be nearly as expensive as copper, and the fastenings would also have to be tinned.

Plain iron is the only metal on which any saving could be effected, even at the cost of additional labour. In this case, perhaps, three times the amount of paint should be taken.

A mixture of red and white lead, with half boiled and half raw linseed oil, should be used rather thickly for painting the inside of every joint, and all the bolts, screws, or nails, should be thrown into boiled oil, then taken out and allowed to drain and dry before they are used. The boat must be thoroughly well painted after completion, and the paint allowed to harden before she is put into the water.

If the boat is built of wood the same size—

Two deals and a half, as before, for keels, keelsons, stems, and stern posts.

Four deals, each to be cut into four $\frac{3}{4}$in. planks, for flat sides, gunwales, and stringers.

Five deals, each to be cut into six $\frac{1}{2}$in. planks, or equal to 230 running feet of plank, to stand, when cleaned, not less than $\frac{5}{8}$, and 630 feet not less than $\frac{3}{8}$.

5000 copper boat nails, 1$\frac{1}{4}$in., with rooves.

28lb. iron nails, assorted, from 1$\frac{1}{2}$in. to 3in.

2000 iron screws, from smallest size to 3in.

90 ½in, screw-bolts and nuts, 6in. grip.
200 ¼in. screw-bolts and nuts, 3in. grip.
  6 rods of ¼in. iron, to cut into lengths for bolts, as required.
Paint, oils, &c., as before.

If the traveller can afford to carry two or four good 12ft. ash oars and one of 14ft., by all means let him do so. Nothing is equal to them for pulling or steering, but let him carefully preserve his treasures, and not put them to any use that will twist or warp. If he engages natives as a permanent crew, they may be taught to pull very well; but if he hires temporary helps, let them bring their own paddles, and they will make the boat go well enough.

For the connecting beams, the masts, yards, &c., we should prefer bamboo, as being exceedingly strong in proportion to its weight. In the Indian islands we have seen oars made of bamboo poles, with a disk of wood about as large as a dinner plate lashed on the outer end, and the men pulled very well with them. If bamboo cannot be obtained, poles may generally be cut in the vicinity of a river; but the traveller in Africa or Australia must not expect to find any wood that will possess all the valuable qualities of good red deal, therefore we would say take as much of this as you can carry, without inconveniently incumbering your vehicles.

In 1864 Mr. Charles Bell, the Surveyor-General at Cape Town, who has built and used double boats since 1850, favoured us with the subjoined description of his method of construction :—

" My boats are only 12ft. long by 9in. wide, and 9in. deep, and 12ft. by 14in. I have never made them more than 15ft. long, with a bearing power of about 800lb. I have now built or directed the building of about five good boats on the principle, easy and swift under oars or before the wind under sail, and not very faulty even on a wind without any false keel, but you can never sail quite close without one. Mine were built to go through heavy surf all fore and aft, so that the wave could strike nothing except sharp edges, and in surf they are first-rate.

" Iron is objectionable both on account of weight for carriage, and liability to oxidysation in heat and moisture; nothing like canvas. A bolt of No. 3, 2lb. of tin tacks, and a few needles and hanks of twine, would be all I would bother myself to carry a mile. My first boat had not an ounce of metal in her barring rowlocks and rowlock sockets, and she cost me 17s. 6d. and some old plank, and carried me safely through wall-sided breakers that would have troubled a whale-boat's crew. Say you want a pair of 30ft. boats of 3ft. beam and depth, tolerably safe even against snags and rocks. For each take a 30ft.

batten, 3in. by 2½in. for keel; strut and erect on it knees' planks and
stem pieces as in Figs. 5 and 6, and section in Fig. 2 below.

" Trust greatly to lashing the frame; let the knees diminish in beam
from the centre to each end as in Fig. 1 : draw in your side pieces
and planks, or rather press them down to your vertical side laid
on a flat surface, and you will have lines that will astonish you. Of
course you can raise stem and stern for the look of the thing, as I have
done, but it gives more trouble than it is worth. If you want to make
a safe lifeboat, tack tight over each knee-frame a piece of canvas
(Fig. 3), leaving an edge loose and broad enough to be sewn on to the
outer canvas, loosely (so as not to interfere with the lines it will
naturally take), and be tacked to boards and battens where they come
in contact with it. I should have first said cover bottom and sides with
tightly-stretched canvas, in which operation a cobbler's pinchers are
most useful, but any others will do, then grease outside and in. If you

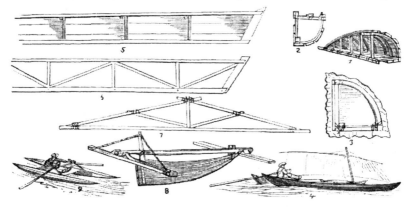

prefer tar and have it, well and good; then cover the deck in the
same manner, stitching knee-piece canvases as you go. You will
thus, if the workmanship be perfect, have in each half boat ten water-
tight compartments, which it will be no easy matter to damage; snags
will be your worst enemies, and they cannot damage more than one at a
time under ordinary circumstances, whereupon the first landing and a
crooked needle with patch of canvas, twine, and grease, will make all
right. In the deck of each such compartment you should pierce a
marlinspike hole, button-hole the edges, and fit a plug, and as a large
boat cannot be so easily turned upside down as ours, you may have a
pipe, and any simple means of sucking out such bilge water as may get
in. Next as to connection of the boats. If you wish it sliding, so as
to increase or diminish the width between them when necessary, make
it on the lattice girder or rafter principle, and avoid weight, as in

Fig. 7; each not more than 6ft. from the centre. Stay and strut them to points near the stem and stern, and they will be quite strong and firm enough to support the mast and the awnings, with the other fittings. The knee-pieces may be left projecting when required to meet the sliding rafter; 4ft. between the boats will be quite enough, so 10ft. of rafter will be quite enough. The sail may be a long low lug, split if you like, to let it pass the mast when on a wind (Fig. 4). An oar will steer, and easily control the extra face of sail on one side when before the wind with the yard squared. But on a wind you must have a keel, one that will slide over sunken rocks, and not be damaged even when it takes them side on. It may fix with free play in the front beam, and lay loose in cleats on the after one with a projecting arm to be held upright by rope, as in Fig. 8.

" Of course there must be an opening between the deck planks, to allow of its rise. Such a boat will carry at least a ton and a half of cargo, if made sufficiently flat in the bottom, and it will require a very stiff breeze and large sail even then to submerge the lee boat. There is this advantage, too, that it cannot be done so quickly as to prevent the remedy by luffing up or otherwise with ordinary vigilance. Your goods and tarpaulins will be quite safe 6in. above the gunwale."

Just before returning from South Africa we found that the clever author of " A Painter's Camp in the Highlands " had also gone through nearly the same course of experiments, and had arrived, like us, at the conclusion that the double form of boat was the most safe, convenient, portable, and roomy on deck; and also that it was objectionable to have the inner sides rounded, for the reasons before given. He therefore finally adopted the flat inner side, and making his boats 30ft. in length and 4ft. apart at the stem, increased the width to 4ft. 1in. aft, so as to let the inclosed body of water glide away more easily. He found, however, that after working out his own idea for his own use, he was served with a notice for infringing a patent of which he had not previously heard; and in like manner, after our return from Africa, a description of a patent tubular life raft was submitted to Captain George, at the Royal Geographical Society, and he immediately saw that this was nearly identical with our own plan.

About 1853, a friend in Graham's Town, with whom we left our model of the inflatable boat subsequently used in Australia, (see p. 42), made one for his own amusement, Making inflatable on a small river. He had but two tubes, each of boats safe. them with a flat side toward the centre, with a small platform between raised on crossed struts, one pair of which on each side were very ingeniously made to carry the rowlocks, as in the next sketch (Fig. 9). And, as he was doubtful of keeping the canvas of his boats sufficiently air-tight, he either filled them, or proposed to do so, with the bladders of oxen previously inflated, so that, even were air to escape from the tubes which formed the boats, they could not collapse. This, in itself, would be a hint which a traveller, who must either shoot game or kill domestic animals for his followers, would do well to bear in mind.

Iron, whether plain or galvanised, is sold in sheets of 2ft. by 6ft., while those of copper are 2ft. by 4ft. We recommend only the copper ; Skiff of iron or but economic or other reasons may very possibly copper. compel the traveller to use iron.

We have, for facility of construction, chosen the form of a Norwegian praam, or wherry, with both ends alike. A semicircular section slightly flattened at the bottom, without a keel, and rising with an easy sheer to a sharp point at either end.

Eleven sheets of iron would be required ; the central one being left of its original shape and size, while the five at either end are cut to the forms shown by the outer lines, and to the dimensions indicated by the figures marked along the lower edge : thus, in No. 1, from the centre there is no perceptible curve along the 6-foot side, but the ends are sloped off, with straight although diagonal lines, so that the side nearest the centre remains 6ft., while the farthest is reduced to 5ft. 9in.

In the next sheet, or No. 2, the side nearest the centre curves very slightly ; the segment taking off only one inch at either end, the curved side (supposing we are now working from the centre forward) overlaps the edge of No. 1 two inches, and it is therefore cut, not to 5ft. 9in., but to 5ft. 10in., as No. 1 would be of that breadth, a couple of inches back ; the front side is left straight, but is reduced in breadth to 5ft. 5in., and the after side of No. 3 is so much more curved that the segment cuts off three inches. The figures in the diagram will render the progressive diminution to the end sufficiently plain. It will be seen that the end remains one foot wide ; this is usually filled in with a semicircular piece of plank, being quite sharp enough for all practical purposes, and affording room for a rowlock for a steering or sculling oar, or for a hole through which the boat's painter may be passed. But, if desired, another piece of iron, which may be called sheet No. 6, may very easily be let in to continue the curve quite up to a point, as in the dotted end of Fig. 2. The half section is given on the side marked iron of Fig. 3, the outer line standing for the two edges of the central sheet, where the skiff is 4ft. wide and 1ft. 10in. deep. The next line, 1½in. smaller all round, is the section at the overlap of sheets Nos. 1 and 2; the third line, two inches within the last, is at the edges of Nos. 2 and 3; the fourth, three inches smaller, is at the contact of Nos. 3 and 4; the fifth, six inches less, is at Nos. 4 and 5; and the sixth, diminishing by nine inches, is the end of No. 5, which is filled in by a semicircle of plank about five inches in diameter.

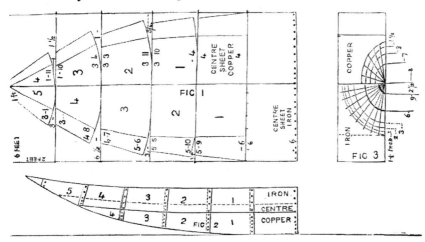

The eleven sheets laid side by side would, of course, present a length of 22ft., but the overlap and the segment of the curve cut from those near the ends would reduce the length of the boat to 19ft.

Our diagram is on a scale of a quarter of an inch to a foot, but this is somewhat small for the needful accuracy; therefore if anyone intends to build, we would advise him to copy it on a scale of at least one inch to a foot, in which case the halves will represent six inches and the quarters three, and if he has a rule divided to one-twelfths, his work will be much facilitated.

It would be better to make, as we have done in preparing this description, a model block on which to test his work; indeed we would

advise this in all cases of intended boat building. If the boat is to have a bow and stern distinct from each other, the model must be of the whole length, but may be of only half the breadth. If both ends are to be alike, it may be half the length and breadth, or one quarter of the boat.

In the present instance, take a piece of deal, as clean and straight-grained as possible, 19in. long (or 21in. if you wish the ends to come to a point), 4in. wide, and 3in. deep. Having smoothed this, draw a line along the centre of the top and bottom, connecting them by perpendiculars at the two ends; then on the top set off the line of one-quarter of the gunwale, or outer line, taking the breadths from the section in Fig. 3 (p. 105), and their distances from the centre, from the elevation in Fig. 2 (p. 105), bearing in mind that the centre means *not* either of the edges, but the middle of that marked as the central sheet. It will save trouble to cut out a piece of card to the size of this quarter, and trace the corresponding ones on the top and bottom of your block; then copy the elevation given in Fig. 2, and trace this, as before, on both sides. Now fix the block, with one end up in a bench vice, and with a narrow frame saw cut along the gunwale lines nearly to the centre, but do not cut them quite off, or you will lose your elevation lines (if a friend helps you by guiding the other end of the saw to the line on his side, you will be more certain to cut truly); then turn the block one-quarter round, and cut the line at top and bottom. Now place the other end uppermost, and repeat the process; and lastly, finish the cuts, and detach the superfluous pieces.

Take a piece of card or thin stuff, and draw on it the midship section, and cut this away, leaving a corresponding hollow; round off the edges of your model until she fits this hollow, and of this size 2in. of the centre must be left. Do the same with the diminishing sections, forward and aft; then cut eleven sheets of card 2in. by 6in., mark a central line across each, and also along the bottom of the model; lay one sheet uncut across the midship section, and tack it there; mark each of the others after the outlines given in the diagram (Fig. 1, p. 105), but test them in their places before cutting them. Take care also that as you go forward each sheet overlaps that which is behind; but as you work aft, insert the front edge under the one before it. You may think this operation would be tedious; but having once gone through it, you will build your full-sized boat with confidence. And let us again assure you that time spent in obtaining a preliminary certainty of your plan is saved over and over again when you come to actual work.

The sheets having been cut to the proper shape, set the two points of the gauge ¼in. apart, and so that the centre of the space between them shall be exactly 1in. from the shoulder, and gauge these lines all round the sheets, then, commencing from the centre of the longest side, mark off spaces of 3in., and with a flat-ended punch, and a dolly or matrix, or, in lack of that, a hard block of end wood, drive ¼in. holes on all the sides except those which are cut with a curve.

Then lay the centre sheet on the rib or mould, which, like the rough frame on which bricklayers construct an arch, gives it its proper curve, and, under one edge, lay the curved edge of the next sheet. Mark where the holes should come; remove it and punch them, and fasten the two sheets together temporarily with three or more of the screw bolts. Do the same with the successive sheets towards each end, and you will find that the copper shell, even without ribs or strengthening of any kind, will assume its proper form and will be tolerably stiff. If the sheets are truly cut, the result may be attained, even without a mould, by driving one hole in the centre of the curved side, bolting it to the straight edge of the other sheet, and then bending both round till the curved edge coincides with the straight one. In this condition you may decide on increasing the width of your boat by forcing the sides farther apart; this will increase her sheer or elevation at either end, and will diminish her depth, or you may incline to reduce her beam, which will give her greater depth and will reduce the sheer till the elevation of the gunwale presents nearly a straight line. It would

be better, however, if circumstances permitted, to adhere very nearly to the form given in the drawing, and set up such a frame for working on as is shown in the illustration above.

Drive as many rough stakes into the ground as the number of sheets in your intended boat requires. Let those near the centre be three and a half or four feet high, and those at the ends slightly lower. Stretch a chalk line fore and aft, and see that all their centres are in true alignment and 1ft. 10in. apart. The line should be fastened to two posts in the same line as, but beyond those required for, the boat. Let it come low enough just to touch the central posts, then measure downwards from the line the amount necessary to be cut off those towards the ends, so as to give the proper sheer. Next, commencing from the centre, face off with a saw, or otherwise, as much of each post as is needful to let each frame lie truly against it, noticing that as the bottom of each is farther from the next than the top or part near the gunwale, it is more convenient to face that side of the post which looks towards the centre; then, with any rough slabs or planks, form two moulds the exact size and form of your midship section, just as bricklayers would do if they were building an arch. Nail these to their proper supports, and on them bend the strips, 2in. broad by ¼in. thick, you intend for ribs, letting only one edge rest on the mould, while the other projects so far that you may have clear space to bore through the centre the holes for your screw-bolts. Do the same with all the others towards the two ends, confining them with a temporary riband where the gunwale is afterwards to be; or, still better, leaving their ends 6in. too long, so that this riband may not interfere with the completion of the boat. Have a chalk line stretched near the ground, along either side, parallel with the centre one above, so that any deviation from the proper form can be measured and corrected. Then lay on the sheets, insert the bolts, and screw them up, adding a keel or centre batten, bilge streaks, and gunwales, externally, and bottom boards to prevent the occupant treading on the copper, and stringers for the thwarts inside. The projecting ends of the ribs can be left where required for rowlocks, or cut off where they are not.

The same process, with attention to the different dimensions, will make you a copper boat, consisting of nine sheets, 2ft. by 4ft.; and this will be 16ft. long, 3ft. 3in. wide, and 10in. deep; but if the gunwales were made of plank, 4½in. wide, or half the width of a deal, the skiff would be quite deep enough to carry three or four persons in moderately smooth water.

If you wish to build the same boat of wood, ⅜in. planks (not more than 4in. wide) will be stout enough. The lines radiating from the centre in the sectional drawing are given for the purpose of showing the progressive diminution of the planks in width, from the central section towards each end. These should be tested by cutting strips of card and tacking them, like planks, on the block that serves as your model.

This would be a very handy form for a dingy for the traveller's personal use, as it might be taken to pieces, and the sheets laid flat, occupying a space of 2ft. by 4in. in extent, and less than 1in. in depth, or they might be rolled up in three bundles, of which each must weigh less than 24lb., as the weight of the whole nine sheets of copper before being cut would be only 72lb. The screw-bolts would weigh probably more than the sheeting, but they could be divided into packets of any convenient weight for carriage by native porters or otherwise; and we should think that half a day would be quite sufficient to put the whole together when wanted, or take it apart when done with. The boat would pull or paddle, and would sail well enough off the wind, but would not compete with a keeled boat close hauled; if the iron sheets were used, she would, of course, be larger and heavier, and the material would be less portable.

In the boat built for Mr. E. D. Young, for use on the Shire river and Lake Nyassa, thin sheets of steel were at first proposed, but as these could not be readily obtained, the best iron was used, and the edges of these being turned upward and inward, formed the ribs of the boat, each sheet being connected by bolts passing through this inward edge to the next sheets before and behind it. This form of construction combines all the elements of lightness, simplicity, and strength; but we do not recommend it to a traveller who has to work up his own material, because none but a skilled workman could turn inward a broad segment of a sheet of metal, the outer surface of which has to present a curve. If anyone doubts this, let him try it by folding half an inch of the edge of a sheet of paper to a right angle with the other part, he will then find it impossible for him to impart a curvature to the sheet without tearing the upturned edge if he bends it outward, or wrinkling it if he gives the contrary curve. If he wished to adopt this form of joining the parts, his plan would be to cut up his sheets of copper into planks 4ft. long, and 8in. broad, then gauging a line all round 2in. within the edge, cut out the squares at the four corners and turn up the borders all round, he would thus have out of one sheet of copper 4ft. by 2in., three planks 4in. wide, and 3ft. 8in. in length, a waste of material that hardly any circumstance could justify.

In 1858 we made a model of a metal boat, about thirty feet long, by six feet beam, to carry a crew of sixteen men, each of whom, when it was taken to pieces, should not find his share of the load to exceed 50lb.; each of the thwarts, and the bow Metal boats. and stern sheets were continued downward so as to form a water-tight box, the lower outline of which coincided with the section of the boat, so as to supply the place of ribs and convert her into a lifeboat. Indeed, we would advise that in all metal boats some such portions should assume the form of lockers or of reservoirs of air, so that, should the boat be swamped or become leaky, she might not sink even when filled with water.

Our model was approved by Captain Washington, R.N., the Secretary at that time of the Lifeboat Institution, and the builder to whom we submitted it estimated the weight of the sheet copper and bolts of the same to be employed in the hull at 260lb. and the cost at 60*l.*, while the internal fittings, somewhat less in weight, would cost 40*l.* This expense Dr. Livingstone considered to be too great; but, when we reached the Zambesi, it was a matter of frequent regret that we had not some form of boat portable enough to be carried over rough country to rivers we wished to explore.

One of the most beautiful little vessels we ever saw was built by the wrecked crew of a French steamer. She was 40ft. long and 8ft. or 10ft. beam, clinker-built, with thin and narrow planks, without a joint in their whole length, sawed out of the mainmast, and flexible ribs about a foot apart and not more than one inch in breadth or thickness. Her deck beams were, of course, somewhat more rigid, to sustain the weight of the men who crowded her. She was said to have sailed eleven knots.

Our friend, Mr. Wilson, an experienced African traveller, recommends a wattled or basket-work boat, and in a country where rattans, osiers, flexible twigs, or green reeds, are obtainable, such a boat would be both light and durable; but it would be open to objection on the score of unavoidable roughness, and inequality of outer surface, which would impede its progress through the water, and expose parts of the canvas covering to constant liability to chafe whenever it touched the ground. Even if a traveller intends to purchase or hire native canoes, it is indispensable that he should have some small portable boat of his own, sufficient at least to show the natives that he is not totally helpless on the water and dependent on them.

Wattled boat.

In the case of our copper boat, illustrated at page 46, we have already remarked that the difficulties of the road, and the mortality among Mr. Chapman's cattle, obliged us to leave behind eight of the sections. The method we adopted with the other four is shown in our full-page illustration, representing boat-building on the Logier River.

On account of the danger from the tsetse, or poisonous cattle fly, our friend's waggons could not be taken to the banks of the Zambesi, and everything had to be carried by the Damara servants and hired natives to Logier Hill, about eighty miles below the Victoria Falls, which we had selected as the first place from which continuous downward navigation was possible.

The building of the house will come more properly under its own heading, and we will now only treat of what concerns the boat.

About the 3rd of October, or towards the close of the dry season, we cut down a motchicheerie tree, which divided a little above the ground into two tolerably straight logs of manageable dimensions. These were first notched with the axe on the side we intended to "fall" them; the cross-cut saw was then "put in" as far as it would go without nipping from the pressure of the wood, and a notch being made on

BOAT BUILDING ON THE LOGIER RIVER.

the other side, the saw was used freely, the weight of the tree on the "falling" side opening the cut as the work proceeded.

Fresh reports, however, caused as much uncertainty whether the Falls of "Moambwa," or the rocks, were not still below the station, and some time was therefore spent in exploring the river down to Sinamane's Island, when, having ascertained that the rapids and other difficulties appeared not quite impracticable, we set up the bow and stern sections of one boat, connecting them by the ribands of red deal we had been able to carry up, and fitting at short intervals a series of frames on central posts, as described at p. 107, and further supported by shorter posts on either side, in a line with the gunwale streak, testing the accuracy of all parts where correctness was required with plumb line and level, and leaving the rest rough.

Our bench consisted of ten stakes, nearly 3ft. high, driven into the ground, and two long straight poles laid fore and aft in their forks; smaller poles were laid across these as closely as possible, and lashed with the inner bark of the young branches of the "kookomboyon"— a kind of sterculia, which, while still moist, answers very well, but becomes brittle in drying. The large smith's vice was firmly lashed to the stoutest upright with raw hide, and forked poles were set diagonally to resist the forward strain to which the bench was subject when wood was being planed up.

It was just possible to get thin poles that would bend, but none were sufficiently flexible to take the true curve required for the ribs, and at the same time strong enough to bear the strain when they became dry. Therefore we had to cut crooks out of the motchicheeries, the wood of which looked something like coarse short-grained cedar; and first burning away the light stuff from the tree cut down a month ago, we found a great many available forks and curves.

We had great difficulty in selecting wood of a suitable size for plank; trees too small, or too crooked, or of unsuitable wood, were in abundance; while those of the wood we wanted were mostly too large and unmanageable. Sometimes, at a distance, one would appear to be small enough, but when we came near it would prove three or four feet thick and sixty or eighty feet high, and had only seemed small by comparison with those around it. One group of motchicheeries had grown to maturity, throwing a wide-spread shadow around them; and a young sapling had shot straight up from near their roots towards the air and light; this was 9in. thick at the base, and 4in. at nearly 30ft. up; it proved impossible to "fall" the top outward, and it was very difficult to clear from the other trees. We would have saved labour by floating it down stream to our building-yard, but the wet season was coming on, and the sap had by this time risen in the wood, so that a small piece sunk when thrown into the water. The labour of sinking a saw-pit would have been great, and besides this the expected rains would have kept it always wet. We therefore erected trestles of primitive construction; two triangles of forked poles, 6½ft. long, supported the ends of a stout cross-beam, firmly lashed to them with buffalo hide, and for greater security lashed also to the stem of a tree. The second trestle was destitute of this support, and therefore had to be shored by longer poles, the forks of which took the necks of the opposite triangles, while their hands were stopped by wedges driven into the ground; for additional firmness, lashings were passed at the points of intersection. Two stout poles were laid fore and aft upon the trestles, and shorter pieces across served to rest the log upon; there was some difficulty in lining the lower side, but by cutting notches in the cross-pieces large enough to let the chalk line pass freely, and "springing" it only by short lengths at a time, this was accomplished. It was difficult to teach a young Dutch lad, strong as an ox, and nearly as stolid, to saw with us; but at length the " sapling " was cut, and one of the larger logs lifted gradually up by forming an inclined plane with strong poles, and supporting it whenever we gained a few inches of elevation by forks of various lengths lying ready for that purpose. This having been felled before the sap was up proved much easier to saw, and we had so far overcome the difficulties in our way, that we had commenced laying the bottom plank of the first boat, when the difficulty of providing food, owing to the retreat of the wild animals to the pools which the rainy season was filling all over the desert, and the fever among the people, seven Damaras, mostly women and children, having died in Chapman's camp, and one of the most useful men in ours, obliged us, for the sake of saving the rest, to retreat to the highlands of the desert, and on the 3rd of February, 1863, we hauled down our colours at Logier Hill, and commenced our return journey.

Two general rules in boat building should be borne in mind. First, that clumsiness is not necessarily strength; and, secondly, that General hints on it is much easier to build a sharp swift boat with boat building. moderate sheer, and clear lines of entrance and run, than a short one with great beam, bluff bows, and wide overhanging stern. The stem and stern post should rake considerably, or even form parts of a curved line connected by the keel, as if they are made too upright, not only is the boat more difficult to steer when sudden alteration of the course is necessary, but if she is built of wood, so much curvature is required in the ends of the planks that it is difficult for an inexperienced hand to lay them. A rudder cannot be nicely fitted to a curved stern-post, but if you decide to steer with one instead of an oar, make the stern-post straight, and if you wish to diminish its "rake" or inclination, make it one foot wide below and only a few inches at the top. A rudder is much more convenient in ordinary cases; but, when great quickness and power is required, nothing is equal to the steering oar.

In constructing a clinker-built boat some practice is required in clenching the nails. First, a hole is bored with a gimlet of such a size that the nail requires some driving, but very little, to force it through. This prevents any lateral curvature, which would be fatal to any attempt at clenching. A roove is then put over the point and driven home to the surface of the plank, and the end of the nail is nipped off nearly close with a pair of cutting pincers. If you have a spring-handled hammer to screw on to the plank so that the face of it just rests on the head of the nail, so much the better, if not, you must hold your heavy hammer with your left hand or get a mate to do so; while with the edge of your little clinch hammer, you tap as sharp and lightly as possible on the centre of the cut end of the nail, causing its sides to overspread the edges of the roove, when it can be nicely smoothed off with the face of the hammer. When one plank has been laid, the outside of its upper edge should be bevelled off so as to let the lower edge of the next lie truly against it in the position required by the curvature of the boat's side; and, to retain it in its place, several pairs of "nippers" should be used. These are made of two pieces of wood—say sixteen inches long and two inches square—cut a mortice ½in. wide by 3in. long in each, and pass through them a piece of hard wood fitting the mortice loosely and 12in. long, so as to project 4in. at either end, in each end of this bore three ½in. holes, not quite in the central line, but one a little on one side of it, and the next on the other, so as to avoid the risk of splitting two into one; have pegs of hard wood or iron to put through these at the distance you may require, then having adjusted one end of the nippers on the planks you wish to hold together, drive a wedge between the other ends till the grip is tight enough. A pair of these is shown in our illustration at page 94. We believe that the traveller will find it generally most advisable to build his boat bottom upwards.

We should think that a traveller in South Africa, using the common ox-waggons of the country, might easily, and without additional weight, carry up with him all the wood necessary for

I

the purposes of boat building. The floor or bed-plank of the *Cape-waggon* waggon is about thirty-six inches in width, and *boats.* from twelve to eighteen feet in length. Four deals might be laid down for this. If they were twenty-one feet long, they would project considerably behind. It is not considered expedient to have the fore and hinder wheels too great a distance apart; but then the projecting ends need not be loaded. The usual holes for the fastenings of a waggon bottom should not be bored in them, but they should be secured by lashings of raw hide, and the parts liable to be chafed should also be protected with the same material. They might be previously sawed into planks or battens of the required size, and then tightly lashed together by thongs of raw hide, especially near the ends, which would otherwise be liable to split with changes of weather and rough usage. The waggon sides are usually a little more than two feet high in front and three or more behind, and the framing of these is an elaborate piece of work. Three deals 9in. wide would give 27in. in height all along. These might be cut into $\frac{3}{4}$in. or $\frac{1}{2}$in. plank, and again bound up with raw hide, like those of the floor, and thus the traveller would have in one waggon nine deals, or more than sufficient, if he built his boat of copper; while, by raising the sides to 36in. with a couple more, he would have enough to construct her entirely of wood.

In building the waggon-tent or tilt, as it would be called in England, two methods are adopted in the Cape. The first is the kap-tent (E on next page), which is regularly framed by the waggon builder with stanchions about five feet high from the floor, neatly fitted to the sides, at intervals of two feet or thirty inches; with bows of flexible wood, forming a flattened arch about nine inches higher, across them, and fore and aft battens, half-checked in, so that the whole presents a smooth external surface to receive the inner sail, or cover of painted canvas, which is laid on before the outer sail, or snow-white neatly-fitted tilt, is drawn over all. The second is that which any competent waggon driver can extemporise for himself with a sufficient quantity of bamboo split into laths two or three fingers broad, stout Spanish reeds, common hogshead hoops, or an adjacent forest, in which flexible poles can be cut. His first care is to lift and shore up his waggon so as to set free one or both of the hinder wheels, on the circumference of which the flexible rods he intends for his bows are bent and fastened down, and in doing this some care is requisite. The rod must not be grasped by both ends and suddenly forced into the curve, for one part may be weaker than the rest, and it may break there, or be forced into an unsightly prominence; but, after having been steamed, if possible, or, as is more commonly the case, laid for two or three days in water or wet earth, the part intended for the centre of the arch should first be bound tight and flat upon the tire of the wheel, then the ends should be gradually pressed down by two assistants, the principal watching the inequalities of the curvature, and reducing them by passing turns of raw hide tightly over any parts that have a tendency to irregular projections. The bows, which should be about twelve or fourteen feet in total length, are now set up. Care having been taken that the waggon sides stand truly, the front and aftermost are first fixed, and the driver, if a man of average height, stands on the centre of the waggon floor, holding the bow as fairly as he can, with the crown of its arch about the level of his eye, say five feet six from the floor, while his assistants, standing

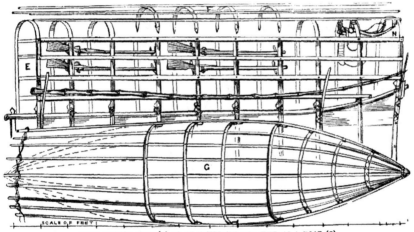

CAPE WAGGON TENT (E) TO BE TAKEN OFF AND USED AS A BOAT (G).

outside, fasten the ends with screws or thongs of raw hide, to the styles or stanchions of the waggon sides. The lifter, the dissel-boom, or other straight and heavy pole, is now laid fore and aft upon the bows to keep them in a level line, and also somewhat to flatten the crown of the arch and expand it laterally. The laths or battens, fore and aft, are now lashed on, and the result is a less sightly but stronger and more durable roof for the exigencies of travel than the kap-tent. In the rear of the tent (letter N) are shown the ribs of an ox or buffalo slung to the roof to hang the saddles on.

Such a tent as either of these might be easily constructed so as to be available for a boat whenever it might be required. First let the stanchions, screwed or lashed to the waggon sides, rise to the usual height of about five feet, and let the bows forming the flattened arch across them be of any flexible material, but preferably of straight-grained ash, such as is used for the better kind of tubs or casks. The hoops of American flour barrels would answer well; they are somewhat thin, but three might be laid together, and would be much more flexible and strong than if one piece only was used.

Of these, supposing nine bows were used, three in the front and three in the rear might be permanently secured to the stanchions, as in the illustration (E, p. 115), while the three central ones should be so fastened as to be readily cast off. The laths or battens, on the contrary, should be securely fastened to the central bows, so as to lift off with them, and only slightly to those at either end.

When the boat is required, it would be but an hour's work to cast off th temporary fastenings. Take off the movable part of the top frame, draw the ends of the battens together, as shown in the illustration (G, p. 115), inserting at pleasure three or four smaller bows at either end, and then taking the under sail—which is generally of oiled canvas—fold down the corners so as to narrow it at either end to the shape of the boat, and stitch or lace it with eyelet-holes to the gunwale. A second thickness of unpainted canvas might always be kept upon the roof between the inner and outer sail; and if this were also laced on the boat, previously reversing the ends of the two parts of canvas, so that if any portions had been chafed while on the waggon they might not coincide with each other, the boat would be as impervious to water as wooden boats generally are.

A few spare laths, previously lashed beneath the front and aftermost bows of the tent, so as to remain there when those required for the boat were removed, and perhaps two or three duplicate bows, would prevent the necessity of leaving the vehicle destitute of cover while the boat was being used.

Very often the explorer may find himself alone in a boat, or he may wish to cross a river or pass from a ship to shore or back again

Sculling. without calling other men from their duties, and in such cases he who has the power of managing a boat with a single oar, has a great advantage over one who must ask the aid of another. We have been on boat trips where the scientific officers have cheerfully manned the oars and pulled against the stream all night, and when we volunteered to take our turn, the answer was, "No; you can scull, and none of us can. Keep the steering-oar, and help us onward with it." The first great difficulty of the novice is to get the blade of his oar under water and keep it there, and to make the loom rest firmly in the rowlock; the natural tendency of the wood to float will at first seem insuperable, but as soon as he has acquired the proper motion of the wrist he will wonder that he ever had the slightest trouble in keeping the oar to its duty.

To learn to scull, go into a boat that is either fast to the shore or vessel, or have a comrade to pull the other oar with you should you fail. Then stand on the stern-sheets on the starboard side, so that the right hand may be toward the bow of the boat; plant the left foot on the starboard side seat, and advance the right to the middle of the aftermost thwart; grasp the small end of the oar with the right hand, and the loom with the left about eight or ten inches from it, so that when the blade of the oar is horizontal the back of the hands and arms may be uppermost and also in a horizontal line. You will find that when the blade is supported by the water, the loom will not lie in the rowlock; but now depress the wrists a little, raise the hands till the blade forms an angle of 40° or 45° with the horizon, the edge farthest from you being the highest; push the oar from you as far as you can without losing your balance, then, as your first stroke ceases, drop the hands and raise the wrists till the blade inclines as much the other way, the raised edge being then nearest you; pull the loom towards you, bending backwards at the same time as far as you safely can, and you will find the arms in the proper position, with the elbows at the side, the wrists lowered, and the hands ready to rise for the stroke from you. Make short strokes at first, and do not hurry. Never mind which way the boat goes, or whether she goes at all; stick her nose in a mudbank, if you like, till you can keep your oar below the surface, then give her her head; if your oar keeps under water she must go forward, and by making a stronger sweep to starboard or to port, you may steer her at your will. If you have a long narrow boat, she will keep a straight course, but with a short dinghy, she will incline at each stroke a little to the right or left, and if you use the oar regularly, her wake will show a series of graceful and equal curves.

In default of an oar, the bottom board may be taken up and used by being laid on the point of the stem, the boat going then stern first. Lightermen, on the Ouse, frequently scull their horse boats in this manner. We have sculled a whale boat with one oar over the quarter, *i.e.*, in the crutch of the stroke oar, much as a gondolier does; but tholes or rowlocks cut in the streak above the gunwale would not admit of this. We give no directions for this or for the use of the plank. When the novice can keep his oar blade under water, he can easily learn how to adapt his new power to any emergency.

In paddling a canoe sit near the stern, looking forward, and with the paddle on your right side make a long fair stroke ; never mind

Paddling.
the deviation of her head to the left ; but just before you lift your paddle from the water, feather the blade of it by turning the right hand inward from the wrist, turn the right elbow outward, and draw the left hand inward across your breast ; this will " port your helm " and bring her to her course again.

If you have a mate who handles another paddle this is less needful ; but it is well to learn to paddle your own canoe practically as well as metaphorically, single handed.

The kroomen about Sierra Leone use a canoe pointed at both ends and with a great sheer ; this, to a novice, is much more difficult to keep to a true course, but a single krooman tossing his paddle from hand to hand, without missing a stroke, will make her fly direct as an arrow the way he means to go.

In the gunning boats on the Norfolk coasts, when strict silence is not needed, and in canoes of some other countries, a double-bladed paddle is used. The pole is grasped by both hands, like the balance-pole of a rope-dancer, and equal strokes are given alternately, or the course is changed by a more powerful stroke on the other side.

We have occasionally found that the power of handling the native paddle has been of great service, for when we have wished to cross a river to secure some specimen of wading bird, and the bargaining over the hire would have occupied half a day, we have cut the matter short by stepping into the canoe, paddling to the other side, shooting our bird, and making the owners a sufficient present on our return ; and, while we advise that all travellers should most scrupulously regard the rights of the natives, we must also intimate that they will not gain the respect of savages by submitting tamely to extortion, or showing themselves in any way afraid to maintain their own.

The proas, or outrigger canoes, of the Malays and Indian islanders, are so proverbially swift that they have fairly earned the title by which

Proas.
they are generally known, of " flying proas." We have seen and admired many varieties of these, as well as their fan-shaped sails, sometimes of matting—bright and yellow while new, and deepening to browner tints with age, and sometimes of snow-white cotton, or of white alternated with cloths of blue or pink, and gay streamers floating from the bending yards. The most common and we may almost say the most beautiful of these, were the little proas sailed by one man only, as represented in our sketch. The hull consisted of a single log, perhaps twenty feet in length, and hardly as many inches in depth and breadth ; the mast was about six feet in height ; and the

sail, of triangular form, was laced to a couple of bamboos nearly as long
as the canoe; the thick ends of these crossed, and were lashed together
at the tack of the sail, and were made fast, loosely enough to give
them sufficient play, a little before the mast thwart; a loop attached
to the upper bamboo, or yard, at about six feet from the tack, was
hitched over a knob on the mast-head, instead of hoisting the sail by
halyards, and the sheet was attached by loops like kite loops, or
bowline bridles, to the lower bamboo or boom; in hauling to the wind,
the simple gathering in of the sheet trimmed the sail nearly down to
the gunwale, as seen in the distant proa, while in going free the
slackening of it allowed the sail to rise to the wind, till in the distance
it reminded us of the beautiful fan-shaped sea-shells, so often found
upon the coast. Stability was imparted under this enormous press of

THE PROA.

sail by two bamboos twelve or fifteen feet long, and from four to six
inches thick, kept parallel to the boat at six or eight feet from her
sides by two beams of the same lashed across her gunwales, bending
slightly downward, but the foremost less so than the after, so that the
fore end of the outrigger might be raised slightly above the water, and
not impede the boat. The rudder was just like that of our own boats,
except in its fittings, which consisted simply of a rope grummet at its
neck, by which it could be hitched on to a timber head on either
quarter, and we believe it made so little difference that the boatman
seldom gave himself the trouble to shift it from one to the other.
Of course a tiller was used, as yokes and lines would have been
inapplicable. We cannot tell exactly their rate of sailing, but they

passed our swift and handy little schooner the "Tom Tough" with ease, even when the breeze was at its freshest. The hull is generally whitened with a mixture of chunam, or coral lime, and cocoa-nut oil, and the raised ends are ornamented with devices in red or green, and sometimes a red streak runs along the side. The tambanga, or waterman's boat for passengers, has more beam, no outrigger, and a smaller though similarly shaped sail.

Some of these proas were much larger, being fifty or more feet in length, and then the sides of the log forming the bottom of the canoe would be raised either by other planks sewn on or by a framework of bamboo, with pieces cross cut from the leaves of the fan-palm, so that the leaf ribs should stand vertically, stitched to them to form the extra height of side, while a roof of the same was built over the centre where cargo would be stowed, or over the after end, to form a kind of cabin. When planks are used for raising the sides, they are not sawn like ours, with economy of time, labour, and material, but are laboriously chopped out of the solid; and, instead of being bent, are patiently dubbed down to the requisite curve with numberless strokes of the keen little Malay adze, projections being left on the inner side through which holes are bored to lash them to the timbers, while rows of holes along the edges admit of their being sewn together with strips of rattan, and shreds of palm leaf laid along the seam and confined by the tightening of the stitches, help to reduce the leakage, which, if the vessel works at all in a sea-way, can never be entirely stopped. They have two large sails similar in form to those of the smaller proas, and sometimes a third, as a mizen. This is small enough to be hitched over the mast head, as before; but the others have to be hoisted by halyards, and the long yards supported by propping them at some distance from the slings by bamboo poles. The stays were formed of slips of bamboo, and sometimes even of the poles, which, being well fastened, would not only resist tension on the weather-side as well as ropes, but on the lee would, by their rigidity, help to support the masts. The outriggers of these were more elaborately framed with a lighter set of beams, which supported stanchions and hand-rails, so that, when the wind freshened, men might run out upon the weather outrigger and, holding on by the hand-rail and stays, which lead from the mast-head, serve as a counterpoise to the immense sails as the boat dashed through the water. Reefing seemed never to be thought of, and our own men soon got into the habit of speaking of a one-man or two-man breeze, according to the number seen on the weather outriggers of the proas that flew past us.

The professional pirate has the outrigger only on the weather-side, and this is frequently a log of light wood trimmed sharp at either end, so that while its specific gravity is small enough to keep it buoyant, it is still so heavy as not to be easily lifted out of the water, like a bamboo, and when requisite, men sent on it, as in the former case, will give it additional weight. But the chief peculiarity is in the hull of the vessel, which is only half a boat, the lee-side being perfectly flat while the weather, or that toward the outrigger, is rounded as usual; they will be frequently more than fifty feet in length, and six

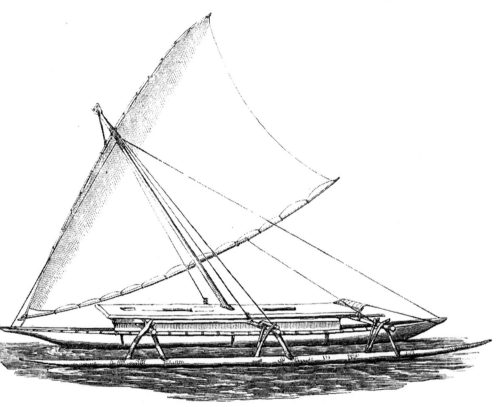

PROA WITH OUTRIGGER ON WEATHER-SIDE ONLY, TO SAIL WITH EITHER END FIRST, AS REQUIRED.

or eight in breadth. We speak of the lee-side, because when the course has to be changed—say in beating to windward—they do not go about like a ship, that must go with her bows forward and be steered from the stern, and therefore turns to receive the wind on the other side. This would be fatal to the proa, as the buoyancy of the outrigger would not prevent her from capsizing; and therefore while the steersman lets that end which is temporarily her bow fall off from the wind, the men who have charge of the tack run round with it on the platform to windward of the mast, the sheet is brought round to leeward, a steersman takes his place at the other end, and that which has been the stern now becomes the bow, and cleaves the waves at the rate of twenty miles per hour. But no one need fear a proa with a double outrigger, for she is not intended to lay alongside and board.

The engraving represents a proa with an outrigger only on the weather-side; and not only would the sail be made to traverse by shifting the tack to that end which, for the time being, was intended to go foremost, but the mast is also fitted to be inclined forward by slackening that which happens to be the back stay, and tightening that which is *pro tempore* the fore. Those which serve for shrouds, being exactly abreast of the mast, are so arranged for the purpose of facilitating this.

The commander of the United States Exploring Expedition, Charles Wilkes, U. S. N., gives the following description of the Feejee canoes :—

" They are superior to those of other islands. They are generally double, and the largest are 100ft. in length; the two canoes are of

Feejee canoes.

different sizes, the smaller serving as an outrigger to the other, and are connected by beams on which a platform is laid, 15ft. wide, and extending 2ft. or 3ft. beyond the sides. The bottom of each canoe is a single plank; the sides are fitted to them by dovetailing and by lashings passed through flanges left on each piece; the joints are closed by the gum of the bread-fruit tree, which is also used for smearing them. They have a depth of hold of about 7ft., and the ends are decked for 20ft., to prevent their shipping seas. Amidships they have a small thatched weather house, above which is a staging on which several people can sit. The canoes of the chiefs are much ornamented with shells. The sails are so large as to appear out of proportion with the vessel, and are of tough and pliable mats; the mast is half the length of the canoe, and is stepped on deck in a chock; the yard and boom are twice as long as the mast; the halyards are carried over a crescent on the mast-head, they are bent on to the yard at a distance from its tack or lower end nearly equal to the length of the mast. The natives manage these vessels very expertly; they require much skill in beating against the wind, for it is necessary that the outrigger should be always on the weather-side, *as, if it gets to leeward, no vessel is so easily capsized ;* in tacking, therefore, the helm is put up instead of down, until the wind is brought abaft the beam, then the tack of the sail is carried to that end which was previously the stern, but which has now become the bow, and the canoe is steered from the other end; they carry sail even when it blows heavily, by sending men on the outrigger to counterbalance the force of the wind. The canoes are of logs hollowed and built upon; they make long sea-voyages, and are provisioned only with yams; they are ornamented with *Cyprœa-ovula* shells, and carry white pennants; they carry water in cocoa-nut shells, and with fire, and an ' ava ' bowl, are equipped for sea. The chief holds the end of the sheet, and it is his duty to prevent the canoe capsizing; the steer oar has a large blade. In smooth water they sail very swiftly, but the force of the sail strains them, and they leak badly, so that the men are constantly baling. The planks are kept in shape by small ribs as with us. The principal tool used is an adze, which is now made by lashing a European plane iron to a crooked handle; they are anxious to possess our tools, and especially the American axe. Their knives are made of bamboo, cut into form while it is still green; after being dried it is charred, which makes it very hard and sharp; a second charring, followed by grinding on a smooth stone, will even fit it for surgical operations."

The balsas, at Guayaquil, as described by Sir E. Belcher, in his journal of the voyage of the "Sulphur," are rafts of ten logs 14in. in diameter, and 60ft. long. The wood is a kind of bombax, *The balsas.* called balsa wood, they bear fifteen or twenty tons, independent of their crew, and bring fresh water down the river in jars of seven gallons each. Houses thirty or forty feet long, and twelve feet wide are built on some of them, and families take passage or live permanently on board.

The balsas, at Arica, in Peru, are differently constructed; they are simply skins, stripped off the animal, with as little cutting as possible; the absolutely necessary incisions are then securely closed, the hides are inflated and allowed to dry and harden, and two being laid alongside each other a platform is laid across them, on which the cargo is kept sufficiently high above the spray or ripple, and brought dry ashore even through a heavy surf. Two ox-hides would make a very serviceable balsa, as would also the skin of a pair of the large seal, the sea-elephant, porpoise, or other marine animal of suitable size.

We will now endeavour to show how the chests that are usually carried in Cape waggons might be converted into Cape waggon a buoyant, roomy, and manageable raft. These chests as rafts. chests are generally about three feet in length, and sixteen inches wide and deep; two of them, the fore and after chests, are indispensable, as the waggon cannot be kept in shape nor the cargo properly secured without them; sometimes more are carried, and others of smaller size are affixed to either side, but the objection to these is that in a densely-wooded country, stumps and stout branches are apt to catch the angles of the side chests, and damage or carry them away.

We propose that, in the waggon used by the traveller for his own conveyance, as many of these chests should be stowed as will stand fairly on the floor beside each other, say ten, as in the illustration (A, p. 125). Then, instead of the two usual square-ended side chests, we would advise that four should be fitted (Nos. 11 to 14), each of them having one end 16in. square like the other chests, but tapering at the other end to the mere thickness of the plank, and with the bottom also sloping, so that the narrow end should be only 8in. deep. Two of these with the broad ends together could be fitted on each side the narrow points, passing well clear within the wheels. Care should be taken to have them water-tight; and, if made of well-seasoned plank and well oiled, they would remain so for a long time. When they are required for a raft, take them from the waggon and place them in two rows about three feet apart, and also with an interval of 3in. between the ends of the boxes in the same line—as shown in the illustration (B, p. 125)—with the tapered side boxes, as indicated by the numbers, forming the four ends. If you have been able to carry a couple of long stout bamboos, lay them along the inner side of each line of boxes, and if you have lighter ones to lay along the outer sides, so much the better; if you have not bamboos, the dissel-booms and lifter poles of the waggons must be pressed into service, or poles sought in the nearest forest, long and as straight as possible; then take the yokes off the oxen and lay them across in the 3in. spaces between the boxes, and passing the "reims" or other thongs cut from raw hide through the holes made for the yoke "skeis," lash each yoke to the fore and aft poles, securing the boxes each in its own compartment by passing a few turns through the handles in the ends and round the yokes. When this is completed, you will have a very serviceable raft or double canoe. The hinges of the chests will, of course, be towards the centre, so that when opened the lids will fall inwards; and if other poles are now laid fore and aft upon the yokes, they will support the lids so as to form the deck, leaving the chests open, so that, if any of them should leak, the water may be at once seen and baled out; but should it be thought preferable to keep the boxes closed, the buik plank or floor of the waggon, or even its sides, may be made use of for the deck. If the traveller contemplates a long voyage, and requires a sharper boat so as to attain more speed, he may make four of his boxes (marked D 7, 8, 9, 10) tapering diagonally to 8in. at one end; but he must take care that they are

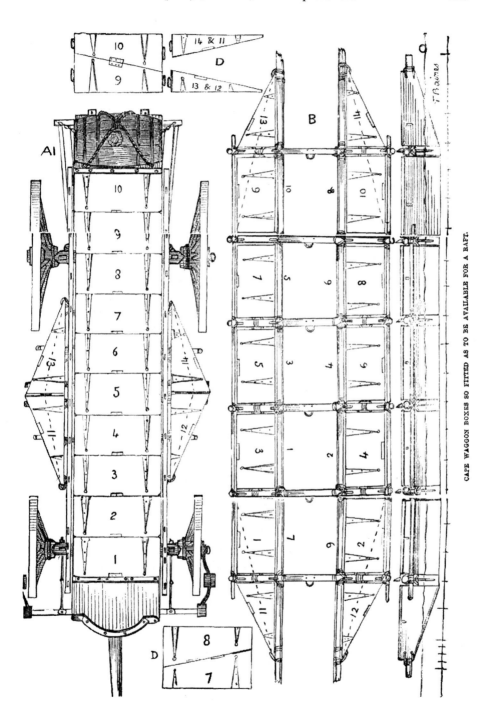

CAPE WAGGON BOXES SO FITTED AS TO BE AVAILABLE FOR A RAFT.

made in pairs, so that he may be able to place the straight and the diagonal side of each in its proper position in the raft. He will then also find that they will be easily arranged so that each pair will stow square in the waggon; then the side boxes (D 11 to 14) must be made only 8in. wide at the larger end, tapering as before at the smaller, and, with a slight diminution of floating power, he will have a sharper and more speedy boat. The figures in the central spaces of B indicate the changes of position in the numbered boxes, and the dotted lines show the increase of sharpness at the ends. It is of importance that in the boxes which taper, one side should be straight and square with the end, and one only diagonal, as it might be necessary in a narrow stream, to place both the lines of boxes close together, and then the line of the inner sides being perfectly straight and the outer tapering, the whole would form one boat sharp enough at either end.

Some of the yoke "skeis" might be left in their sockets where required, as shown in the elevation, or other pieces might be cut to a proper length, to serve for tholes or rowlocks, awning stanchions, or belaying pins. If a mast were needed, it might be stepped by cutting jaws like those on the gaff of a cutter, and setting them across one of the yokes. The fork of a branch might serve; but as poles generally become thinner upward, and the natural position would be thus reversed, it would be less laborious to cut or fit on jaws to the butt of the pole, and leave the fork at top for the halyards to run over. Two back stays would be required, spreading at a considerable angle; and one or two fore stays, with sufficient spread not to interfere with the free motion of the yard: two, three, or four poles, set up as a triangle or sheer legs, would also serve, and then only one stay, stretching perpendicularly downwards between them, would be required.

In ferrying wheels over, the readiest way (if the breadth of the boat permits) is to keep each pair on their own axle, which is laid across the boat, with the wheels overhanging each side.

Even if the traveller be not provided with a waggon, he must have with him a quantity of stores, or materials for whatever scientific pursuit he is engaged in, as well as beads, calico, or other currency of the country, to pay for service, or purchase food; and if his boxes for containing these were all of uniform size, they would serve equally well as a raft; the copper boxes described at pages 8 and 9 are expressly designed for this service.

In floating a waggon over without extraneous assistance, the buik plank or floor, the water cask, the fore and after chests, and the side boxes, will be sufficient, if tolerably water-tight—and if not, they may easily be made so, either by covering them with canvas, by caulking them or even laying them in the river all night to let the wood swell, which will generally have the desired effect. But it would be well, if this is at all doubtful, to remove the drag chains, "reim-schoens," and all easily detachable ironwork, and first float over only the under carriage and its wheels. If a line can be previously stretched across the river, and the oxen ready in their yokes on the other side attached to it, they may save much trouble by towing it across, while one or two men steer till the wheels take the ground, and it is drawn on shore in the natural way. The buik plank, with the casks and chests still fast to it, can be taken back for the rest of the heavy gear, and as much of the cargo as it will carry. If large hollow reeds—the drier the better —can be obtained, faggots of these can be fastened fore and aft, within the side chests, filling up nearly the whole space, except sufficient for the men to stand on in the centre; and a light platform can be laid above the top of the chests, on which to lay light goods which require to be kept dry. But bear in mind that the cargo a raft can carry above water is always small, and not at all like the mountain of treasure invariably represented on that of Robinson Crusoe,

To float waggons.

About 1849 or 1850, while staying with our fellow-traveller, Joseph Macabe, at Vaal River, an extraordinary drought prevailed; the great river could be crossed dryshod at the "drift" by means of stepping-stones, though there were long reaches above and below in which a good-sized vessel might have floated, and on one of the sand-banks then laid bare appeared an upright pole, belonging to a waggon which the owner had attempted to float over with bundles of green reeds, leaving the "rein-schoems" and drag-chains on as ballast, and previously removing the sides, the chests, buik plank, and everything else that could impede its passage to the bottom.

Whilst gazing at this odd landmark Mynheer appeared; with him came a goodly staff of tall athletic sons and nephews, attended by a numerous train of native helpers. On digging for the waggon, it was found to have settled so far below the sand that when the tallest of the family stood on the tire of the wheel his shoulders were barely at the surface of the water, and Mynheer had yoked his oxen and was attempting to draw out the waggon by a horizontal strain. We forbore to offer advice which would certainly have been rejected, but retired to the house, and when one of the sons visited us after the day's fruitless labour we rigged a pair of miniature shears, and, letting them incline over a weight, showed

Extricating waggons from quicksands, &c.

how easily it might be lifted by applying a horizontal strain to cause the shears to rise to a vertical position. The result of this was that Mynheer sent up a request that, as " een groote zee-water's men," we would come and give him a bit of advice. We accordingly suggested that, as the sand was not firm enough to set the shear legs upon, he should cut three good-sized beams, and laying one horizontally, cut mortices in the ends, while tenons were cut on the other two to fit in them, the apex of the triangle being firmly lashed with the "reims" or thongs of softened hide, used for spanning in the oxen. The triangle was now set up sloping somewhat over the fore-stell, or carriage of the buried waggon, and one of the drag-chains was fastened to the wheel

EXTEMPORE SHEARS.

and led over the top of the shears, whence, lengthened out by the other chain and spare rope, it was bent on to the " trek-touw " to which the oxen were already yoked. At length the cattle bent them to the yokes, the gear tightened and strained, the dissel-boom, that so long had been our beacon, began to rise, when some fastening gave way and all came down by the run ; the pole, however, remaining a foot higher than it was before. A native was desired to refasten the chain ; and, sticking two fingers of his left hand into his nostrils in a manner no European could imitate, he settled down below the water, and worked with his right hand only. Piece by piece the waggon was hauled out during the succeeding days, after having been three years and three days imbedded.

In exploring countries covered with dense forests or difficult to be traversed, rafts are wonderfully useful for navigating lakes and rivers, or for conveying your goods. Dr. R. Brown, commander of the expedition in Vancouver's Island, favours us with the following note :—

" We travelled long distances by rafts in Vancouver's Island, and, in order to have facilities for making them, we caused an augur (2in.) to be constructed with a ring-head instead of the usual spike with a nut, so that, by a piece of wood being Trenneled rafts. put through it, a handle might be extemporised. Generally speaking we could find dry fallen cedar (*Thuja gigantea*) by the borders of lakes or rivers, or if not, living cotton wood (*Salix Scouleriana*) will do ; and in fact any wood, though pine is rather too heavy and apt to get waterlogged

" Cutting two lengths of logs, the length of the raft required, sharpening the ' bows ' off roughly, we laid them on the ground, parallel, and as far apart as we wished them. Then two cross-pieces, composed of a log split in two, were pegged by means of the auger across near the ends, over them was built a floor of split cedar boards. Two rowlocks were pegged in here and there according to the number of rowers required, and one pair at the end for a steering oar. Oars were soon extemporised by means of the axe, and the raft moved lazily along at about one and a half or two miles an hour on a lake, but the labour was infinitely easier than working through the wood with a seventy or eighty pound load on your back.

" Sometimes we constructed even ruder rafts than these. Mr. Frederick Whymper and Mr. Ranald M'Donald once descended twenty miles of a river on a little raft composed of the boards out of an Indian's hunting lodge, tying it together with withes of cedar twigs, which are very tough, and used by the Indians for sewing their canoes and fastening their lodge planks together. The holes they made with pistol bullets."

The general principal on which all rafts are or ought to be constructed is nearly the same; that is, if they are intended to be worked or to make progress through the water, as in most Principles of raft building. cases is desirable. The exceptions to this are generally when it is merely desired to float down a stream, abandoning the raft as worthless when the voyage is completed, or when produce or manufacture of any kind has to be brought down from a higher country to a lower, and, from its buoyancy it may be collected into a raft, which on reaching its destination, may be reduced to its component parts and sold ; or where, as in still more exceptional cases, it is necessary to provide floating habitations for families or small communities without reference to locomotion, which is effected by other means.

In the first and most general case, the object is to obtain sufficient

K

carrying power with as little resistance to progression as possible; and to this end the larger spars, on which the buoyancy of the whole depends, ought to be laid parallel to, and at such a distance from, each other as seems necessary either to insure the requisite stability, to give sufficient room on deck, or to suit the length of those that are to be used as cross-beams; but they should never be laid close together so as to present a broad united surface to be forced through the water, nor even so close as to convert that portion of fluid between them into dead water to be dragged like a solid body with the raft. We would say, if there be two or more spars of equal size, let the interval between them be at least three times as broad as their diameter, and generally let the width of your raft be not more than one-sixth of its length. If you have only one large spar, let that form the centre, or, as it may be called, the keel, and let the smaller ones, either singly or lashed together in bundles of convenient size, be laid parallel to it at proper distances on either side. Endeavour as much as possible to keep your cross-beams as high above the water as possible, for if these are submerged, their sides will offer as much resistance to your progress as if the whole raft had been filled up with solid logs. On this account, therefore, it would be advisable to lash or pin on the top of each of the main beams either a smaller one to increase its height, or short pieces at intervals, as chocks on which to lay the cross-beams.

Let the ends of the spars that form your floats be pointed to an acute angle by either sawing off wedge-shaped pieces of about 15° or 20° in the sides, or chopping them with axe or adze.

The cross-beams at each end and one in the centre must be securely fastened. Do not have too many, nor keep them too close together; but let the others cross diagonally in opposite directions, or even brace the frame thus formed by stout ropes stretched diagonally from corner to corner, and seized together with smaller lines where they cross each other in the centre, which will give great firmness and rigidity to the structure.

Let us suppose, for instance, the case of a stranded or water-logged brig of about 200 tons, of which the lower masts and the wreck of some of the other spars are still available. If the masts can be got out so much the better, for they would be in the whole not much short of 60ft. long; but it is much more probable they would have to be cut by the board, and perhaps also below the hounds, which would still leave clean spars between 30ft. and 40ft. in length, and most likely 14in. thick. If the mast-heads were left on they would be at least 10ft. longer, but the tops should be removed, and the projecting portion of the hounds chopped down so as to offer as little impediment to progress as possible; the masts should be laid parallel to each other about 8ft. apart, and the main boom, lower yards and jib boom, or spare topmast, if available, lashed together as a faggot, and laid between them as a central spar. A short, stout spar, such as the heel of a broken topmast, should then be laid across at 6ft. or 8ft. from either end, and firmly lashed to them, and one, or at most two, more may be laid across in like manner near the centre; the intervals between these should be occupied by small spars laid across diagonally, or by cross bracings of rope as before described; it is of little use to peg or treenail the parts together, unless the water is very smooth, for the pegs would be sure to break with the working of the raft in a heavy sea. We have suggested the heels of the topmasts as cross-beams, because their thickness would help to raise the platform above the level of the sea, and this might be farther raised by laying a couple of studding sail booms fore and aft upon the masts under them, and laying the deck with short spars or pieces of plank across the booms. If tools can be got at or used, mortices may be sunk in the masts, or fore and aft spars, and handspikes or capstan bars set upright in them at intervals of 6ft.; these will carry a light rail to prevent men being washed off, and will serve to spread an awning when such a luxury can be attempted, and also as supports to which rowlocks can conveniently be fastened.

If the vessel is provided with sleeping bunks, which are sometimes lashed to ring-bolts on the deck, it might be well to secure at least one of them; if not an empty hogshead or anything that can serve as a place of temporary shelter for a wearied man, or for the commander to consult his charts and compass in, should be fitted on the platform. A sheet of iron, or non-combustible material of any kind, should be taken to form the foundation of a fire-place; and if there is choice of provisions, preserved fresh meat should be taken in preference to salt, with as much biscuit, vegetables, vinegar, sugar, tea or coffee, and fresh water, as circumstances permit. If canvas is at hand, sails will be easily made, if not, any flat surface, sheets of iron or planks, either separate or framed together, may be set up that the raft may sail free, or trimmed for her to go as near the wind as she will lie.

If three casks are available as floating power, make a triangle of studding sail booms, and lash each angle firmly on the top of one of the casks, taking care to keep their heads pointing forward to that which is intended to be the bow; then on these spars build such platform as you need, and erect your mast and sail.

A couple of spare topmasts brought together at their heads, and extended by a shorter spar at their heels, so as to form a triangle more or less acute, form a good foundation for a raft; the space between may then be filled with whatever buoyant material you possess, whether casks, boxes, or smaller spars.   No rules can be considered absolute in raft making; anything that will float, and can be lashed together in any manner, must be used; if a portion of the vessel's deck can be cut out by axe or saw it may form a good foundation; if the raft can be built on board the wreck, or on the beach beside her, so much the better, but it would be better to throw the materials

overboard, and, at the cost of any extra labour, construct it in the water, than not be able fairly to launch it when completed.   We have seen the waist stanchions of a waterlogged vessel cut away for such a purpose, or in extreme cases the hull may be expected to go down, and then the only anxiety will be to complete the raft so that it may be capable of floating off the sinking vessel.   In the water a rectangular raft is best built alongside the vessel, but the triangular one must be built astern.

Of buoyant merchandise formed into rafts for the purpose of floating down rivers to the markets, we have an example in the Pot raft.   pottery floats upon the Nile, where a number of jars having been made, are bound together, and a platform of reeds laid on them.   The long timber rafts upon the Rhine and on the rivers of Canada and North America are also examples of this principle.

On some of the larger rivers of Africa, as the Okovango, discovered by our late friend C. J. Andersson, the Teoughe and others, rafts of sedge grass are used; sometimes these, if only intended to carry a few persons Sedge-grass   across a river are small and comparatively manageable, rafts.   and have even an attempt at comfort and security in a kind of rail raised round them of faggots of the same material.   Others, used in hippopotamus hunting, are mere floats on which the small canoes are drawn up, and their chief merit is that they are so like natural accumulations that the animal does not think of getting out of their way.

On a still larger heap of these Mr. Andersson descended the tortuous course of the Teoughe for many miles; and Mr. Oscar T. Lindholm, who accompained the eminent but unfortunate Swedish naturalist Wahlberg, gave us a most graphic account of a similar voyage. Immense quantities of sedge was collected, and bundles of it were thrown upon the water in some quiet nook, without any regularity and with no other fastening than its own natural cohesion and entanglement when one layer was thrown almost at random across another. A small hut was built upon the heap when it had acquired sufficient size, and the whole, when ready, was forced out into the stream, which brought it down at an average rate of two and a half miles per hour. If it took the ground, the only consequence was the loss of a few reeds from the bottom layer as the mass swung round and cleared itself. Snags, projecting points, or other impediments might tear off more, but nothing could stay the quiet but irresistible movement of the great raft, which, as the grass below became densely pressed and sodden, began to draw nearly 6ft. of water, and sank deeper every day; to remedy which, fresh grass was cut and thrown daily upon the upper layers. Frequently overhanging trees tore off portions, and once a large trunk lay so close to the water that it fairly swept the decks fore and aft; the occupants saved themselves by climbing over the tree, but the hut, with many valuables, was carried right away. With this exception the voyage was accomplished safely, but it was a task of great difficulty to prevent the unwieldy mass being swept by the stream into Lake Ngami, in the still waters of which it might have floated for an indefinite period without coming nearer to the shore.

The obelisk of Luxor was removed by laying a vessel ashore, with her head towards it, when the river was at its highest; the masts were lifted and shored up from the deck, so as to allow an immense packing case to be built upon the keelson; ways like those for launching a ship were built, and on them the heavy monolith was forced onward till it lay at length fairly in the vessel, occupying nearly her entire length; a deep channel cut from the vessel to the river, and at the next rise of the water she floated off. But without forgetting this, we do not remember a case of more ingenious and persevering adaptation of apparently insufficient means to great and important ends, than that of the conveyance by our countryman, Layard, of the great human-headed bulls and lions from the magnificent ruins in which he found them to the point of embarkation on the Tigris, and thence, by rafts so frail that we almost wonder how the ponderous masses were supported, to a place where vessels more adequate to the carriage of such a burden could receive them. It would be a pity to curtail the brief and graphic description, and we therefore give it in his own words :—

" I did not doubt that the skins, once blown up, would support the sculptures without difficulty as far as Baghdad. The journey would take eight or ten days, under favourable circumstances. But there they would require to be opened and refilled, or the rafts would scarcely sustain so heavy a weight all the way to Busrak; the voyage from Baghdad to that port being considerably longer, in point of time, than that from Mosul to Baghdad. However carefully the skins are filled, the air gradually escapes. Rafts bearing merchandise are generally detained several times during their descent to enable the raftmen to examine and refill the skins. If the sculptures rested upon only one framework, the beams being almost on a level with the water, the raftmen would be unable to get beneath them to reach the mouths of the skins, when they require replenishing, without moving the cargo. This would have been both inconvenient and difficult to accomplish; I was, therefore, desirous of raising the lion and bull as much as possible above the water, so as to leave room for the men to creep under them.

" It may interest the reader to know how these rafts, which have probably formed for ages the only means of traffic on the upper parts of the rivers of Mesopotamia, are constructed. The skins of full-grown sheep and goats are used. They are taken off with as few incisions as possible, and then dried and prepared. The air is forced in by the lungs through an aperture, which is afterwards tied up with string. A square framework, formed of poplar beams, branches of trees, and reeds, having been constructed of the size of the intended raft, the inflated skins are tied to it by osier and other twigs, the whole being firmly bound together. The raft is then removed to the water and launched. Care is taken to place the skins with their mouths upwards, that, in case any should burst or require filling, they can be easily opened by the raftmen. Upon the framework of wood

INFLATED FLOATS.

are piled bales of goods and property belonging to merchants and travellers. When any person of rank or wealth descends the river in this fashion, small huts are constructed on the raft, by covering a common wooden "takht," or bedstead of the country, with a hood formed of reeds and lined with felt. In these huts the travellers live and sleep during the journey. The poorer passengers seek shade or warmth by burying themselves amongst bales of goods and other merchandise, and sit patiently, almost in one position, until they reach their destination. They carry with them a small earthen "mangal," or chafing-fish, containing a charcoal fire, which serves to light their pipes and to cook their coffee and food. The only real danger to be apprehended on the river is from the Arabs, who, when the country is in a disturbed state, invariably attack and pillage the rafts.

"The raftmen guide their rude vessels by long oars—straight poles, at the end of which a few split canes are fastened by a piece of twine. They skilfully avoid the rapids, and, seated on the bales of goods, work continually, even in the hottest sun. They will seldom travel after dark before reaching Tekrit, on account of the rocks and shoals which abound in the upper part of the river; but when they have passed that place they resign themselves, night and day, to the sluggish stream. During the floods in the spring, or after violent rains, small rafts may float from Mosul to Baghdad in about eighty-four hours; but the large rafts are generally six or seven days in performing the voyage. In summer, and when the river is low, they are frequently nearly a month in reaching their destination. When the rafts have been unloaded, they are broken up, and the beams, wood, and twigs are sold at a considerable profit, forming one of the principle branches of trade between Mosul and Baghdad. The skins are washed and afterwards rubbed with a preparation of pounded pomegranate skins, to keep them from cracking and rotting. They are then brought back, either upon the shoulders of the raftmen or upon donkeys, to Mosul or Tekrit, where the men engaged in navigation of the Tigris usually reside."

In one of the sculptures thus brought to our own country by the energetic traveller, an army is represented crossing a river, and the soldiers are supported each by an inflated goatskin held under the chest, while one of the legs being led upwards to the swimmer's mouth enables him to keep it distended, should any air escape. In making these bags, the only sewing necessary is at the aperture  through which the animal is skinned; the neck, cut close to the heap, may be tightly bound up with a thong, and an over-hand knot cast in the three legs; the fourth being left with a tube for re-inflation.

Sir Samuel Baker says, when speaking of crossing the Atbara River, "I had eight inflated skins attached to the bedstead, on which I lashed our large circular sponging bath, 3ft. 8in. in diameter. This was perfectly safe for my wife, and dry for the baggage; the watertight iron box that contained the gunpowder was towed as a pinnace behind the raft. Four hippopotamus hunters harnessed themselves as tug steamers, and there were relays of swimmers. The raft answered well, and would support about 300lb.; the sponging bath would carry 190lb.

Colonel R. C. Buchanan, of the United States service, is the American portable inventor of a very useful form of portable boat. It boat. was used in several expeditions, in Oregon and Washington territory, with much advantage. It is thus described :—

"It consists of an exceedingly light framework of thin and narrow boards, in lengths suitable for packing, connected by hinges, the different sections folding into so small a compass as to be conveniently carried upon mules. The frame is covered with a sheet of stout cotton canvas or duck, secured to the gunwales with a cord running diagonally back, and put through eyelet holes in the upper edge.

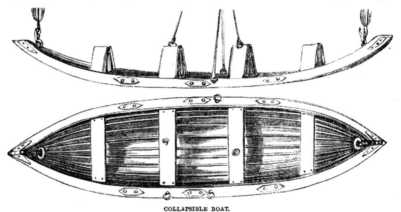

COLLAPSIBLE BOAT.

When first placed in the water, the boat leaks a little, but the canvas soon swells, so as to make it sufficiently tight for all practical purposes. The great advantage to be derived from the use of this boat is, that it is so compact and portable as to be admirably adapted to the requirements of campaigning in a country where the streams are liable to rise above a fordable depth, and where the allowance of transportation is small. It may be put together or taken apart and packed in a very few minutes, and one mule suffices to transport a boat, with all its appurtenances, capable of sustaining ten men. Should the canvas become torn, it is easily repaired by putting on a patch, and it does not rot or crack, like india-rubber or gutta-percha; moreover it is not affected by changes of climate or temperature."

We have not seen Colonel Buchanan's boat, but we remember one perhaps not very dissimilar, it was, in fact, a collapsible boat—the gun-

wales, the keel, and all the intermediate pieces being exactly alike, and
made of ¾in. plank from 4in. to 6in. wide ; these were hinged together
at the two ends, just as are the frames of the oval reti- Collapsible
cules, and covered with stout canvas ; the thwarts have boat.
hinges below the centre, from which also the third board, serving as a
stanchion, reaches downward to rest upon the keel.   There is a ring-
bolt near the centre of each of the midship thwarts, and when the boat
is hoisted out of the water by tackles at either end, a couple of small
lines from these rings jerk up the centre of the thwarts and allow the
gunwales and all the corresponding boards on either side to fall down
beside the keel, as shown in the upper figure of our illustration (p.136).
There are also ring-bolts to the gunwales, and a couple of lines from
these are held fast while the boat is lowered ; the gunwales rise, and
a man sitting on the thwarts presses them into their place and the
boat assumes its proper shape ; of course the segments of plank
below the gunwales have to be cut a little shorter at each end as they
come nearer to the keel, or the boat would not shut up on its hinges.
A boat 4ft. wide would collapse into a width of not more than 1ft.
Such a frame could be readily taken to pieces by withdrawing the
bolts of the hinges, and if each piece, supposing the boat to be 4ft.
wide and 16ft. long were hinged in its centre, it would not be much
too long to carry on a mule, except the country were more than ordinarily difficult, when it might be hinged in three lengths.

At the meeting of the British Association, in Birmingham, we saw
some model boats of good form, but with very little projection of keel or
stem or stern post, so that one might be fitted into the other without
rising more than a few inches above the gunwale of the first; the thwarts
of the lower one are stowed between the two very conveniently, and
three or four may be thus packed, the uppermost, however, retaining
all her fittings in readiness for immediate use.

The aborigines of many countries make use of the bark of certain
trees for the purpose of canoe building.   The most important of these
is the canoe birch (*Betula papyracea*) ; its range may be Canoe birch.
estimated at 37° north to 43° south. Trees of this
description not unfrequently grow to 70ft. in height, and are proportionately thick, so that sheets of bark of very large size can be readily
stripped from them.   The bark canoes of the Canadians and Indian
traders are often of a very large size.

In the absence of forest conservators, economic considerations
go for very little.   It may be convenient, when canoe building or
repairing is the object, to " fall" the tree, and, in doing so, care
must be taken that the bark shall not be rent or bruised, either by

fracture of the tree or by falling across a rock or stump, while the log ought to lie with both ends somewhat supported, so that the required sheet of bark may not be crushed between it and the ground. Perhaps it will be found generally easier to detach the bark while the tree is standing, and in this case a cut must be made all round the tree at the lower end of the sheet; the most perfect side should be left for the bottom of the canoe, and the longitudinal slit should be so made as to cut right through any defective portion which may thus be cut out with the least possible waste of material. If the tree has an inclination, it will be easier work to make the slit on the upper side. The bark should be detached by broad round-edged spuds of soft wood, thrust gently and cautiously between it and the tree, and it may also be previously loosened by striking it with a broad log or mallet on the outside, taking care not to break its texture. Steps may be cut in the wood to stand in, and hand-holds also as the work proceeds; and the lower part of the bark should be made fast with cord or slips of bark, passed loosely round, so that it may not swing clear of the tree and split the upper part before it is finally detached.

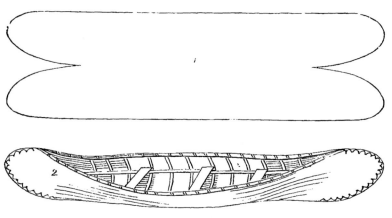

CANADIAN BARK CANOE.

The sheet should now be taken to a plot of level ground, carefully spread out with the inside downward, and the outside should be cleaned from any knots, excrescences, or hard and brittle Canadian bark layers that increase its weight without adding to   canoe. its strength; and it should then be cut nearly to the form shown in the sketch (Fig. 1). A sufficient number of ribs or hoops of light flexible wood should be provided, and great care should be taken, in bending it, not to split or unduly to force any part so as to make an unsightly protuberance, which would also most probably become a leak. The holes should be carefully bored along the edges that come in contact, and they may be sewn with fibres from the roots of pine trees or from small cedar twigs, and rendered water-tight by the use of pine-tree gum. Flexible poles or laths are then stitched in for gunwales or thwart stringers, and the canoe is more or less tastefully trimmed off and ornamented, according to the taste of the builder, as in Fig. 2 (p. 138).

Canoes of this description are wonderfully buoyant, and draw very little water; and, when managed by skilful hands, few boats are more reliable. Our friend, Mr. F. Poole, who has spent many years among the Indians of

Queen Charlotte's Island canoe.

BIRCH BARK CANOE OF QUEEN CHARLOTTE'S ISLAND.

North-West America, and is a canoeman of no ordinary skill, has recently completed a tour of extraordinary extent and interest, paddling fearlessly, and alone, far out to sea. The dimensions of the canoe he uses, which was made expressly for him by the Indians of Queen Charlotte's Island, are as follows : Length, 15ft.; width across beam, 3½ft.; depth, 15in.; weight, 100lb.

In her Mr. Poole started from Liverpool, paddling to New Brighton, from thence to Southport, Blackpool, Fleetwood, Dutton Sands, Whitehaven, Kirkcudbright, Whitehorn, Port William and Glen Luce. From thence by the use of wheels—two pairs of which, composed of iron, mounted on iron axles, are kept, until required, stowed away in the canoe—Mr. Poole proceeded overland to Stranraer; from thence paddled along the coast and up the river to Glasgow; then by canal to Grangemouth, and by sea to Leith. For two nights and the greater part of two days Mr. Poole was out of sight of land, and the voyage was prosecuted during the prevalence of the equinoctial gales. Such of our readers as may contemplate canoe voyaging will do well to borrow a few hints from Mr. Poole's equipment. A powerful bull's-eye lamp was always carried, lashed fast to the stem at night, and a mariner's compass was provided to steer by.

The wheels before referred to are extremely useful in many ways. They are like those of an ordinary perambulator, only of light wrought iron; they are 1ft. in diameter; the axle is also of wrought iron, ¾in. square, and long enough to carry the wheels clear of the canoe's sides when mounted on them.   To travel the canoe on dry land, the axles, each covered with a strong common pillow, are brought under the fore and after portions of the canoe, like the axles of a long narrow carriage.   Rope lashings are now brought from the thwarts down to the axle bars, through which iron belaying pins pass; these keep the lashings from shifting, and keep all secure when the canoe is pushed or drawn onwards.   The wheels are an immense assistance in beaching the canoe and getting her above high-water mark, when there is but one voyager.   They also serve as ballast, and are useful for a number of camping and makeshift purposes.

The paddle shown in the accompanying illustration, kindly furnished by Mr. Poole, is of the exact form requisite to obtain perfect efficiency. It is composed of red cedar, and is exactly onetenth, diminished scale.

The bark of the cedar (*Thuja gigantea*) is also much used by certain Indians of North-West America for canoe building; but the form usually made from it differs materially from that just described.   The cedar-bark canoes are in shape much like some of our iron-clad rams, having projecting beaks, or prows, almost in a line with their keels.   The Indian paddling one of these frail craft, sits, or rather squats, at one extreme end of the bottom, which has the effect of tilting the bow end up in the air, burying the stern end deeply in the water.   The sharp taillike point thus immersed seems to impart speed and capability of evolution to a remarkable degree; much practice is required before the exact poise and adjustment of weight are acquired. The Indians, who half live in their canoes, manage them with extraordinary dexterity, ascend and descend rapid rivers, and cross wide

Cedar-bark canoe.

stretches of lake fearlessly. The form of these canoes, and of the bark sheet used for making them, is shown in the above illustration.

CEDAR-BARK CANOE.

The mode of sinking the stern of a canoe is also had recourse to by the Rockingham Bay savages, who manage the so-called shoe canoe with

much skill. The frame is of rough wicker-work, the covering of hide, and the two short shovel-shaped paddles made use of are shown in our

illustration. A canoe of this kind is very easily made, and is not difficult to manage.

We have just seen a small canoe sent from Terra del Fuego by the Governor of the Falkland Islands to the Royal Geographical Society. It is small, and was paddled by a

SHOE CANOE.

girl eight years of age ; it is chiefly interesting as showing how small pieces of bark may be utilised. It is about 8ft. long, 22in. wide, and 18in. or 20in. deep ; the centrepiece of the bottom is nearly 3ft. long and 10in. wide, and to this are stitched two pieces, each about

4ft. long, tapering to a point, and curving upward to a high peak at either end. The sides are pieces of bark nearly 8ft. long and 18in.

Fuegian canoe. deep, straight on the upper edge, and cut to the curve of the bottom on the lower. The whole are stitched together with wood fibre, for which sometimes strips of whalebone are substituted, and caulked with the fibre of the wild celery. The boat is kept in shape by ribs of winter bark twigs, not thicker than the little finger, and packed closely side by side through the whole length; nine small sticks lashed athwart the gunwales keep them in their proper shape, and a sheet of bark midships serves to sustain a patch of clay on which to keep a small fire. A bundle of weapons of he chase accompany this canoe.

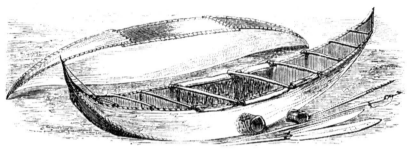

FUEGIAN CANOE.

The spears are pointed with bone, and the barbed one used for fish and cetaceans is only shipped loosely into the shaft, to which it is attached by a lanyard, so as to remain fast during the struggles of the animal; while that used for birds is serrated, and is firmly fastened into the shaft.

The tea-tree bark is sometimes used in Australia for canoes. We have seen a length of it roughly tied up at the ends, and strengthened

Australian a little by poles along the gunwales, in use at Moreton
bark canoe. Bay, as shown in our illustration. It is just possible to make the bark of the gum tree answer the purpose in the absence of better material. We have often searched in Africa for a tree with bark fit to make a canoe of, but never succeeded in finding one. Along the eastern coast of Australia, especially towards Torres Strait, we frequently fell in with canoes, some with outriggers and others double. They were generally long straight logs, of very little breadth or depth; and the advantage of this seemed to be that though the ripple would frequently wash into them, yet, if they pitched ever so little, their great length and shallowness would tilt out the greater portion of the water. The outriggers were mostly logs of wood

sharpened at either end, and with pegs set up in them, so that the outrigger beams might not dip into the water and impede the motion of the canoe.

AUSTRALIAN BARK CANOE.

When we reached the Victoria River we found that the natives were accustomed to support themselves in crossing on logs of the light mangrove wood, either singly or tied up in bundles. The part near

MANGROVE FLOATS.

the roots seemed to be the favourite, as the stumps of the roots formed pegs on which to hang their spears, skins, or other possessions. The wood of the milk bush, which is about half the specific gravity of cork, is much used by the natives of equatorial Africa for the above purpose.

At Shupanga, on the Zambesi, we have seen dug-out canoes

50ft. long and about 5ft. wide and deep; at all events, a tall man
standing beside them did not stoop much when he
rested his arms upon the gunwale. These were
hollowed and roughly shaped in their native forests, and hauled
along nearly thirty miles, on rollers, by the long rope-like stems
of the vines and creepers common in tropical forests. They were
made only for the Portuguese. The upper part of the bows .
expanded into a platform sufficiently large for the chief boatman to
stand on, while the stern was cut into an imitation of a run and dead
wood, with a couple of holes in the after part, to which a rudder was
secured by lashings. Nothing can be better for hollowing a canoe
than the adze, but our Kroomen used a broad spud or chisel on a staff
about 6ft. long, driven in a manner which will be best understood by
a glance at the statue of "Michael overthrowing Satan." The
Krooman's method of baling is characteristic. Should the canoe fill,
all hands jump overboard, seize the gunwales, and sally her fore and
aft till the water flies out at either end and leaves her absolutely free.
We have seen a canoeman, near Lake Ngami, walk to one end of
his leaky craft and, thus depressing it, cause the water to flow
towards him, when, making his broad foot do duty for a scoop, by a
succession of vigorous kicks, he soon had his canoe as free as he
desired.

Long canoes.

In many parts of the world, boats of almost any size are built
without metal fastenings, and the Massoolah boat of Madras may be
taken as a fair type of those which are sewn or laced
together. It will be seen in our illustration, copied
by permission from a model in the United Service Museum, that
the bottom boards are flat and form an oval elongated and pointed
at the ends, so that the side planks curve naturally to meet the
stem and stern-post, and give the boat an easy sheer. They are
sewn together with coir yarn (or cocoa-nut husk fibre), the stitches
crossing over a wadding of coir or straw, which presses on the
seam and prevents much leakage. They are very elastic and give
to the shock as they take the ground in the surf, which runs
sometimes nearly 16ft. high; they are from 30ft. to 35ft. long, 10ft.
or 11ft. wide, and 7ft. or 8ft. in depth; they pull double banked,
six oars on a side, made of long rough poles with oval pieces
of board lashed to the ends; they are steered by an oar. Our
illustration shows also the catamaran or log float, on which the
natives will pass to and from the shore when no other craft, not
even the Massoolah boat, would venture. It must be remembered,
however, that the men are themselves nearly amphibious, and care

Massoolah boats.

as little for being washed off their rafts as so many frogs; while the letters or small parcels they carry are kept dry only by being worn in a kind of oil-cloth turban.

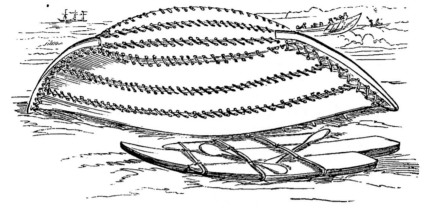

MASSOOLAH BOATS.

We have seen very nice boats built in Norway with dowels instead of nails; they are clinker built, and the dowels were about ½in., or fully as thick as the planking. A number of rods, from *Norwegian boats.* 3ft. to 4ft. long, are planed up to the required size, and cut into lengths say, when two thicknesses of ½in. plank are to be clinched, to 1½in., or, when the two planks and a timber of perhaps 1in. are to be fastened, to 2½in., so that both ends may project a little beyond the wood they are to fasten; the dowel is then split at each end with a sharp chisel, taking care that the cut is made at right angles to the grain of the plank or rib, wedges are driven in, and the end, being slightly spread out by the use of the clench hammer, is trimmed off not too close; the wedges should be all neatly cut with a fine saw, and by sawing them in breadths from a board, and then splitting them to the required size, labour may be greatly economised. The holes should be bored with a sharp centre-bit; and if the dowels fit tightly the wedges may be dispensed with, as the ends will spread sufficiently under the clench hammer without breaking the grain.

In building, if any difficulty should be found in drawing down the end of the plank to the stem, it will be advisable, after having fitted it carefully, to slack up the centre, let the end come to its place, fasten it, and then again bend the plank downwards. In some boats, especially in the navy, the planks do not run fore and aft, but two thin layers are crossed over each other diagonally, and clenched together; this leaves the outside perfectly smooth, and is perhaps the strongest known method of boat building. In planing up the edges of planks, &c., it is absolutely necessary to have a vice of some kind, and nothing is better than a tree vice, unless you have a blacksmith's. Saw off a young tree from 6in. to 8in. thick, at about 3½ft. from the ground; saw the stump down the middle as low as you can; bind the lower part tightly with thongs of raw hide to prevent its splitting, then insert wedges to open the upper part, put your planks in, withdraw the wedges, and it will hold tight enough. It is as well to cut the upper part of the opening sufficiently wide to admit an inch plank, as short

pieces can easily be put in to fill up should you wish to hold a thinner one.

We have already mentioned the principle on which Mr. E. D. Young's portable steel boat for the Livingstone Search Expedition was built; and although, as we then said, none but a skilled workman could hope to turn up the edges of a curved sheet of metal, we think the principle

Portable steel boat.

might be applied to a flat-bottomed boat by merely snipping the flanges at the turn of the bilge, and bending upward the sides at any convenient angle; by cutting these more and more diagonally from the centre, the boat might be tapered to each end —not, indeed, in a true curve, but in a succession of short straight lines, which would tolerably represent one.

The number of pieces composing the "Search"—the boat used in the expedition sent in quest of Dr. Livingstone—were as follows: Thirty-six side pieces of steel, each being a load for one man; the midship piece required 2; the stern piece, 3; the bow piece, 3; the mast, 2; the boom, 2; the sails, 2; chain cable, 6; anchor, 1; and the whole with provisions, luggage, &c., made up 180 loads.

Captain Faulkner, who, as a volunteer, accompanied Mr. Young on the Search Expedition, has determined on returning with a party of ardent hunters and explorers, and an engineer, to Lake Nyassa, and for this purpose an iron steamer has been built 50ft. long, 5½ft. deep, and 11½ft. broad. The little craft, appropriately named the "Faugh-aballagh," is composed of 75 sections, put together with 8000 screws, so that she may be carried, as was the "Search," past the rapids and cataracts of the Shire River.

The American life raft "Nonpareil," which some time ago made the voyage across the Atlantic, may be taken as a successful application of the tubular system. It will be seen that she was constructed of three parallel inflatable tubes, covered American life raft.
with stout canvas, connected by breadths of the same, and with a rectangular frame laid over all to support the masts and rudder

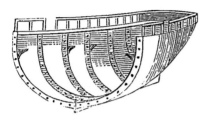

fittings; but the sketch is introduced here also to show the use of the droge, by which the little craft may in effect be anchored in the open sea, or at least may have her drift effectually checked, while the sea itself is broken before it reaches her. The droge in the present instance is of canvas, stretched on a large hoop with four lines, so attached to its circumference that when the strain comes on it it stands vertically in the water, and opposes the resistance of its entire surface. The oars or mast, and sails of a boat, will also answer this purpose; and we have heard of one instance in which the imperilled crew added also a number of the skins of
freshly-killed seals, the
oil working out of which
calmed the water for a
considerable distance. It
is necessary to watch
the length of the sea, so

that the boat may be veered as far from the droge or raft as it will serve to protect her against the breaking waves. We have heard the captain of a vessel say that he would never incur the risk of wearing in a gale, but would rather sacrifice some spar or piece of lumber to bring the ship's head to the wind. In doing this, the hawser would be carried round from the droge on the weather bow, under the bobstays and bowsprit rigging to the lee bow, and finally to the quarter; the droge would be thrown over, sufficient line paid out, and then held on to till the ship's head came to the wind ; the strain would be then changed for a moment to the lee bow, and then to the quarter, whence it would be cut away as the ship fell off upon the other tack. A spar held by a hawser, and bridle, with a stout sail bent to it—the clews, or lower corners, being weighted with shot, lead, or iron, to make them heavy—forms an excellent droge for a small craft to lie to under.

Although this subject may seem almost beyond the province of our work, it is by no means improbable that explorers may have to turn their attention to it, or that shipwrecked crews, or dwellers on a lonely coast, may have to repair or build small craft for themselves. We have seen first-class waggons built by missionaries, and others have built vessels ; and the reader may remember with advantage the description given by Ulysses of his laying down side by side ten or a dozen pine trees more or less smoothed off as a foundation on which to build his upper works.

Temporary repairs of vessels.

During the progress of the North Australian Expedition, we were ascending the Victoria River with our little schooner, the "Tom Tough." There was little or no wind, and with the boat ahead towing and the lead going we were drifting up with a strong flood-tide, and the captain, elated by success, and anxious to make the most of his opportunity, kept going onward instead of prudently anchoring while the tide was still rising.   In consequence of this, when the vessel touched the ground, there was no subsequent rise of water to float her off ; indeed, it was remarked that the water began to fall while the tide was still running upward, and she was left at low water on the 27th of September, 1855, on a mud bank, with her bows uncomfortably propped up by a projecting rock.

On the 29th she floated ; but the flood-tide was so nearly done, that we had no time to choose an anchorage, and the schooner grounding with the ebb, parted her chain cable and heeled over with the force of the tide till we could barely stand upon her decks.

Day after day the schooner drifted to and fro upon this sand bank, sometimes moving a length or two, and sometimes only a few feet during a tide ; the sand scoured out from beneath her bow and stern, leaving holes with 6ft. or more of water there, while hillocks accumulated under her in midship ; and the sand seemed to travel so evenly with her, that the usual criterion—a hand lead, allowed to trail upon the ground—was of no service in enabling us to estimate the distance she had moved.

On the 10th of October the decks had rifted, the combings of the main hatch had started up, the starboard side between the masts was hogged up 18in., and at the turn of the bilge, where the floor timbers join the ribs, one of the planks had split for 15ft. or more, leaving spaces into which the flat hand might easily be passed.

We laid broad strips of blanket and sheepskin well tarred on the principal rents, and nailed thin planks over them (Fig. 8, below), but in another day or two she was just as bad on the other side; her stern was peaked into the air, while her bows dipped about 7ft. into a hole, the water pouring out of the fresh rifted planking as the tide fell. The mainmast rose up through the partners, so that we were obliged to slack off the rigging, and it became a question whether the stanchion under the main hatch should be knocked away to prevent its bursting up the deck, or whether it should remain so that the strength of the deck might keep the bottom a little longer from breaking.

On the 25th we again floated, after nearly a month of straining to and fro upon the sand banks, and drifted rather than navigated the vessel up to the camp we had established below Steep-head.

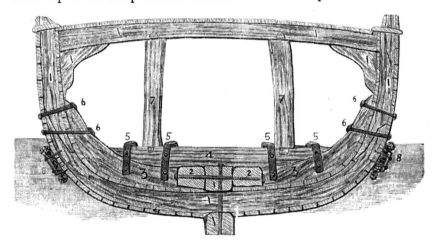

Captain Gourlay with his crew, and some of the expedition men, found suitable trees some little distance up the river at Timber Creek, which, however, after a rather exciting adventure with some wandering natives, acquired the name of Cut-Stick Creek instead. Two long heavy gum trees as straight as possible were selected, brought to the vessel, and laid as sister keelsons (Fig. 2) alongside the real one, which, as well as all the original framework, is marked Fig. 1 in our illustration. Three or four pair of heavy crooks, each representing the half of a floor timber (Fig. 3), were then laid on the inner skin, with the inner ends abutting on the sister keelson, and the outer reaching up above the junction of the ribs with the floor heads. Heavy riders (Fig. 4) were placed upon them crossing the three keelsons, and were secured by clamps (Fig. 5) made of the tires of our dray wheels, which we had no hope of being able to put to their proper use. Being now above the rise and fall of the tide we could not beach the vessel, and, therefore, the frame could only be bolted to the true sides above the water line (Fig 6), but it was pressed down upon the bottom not only by its own weight but by stanchions (Fig. 7) between it and the deck beams.

The schooner being detained for repairs, it was decided to under-take an expedition to the Albert River in the long boat; and thus, by reaching Mr. Gregory in time to assure him that a vessel was coming, prevent his starting for the colony with insufficient supplies; Mr. George Phibbs, the overseer of the expedition, and Mr. Graham, the mate of the "Messenger," volunteering for the trip, we com-menced our preparations. The boat was cleaned, repainted, the leaks stopped; and two inflatable tubes were made, each of them of one piece of canvas, 14ft. long, lined with waterproof calico, folded so that the two sides should come together, a rope along the seam, with eyes turned in at the corners, to make it fast by, and, with one of the screw valves from our worn-out boat (p. 42), let into the after end, to receive the nozzle of the bellows. These we at first intended to stretch beneath the thwarts, inside, but eventually laced them outside each gunwale, where they were less in the way, and, when kept in a state of semi-inflation, projected sufficiently to prevent a great deal of the ripple of the sea washing into the boat, and this advantage we made the most of when we were fairly at sea, by fitting light bamboo stanchions forward, and securing the tubes to them, so as to make a kind of raised wash streak round the bows.

We cannot dismiss the subject of boats without appending a few remarks on such simple forms of sails as are likely to be of service in such small craft as a traveller might Sails and their substitutes. possess, and we shall take, as the maximum, one of those swift and handy fore and aft schooners in which the Americans push their trade in all quarters of the world. Each lower mast and topmast would most likely be in one piece, combining great strength with neatness, and obviating the necessity for much staying. The bowsprit is also of a single piece; the sails are a jib from the foremast head to the bowsprit end, a forestaysail set to the stem head, a foresail and mainsail on gaffs made to lower when the sail is reefed or taken in; the foot of the mainsail is always extended by a boom, and that of the foresail sometimes ; if they are laced to the boom, as in the yacht "America," which had booms even to the foot of her jibs, the sails sit flatter and better on a wind, but if they are not, there is the advantage of being able to reduce the sails without the trouble of reefing, by tricing up the foot ; gaff topsails may be either jib-headed, like the fore, or on a gaff, like the main, in Fig. 1, p. 152. The mainstay causes some little difficulty ; if it goes from mast to mast, the tack and sheet of the fore gaff topsail must be passed over to leeward of it when the vessel goes about ; if it leads down to the deck there must be two parts, one on each side the foresail, and the lee one ought to be slacked, and the weather one set up on each tack. If a foreyard, or rather a cross-jack, is carried, a flying squaresail, half the width of the yard, may be sent up on the weather side, and a topsail may be set in the same manner, the fore and aft sails supplying canvas enough on the lee side.

The cutter (No. 2) has a jib, a foresail on the stay, and a mainsail ;

BOAT FITTED WITH INFLATED TUBES.

the jib topsail runs with grummets on the topmast stay, but the halyards only reach the lowermast head ; a lug-headed gaff topsail gives opportunity for a greater spread of canvas.

The boat (No. 3) is rigged with foresail and spritsail. An eye in the peak of the latter receives the upper point of the sprit, while the lower end is set into the eye of a snorter, a bight of rope passing round the mast and tightened chiefly by the strain of the sail upon it. Sometimes it is pushed up by hand while the sail shakes, so as to set it properly up, but it is better to have a small tackle as seen on page 151 to set it up with.

No. 4 has shoulder-of-mutton sails, the peaks of which are bent on

to small taper yards which slide up and down on and abaft the lower masts like gunter topmasts; this facilitates the reefing of the sails, and also the setting of the jib from the foremast head.

No. 5 is a lugger, the yards are slung in the thirds, the shortest and thickest arm is forward, and the longest tapers aft; the foremost leach of the sail is very strongly roped, so that the tack holds down the forearm and elevates the peak. Sometimes in well-manned vessels the lugs are dipped so as to pass to leeward of the mast whenever they go about, and in this case the tack may be bowsed down considerably in front of the mast and a large sail carried; but in short-handed craft the tacks are brought down to the mast, and the foresail and mizen are set on one side and the mainsail on the other, and are not dipped. The after leach of the jib must be cut so as to go clear of the foreyard, the topmasts to slide abaft the lower masts; and there is always some difficulty in setting a fore topsail, and there must either be a double tack to pass the sail over the jib halyard in going about, or its fore leach must remain to leeward of it.

The lateen (No. 6) has triangular sails with very long taper yards, the head and fore leach becoming one; indeed if there be any distinct fore leach, the sail becomes an ill-shaped lug, and not a lateen. The masts are somewhat short; sometimes mere stumps, but then the halyards and the tacks must be enormously strong to counterpoise the immense length of the yard.

The proa sail (Figs. 7 and 8), a triangle spread upon two bamboos, hitched upon a stump mast in small boats, we have described at p. 119. No. 9 is a modification of it, by which a boat sets jib and mainsail in one, the angle formed by the yard and boom becomes more acute at each reef as indicated by the lines. It would be difficult, however, to work the boat without a small mizen to help her round in staying. No. 10 is the shoulder-of-mutton sail, set on a single taper yard or mast.

Palm leaves are sometimes used as sails; our sketch represents three or more cocoanut leaves, so woven together as to present a surface to receive the wind. Blankets and articles of clothing are used in emergencies. Oars are set up, and a boat will gather considerable way under them. Planks, the broader and flatter the better, are excellent substitutes, and may be trimmed at pleasure. It must not be forgotten that, however graceful in art and poetry the bellying canvas may be, the chief object of the sailmaker is to get it " to sit like a board."

Sometimes when a sail is split, or otherwise rendered unserviceable, it is desirable to use another for a substitute without Reefing of sails spoiling it by cutting. We remember reading of a from the sides. vessel in which the topsail was split in a heavy gale; a spare foresail was got out and stout bands sewed on it, from the clews to the reef-band, diminishing upwards to the width the topsail head ought to be; eyelet holes were worked in, points or lacings inserted, and the sail, thus reduced, sent up to do duty as a topsail.

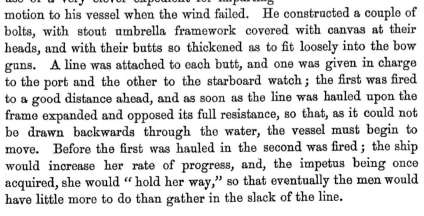

Captain (now Admiral Sir E.) Belcher, when in command of H.M.S. " Sulphur," made use of a very clever expedient for imparting motion to his vessel when the wind failed. He constructed a couple of bolts, with stout umbrella framework covered with canvas at their heads, and with their butts so thickened as to fit loosely into the bow guns. A line was attached to each butt, and one was given in charge to the port and the other to the starboard watch; the first was fired to a good distance ahead, and as soon as the line was hauled upon the frame expanded and opposed its full resistance, so that, as it could not be drawn backwards through the water, the vessel must begin to move. Before the first was hauled in the second was fired; the ship would increase her rate of progress, and, the impetus being once acquired, she would " hold her way," so that eventually the men would have little more to do than gather in the slack of the line.

Paddles worked by mill sails have been proposed; but of these it will be sufficient to remark that the power of the paddles to drive the vessel's head to wind will be less than that of the wind to drive her backward by the full amount of all that is expended in overcoming the friction of the machinery; in every other position the wind on the sails would do its work without the paddles.

A Prussian vessel, with the leaks gaining on her and her crew exhausted, was saved by lashing a spar across the mainmast, with one end projecting overboard with a barrel half full *Hints on emergencies.* of water fast to it, so as to rise and fall with the sea. The pump brakes were made fast to the spar, and the vessel was thus kept afloat, while the crew were relieved from their labour.

A boat has been known to come ashore safe through a heavy sea by means of a handful of oil judiciously thrown over by one of the men whenever a wave threatened to break near her; and Captain Basil Hall relates how one of his boats was hove to all night under a droge of all her spars and sails and two or three seal skins, the oil of which working out calmed the water for a considerable distance.

Instances of this kind might be indefinitely multiplied; but we note only a few as suggestions. No amount that we could give would supply the want of presence of mind and the ready power of adapting the means at hand to the emergency.

Our space will not allow us to go into all the details of boat sailing, but we must find room for one or two general rules. In seeking to land through breakers, which must always be effected by the oars, wait just outside them till you find the heaviest roller coming in ; then give way and come in upon it, with your boat's bow all but overhanging its crest, and, as it lands, you jump out and haul your boat beyond the power of reflux. Some crews are in the habit of giving two or three powerful strokes just before they reach the shore, and then pitching their oars simultaneously as far from them as possible, picking them up again when they have secured their boat. It is well, however, to know that there is no current to set the oars out to sea before doing this.

In coming off, face the breakers boldly, but judiciously watch the smaller waves, and give her good way through them. Keep your boat's head on to the sea, and never let her take a breaker more than two points on either bow.

Trim the sails so that when brought to the wind the boat will very nearly steer herself, and she will attain her utmost speed. The action of the rudder has always a slightly-retarding influence, but if there is any want of balance let it be on the side of ardency or tendency to fly up in the wind, so that she may carry a little weather helm rather than want helping up by a lee one, and thus, in case of sudden squalls, the boat will, as if by instinct, obey the first touch of the lee helm, and, shaking the wind out of her sails, will right herself. The main sheet of an open boat should never be made fast, but held either by the steersman, or some one near him, in readiness to ease off. A squall seldom comes so suddenly that the first puff, if well watched, will not help the boat into the wind before the full strength comes ; but on the coast of Australia we have known a squall come so suddenly through the dead calm of the night that it struck us at once like a blow from a sledge-hammer, and, though we had taken all the usual precautions, the sea was pouring like a jet-black cataract flecked with diamonds over 8ft. of the lee gunwale before the boat came to the wind ; and we would say, therefore, if there is not an air to bring the boat's head up when you expect a squall, help her with the sweep of an oar into the best position to receive it.

If you want to carry on sail do not attempt to stiffen the boat by making all the crew sit to windward ; for, should the mast break, as is not unlikely with the increased strain, nothing can prevent her capsizing ; let them sit in the bottom. In the way of ballast, nothing can be better than bags nearly filled with fresh water. They will assume the form of any place you want to stow them in, and will not sink the boat if she should fill; in fact, being lighter than salt water, they would impart a trifling buoyancy.

The loss of the rudder, an accident which is by no means so unfrequent at sea as may be imagined, involves also, for a time at least, Temporary the loss of control over the vessel's course. Even in rudders. the open sea this must be attended with considerable peril; but when it happens in the vicinity of rocks or shoals, and the vessel has not sea-room, the danger becomes appalling. The careful and vigilant trimming of the sails is the readiest means of regaining command of the vessel, and we believe the "Wager" was extricated from a most perilous position by this alone; but it is a work of immense labour, and harasses the crew severely. A stream cable payed out astern, and veered to either quarter, is sometimes used; or, if the accident should occur in moderate weather, by striking on a bar, the jolly boat with the plug out may be lowered and towed astern, but both these plans check the speed of the vessel, and are only useful when they can be made to impede one side more than the other; and this is not the true principle of steering. The rudder may be considered as a continuation of the keel, capable of moving on a hinge to an angle of $22\frac{1}{2}°$ on either side, and when the vessel moves forward, and the helm, for instance, is put to port, the water impinging on the starboard side of the rudder is reflected from it at an equal square to that of its incidence, and the resulting force tends to drive the stern to port and incline the head to starboard. But as the force acts in the direction of a line midway between the angles of incidence and of reflection, it has also a retarding tendency, and if the helm were put over to an angle of 45° the greater part of the power would be expended in stopping rather than in steering the vessel. If a ship could be made so flexible as to be converted like a fish into the segment of a circle either way at pleasure, the very perfection of steering would be attained, and the rudder is merely the best imitation of this that can be devised.

Our illustration shows one expedient for the remedy of the misfortunes we have named. A warp or cable is faked down upon the deck in lengths equal to that of the required rudder, all the parts are then so closely pressed together that it resembles a board of the required breadth; it is then stiffened by longitudinal and cross bars, a weight is attached to the bottom, and a tiller projects aft, from the extremity of which the steering tackles (A) lead in over each quarter. When lowered into its place, the heel is confined to the stern-post by chains or hawsers leading to the gangway on either side, and in the present instance ropes are reeved through the gudgeons on the stern-post. Sometimes two parts of the cable are left longer than the rest to come up the rudder trunk and form the neck of the rudder, a short spar passed through the bight on deck serves to suspend the whole. Very frequently, however, when the rudder goes, the gudgeons, and perhaps also part of the stern-post, are carried away, and it then becomes necessary to devise some plan which shall supply their loss.

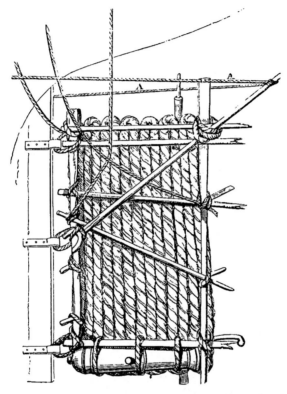

Several expedients are given in the *Nautical Magazine* for 1836, and from these we extract two or three examples. A spar, such as the spanker-boom or jibboom, is first passed over the stern, secured to the centre of the taffrail by temporary " partners," and to the heel of the stern-post by stout guys leading forward to the gangways on either side ; the gaff is then fitted on this, just as it would be on a mast, and one of the smallest and stoutest storm staysails is laced, with the head downwards, to the upright spar, and also to the gaff, the foot of the sail being cut off, if it be too large. It is then hauled down to the lower end by a halyard previously reeved, and the gaff, which should go a little below the surface of the water, is hoisted until the sail sits " as flat " as a board. If greater power is thought necessary, the outer end of the gaff can be sawn vertically down the centre, and boards clinched in, as shown in the sketch (Fig. 3, p. 159) ; or either the sail or boards might be used separately. The ship is steered by guys leading from near the end of the gaff over each quarter. Sometimes the principle of the steering oar is adopted : a spar, with planks fastened on its outer end, is got over, and the foremost end is fitted to the stern by ring-bolts or lashings, so as to allow it to work freely without too much play. The outer end is kept down either by a lower guy or by a piece of pig ballast or other weight; and if a topping-lift be attached, leading to a boom over the stern and thence to the mizen topmast-head, the oar may be lifted out of the water when one stroke has been completed, carried back again to the other side, and thus bring the ship's head round by a succession of sweeps.

Sometimes it is necessary to make a temporary stern-post, and the spare lower cap (which, however, we may remark, is generally stowed away where it is least likely to be found on an emergency) can be fitted on this by enlarging the masthead hole and securing it, as before, by lower guys. A topmast, with its heel upwards, may be passed down through it, and such additional spars or planking bolted on as will give the needful increase of breadth. The surface should be as smooth as circumstances permit, so that the water may glance off readily ; the fid-hole will then receive the tiller, but the spar must be well banded or lashed round to prevent its splitting with the strain, or perhaps breaking off where the sheave-hole weakens it.

The captain of our battered little vessel, " Tom Tough," had always some rough and ready expedient at his finger-ends. When one of the

Scarfing or fishing of broken spars.

iron davits of the quarter boat was bent by a colli-sion, he extemporised a forge with some pig ballast, on deck, and, though the planks beneath were somewhat scorched, he rendered the davit again effective. Once, when running before the wind, the mainsail jibed in consequence of careless steering, and the boom, being fastened by a " lazy guy," a slovenly shift a little too common among us, broke short off; however, a good stout plank was found, cut into four pieces, which were laid round the fractured part so as to inclose it in a kind of packing-case, of which the four sides did not meet at their edges ; wooldings of rope were passed round at intervals and tightened by driving in wedges, and the boom, though somewhat clumsy, was again fit for duty. (See illustration in next page.)

If a spar, with both ends alike, breaks at either end, a very neat and effective scarf may be made by sawing it down the centre and reversing the two parts, end for end, so that the fracture in one half may come against the unbroken part of the other, as in our sketch below. If a fracture is long, there may be no need for that

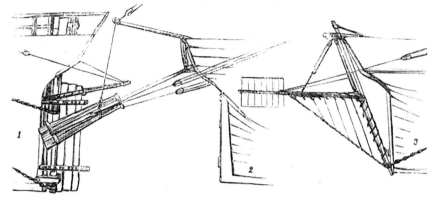

unsightly appendage called a fish, and, even if it is short, a very small one will serve the purpose.

If a mast breaks, much above the deck, it may be again used, with little or no diminution of its strength, by reversing it, and stepping what used to be the masthead upon the keelson, so that the fractured

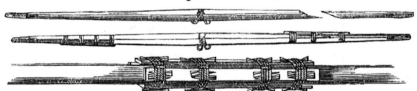

part may come below the deck, while that which was the heel is shaped and fitted to become the head. It will be evident from the sketches we give that in a ship with a very deep hold, where very nearly half the mast is below the deck, this plan is more likely to be of service than in a shallow one, where the part below bears but a small proportion to that above.

As a substitute or as an auxiliary to the common sails, or as a means of send-ing up a signal or effecting com-munication between a ship and a lee shore, a kite of sufficient power would frequently be useful.

Kites.

Every voyager knows how frequently all the lower and larger sails of a vessel are becalmed, the uppermost and smallest catching only a gentle air, while at a little height above them the wind, as indicated by the fleecy clouds, may be blowing much more briskly.

In this case, when even the flying kites, as the upper sails are figuratively called, have become useless, real kites flying at a sufficient elevation would do good service; and even though the wind might not be fair, still so long as it was a little abaft the beam the vessel might be steered to her course. One thing must be kept in mind, and that is, that when it has once fallen calm below the kites cannot be raised to the breeze that is blowing above, therefore it would be well either to send them up before the breeze fails, or at least to send up in preparation a small one, to the line of which the larger could be hitched, and jerked clear when it had been carried to a sufficient altitude.

A kite of 12ft. in height spreads about 50ft. square of canvas, and will pull, in a fresh breeze, with a strength of about 200lb., if the height were doubled the strength would, of course, be fourfold; and as it would act as a lifting or buoyant instead of a depressing sail, the only risk in " carrying on " would be the parting of the line connecting it with the vessel; on this account it would be the best possible form of sail to rig in an open and over-crowded boat when leaving a wreck, for its tendency would be to lift the bows over the seas instead of depressing them. And even if a man about to risk the passage by swimming from a stranded ship to a lee shore could send up a small kite, such as he could make with a cotton shirt, a couple of sticks, and a few fathoms of fishing line, it would most likely buoy him over the crests of the breakers in which he would otherwise be overwhelmed. But the greatest objection to the general use of the kite is, that in the usual mode of flying we have no command of it except that of letting it go higher or hauling it in at the risk of breaking the line; this has been met by a very ingenious invention, and although it is patented, we think that we may do the public some service, and Mr. Pocock, the patentee, no harm, by describing it.

The common form of kite is best. The standard is made into two or three equal lengths, connected either by fishing-rod, by tent-pole, or by parasol joints; the wings have hinges at the head of the standard, and, if large, joints in each pinion. The flight band consists of two lines, the uppermost of which has an eye upon it through which the lower, called the brace line, reeves, and both come down to the hand of the conductor, and by these the deviation of the standard from the perpendicular is controlled. By hauling on the brace line the surface is opposed fairly to the full strength of the wind (Fig. 1); by slackening it the kite floats more horizontally, allowing the wind to pass gently beneath it, so that even in the strongest gale the power may be regulated at pleasure (Fig. 3). The power may be increased by backing the first with a second kite as in Fig. 2, all the lines of the second kite being made fast to their corresponding places on the first, so that both assume the same relative position in all cases. Two smaller lines from the wings, also passing through eyes on the upper line, act as braces by which to trim the kite upon a wind; and it appears from a diagram given by the inventor that a vessel braced sharp up will lie within about five and a half points of the wind, or as close as most vessels can with their usual sails, and, therefore, may turn to windward. With a kite the operation of tacking would be very easy. Even should the boat not answer her helm, the kite line taken aft would bring her head up to the wind, and, being carried round on the other quarter, and again forward to its proper

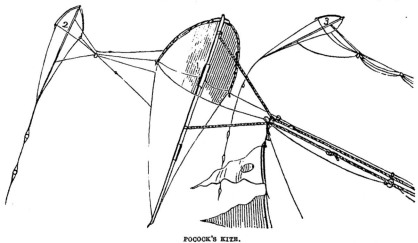

POCOCK'S KITE.

place, would help her to her proper course; and in manœuvring the absence of masts would be an advantage rather than not. A carriage with the fore wheels capable of being turned by a tiller would also turn to windward, and the draught power might be increased at pleasure by backing one kite with another, the connecting lines all being fastened in their proper places, as in the illustration, so that whatever change of position was imparted to the lowermost kite might be also assumed by all that were harnessed to it.

Signals by day or night might be sent up with great facility by hitching the halyard block upon any part of the kite line, when the flags or lanterns might be sent far above any spars or sails that could obstruct the view of them. In case of shipwreck, even a common kite extemporised with the roughest materials would very generally be useful.

M

When the ship is on a lee shore, a common kite, flown from on board, could not fail to bring a line to land, and, with this communication once established, all hands could probably be saved. Their own boat might be veered ashore, or the men sling themselves with grummets and warp themselves hand over hand; or if passengers are on board, a cot or hammock, slung to notched blocks running on a hawser with a line to haul it back to the vessel, and one to bring it again towards the shore, might be employed.

But with kites rigged as we have described, there would have been a greater chance of safety, for they may be braced to fly three and a half points either way from the direction of the wind, and if they are employed to carry a grapnel or small kedge, they may be braced and veered within a limit of seven points of the compass towards a suitable spot; may be lowered gradually by the slacking of the brace line, and, if the hold is not good, again elevated by hauling it in, to drop the anchor in a more suitable spot.

In our full-page illustration the extemporised kite is not so completely rigged, but the flight line is led through a block, so that the wrecked crew could make fast to one end a stronger line; and, having hauled that through, could next bend on a sufficiently stout hawser.

The inventor states that he has travelled in a carriage, at twenty miles per hour; that a boat so drawn outsailed the speediest vessels of the usual rig; that a lady ascended to a height of a hundred yards; and that his son, with a 30ft. kite, scaled a clift 200ft. high. The main and brace line of a kite of this size were ½in. in diameter, the braces (proper) were somewhat smaller. The discovery that a statue once stood on Pompey's Pillar was made by some merchant captains who ascended it by means of a line carried over by a kite.

The canoe or boat voyageur should at all times pay particular attention to the instructions which foretell the approach of storms; these are not
Weather signs. at all times so unmistakable as to enable him to surely count on the kind of day or night which he has to pass through; still, the remarks of the late Admiral Fitzroy, published by the Board of Trade, are of much practical value:

" Whether clear or cloudy, a rosy sky at sunset presages fine weather; a red sky in the morning, bad weather, or much wind (perhaps rain); a grey sky in the morning, fine weather; a high dawn, wind; a low dawn, fair weather. Soft-looking or delicate clouds foretell fine weather, with moderate or light breezes; hard-edged oily-looking clouds, wind. A dark, gloomy blue sky is windy; but a light,

SENDING LINE FROM WRECK TO LEE SHORE BY MEANS OF A KITE.

bright blue sky indicates fine weather.   Generally, the softer the clouds look, the less wind (but, perhaps, more rain) may be expected; and the harder, more 'greasy,' rolled, tufted, or ragged, the stronger the coming wind will prove.   Also, a bright yellow sky at sunset presages wind; a pale yellow, wet; and thus, by the prevalence of red, yellow, or grey tints, the coming weather may be foretold very nearly, indeed if aided by instruments, almost exactly.   Small inky-looking clouds foretell rain; light scud-clouds driving across heavy masses show wind and rain; but, if alone, may indicate wind only.   High upper clouds crossing the sun, moon, or stars, in a direction different from that of the lower clouds, or the wind then felt below, foretell a change of wind. When sea-birds fly out early, and far to seaward, moderate wind and fair weather may be expected; when they hang about the land, or over it, sometimes flying inland, expect a strong wind with stormy weather. There are other signs of a coming change in the weather known less generally than may be desirable, and, therefore, worth notice; such as when birds of long flight, rooks, swallows, or others hang about home, or fly up and down or low—rain or wind may be expected.   Also, when animals seek sheltered places, instead of spreading over their usual range; when pigs carry straw to their styes; when smoke from chimneys does not ascend readily (or straight upwards during calm), an unfavourable change is probable.   Dew is an indication of fine weather: so is fog.   Neither of these two formations occur under an overcast sky, or when there is much wind.   One sees fog occasionally rolled away, as it were, by wind; but seldom or never formed while it is blowing."

The traveller will not unfrequently wish to render sailcloth, duck, calico, and other materials water-proof; few handy methods surpass that of the Chinese. They   Waterproofing. proceed as follows: to every ounce of melted white wax is added one quart of spirits of turpentine.   The mixture must be stirred with a stick until quite cold, when the material to be treated is thoroughly dipped, allowed to drain out, and then finally hung by the corners in a current of air to dry.   In making common tarpaulins it is well to soak the canvas thoroughly in sea-water before laying on the dressing, and as the water evaporates the tar penetrates the fabric.   In Africa we used the acrid milky juice of the *Euphorbium* mixed with a little boiled oil, on calico.   It was very flexible, and perfectly protected a common open packing-case, with books and papers, on the deck of the vessel from the Cape to London.   Boiled linseed oil, when allowed to soak into linen or cotton cloth, much increases its power of resisting the action of water.

To those who are engaged in boat expeditions, researches along the sea-coast, or lake investigations, it is of the greatest importance to be

The deep-water glass.

able to see far down into the depths below; as, for example, for the recovery of sunken seals, which often go to the bottom like lead when struck dead by a shot, the examination of rocks, and the detection of lost objects. The late Mr. Wheelwright gives such a thoroughly practical account of his deep-water glass that we insert it in his own words : " I have had a little experience myself in seal-shooting off our north-west coast, and when I first began I had the mortification of seeing many a seal which I had shot stone dead go down like a plummet and we lost him. But afterwards we used a seal-glass, a kind of machine very similar to a small hand-churn, like a bucket, about one yard high, tapering towards the top, about 9in. wide at the top, and 18in. at the bottom. Of course the top was open, and in the middle of the bottom was fitted a square piece of glass (I believe common window glass). As soon as a seal sunk dead, we cast over a small buoy, kept in its place by a grapnel, as near the spot where the seal sank as possible, and then we examined the bottom after this fashion : We sunk the glass over the boat's side (just where we fancied the dead seal lay) into the water, within about two inches of the top (glass downwards), and by steadily looking down through the little glass window we could distinctly see the bottom of the sea and what lay on it. As soon as we saw the dead seal we hooked him up with a line and a drag. I don't know what is the greatest depth of water in which such a glass is available, and it is now some time since I used one; but I am sure I have often seen a dead seal lying in eight or ten fathoms; and just round the rocks where we shot the seals the water was never very deep, but still we rarely could see the bottom with the naked eye. I do not believe the glass at all has any magnifying properties, but I suppose the focus of vision is better concentrated below the surface of the waves in the comparatively still water. I was at this time living with one of the Customs' officers on the coast, who often used such a glass with great success in finding kegs that were sunk by smugglers off this coast."

Our remarks and directions concerning the various means which may be had recourse to for traversing rivers, lakes, and the sea would

Treatment of the apparently drowned.

be incomplete without instructions for the restoration of the apparently drowned. None that can be drawn up are more perfect than those given by the authority of the Royal Lifeboat Institution, which were published, with some of the following remarks, in the *Field* newspaper some short time since :—Hanging the body up by the heels to drain out the water which is supposed to have been swallowed, is not one of the least injurious of the popular expedients in cases of suspended animation, and it is, in itself, sufficient to keep up the engorgement of the brain, which is one of the chief dangers to be apprehended. So, also, warm baths, tobacco smoke, and other depressing influences, should be strictly prohibited; and also that horrible practice of rolling the body over and over, which is so frequently adopted by those who are ignorant of its effects. The Royal National Lifeboat Institution and Humane Society constantly circulate printed papers containing cautions against the adoption of these expedients; but, unfortunately, they are seldom to be met with when they are wanted, and, on that account, we venture to impress upon our readers the importance of making themselves intimately acquainted, not only with the objectionable practices to which we have alluded, but also with the methods which scientific men are agreed upon as those most likely to restore the circulation and respiration.

" In the first place, it may be observed that for several hours after the submersion all hope of recovery should not be given up, unless it is declared by a medical man of experience that life is extinct. The signs by which this opinion may be formed are pretty clear to him, but by an ordinary spectator they are liable to be mistaken, since they are all more or less comparative in their nature. When, however, for half an hour there is not the slightest evidence of breathing, or of the action of the heart—when the eyelids are half closed, with the pupils turned upwards and dilated, the jaws clenched, and the fingers semi-contracted—there is little doubt about the result, especially if the tongue is partially protruded, and the lips and nostrils are covered with frothy mucus. The temperature of the body is often not a reliable sign, because that is kept up by artificial means; but if, in spite of these, and in addition to the existence of the above symptoms, the coldness of the surface is very manifest, even if there is no medical authority for the relaxation of all efforts at restoration, it can serve little purpose to persevere. Still it is better to err on the safe side, and in this country there is seldom a long interval of doubt.

" But supposing a body to be brought out of the water, it becomes a question, What shall be done? Shall it be taken to the nearest house, or at once be treated on the spot? The answer is, proceed at once in the open air, whether on shore or afloat, and lose not a moment in the attempt to *restore breathing*, and *keep up the temperature of the body by the application of dry heat.* The first of these is the main object, and the second must be for a short time sacrificed to it but only for a few minutes, after which the two objects must be jointly pursued. These efforts must be continued energetically till they are either found to be successful, or declared to be useless. Should the breathing be restored, the circulation should next be encouraged by rubbing the limbs in the direction of the heart, with firm and steady pressure, and with the aid, if possible, of warm flannels or silk hand-kerchiefs, protected by a blanket over all. Beyond these general directions, however, it is necessary to give others more minute, and this will be best done in the words used in the printed directions of the Royal National Lifeboat Institution, which are given in a succinct tabular form, and should be hung up in every public place near which accidental drowning is at all likely to occur." These directions are as follow :

TO RESTORE BREATHING.

To clear the Throat.

1. Place the patient on the floor or ground with his face downwards, and one of his arms under the forehead, in which position all fluids will escape by the mouth, and the tongue itself will fall forward, leaving the entrance into the windpipe free. Assist this operation by wiping and cleansing the mouth.

2. If satisfactory breathing commences, adopt the treatment described below to promote warmth and natural breathing. If there be only slight breathing, or no breathing, or if it fail, then—

To excite Breathing—

3. Turn the patient well and instantly on the side, and—

4. Excite the nostrils with snuff, hartshorn, smelling salts, or tickle the throat with a feather, &c., if they are at hand. Rub the chest and face warm, and dash cold water on it.

5. If there be no success, lose not a moment, but instantly

To imitate Breathing—

6. Replace the patient on the face, raising and supporting the chest well on a folded coat or other article of dress.

7. Turn the body very gently on the side and a little beyond, and then briskly on the face, back again ; repeating these measures deliberately, effi-ciently, and perseveringly about fifteen times in the minute, or once every four seconds, occasionally varying the side :

[*by placing the patient on the chest, the weight of the body forces the air out; when turned on the side, this pressure is removed, and air enters the chest.*]

TO PREVENT ANY FURTHER DIMINUTION OF WARMTH.

N.B.—These efforts must be made very cautiously, and must not be such as to pro-mote *Warmth* and *circulation rapidly* ; for if circulation is induced before breathing has been restored, the life of the patient will be endangered. No other effect, therefore, should be sought from them, than the prevention of evapo-ration, and its result, the diminution of the warmth of the body.

1. Expose the face, neck, and chest, except in severe weather (such as heavy rain, frost, or snow).

2. Dry the face, neck, and chest, as soon as possible with handkerchiefs or any-thing at hand ; and then dry the hands and feet.

3. As soon as a blanket or other covering can be ob-tained, strip the body ; but if no covering can be imme-diately procured, take dry clothing from the bystanders, dry and reclothe the body, taking care not to interfere

8. On each occasion that the body is replaced on the face, make uniform but efficient pressure with brisk movement, on the back between and below the shoulder blades or bones on each side, removing the pressure immediately before turning the body on the side :

[*the first measure increases the expiration, the second commences inspiration.*]

⁎ The result is—*Respiration* or *Natural Breathing;* and, if not too late, *Life.*

with the efforts to restore breathing.

Cautions.

1. Be particularly careful to prevent persons crowding round the body.

2. Avoid all rough usage and turning the body on the back.

3. Under no circumstances hold the body up by the feet.

N.B. The directions are printed in parallel columns to avoid confusion, and to insure that the efforts to obtain both objects shall be carried on at the same time.

CHAPTER III.

———

WORKING IN METALS.

It would be of great advantage to every traveller if before
starting on an expedition he were to spend a few hours in learning
from a blacksmith how to weld together two pieces of iron, and
from a tinman how to solder tin or copper. In the absence of
this experience, a man who is determined to help himself need not
despair of success if he will bear in mind that the chief essentials,
in both cases are proper heat, strict cleanliness, and sufficient
quickness of manipulation without hurry. If the traveller possesses a
portable forge, it is most likely he will have learned how to use
it before starting; if not, he may in many countries, South Africa
especially, find almost in every tribe some native who could make one;
or if not, he might adopt some of the expedients described under
that head. His first care should be to see that his fire burns clearly
and with sufficient intensity, and this he may aid by occasionally
dashing in a little water, which, by the decomposition of the gases,
will increase the heat under the direct blast, while the surplus, falling
on the surrounding coal, will prevent the fire spreading farther than is
requisite. The broken ends of the iron to be rejoined should then be
placed in the fire, one of them in the centre of the heat, and the other
near enough to acquire a preparatory warmth; the first, heated to a
bright orange red, should be taken out and thickened by stamping
the broken point upon the anvil till it is considerably shorter than
before; if the heat is sufficient, the scarf, or smooth diagonal surface
which is to form one part of the welded joint, may be worked upon it;
if not, it must be returned to the fire while the other part is taken out
and driven up in the same manner. In using the hammer, some care
is needful to proportion the force of the blow to the size and
comparative heat of the metal you are working, and also to turn the
iron under the hammer so that each stroke shall help to consolidate
the mass instead of splitting it into fibres. When the surfaces of the
scarf are worked smooth, fair, and perfectly free from scales or dirt

of any kind, place them side by side in the fire and bring them to an intense white heat, so that when drawn forth they may almost spontaneously give off small white sparks. We would add a caution against burning the iron, or partially fusing it, by too much heat, but we do not think a traveller with an extempore forge is in much danger of doing this. The anvil should now be perfectly clean; the " smith," with his hammer ready in his right hand, should grasp with his left one of the pieces while his attendant draws out the other and lays it with the scarfed side uppermost on the anvil; prompt action without hurry is now the one thing needful: the smith withdraws his piece, lays it with its scarf turned downwards on that of the assistant's and with one decisive stroke of the hand-hammer unites them; a few more smart and rapid strokes while the iron is slightly turned to and fro to receive them properly, complete the union; and when the first heat is lost the iron is again put into the fire, and the joint which, owing to the thickening and shortening previously described, should present a clumsy appearance, may be trimmed and hammered down to its proper dimensions, the iron, if this is neatly done, having lost but little of its original length; and it is now for the operator to judge whether he will restore this by beating the metal a little thinner or sacrifice a little of it for the sake of retaining the original thickness. Among the Kafirs a rock is most frequently used for an anvil, and a smaller stone for a hammer. The West Africans use a conical block of iron, about the size and shape of the link extinguishers, some of which may yet be seen before old houses in London. The work has, in consequence, a slightly indented appearance, which distinguishes it from the smooth-faced hammer-work of England; but their weapons are of excellent metal, and so flexible, that they will almost tie in a knot rather than break. The Abyssinians also use weapons of this temper; for they say if a steel sword breaks, who can mend it, but if it bends we can sit on it and straighten it.

We have often made very good knives for skinning or cutting up animals from the handles of broken gridirons, frying-pans, stout hoop, or other bits of iron. Broken sheep-shears are also excellent substitutes. The hoop iron used to bind the bundles of compressed hay issued to troop horses can be made use of for an Scrap and immense number of useful purposes. The walls of hoop iron. many of the stables we erected in the Crimea were composed entirely of this material, closely interwoven, like basketwork. Excellent gabions can be made from it, as can the framework of hut roofs. A piece a couple of yards long, doubled forward and back in zigzag form, makes an excellent gridiron. Short pieces,

straightened out by hammering, form useful make-shift knife blades
for the use of native servants.   Tent poles are greatly strengthened
by having a spiral strapping of this iron nailed to them.   Saws for
cutting or rather fretting blocks of stone can be made by stretching
a strip of this material edgewise in a wooden frame, aided by water,
sharp sand, and a suitable balance weight, such as marble masons use.
Excellent eel traps are made by arranging long strips of hoop for a
body, and then securing them by small nails, as rivets, to hoops made
from the same material.   Eel traps will be fully described under the
head of " Fishing. "   We once made a complete set of bars for the
bottom and front of a camp stove entirely of forage hoop iron, made a
scraper for the door, a set of hooks for a gun rack, and a range of
shamble hooks to hang meat on.   Never heedlessly throw away forage
iron.

Trimming and filing up are matters which may be left very much to
the taste and opportunities of the traveller, but it should be remembered
that, *cæteris paribus,* a neatly finished piece of work, besides being more
satisfactory to the eye, is in itself stronger, as the inequalities, flakes,
flaws, or roughnesses of the surface, which, under any strain, might
form the commencement of a fracture, are removed; and besides this,
especially in wet climates, a well smoothed piece of work is less liable
to rust in patches than one of unequal surface.   If you intend to file-
finish your work, remember to let it cool slowly, and do not harden it
by immersion in water.

In some cases incisions may be required, too sharp or clean to be
The use of cold or of cut with a file, and, if proper care be taken, a fine,
joiners' chisels.   sharp, joiner's chisel may be used without more injury
than may be set right by fresh grinding it; it is advisable, however,
first to render the angle at which the edge is set a little more obtuse,
so as to lessen the danger of flawing it, taking care at the same time to
keep it as keen as possible.

In all expeditions in which wheeled vehicles are used, nothing
causes more trouble than the loosening of the tires, owing to the
        Tires   shrinking of the woodwork, and possibly some slight
    and wheels.   expansion of the metal, from the heavy pressure on
the rough roads, as well as from the intense heat of a tropical climate.
If sufficient skill be available, the proper course is to cut and shorten
the tire, for all other make-shifts have the disadvantage either of
being insecure, or positively injurious to the fabric of the wheel.
Supposing the shortening to be determined on, the tire must be
taken off, and if, as is frequently the case, it be fastened with rivets
through the felloes, the clinch on the inner ends of the bolts must

be first cut or filed away, the "washers" or iron rings taken off, and the rivets themselves driven back with a long punch or drift pin; the "band" or tire will then either fall off or require but a few blows to detach it. The streaks used to protect the wheels of field artillery guns and waggons are removed and replaced separately.

It is impossible to measure the relative circumference of the felloes and the *inner side* of the band without an instrument similar to the perambulator; *i.e.* a wheel or disc of wood or metal, mounted on a handle. A chalk mark is made on the felloe and a corresponding one on the edge of the disc; the two are set together, and the disc—say 1ft. 6in. in circumference—will then revolve perhaps ten and a half times in going round the hinder wheel of a Cape waggon of about 5ft. diameter. As soon as the disc has again reached the starting point another chalk mark is to be made upon it, and the distance between the two marks on the disc, say 9in., is to be added to the number of revolutions counted; it is then to be applied to the inner side of the band, the ten revolutions counted off, the additional 9in. to be run, and the distance between the starting point and the finish of its course is the amount by which the band is too long. Some judgment is required to decide whether more or less than this piece shall be taken out. If the wheel looks very firm and close in its joints, perhaps a little less should be cut, as the overlapping of the weld will take up a trifle—especially if it be not very skilfully and neatly done; if the wheel is loose and the spokes not firmly shouldered up to the nave, a little more may be taken away; and in this case it is proper to estimate whether the felloes will close up sufficiently to force the spokes home upon the nave; if not, the ends of four or more felloes opposite each other should be cut a trifle shorter with a fine tenon saw, great care being taken not to cut the dowels by which the ends of the felloes are kept true to each other. A smooth, hard place must now be sought out, on which the wheel can be laid flat, the front downwards, a hole being dug, if necessary, for the reception of the nave; flat stones, plates of iron, or slabs of hard wood, laid evenly under the circumference, would be of advantage when the shortened band is to be driven on. The next essentials are plenty of water and abundance of heating power. The ends of the band must now be heated, and the smith will bevel off each of them, one from the inside and the other from the out, so as to form the scarf; an attendant or two holding the band, as he directs, upon the anvil. The tire should now be reversed, and the curvature increased by resting it on two points of support and striking heavily between them on its inner surface till the scarfed ends close upon and begin to overlap each other. It is again placed in the fire with the ends equally exposed to the intense heat, and at the proper moment is lifted out by two attendants and promptly, but carefully, placed upon the anvil; a few smart decisive blows are given, and the joint is made. The hammer man now comes to the assistance of the smith and consolidates it by striking alternate blows with the " sledge," under his direction.   The circumference is again tried with the revolving disc, and if it be too short, as it ought rather to be, it is again heated and hammered out, the weld, if this be rightly done, gaining solidity in the process.   The band is then laid upon the ground and a fire of wood, dry cow dung, or other material made, so as to heat it to redness through its whole circumference.   It is then lifted by tongs or other means (if hooks are used they must be applied from the outside), and placed upon the wheel, and, as quickly as possible, hammered down nearly into its true position.   The workmen will soon find what " smoke to the eyes " is like, but they must disregard this, and, before the wood is too much burned away, quantities of cold water must be dashed on, the hammer men all the while beating down the shrinking band to a level with the felloes; before it is quite cold the wheel should be caught up and brought to the anvil, or a smooth rock, where the tyre is faced up true to the felloe front by heavy blows, and finally cooled off and tightened by another deluge of cold water.

Everything depends upon prompt action; and the tiring of a set of waggon wheels at some out station is really an exciting event, at which all hands are required to work with a will.

Not unfrequently the " schammel-bolt " or perch-bolt will give way in the grip, and if this flaw be detected in time, and the bolt be long

Repair of perch-bolts.

enough, the evil day may be staved off by removing it, boring a hole through the "buik" plank or floor of the waggon, right above, and dropping the bolt down through it so that its head remains 3in. or 4in. higher than before, and the nip is brought upon a fresh place, as shown by the dotted line above H (p. 188).

For small work, the "reim schoen," or drag, turned up upon a block of wood, will form a very decent anvil; and the next essential

Extempore anvils and vices.

is a vice, which ought to be as large and powerful as can be carried.   A weak inefficient vice is worse than useless.   The means of attaching it ought also to be good, for if it is not firmly fixed no work can be properly finished in it.   No part of the waggon ought to be used as a holdfast for the vice, unless indeed it were properly fitted with iron guards for that purpose before starting for the claws and screw-bolts would speedily tear and split the wood, and only damage the vehicle to no purpose.   It would generally be better to cut down a convenient tree, leaving a stump about 3½ft. high, and in this to cut a niche, partly to let the vice in : it might then be secured by hoops of iron, if available, such as the nave bands, or anything similar, tightened with wedges, and lashed in its place by thongs of raw hide, which, when they dry, acquire almost the rigidity of iron.

If the vice cannot be fixed firmly, it is better to cut with the saw a deep groove down into the solid stump, and, having inserted the iron you wish to file, to tighten it with wedges, screws, lashings, or such other appliances as you may have at hand (p. 146).

The tapping of screws on bolts or nuts, especially if of any size, requires that the work be firmly held ; but we should rather advise

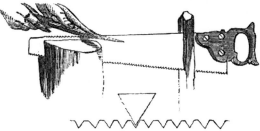

that duplicate bolts and nuts of the principal sizes used in waggon work—½in., ¾in., ⅞in., and 1in.—be carried, as a set of taps and dies could not be had even in Cape Town for much less than £5, and an unskilled hand would be more likely to break the instruments than use them to advantage. For the smaller sizes, suitable for gun-locks, &c., a plate and set of taps might advantageously be carried.

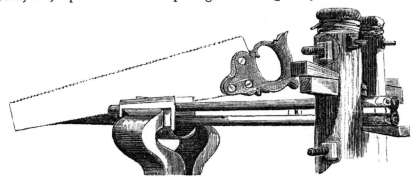

Sometimes a bolt, rod of iron, or a gun-barrel, has to be cut off to a given length, and the most convenient way of doing this is to file Cutting bolts and a row of small teeth upon the back of a handsaw, gun-barrels. and with it to saw off the superfluous iron : the first illustration shows the manner of cutting the teeth, and their exact size and shape.   Always put in a bit of copper, lead, or leather to protect the gun-barrels from the grip of the vice.   It may, perhaps, be well to remark here, that nearly all Russian saws are made to cut backwards, and all the gun breech-screws made in that country are cut the reverse way to ours.

For repairs of guns, it is well to have sufficient wire of different thicknesses; but when a hardened pivot is required, a broken gimlet or a bradawl will often supply the material; and we have before now earned a goat or sheep for dinner by supplying in this manner some deficiency in the arms brought to the white man to be repaired.   It is convenient to buy a musket-lock or two before starting, and to save all sorts of screws, tumblers, springs, &c., out of old locks.

We were once asked, far away in Namaqualand, to perform no less a service for a friend than to put a new hammer on his gun. Modest disclaimers of ability were not received, and there was nothing left but to do our best.   We found a bit of flat iron, which, fortunately, had a hole in it : this we first squared up with a small " three-square " file, and then fitting it to the tumbler, and making sure that the flat surface of the hammer should strike upon the nipple, laboriously cut and filed away the intermediate parts, and before morning the hammer was fixed.   Mr. Rae, the engineer of the Zambesi expedition, proceeded more scientifically ; he employed a native to weld up a quantity of iron hooping into a plate quite thick and large enough to make the hammer, then, drawing the outline, he bored small holes close together all round it, broke off the superfluous iron, and finished with the file.

On one occasian we were unfortunate enough to break the little S-shaped bridle which connects the claw of the mainspring with the arm of the tumbler.   Most of our readers will remember that this portion of a gun-lock is of a most peculiar form, being not only S-shaped, but flat-cheeked and T-ended.   Notwithstanding the apparently complicated nature of the undertaking, a new one had to be made : so we proceeded as follows:—One of our small mining picks chanced to have an iron wedge (which had originally been cut from an old patten iron) in the handle.   This we softened in the fire, worked into form on the head of an upturned hammer with one of smaller size, and then roughly finished it up with a handsaw file.   The screw hole had then to be made, and, as we had no drill, we took the scissors from our fishing-book, ground down the point on our bit of Turkey hone, tempered it in the candle, and then, by dint of hard labour and persistent boring, made a hole through the end of the bridle.   We then gave our work a few finishing touches, tied it up in a bit of old leather, heated it in the fire, plunged it in water to case-harden, and then secured it in the lock, where it performed its work well until we parted with the gun so repaired.

Most of the hunters in South Africa find that ivory, from its agreeable creamy white, is better adapted for the "korel," or front sight of a gun, than the polished metal used for that purpose by the maker. Sometimes the sight is Sighting guns. accidentally lost, and has to be replaced; but more frequently the dazzling bit of metal is purposely knocked off.

A broad flat groove, say $\frac{1}{2}$in. broad, or as wide as a handsaw file, and $\frac{1}{16}$in. deep, is cut across the midrib of the gun (Fig. 1), and the edges of this are under cut, either with a sharp-edged file, or, if the operator

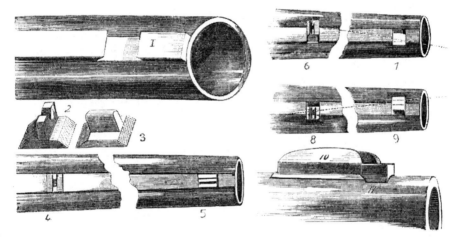

is expert in the use of tools, with a chisel and mallet. A piece of ivory (Fig. 3), cut so that the grain runs with the length of the barrel, and with an elevated ridge left in the centre, is then fitted tightly in, adjusted as nearly as possible, and the metal clinched down upon it; then the central ridge is filed on either side until, by occasionally firing at a mark, the gun is found to shoot without lateral deviation. It should, in the beginning, be considerably too high, and should then be filed down so as to carry the bullet point blank to its mark at a hundred yards.

If the back sight is lost, cut a notch across the midrib as before, and fashion a piece of iron (Fig. 2) to the same shape as you did your ivory, only let the elevated ridge in this case be across the barrel. File a notch in the centre, and leave the iron a little wider than the rib, so that it may admit of being driven a little to either side, and the superfluous metal filed off when the adjustment is nearly perfected. Mark it, and take it out to do this; then put it in again, clinch it, and test it by firing at a mark.

Figs. 4 and 5 (p. 175) represent the position of the two sights. If the gun shoots to the right, shift the back sight (Fig. 6) to the left and the front sight (Fig. 7) to the right; if to the left, shift the back sight (Fig. 8) to the right, and the front one (Fig. 9) to the left. If the gun shoots too low, file down the front. sight; if too high, file down the notch of the back sight.

In one of our own rifles the front sight was, as usual in military patterns, based on the block of iron which forms the check for the bayonet (Fig. 11). We did not remove this, but cut behind it a very shallow groove an inch broad, and in this fixed and soldered a piece of iron with a longitudinal groove, to carry a knife-edged sight of ivory, as seen in Fig. 10.

For night shooting, we used the only sixpence to be found amongst our party; bending and polishing it and clinching it on to a saddle of zinc painted black. Holes were punched in this for leather thongs, and in front was a notch cut to fit the actual sight, and so insure the central position of the silver one when in use (Fig. 13, p. 177). By day the saddle was turned beneath the barrel (Fig. 12), and the little flat thongs of antelope hide were not at all in the way. With guns not of military patterns the sight could not so conveniently be turned under, but would have to be removed by day; but we should think a broad silver sight might be fixed on a steel spring on the rib behind the sight, with a broad ring to slip over and keep it down by day, as in Fig. 15, or to draw back and let it rise into view by night, as in Fig. 14. For the same purpose our late friend, C. J. Andersson, used to wrap a bit of white paper round the muzzle of his gun, pinching it up in the centre, or laying a cord under it to give it a little elevation (Fig. 16).

As a protection, and also for the contrast of the colours, the Dutch, and many of the English colonists, stitch very tightly over all a bit of skin from the inside of the elephant's ear (Fig. 17). This is very fine, exceedingly strong, and, when rubbed with a little grease, intensely black; it is then carefully cut, to allow the front sight to appear through, and left to dry. Another advantage of this plan is, that it corrects the errors often caused by the mirage or refraction of the sun's rays from the polished barrel, which, especially in the tropics, causes the object aimed at to become indistinct, to assume the appearance of motion, and to be seen sometimes considerably above its true position, thereby causing the marksman to miss by shooting over it.

No wise traveller ever encumbers himself with a long sword or bayonet of ordinary pattern; but every one carries a sheath knife, of from 6in. to 12in. in the blade; and the handle of this ought to be made so that it may fix as a bayonet on his gun. We have seen natives considerably astonished by this sudden conver- Sheath knives sion of our gun into a spear to kill a wounded animal. or bayonets.

If the knife handle were simply made round, so as to stick into the barrel, like the bayonet of old times, it would be better than nothing; but if the side-springs were generally adopted, it might be well to arm our troops, intended for service in wild countries, with a good serviceable sheath knife, of 8in. or 10in. in the blade, to be used for general purposes, and fixed as a bayonet when wanted, rather than with the orthodox triangular needle, that is only of use in opportunities that occur but rarely. We remember a party of a certain line regiment coming upon a number of Hottentots, when their officer ordered them to fix bayonets, forgetting for the moment that as usual they had been left at home—just as were the swords and steel scabbards of the Cape Corps—lest their rattling should give warning to the crafty foe. It is a common custom in India, when real work has to be done, to throw aside the steel scabbards and replace them with wooden ones, which have the double advantage of being noiseless

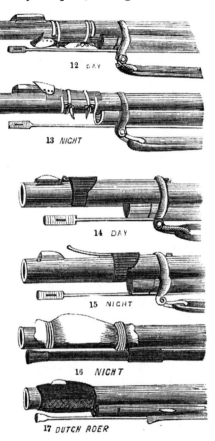

and a preservative to the edge of the sword. We have heard a man of the Rifle Brigade say, he should not fear even though lost in the bush. "Shoot the first Kafir that attacks you," said he, "and arm yourself with his assegai, and no other will come near you."

Our allies, the Fingoes, in the war of 1850-53, generally carried one or more assegais, using the shaft as a ramrod, or holding two of them crosswise in the left hand as a rest for the musket. The Kafirs, when hard pressed, retain the largest assegai, and, breaking off the shaft, use it as a sword or dagger. The contest is often prolonged by picking up the assegais thrown by the other party, and sending them back again. To prevent this, sometimes a tribe, bent on a sharp decisive conflict, will cut the shaft half through, so that it may break when it strikes, and become useless to the enemy.

The Dutch Boer sits down, rests his elbows on his knees, and extending his left arm, with the ramrod grasped firmly and planted on the ground, obtains an almost immovable rest for his heavy roer. Many of them shoot from the left shoulder, and some few can shoot from either shoulder equally well—an immense advantage if a man on horseback is surrounded by enemies.

In an out-of-the way corner of Central India we were so unfortunate as to loose our watch-key—the last of three. This we replaced as

Watch-key, to make. follows : We first routed out a piece of soft steel about the size of a small black-lead pencil. After filing off one end perfectly flush, we placed it in the fire, whilst we prepared the square end of a saddler's awl by grinding it to the exact size of the key-square of the fusee of the watch. When the steel was heated to a cherry red, we fixed it upright in the vice, and then supporting the bit of awl with a pair of pliers we, with a light hammer, drove it a fair distance into the steel bar. When it cooled, it was reheated, and the bit of awl driven deeper, until a square hole of sufficient depth was formed. The bar was then filed down to the size of the key-hole of the watch. The requisite length was then cut off; the end flattened out for a thumb-piece ; and a hole drilled in it to pass a thin strip of tendon through. A few finishing touches were given with a fine file ; the work was heated to a blue heat on a bit of red-hot iron, and was then dropped into a cup of water. So we made our watch-key, which did its work well through about 4000 miles of travelling, and was as good as new when we returned to England with it hanging to our whip-cord watch-guard.

In all cases in which heat is required for iron work care should be taken that the fire is perfectly clear, especially if it has been previously

Tools, to temper. used for melting lead, when any dross or other extraneous matter should be scrupulously cleared out. Sulphur in any form is most destructive. It would be well that the operator should learn before starting how to work up and fresh temper a cold chisel or punch, or even to make one if needful out of a broken file or rasp ; of course, the punch is round, square, or octagonal, according to circumstances, and generally flat at the end to drive back the nail or bolt that is to be withdrawn. Sometimes a tapered point on a triangular instrument, such as a hand saw file, with the edges sharpened, is useful for driving into a broken nipple, and by turning it against the sun to extract it when sufficient hold has not been left for the usual nipple key. The cold chisel is first forged to a chisel edge, more or less finely tapering according to the strength required, the two sides forming an angle of about 15° to 20° with each other; the cantle is then filed or ground till its sides form an angle of from 45° to 90°; it is then heated to a cherry red, and dipped in water, cautiously at first, being frequently taken out and watched during the process till it assumes a pale straw colour, a deeper tint or even a deep blue or purple, according to the degree of hardness required, and is finally ground sharp upon a stone with plenty of cold water. Small tools may be tempered by laying them on a piece of

THE ASSEGAI GUN REST.

red-hot iron, such as a bit of waggon-wheel tire; the changing colours should be watched, and when the desired tint appears the tool may be plunged into water. Should it be too hard the temper may be reduced by dry grinding; when a temper not quite so hard and less liable to fly is required, it may be given by cooling the steel in grease or oil. The tools carried for this purpose must vary according to the means of conveyance. On the North Australian Expedition we had a portable forge, which remained at the main camp, but on our inland journeys with packed horses we took as many horse-shoes as were thought requisite, a small hand hammer, a pair of tongs, a few files, rasps and punches, and a supply of nails.

RAMROD GUN REST.

It not unfrequently happens that some object, such as a fish-hook, key, portion of a gun-lock, or gun furniture, will require being so treated as to harden the surface whilst toughness of texture is retained. This process is known as case-hardening, which is, as its name

Case-hardening. implies, one by which a hard case or crust is formed over the surfaces of the articles operated on. There are numerous instruments and contrivances in constant use in the construction of which the toughness of iron combined with the hardness of steel, communicated by the process about to be described, is taken advantage of. Gun-furniture, fish-hooks, and handcuffs are examples, the latter most remarkably so, as, were they composed of ordinary iron, nothing would be more easy than to file or saw them through ; if of steel, a blow with a stone, or any other heavy substance, would break them as though made of earthenware. When case-hardened neither of these devices is available. Too hard to cut, too tough to break, the metal is all that can be desired. Having fashioned, filed up, and finished the article or articles in hand, procure a fair quantity of leather cuttings, or horsehoof parings. These should be roasted crisp, and pounded up until a sufficient quantity of coarse powder is obtained to bury the " work " when laid in a little iron box, which can be conveniently made by doubling up the edges and ends of a bit of sheet iron. In the absence of iron, clay may be used to form the box. This, when filled and gently pressed down, must be placed, when dry, in a clear bright fire, and heated up to a blood red heat, at which temperature it should be allowed to remain for a short time, taking care not to increase it. The box and its contents may then be withdrawn with the tongs, and thrown into a pail of cold water. The work may, when cold, be washed and brushed clean, made thoroughly dry, oiled, and put aside for use. Ferrocyanide of potassium is also extensively used for case-hardening, being either sprinkled over the work when hot, or mixed with some convenient substance, such as dried cow dung, and placed in the box ; but, unless in the hands of those accustomed to use it, the surfaces of the work at times becomes " pitted " from the contact of stray particles of the salt.

Professor Church gives the following directions for covering the surfaces of metallic objects with a film of platinum : "Dissolve in 1oz.

To platinise iron, of distilled water 60grs. of bichloride of platinum and
&c. 60grs. of pure honey. Add to the above solution ¾oz. of spirits of wine, and ¼oz. of ether. The mixed liquids, if not quite clear, must be filtered through a piece of white blotting-paper. The objects to be platinised, which may be of iron, steel, copper, bronze, or brass, are to be thoroughly cleaned by washing them in soda, then in water. When they have been dried they require heating over a lamp to a heat below redness. For this purpose they may be

suspended, by means of a fine wire, over a spirit or an oil lamp, in such a way as not to touch the flame. Suddenly, before they have had time to cool, the objects are to be completely plunged beneath the surface of the platinising liquid. One immersion for a single minute generally suffices, but the process may be repeated if necessary, care being taken to wash and dry the pieces operated upon before re-heating them. The composition of the solution may vary considerably, and yet good results be obtained. Sometimes the addition of more honey improves it; sometimes the proportion of bichloride of platinum may be increased or diminished with advantage. Indeed, it will be found that the appearance of the platinum film deposited upon the objects may be altered by changing the proportion of the bichloride present. The solution may be used several times; gradually, however, it loses all its platinum, the place of this element being taken by the iron or copper dissolved off the immersed objects."

If the film of platinum deposited by this method is found to be permanently adherent, the plan promises to be very valuable. It would be a great boon to travellers in warm, damp countries to be able to protect iron and steel articles by so simple a process. In the same article Professor Church describes a new and very simple plan of inlaying iron with silver, and also for enamelling metals with different colours. Both these processes really come within the scope of amateurs, and we can strongly recommend the entire paper to those interested in the chemical arts.

We may now appropriately mention a few examples where this platinising process seems to furnish desirable results. Articles made of iron or steel—watch-chains, seals, sword-handles, keys, and similar useful or ornamental objects—are greatly improved in appearance, and, moreover, preserved from all chance of rusting, by this treatment. The colour of the platinum film is of a neutral greyish black, and it often shows at the same time a faint iridescence. Iron or steel which has been inlaid with gold or silver, forming what is known as damascene work, is greatly improved by platinising. Neither the gold nor the silver are in the least degree affected, and they will be found to afford a better contrast with the colour of the platinised than with that of the original iron.

Iron which has become deeply rusted cannot be platinised by our process. In order, however, to preserve from further destruction objects of steel or iron having an archæological or artistic interest, a very excellent plan may be used as a substitute. The purest white paraffine is to be melted in a clean pan, and maintained at about the temperature of boiling water. The rusted and corroded specimens are to be immersed in this paraffine bath till they cease to froth from escape of moisture. They are then withdrawn, wrapped in blotting paper, and kept in a warm place till the excess of paraffine has been absorbed. The objects thus treated, while preserved from further decay, do not acquire that disagreeable greasy aspect which the varnish ordinarily used imparts. We have been obliged to tar our saw blades, which was very inconvenient in working, but this was better than having them spoiled by rust.

If the traveller has a waggon, as in South Africa, he may either carry a portable forge or trust to finding natives capable of building one and supplying bellows of their own manufacture.

Smith's tools.

If he thinks the weight of a small anvil too great, he should carry a heavy sledge hammer, which will serve as an anvil for ordinary purposes; two hand hammers of different weights; half-a-dozen pair of tongs, of such form and size as will enable him conveniently to hold the different sizes of work he may find necessary to do; at least a dozen files or more—square, flat, half-round, or rat-tail; and of these the temper should never be destroyed by working with them on iron that has not yet become cool, though occasionally time may be saved by using a worn-out file to work on iron while it is yet hot and comparatively soft; cold chisels of different sizes, from small ones of $\frac{1}{4}$in. or $\frac{1}{2}$in. wide, to be tapped with a small hand hammer, to others of $1\frac{1}{2}$in., to be held by pieces of rod iron coiled round them, or still better by rods of osier, and to be struck with the sledge hammer; if there is an anvil, of course a chisel to fix upright in the hole provided will be taken with it; punches of various sizes, and a stock and set of drills for boring holes up to $\frac{1}{2}$in. in diameter, with rymers or tapering four-edged tools for gradually enlarging them, and countersinks for letting in the heads of screws, &c., to the surface level. For small work, such as gun-locks, &c., an Archimedean drill and set of bits are very convenient, a hand-vice and set of gunsmith's small files—triangular, square, flat, half-round, round, and knife-edged— should accompany them.

A traveller will frequently have occasion, either for his own servants or for the natives of the country, to put "fresh fire" into the pan cover of a musket; for this purpose nothing is better

Muskets, to repair.

than the blade of an old saw, the thinner the better; a piece is broken off, softened and filed down to the exact size; it is then bent so as to fit the face of the pan-cover, and is bound to it by several turns of iron wire, not drawn so tightly but that bits of brass wire may be thrust beneath them all round the edges that are to be joined; borax, dissolved in water, is now laid on with an old brush, and, if necessary, small lumps are also added, and the whole is placed in the fire and heated till the brass melts and brazes the two parts firmly together; let it cool slowly, finish it carefully with the file, heat it to a dull red, and temper by cooling it in water. Half-civilised Hottentots frequently do this.

The snoek-hook used in Table Bay is a bit of brass wire as thick as a quill and 7in. long; the point is filed sharp, and the barb is merely such a triangular notch as might be made with a handsaw file. It is not bent in a true sweeping curve, like our fish-hooks, but turned sharply up at about 2in. from the point, so that when the lip is pierced, it slips at once into the sharp bend of the hook, and the struggles of the fish are less likely to break it than they would be if it afforded the leverage that the usual form of fish-hook gives. (See Fig. 20, p. 185.)

Fish-hooks can be made by taking a wire or rod of the required size and softening it by heating it to a bright red and letting it cool very slowly in sawdust or leaving it till the fire dies out; let the soft end abut against something solid, and, with a sharp chisel and mallet, make a deep cut at such an angle as to form the barb; file up the point, heat it again, and bend it round a stick of the proper size so that the curve may be true. We have, before now, broken up a gridiron at the galley fire, and with a hook thus formed from one of the bars caught a young shark, whose flesh formed a very desirable addition to our fare. On another occasion, while exploring a branch of the Victoria River, in North Australia, we halted, as usual, at noon, with scanty rations, which Mr. Gregory improved by taking from his hat a stout sewing needle, softening it in the fire, and bending it into a fish-hook, baited with grasshoppers; a few strands of thread made a sufficiently strong line, a small sapling formed a rod, and, in a few minutes, he had caught three fish, resembling mullet, nearly 18in. long. The needle had done good service, but was too precious to be thrown away, so Mr. Gregory carefully restored it to its pristine straightness, tempered it, and again stuck it in his hat, to be used, when required, for its legitimate purpose.

It is rather curious that with brass the softening process is the very reverse of that we use with iron. Heat a bit of brass and plunge it into cold water, and, with a sharp knife or chisel, you may carve it almost like pewter; heat it again when finished, let it cool slowly, and it becomes as hard as before.

A traveller in Africa should be well provided with brass, the best form being that of stout wire as thick as stair carpet rods; this will serve for many useful purposes: hooks, rings, ramrods for guns, or almost anything can be made of it.　While, in lengths sufficient to make armlets, it is always a convenient medium of barter, or payment for the services of the natives, who, though they will give nothing for hollow lacquered curtain rings, will always appreciate solid metal, that may be cut, worn away, or broken, and remains the same throughout.

To tin copper : first clean the surface carefully by rubbing it with sandpaper or stone, or washing it with diluted nitric acid or aquafortis; *Tinning copper.* heat it till it is rather too warm to handle, by placing a hot iron or pan of fire under the part to be tinned; rub on, with a feather, a little hydrochloric acid (commonly called spirits of salt) with zinc dissolved in it; then, with a soldering bolt previously rubbed on sal-ammoniac, touch the bit of tin you hold upon the copper, and, as you melt it, spread it evenly with a bit of rag over the surface you wish to tin ; this ought to be done with the insides of all copper vessels that are to be used for containing liquids or for cooking, and also for the edges of sheets that are afterwards to be soldered together.　Even if the edges were to be riveted, it would still be advisable to tin them, as they might then also be soldered by slightly heating them and running a little tin into the joint, by means of the heated bolt rubbed on sal-ammoniac, as before.

Small iron nails, tacks, fish-hooks, &c., are protected from the effects of rust by tinning.　The process is carried out as follows : First cleanse the objects to be operated on in diluted sulphuric acid, then place them with broken fragments of tin and sal-ammoniac in an earthenware bottle over a strong charcoal fire.　When the coating of tin is found to be complete, they are first washed in clean water, and then dried in hot bran or sawdust.

A very strong joint may be made by turning up, say ½in., more or less, of the edge of one sheet (Fig 1), then laying in it the edge of the *Sheet metal, to join.* other (Fig. 2), and turning up the edges of both (Fig. 3); then, keeping the joint pressed down, lift up the second sheet as you would open a book, and press it out flat and open (Fig. 4).　You cannot make this joint in the two edges of the same sheet, turned round upon each other (Fig. 5), unless you first nearly flatten the two parts (Fig. 6), when they may be doubled upon each other, and the sheet restored to its cylindrical form by the insertion of any pointed cylinder, such as, for instance, the horn of the anvil or a block of wood rounded and tapered at the end (Fig. 7). Suppose it is required to make a pannikin, this joint, whether previously tinned so that it may be soldered or not, is the only proper one, but the corners should previously have been cut away, so that only a single or, at most, a slightly overlopping double thickness may be left at top and bottom (Fig. 8). The bottom edge is now turned outwards by gently tapping it on the block or anvil edge with a hammer till it resembles a narrow flange (Fig. 9). A circular piece is now cut for the bottom so much larger as to allow a rim to be turned up all round (Fig. 10), and to admit the flange within it (Fig. 11); then setting it flat upon the anvil, and forcing into it a block of wood that has been cut perfectly to fit it, clinch down the rim of the bottom upon the flange (Fig 12), and turn them both up against the side together (Fig. 13). The top edge may now be rolled over in the same manner, and it will give additional strength if the rim

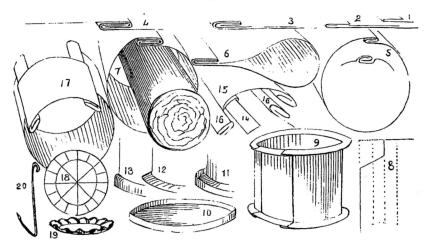

is strengthened by the insertion of a piece of wire. If the foregoing joints have been carefully made you will have a water-tight and, what is more, a fireproof pannikin with or without the aid of solder, and a handle can be riveted on or not just as suits your convenience. One great advantage of the folded joint is, that if it is not too tightly hammered down, the parts will slide freely on each other, and advantage may be taken of this for making an opening in one side of a cannister to be closed by a sliding lid; or, if you are making a pannikin or other vessel, and your metal is not large enough to make the whole circumference in one piece, cut a small strip (Fig. 14.) of the breadth you wish the joint, say $\frac{3}{16}$in. or $\frac{1}{4}$in., and fold the edge of the metal twice over it (Fig. 15), then draw it out; do the same with the other edge, and also with the edges of the piece you intend to insert

(Fig. 16), and you may then, with a little care, slip the parts together and clinch down the joints as closely as you wish (Fig. 17). If the corners have previously been snipped off, or smoothed with a file, it will considerably increase the facility of doing this.

During the North Australian Expedition, when Mr. Gregory was preparing for the journey from the Victoria River to the Albert, in the Utilisation of Gulf of Carpentaria, he collected all the emptied pre-meat tin cases. served meat tins, and burning off the old paint by placing them above the forge fire, smoothed down the tin upon the surface with a piece of *greasy* rag, trimmed up the ragged edges, and, in most cases, obtained sheets of tinned iron nearly equal to new; from these he made pannikins of graduated sizes, in fact a nest of them, one fitting into the other from the largest to the least, thus securing comfort and convenience to his party, and utilising material which many persons would have thrown away as useless.

In opening a packing case lined with tin, care should be taken to cut the edges as clean as possible, for not only are ragged points liable to tear the hands very disagreeably, but if you wish to make use of the tin in any other manner, it is of great importance that it should be kept quite clean, flat, and free from unsightly wrinkles; a smooth sheet of tin may be cut, turned, or bent almost at will, but if it has previously been wrinkled, it is absolutely impossible to restore it to flatness, and to make a true joint in it is as much out of the question as to write freely on note paper full of unsightly folds or creases. For cutting tin or other sheet metal, a pair of small tin snips, say 8in. or 9in. in total length, will be found exceedingly useful: stout copper or sheet iron may be cut with them.

To make plates or dishes of sheet iron or other metal, cut out a disc or oval, of the size you wish, and then draw a line parallel to the Dishes and plates, edge all round it (Fig. 18); then draw lines radi-to make. ating from the centre, like points on a compass card, as many as you please, say twelve, which will divide each quarter into three parts, answering to the hours on a clock face.

Make a small hollow across the end of a block of wood, the stem of the nearest small tree cut off at a convenient length for instance, lay the edge of your plate on it with one of the radiating lines corresponding with the hollow; strike it with the edge of your hammer till you have slightly indented it, do the same on the opposite side, and then with the other two quarters; repeat this all round, and you will have a very neat and useful plate, with scolloped edges like the patty pans usually sold by tinmen (Fig. 19).

A few rivets of various sizes, of iron, tin, and copper, should be taken; but, if the work is to be exposed to the action of the water, care should be taken not to fasten iron sheets   Rivets. with copper rivets, as the action of the metals on each other will be most destructive.

Tin rivets may be used to fasten any other metal where great strength is not required, and they are very advantageous for many purposes, as handles of tin or copper pannikins. By these we mean rivets of tin, not of iron tinned over, which also are useful, but not so easily worked.

To extemporise a forge and bellows, the natives of Africa and India, who invariably squat down to their work, simply make their fire on the ground, which is previously smoothed and clayed   Make-shift forge over; behind this is raised a bank or fence of clay,   and bellows. perforated for the admission of a tube, either of wood of the bark of a small tree, or of the horn of an ox, or other large animal.

Their bellows are variously formed, but in every instance a pair are used, being worked alternately, one with the right hand and the other

with the left, so as to keep up a continuous blast. They are generally formed of goat or antelope skins of about the same size, which are skinned off as "sacks," and "braiied" or softened in the usual manner.

The sack is made by cutting the skin of the animal along the inside of the thighs, and then, with-

NATIVE INDIAN BLACKSMITH.

out making any other incision, stripping it over the fore part of the body, the head being previously cut off, the skin of the legs is sewn, or knotted up to prevent the escape of air. In one of the hinder legs of each bag is fitted a smaller tube, frequently of gemsbok horn, and to the sides of the aperture of the neck are sewn two pieces of stick with loops upon them for the insertion in one of the thumbs, and in the other of the fingers, so that by expanding the hand the neck can be opened while it is raised to inflate the bag, and closed up by grasping it tightly when it is pressed down to force the stream of air upon the fire; then by inflating and compressing the bags alternately, the primary object of a continuous and sufficient supply of air is obtained.

There are various modifications of form, in some of which more or less wood is very ingeniously used; but as the power of the whole depends entirely on the amount of air that can be inclosed in and forcibly expelled from the skin bags, we think the foregoing description will sufficiently answer the purpose.

If the traveller wishes—as an Englishman generally does—to stand up to his work, he can build up for his forge a square of rough stones, and then smooth over the top with a mixture of cattle dung and clay, of which last anthills broken up afford the finest quality ; or if the hills are sufficiently large, he may at once smooth off the top of one and shape the embankment in the rear. But in this case he will also have to raise another platform, not only to carry his bellows, but for the blower to sit upon ; for we doubt whether a native in the wilderness could be prevailed upon to blow them in any other position.

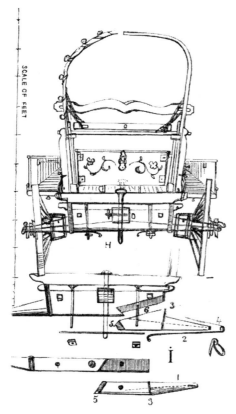

One of the most important portions of a waggon, and at the same time one most liable to damage, is the axle, and it is therefore of vital consequence that the traveller should understand properly how to set about repairing it.

Suppose it be necessary to condemn the broken axle and make a new one ; the first care is to seek out a tree of good hard wood—"kameel doorn" (*Acacia giraffæ*) is about the best a traveller is generally likely to find, though many other varieties may be used)—and in thinly wooded countries this may imply a day or more spent in searching for miles around, for the trunk should be of tolerably straight grain, solid, and capable of affording a log 6ft. or 7ft. in length, 10in. in depth, and 4in. in thick-

New axles.

NOTE.—The sketch above shows, on one side, the kap tent, or properly-built roof, and on the other, the wattled substitute. O is the front of the "kadel," or swinging bed-frame. L, 8, M, on the next page, are the yokes, skeis, and trek gear, drawn to the scale given at the side.

ness. A yoke of oxen may be sent to draw it home, and it should then be truly, however roughly, squared up to the above dimensions.

The size of the aperture in the nave, both at the back and front of the wheel, should then be taken, they will generally be about 4in., tapering to 3in. or 2½in.; the length of the arm will probably be from 14in. to 16in. In cutting the arm *nothing* is to be tapered off from the front (Fig. 1) or from the lower part (Fig. 2), all the taper being cut from above and from behind, so that the wheels may incline a little inward in front and below, and if the axle arms should bend a little with the weight of cargo and with the forward draught, they may only have a tendency to resume a true position.

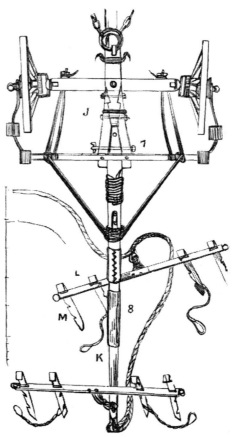

The arms should be carefully lined off in accordance with these rules, and in cutting the shoulder (Fig. 3) it should be squared, not from the edge of the axle, but from a line (dotted in the illustration) drawn along the centre of the arm, so that the back of the nave may bear truly against it. In cutting the shoulder be sure not to weaken the arm by letting the saw go, however little, beyond the proper depth, for where so great a pressure has to be borne the slightest cut would become the beginning of a fracture. When the arms have been cut and roughly rounded by saw and adze or axe, trim them with the spoke-shave, and occasionally try on the wheel, whirling it round to test the truthfulness of the work—there is almost sure to be sufficient grease or tar left in it to mark all the undue projections, and to leave clean the hollows on the arm, and the marks should be carefully examined that you may know what parts require to be trimmed away. It is now time to take off the iron work from the condemned axle; and sufficient notice should be taken of every piece, to know exactly to what portion of the woodwork it is to be restored, for much extra difficulty is occasioned by any uncertainty on this point. Bolts, though of the same apparent size, should not be transferred at random from one side to the other, and every nut, when once removed, should be scrupulously restored to the individual bolt it belongs to. These injunctions may seem needlessly strict; but we speak from experience, and if the reader has to attempt the work now under consideration he will do well to attend as strictly to them.

The iron skeins, or friction guards (Fig. 4), should be removed from the arms of the old axle and carefully let into the corresponding ones of the new; and when nearly fitted they may be slightly heated so as to char and smooth the bed for themselves, as well as to grip more tightly, in cooling, the wood they are meant to protect. Before fastening them with their proper bolts the wheels should be tried on to ascertain that they have been truly fitted.

If, as is most frequently the case, the new axle is a front one, it must now be fitted under the rest of the fore " stell " or " carriage " (H), the holes for the connecting bolts and perch-bolt marked and truly bored, and the clamps which bind it to the upper portion heated, driven into their place, and tightened by being suddenly cooled with water.

Sometimes, when it is not necessary, or wood sufficiently large cannot be procured, to make a new axle, a new arm (I) may be let in, and this should be scarfed and checked in, and the inner end (Fig. 5), which reaches nearly to the centre of the axle, cut, not square, but diagonally across, so that the after side is somewhat longer than the front, and this, preventing the inner end from coming forward, will also counteract the natural tendency of the draught to force the arm backward.

If the longitudinal cut (Fig. 6) for the scarf is also made not square across, but a little inclined upwards in front, it will also help to resist the backward pressure of the wheel. No fastening beyond the bolt which passes through the quarter of the axle and the band at the shoulder is absolutely necessary for the fixing of a new arm. We have, upon one occassion, not only made a new axle, but when, from unsoundness of timber, a new arm was necessary, have put in one on which the heavily-loaded waggon ran nearly 1000 miles; and besides this, the fore " tong " (J), or socket in which the dissel-boom or pole (K) works being much broken, we cut off the jaws on either side, and fitted new ones in a manner that will be much better understood by the above sketch than by description; and these, after running from the Zambesi to Otjimbengue, were still so firm that the professional waggon-wright, deemed it necessary only to secure them by the addition of a couple of bands put on hot, and shrunk down on them with water.

Frequently the "dissel-boom" or pole will break, but the cutting and fitting of a new one is too simple a matter to need much more instruction than a careful inspection of the old one will Repairing afford ; it was our practice, however, to bore a hole per- poles. pendicularly downward behind the dissel-bolt (Fig. 7), and by means of a ½in. bolt and nut, tightly screwed, preserve the pole from splitting when subjected to a heavy strain.

Mr. Reeder, whom we met near the Zambesi, showed us a very ingenious plan of staying the dissel-boom when the fore tong was weakened. Chapman went out and shot a rhinoceros, and Reeder first nailed a chock upon the dissel-boom, and fixed on it a grummet of rhinoceros hide as tight as possible, then, taking a long, stout strip of the same, he hitched the middle of it on in front of the grummet, leading the parts to each side of the splinter bar, and thence under the axle to the bolts behind it, where the ends were thinned off sufficiently to admit of their being easily made fast. These stays did not come forward enough to gall the after oxen. The great virtue of raw hide is that, instead of slackening like rope when it dries, it shrinks, and becomes as hard as iron. Suppose a dissel-boom sprung where another could not be procured, the skin from the leg of an ox, or a wild animal of corresponding size—say a buffalo or quagga—drawn on while wet and allowed to dry, would make the joint firmer even than the unfractured part (Fig. 8). The skin from the tail of an ox will, in the same manner, mend a broken waggon whip; and that of a calf's tail is in like manner used by the Kafirs to bind the part where the iron of their assegais or light javelins is inserted into the shaft. Quagga skin, indeed, is especially used for this purpose, and hardly for any other, as it is so rigid that the ordinary means for softening leather are of no avail. Sometimes the Dutch farmers use the skin, just as it is stripped off, as a jar or barrel to hold corn or other produce.

A long journey over rough roads and in an intensely hot country, like Africa in the dry season, will tell upon the best-made wheels, and the spokes and tires will become loose most frequently where it is impossible properly to rectify the defect. In such cases a number of wedges of dry, straight-grained wood must be pre- The repair pared, and for this purpose some box or packing- of wheels. case, made of deal, must be sacrificed, as it will be almost impossible to procure anything so suitable in the bush; the plank must be cut into pieces between 3in. and 4in. long, and, if these are again sawn diagonally along their length, material will be saved by the production of two wedges, where only one could have been made by the whittling process. These must be driven tightly in from back and front, between the felloe and the tire, and as equally as possible all round the wheel; if they are then wetted with, and allowed to absorb, a strong solution of salt in water, they will swell, and will not again shrink as they would if wetted with water only. We knew one very practical Englishman who used to soak his wedges in salt and water before driving them in, but what he gained by thus previously swelling them we never were able to learn. If the spokes become loose in the nave the temporary remedy is to cut two stout bars, in length just equal to the diameter of the wheel; half check them so as to give them a better hold on the felloe; lay them parallel

to each other on the front of the wheel, one on each side the nave, and bind every spoke as firmly as possible to them with thongs of raw hide, taking care to keep the lashings quite close to the centre of the wheel; the drying up of the thongs will shrink them so much that the fabric of the wheel will be as firmly bound together as if clamped with iron.

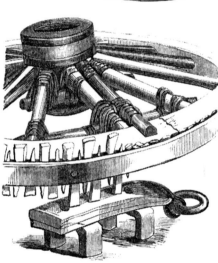

If a spoke be broken, cut a new one much thicker than the rest, half check it on to the back of the felloe, and let the other end abut upon the nave, filling up nearly the space between the sound spokes on either side; it should need to be driven in tightly, and, when in position, should be secured by thongs of raw hide, both at the nave and at the felloe, to sticks laid across the front of the spokes on either side, and securely lashed to them.

Lead is useful for a multitude of purposes; its great specific gravity, and the ease with which it can be melted, cut, hammered, moulded, and *Lead, and* bent, render it especially valuable as a handy metal. Our *its uses.* space will not admit of our giving more than a few of the most noteworthy purposes to which it can be applied by the hunter and explorer. Projectiles of all sizes can be made from it, from the ponderous cannon shot to the small sizes used by the hunter naturalist.

Round shot for artillery, of excellent quality, can be manufactured from lead; and there is no doubt that for certain purposes it is far superior to the iron missiles in general use, the cheapness of the latter material being its great recommendation. It Cannon shot. will sometimes happen in wild countries that although regular cannon balls are not obtainable lead is, and to make round shot from it two or three methods may be adopted.   The first is to form a ball from well-mixed clay, or carve one from wood, of size to fit the bore of the piece easily, but not too loosely.   The clay ball will require thorough drying in the sun or before a slow fire before use.   The wooden one will merely require sprinkling over with fine ashes from the camp fire to fit it for use.   Two large calabashes, wooden boxes, bowls, or cooking pots, are now to be rather more than filled with well-kneaded clay, which has been carefully freed from stones or grit, pressing it well down with a flat board until it is quite even at the surface and is perfectly compact. The clay round the edges of the two clay holders must now be trimmed off with a knife even with the sides of the holders, but projecting about an inch beyond the brim.   The surface of each is now to be sprinkled with very fine ashes, and the ball pressed into the centre of the clay until it is half imbedded.   It is then to be carefully removed, and pressed in like manner on the other holder.   The ball is then taken out and laid aside, the two holders being allowed to dry slowly, care being taken that the clay is not cracked by the too sudden application of heat.   When thoroughly dry, the vessels or holders are to be placed mouth to mouth, and so fitted, by scraping the clay, that the two indentations formed by the ball fit exactly facing each other; when this has been done, a funnel-shaped inlet must be cut for the admission of the molten lead.   The two holders may now be put together, secured with a lashing of cord or strips of hide, and the metal run in at the inlet. Some time must be allowed to elapse before the mould is disturbed, or the lead will not have sufficiently settled to admit of the shot being removed without injury to the apparatus.   The tail of lead formed by the inlet serves to lift the shot out by, and is then cut off flush with the surface.   A number of balls may with care be made with the same pair of holders, only the greatest caution is needed in this, as with all other operations in which molten lead is used, to guard against the presence of moisture in the mould, or most serious accidents will happen.

Soft stones of many kinds can be conveniently made use of for casting in, taking two of equal size, scooping out the cavity in each stone of the form intended to be given to the casting, and then cutting

o

an inlet. Common Bath scouring bricks answer this purpose admirably. We constantly use them for casting fishing leads, plummets, bodies for artificial baits, &c. &c. Two bricks, or portions of brick, are made use of. The surfaces are rendered smooth by rubbing them together. The intended cavity is then marked with a sharp point on each half, and scooped neatly out with a knife, chisel, or other convenient instrument; when finished, notched, and the inlet cut, the two halves are tied together with tape and the lead poured in. Objects of six or seven pounds weight can be made by the use of two common scouring bricks. Balls of large size are often made in the East by hammering square masses of lead, or iron, on an anvil until sufficiently round for use. Great labour and no little skill are required to perform the operation, which after all leads to very unsatisfactory results, the balls being rough and untrue, corresponding with the interiors of the barrels they are intended to be fired from. We have seen heavy stones and bits of iron covered with lead, fired from the most unpromising looking matchlocks, which, somehow or another, deliver their charge with greater force and accuracy than would be anticipated on a first examination. The best moulds for casting bullets of all sizes and forms are those made from gun-metal, bronze, or brass.

A buck-shot mould of either of these materials will be found of great value. We have one which has proved on many occasions of the greatest service; it is constructed to contain two rows of cavities for the shot, seven in each row, one above the other; so that when the groove leading to the inlets is filled with lead, and all the cavities are charged, the second row is turned upwards and treated in the same manner. The shot, when cold, are cut from their necks with a knife or strong pair of scissors, and are then fit for use. They should be about the size of common peas, and a charge of them from a large powerful gun is tremendously effective; they are extremely useful for deer jumping, antelope shooting, wild goose or bustard stalking. At very short distances, and in close encounter with a large animal, they may be used with destructive effect, but must be only considered in the light of a makeshift when the true large game of the forest has to be dealt with. Against attacking hordes of savages, in a bush fight, or canoe encounter, they are invaluable. The charge must be proportioned to the size of the guns; those of heavy metal and large bore generally deliver them best.

Slugs are to be made by filling a box or a large pot with fine clean sand, forcing it down tight, and then with a smooth round stick, about the size of a small pencil, making a number of holes from the surface to the bottom of the vessel or receiver in which the sand has been placed. When as many are made as the space will admit of, pour the moulten lead steadily into them until they are filled; when cold, the sand can be thrown out, and the leaden rods or pencils separated from it. These, when laid on a board in rows, can be cut up into short junks by placing a strong knife on them, and striking it on the back with any convenient instrument. Thick sheets of lead are cut up into dice in much the same manner. These are usually shaken about in a tin box or an iron pot, in order to round off the corners.

The manufacture of shot by the amateur, although not quite as easy of accomplishment as the preparation of slugs, may be, with the exercise of a little ingenuity, successfully carried out; and although the produce of his labours will **Shot, to make.** not equal the perfect spheres produced by the professional shot manufacturer, by the aid of his costly tower, yet it will be good enough for the description of shooting he will be likely to obtain in situations where the making of shot is rendered necessary. We were driven to the necessity of devising the plan we are about to describe by the impossibility of obtaining shot, coupled with the urgent want of that to be procured with it. Thus is the operation to be conducted :—A piece of iron, such as horse-shoes are made from, is to be obtained if possible, if not, any other piece of iron, about 2ft. long and of moderate width and thickness, will answer the purpose. About an inch from the end of this drill a wide-mouthed, funnel-shaped hole, of the form known as a *countersink*, until within about the eighth of an inch of going through the bar; then, with a drill about the size of a knitting-needle, extend the hole quite through; next, get a piece of dry plank, about 3ft. long, and in it, with a handsaw, cut as many longitudinal cuts as the width of the board will admit of, making them a little over the eighth of an inch deep and the thickness of the saw wide. The board, when placed slightly on the incline, must be so treated with a charge of molten lead that all the cuts are filled with it from the upper end; the result will be the formation of a great number of long lead wires. These are to be taken from the grooves and fresh batches run, until as many pounds have been made as it is intended to make shot. A preserved-meat tin, or an ordinary tin pot, must now be about one-third filled with water, and the remaining two-thirds filled up with oil; the pot must be placed on a plate or dish, in order to catch any oil which may run over as the work proceeds. The end of the iron bar which has the hole in it is now to be placed in the fire and heated to a bright-red heat: when the other end, round which a piece of cloth may be bound, is grasped with the left hand, and the bar quickly withdrawn from the fire, struck

smartly against some solid body, in order to remove adhering dust and
ashes, and then held with the wide mouth of the hole upward, a short
distance above the surface of the oil in the pot.   A lead wire is now to
be quickly taken up in the right hand and its end pressed well down
into the hole (as shown in the above illustration); if the iron
is well heated, the wire will melt away very rapidly and run in a success-
sion of drops into the oil: wire after wire is to be thus melted, until
the iron requires reheating.   (It is a good plan to have two or more
irons at work, but it is not essential.)   This wire-melting process must
be continued until all the stock has been expended, when the solid
contents of the pot may be taken out.   If the operation of *dropping*
has been properly performed the result will be shot of about three
sizes—No. 7, No. 4, and duck shot.   Certain conditional circum-

stances somewhat alter these sizes, but approximately they are to be
expected, and a certain number more or less *tailed* will generally be
found amongst the rest.   To separate the three sizes of round shot two
flat tin boxes or empty sardine tins are required.   With a piece of nail
filed down, so as to make a hole the size to just let No. 7 shot
through, punch a number of holes in the bottom of one of the boxes,
so as to make a sort of sieve of it; then with another nail make holes
in the bottom of the second box, just large enough to let your No. 4
through.   When these are prepared, wash your mixed shot in water
with wood ashes in it; this removes all the oil in the form of soap.
The shot, when dry, is ready for sifting with the boxes.   The first box
lets only No. 7 or a size or so smaller through, keeping back the No. 4.
The second box lets the No. 4 through, retaining the duck shot.   Each

size may now have its own respective *tailers*, or pear-shaped shot, mixed with it; these can be got rid of by allowing the shot to run down over a sloping board, when the round shot run straight to the bottom, whilst the *tailers* run off at the sides, and can be collected to melt up again.

Plates of lead for writing inscriptions on can be cast by turning up the edges of a piece of sheet copper, iron, or tin, just high enough to form a sort of shallow tray to hold the molten lead. In the absence of sheet metal, the surface of a box of sand, or a flat stone with a little wall of clay round it, may be made use of. Lead plates, to make.

Lead pencils, for rough carpenter's work, can be made by filling joints of small cane, marsh reeds, or weed stalks, with melted lead, and then pointing them with a knife. The handles of stock whips and some other implements are weighted, and prevented from splitting, by having lead run into them; Lead pencils and stock whip handles. some of the former are occasionally very elaborately ornamented. The operation is performed by first cutting out the intended pattern on the handle with a sharp-pointed knife or other instrument, taking care that the cutting penetrates the wood deeply, that the form of the groove is slightly undercut, and that each ring of the pattern communicates with the one below it. The first ring on the stick must have an *inlet* made in it; strips of stout brown paper are now, after being slightly moistened and touched over with paste, rolled round the stick, layer after layer in spiral form, until its whole length has been thickly covered like the case of a rocket. When thoroughly dry the lead is run in at the inlet, and when cold the paper can be stripped off, and the handle finished off and polished with sand-paper or a bit of fish-skin.

Indentations in the sides of gun or rifle barrels can be taken out by the following process:—Take the barrel out of the stock; cut a cork so as to fit the muzzle tightly, and then force it down three inches, ram in about a Bruised gun-barrels to repair. quarter of an inch of dry powdered clay on the cork, twist a cloth dipped in cold water several times round the barrel in order to prevent the rib from becoming unsoldered by heat, and then fill up the space above the clay with molten *hardened lead*. (See " To harden bullets," p. 200.) You will then have a metal plug exactly fitting the barrel. Remove the cork and clay, and fashion from strong hard wood a rod just long enough to reach a few inches beyond the indentation. A bar of iron is now to be heated to a red heat, and placed against the indented spot on the outside of the barrel; the wet cloth being at the same time wound above and below it. The metal plug is now to be forced down the tube with the rod until it rests on the obstruction, when a few blows with a piece of heavy wood on the upper end of the rod will generally pass the plug onwards by forcing the tube back to its proper position. It will be well to reverse ends with the plug and force it up and down several times, until it travels quite freely past the place of obstruction.

Rifle shells may be extemporised by having little tin tubes the length of the conical bullet and the size of the gun nipple made.

Make-shift rifle shells. These, when their ends have been plugged with wood, are placed one by one in the mould, held upright by a bit of very fine brass wire, and the lead cast round them, so that the lead at the base of the bullet may extend beyond the end of the tube and cover it. The thin end of the tube should project just a trifle beyond the apex of the cone, as a rest for the cap. The wooden plug at this end is now taken out; the tube filled with the best sporting powder, and a strong, well made percussion-cap put on the tube, and secured there with strong varnish, sealing-wax, or pitch. The loading of a breech-loader with these is accomplished with no danger, but with a muzzle-loader the very greatest caution is required. The end of the ramrod or loading stick should be very deeply countersunk, in order to take all pressure off the cap; and even with this precaution it is well to make use of an overhanging branch of a tree to place the rod against, whilst the rifle is thrust muzzle upwards until the ball is home. Shells somewhat on this principle were first brought into notice by the late General Jacob, of the Scinde Irregular Horse. They are tremendously destructive when skilfully used: destroying large animals by exploding in them, and blowing up magazines of gunpowder at all but incredible distances; but we have known them explode *outside* the elephant and other large pachyderms, thus failing completely in the object they were used for. Mr. Metford's improvement on the Jacob shell is worthy of remark. Finding that it did not always explode, he mixed equal parts of chlorate of potass and sulphate of antimony; the two can be mixed on a plate with a *bone* paper-cutter or a quill pen. The more they are mixed, the more sensitive is their detonating power. The bullets are moulded with a hole from point nearly to base, as for Jacob's shells, but no copper tube is used. The powder is filled in with a quill to the top, and settled down by a few taps of the base of the bullet on a table and the end is then stopped with wax. But it is very questionable whether, in close encounter with large animals, it is not better, after all, to rely on the more certain effects of heavy balls of ordinary construction, with strong charges of powder behind them. With the numerous improvements in rifle shells we cannot deal, as

LEAD SMELTING IN THE FOREST.

many of them are too complex in their component parts for a wandering hunter or explorer to be able to imitate successfully.

Small ladles or iron spoons are usually used to melt lead in, but, in the absence of these, bullets and other small matters may be cast in the following manner, which is a favourite one amongst the Indians:—A piece of dry hard wood, about 16in. long, 3in. broad, and 2in. thick, is prepared; on one end of this a spoon-shaped cavity, with a lip-shaped groove in the end, is made; in the bottom of this a few red-hot wood embers from the fire are placed on these same fragments of flattened lead, and on the lead, some good-sized pieces of red-hot embers. A bit of bark is now twisted into a blow-pipe, from which a steady stream of air is directed to the miniature furnace, which almost instantly melts the lead, and fits it for running by the lip into the mould, just as it would from a spoon. Clean, excellent bullets are to be made in this way.

Ladles, spoons, and other substitutes.

It sometimes happens that lead ore or galena is discovered. Lead as a metal, except in very rare instances, is not found in a native or malleable form; and as the ore is a sulphuret, brittle, and easily pulverised, some method must be had recourse to in order to smelt and render it fit for use. Some Indians do it in the following manner:—After reducing a large quantity of the ore to powder, between heavy stones, they seek out a hollow tree stump, clear out the bottom flush with the ground, and dig a pit just outside it. Then on the bottom or floor of the stump a thick layer of dry wood is placed, evenly on this a layer of the powdered ore, then another layer of wood, then one of ore, and so on until the stump is quite full. A small hole is then chopped with a tomahawk through the side of the stump, level with the ground and opposite the pit. Through this orifice fire is introduced, and the stump soon becomes a mass of glowing heat as the air rushes in at the hole at the bottom; so fast as the galena (which is usually very pure) is reduced to melted lead it trickles through the interstices of the heated pile, and runs out into the pit, where it is allowed to settle and cool.

Lead ore smelting.

The Dutch-Africans like to have their bullets of such a size that when one is put into a clean barrel it passes slowly down without rattling, the slight noise of the escaping air being heard as it descends. In a skirmish they load very quickly; the powder is poured from the large ox-horn into the hollow of the hand, and thence into the gun: a number of bullets are held in the mouth, one is dropped in, and the moisture cakes the powder round and holds it in its place with a very slight tap from the ramrod, or sometimes perhaps without; though we should never advise any one to incur so great a risk of bursting his gun.

For such game as the elephant or rhinoceros the hunters harden their bullets with a little tin—not more than one tenth; if too much is
To harden bullets.   added it makes the bullet brittle, and detracts from its specific gravity; it should be just hard enough to show a slight indentation when bitten. The lead must be first melted as requiring the greater heat, and the tin added afterwards. Type metal, or worn-out type from printing offices, is much used for this purpose; but quicksilver, which, from its own great specific gravity, does not detract from the weight of the bullet, is the best alloy. Sir S. Baker says :—"The lead is melted in a pot, which is kept at red heat. Enough to make three or four bullets is taken in a smaller ladle, and one-tenth of quicksilver added and stirred into it with a bit of iron, as if the quicksilver is exposed to the great heat of the larger pot it will soon evaporate. The rifle bullets used in the army, being compressed instead of cast, are hard enough without alloy; and in breech-loaders, where the bullet has to pass through a barrel which is generally a trifle smaller than the chamber, it would be unsafe to harden it too much."

The Fingoes and Kafirs cut a small piece off two bullets, so as to produce flat surfaces (Fig. 1); then, while the lead is still clean, press
Cleft bullets.   them strongly together, giving them a half turn to expel the air and bring them perfectly in contact. They will adhere so strongly as to bear throwing on the ground, and when fired at a hundred yards will separate only a few inches. A bullet cleft very nearly through with two cuts, so that it spreads into four parts (Fig. 2), makes a fearful wound at close quarters—a conical cut from its base (Fig. 3) particularly so. Sometimes two bullets are connected by a bit of bell wire rolled up spirally as a spring (Fig. 4). We have seen bundles of nails bound together with wire by the rebel Hottentots in imitation of conical bullets. The Kafirs use bits of the legs of iron pots. Some of the native hunters use iron bullets, or rather bolts twice as long as their diameter; but they creep so close that they cannot miss, and follow the wounded animal till he dies, so that they always recover their bullet. A bullet of the ordinary "Enfield" pattern so cast as to have a small tubular cavity left in its centre extending from its apex downwards expands to a great size when striking the object against which it is directed. It is well to stop the mouth of the orifice with a bit of softened beeswax before loading, to exclude air. By partially filling this cavity with a charge composed of equal parts of sulphuret of antimony and chlorate of potash in powder,

and stopping with beeswax as before directed, the ball is converted into a most destructive form of shell which can be discharged from either gun, rifle, or pistol, provided the arm is a breech-loader. The chemicals must be kept separate in bottles and only mixed in small quantities when required for use. A quill cut like a pen is a convenient instrument to charge the hollows in the balls with.

Bullet moulds may be extemporised in many ways. Two shallow boxes may be made and filled with loam or clay, much as the moulds for cannon shot, before described, are made (of which last no material is better than a pounded anthill), and the surface of the lower one must be smooth. A piece of stiff paper pierced with holes the size of the bullet laid on it, and as many bullets as convenient pressed half way into the clay,

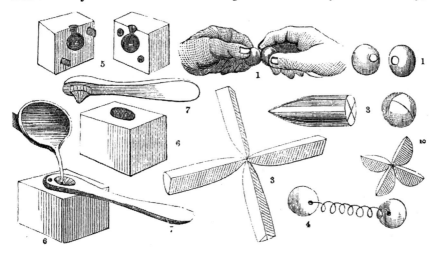

the other half must then be pressed down upon it, and when nearly dry the bullets must be taken out, holes made through to the outer surface, on which a small channel should be cut, so that the lead may run to the entrance and not waste itself by spreading. Most likely the mould would be damaged after two or three castings, but it is easy to make a new one. The Dutch boers frequently use blocks of steatite or soapstone, with half the bullet cut into each, and pegs or projections on one half, with corresponding hollows in the other, keep the two parts in true position (Fig. 5).

In Sydney we required a conical bullet mould; and, as such things were not generally kept for sale, we engaged a founder to make a solid block of brass, as in Fig. 6, and in this to bore a cylindro-conical hole, point downwards, about ½in. deeper than the length of the bullet; another piece was made with a handle at one end, and at the other a projection (Fig. 7), to fit into the block and give the form of the hollow back of the bullet ; a hole was bored through this a little smaller above than below, so that when the superfluous lead was cut off the bullet would come away with a tail about 1in. long, tapering to the end ; this was easily cut off with proper pincers ; there was a small notch cut up the side of the inserted block so as to allow of the escape of air as the lead was poured in. In some conical moulds the lead is poured in from the side, and in others from the point. We do not approve of either of these methods. The greatest hardness, weight, and density should be at the point, and therefore this should be downward in the mould, while the metal is poured in at the base.

Of course the great range acquired by some of our most perfect rifles with cylinder conical bullets is an immense advantage, for if animals cannot be approached they may be shot at long ranges ; and very frequently during the last Kafir war, while parties with the common musket have been defending themselves against savages who occupied almost impregnable positions, those among the colonists who possessed long-range rifles would occupy a hill perhaps a couple of thousand yards off, and send bullets among the enemy with quite sufficient accuracy to create a very uncomfortable feeling of insecurity.

A very favourite form of gun was a double-barrel, with one barrel rifled, and very carefully sighted for long ranges, and the other plain, and capable of throwing a good charge of buck shot, which we have seen very effectively used at thirty or forty yards.

When the elephant hunters lie at the water by night, and shoot at very close quarters, they find that a sharp-pointed conical with very high velocity, pierces so suddenly and sharply, that the animal feels no shock to the nervous system, and gets away for many miles, and dies beyond their reach. They therefore choose a short, smooth-bore gun, with a very large round bullet. We have seen them as large as half a pound; and this, with a comparatively small charge of powder, say 9drs. or 10drs., bruises rather than pierces, communicating such a shock to the adjacent parts that the creature is stunned as well as wounded, and is not able to make those marvellous last efforts that in the former case would enable him at least to die in peace far out of reach of his pursuers. We, after a fair trial of the conical ball in India, abandoned it on account of the quantity of wounded game lost, and returned to the old spherical projectile.

Sporting rifles.

Improvements in guns are long before they are generally adopted in wild and distant countries. The old flint musket is to this day the favoured weapon of most of the border tribes of South Africa,

America, and the East; it will shoot quite well enough for them, and, if of military make, it lasts a. long time in comparatively good order. Percussion guns found their way very slowly even among the Dutch colonists; many admitted their superiority, but there was always the uncertainty of being able to obtain a supply of caps, and, in the same way, many excellent forms of breech-loaders cannot be adopted by persons travelling or residing far from civilisation, because complicated and expensive cartridges are required, and when the supply runs short the gun is useless. And sometimes, because however perfect the gun may be while well taken care of, its delicate adjustments soon give way under the rough wear and tear of actual hard service. The advantages of facility in reloading, especially on horseback, or while running after or away from the game or enemy, are so great, that if a breech-loader can be made sufficiently strong and simple in all its parts, capable of being used as a muzzle-loader on emergencies, or with cartridges so simple that a person of ordinary skill can make them for himself, it will surely commend itself to men whose lives, in many cases, depend upon the effectiveness of their guns. It would be invidious in us to compare the merits of the various forms. We have already mentioned the satisfaction with which we used the single-barrelled Wilson breech-loader, the simplicity and strength of which, combined with facility of loading, were all that could be desired, unless, indeed, it were made self-capping, which we believe could easily be done. A metal breech-plug, to be inserted when required, converts it into a muzzle-loader; but then a smaller size of bullet must be used, and the cartridges are so simple and inexpensive, that we found it more easy to make them on the spot. The materials required were a few sheets of tissue paper, a quantity of felt wads, tolerably stout, half of them the exact size of the bore, and the rest a little smaller. A piece of tin of the form and size indicated by

Cartridge making. the diagonal lines (Fig. 1) in our illustration was used as a pattern by which to cut the paper. The straight edge that was to surround the bullet, and the farthest diagonal side, were touched with a little gum, gathered from the nearest mimosa. A small cylinder of wood (Fig. 3) was then taken by the knob, in the left hand, and, with the right, the hollow base of the bullet (Fig. 2) was fitted on to the convex end, laid fairly on the paper (Fig. 6) and rolled forward until the cartridge case was formed. The wood was then withdrawn, and the paper, adhering to the bullet, left to dry. When a sufficient number were completed, they were set upright in any convenient trough, or in a block of wood (Fig. 7), 3in. deep, bored with holes of the proper size (Fig. 11). The charge of powder was poured into each

and covered with a small disc of card or paper.   One of the small wads,
saturated with grease, was next put in (Fig. 8), the superfluous paper
folded down on it (Fig. 9), and a full-sized wad was then affixed to the
end with a drop of gum (Fig. 10).   The tissue paper was quite strong
enough to confine the powder, and a military cap, of fair average quality,
never failed to drive the fire through it to the charge.   We found it best
to saturate our wads by melting, or rather heating, our hardest fat nearly

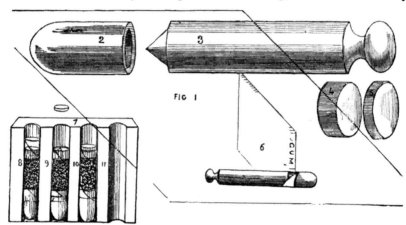

to boiling point, throwing them in and letting them absorb as much as
possible, and then spreading them out on a clean surface to cool.   Of
course we carried a couple of wad punches of the proper size in case
our supply should run short.   In making a cartridge for a muzzle-
loading rifle, the wooden roller should have a hollow to receive the point
of the bullet; the bullet is placed on the paper with the base towards
the right hand, just so far within the edge as to allow a wad to be
put behind, and the paper turned down over it.   The powder

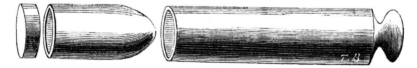

is then measured into the case on the point, and, in loading, the
powder is first poured into the gun, then the bullet is reversed and
the paper torn off before it is rammed down.   It is questionable,
however, whether any form of single-barrelled rifle or shot gun can
compete with a double barrel for general usefulness and efficiency.
Whilst on the subject of cartridges, it may not be amiss to refer
to the tallow cartridges used for shot guns.   They add greatly

to the length of range, and are extremely valuable for wildfowl shooting.

The following communication to the *Field* newspaper will serve to explain the mode to be observed in their manufacture :—

" A represents a piece of common cartridge paper ; B a roller of boxwood, or any hard wood, turned to the size to admit the paper A being rolled once round it, and then fitting into Grease cartridges, the chamber C; C a chamber turned out of a   to make. solid piece of wood, the chamber to be the exact size of bore of gun the cartridges are intended for. To make the cartridges,

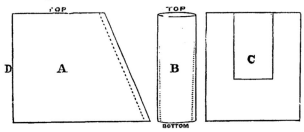

cut a piece of paper in the shape of the drawing A, cutting the top to the width requisite, to allow the paper at top to overlap nearly a quarter of an inch ; then gum the edge of the paper to about the eighth of an inch, as marked by the dotted line on the drawing A. Place the roller B on to the paper at D, and roll up firmly ; wind round it a little thread, to keep the paper from slipping. In a few minutes it will be dry. You can then push the roller out of the case, and proceed in the same way till you have enough cases. Secondly, take the roller and return it to the case, excepting that you leave the roller exposed at the top, say for 16-gauge about $\frac{3}{8}$in.; place the case and roller in the chamber, bottom upwards, then take some fine strong twine and place round as in draw-

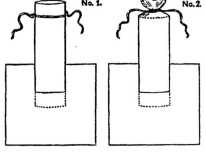

ing No. 1. When drawn tight, tie firmly, and it will appear as in No. 2 : then reverse the roller and case, bringing the tied end down to bottom of chamber, press down hard to flatten the bottom of case, draw out the roller, pour into the case some melted tallow of about the consistency of cream, and then put in your charge of shot, having sufficient quantity of tallow to just cover the shot. Put by until cool ; when set firm, place on the top of the tallow a leather wad (the size for 16-gauge cartridge will be 18-gauge). Any leather not too thick will do, and you can cut the wads out with a punch. Turn down the case neatly over the leather wad, and make fast with sealing-wax. When loading place the tied end of the cartridge next to the powder. These directions are for both muzzle and breech-loaders, the only difference being in the roller, which for muzzle-loaders must be made $\frac{1}{16}$in. smaller at the bottom end, as marked by the dots in drawing B. After a little practice the cartridges do not take long to make."

Wherever the means of transport will permit, take plenty of Ely's wire cartridges, but when they cannot be obtained, a make-shift form, well adapted for general use, may be made as follows:—Prepare a stick, about 18in. long, by rounding it carefully and making it fit the bore of your gun loosely. Round this take two or three turns of oiled silk, such as chemists sell. Then draw off the end of the stick tube enough to hold the charge of shot and admit of two ties being made round it. Now, with a piece of fine twine, put on the first tie close to the stick; then put in your charge of shot, and when it is shaken into place, put the other tie on the outer end, just as sausage skins are secured. The cartridge is now complete, and can be cut off next the stick, when you proceed as before until all the tube has been used. We manufactured a great number of these in Tartary, and found them hard-hitting and durable. We usually carried a waistcoat pocket full of them, and rammed one down on each charge of powder without any wad between the cartridge and powder, but always placed one over the cartridge, in order to prevent it from rising in the barrel. Cartridges of this description kill considerably farther than a loose charge, and are exceedingly handy when shooting from the horse's back. We, with 1oz. of No. 4, killed in this way, near Phoros Pass, an eagle, which we gave Captain Blackiston, R.A., who, we believe, deposited it in the Royal Artillery Institution at Woolwich. The fingers of old kid gloves should always be kept, as they serve as excellent covers both for shot and ball. Shot will require one tie to keep it in; balls will remain in without fastening. A little grease or oil should be smeared over them when first made.

The range of a common breech-loader cartridge, may be consider-ably increased by placing within it that which is known as a concen-trator. This is simply a cylinder of paper the same substance as the cartridge it is to be used with, open at each end, of half an inch in length, and of sufficient diameter to fit nicely into the bore or chamber of the cartridge to be altered, a cylinder cut from a 16-gauge case will just fit one of 12

Makeshift cartridges.

Concentrating cartridges for breech-loaders.

bore. In the absence of odd cases the cylinders can be easily made from stout paper rolled round a stick of suitable size and gummed or pasted. The accompanying illustration represents a section of a charged cartridge, with the concentrator fitted to it. Load as follows: Introduce the charge of

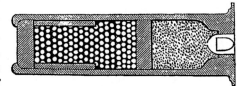

powder and the thick wad in the usual way; insert the concentrator and thrust it down until it is just far enough entered to allow for the thickness of the covering wad, charge with shot wad, and close in the usual way. A weak shooting gun may be made to hit extremely hard by the use of this simple contrivance.

On many occasions we have been obliged to fire shot from a rifle, for the purpose of obtaining birds, when the smooth-bores were not at hand. Either the oiled silk or glove-finger cartridge is very far superior to a loose charge. In loading ordinary guns with loose shot, it sometimes happens that a few grains get dropped into the loaded barrel between the ramrod head and the barrel. When this happens, invert the gun, pass the rod upwards, and the shot will fall out, when the rod can be withdrawn. The ramrod will also at times get firmly fixed in a foul barrel, and defy every ordinary effort to get it out. A little water, spirit, or any other fluid poured down the barrel almost instantly releases it. Should a gun or rifle miss fire, or be exposed for any time to damp, cut a small peg of dry, soft wood, hammer it well down into the nipple, cut it off flush, put on a new cap, and pull the trigger, when the weapon is almost certain to go off. We first saw this plan in use among the Sardinian Bersigliari, and have since found it answer perfectly.

Hints on firearms.

When hunting through wet jungles, or the reeds of the marsh, percussion caps can be rendered almost waterproof by melting a little beeswax on a piece of tin and then dipping the mouth of each separate cap in it. These, when cold, are set aside for use. When placed on the nipple, the wax forms a shield between the cap and nipple, which prevents the water from working its way up. All vegetable oil used about gun-locks should be prepared as follows:—Partly fill a common vial with oil, throw in a half charge of shot, hang it in the air with the cork out, and in a few days drain off all the clear oil from the top for use.

Spirits of turpentine, when it can be procured, is very valuable for cleaning the interiors of guns, pistols, and rifles. When water is used,

wash the barrels out thoroughly with cold water, making use of
a tough wooden rod with a number of notches at the end. Round
this a piece of woollen cloth may be twisted until of a size to
act as a sucker in the barrel. Woollen is better

Gun cleaning.

than tow, linen, or cotton, as there is no danger
of ignitable threads being left behind, and it can be used repeatedly
by washing and drying it. When the barrels are thoroughly clean,
fill them with boiling water. When this has all run off through
the nipple holes, commence with a fresh strip of cloth to dry out the
barrels, which must be held in a folded cloth, in order to guard the
hand from the heat of the water. When quite dry, and before the
barrels are cold, finish off with a little spirits of turpentine. Lead may
be removed by the use of a little quicksilver. The cleaning of fire-arms
in a wild country is a matter of the very greatest importance, and
should never be entrusted to servants, unless, from long service and
great experience, they may be implicitly depended on. Even with such
followers about us, we always, however fatigued, clean our own guns.

It not unfrequently happens that white men residing alone or in
small communities in the vicinity of numerous and powerful native
tribes possess cannon of some kind or other, generally small signal
guns from merchant ships, perhaps recovered from wrecks upon the
coast, or field pieces abandoned as not worth the trouble of bringing
away when some military outpost has ceased to be occupied.

. During 1863 and 1864 the barbarous and desultory war between
the Namaqua Hottentots and the Damaras, whom they had so long

Mounting cannon.

oppressed, was keeping the country in a state of
alarm for many hundred miles around, and we were
requested to take charge of a couple of brass yacht guns. It was
necessary to mount them, so that they might be easily moved from
point to point on the plain around the village; and for this purpose we
took for each the hinder wheels and axle of a Cape waggon, inserting a
pole to serve as the "trail" into the socket of the "lang-wagen" in
the centre of the axle; we then took a plank of stinkwood, 1ft. wide,
3in. thick, and about 4ft. long. About 1ft. from the foremost end a
stout bolt passed through it and the centre of the axle so as to let
it work freely, the after end was tapered to a point and travelled on
a quadrant, made from the felloe of an after wheel.

On this, as a swivel bed, we bolted down a pair of cheeks of 2in.
stinkwood to carry the guns. The quoins and wedges ran in grooves,
formed by 1in. slips of stinkwood nailed upon the bed, to which they
were secured by lanyards of raw hide; the boxes for ammunition on
either side were covered with raw hide, and that containing the

powder was thickly lined with green baize; the matches were kept in a small box in front of the gun-carriage; the fuze-holder was made from the segment of a hollow brass curtain ring fixed to a handle of hard wood; the fuze itself was a strip of calico 1in. broad, doubled and loosely twisted into a two-stranded rope; it was steeped in a solution of gunpowder, and the colour indicated its strength—light grey was slow match, and dark grey was quick.

As we did not contemplate moving the guns farther than necessary for the defence of the village, we made no provision for yoking draught oxen, but this could easily have been done if needed. It was enough for our purpose to provide man ropes, one pair behind the gun and one before, so that, either in advance or retreat, its muzzle might be towards the enemy.

TIME GUN.

The bullets were all tied up in calico, with wads made by cutting off sections of soft deal rods, and cartridges of twelve or fourteen musket balls or fifty revolver bullets were made up.

One use to which one of our guns was put is shown in the illustration. We were asked to repair the clock, but this was always difficult, and it was uncertain how long it may go correctly afterwards. We therefore erected a frame over the gun, and fitted the lens of a camera on an axle placed due east and west, so that it could turn in the plain of the meridian, and so be adapted to the sun's gradual change of declination. Below the lens we fitted a piece of tin with its edges turned downwards, to hold a piece of quick match, a strip of calico, steeped in a strong solution of gunpowder, beneath it; a small slit in the tin was then so adjusted as to let the focus of light fall through it exactly at

Time guns.

P

12 o'clock: a small clip of tin confined the other end of the match over the vent. The moment of noon was announced with a regularity that no clock in our possession could have attained; and one great advantage was, that if by the interposition of a cloud, which would not happen once in nine months, the gun should fail to fire at the proper moment, it could not go wrong, for the speck of light would pass the narrow slit, and no discharge would take place till the next day.

The absence of the cap squares of a gun can be remedied by lashing the metal firmly down to the carriage with a raw hide rope, and then twisting it up tight with a stick, as shown in the above illustration; which also exhibits the mode of raising a gun by making use of the trail as a lever. A heavy gun may be mounted by letting its muzzle into a hole in the ground while the carriage is run under it.

During the continuance of the Damara and Hottentot war we Percussion caps were becoming exceedingly short of percussion caps, and substitutes. and were obliged not only very carefully to husband the few that were left, but to turn our attention to the manufacture of substitutes. The tips of Congreve matches, with the wood cut to a point so as to stick in the nipple of the gun, proved very effective, but were liable to be brushed or shaken off, or to become damp if carried for any length of time before firing. We, therefore, first inclosed the end of the match in the shell of an expended cap, and finding this answer, we dissolved the composition, and put a drop into the cap without the wood; we then dissolved it off a whole box of matches at a time, and with a camel-hair pencil put small drops into as many cap shells as it would serve. This answered admirably; but our next fear was that the supply of matches would run short, and therefore, drawing on our own artificial horizon for the quicksilver, on the photographic stores for nitric acid, and on our friends, the missionaries, for a supply of alcohol from their natural-history department, we set about the manufacture of fulminate of mercury according to the following recipe:—Dissolve 10 grs. of mercury in 1½ oz., by measure, of nitric acid; the solution is poured cold into 2 oz., by measure, of alcohol in a glass vessel, and gentle heat is applied till effervescence is excited, though it ordinarily comes on at common temperatures, a white vapour undulates on the surface, and a powder is gradually precipitated, which is immediately to be collected in a filter, well washed, and cautiously dried. It detonates by gentle heat or slight friction. Two grains and a half, with one-sixth of gunpowder, form the quantity for one percussion cap. We used a conical twist of blotting-paper for the filter, and mixed the fulminate, while still moist, with a small palette knife upon a plate with the gunpowder, treating it very gently, and in small quantities. We collected all the shells of expended caps, and for new ones cut out a cross of thin copper; then, making a hole in a piece of iron and a punch the size of the nipple, we drove the centre of the cross in, and the shell was formed. Stiff cartridge-paper stiffened with gum would have answered for dry weather, but would not have been secure against wet.

The block-houses erected by the Hudson's Bay Company, as depôts and forts in connection with the fur trade, usually have guns mounted in them. Brass field guns and howitzers are also at times to be met with at the border stations of wild countries, and it may, therefore, be well to know the charges and ranges of the ordinary kinds, which are as follows:

Brass guns and their charges.

BRASS FIELD GUNS.

6-POUNDER GUN.   WEIGHT, 6CWT.   SERVICE CHARGE, 1¼LB.

Elevation.	Ranges.			Length of fuse.
	Round Shot.	Shrapnel.	Case.	
P.B.	310	—	100	·3
0½°	470	450	150	·4
1	620	600	200	·5
1½	760	710	250	·6
2	890	820	300	·7
2½	1000	920	—	·8
3	1100	1020	—	·9
3½	1190	1110	—	1·
4	1280	1180	—	1.
4½	1370	1250	—	—
5	1450	1320	—	—
5½	1530	1380	—	—
6	1600	1440	—	—

9-POUNDER GUN.   WEIGHT, 13·5CWT.   SERVICE CHARGE, 2½LB.

Elevation.	Ranges.			Length of fuse.
	Round Shot.	Shrapnel.	Case.	
P.B.	300	—	150	—
0½°	500	—	200	—
1	680	670	250	·3
1½	830	800	300	·4
2	960	910	—	·5
2½	1080	1020	—	·6
3	1190	1120	—	·7
3½	1300	1220	—	·8
4	1400	1320	—	·9
4½	1500	1410	—	·9
5	1590	1500	—	1·0
5½	1680	1590	—	1·0
6	1760	1680	—	

BRASS HOWITZERS.

12-POUNDER HOWITZER.   WEIGHT, 6·5CWT.   SERVICE CHARGE, 1¼LB.

Elevation.	Ranges.			Length of fuse.
	Common Shell.	Shrapnel.	Case.	
P.B.	200	—	100	—
0½°	310	—	150	—
1	420	400	200	·3
1½	530	520	250	·4
2	630	630	300	·5
2½	715	725		·6
3	800	820		·7
3½	885	910		·8
4	970	1000	Ricochet.	·9
4½	1050	1090		1·0
5	1135	1180	Charge 6oz., el. ·7°. 600	1·1
5½	1220	1270	„ 8oz., „ ·6 . 600	1·2
6	1290	1350	„ 10oz., „ ·5 . 600	1·3

24-POUNDER HOWITZER.   WEIGHT, 12·5CWT.   SERVICE CHARGE, 2½LB.

Elevation.	Ranges.			Length of fuse.
	Common Shell.	Shrapnel.	Case.	
P.B.	270	—	150	—
0½°	390	—	200	—
1	520	500	250	·3
1½	640	630	300	·4
2	760	760		·5
2½	860	870		·6
3	960	980		·7
3½	1060	1090		·8
4	1160	1200	Ricochet.	·9
4½	1260	1300		1·0
5	1350	1400	See Table B.	1·1
5½	1440	1500		1.2
6	1520	1600		

TABLE B.

RICOCHET.	24-POUNDER HOWITZER.		RICOCHET.	24-POUNDER HOWITZER.	
Charge.	Elevation.	Pitch.	Charge.	Elevation.	Pitch.
oz.	deg.		oz.	deg.	
6	7·5	400	12	5·25	—
9	4·38	—	14	5·	—
8	9·	500	9	7·75	600
10	7·5	—	12	6·5	—
11	6·	—	16	4·75	—
11½	5·5	—			

Cartridges for either brass or iron guns are best made of some woollen material; trade serge or old blanketing answers very well for the purpose. Bags should be made a little less than the bore, and into these the charge of powder is to be poured. A piece of woollen thread, double worsted, or twine should now be used to close the end of the bag, after which it is to be passed two or three times round the bag, giving it at the same time a compact cylindrical form by rolling on a board or table under the hand. Passing the thread through the substance of the cartridge aids much in keeping its form and facilitates loading. A cartridge needle should be used to perform this operation. This needle can be easily made from a piece of stout copper or brass wire. Flatten out one end, drill or punch a hole in it to form the eye, and file the other end sharp for a point. Fourteen inches is a convenient length for a cartridge needle. It is said that a sailor's wife enabled a British vessel to continue a long and desperate fight by pillaging the officers' quarters of all the stockings she could find, and handing them up to be filled for cartridges. The intestines of animals, according to their size, would make as good cartridge cases as could be desired. Wads may be made of picked oakum twisted in a flat spiral to the proper size of the bore, when they are made to retain their shape by being secured here and there with fine twine passed through with the needle. In the absence of oakum, wooden wads may be made by first spokeshaving a stout pole to the size of the bore, and then sawing it up into convenient lengths.

Old guns which have been laid by will not uncommonly be found spiked, by having a common nail driven into the vent. If efficient tools are at hand this may be drilled out, if not, put a charge of powder in the gun, bore a gimlet hole in one of your wooden wads, through which pass a loosely-twisted string well impregnated with dissolved gunpowder, and afterwards dried. Cut the end of your prepared string just at the muzzle of the gun, light it, and get out of the way, when the explosion, which soon takes place, will not unfrequently expel the spike. A gun which has had its trunnions knocked off, with a view to rendering it useless, may be made nearly as effective as ever by cutting with the axe or adze a bed for it in a stout piece of log, of such a form that the cascabel of the gun and the breech end are rather more than half buried in solid wood. The log may now be trimmed off to convenient dimensions, and all made secure by a lashing of wet raw hide rope, which rests in a broad shallow notch cut in the log to receive it. The gun and its bed are thus, as the rope dries, held together by a material little less rigid than iron.

The bed log and gun may now be mounted by placing a very strong round bar of hard tough wood across the slide or carriage immediately below where the trunnions would have rested. This receives a deep semicircular notch, cut to exactly correspond with it on the under side of the bed log. The gun can now be elevated and depressed in the usual manner by placing wedges under the log. The common mode of priming a gun from a flask or horn, when there are no percussion or friction tubes to be obtained, is, to say the least of it, inconvenient and dangerous. It is far better to keep on hand a few priming cups. These are made as follows:
Priming cups, to make. From the joints of a bamboo cut a number of little cups, the bottoms being formed by the knots of the cane; in the centre of the bottom bore a hole, with a gimlet or red hot wire, large enough to admit a piece of marsh reed, hollow cane, weed stalk, or quill, about 3in. long, and small enough in diameter to pass down into the vent of the gun easily; stop the small end with a bit of melted sealing-wax; secure the large end in the cup by the same agency.

The cup becomes now a sort of funnel, through which common fine sporting powder should be poured until both tube and cup are full, when a piece of oiled paper is strained over the top of the cup like the head of a drum, and is tied fast with twine. When the gun is to be fired, the cartridge is pierced in the usual way with the priming wire. The tube of the priming cup is now to be inserted at the mouth of the vent, and pressed down until the bottom of the cup rests on the metal of the gun, when on the port fire or linstock being applied, the paper lid is instantly burned through, and the gun discharged. In windy weather, heavy tropical rains, or at night, these cups are extremely useful.

A cannon, of very tolerable efficiency for close quarters, and slug or bullet charges, may be made by boring a hole partly through a piece of tough strong log, with a pump auger; Makeshift firearms. bore a vent with a gimlet, put on one or two hoops or rings of iron or raw hide, and the gun is ready for use. We have seen several of these, which were effectually used during the rebellion in Canada.

In 1838, at the siege of Herat, Mahomed Shah brought up a quantity of metal on the backs of camels, and had a heavy bronze gun cast, and completely finished before the town ; and when the siege was raised the king had his gun sawn to pieces and taken to Teheran. Shah Abbas, of Ispahan, had a heavy piece of artillery, but said it would delay his march, and he would much rather carry metal on camels and cast artillery before the enemy's town.

During the Indian mutiny, the rebels pulled down the telegraph-posts which had iron tube sockets fitted to them in order to keep off the white ants. These sockets were taken off, and vents drilled in them. They were then loaded with powder, and charges of slugs made from doubled up and hammered pieces of the telegraph wire. We have seen a piece of common iron gas-pipe, a piece of wood, and a few bits of sheet copper, converted into a very formidable matchlock pistol.

In our Australian boat voyage we had a small 1lb. swivel carronade. We jammed a pole about 6ft. long into the fork of the swivel, and had we met any of the Malay trepang fishers, who go in companies of a hundred or more, we should have made the swivel-bolt fast to the bowsprit just outside the stem of our boat, and, letting the trail rest on the mast thwart, have defended ourselves with heavy charges of musket bullets. Of course the fishers might have been friendly, or, if not, the knowledge that we had a gun would have made them so, and we should not in any case have been the aggressors.

Light guns mounted on dromedaries or camels are valuable for the defence of caravans, &c. The Afghans first used these in an emergency against the Persians. A number of pivoted The Zemboureks, or arquebuses were mounted on the saddles of dromedary artillery. dromedaries, which were taught to kneel while the pieces were fired from their backs. The Persians, profiting by the lessons of their defeat, also organised a similar force, the guns weighing not more than 75lb. The saddle was originally constructed of two-forked branches connected by wooden bars, and if the gun was slightly overloaded the recoil would injure the fittings, and disturb the animal; but subsequently the saddle was much improved, and wheels were added, so that it might be taken from the animal's back and used as a field gun. It will be seen that the staff of the bannerol carries a little tent, and this covers the ammunition bags. A skin of water hangs under the belly of the camel. The Persians have sought out with eagerness and perseverance the best form of artillery to be carried on the backs of animals ; and, as it seems that dromedaries have been successfully imported into America and Australia, it may be of advantage to know that they are capable of being utilised in this way. Other animals, perhaps oxen, might be trained to carry smaller guns.

Very efficient common case shot can be made by filling empty preserved-meat tins with rifle or pistol balls. A bag of cooper's iron hoop rivets is a very favourite charge among the South-Sea whalers. Round shot can be made as directed under the head " Lead, and its uses."

Extempore grenades can be made from empty soda-water bottles or old ink jars. On one occasion we made a number from the latter

Grenades and rocket arrows.

vessels by filling them with a mixture of buck shot and strong sporting powder; stoppers of wood were then fitted by notching the upper ends, and fastening them down with wire, like the corks of champagne bottles, a gimlet hole was then bored in each, and a few inches of quick match put in. When the fuse has been lighted, these vessels are either hurled from the hand or fired from large powerful cross-bows, when they, by exploding in full flight or on the ground, cause no trifling confusion among an undisciplined enemy, a pack of wolves, or a sounder of hog in a cactus brake.

An unarmed merchantman was chased by a pirate galley ; she hove to, and pretended to surrender, but two men stood at the gangway with a cask of powder. As soon as the long low open boat came alongside they threw it into her, and the cook, running out of the galley, threw a shovelful of hot coals after it. The ship forged ahead before the smoke had cleared away, and escaped, leaving the desperadoes to their fate.

Large arrows tipped with strong paper cases, such as are made for rockets, only choked at the bottom, become most formidable projectiles. The cases are partly filled with powder, a wad, with a hole in it, is rammed down on the charge, a quill is put in the hole, about thirty buck shot is deposited round the quill, which is filled with meal powder. The case and quill head are then capped with paper which has been soaked in dissolved gunpowder or nitre. Arrows thus made are to be fired from powerful hand-bows, after the match has been lighted. In the true rocket arrow the touchpaper is ignited just before the arrow is fixed in the bow, and it is shot just before the fire reaches the composition; the combustion then aids the flight rather than retards it. The head is strongly barbed, so that it may not easily be drawn from thatched roofs, &c.; the Chinese and Indian tribes often use these.

It is not uncommon, in cases of petty pilfering by light heeled natives or troublesome juveniles, to hear irritated travellers threaten to make them smart for it with a charge of peas. Caution as to the use of Beware, however, of trying the experiment. Peas   peas as projectiles. will at times do more than cause a smart, and as effectually destroy life as buck shot. Mr. G. M. Sproat relates, that when in the neighbourhood of Barclay Sound, Vancouver Island, a fugitive Indian potato thief was unintentionally shot dead by one of his men, who had, as a caution to depredators, loaded his gun with a charge of powder and five peas, one of which was, on a post mortem examination being made, found to have entered the cavity of the chest, and imbedded itself in the substance of the lungs.

It sometimes happens that the hunter or explorer has, like many members of the Algerian, Tartar, and Mongolian tribes, to turn gunpowder manufacturer. To make gunpowder Gunpowder, to make. three ingredients are requisite: viz., saltpetre (nitrate of potash), sulphur, and charcoal. The two former ingredients should form a part of the equipment of an expedition (see "Farrier's Stores," p. 74). Still, where such stores are not carried, sulphur and saltpetre are usually to be obtained, more or less pure, from the natives of all but the most unfrequented and isolated countries. The saltpetre will require recrystallisation, which is carried out as follows: Take equal quantities, by measure, of the saltpetre and boiling water, stir them well about with a stick until all the lumps are thoroughly dissolved; strain the resulting fluid through a coarse cloth in order to get rid of sticks, chips, and stones, and set it aside to crystallise; when the process is complete drain the water from the crystals, set them to dry on a skin or a cloth. The sulphur, if in lumps as imported, will require purification by melting. This operation must be conducted over a very slow fire, and immediately the mass becomes liquid in the pot it should be put to stand for a few minutes in hot wood ashes in order that impurities may settle to the bottom. The neck of the vessel may then be held fast in a twisted stick, and the contents poured dexterously out into a convenient mould until the sediment at the bottom, which is useless, is left. Flowers of sulphur will not require this treatment. The charcoal (see " Charcoal Burning," p. 234) should for gunpowder making, be prepared from some light, clean-grained wood. In this country willow, withy, alder, hazel, linden, &c., are held in high esteem for the purpose; but in wild countries the nearest approach to these within reach should be obtained. The three ingredients must be first separately ground, either in a native quern or stone hand-mill, between two conveniently-formed stones, or in an extempore pestle and mortar, until reduced to perfect powder, quite free from lumps or grit. The three powders are to be now weighed out carefully in the following proportions : One part sulphur, one part charcoal, and six parts saltpetre. Mix these on a skin pegged out on the ground, and rub the mixture together with the palms of the hands until most intimately and thoroughly blended; then, with an empty percussion-cap box or drinking cup, measure your mixture, and for every ten cups or boxes of powder put down a stone or make a mark, and for every mark put aside a cup full of warm water, so that you have just one tenth of fluid. This you sprinkle with a bunch of feathers or grass, a little at a time, on the powders, until, by constant and persistent working and kneading, a smooth homogeneous paste is formed. Two well-selected stones much facilitate this stage of the process; one should be large and flat, the other water-rounded and oval; in fact, a water-worn pebble of about 2lb. weight. By sitting on the stretched skin with the flat stone between the legs, the water and sprinkler at the side, and the pebble between the hands, the paste can be effectually worked up; and it is well to bear in mind that on the perfect homogeneity of this paste depends, in great measure, the quality of the gunpowder. The paste—or devil as it is sometimes called—being thoroughly elaborated, make square flat cakes of it 6in. square and 2in. thick, and wrap them compactly up in cotton cloth or old sheeting four or five times doubled; then stitch up a stout hide bag just large enough to contain all your cakes and their coverings when built in compactly one on the other, and sew up the opening; then, with

a chisel, scoop out a cavity in the end of a log just deep enough to half
bury your case of cakes; then with the aid of a neighbouring tree, and
a few suitable pieces of wood, which are easily fashioned with the axe,
prepare such a press as is shown in the illustration below. The
weight should be increased gradually, and the pressure intensified
until the cakes are pressed into compact masses. The coverings are
now to be removed, and then the process of corning begins, and the
help of a corning sieve is required. This is made as follows : Make
a wide stout hoop of any pliant wood, and over one of its edges stretch
a head of parchment, like that of a banjo, nail or lace it on wet, and
when dry it will become perfectly tight, like the head of a tambourine.
Now, take a very small-sized key, file off the wards and bow, sharpen
the lower edges round the tube with the file until it is converted into a
sharp hollow punch. Turn your tambourine upside down on a smooth-

faced log of suitable size, and, with a small hammer and your little
punch, proceed to perforate the parchment until the head is covered
with small round holes. Now fashion from any dry, hard, heavy wood
a flat disc 1½in. thick and 4½in. in diameter; this, with the broken
cake, is put in the sieve and rattled about forward and back until the
small broken granular fragments are in numbers forced through the holes
in the parchment, and fall on the skin stretched to receive them. It will
be found that among the grains thus formed there will be a certain
quantity of fine dust; this can be separated by sweeping the grains
over a sloping board on which flannel has been stretched, the grains
pass on, the dust remains amongst the fibres of the wool, and can be
collected to work up again. The granules can now be placed in a
little wooden box and shaken about until rubbed smooth against each

other. To finish them off it is well to place a large sheet of iron, copper, tin, or any other metal over a pot of boiling-hot water, throw the now all-but-finished gunpowder on the plate and stir it about until completely dry. A clean frying pan is by no means a bad instrument for powder drying; take care that it is only placed on hot water, and not subjected to fire heat, or a blow-up will probably follow. Too much caution cannot be used after the powder has been subjected to the granulating process; before that there is little to fear, after it a great deal.

In travelling through little known or comparatively undescribed countries, it will be well for the experienced traveller to closely

Geology for travellers.

investigate and carefully study the geology of the region he is passing through; outcropping rocks and the stones of the river beds should be closely investigated. Sand should be gathered on the borders of the deep pools, dried, spread out on paper, and examined under the lens. Thus will the formation of inaccessible mountain regions be often brought to light. The winter ices and spring floods, by breaking up and disintegrating the rocks they flow through, gradually, by friction and the grinding power of water-moved boulders, reduce the detritus which accompanies them to sand, more or less ponderous according to the metallic elements of which it is formed. Thus, by the breaking up of quartz veins by the agencies just referred to, gold is released from its matrix to enrich the sands and shingle beds of certain rivers. Alluvial tin is in the same way set free in grains and nodules from the granitic or other formations in which it resides, and, water borne, travels onward until arrested by some deep pit or crevice in the river bed, where it remains until disturbed by floods of more than ordinary magnitude, or the pick and shovel of the miner. Our space will not admit of our dealing at length with the indications of gold or other metals, or of the regions in which the precious metals and gems are to be sought. We shall, therefore, content ourselves by giving a few plain, and we trust practical, hints for the finding and identi-

Metals, to identify.

fication of such metals, stones, &c., as the traveller is likely to meet with. First in importance we class gold; and, although precarious and uncertain in the bulk of its deposits, is more generally distributed throughout the earth's surface than any other metal. Clay slate formations, traversed by iron-stained quartz dykes, are well worth investigating; and

Hints to gold searchers.

most of the streams which flow through such formations will be found, on careful examination, more or less auriferous. In prospecting a stream, or river bed, choose

SEARCHING FOR GOLD.

localities where the stream, after a sharp descending run, has impinged against a perpendicular bank, forming an eddy before flowing onward. Dig away boldly all the top deposit until the bed rock is reached. Rout out all the depressions, crevices, and holes in this, scooping up all the clay, gravel, and grit they may contain. Place all this in convenient quantities in a broad shallow metal pan or dish, add water to it, rub it about briskly with the hand, pour away all the dirty water, add more, shake it about, give a sweeping rotatory motion to your pan, pick out all large lumps of stone or quartz, giving a sharp look at the latter; still add water, and work the pan until nothing but fine clear sand remains in it. A dexterous rolling, tilting motion is given by the initiated, which at once clears away the baser fragments, and reveals the "colour," as the gold dust is called by the miners. A broad shovel is at times used somewhat in the same manner, the handle being held as shown in the full-page illustration "Searching for Gold," when the process is called vanning.

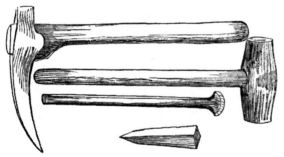

To carry out a regular system of investigation among quartz reefs, mineral veins, and metalliferous rocks, certain tools and appliances
Mining and miner's tools. will be needed—picks of Cornish pattern, such as is represented in the above illustration, sets of steel borers, with cockscomb ends, sets of steel gads or wedges, borer, steel and gad steel in bars, blasting powder, safety match in coils, some heavy hammers, a portable forge (such as is represented on p. 222), set of smith's tools, shovel blades, spare pick-heads, and hilts of ash, &c. When it is deemed requisite to blast a portion of rock, the borer and hammer are used much as shown in the illustration on p. 223. One man, sitting on the ground, holds the borer upright and turns it freely round, whilst his assistant strikes it with the hammer. A little water dropped from time to time down the hole keeps the bit cool, and facilitates the operation. As sludge collects, it is removed with a species of scraper, fashioned from the end of an iron

bar. A small rod or stick, with its end fibres frayed and set up like a mop, is used for drying out the hole. Should it be in wet ground, where moisture remains in spite of swabbing out, a cartridge composed of tallowed cotton or oiled paper, may be used to inclose the powder in. According to the old-fashioned plan, which some miners still follow, a long pointed copper rod or needle was pressed into the charge after it had been rammed into the bottom of the hole. Round this rod clay, pulverised clay, slate, &c., was closely packed, and driven with a copper tamping rod until the hole was compactly filled up. The needle was now withdrawn, and a match, composed of a long marsh reed filled with mealed powder, thrust down the orifice until the charge was reached, when the upper end was held in its place by clay. A bit of rag, smeared with moistened powder, was attached to the head of the

reed, which, when fired, burned long enough to afford time for the miners to shelter themselves from the effects of the explosion. Since the introduction of the so-called patent safety match, it has been with great advantage substituted for the reed; the burning of this match or fuse is generally so uniform, that it has only to be cut according to the distance between the hole and the place of shelter. Even this great improvement in the means of ignition falls very short of exploding by voltaic electricity, which should always, when practicable, be had recourse to. The wandering miner and explorer will, however, seldom be able to avail himself of its valuable aid, or the use of gun cotton or nitrate of glycerine, which agents have of late been much lauded as substitutes for gunpowder in mining operations.

It not unfrequently happens that diamonds and other precious stones are found in river beds, and such other localities as miners are in the habit of examining. We therefore offer a few hints and directions for the identification of these in their rough state, as given by Professor Tennant :

"Fig. 1 (on. p. 225) is an octahedron; Fig. 2 an octahedron having six planes on the edges; Fig. 3, dodecahedron with rhombic faces; Figs. 4, 5, and 6, are rarer forms. Out of 1000 Precious stones, to diamonds we have generally found about one of the identify. form of Fig. 6; about ten like Fig. 5; fifty like Fig. 4; and the remainder like 1, 2, 3, in about an equal proportion. With regard to the size and weight of diamonds, 500 out of 1000 which came in the same parcel were found smaller than Fig. 1, which is the exact size of a diamond weighing half a carat; 300 were of the size 3, 4, 5, and 6—none of these exceeded a carat in weight; eighty of the size 2 weighed a carat and a half; only one was as large as Fig. 16 —this weighed 24 carats. The remainder varied from 2 to 20 carats, a carat being equal to three grains and one-sixth troy. Fig. 7 consists of a conglomerated mass of quartz pebbles rounded through having been water-worn, a crystal

of diamond, the size of a small pea, and various grains of gold, the whole cemented together by oxide of iron. This specimen is peculiarly interesting at the present time, as showing the association of diamonds with gold. In 1844 a slave was searching for gold in the bed of a river in the province of Bahia, and discovered diamonds. It being a new locality for diamonds, 297,000 carats were collected in two years, which produced upwards of 300,000*l*. We see no reason why diamonds should not be found in Australia, Canada, California, as well as in those other gold districts from which they have hitherto been obtained. The value of the most inferior diamonds, unfit for jewellery, is 50*l*. per ounce. Could they be found in sufficient abundance to be sold at 5*l*. per ounce, the benefit to the arts would be incalculable. Not only would the seal engraver, watchmaker, lapidary, glazier, &c., be able to procure them at easier prices, but numerous substances would be rendered useful which at present cannot be profitably worked owing to the high price of diamonds.

"Figs. 8 to 11 represent four crystals of corundum. This substance is commonly found in six-sided prismatic crystals, and frequently terminated at each end by six-sided pyramids. When transparent, and of a blue colour, it is known in jewellery as the sapphire; when merely of a red colour, it is called Oriental ruby; and when this colour is of a rich depth, the stone is more valuable than even the diamond.

"Figs. 12 to 14. Three crystals of spinel-ruby. It is of various shades of red, and is easily distinguished from corundum by the peculiarity of its crystalline form and inferior hardness.

"Figs. 15 and 16. Crystals of garnet. These are chiefly found in the form of the rhombic dodecahedron; are occasionally of a beautiful red colour; when semi-transparent, are called by the jewellers "carbuncles." They are of comparatively little value.

"Figs. 17 and 18. Two rhombic prisms of topaz. It is found in rivers, frequently with all the edges and angles of the original crystal worn off, and presenting a round appearance, in which state it is often mistaken for the diamond, owing to the colour and specific gravity of each being the same. It may, however, easily be distinguished from it by the difference of the hardness and fracture. The diamond yields readily to mechanical division parallel to all the planes of the regular octahedron, the topaz only at right angles to the axis of the crystal.

"Fig. 20. Tourmaline. A crystal having six sides, deeply striated in the longitudinal direction, and terminated by a three-sided pyramid; colour varying from black to brown and green. Transparent specimens are useful to the philosopher in experiments on polarised light.

"Fig. 21. Crystal of transparent quartz or 'rock crystal,' frequently called a 'diamond' in the mining districts, as 'Bristol diamond,' a 'Cornish diamond,' &c. The crystal represented by this figure was brought from California by a person who refused 200*l*. for it under the impression that it was a real diamond, because it scratched glass and could not be scratched with a file. Its real value, however, is not more than 2*s*. 6*d*.

"Fig. 22. Beryl, presents a six-sided prism, and is usually of a green colour."

When substances are found which are supposed to be precious

stones, the file test should be at once applied; if the teeth of the instrument "bite," as it is called, or cut into the substance, it will be at once fair to infer that some inferior mineral has been discovered. The bit of sapphire from the case may also be called into use, and if the stone you have found is of white colour, and a corner of your sapphire bites or scratches it, there is no hope of its being a diamond. If on weighing it the specific gravity of the specimen is found to be less than 3·9, it will not turn out to be a ruby or sapphire. The application of heat is another test, as if no electricity is manifested it will not turn out to be a gargoon or a topaz. If, on testing it on your piece of flint glass, the surface of that is bitten by the specimen, it will probably be found to be either rock crystal, quartz, or per-

chance beryl. The rivers of many countries, our own amongst the number, not unfrequently contain large mussel-like shells; these are the fresh-water pearl mussels (*Unio margaritiferus*), and the pearls which these at times contain are of considerable value, and well repay being looked for when the rivers are low.

River pearls, to find.

"All is not gold that glitters." Sulphuret of iron and yellow mica are not unfrequently mistaken by the inexperienced for gold, and we have not unfrequently had some little difficulty in convincing the sanguine discoverer of his error. Sulphuret of iron, pyrites, or the mundic of the miners, is a bright yellow glittering mineral, which sometimes has gold associated with it. The differences between it and gold are sufficiently marked. Strike the suspected fragment on a hard substance with a hammer, and if "mundic," it at once becomes reduced to minute fragments, whilst gold would be only slightly

Q

flattened. Gold is malleable; mundic is not. Gold can be cut with the pocket-knife just as easily as copper; mundic resists the knife, turns its edge, and will strike fire against its back, giving out sulphurous fumes. Mundic, after being made red hot, is attracted by the magnet; gold never is. Hot nitric acid causes it to decompose with much effervescence, leaving such spangles of gold as it may contain free in the bottom of the test tube. Gold dust is readily taken up by quicksilver; mundic is not. Yellow mica is so much lighter than gold that its comparative want of ponderability should at once distinguish it; a small portion placed on an iron bar, and heated in the fire to redness, becomes, on cooling, flakey and lustreless, whilst gold would remain unaltered; it floats on the surface of mercury, refusing to unite with it, whilst gold is immediately converted into an amalgam. Sulphuret of copper, or copper ore as it is usually called, breaks freely under the hammer, but can be cut easily with the knife, only, instead of producing a solid metallic chip, it crumbles into powder, just as soft stone or chalk would. Alluvial tin can in no case be mistaken for either gold, silver, or copper. It is dark coloured, breaks into powder under the hammer, and is exceedingly ponderous. With the so-called *rosin* and *wood* tin we cannot deal here, as the explorer is not very likely to find them. Minute fragments of stream tin are to be easily distinguished from small bits of iron ore by first heating them red hot, and then subjecting them to the magnet; iron will be attracted, tin will not.

Many wild countries produce iron ore of remarkable purity, and a number of native tribes, by a rough system of smelting, contrive to obtain enough metal for the manufacture of their weapons, implements, &c. The greater the purity of the ore, the less difficulty
Iron ore, to smelt. will be experienced in dealing with it. Should the explorer at any time be called on to smelt a little iron ore, he may proceed as follows: Build a turret-shaped furnace, proportioned to the quantity of ore to be treated, line it with ant-hill clay, or common clay and sand, leaving a hole in the front near the bottom, which has a temporary stopper of clay placed in it, and another orifice about 2ft. up the back for the air blast to enter at. Either a large pair of double bellows, compressible skin air-bags, such as we have before described, or blowing cylinders, such as are represented in the illustration on p. 227, must be set up at a convenient distance from the back of the furnace. These cylinders are used by the inhabitants of New Guinea instead of bellows, and answer remarkably well. They are composed of two hollow tree trunks, placed side by side; a wooden tube, which serves to let the air out unites them; and a man or boy sits on the tops of the tubes, and

works alternately up and down a couple of mop-shaped pistons, which are made from poles armed at the ends with bundles of fibre, feathers, or dry grass, so adjusted that they expand on being thrust down and collapse on being drawn up. As one piston man gets fatigued, another takes his place; thus a continuous stream of air is kept up. Whatever method of blast is decided on, it must be so arranged as to be continuous and powerful. When the interior of the furnace is quite dry, throw in a good quantity of well-burned charcoal; then a layer of split dry wood until it reaches about 1ft. above the entrance of the blast; then another layer of charcoal and dry cowdung, a few inches deep; then sprinkle in loosely a layer of broken iron ore, mixed with a little limestone if you can get it; then another layer of charcoal and dry cowdung, and another of ore; and so on until the furnace is all but full, only one layer of wood being used. Now through the blast entrance introduce some well-ignited and glowing embers from your fire; put in the tube of your blast, which may be of baked clay; lute it fast in its place, so as to prevent any escape of air; and proceed to blow, when your furnace will soon be in a state of active ignition and glow. Keep up the blast steadily, and as the contents

of the furnace sink down add to them from above layer by layer as before directed, until it is considered that enough metal has been cast in. So soon as it is thought probable that the iron has melted, a small portion of the clay of the taphole may be removed with an iron bar, when, if in a sufficiently fluxed condition, the iron will run freely out into long shallow pits dug to receive it. The iron thus procured is called bloom, and has to be heated in pieces in the forge fire, and thoroughly roasted and thumped about until it is soft and tough enough for general use. The natives do not as a rule wait for their iron to flow, but open the furnace when it cools down, and then drag out such bloom as may have settled to the bottom. Excellent steel is made from the iron thus procured by the natives of the hill districts of India, by putting it in small earthen crucibles with charcoal, rice, chaff, peroxide of manganese, and green leaves. These pots are then luted down with clay, and placed in a clay furnace heated with dry cow dung and charcoal. Here they remain for a considerable time, when the fire is allowed to burn out; the pots are then, when cool, removed, and the steel taken out to be fashioned by the hand of the smith into any form required. We have used a great deal of both iron and steel prepared as above described, and found both of admirable quality.

A common horse-shoe magnet, such as can be bought for a mere trifle at any toyshop, will be found very useful for extract-Chemical tests for ing particles of iron from other mineral. Whenever the means of transport will admit, it is well to take a small compact case of simple appliances, tests, and reagents. The whole, by a little ingenuity, may be easily packed in a solid leather case very little larger than an ordinary sandwich box. Its contents should be as follows: Small glassstoppered and capped bottle of nitric acid, ditto hydrochloric acid, ditto liq. ammonia, ditto quicksilver, small corked bottles of ferrocyanide of potassium, bi-chromate of potash, fused borax, and common salt; a small jointed blowpipe, a pair of forceps, a small pair of scales, fitted for taking specific gravities, and a set of weights, a bit of flint glass, a piece of sapphire, which can be obtained from any lapidary; half a dozen test tubes to nest one within the other; half a dozen old watch glasses, to be obtained for a few pence from any watchmaker; half a dozen narrow strips of window glass, cut to a thickness little greater than stout wire, and 5in. long (these are for stirring up hot acids, &c.); a piece of stout copper wire, shaped like the figure 9, to hold the watch glasses on whilst they are over the lamp or candle flame; a small fine file and a few narrow slips of well burnt light charcoal; a common wire cigar-holder, to hold the test tubes in whilst heated; and a very small bright-faced hammer, such as watchmakers use. It is truly astonishing how much qualitative analysis can be carried out with these comparatively limited means. These cases complete, together with the key or guide book, can now be obtained from J. W. Silver and Co., 7, Cornhill, who have the sole authority from us to supply them. We will suppose that a little bag of sand has been obtained; that it shows, on being spread out, a number of particles of a glittering yellow substance, as well as black-coloured grains, mixed with common quartz and minute fragments of stone. We first place our sand on a sheet of white paper, and with our pocket lens have a thorough examination of the various constituents. Should any grains of sufficient size and questionable character present themselves, they may be at once taken up on the moistened point of a pin. If one of them should look like gold, place it on some hard substance and give it a blow with your hammer. If it flattens without powdering, drop it into one of your test tubes, pour in a little nitric acid, and hold it in the flame until it boils thoroughly. If your particle gives off a train of minute bubbles and gradually dissolves, pour a little of the contents of your tube into two separate watch glasses placed side by side, add a little water to each. Add a little common salt to No. 1 ; if the particle is silver, you will at once have a thick white precipitate—chloride of silver. Drop a few drops of your liquor ammonia into No. 2 ; and if copper, the beautiful and well-marked blue colour of ammonuret of copper will at once appear. Should the particle have crushed under the blow, it is probably either sulphuret of iron or copper ore. To distinguish these two substances when in a minute state of division, proceed with the acid as just described, and test one watch glass with a small fragment of ferrocyanide of potassium, when, if sulphuret of iron or " mundic," you will have a dense cloud of Prussian blue in your watch glass. Treat the other with your liquor ammonia, and you will have the same brilliant ammonuret of copper colour as if the particle had been native or malleable copper. Having satisfied ourselves as to the selected particles—for should the flattened grain resist the action of the hot acid and remain bright, it is surely gold—we place our sand on a shovel, and hold it there until the whole is red hot; it may then be taken from the fire, and allowed to cool on the shovel. The magnet will now take out all the bits of iron. Now with a hammer-face or smooth water-worn pebble proceed to crush all the substances on the shovel fine. Then at the nearest stream of water, or in a large tub, carefully *van* and wash your sample until all the earthy and worthless matters have been washed away; then the practised eye will instantly distinguish the gold, if any. The utterly inexperienced may, however, be deceived by remaining fragments of mundic or copper ore before referred to ; therefore, to make assurance doubly sure, let him dry his washed metal powder on the shovel over the fire, then carefully place it in a small, clean, dry vial-bottle with a little quicksilver. Shake and rattle it well about until all the particles have been brought well in contact with the mercury. Such fragments as it will not take up are not gold; but to find that which it has converted into an amalgam, place the mercury in a piece of clean chamois leather, press it carefully, and the mercury will force its way in minute globules through the leather, leaving the gold in a soft mass within. This, by being heated to redness, throws off the remaining quicksilver, and can be estimated as gold. Silver will also amalgamate with mercury, but can always be distinguished from gold by the nitric acid and salt test before described. Lead ore is rarely mistaken for anything else, its peculiar colour, cubical form of crystallisation, and gravity being generally sufficient to identify it. A small quantity, reduced to a fine powder and mixed with a little fused borax, readily fuses on a charcoal slip before the blowpipe, and is then ordinary lead. The silver often associated with lead ores can alone be estimated by a regular assay, requiring the use of crucibles, cupels, furnace, &c., Sulphuret of antimony, although massive and somewhat lead-coloured, leaves a thick rough deposit on the charcoal, and fuses into a brittle crystalline regulus, in no way resembling lead. Small specimens of galena, or lead ore, should always be preserved for future investigation, as it is at times extremely rich in silver, whilst at others a mere trace only remains. We have analysed lead ore from Cornwall which yielded between 90oz. and 100oz. of silver to the ton, whilst other samples, raised in Wisconsin, although yielding 85 per cent. of lead, did not contain enough silver to render its extraction remunerative. The points of distinction between minerals and metals we have thus been briefly laying down do not properly apply to the investigations of the regular gold-digger, but are mainly intended for the use of those who are engaged in exploration and research. The professional gold-seeker, as a rule, casts all aside save the one great centre of his hopes and pursuit. He, in his prospecting expeditions, makes use of the broad shallow metal pan shown in the illustration which represents " Searching for Gold." The quantity of gold brought to light by its aid guides him in his choice of a locality. If it is considered rich enough, he, with his mates, sinks down to " *the pay dirt,*" or deposit containing the gold; this is either washed out at once on the cradle, or piled in heaps for future treatment. With gold quartz-crushing, amalgamation on a large scale, or the washing down of drift by hydraulic power and the use of flumes as practised in California, we cannot deal here, as the appliances are far more complicated and ponderous than the mere traveller could carry with him.

It sometimes happens that imposition is attempted in far-off lands, and imitation gold ornaments offered to the traveller. To test the quality of these, it will be requisite to have a bit of black terracotta pot, or a fragment of any hard smooth black stone. Rub the suspected ornament on this until a metallic streak is left, dip one of your bits of glass rod in your nitric acid, and let a drop or two fall on the track left by Base metal, to detect. the metal. If of base material, the particles will rapidly turn green and dissolve; if gold, they will remain unchanged; and if an alloy, the combined metal will be removed, and the gold will remain stationary on the black surface. The exact standard of mixture or combination can only be arrived at by the use of a set of touch-needles, which are rubbed and compared with the doubtful marks on the stone.

There are many situations in which stone may be advantageously used for the erection of houses, forts, or defensible depôts. On the discovery of a bed of rock adapted for the pur- Stone, to quarry. pose, the head or covering earth should be removed either by the agency of water obtained by diverting some neighbouring stream for the purpose, or by digging with the spade or shovel. Careful examination will now generally disclose veins or seams traversing the stone, such of these as run in favourable directions should be selected, and the gads or wedges before described had recourse to. It is well to have, at least, a dozen of these for stone splitting. They should be about 5in. long, 1½in. wide, and ½in. thick, tapering to the edge, which should not be too sharp. All gads should be made of the best gad steel, carefully pointed and tempered. In entering the gads, it will be well to insert them in the selected seam at about 1ft. apart: then, with the heavy hammer or pickhead, strike each gad a blow or two in succession, which will serve to open the seam, and not unfrequently detach the required fragment. When large square or oblong blocks are required, it is well to first mark out the size required on the rock with the pick's point, and then with either the borer before described, or a jumping bar (of form shown in the annexed illustration), drill a row of holes about 8in. apart on the line before marked out, in depth proportioned to the intended thickness of the stone, in each hole should be placed a pair of gad cheeks—these are pieces of half-round iron bar. The rounded sides rest against the sides of the holes as the gad is driven between the flat surfaces, thus forcing open the grain of the rock without breaking away the sides of the holes by gad clinching. As in the former case, each gad is gradually driven home until the line of holes run into one long fissure and the block is detached. In breaking out flat slabs of comparatively thin stone, it will be found a good plan, after measuring and marking the size decided on, to sink a shallow groove either with the pick's point or a stonecutter's chisel across the extreme length of the slab; then, by inserting the gads at the outer face or edge of the deposit, the slab will not only be raised but evenly broken off. Fire is a most powerful agent and aid in stone-breaking, especially when assisted by water. The huge and massive boulder of rock which bids defiance to the sledge-hammer may very soon be reduced to fragments by making a strong fire round it, and, when thoroughly heated, throwing buckets of water over it.

Some Indians are particularly clever in the art of stone dividing. They build a double wall of clay the whole length of the stone,
The treatment of   leaving about six inches of bare rock between
stone.   them. They then lay more clay on the outsides of the walls, nearly the width of the stone. Then between the walls of clay they make a long line of fire with dry cowdung and chips of hard, dry wood. An incredibly short space of time elapses before the division of the stone is completed, when the fire is carefully extinguished with earth or sand, and the stone allowed to cool. Rocks, so placed as to prevent recourse being had to either of the expedients described, may be split out by the action of a small charge of powder, fired, as before directed, in a hole made by the jumping bar. To drill a hole with this no hammer man is required, but the weight of the protuberance on the instrument, when aided by a jumping and rotatory motion, is sufficient to cut away the rock. Water swab, shell scraper, &c., are used with these implement, just as they are with the miner's borer, which can be used in confined spaces and under outlying works, where the jumper would be useless. A crowbar or two will be found very useful for lifting out broken pieces of stone, &c. There is also an instrument much used in America called a "canthook," which is here represented. It is extremely valuable for moving both stones of large size and logs of unwieldy dimensions. The handle, or lever, is made of tough, well-seasoned timber, and is usually from 6ft. to 7ft. long. The claw is of sound, tough, wrought iron, and proportioned in weight

and spread to the bodies it is applied to. Two or three sizes of claws fit one handle, just as a dentist's key is adapted to the size of the tooth it is to grasp. An oblong square hole is cut through the lever for the claw's end to pass through, and a stout iron pin, with a hole in the end for a split stop to go into, keeps the claw at its proper point of adjustment. The boulder claw is another most useful implement. It is used for turning over and rolling out large boulders of rock, lifting out logs, &c. These claws, and the chains and rings to which they are attached, should be made of the best Swedish iron; the claw point should be of gad steel, welded in. The form of the hook or claw is very important, as, if not turned to the exact bend, it will not grip or hold. The annexed illustrations will serve to show both the form of the claw and its mode of action when in use.

When water settles in a comparatively shallow pit, too large to be conveniently emptied by the aid of buckets, a very simple form of pump will be found useful. Nail four long planks together

in the form of a narrow square box or tube, say 1ft. square; now procure a stout pole a little longer than the box, nail a flat board to one end of it just as a table is attached to its stand, cut away the edges until

Miners' pump, to make.

it fits the box loosely, then nail a bordering of old boot leather or hide round the edges until it fits tight enough to suck; cut a large square hole in it, and fasten over this with tacks a piece of tapping leather or raw hide backed with wood for a valve; bore a hole in the upper end of the pole to put a cross handle through; bore an auger hole through the lower end of your box about 1ft. from the opening, and through this drive a stout stick to keep the sucker from coming too far down; your pump is now complete. Place it in a slightly slanting direction in the pond, and secure it with a crooked stick driven in by its side; push the sucker to the bottom, pour a bucket of water or so in to make it draw, and you will, by working the piston steadily up and down, soon have the water pouring in a flood over the upper edge of the box, where it can be caught in a hollow log or a pit lined with clay. One of these box pumps is shown in the full page illustration "Searching for Gold."

The traveller will find it extremely useful to be able to manu-

facture his own charcoal. There are several methods by which he can do this, all depending on the same general principles. Pieces of wood of suitable length and convenient size are prepared. We show here the most effective arrangements.

Charcoal burning.

The pile, when evenly and completely built up, is covered with turf and a little sand or earth—leaving one fair-sized orifice as a draught hole. Fire is introduced either at the bottom of the pile through a hole left for it, or dropped down through the space left by the withdrawal of the centre post. The orifices of all charcoal pits or chambers should remain open until the fire has become well distributed through the mass of wood, but should be covered with a stopper of turf or clay

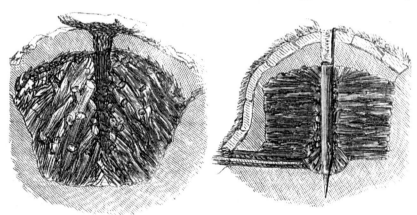

directly the light grey smoke of active combustion shows itself. The contents of the pile may from time to time be tested by removing a small portion of the stopping or covering turf and inserting a hooked iron rod, by the aid of which a sample of the baking may be withdrawn for examination. Immediately on being satisfied that the charcoal has been sufficiently burned, more earth, turf, sand, &c., should be heaped on the top of the pile, until every crevice is stopped completely. The fire will then soon die out, and the contents of the pile can be removed. We also represent a contrivance for preparing charcoal for gunpowder making. A small cask has one head removed, a stout pole run through the bung-hole, and is then evenly packed with selected billets of light suitable wood. (See "Gunpowder, to make," p. 217.) The head is

then replaced, the cask covered with well-worked clay, and then sunk in a pit prepared for its reception. The pole is then withdrawn, and a good quantity of red-hot embers thrown down the hole. The cask, after being used for charcoal making, is very useful for an oven, as will be shown when cookery is under consideration.

CHAPTER IV.

HUTS AND HOUSES.

BEFORE proceeding to give directions for building huts and houses, it may not be amiss to give a few hints on felling trees. Hints they Timber felling. can only be, as it is just as impossible to teach the art of wielding the backwoodsman's axe by writing as it is to communicate the faculty of tracking wild animals through the forest by verbal directions. Experience and close observation are the only two true masters in both cases; still, we may be enabled to give such general directions as may save our readers from some of the humiliating predicaments we have seen the inexperienced wood-chopper placed in. Nothing is more

common than to see one of this class hopelessly pinching his axe at every cut, from having commenced his chop too narrow. The length of the chop, or chip as it is sometimes called, will, of course, depend on the size of the tree; but in all cases it should be made in a long wedge form, as shown in the annexed illustration. By cutting in this way, the surface of the stump is left as level as a planed board, and the log which is separated from it has, when it falls, a wedge-shaped end. It will, in most cases, be found that the tree which you are about to fell will lean more or less in one direction. Station yourself, axe in hand, on the side towards which the tree leans; then measure your distance by placing the edge of your axe on the centre of the boll of the tree, at such a height from the ground that the axe lays in a straight and true line

according to the stature of the axe man. The check or flange at
the end of the axe helve should rest in the hands as the arms are
extended towards the tree. This will give the distance at which
the axe blade may be best brought to bear on the tree trunk. In
delivering the cuts, which should follow the distance test, the axe
should be dexterously and powerfully whirled round the head; sometimes obliquely from above downwards, and at others in a straight and
direct sweep across the line of the log. The horizontal form of the
lower cut and the wedge shape of the upper will be thus preserved
until the tree is half cut through, when exactly the same system of
operation should be followed out on the side of the tree opposite
to that on which the first incision was made. On the second chop
being nearly completed, the tree will fall directly away from the axe
man in the line of its inclination. On all the tops, lops, and branches
being removed, and the log cleared from surrounding impediments, it
may become a question as to what purpose it is to be applied. If it is
of great length, and comparatively short pieces are required, the
process known as "logging up" must be had recourse to. This is
carried out as follows: After measuring the length of the log, and
dividing it into the requisite number of pieces by marking it with the
axe, stand on the tree trunk, with your feet pointing across the grain
of the wood, then with your
axe proceed to cut two sloping
or wedge-shaped cuts, as
shown in the annexed illustration, carrying them into
the log until half through it;
then face about, and make
two on the other side, which,
when finished, should meet
the others at their widest
diameter, which will be that
of the tree. Some settlers in
wild countries burn down the
trees in order to save labour; others girdle them. To perform
this latter process, it is necessary to cut a wide band of bark from
the butt of the tree near the ground. This prevents the sap from
ascending, and thus quickly destroys vegetation. Where timber
is scarce and valuable, the cross-cut saw may be made to aid the
axe, and the tree taken off almost level with the ground. It sometimes, although not frequently, happens that trees are found too large
to be felled by the axe or saw. This was the case with the so-called

" big tree," one of the " mammoth trees " of California. It was felled by boring a complete circle of holes round and into its immense trunk with augers. Five men were occupied during twenty-two days in completing the final overthrow of the tree, which was effected, after all the holes had converged, by the introduction of a number of wedges. Its period of growth was estimated at 3000 years ; it measured 302ft. high, and was 96ft. in circumference at the butt. The bark measured nearly 1ft. in thickness.

The quality, strength, and durability of timber are much influenced by the season of the year in which it is felled. In all temperate *When to cut* regions the autumn or winter season should be chosen, *timber.* as at that time little sap is flowing through the vessels of the tree. In this country it but too often happens that well-grown oak timber is all but sacrificed in order that the bark may be procured. Early spring, the season for bark rending, is the very worst that could by any possibility be chosen for cutting timber. Charged as it is with vegetable juices, rich in saccharine matter and albumen, the seeds of dry rot and decay are carried with it, which no after treatment will serve to eradicate. In tropical climates it is well to fell such timber as is intended to be kept for future use at the end of the dry season and before the setting in of the rains ; all logs intended for rails, posts, &c., should be split up, immediately after felling, into the rough forms of the objects into which, when fully seasoned, they will be converted. The bark should be all stripped off, and the rough timber placed under cover in such a situation as will admit of light and air penetrating freely through it. Timber cut and thus treated one season, should not be used until the next. The durability of seasoned timber is infinitely greater than that of green.

For efficient timber splitting, a set of thoroughly well-made and correctly-formed iron wedges, and a number of equally well-shaped *Timber, to* wooden wedges or gluts, are needed. The iron wedges *split.* should be made of the very best tough iron, tipped with gad steel, as in the form of the annexed illustration. All the edges and corners should be slightly rounded off in order to give freedom in

driving ; the length, from head to point, should be 10in., the width across the wedge 2½in., and the thickness of metal across the edge at the head 2in. Some judgment is required in tempering wedges, as they must be hard enough at the point to prevent bending, and yet not hard enough to break. The file test is as good as any. The edge of the wedge point should never be hammered thin before tempering, but left rather thick to be reduced to the proper degree of sharpness on the grinding stone. The wooden gluts are usually considerably larger than the iron wedges; these are to be made from hard, tough, well-seasoned timber—round stout poles are convenient for making them. The proper lengths, which are mainly dependent on the size of the logs to be operated on, are sawn off. The sides or cheeks of these pieces are then chopped off with the axe in approximately true wedge form, an even surface and exact pitch is afterwards given to them with a cooper's drawing knife or a spoke shave. Wedges, whether of iron or

wood, should never be driven with an iron hammer. A wedging beetle, of form shown in the accompanying illustration, should be always made use of. The hardest and toughest wood to be obtained should be used to form the head; the ends are usually hooped with flat iron rings, and the handle fashioned from some tough elastic wood, such as ash or hickory. Scarcely any two men use the same size beetle, but the following will be found fair average dimensions from which to make one: Length of beetle head 9in., binding hoops 1¼in. wide and ½in. thick, diameter of beetle head

5½in., length of handle 2ft. 8in.

Great care should be taken in fitting in the handle, as it is essential to the efficiency of the instrument that it and the head should be exactly true with each other. A slightly flattened handle lies in the hand more compactly, and works more freely, than a perfectly round one. Nearly all logs split best from the small or crown end towards the butt. If it is intended to divide the log into four pieces, the wedges must be inserted as

shown in the annexed illustration (A), if into three they are placed as at B. When rails, &c., are to be made, the logs must be divided into quarters by first making a cross-shaped cut in the end of the log, and striking the back of the axe with the beetle until the edge enters deep enough to afford a hold for the iron wedges. Longitudinal cuts with the axe are now to be made, the whole length of the log corresponding with the cross. The wedges, gluts, and beetle do the rest when the latter implement is properly wielded. Logs for shingle making are quartered much in the same way, only instead of being

split out in the full length, the log is cut up into short lengths before quartering. The shingles may be 15in. long by 9in. wide, and in form like that represented in the annexed illustration. The axe and beetle may be used for splitting of these wooden flakes, but the lath render's *froe* is a far more convenient instrument for the purpose.

The diagrams given below will serve to show the mode by which the long log quarters are split up into rails, &c. Some

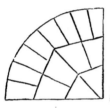
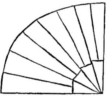

particular species of tree will split without the aid of wedges; the axe alone being used to cleave them. Two axe men attack a log, one chops in his axe blade in the line of grain, the other follows behind and chops in his, when the first man becomes the second, and so on until the cut is complete and the log is split.

Such posts as are intended to be driven into the earth require accurate and careful pointing. Each cheek of the timber should be smoothly and evenly sloped off to about the proportion shown in the

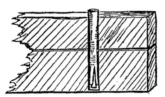

illustration representing the wedge. The centre of the post will thus become the point.

The Fox Wedge.

Tree nails or wooden bolts driven into timber through auger holes, are caused to hold with extraordinary tenacity, by splitting the inside end slightly, and then introducing the point of a small hard wood wedge, (as shown in the annexed illustration), as the tree nail is driven home, its wedged end expands, and so fills the hole it is placed in, with great tightness and solidity.

The accompanying illustration represents a log clip for holding a post whilst undergoing the process of pointing. The side wedge holds the post securely in the notched piece of log laid to receive it. A camp, garden, or cattle inclosure may be easily and expeditiously fenced in by either of the plans shown in the following illustrations. The first system of railing consists in driving double posts into the earth at equal distances, and then dropping trimmed poles and pieces of wood or stones alternately between them. A wooden pin driven through the heads of

both posts at each nip keeps all compact and secure. To erect a fence by the second plan, posts are driven into the ground singly, in the position shown in the diagram on the next page, and then poles are laid with their ends crossing at a sufficient inclination to rest against and be held by the posts. The rails can be adjusted to any distance apart, by fitting in short pieces or junks of pole between the ends of the long bars. A very simple and useful fence for marking the bounds of a camp, or piece of cultivated ground, is formed by planting short stout poles obliquely in the earth, so that they may cross each other like the letters XX. The points at which the poles

cross are secured with a twisted withy, a bit of raw hide, a strip of twisted bark or root. Fences of this kind are very useful to show natives the nearest point to which they may stray towards the packs and bales of goods.

The natives of British Columbia and some other countries labouriously hew and chop away the two cheeks of a log with their

primitive hatchets until they form a plank by the reduction of a whole tree. In India and China the natives make use of a long cross-handled saw, not unlike our pit saw, for the division of a log into planks. They do not, however, sink a sawpit as we do in this country, but set up a pair of cross legs or shears, and run the log obliquely across the upper fork until it is some distance in the air. They then saw down to the fork of the shears, and, when that is reached, reverse the log, end for end, by tilting it, and commence at the other extremity. The hunter or explorer will, as a rule, be mainly dependent on his skill as a woodsman, and wielder of the axe, for a comfortable dwelling among the forests. The number of a party and the duration of a visit to any particular locality will influence the kind of structure it will be best to erect. A single trapper or hunter naturalist can content himself with very moderate accommodation.

A simple form of wigwam can be thus built with the aid of the axe only, in a very short time; search out and cut four stout fork ended posts between 6ft. and 7ft. long, sharpen their ends, drive two of them into the earth firmly at 9ft. apart, then cut a couple of straight strong poles of about 1ft. girth and 10ft. long, lay one of these in the forks of the two posts and fasten it there with a twisted withy or a bit of raw hide; then measure off 5ft. from one of the posts, and, parallel with it, set up one of the others; plant the remaining one at the other end, lay in the second pole, secure it as before, and the framework is complete. Now look out for a free-splitting tree, log it up into 13ft. lengths, split these into boards, place them in a sloping direction against the poles which rest in the forks, and arrange them so that the upper ends do not meet, but leave a good wide opening for the smoke to come out. Split up a log or two the length required to board up the ends of the wigwam; this can be done by setting the boards upright, leaving a wide one movable to form a door, drive in a few hard wood pegs so as to catch the bottoms of the boards and all is made secure. During the day a board or two to leeward may be slid aside to let in light, by night air enough comes in through the chinks. As a more permanent home for a party who are about wintering in the woods, it is best to construct a log hut of the description represented in the following illustration; its size must, of course, depend on the number of its proposed occupants; it can be made either oblong or square. When a sufficient number of trees of convenient bulk for handling have been felled and logged up into proper lengths, the ends should be notched with the axe, as shown in the opposite illustration. The four ground logs are then laid and keyed together by their notches; the second row are then placed on these, either by the aid of skid bars placed in a slanting direction on the lower logs, or by manual labour. When all the walls are high enough, the doorway must be cut in the following manner: Begin on the upper log and chop through at each end, the exact width

Board wigwam.

Log house, to build.

of the proposed opening; follow down, cutting log by log until the ground log is reached; cut this nearly half through and then split out the piece, the other portion below forms your threshold. Take a fresh log, and in it split out a space exactly to correspond with that in the ground log, place this as a crowning log with three others, uncut, to

form your wall plate, the split-out piece will form the top of your doorway; the square hole for the window or shutter is chopped out in the same way. The gable ends and ridge log must be adjusted at such a pitch as to insure a free run for rain water or melted snow; the four ends or butts of the gable angles should rest and be firmly wedged in four holes axed out for them in the ends of the upper row of wall-plate logs; where the gable peak crosses, the logs should be notched together and pinned; the ridge log will then rest in the crutches formed by the intersection. Now, after having selected the most convenient spot for a fire-place, chop a hole through the logs, including that on the ground, about 3ft. wide and 4ft. 6in.

high. There are several ways of forming a chimney and fireback; one is to build a beehive shaped wall outside the opening, plastering the inside with clay, and forming a rough chimney stack with turf and stones. All chinks or crevices between the logs are stopped with clay and moss. Some American trappers and hunters proceed as follows: They cut a number of poles long enough to reach the top of the proposed chimney, which is, of course, a little higher than the ridge of the roof; they then plant the sharpened ends of the poles

in the earth in such a way as to form a semicircular hedge surrounding the back of the hole in the logs, and about 6ft. at its
widest part from them. An inner hedge of sticks about 6ft. long is
now planted within the row of long poles, at about 8in. from them; a
number of bushy twigs are now collected and interwoven between
the poles and sticks until a sort of double wall of basket work is
formed between these wicker partitions; a quantity of wet clay and
small gravel is firmly impacted, and rammed down until the space
will hold no more. The long poles are then gathered together into a
sort of inverted funnel form, a hole being left where their small ends
meet for the smoke to pass through; a thorough slap-dashing with
thin wet clay within and without finishes the affair. The inner layer
of basket work consumes in time, but leaves the clay and stone hard
enough to resist an ordinary heat. Huts of this description are either
half log-roofed or shingled; that represented in the illustration is
covered by the former mode. Logs of fitting size and length are split
in halves; the surfaces of one-half of these are slightly hollowed with
the axe or adze, and then placed side by side with the round surface
downward on the ridge bar and wall plate; on the hollowed faces of
these over every interval is laid face downward one of the flat-faced
pieces. (See illustration, p. 243.)

To roof-in one of these log huts with the shingles we have before
described, the builder must proceed in a different manner; rows of
rafters must be pinned on to catch the shingles. The first row, or that
at the wall plate, should project some inches beyond it; on the
heels of these a long flat lath or batten of wood is secured by wood

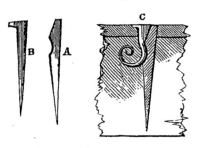

pegs driven in here and there, this
nips the row of shingles and keeps
them in place. The second row is
laid over and beyond the batten and
so on, much as slates or tiles are laid
for the roof of an English house.
Doors and shutters for log houses
are usually made of boards obtained
from split logs pinned together with
cross-bars, and are generally called *dowel hinged;* an auger hole is
bored a few inches into both frame and door, a hard wood peg placed
half-way into each hole gives perfect freedom of motion, and will last
as long as the house.

The shingles of roofs, flooring boards, or the planks used in the
construction of huts are very securely attached to the wood work on
which they are intended to rest, by the use of the contrivance shown

in the illustration on page 244. A, is a straight flat nail without a head, but with a shallow half moon-shaped indentation Shingle spike and made in one of its edges; B, is a common wrought rail. iron brad, A is first driven through the two pieces of wood to be secured'

B is then entered with its point resting against the edge of A at its crown, and above the crescent shaped cut, when B is driven home with the hammer it will clench itself as at C, and hold with extraordinary tenacity.

A flooring is very easily made by splitting a large log into rough boards, and much increases the comfort of the establishment. The above illustration represents a rough temporary wigwam, Temporary which may be easily made as follows : Select either a wigwams. large fallen log or high bank for a back ; drive two stout forked pieces sufficiently far from the back and far apart to give space for the interior ; lay another pole across the crutches for a front wall plate, and two side poles from the back, long enough to rest on and be secured to this. Thatch with hemlock or balsam fir branches, arranging

them layer upon layer, butt end upwards. The gable ends can be closed with either branches or grass-covered hurdles or frames. Another kind is made by placing all the posts double, and then dropping the planks down between them, so that they are nipped by the uprights, as shown in the accompanying sketch.

Roof-riders are very useful and easily constructed contrivances, and serve to keep the sheets of bark or other material used in forming a roof, from being loosened or blown away by the wind. Six roughly Roof-riders. trimmed and partially squared poles, of tolerable size and weight are fitted together as shown in the illustration on next page.

Auger holes and wooden pins are alone used to secure them to each other, and from the comparative ease with which a pinned joint can be moved the rider can be caused to fit any pitch of roof, just as a pair of scissors are opened and shut. In very rough weather it is a good plan to lash fast a tolerably heavy stone or bag of sand or earth to the centre of each long bar of the contrivance.

As an almost invariable rule, the huts built by savage nations are round, or approximate more or less to the circular form. But The huts of sometimes they are shapeless things, like the rude savages. "gunyah" of the Australian, which consists merely of a sheet of bark of the tea-tree (one of the Eucalypti) broken across the middle and set up in a triangular form to shelter "the body" from the inclemency of the weather; while small fires are lighted all around for warmth and defence against the mosquitoes, or a dry log, 6ft. or 8ft. long, is laid on either side, and set on fire in several places. Equally simple is the hut of the desert bushman. A few sticks are set up against each other, so as to form an

irregular cone, with one side left open to admit "the body" of the sleeper, as shown in the illustration on p. 247. In almost all tribes the commencement is made in the same manner. A circle is traced or imagined on the ground, and the women squatting down, with sharp pointed sticks work holes a foot or more apart all round it; long flexible wands are inserted, and their tops bent over and lashed together, and if the hut be large, one or more poles are placed inside the circle as supports. In Kafirland the fireplace is simply a flat hearth, occupying the centre, so that the poles, when there are any, are arranged round it. Smaller rods are wattled all round, or bound tightly to the ribs with strips of the inner bark of the mimosa, or other tree, and the hut is thatched with reeds, grass, or whatever may be the favourite or most convenient material of the country.

In Kafirland the huts are hemispherical, like beehives, or rather like inverted bowls slightly flattened on the top. The thatching is very neatly and compactly done, and generally small ropes of grass are carried many times round and round outside the hut, and laced with smaller strips through the thatching to the *inner* frame. The floor is nicely clayed with a compost of "kraal mist" or cattle dung, and the fine clay of ant-hills broken up and well mixed. Sometimes the inner wall for 2ft. or 3ft. high is plastered with the same, and pumpkin seeds stuck into it in fanciful patterns, and picked off again, when the clay is dry, leaving a glazed film sparkling in the hollow.

There is one fault in these Kafir huts. They resemble an inverted bowl; the door is cut out of the edge, and there is no other aperture

extremities may be absolutely chilled, while from the waist upward he is immersed in a bath of smoke or heated air; and when the fire has gone low, and the intensely cold air of the early morning fills the lower part, driving the warm air above the level of the doorway, the sleeper is glad to wrap himself more closely in his mantle.

In countries where stratified rocks, as sandstone, &c., which split easily into flat slabs, abound, huts are frequently built of stone. A circle of blocks is laid on the ground, then another on them, with the edges projecting a little inward, so that the circumference of each course is less than that of the one immediately beneath it; a large slab covers the top, and finishes the building. Such

huts are found in the north-eastern part of the Free State in South Africa, formerly the Orange River Sovereignty.

Among the various Bechuana tribes in and beyond the Free State, the building of a hut is a more elaborate and artistic affair; in fact, it deserves rather to be called a house, consisting, as it does, of walls and a roof perfectly distinct from each other. In its simplest form it consists of a row of stakes from 4ft. to 7ft. high, set up in a circular form, and of a conical roof, the frame of which is mostly made separately on the ground, and then lifted into its place, and bound firmly upon the upright wall. In the larger huts a smaller concentric circle of stakes (of course much longer than the first, as they have to reach the roof at a higher point) forms an inner chamber, and generally the eaves of the roof are extended, so as to form also a verandah, or shade, all round; and, besides this, there will be a larger circular wall inclosing a courtyard, frequently of considerable dimensions.

Sometimes, as on the Lower Zambesi, the row of stakes forming the outer wall of the house is plastered round with a broad central horizontal band of red or yellow clay, leaving about a third above and below it open for ventilation, and sometimes the whole is elaborately smoothed with a mixture of the fine clay of broken ant-hills and cattle dung, which, being left of its natural colour, has the appearance of a light greyish stone. All this is performed by the women, who put it down and smooth it with their hands, finishing not only the house, but the outer walls and even the floor of the courtyard, with so much nicety that, as good housewives say at home, " you might eat off it." Raised seats are generally built in the form of segments of a circle, and these are as carefully smoothed over as the rest. The hut of a Bechuana chief at Vaal River was a model of neatness in its way; the walls had been marked off into blocks, zigzag lines had been traced on them, and uncouth patterns were painted in black or coloured clay over the low door of his inner chamber, which, hung round with antelope skins, was, as he said, very nice and warm—in fact, insufferably hot. The outer apartment was 3ft. or 4ft. broad, and ran all round the inner. The part nearest the door served as a reception room, and the remoter regions were used for the stowage of rough skins, household gear, the muskets and ammunition, and large pots and calabashes of outchulla or native beer, which kept up a constant simmering as it fermented, and to the taste seemed very like spoiled vinegar. Large frames are made of wattled work, and coated with clay till they resemble capacious jars; in these the corn is stored, small roofs are raised over them, and the timber around is wastefully heaped up to form a kind of shelter from the sun for its chief and council to sit under.

The hartebeeste hut shown in the full-page camp scene in Kafirland, mostly used by colonial Hottentots, is simple and easy enough to make. It has one straight side, and one lean-to, and derives its name from its resemblance to the sloping back of the animal.

The huts of the Damaras are generally of very rude construction. A circle of sticks is planted in the ground, and the tops bent over and lashed together, generally with their own bark; they are then roughly wattled, and plastered over with clay and "kraal mist." Rain so

CHIEF'S HUT, VAAL RIVER.

seldom falls that they seem to take no precaution against it, preferring rather to risk the few drenching showers of the wet season than to take the trouble of making their huts waterproof. Sometimes the hides of the few cattle they slaughter are spread over their huts, and kept in their places by stones or heavy poles laid on them. In one respect only they have an advantage over the Kafir hut, and that is, the smoke escapes through the cracks and interstices of the roof. Internally there may be a dried hide to sit and sleep on, an earthen pot for cooking, a calabash or two, or a bamboo or wooden bowl for milk or water; two or three skins stripped off whole, as sacks for "uintjies" or earth nuts; and it may be an axe, of Ovampo, or more rarely of European manufacture.

The box made of stiff leather, in which they carry grease and red ochre, may also be here; but, with the exception of their cattle, the Damaras seldom possess much more property than can be carried on the person.

The huts of the Berg Damaras are still more primitive; and sometimes they seek no other shelter than one or two small bushes, the lower branches of which are cut away, while the upper ones are brought together and interwoven—others being added if needful—and grass thrown loosely over all.

Indeed, small trees, with the lower branches cleared away, and the upper ones drawn together and interlaced, form very convenient huts or arbours. The Bechuana women, in making a kraal, beat the mimosa branches on the ground till they flatten them into a fan-like form, then they plant them side by side and interlace the branches.

The Namaqua Hottentots, the Makobas or canoemen of the Bō-tlét-tē River, and many of the Bechuana tribes in the Orange River Sovereignty and elsewhere, build hemispherical frames of flexible wands, and cover them with mats of rushes like cheese mats. These are very neatly made. The Hottentots use flat awls, 18in. or 20in. long, for this purpose, but the Makoba awl is not more than 5in. or 6in.

Small thongs of dressed antelope skin, or cords twisted from the fibres of different plants are used for sewing the mats. These might be easily made by a traveller needing them, and he could best do it by having two or three needles of any convenient length, from 4in. or 5in. to 20in.; they should be flattened at the point, and pierced with an eye to carry the cord on which the reeds are strung. The most convenient method would be to fix the needles upright at the proper distance from each other, and then press upon them as many rushes as their length would allow; these, with the strings drawn through, should then be removed, and a fresh set threaded on, care being taken to see that the strings are kept clear, so that they reeve consecutively through all the rushes, and make a smooth uniform mat. Generally, however, it will be found that, where the proper materials grow, the natives will make and sell them cheaply enough. Mats of this description are much used by the natives of North-West America in hut building; the needles used in that country are not unfrequently 5ft. long.

It often becomes necessary for the traveller, if he contemplates a stay of a few months, or even weeks, in any one place, to build his own hut; and it is as well that this should be, if possible, somewhat

superior in size and form to the dwellings of the natives around him.
If the nature of the ground and the materials at hand   Crook and prong
will admit of it, this may as well be a house regularly   house, to build.
walled and roofed, and at least the four corner posts, as well as the two
which support the gables, should be firmly let into the ground. If
care is taken to cut all these with a fork, so that the ridge pole of the
roof may rest in the forks of the gable poles, and the wall plates
in those of the four corner posts, the building will be much
stronger, and the work greatly facilitated. The rafters may also have
forks, which can rest upon the wall plate, but this would leave the
thickest part of the branches upwards; a little labour in thinning them
off would remedy this, or they might, in favourable localities, be so
chosen that it would be of very little consequence. Every alternate

rafter should be reversed, so that its forks might help to support the
battens. All the poles forming the side walls should have forks to
help to support the wall plate, and those which form the sides of the
doors or windows should be so selected that smaller forks, at the
proper height, would serve to receive the sills of the door and windows.
Such a frame as this would present the greatest amount of strength
and firmness with the least possible necessity for lashing, pegging, or
other fastening.

The sketch of the framework of a house indicates the manner in
which the forks and branches may be used to the best advantage. If
trees of proper size are abundant, the builder will be able to choose
them so as to suit their places, with as much regularity as indicated in
the drawing; if not, he must make the best of the materials.

The smaller framework beside it represents that of a hut we built at Depôt Creek. We set up three forked poles as a triangle at either end, laid a ridge pole between them, and lashed it firmly there. Rafters and battens were added, and we stripped off large sheets of tea-tree bark (*Eucalyptus melaleuca?*) to cover it. We also obtained some of the white-barked red-gum tree (*Eucalyptus resinifera*); but this is more brittle, and did not answer so well.

The roof may be covered with the reed mats already spoken of, one or two thicknesses of which, if the roof has a pitch of *not less* than 45°, will suffice to keep out rain; or it may be thatched with grass, reeds, or the broad leaves of the fan palm—remembering that, whatever material is used, it will cast off water much better if the point of the leaf is downward. The lowest course will be laid and securely fastened first; then the next, overlapping it; and so on to the top. This may be done by simply lashing the stalks of each course to the proper batten; or a thatching needle may be made of wood, smooth and flat, an inch or more in breadth, and pierced near the point with an eye to carry the lashing. The inner bark of many trees, though unfit to make cord which is to remain permanently flexible, will answer very well for this purpose; for if stripped as required, and used while still wet, it will tie in any knot, and bear straining tightly. It will hold well enough when dry, though it would not again bear working up, on account of its brittleness. The leaves of the *Phormium tenax*, of New Zealand, which grow much like those of the common flag, are very generally used in that country, just as they are gathered for binding various matters. Excellent twine, thread, cloth, and rope are made from the fibre, as will be seen as our work proceeds.

The walls may be filled up, according to taste or necessity, with mats or reeds; or, if permanent shelter from bad weather is required, nothing is better than wattle and daub, and if the wattling is carefully done, and good clay or broken ant-hills and " kraal mist" used for the daub, a very neat job may be made of it. We have shared the hut of a sergeant of Sappers in the forest of the Pierie Hills in Kafirland, where he had a clay hearth, and wattle and daub chimney, and, though a roaring fire was kept up, he did not anticipate any danger. He had charge of a party who were cutting timber, and one noble " yellow wood" they had just felled was no less than 7ft. diameter at its base. The bush vines hung in long straight lines, like ropes from the upper branches of this tree; and on one of these, 60ft. or 80ft. long, and not more than an inch thick, the sergeant, who was a heavy man, raised himself, and swung to and fro without fear of breaking it. In fact, these vines may be used while green for many of the purposes of rope or cord. We have disentangled nearly 30ft., as fine and almost as tough as a small fishing line, from the forest in front of the Victoria Falls, and rolled it into a small coil; but once dry, it becomes brittle, and cannot be straightened. Some of these vines bear fruit, which, though not equal to the cultivated grape, is by no means to be despised.

When looking for a spot along the banks of the Zambesi on which to establish a camp and rebuild our boat, in September, 1862, we were warned by the natives who came to meet us against the pretty little sequestered spots beside the tributary rivulets, as they were certain to be infested by mosquitoes. We, therefore, having in view also the probability of being obliged to stay far into the unhealthy season, tried back about a mile, and selected a limestone spur which

had a small valley between it and the higher range in its rear.

This we named Logier Hill, after our old and steadfast friend in Cape Town; and, setting to work with a keen American felling axe, cut down the thorns and brushwood on the top, while the people assisted us in cutting or dragging the fallen bushes to the verge. Three mimosas, which were in a good position, we left standing, and added one for

Roof, to raise.

the fourth corner post. Then selecting flexible branches, we framed upon the ground an oval of corresponding size; on this with lighter poles (most of them the young straight branches of the "kookom boyou," a gigantic sterculia in general appearance, somewhat resembling the baobab), we framed a roof similar in form to that of a marquee, using for lashings the inner bark, stripped from the branches just mentioned. To lift this, as its weight was considerable in proportion to its strength, and all the people were away collecting poles or grass for the completion of our huts, was rather difficult, but we had fortunately a small coil of manilla line and a few blocks. With two of these we made a tackle, and lifting one side of the roof 2ft., supported it by a forked branch while we raised the rest, shoring it in the same manner all round, and then lifting it again and supporting it on longer forks till it was high enough to be fastened securely in its place (see page 255). We placed forked uprights under it at proper intervals, but as the eaves projected considerably we did not find it necessary to close in the walls, but when the rain came on laid fresh poles upon the roof and thatched it with grass and reeds to the ground. For central supports we took two forked poles, and instead of setting them upright at the two ends of the ridge pole gained additional rigidity by crossing them like an X, and lashing them together in the centre. At one end, raised upon forks above 18in. high, we made a platform of small poles as straight as we could get them to serve for a bed, and when a buffalo was shot spread over it the dried hide to level it a little more. This platform was continued all round between the uprights and the eaves, and various stores were laid on it.

One advantage here was the immunity from the ravages of the white ant, which is seldom found in a limestone country. But as the rainy season came on hosts of the destructive little white-shouldered beetle that feeds on skins, preserved hides, and specimens of all kinds— seeming rather to enjoy arsenic soap and other preservatives—ravaged everything made of untanned leather ; while other kinds, larger and still more unpleasant to the eye and touch, would actually commence eating the velschoens off our feet during the short meal time.

We should have preferred reeds for thatching, as when laid at a sufficient angle, say anything above 45°, they cast off water perfectly, although if laid at a lower angle they might be by no means water-proof. Of course the cut ends of the stems must be upward, and the leaves pointing down, or the water will be retained, and allowed to leak through instead of being thrown off; and this rule holds good when grass or such like material is used. If the roof of the hut be conical, the ends may simply be brought up and tied tightly together, or they may be worked into an ornamental form like those of the Bechuana hut (see p. 249). If it has a ridge, as ours had, it must be covered with a horizontal layer, sufficiently thick to keep the water from insinuating itself between the meeting of the two sides.

In our own house we stretched the sails of our boat and calico tent within the roof to keep off any leakage during heavy showers, and added fresh poles and grass to the outside. Sir Richard Glyn, who visited the hill after we had been compelled to abandon it, and who returned to England before us, reported that our house was the strongest building of the kind he had ever seen.

In countries like the Indian islands, where bamboo can be obtained in any quantity and of any size, from a reed fit for a lady's arrow to one big enough for the mast of a small sloop, it is easy enough to build a house; the extreme strength and lightness of the material, with its glossy surface and neat and uniform appearance, rendering it in every sense most valuable for such purposes. Bamboos, for Poles of uniform size may be planted closely so as building. to form a wall, or pillars may be placed more or less apart, and mats or blinds of smaller reeds, or larger ones split up, may occupy the intervals. Balconies, strong and sufficiently ornamental, may be formed; and the eaves of the roof may be made to project to any distance, so as to form an effectual verandah; while palisades or fences of any form or height may be constructed *ad libitum.*

Bamboos from its polished siliceous covering, is, externally at least, proof against the ravages of the white ant, which destroys without mercy all the softer kinds of wood and vegetable or animal

fibre, whether in the form of boxes, furniture, books, clothing, specimens of natural history or botany, drawings, or articles of necessity or luxury of any kind.

If thunderstorms are frequent or dangerous, a glass bottle on the highest point of the roof will act as a non-conductor, and may not unfrequently avert the flash that might otherwise destroy the building. It is not always, however, effectual.

Doors or gates may be made as closely worked or as open as may be desired; and, while upon this subject, it Doors and gates, to may be as well to mention a very convenient make and hang. way of hanging them in the absence of regular hinges. The hinge side of the door or gate should be a standard of some strength, to which all the rest is framed and securely fastened with pegs or lashings; round this and the corresponding doorpost a strap or thong of leather or cord should be passed in figure of 8 fashion to form each hinge, or it may simply be passed round both and "seized" between them with smaller cords. This, however, will not hold the door with sufficient stiffness to let it swing true and easily; therefore, take a common ale or porter bottle, bury it neck downwards in the ground, leave the lower end of the standard somewhat longer than the door, point it a little, and insert it in the hollow at the bottom of the bottle—the gate will swing fairly on such a pivot, as it never gets out of order, and it may almost be said will never wear out.

The gate itself (Fig. 1, page 257) may be built of rough branches—one tolerably stout limb, for the hinge or swinging side, should have a good branch projecting from its lower part diagonally upwards to the upper part of the latch side; another fork, with its branches as nearly at right angles as possible, will form the latch side and top rail; and a third will make the lower one. Never be in a hurry to trim off small branches; generally they will weave in and add to the strength; and if not, they are easily cut off afterwards. When the posts are set up on the ground, it is as well to char the ends as a protection against damp or wood-destroying insects; cut notches near the ends, and in them wedge good heavy stones—they will keep the posts firm, and in countries where there is frost nothing else can prevent their rising out of the ground. We found this arrangement very valuable in the Crimea. It is not necessary that the bottle should be whole; if the " cup " under the bottom is perfect, the broken edges of the sides will give it additional firmness.

In Fig. 2 the gate post has a fork, and another on the branch serving as the top rail makes the upper hinge. One of the other branches has a fork projecting from the lower angle and working on the gate post as a cutter's gaff does on the mast. This is easy to make, can be unshipped at a moment's notice, and hung up again as readily. Fig. 3 is a more regularly made gate on the same principle. The top rail has a hole working on the thinned upper part of the gate post, which is pierced with holes, and has a peg so that the gates may be raised or lowered as required; the lower part works on the gaff principle.

It is generally desirable to hang a gate so that it may shut of itself after it has been opened; and to insure this, if iron hook and staple hinges can be had, let the hook of the upper hinge project a little farther from the gate post than the lower one, as in Fig. 5. If it is requisite that the gate should remain open—which is sometimes, though not often, the case—the upper hook should project less than the lower, as in Fig. 4. Generally, if the hinges be equal, the gate will hang in whatever position it may be left; but if the post inclines from the perpendicular to right or left, the gate will swing to the same side.

Very good standards for fences may be made by cutting half mortices in the opposite sides of a squared log, 4ft. or 5ft. long, as in Fig. 6, then cutting it into planks, and, before these are quite detached, sawing it down in the direction of the diagonal line; a pair of these are matched together, as in Fig. 7, and the lower end morticed into a flat plank so far as to let one hole come below it to receive a key to fix it there. The horizontal plank should rest upon a short log at each end, and it may be held in place by a couple of notched pegs driven into the ground.

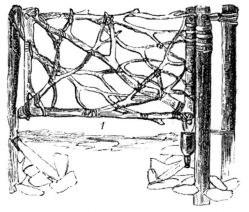

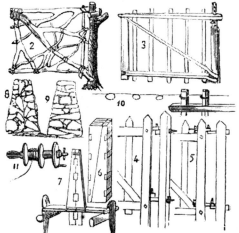

The sparsely scattered settlers amongst the great northern forests, construct self closing Lapmark gate gates in a closer. most ingenious manner. The object being to prevent such cattle or reindeer, as may be brought to the homestead for use or domestication from straying away into the interminable woods and thickets. To the centre of a strong wooden gate, set in the usual "pole and post" fence, a long link of twisted birch sticks is fastened by one end, in the manner shewn in the annexed illustration. The other end has a tolerably large loop made in it. This passes through a hole made in the end of a lever, which is much heavier at one end than the other, rests in a slot made in the end of a post, and moves freely up and down as the gate is drawn

forward or falls back again, when the force requisite to overcome the lever is removed.

Many of the natives of South Africa are very handy at building rough stone walls; but they require an overseer to insure the proper Walls to binding of the stones as they are laid. Some of their build. own countrymen may be found with skill enough for this. It is no use to build up two fair faces, as in Fig. 8 (p. 257), and then fill up the middle with loose stones—their weight would be sure to force out the sides and bring down the whole structure; but large flat stones should be chosen, as in Fig. 9, to reach either quite through the wall, or at least so far that the stones on the other side may meet and have a bond with them. Such walls, miles in length, are built without cement of any kind. If galvanised iron wire is to be used for fencing, to support upright rails, it is a good plan to have two rail-heads fixed at the proper distance, and to make the turns of the wire on these to insure each loop being equidistant, as in Fig. 10.

Chalk lines and measuring lines of all kinds suffer from being coiled or rolled up by hand—turns and kinks are put on or taken out of them; and it is much better to have reels, either like the log-reel of a ship, or like Fig. 11 (see p. 257), where a peg in the circumference of the disc serves as the crank by which to wind it up.

Effective screens can be readily extemporised with planks of any kind and ropes; the simplest plan is to double the rope, making one Plank screens, part somewhat longer than the breadth of all the to make. planks to be used, and leaving whatever spare end may be upon the other to hoist the screen by when finished. The first plank is laid in the bight of the rope, the two parts of which are then crossed and the next plank laid between them; they are crossed again for the third plank, and so on till all are inclosed. If there is not an eye on the shorter end of the rope, make a bow-line knot or two half hitches on it (see " Knots and Hitches "), and pass the longer end through; then lead the spare line at each end of your screen over the forks of trees, or sheer legs, or whatever support you mean to use, and hoist away simultaneously and carefully; for this arrangement, though perfectly strong and secure while every part remains in its proper place, is most easily disarranged; and in fact the great advantage of it is that, when no longer required, it can be shaken to pieces like a house of cards, leaving neither holes or imperfections in the planks nor kinks or knots in the rope. We have shown the boards rather far apart in our illustration for the sake of distinctness, they will lie closer, but they must always be separate by more than the thickness of the rope. They may be made to lie closer by omitting to cross the ropes and "stopping" them together with small cord, as in Fig. 2; or a perfectly weather-proof wall with overlapping edges may be obtained by looping the rope into a chain, as in Fig. 3, taking care to make the lower link well fast, for on this the security of the whole depends.   To

take this to pieces nothing more is necessary than to slip each loop off the end of the plank; let go the fastening of the lower end, and all the links of the rope chain will shake out.

Great firmness may be imparted to any of these arrangements by placing a small pole inside, and securing every plank to it by successive hitches of a smaller line, as in Fig. 4; or, if stouter poles be used, the walls may be built up in this manner, commencing from the bottom plank and fastening the upper ones as you go on.   Each plan will have its advantages under peculiar circumstances.   In the Indian islands, large hollow bamboos are either split into three or four parts, making somewhat rounded narrow planks, or an incision is made in the side of the cane, when it is opened out, laid flat, pressed, and converted into a

single plank.   Movable screens of considerable size are made in the same manner as in Figs. 1 and 2 already referred to.

A shelf is easily made by piercing holes in the four corners of a plank, passing lines through, and sus- Makeshift pending it to a shelves. beam.   A very neat set of bookshelves may be obtained by doubling two cords of sufficient length, working an eye in the bight of each, passing the ends down through the

holes in the first plank, and turning double knots on them, so that it hangs fairly; then passing them through the next and knotting them, and successively through as many more planks as you require shelves.

We have seen houses built by traders or missionaries almost entirely of reeds, some of which grow from 10ft. to 20ft. long and more than 1in. thick. Bundles of these, with the thin ends and butts reversed, and overlapping each other so as to equalise their strength as much as possible, are laid on the ground to serve for top, bottom, and centre battens; then across these the reeds are distributed in two or three layers, according to the required thickness of the wall; other battens are laid on the upper side to correspond with those below, and the cords —slips of bark, palm leaf, twisted grass rope, or thin and flexible forest creepers—are passed through to bind the whole tightly together. If a number of these are made, say 12ft. or 15ft. square, they may easily be arranged on the framework of a house, or set up as a continuous fence. A trench is dug about 1ft. deep, the screen inserted in it, the earth well pressed down, and support is given either by shores, if needful, or by the next screen forming an angle with the

Reed houses, screens, and sheds.

first. If the wood of the country is more available for making hurdles, they can be used in the same manner.

We have had very excellent temporary stables, and sheds erected in Central India, composed entirely of poles, cords, and grass, forming what is called "chupper" screens. These are formed by laying together double poles; in the space left between these poles long tufts of jungle grass are arranged, until the whole frame is filled up, when the sticks or poles, being tightly drawn together with cord, the grass is nipped between them, as shown in the above illustration. When in the Tartar country, we saw a number of very comfortable huts made by cutting out a kind of notch in the hill side. The space thus formed was first framed over with strong poles, and then covered with brushwood; a layer of turf covered all, and soon took root, forming feeding grounds for whole families of goats, which walked about on the houses quite at home. The fronts of these hill dwellings were composed of wicker work, plastered with clay. Logs were hollowed out by the Tartars almost as thin as paper, when their ends were stopped with clay. In these the bees laid up their stores of honey, which was taken as required, without disturbing the industrious swarm in the next log.

The annexed illustration represents one of these huts and a pile of bee logs.

During the Kafir war we visited the homestead of a Scottish farmer, who, although upon the very border, had gallantly determined to stand his ground, and to that end he had built a small defensible tower; the flat roof covered with raw Defensible farmhouses. hides, and surrounded by a loopholed parapet, and the only door fronted by a solid shield of brickwork, with a small aperture on one side, so that an enemy attempting to enter must do it in a stooping position, and before he could turn and straighten himself in the doorway, must present his head in the most convenient possible position to have it split by the defenders. A large water cask was kept filled in the fort, and even should the enemy gain possession of the lower room the women and children could still be tolerably safe in the upper, except from random shots fired upwards through the floor, and which of course could be returned  in the same manner from above. Against fire their only defence lay in the supply of water we have already mentioned, but care was taken to have nothing inflammable in the lower room. There was no staircase; the ladder would be drawn up through the trap. The beams and flooring would require a considerable blaze to ignite them, and against any quantity of material being brought in for that purpose the defenders relied upon their rifles, or no less deadly smooth bores, loaded with loopers or buck shot.

Blockhouse, among military edifices, is, as its name implies, a

building constructed chiefly of timber. If alone, it constitutes an
independent fort; if formed in the interior of a field-
work, it becomes a retrenchment or redoubt, and serves
to protect the defenders from the inclemency of the weather when
the work is occupied during a considerable time, or to prolong the
defence when the work is attacked, and after it is taken to enable the
garrison to obtain a capitulation. When the blockhouse is to be
employed only as a retrenchment, its plan is generally a simple
rectangle, and its walls consist of a single row of piles placed upright
in the ground. These are pierced with loopholes at the distance of
3ft. from each other, in order that the building may be defended by
a fire of rifles from within. The roof is formed by laying timbers
horizontally across the inclosed area and covering them with fascines
and earth. The interior breadth of the building may be from 18ft.
to 20ft., in order to allow a passage between the two rows of bed-
steads. These are placed with their heads to the side walls, and serve
as stages on which the men may stand to fire through the loopholes
when the latter are much elevated above the floor. In a mountainous
country the blockhouse possesses great advantages over an ordinary
field fort, inasmuch as the interior of the latter would be incessantly
ploughed up by the fire of artillery directed into it by the enemy
from the surrounding heights. Here, then, the blockhouse may with
propriety be constructed as an independent work; its plan may have
re-entering angles, or be in the form of a cross, in order to allow the
faces to be defended by flanking fires from the rifles and revolvers
from within; and the walls may be thick enough to resist even the
shot from 9-pounder guns. For this purpose they must be made by
planting parallel to each other, at a distance of 3ft. or 4ft., two rows of
strong piles, those in each row being close together, and the interval
between the rows being filled with earth up to the height of the loopholes, which should never be immediately under the roof of the
building. The roof must be made shell proof, as before; but it has
been recommended, when the work is not overlooked by the enemy,
and when its breadth will permit, to have the piles forming the side
walls long enough to rise above the roof, and, either alone or with a
mass of earth behind them, to serve as a parapet.

Where blockhouses have to be constructed among hostile or
doubtful Indian tribes, who are not the possessors of artillery, the
fascine and earth roof and double rows of piles may be easily and
safely dispensed with.

Logs, squared with the axe and laid on each other, may be substituted for piles with advantage, as the labour of planting firmly in

the earth so many ponderous beams of wood is considerable. It is well, in building a blockhouse, to construct a raised breastwork of small logs round the margin of the roof; these may be roughly squared and dowelled together with short wooden pins. The roof itself should, after shingling, have a goodly layer of sand, earth, or raw hides laid over it in order to guard against the fire-tipped arrows of hostile savages. A few auger holes here and there serve to carry off rain water or melted snow, and the log breastwork can be both loopholed and fired over with ease.

Frontier blockhouses are usually built of squared logs of timber dowelled together; loopholes are made for firing rifles through, and portholes for one or two iron guns. Some frontier posts are merely squares of heavy log palisades, with all the requisite offices and buildings erected within them. A banquet runs from end to end of each side of the square in order that the defenders may command the attacking force. All trees and bushes within long shooting range are carefully removed so that there shall be no cover.

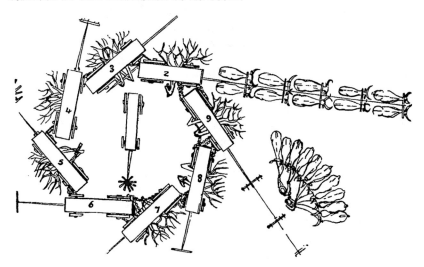

Bands of travellers in Africa not unfrequently so arrange their waggons as to form substantial defences against the attacks of hostile natives. We have often assisted in forming these Waggon burgs, so-called "waggon burgs." They are made as to make. follows: One waggon, with all the women, children, and ammunition, is placed in the centre. Others are drawn up, each with its inner fore wheel nearly touching the outer hind wheel of the one before it, and forming just such an angle with it that the dozen or thereabouts of vehicles form an almost perfect circle, their poles and trek gear extending on the outside, so that the oxen can again be yoked to each without disorder or confusion. There is room inside for the horses and cattle beside the defenders; and, should danger be imminent, the waggons can be locked together by the drag chains, and all the interstices choked with thorn bushes, the stems of which thrust inward would be securely fastened by pegs driven into the ground, or by lashing branches, cut short for the purpose, to the inner wheels, or by "reims" or thongs reeved through the bifurcations; while the tangled branches would oppose a barrier that no enemy could force in the face of the bullets or the small shot that would be poured through. The gear of the oxen would also be brought in and used in strengthening the defences.

In rendering a farmhouse defensible regard must be had to the character of the expected enemy. In countries like South Africa,

Farm and village, to fortify.

where the main object of the Kafir is the acquisition of cattle, the house ought to command and protect the kraal, the fence of which will often of itself form a shelter for the crafty foe. It is usually circular, as this form is most easily made, and will inclose the greatest number of cattle, with a given amount of material; but, if it were made triangular, with bastions on the two angles nearest, the guns of the defenders would sweep the other two sides, their fire crossing at the farthest angle, and leaving no place for an enemy to conceal himself. The house itself, with its outbuildings, should if possible be in the form of a square, inclosing as large a courtyard as is convenient for the accommodation of the defenders and their allies, and on emergencies for their horses, with a few sheep or oxen. If there be a spring or well in it so much the better; a ledge or bank, 18in. or 2ft. high, should run along the inside of the wall, so that the loopholes may be too high for the enemy to look in at or fire through; and there should be small chambers projecting from the angles, or at least from two diagonally opposite loopholed, so that each can enfilade two sides of the wall.

But perhaps it will be better, instead of describing an ideal defensible homestead, to give an example of a real one, which, though not quite perfect in a military point of view, was as nearly so as the accommodation required for the traffic and the work carried on there would allow. Our illustration is a plan, drawn from memory, of the village of Objimbengue, to the south of which (Fig. 1) is the flat sandy bed, 400yds. wide, of the Swakop River, filled only during the flooded season, but in the dry retaining a vast amount of water beneath the sand, while a little rivulet, represented by the faint line, appears here and there upon the surface. Fig. 2 is a low bank or foreshore, overgrown with wild tamarisks or dabbie bushes, and partly cleared for a garden (Fig. 3) in which is a well, and used in other places for corn land, care being taken to reap the crop before there is any possibility of its being swept away by the floods of the next season On the east of the village is a small tributary, generally dry, called the Artip (Fig. 4), and beyond this, and the limits of the picture, would be the Mission House of Regterveldt and the Damara village, with its curious entrenchments scattered without order, but not without great judgment, over the face of the hill wherever a few men could find a place to shoot from. The trench (Fig. 5), fronted by the mound of earth thrown out of it, and by a breastwork of dabbie logs, made by the Damaras, formed the outer line of defence of the homestead, and the owner could in emergency have depended on a thousand men to man it. Fig. 6 is the opening for the southern road leading across the river from the country of the hostile Namaquas. Fig. 7, the road

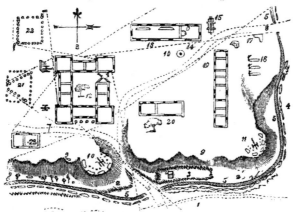

ENTRENCHED VILLAGE OF OBJIMBENGUE.

leading from Walvisch Bay; and Fig. 8, the continuation of it toward Lake Ngami, and Fig. 9 is the steep edge, 15ft. or 20ft. high, of the plain, on which the village is built. Fig. 10 is a small breastwork for a brass 1-pounder gun commanding the southern road, and Fig. 11 for another gun sweeping the open space to the south-east, where, in fact, an attack actually took place. The guns were, however, usually kept beside the house, where one served as a time gun, and they could easily be moved whenever they were wanted. Fig. 12 was a dwelling-house; the central space is open and would serve as a shelter for native fugitives, for horses, sheep, and a few of the most valuable working oxen; the front is composed of a voor-house or entrance-hall usually occupied for general family purposes and reception of visitors, and before it is a verandah.

At each angle are rooms used as sitting or bed chambers: on the western side are spare chambers for the reception of guests ; in the rear are kitchen, bath-room, and other offices; and on the east are store-rooms and the entrance gate. Fig. 13 is the wheelwright and waggon maker's shop; Fig. 14, the smithy; Fig. 15, the sawpit; Fig. 16, the tiring plate; Fig. 17, small trenches with angular mounds before them, commanding the eastern gate of the village ; Fig. 18, the graveyard; Fig. 19, the workmen's cottages; Fig. 20, the slaughter-house and waggon-shed ; the walls of all these buildings being musket-proof, and the windows more or less convenient for firing from. Figs. 21 and 22 are stoutly stockaded cattle kraals ; they were both square, but the triangular outline of Fig. 21 shows what would be gained in defensibility and lost in accommodation by adopting that form ; Fig. 22 has small " scherms " at the angles protected by the fire from the house, and commanding the other two sides ; Fig. 23 is a storehouse, adding but little to the strength of the position, but indispensable for its use. The dotted lines indicate the directions of effective fire from the dwelling-house.

In most frontier villages the church, as the most substantial building, is used as a place of refuge, and as a last stronghold against savage assailants ; and on the east coast, the natives, when they throw up a rough tower of defence, always call it by the Portuguese name, " Egregia," or church.

We have seen the church at Shiloh converted into a very pretty little Churches, fortification by one of our own engineer officers. Bastions to fortify. were raised at the angles of the outer wall, the building itself was unthatched, and a breastwork, with loopholes, raised upon the walls.

We have known friends who have had to entrench their waggons for months among tribes whose friendship was dubious ; and they seemed to prefer that, especially for a night attack, or for a sentry's accommodation, the embankment should be behind the trench, and not before it, so that they might look from the very edge of the pit and see the dark figure of an approaching enemy against the sky, whilst they would be invisible against the mound behind them ; whereas, if the mound were in front, they would have to raise their heads to look over it, and an enemy creeping close to the ground, would be absolutely invisible, and would, moreover, be able to see clearly the elevated figure of the sentry.

We have on several occasions been asked to draw plans for churches on remote stations, and for defensible farmhouses ; in the former Mission churches, case, regard must be had to the nature of the plans for building. materials at the disposal of the missionary, to the number of the congregation he wishes to accommodate, and also to the number and skill of the assistants, whether European or native, he can employ or persuade to join in the work. Generally, it is better so to draw the plan that a portion of the church may be commenced, and sufficiently furnished for almost immediate use; while the remainder is left to be finished as the congregation increases, and as the tribe become more and more alive to the benefit conferred on them by religion and civilisation. Some regard must also be had to the doctrinal views of the missionary requiring the plan.

If, as is frequently required, the men and women of the congregation are to be separately seated, the best form is that of the Greek cross, and the seats of the men must be placed in one arm and those of the women in the other; while the position of the pulpit, with its back against the angle of the other two, gives every individual a fair opportunity of seeing and hearing the minister.

Where this regulation does not prevail, the Latin cross is the best form; the longest limb lying east and west affords space for the congregation and the preacher. The wings or shorter limbs on the north and south give very great support to the walls, and serve for vestries or other offices; the tower and porch at the eastern end form the continuation of the longer limb, and it should also be capable of increase if necessary, by the addition of a smaller continuation at the western end.

In this case, too, it is the part intended for the congregation that should be first built. It is most probable that the materials would be rough unhewn surface stones, for powder to blast out more solid material would be expensive. Tools for quarrying would be unattainable, and men with skill or industry to work them even still more so, while ant-hill clay would be the only available cement, unless the erection should be in a limestone district, or near a beach, where shells in abundance could be procured and burnt into lime.

Bricks are often made, but they are frequently of inferior clay, and often merely sun-dried or inefficiently burned, and are in no case equal to the well-squared and hardened article known by the same name in England.

It would, therefore, be prudent not to make the walls more than 10ft. or 15ft. in height, and to allow at least 2ft. of thickness at the base for every 10ft. of height, and even then they ought to be supported by buttresses not more than 20ft. apart; the top should not be less than 12in. or 15in. in width, and if good planks for wall plates cannot be procured, they ought to be rather more to allow for the proper bedding in of rough substitutes. The roof must have a pitch of 45° to enable it to throw off water in the rainy season, and each rafter must be two-thirds the width of the building to the outside of the walls, and so much more as is required for the projection of the eaves.

If, therefore, rafters can be procured 20ft. in length, of which 2ft. are required for projection, this will leave 18ft., and the possible width of the church may be found by adding half the length of the rafter thus— 18+9=27—27ft. to the outside of the walls, or about 24ft. in the clear; this, with 4ft. of passage down the centre will give two benches of 10ft. capable of accommodating six persons each. Each sitter ought to have 3ft. of space from front to rear, although it is possible to sit in 2ft. ; thus, a space of 60ft. would accommodate a congregation of 240 or 360 persons, according to the room allowed.

In many cases the fitting-up of benches may be deferred, as the natives will sit naturally on the ground, or will bring their own seats with them. At least 15ft. or 20ft. ought to be reserved for the pulpit and the communion table, and this would give an aisle of 80ft. long by 24ft. wide.

A high gable and Gothic window is doubtless a great ornament to a church, but it would be dangerous to build the wall 15ft. higher for that purpose; and it is much better, therefore, to make the end no higher than the sides, and let the roof incline at an angle of 45° instead of having a gable end.

The windows must be small, and it is better to make them lancet-shaped and narrow; if the buttresses are 20ft. apart there may be two

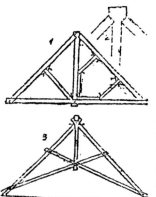

windows, 2ft. wide between each. The rafters ought not to come over the windows, even if the wall plates be good, but ought to rest on the solid space between them.

The rafters are half checked at each end to the cross-beam and let into checks on the king-post; thus (Fig. 1) struts to the beam will considerably strengthen them, and if these are fitted into checks nailed on instead of being mortised or half checked in, the strength will not be impaired. Fig. 2 shows more clearly the manner in which the square ends of the rafters abut on the king-post. If it should be desirable to avoid having cross-beams the rafters may be framed as in Fig. 3; but unless this is very substantially done the weight of the roof is apt to expand them and force the walls outward. We, therefore, advise the common form, at least until the assistance of skilled workmen can be procured. The upper part of the king-posts may be a forked branch, and the ridge pole will lie very nicely in this.

In extemporising rough frame-houses in dry countries, the foundation is a matter of small importance; generally, when the ground is cleared, a place sufficiently hard and smooth, and a little elevated so that rain may not flood the house, is easily found. But sometimes a foundation must be formed, not only to afford a support to the fabric, but to raise the floor above the influence of damp or of low-lying noxious vapours. We have heard of barges or vessels being grounded and houses built upon them, and have in fact seen instances of this as well as of the deck houses being removed from wrecks and set up, sometimes raised on low walls, forming very comfortable habitations ashore, and of tents being set up as roofs over walls of rough stone. We have heard of the foundations of a house in San Francisco being laid with the 21lb.-sized oblong boxes of tobacco with which the market had been glutted. In Cape Town, when meat was a few halfpence a pound, we have seen bullocks' heads used as stop-gaps in the fences near Green Point. The cores of bullocks' horns are not unfrequently used for the same purpose in this country. In Walvisch Bay we saw bags of coarse salt used as part of the foundation of the original wooden shed in which, notwithstanding its lowly appearance many a traveller has found a hospitable reception.

We wondered a little at first at the use of such a material on a beach overflowing for miles at every spring tide, but found it was protected from actual contact with the sea by an embankment of sand, supported by posts and planking. Rain would not occur perhaps once in two years, and the fresh water from the Kuisip overspread the flats so rarely that such a contingency was hardly taken into account. The bags and their contents seemed to be in a normal state of dampness, but did not appear to waste in consequence of it.

When more commodious houses were required, the samphire, that formed the only vegetation on the flats, was collected by the Hottentot women, spread in layers alternated with sand well trodden down into it until mounds were formed about 4ft. high. On one of these a store was erected of corrugated iron, and on another the Rhenish missionaries built a wooden house they had brought out in frame. Perhaps for parties who can afford the carriage, corrugated galvanised iron houses offer as convenient a method as any of obtaining accommodation sufficiently permanent, and yet easily removable. The rigidity imparted by the corrugation could not be attained by any thickening of plain sheets, while scarcely more room is required in packing ; for although one sheet of plain iron occupies much less room than one of corrugated, the sheets of the latter fit so closely one upon the other that a dozen or twenty require not much more space than one. Dr. Livingstone took a house of this kind to the Zambesi in 1858; it formed a very efficient shelter for our stores on Expedition Island, but, as we never made any permanent camp beyond the Portuguese town of Tette, it was not again required. The sheets, however, used separately or together in any number according to the weight they were to support, formed excellent bases for tables, beds, settees, as well as benches, raised a few inches from the floor, on which to store such things as we wished to preserve from the white ants.

At Tette, on the Zambesi, there are ridges running parallel to the banks of the river, with hollows between them, which may have served as supplementary channels during extraordinary floods ; and, to avoid the low-lying malaria, which is of greater specific gravity than common air, the Portuguese colonists erect their houses on these ridges. The hollows serve as streets or roadways, and also as channels to carry off the deadly exhalations, which, being heavier than air, naturally seek the lowest level. The dwelling rooms are also further elevated by being built over a basement, which serves as a store-room, the elevation of a few feet frequently making all the difference between the chance of catching fever and of escaping it. In these store rooms they build isolated platforms about 3ft. high, on forked posts of hard wood, which are carefully swept every morning, while salt is strewed around their base to prevent the white ants approaching. Probably tar or turpentine would have the same effect

Buildings of the Portuguese in Africa.

PORTUGUESE HOUSE—ZAMBESI RIVER.

but in remote regions these are not always at command. The tarred wood of our iron house was never touched; and the camphor wood of India is valued very much on account of its immunity from their attacks.

When the Portuguese on the Zambesi build large houses that are to be divided into rooms, they build into the central and side walls a row of pillars, into the thickness of which stout poles are built, with the forks left upon them, and perhaps other rows of pillars without the connecting walls are built for the verandah.

Dr. Kirk, when consulted as to the best method of colonising the Shire, or Sheeree River, gave it as his opinion that the estates lying low in the fertile valleys should be cultivated by natives only (who in their *own country* do not seem susceptible to the deadly influence of fever, though when removed to another locality that is not perceptibly worse, they are as liable to be attacked as Europeans), and that the proprietors should have their residences upon the hills, as far as possible above the level of the malaria, with a small military force at their disposal, to keep order when necessary among the inhabitants of the valley. This certainly appears to be the only feasible plan of occupying such a country with any benefit to the various parties concerned.

An Indian cottage, on the banks of the Rio Negro, has been thus described:—"The main supports are trunks of some forest tree, of heavy and durable wood; but the light rafters are the straight, cylindrical, and uniform stems of the Jará palm. The roof is thatched with the large triangular leaves of the Caraná palm in regular alternate rows, neatly bound with sipos or forest creepers. The door is a frame of thin strips of wood neatly thatched over. It is of the split stems of the Pashiuba palm. In one corner is a heavy harpoon for cow-fish; it is of the black wood of the Pashiuba barriguda. By its side is a blowpipe, 10ft. or 12ft. long, and a little quiver of small poisoned arrows hangs near it. With these the Indian procures birds for food or for gay feathers, or shoots the hog or tapir; and it is from the stem and spines of two palms that they are made. His great bassoon-like musical instruments are of palm stems; the cloth to wrap his valued feather ornaments is a fibrous palm spathe, and the rude chest for his treasures is woven from palm leaves. His hammock, his bowstring, and his fishing line are fibres of palm leaves; the first from the miriti, and the other two from the tucum. The comb on his head is the hard bark of a palm. He makes fish-hooks of the spines, or uses them to puncture on his skin the peculiar markings of his tribe. His children eat the agreeable red and yellow fruit of the pupunha or peach palm, and from the assai he has prepared a favourite drink. A carefully-suspended gourd contains oil from the fruit of another, and the long elastic-plaited cylinder used for squeezing dry the mondiocca pulp to make his bread is of the bark of one of the singular climbing palms which alone can resist for any considerable time the action of the poisonous juice. In each of these cases a species is chosen adapted to the special object to which it is

Rio Negro huts.

to be applied, and often having different uses which no other plant can serve so well."

The arboreal dwellings of the Horaforo tribe in New Guinea have been thus described by Dr. J. Coulter:—"Against each tree rested a notched pole, and at a whistle from the chief, answered by hundreds of similar sounds in every direction,

Papuan tree houses. natives with flambeaux flitted down the poles till the whole forest was brilliantly illuminated. In fact they had their houses, or rather nests, in the trees, and when they retired for the night the pole was hauled up to prevent surprise. These abodes were made by thinning away some of the branches, and

laying horizontal poles on others sufficiently stout to bear them; the uprights are cut with forks, which rest on the lower branches, while their upper ends are lashed with cocoa-nut fibre to those above; the sides are formed by bamboos lashed closely together; the roofing is also of cane covered by sheets of thick bark sewn together, and perfectly proof against the heavy rains. The flooring is laid with split bamboos and light wood, and the walls are lined with stout matting, which

PAPUAN TREE HOUSE.

gives sufficient shelter against the piercing winds. The shape varies according to the spread of the tree; sometimes when the branches extend all round a house is made to inclose the whole tree; the smallest will measure 16ft. square, but sometimes they are longer and less wide; and when the whole tree is built in they are three times as large. They are perfectly safe, for the lower branches are as thick as an ordinary tree."

The lodges of the North-American Indians are perhaps the most convenient residences which could be devised for people of their

American nomadic habits. The lodge poles, or supports, are
Indian lodges. made from tough durable wood, well-grown young saplings being selected for the purpose. On the line of march they are, by fastening them to a sort of pad, secured on each side of a horse, or even dog. The ends trail on the ground like the skids of a sledge, and are packed with various odds and ends, which are prevented from falling off by cross-bars and a lashing of hide or twisted bark rope, as shown in the full-page illustration. When the camp is about being formed, the poles are freed from their attachments and set up in a circle, forming an irregular cone, the apex

INDIAN LODGES.

of which consists of the converging and collected ends of the poles, through which the smoke escapes. The lodge covers are made from prepared skins, on which are depicted, in rough outline, some of the most noteworthy achievements and events in the life of the owner. The lower borders of the skin covers are secured to the ground with pegs whilst thongs are made use of for binding the poles in their places and uniting the skins. The tracks of the trailing lodge poles in the sand, or across the plains, may be looked on by the traveller as peaceful indications, as, where the lodge gear is, the squaws and papooses will be found. On the war-path all such impedimenta are left behind in some place of safety.

The full-page illustration, representing " Indian Lodges," will serve to explain the manner in which dwelling-places of this description are set up.

Some of the natives of Terra del Fuego construct small but tolerably comfortable huts from straight trimmed poles; these are arranged in a shallow pit, the exact size of the Fuegean pole floor of the intended hut; they are arranged side houses by side in conical form, the tops of all the poles being brought together become self-supporting. All the interstices, except those where the heads of the poles come together (which form exits for the smoke), are filled in tightly with a mixture of clay and thick soft moss. Huts thus built will resist the action of the heaviest storms and are tolerably dry.

Peat, when cut in slabs or blocks makes a valuable building material. We once built a shooting house, or rather hut, near the banks of a large river with this substance. We thatched it with reeds laid over willow poles. The door was made of wicker work covered with clay; the hinges were twisted willow. The window was made of oiled paper; the fireplace was plastered with clay, and we mounted a small barrel in lieu of a chimney pot. The fuel used was peat, so there was no danger of its taking fire.

In a continuous Arctic winter the usual relations of fluids and solids are so completely changed that entirely new necessities arise, accompanied by as novel means for supplying them. Hutting in the Water, either for drinking or other purposes, is as Arctic regions. scarce as in the driest parts of India or Africa; for though in temperate countries it may be a luxury to let a piece of ice melt in the mouth, the expenditure of animal heat in thawing a mouthful of snow in the Arctic regions would be greater than even the most robust constitution could afford.

Water, in fact, unless kept in constant agitation, loses its fluidity.

T

A sheet of ice is as dry as a piece of glass, and snow seems to have no more moisture in it than the dust of the highway on a Derby day.

Owing to this quality snow does not accumulate on small surfaces elevated and exposed to the wind. Captain Parry found that from the roof of his vessel a fresh breeze invariably carried off any snow that had settled on it in calm weather, and also from the masts, yards, sails, and rigging. His opinion is that in high latitudes the less the ship is dismantled the better, for the frost does not hurt the gear, and no harm can occur from thawing till the season for refitting arrives.

Should you at any time be so situated as to be compelled to winter on board ship in the Arctic regions, it will be well to follow the plan pursued by Dr. Kane to render his ship and cabin as cold proof as possible. He procured large quantities of moss and turf, with which the quarter-deck was thickly covered. Down below he inclosed a space about 18 ft. square, and packed the walls forming it, from floor to ceiling, with the same materials. The floor was carefully caulked with plaster of Paris and common paste, on this was laid a stratum of Manilla oakum 2in. thick, and over this deposit a canvas carpet was spread. The entrance was from the hold, by a long moss-lined passage or tunnel, formed after the manner in which the Esquimaux arrange the " topsut," or rabbit-burrow like passage which leads to their huts, as shown in the illustrations at pp. 277 and 278. A number of doors and curtains were then constructed at such points as afforded a chance for the ingress of cold. This moss nest, or den, was constructed to accommodate ten men.

The outside of the ship was banked up with moss, and over that a thick bank of snow was made.

The snow, indeed, when lying in proper thickness, and sufficiently compressed, forms the best possible material for building. Cold as it is in itself, it seems to act as a non-conductor of heat; and if an internal structure, however slight, can be set up, the thicker the outer wall of snow is made the better. Captain Parry's men proceeded in the following manner: In banking the snow against the ship's sides, a wall of sufficient height was built about 4ft. from them, and loose snow was thrown in till it covered nearly the whole of the upper works; about 8in. of snow was also laid on the decks and hatches, and above this a layer of sand cemented by water for the double purpose of preventing the escape of heat from below, and saving the planks from being rifted by the frost; and the waste heat of the galley fire was utilised by making the funnel pass up through a tank, which was kept filled with snow, thus without any extra fuel producing 65galls. of water per diem. A wall of snow 12ft. high was built at a distance of 25yds. all round the ship, to afford a comfortable shelter from the wind. It is also essential to make and keep always clear of ice a 'fire-hole,' from which water can be procured at any moment in case of need.

The observatory was built on shore: first of planking lined with canvas, with a layer of turf outside, and completed by an extra thickness of solid slabs of snow; it was flat-roofed, and as small as possible, the instrument room being 8ft. square, and the working room 5ft. by 8ft., thus economising either natural or artificial heat. In fact, it seems that the primary object in building a house is to make the actual dwelling room as small as possible, and the passage to it so long and narrow, that it requires almost a long journey to reach the external air. Dr. Hayes describes a snow house, or rather cave, dug by an Esquimaux in a snow drift that had collected in a sheltered hollow. He dug downwards first about 5ft., then horizontally about 10ft. more, tossing the detached snow blocks out behind him, and then began to excavate his cabin, to which, when finished, he built a doorway just large enough to crawl through. The floor was covered with a layer of stones, and then with several layers of reindeer skins; the walls were also hung with skins; two native lamps lighted, a skin hung across the doorway, and he and his family were "at home," the temperature soon rising to the freezing point.

The doctor's temporary encampments were thus formed: A pit was dug 18ft. long by 8ft. wide and 4ft. deep; over the top were placed the oars to support the sledge; over the sledge the boat's sail, and on that was thrown loose snow. In one end of this den was a small entrance hole, closed with blocks of snow; over the floor a strip of india-rubber cloth; over this two buffalo skins, between which the whole party of twelve packed themselves as closly as possible, the only change of costume being to take off the boots and stockings and replace them with sleeping hose of reindeer skin. A pot of hot coffee, or a hash of dried meat and preserved potatoes, cooked over a lamp of oil or alcohol, forming the repast, of which the most estimable quality is its warmth. Captain Parry, being rather surprised at the short time in which an Esquimaux village sprung up near the vessel, induced some of the natives to build a hut, and found that two or three hours were enough to complete the establishment. The only materials are snow and ice the latter being only used for windows. A number of slabs of compact snow, 6in. or 7in. thick and 2ft. long, are cut and laid edgewise in a circle on a level spot, covered with snow, from 8ft. to 15ft. in diameter; on this is a second tier, sloping a little inward, each slab made to fit closely by running a knife along its edges, the top is then smoothed off with the knife, and the builder, standing in the centre, receives the slabs for the successive tiers from the men outside. When the walls are 4ft. or 5ft. high they begin to lean inward, so that it appears as if the blocks laid on them would fall; but the workman still goes on raising and closing in the hemispherical walls, and when they have become too high for the slabs to be handed over to him he cuts a hole at the bottom with his knife and has them passed through. The dome is often 9ft. or 10ft. high, and it is carefully finished by the men outside dropping the nicely rounded block that serves as a keystone,

SNOW HUT—ARCTIC REGIONS.

to be received and fitted by the man within. The outside workers heap snow round the foundations, and carefully stop up any accidental holes between the blocks. The builder lets himself out by cutting an arch 3ft. high and 2½ft. wide, and from this they construct two passages— end to end—each 10ft. or 12ft. long and 4ft. or 5ft. high, the lowest being next the hut, as shown in the outline ground plan. The roofs of these passages are sometimes arched, and at others covered with flat slabs.

If a single apartment is required the hut is now complete, but if several families are to reside together the passage is made common to all, the first hut becoming a kind of antechamber, and is commonly a little smaller than the rest, which are entered by arched doors, 5ft. high. Sometimes the ground plan assumes the form of a cross, as in the instance we now illustrate. A hole is cut into the side of each compartment, and a circular plate of ice 3in. or 4in. thick, and 2ft. in diameter, let into it. The light is like that transmitted through ground glass, and is quite sufficient.

A bank of snow, 2½ft. high, round the interior of each room, except near the door, forms the bed and fireplace, the former occupying the sides and the latter the end opposite the door. The beds are made by covering the snow with a layer of stones, on which are spare paddles, tent poles, whalebone, pieces of network, and a quantity of birch twigs, reindeer skins in profusion are heaped on these, creating not only a comfortable but a luxurious resting place.

The fireplace is a shallow vessel of stone, the wick is of moss rubbed dry between the hands, disposed along the straight edge for about 18in., it supplies itself from a long strip of blubber hung near enough to be melted gradually, and drop slowly into the hollow of the stone: over the lamp is a network, on which wet boots or mittens are usually laid. Frequently there are two other lamps in the corners next the door, for no married woman or widow can be without her separate fire.

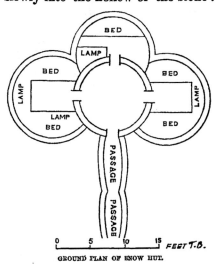

GROUND PLAN OF SNOW HUT.

With all the lamps lighted, and the room full of people and dogs, the thermometer on the net over the fire stands at 58°; 2ft. or 3ft. away it falls to 32°, close to the wall it is 23°, the temperature of the open air being at the same time 25° below zero. If the temperature is raised higher than this, the melting of the roof causes great inconvenience; but when an inclination to drip is observed, a patch of cold snow is plastered on to absorb the superfluous heat. In the time between the extreme cold of winter, and the season when it is possible to live in tents, the natives suffer much from this melting of their walls.

The cooking is done in pots of hollowed stone (*Lapis ollaris*), slung over the lamps. Many of these are cracked, but are joined by lacings of sinew, or rivets of copper, iron, or lead, which, with a sufficient coating of dirt, makes them again watertight. Their knives are sometimes of ivory, but the best are of iron, obtained from the Hudson's Bay Company.

They procure fire by striking two pieces of iron pyrites over a leather case with dried moss in it, and a little floss from the seed of

the ground willow helps to convey the flame to a bit of oiled wick—
sometimes the wick for the lamp is made of asbestos.

At times, especially in the commencement of the winter, the huts
are built of ice instead of snow. They approximate to a circular
form, but from the flatness of the material necessarily present a number
of flat sides and obtuse angles. They are cemented entirely with snow

ESQUIMAUX HUT OF ICE SLABS.

and water, and roofed with skins, which are replaced by snow as
winter advances. The entering tunnels are also of slabs of ice, as are
the kennels for bitches and puppies. The skin canoes are propped
up on slabs of ice high enough to be out of the reach of the dogs. The
semi-transparency of the walls give these huts a strange effect, and
some of our late voyagers have called them crystal palaces ; but all the
purity, either of ice or snow, disappears, and whatever cleanliness the
Esquimaux possess is forced upon them by the annual thawing of their
houses.

The summer tents are made of several seal or walrus skins, the
former without the hair, and the latter with the thick outer coat taken
off, and the rest shaved down so thin as to admit light through them.
They are irregularly sewn together, forming a kind of oval bag,
supported in the middle by a pole of several deers' horns or bones of
other animals lashed together. On the top of this is a cross or T-piece,
which serves to extend the top of the tent, 6ft. or 7ft. from the ground
the lower part of the tent pole rests loosely on a large stone, from which
any accident will knock it off. The borders of the skins are kept
down by stones laid on them, and the top is stayed by a thong on the
outer side, stretching to a heavy stone at some distance. The door is

merely two flaps, one of which overlaps the other, secured by another stone.

Sometimes a little shelter from the wind is given by an outer wall of stone.

If a larger tent is required, two of these bags are made to overlap at the edges, and are set up with a couple of poles.

The accumulation of seal and walrus flesh and blubber during the summer months makes these habitations disgustingly filthy; but it is to be remembered that the great necessity of the Esquimaux is to keep himself warm, and he cannot afford to lower the temperature of his skin by washing off the grease and dirt which encrust it.

On one experimental trip Captain Parry was compelled by a sudden decrease of temperature to shelter his party in a small tent. They attempted to warm themselves by smoking, and found the temperature at their feet to be 1° below zero, while overhead the smoke had raised it to + 7°, the outer air being − 5°, soon falling to − 15°. It was then found possible to dig a kind of cavern in the snow, the spade being lent as a favour to the men who most required to warm themselves, a small fire and a pot of soup were made, and by confining the smoke and hot air the temperature was raised to + 20°, while outside it was − 25°.

CHAPTER V.

EXTEMPORE BRIDGES AND MAKESHIFTS FOR CROSSING RIVERS OR RAVINES.

THE solitary traveller in a wild country will be very rarely compelled to construct his own bridge, for, as a general rule, he will only have to pass once, or at most to return by the same route. The labour of making a bridge would be greater, and more time would be lost, than by seeking for a practicable passage at some distant point, or, in case a river was the impediment, forming a float of some kind.

There are, however, occasions when there is no alternative but bridge-making, as when exploring expeditions, accompanied by pack animals or a field force on the march, have rivers, swamps, ravines, or, perchance, rotten ice, to pass over. Where there is not water enough to float a canoe, but where there is sufficient to cause the formation of Swamp roads, deep pools and dangerous mire, over which few ani-
to make. mals used for the conveyance of baggage could pass without the aid of some artificial footway, narrow deep channels may be very often rendered comparatively easy to cross by filling them up with bundles of brushwood or marsh reeds. We were constantly in the habit, when engaged in making forced marches through Central India, of making use of the stalks of the recently cut juhari for this purpose. Unsafe ice can be rendered firm and secure by strewing a thick layer of reeds over it, and then throwing water enough to cause the whole to freeze into a compact mass.

Before, however, proceeding to describe the various modes usually had recourse to for rendering trees available for bridging purposes, it will be well to give a few plain and practical directions for ascertaining the width of rivers, ravines, and the arms of swamps, without the aid of scientific instruments, and also for finding, by makeshift modes, the altitude of trees.

To find the Width of a River without Instruments.

Fig. 1. If you have a pocket compass, and the river runs, say east and west, and you are on the south side, choose a well defined tree, A, or other object on the opposite shore, and bring it to bear north of you; mark your position by putting in a stake or peg, B, turn to one side, say the left, and walk west-

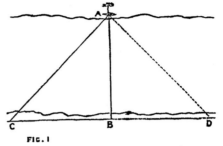

FIG. I

ward till A bears north-east, which will be the case at C; then C B will be exactly equal to B A, or the breadth of the river, because from the point C, A will bear north-east, and B will bear east, subtending an angle of 45°, and as the line C B is east, and B A is north, they subtend an angle of 90°, or a right angle, and must be of equal length; the triangle you have formed being the half of a square, divided by a diagonal line from corner to corner.

If you have room repeat this by walking east till A bears north-west from D; and if the first operation has been correctly performed, the second will confirm it; or if the first be in error, it is likely that the second will be exactly as much in error the opposite way, and the mean of the two observations will be approximately correct.

Fig. 2. If you have not a compass, choose A as before, set in a stake at B, and prolong the line to C; then on this line erect a perpendicular by looping a cord on the stake at C, and with a sharpened peg held at

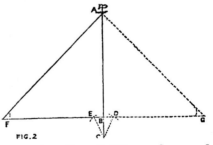

FIG. 2

the other end of it drawing the arc, D E; then, making D and E equidistant from B, draw through these three points the line D B E F; on this line retire toward F till A and B form an angle of 45°, which may be measured either by folding a square of paper diagonally, or by pegging out a piece of string divided into two lengths of 24in. and one of 32in. See that the longest or diagonal side bears truly upon A, and one of the shorter sides on B, which will take place at the point F, then F B will be equal to B A, or the breadth of the river. Repeat this also if the ground allows, on the opposite side, G, and take the mean of the two observations.

The correctness of all these observations may be greatly increased by resting your rifle on each successive point, and carefully sighting all the lines with it.

Fig. 3. Another excellent and simple plan is—choose A ; set in B ; from B erect the perpendicular B C, C D, divided equally at C ; from D erect the perpendicular D E ; retire along it till the stake C bears truly upon A, which will be at F, then F D will equal B A.

Fig. 4. If the river bank is so curved that you cannot draw B C D at right angles, you have two alternatives. If there is plenty of room retire as far as you please from the bank before planting the stake B, and deduct from the result the distance you retire from the bank.

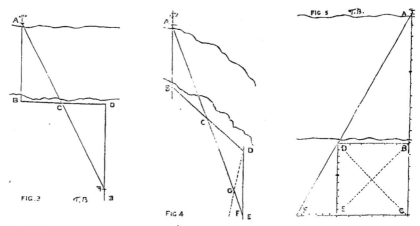

Or, if there is not room, you may draw B C D, as in Fig. 4, diagonally, and contrive to keep D E as nearly parallel to A B as you can ; but any defect in parallelism will greatly affect the correctness of your measurement, as will be evident from the dotted line G.

Fig. 5. If the river is wide, choose A as before ; set in B, and retire any measured distance, say 6yds., to C ; then from B and C erect perpendiculars of equal length, and draw the square B C, D E ; test it by stretching a cord from corner to corner ; then, prolonging the line C E, bring the stake D in one with A, and produce the line A D till it intersects C E at F ; then divide F E into six parts, measure as many of them as you can on the line E D, and you will find as many of them as there are yards on the line B A ; therefore, in the present instance, 11yds. will be the breadth of the river, and one may be deducted because the marks are not close to the edge of the banks ; or say, as E F is to E D so is B D to B A.

Fig. 6. To erect a perpendicular on a given point on any line, measure equal distances on either side ; set in pegs, loop a cord on them alternately, and strike two arcs, their intersection will be perpendicular to the given point. To cross the end of a line by another at right angles, set a peg some distance back, loop a cord on it, and strike an arc. Measure equal distances from the end of your given line to the arc, then a line drawn through the three points will be at right angles to the first.

A scale of equal parts may be made by folding a slip of paper in half, then folding each part in half, and so subdividing it as much as you wish, but do not fold it in half, and then double the two parts to get the quarters at one operation, and then double the four parts to get the eighths, or you will find them come out very unequally.

A measuring tape may be made by taking a narrow white tape, say $\frac{1}{4}$in., and winding it on a

FIG.6

slip of card barely an inch wide, just so little spirally that each turn may not half cover the preceding one, then carefully blacken the edges, and, when you unwind the tape, mark every twelfth inch with figures to denote feet, and every sixth with an extra line.

A square is made by taking a sheet of paper, folding the corner down so that the edge of the end coincides with the edge of the side, and then cutting off the superfluous length, each corner of the square is an angle of 90°, *i. e.*, a right angle or a quarter of the compass, say from north to east. The diagonal fold makes at each corner an angle of 45°, or four points of the compass, say from north to north-east; fold this again, and it will give 22½°, or two points of the compass, from north to north-north-east, and this may again be subdivided if needful.

We have often tried the breadth of rivers by firing a rifle ball at some well-defined mark on the other side, with the sight adjusted to 100yds. or more, according to the estimated distance, and noticing whether the ball reached beyond or fell short of the mark. The habit of doing this very greatly corrects and assists the eye in forming estimates of distance. A good stone thrower ought to know the range he can make with pebbles of different sizes. If a native is near buy one of his least valued arrows or spears, and get him to throw it across, and then ask him to throw a similar one on ground where you can recover it and measure the distance, but never ask a savage to throw away weapons of the chase for nothing. In calm weather, we have fired a rifle ball, with its utmost range, on the surface of a lake, and have counted seconds from the time we saw the splash till we heard the sound of its fall. Sound travels 1142ft. in a second, or about a statute mile in 4¾ seconds, or a geographical mile—or rather one minute of latitude, or of longitude *on the equator*—in 5¾ seconds.

To find, without Instruments, the Height of a Tree or other Object, whose Base is accessible.

Fig. 1. Fold down a square of paper from corner to corner, and you will obtain a triangle, of which two of the sides form a right angle, and the third, or diagonal, forms an angle of 45° with each of them (see below). Make a mark upon the tree 5ft., or the height of your eye, from the ground, and retire from the tree till, holding the paper steadily with one short side horizontal and the other vertical, you can take sight along its lower edge at the mark, and along the diagonal side at the topmost branches; then pace or measure the distance from the tree, add 5ft. for the height of the

FINDING THE HEIGHT OF A TREE BY RIFLE OR FOLDED PAPER.

eye, and you will have the height of the tree; because, if the two angles of the diagonal be 45°, the base and the perpendicular must be equal. A piece of thin board, with pins set in at each angle to serve as sights, would be better than the paper, but is not so readily extemporised. If you split the end of a wand so as to hold the paper or board quite up to the height of your eye, it will give additional steadiness. The observer in our illustration is unavoidably represented a little too near his work, but he is probably taking the height of the first bifurcation, which is often more important than the height of the tree.

Fig. 2. Or, sticking a branch into the ground, select one of its forks, or lash on a cross piece which shall pass through the trigger guard behind the trigger, so that the gun may be about the height of your eye when you aim horizontally at the mark on the tree, the trigger finger grasping the stick for greater steadiness. Take another stick, with a fork or cross rest of equal height with the first, and connect them by a smaller stick of any length, say 18in. or 2ft., and at exactly the same height above the lower rest lash another on the second stick, so that, the base and perpendicular being equal, the gun, when its muzzle is laid on the higher rest, shall form exactly an angle of 45° with its line when previously laid upon the lower one. Now retire until from the lower rest you can sight the mark upon the tree, and from the upper its highest branches; then the distance from your pivot stick, plus 5ft., will be the height of the tree. Our illustration purposely shows this operation in the simplest possible form; but the

frame might be steadied by lashing on other cross bars (X fashion), and a friend to help in moving it to a greater or less distance from the tree would greatly assist the observer. It would be inconvenient to make this observation kneeling. A telescope, a long straight reed, a roll of paper, or a  straight tube of any material, will answer almost as well as the rifle. Even a clasp knife (Fig. 3), with a bit of reed stuck into the handle where the point should reach, and resting on the point of the half-opened blade, is better than nothing.

FIG. 3

If the ground is perfectly level, and you have a looking-glass, lay it down and level it by setting on it a basin full of water; retire till you see the top of the tree reflected in it, then if your distance from the mirror equals the height of your eye, the distance from the mirror to the tree will be equal to its height. In perfectly calm weather the basin of water will do without the mirror, or a shallow pool or river will give an approximation; but, as the ground is always depressed where water settles, there will be some uncertainty about the height of the eye, which will more or less vitiate the observation, and this will also be the case if thirsty animals rush in to disturb it. Or if the sun or moon is shining, set up a stick, and watch till its shadow is equal to its height, or note when your own shadow equals your height, and the height of the tree and the length of its shadow will also be equal. But, as it may not be always convenient to wait for this moment, the height of the tree may be found by proportion. If the stick is 5ft. and its shadow 7ft., then if the shadow of the tree be 70ft., its height will be 50ft.; or if in looking at its reflection in the mirror, the height of your eye be 5ft., and the distance 8ft., then if the distance from the mirror to the tree be 80ft., its height is 50ft. In either of the first two methods the same rule must be observed; the paper may be folded to a greater angle if you cannot get far enough from the tree, or a smaller one if you must go farther, and the same with the elevation of the rifle. In these cases, carefully measure the base and perpendicular of your smaller angle, and say, " as the base of the small angle is to its perpendicular, so is the distance from the tree to its height."

Thus, as in Fig. 4, if the distance between the two rests is 2ft. and the elevation of the rifle 1ft., the distance from the tree must be

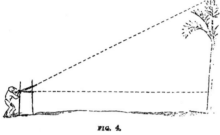

equal to double its height.

All these observations will apply to any object of which the highest point is perpendicular to the accessible base, such as a precipice, the wall of a fort, or the gable end of a house, but not to the peak of a mountain, two or three miles

FIG. 4.

beyond its base, nor to the pitched roof of a house seen sideways, nor to the spire of a church, or flagstaff on the central tower of a castle, unless the doors of these buildings be opened so that you can continue to measure your base to a point exactly beneath that of which you have taken the angular height. Still, if the base be not accessible, it is not impossible to measure the height, for the distance of the object

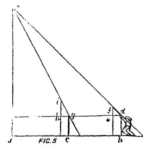

may be taken by any of the plans for ascertaining the breadth of a river, or any of the above methods may be performed twice over, as in Fig. 5; first, at any convenient distance, *b*, and secondly, at a measured distance, *c*, nearer to or farther from the object; and the easiest way of obtaining the result is to lay down on paper the obtained angles, *d*, *e*, *f*, and *g*, *h*, *i*, in due proportion to the measured

FIG. 5.

distance, *b*, *c*, between them; then from them to protract the angle, *d*, *g*, *a*, and continuing the base line, find on it the point *j*, from which a perpendicular would meet the top of the object, *a*. The distance, *b*, *c*, being known, that of the base, *b*, *j*, and the height of the tree, *j*, *a*, will be best found by measurement of equal parts, but bear in mind that the result can only be an approximation to truth, for every additional operation involves an increase of possible error.

The lumberers and backwoodsmen of North-West America adopt a useful rough-and-ready mode for ascertaining the altitude of trees. The plan is to walk off from the selected tree until its topmost branches or first fork can be viewed by look- Trees, to measure. ing backwards between the outstretched legs; a little practice serves to impart much accuracy in measurement by this plan. The distance from the trunk is the height of the tree.

CORDWAY AND ONE-TREE BRIDGE.

In passing extensive marsh tracks, few expedients surpass the so-called American cordway, the subject of the annexed illustration. It is constructed as follows from the description of material usually abounding in marsh tracks : Trees and poles of almost any description will be found to answer. Cut as many as is thought requisite. Divide them into three classes—*ground poles, cross poles*, and *stringers*. The ground poles should be the largest and heaviest. The cross poles are comparatively short lengths, and lay across the ground poles with their ends projecting some distance beyond. They are laid closely together, and then secured and bound down by the stringers which lay on them. A treenail driven in here and there serves to keep all in place by nipping the cross poles tightly. The ends of the ground poles and stringers may be either scarfed and treenailed, or laid side by side and tied with withies or strips of suitable bark. It will be seen, on examining the illustration, that where the roadway ends a bridge begins. This is of the description known as a one-tree bridge, and is made as follows : Select a tree of sufficient length to reach, when Cordway and one-tree felled, across the stream, and of fair average bridge, to make. girth, say 9ft.; fell it with the axe in the manner before directed, and then walk out on the trunk and cut away all the branches from the upper surface; then log up into lengths of about 10ft. a sufficient number of transverse pieces to reach, when placed side by side, from one end of the bridge log to the other. Then in the centre of each of these make a shallow notch by delivering right and left cuts with the axe. Next with your auger bore two holes as wide apart as the diameter of the bridge log will admit of. Lay your transverse piece on the main log, so that it shall rest in the form of a true cross, with the notch in the centre resting on the main log; then, whilst keeping the cross piece steady with one foot, bore down the auger holes about a foot into the solid timber. Treenails (see "Treenails, to make") are then to be placed in the holes and driven home with a mallet or the head of the axe.

Another form of tree-nailed bridge, calculated for very wet or dangerously swampy ground, is formed by laying down two lines of stouter ground logs than those used to form the Swamp bridge, "cordway" just described, scarfing and tree-nailing to make. the ends together as they are laid down. The transverse bars for the footway have a right and left chip taken out each end from the surface which is to lay next the ground log. They are then bored with the auger, one hole at each end being sufficient. They are

TREE-NAILED SWAMP BRIDGE.

then placed closely side by side. One man completes the hole which passes down into the log, whilst another drives home the treenails, as shown in the annexed illustration. Earth or sand thrown with a shovel between the cross pieces increases the stability of the arrangement.

Treenails have been, and will be, frequently mentioned in the course of this work; it will, therefore, be well here to give directions for making and using them. To the shipwright they are Treenails, invaluable, as by their aid he unites the various planks to make. and timbers made use of in the carrying out of his art. In England they are usually made from straight-grained oak, which, after being sawn into proper lengths, is split up into the rough form of the required treenail. This, after being faced and hewn with the adze, is passed through a double-handed cutting instrument known as a treenail tool. A skilfully-handled axe, a spokeshave, or a drawing knife, will, although less expeditiously, produce with ease well rounded and serviceable treenails. In wild countries any tough straight-grained wood may be selected for treenail making. For bridge and roadway work pine wood will answer the purpose very fairly. A dead log is best when it can be obtained for making these wooden holdfasts. Cut it up into pieces the length of the proposed treenail, chop off the bark, and split them into either three or four (as directed at p. 239), according to the size of the log; then, with the *froe* or axe, split them into rough squares the length of the required treenail, round off the curves and corners, chop off the edges at the end, so that it may enter the auger hole freely, and the treenail is ready for use.

Many of the Lapland fens and marshes we have traversed would be impassable without the aid of "spong" roads. These are formed by placing good sized pine poles or young fir trees end to The spong end, and in the line of direction to be travelled over. Two road. sticks with round, wooden, bung-like discs fitted to their ends, are usually used as a means by which the traveller balances himself in walking; some little practice is required before a rapid pace can be attempted safely, as the feet have to be turned out right and left, just as they are in tight-rope dancing. The Lapland boots, described under the head of foot gear, are far better adapted for "spong" walking, than the hard-soled stiff foot coverings known as "shooting boots." Many of these "spong" ways are over a quarter of a mile in length, and traverse fens of unknown depth and dangerous instability.

Rivers which are too wide to be crossed by the one-tree bridge, and yet of inconsiderable breadth, may be crossed by the use of the gabion bridge, which is thus constructed: First, Gabion bridge, prepare as many strong wicker gabions as the width to make. of the stream will render necessary. About 14ft. apart will be found a convenient distance to place them. Their height will depend on the depth of the water. Three feet at least should be

υ

allowed between the surface of the stream and the upper edge of the gabion. Where suitable poles and sticks for gabion making cannot be obtained trees should be felled and split up, as for rails (see p. 240). The bars thus obtained should be cut up into proper lengths, and, by the use of the axe and auger, converted into large deep crates, such as are used for packing earthenware. These are made by boring rows of auger holes in strong wooden bars, and then driving the sharpened ends of the lesser bars into them until the crate is finished, no nails or metal fastenings being required. Whether the crate or gabion is used, the principle of construction

GABION BRIDGE.

observed in making the bridge is the same. The first gabion, after being secured to the end of a stout rope, is launched from the bank, and then guided, end upward, by the aid of forked setting poles, to its proper position. Stones, pebbles, or pieces of broken rock, are now cast pell-mell by hand into the open mouth of the gabion, which is held down by the setting pole until fixed in its position by the weight of the mass within it. When quite full two or three stout poles are laid side by side for a man to walk over. He takes up his station on the gabion, and aids in arranging the ends of two side logs which are pushed out to him from the shore, and placed wide enough apart to give sufficient width to the intended bridge. Transverse bars formed of split logs are now rapidly tree-nailed on, as shown in the accompanying illustration. The second gabion is now launched from the first, the stone collectors with bags and baskets walk out, cast their loads, and return for more, proceeding in the same manner until the bridge is finished.

When travelling among the Tartars we had on more than one occasion to pass our mules and horses over rather insecure-looking bridges formed by the natives. They were alike in construction, and were made by laying three long strong poles, or rather small tree trunks, side by side from bank to bank. Across these alternately (butt-end and top), as shown in the engraving, was laid a close row of tightly-bound bundles or faggots of small brushwood. On these bundles of twigs, large flat slabs of turf, grass side upward, were placed and stamped compactly down, forming serviceable and really good bridge ways.

Tartar bridge, to make,

A small river can be easily crossed by men on foot by simply felling a tree of sufficient girth and length across it. Should there be a number of packs or loads to pass across, it will be well, if the party is a large

TARTAR POLE AND FAGGOT BRIDGE.

one, to so station men along the tree trunk that they can pass the bundles or articles from hand to hand, just as firemen hand buckets of water, thus saving unnecessary labour. A rope stretched across greatly aids the men in keeping their balance.

We, on one occasion, when encamped on the banks of a large Indian river, were called on to provide for the immediate transport of a battery of field guns, waggons, horses, &c., to the opposite side. Some large native boats were procured, but they, even when empty drew so much water, that they could not be made to approach within some distance of the shore. We therefore felled two trees, which fortunately stood side by side, letting their crowns fall from the bank, well out into the stream. We soon foraged out three large dug-out canoes, which were concealed among the reeds hard by. These, with our own axe, and those of two stalwart-limbed gunners, we split into lengths of uneven plank. Whilst we were doing this, a party had been at work forcing down large heavy branches between the two tree trunks, and on these compactly-bound faggots of brushwood (which a number of natives attached to the expedition prepared close at hand) were rammed and stamped down. The boards procured by cutting up the canoes were arranged side by side on this

Extempore jetty, to build.

bed, their ends being secured by burden ropes knotted together and hitched over them, as shown at Fig. 1, p. 259. We now employed the natives in throwing buckets and bags of earth and sand thickly over and between the planks. Over this extempore jetty—which reached out to the boats, on some of which platforms had been erected—all our battery, consisting of two 12-pounder howitzers and four 6-pounder guns, with all their equipment, passed in perfect safety. The work was not commenced until late in the afternoon, and all had crossed long before morning.

The Japanese form dams and strengthen river banks by the employment of long narrow cylinders or tubes of about 2ft. in diameter, and composed of split bamboos and other canes. These are woven into a sort of coarse network. On completion these basket pipes are filled with water worn pebbles piled on each other, and then secured by crossed poles, as shown in the accompanying illustration.

Stone ropes.

It not unfrequently happens that there is greater difficulty in transporting the baggage of an expedition across a river than in getting over the men and animals. This was the case in the following instance. We were exploring the Victoria River, in North Australia, when we came to a branch of one of its tributaries (Jasper Creek) so much swollen that it was unsafe to attempt crossing it with loaded horses. We found, however, a passage to an island, on which stood a couple of tall overhanging gum trees. We had with us several fathoms of Manilla line, about ½in. in diameter, this was passed over a fork of one of the highest and most projecting branches. Mr. Gregory swung himself across, we followed; and while our head stockman, with a fatigue party of five horses, brought the packs to the island, one man lifted the pack that had been bent on to the line as high as possible; another gave an extra pull upon the other part to lift it as clear of the water as possible during its passage, letting go by the run as it swung to the other shore, where one of the party stood ready to catch the pack, while we, making a sharp run with a small line, helped it across, and checked any tendency to swing back again. In this manner we brought over a ton and a half of provisions and stores in between two and three hours; the unloaded horses found a practicable ford a little higher up.

Extempore baggage derrick.

Sometimes the interlacing of overhanging branches answered our purpose; or we found it possible to fell a tree so that its head might fall on the other shore, or into the water pointing up stream, so that it would drift and jam against the opposite bank.

Tree footways.

On another occasion, coming to the Lua, a tributary of the Zambesi, rushing through a narrow place, we went to the edge of the forest, and with a small tomahawk cut down the best tree we could find, and, assisted by three or four Makololo, carried it to the brink, raised it, and let it fall across.

In many of the colonial streams it is necessary to provide the means of passage, for the fords may be inconveniently far apart. In such cases the general expedient is to purchase the chain cables of some wrecked ship, and stretch them across, securing the ends either to stout posts or bars wedged into clefts in the rocks, or to tolerably broad surfaces of timber buried 6ft. or 8ft. in the earth. Of course strong purchases are required to stretch the chains, especially if the distance between the river banks is great; but the buyer would most likely take care also to provide himself, when he obtained the chains, with a pair of large double blocks with iron-hooked straps, and twenty or thirty fathoms of stout rope; so that, when such a tackle is hooked on, and the fall made fast to the trek gear of a span of well-trained oxen, the chain must come or something give way.

Chain bridges, to construct.

Two parts of the chain must be stretched so as to assume perfectly parallel curves, and on these the planks for the roadway are laid, the lashings passing conveniently through the links and preventing any possibility of slipping; other chains or ropes are stretched as hand-rails, and for the supports of these it is a good plan to cut young trees, say 12ft. long, sling them about 4ft. from the top, and fasten them to the chain, so that the upper part will support the rope, while the 8ft. of butt hanging below serves as a counterpoise to keep it upright. This, however, must depend on the height of the bridge; for if the water catches any part of it during the rainy season, there is great danger of the whole being swept away; and it is therefore advisable to make all the fittings as light as is consistent with the safety of passengers, so that in case of extraordinary floods they may be swept off before they communicate strain enough to break the chain—just as the masts of a vessel ought to be of such strength as to be carried away before they capsize the ship. We have seen a bridge built of planks and trestles, very slightly fastened together, but every part was moored by a long line to one or other of the banks.

The whole affair would go to pieces when the floods came, and when
they subsided the pieces were hauled in, and the bridge reconstructed.
In broader rivers the chain is carried across, and a barge is built
Fly bridges
and ferries. with a winch at either end, round the barrels of which
a turn of the chain is taken; the waggon about to cross
is drawn upon the platform by two or more of its own oxen, the
winches are hove round, and the oxen draw the waggon up the other
shore, without even having been unyoked during the passage.

In strong rapid streams an anchor and cable is laid high up the
stream, and the lower end terminates in a bridle. The boat is alike at
either end, and when about to leave the shore the end of the bridle
which happens to be forward is gathered in, while the after one is some-

FLYING FERRIES.

what slackened. The boat shoots over to the other shore, and is kept
there by the force of the stream, so long as the bridle nearest the
bank keeps her head more up than the farther one allows her stem
to be. To bring her back again, haul in that which is farthest from
the shore; slack off the other, and she will recross the river as if of
her own volition.

The same may be effected by means of the rudder. Have a short
mast, to which the cable is attached just high enough to clear the
heads of passengers, &c., and about one-fourth or one-third from the
bows. Then, if the boat be lying on the right bank of the river, her
port side will be to the shore; and as long as the helm is to
starboard, or away from the shore, the rudder will incline the boat's
head inward, and the force of the stream will keep her there. But
put the helm aport, her head will fall off, she will shoot over to the left

bank, and remain there. In fact, this flying bridge, or ferry,—for it partakes of the nature of both—acts in the water on the very same principle that a kite does in the air. The line being made fast, not to the stem of the boat, but to a point about one-third aft, would allow her to ride straight on end with the stream only so long as by careful steering her head was kept exactly to it; but the moment an inclination is made, by putting the helm, say "aport," the boat's head inclines to starboard; she receives the stream upon her port side, which should make an angle of about 22° with the line of the current, and she at once

WIRE ROPE FERRY.

sheers to starboard or to the left bank—remembering always that in speaking of a river, the observer is supposed to face down stream, and the banks are named as they are on his right or left hand. A wire rope ferry of this kind is stretched across the united rivers "Moola Moola" and "Moola Moota," near Poona. We have crossed by it often, and found it to answer admirably.

Sometimes it may be of importance to bridge a ravine, which, though not impassable for an active man, is difficult for average passengers. The first requisite is to get a line across. If the nearest bank is a precipice a man may be lowered down with a rope, and he may then climb the opposite cliff, taking the rope with him; but if the farthest bank is precipitous also the case is more difficult, as the rope will not help him to ascend. Perhaps by walking up or down the bed of the gorge while his friends above follow him with the rope, he may find a practicable route; or another party may be sent many miles up or down to find a crossing, and, by lowering another rope, haul him up with the first still fast.

If neither of these plans is possible, a stone or leaden weight may
Line slings and be slung over with a small line, much as sailors heave
lobsticks. the lead. We usually employ for this purpose a contrivance known among hunters as a " squailer," or " lobstick."

There are several ways of making a lobstick ; the best, perhaps, being
those represented by Figs. 2 and 3 in the engraving below. An oval
ball of lead, with a hole through the centre, and about 6oz. in weight, is

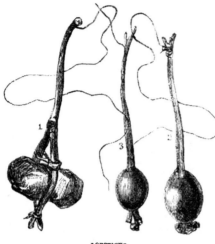

prepared. A strong, tough,
and slightly flexible stick is
now fitted to the hole in the
lead, in which it is held by a
wedge driven into its cleft
end. A long light line, either
twine or fishing line, is now
coiled evenly down on the
bank, one end is firmly knotted
to the extremity of the handle
of the lobstick, and the other
to a peg driven into the
ground. The end of the stick
where the twine is made fast
is now held lightly in the hand

LOBSTICKS.

with the ball downwards ; two
or three rapid and powerful turns round the head are now taken in
such a way as to cause the stick to bend. It is then hurled, at a good
elevation, across the stream or gorge, where a man who has previously
crossed is waiting for it. The string once across, a rope
attached to it follows. No one unacquainted with the
use of these implements would believe that they could be
thrown to the incredible distances which they at times
reach. Fig. 1 is an extempore lobstick, made by splitting
the handle, inserting a pebble or suitable stone, and then
lashing the divided stick fast with twine. The Swedes
Swedish make use of a very handy little con-
throwing bag. trivance for casting a light line ashore,
or from one vessel to another. A little flat oval bag is

SWEDISH THROWING
BAG.
made from canvas, looped at one end with rope, filled
with fine sand, and then sewn up. When in use it is
attached to the end of the line by a common knot. The inner end of
the rope is coiled down in the usual way, and the bag, after being
turned two or three times round the head, is cast at the object to be
reached. In throwing a rope against the wind, the sand bag is of

great help. Fig. 4 in the preceding page shows the form of the arrangement. A line may be sent over also by an arrow or rocket, taking care that the attachment is made with wire or raw hide, so that it may not be burned through. Or, if the ravine be wide, it may be carried over by a kite, and if materials are at hand this kite may be made large enough to carry a man also. There is no fear of the kite line breaking. If there is rope enough to make a bridge, there must be enough to fly a kite strong enough to carry a man.

The communication being effected by any of these means, the next thing is to haul ropes of increasing weight and power across till they are strong enough to haul over the actual cables, and these may be made of various indigenous materials: the bark of Makeshift fastenings. the mimosa, of the baobab, and other trees; the fibre of yucca or aloe leaves, or, still better, of those of the *Phormium tenax*; bush vines,

bind weed, or creeping plants; rattans, grass, or strips of palm leaf, may be twisted into ropes; or poles of any straight wood, of nearly even thickness, may be cut and used as links of a chain, by being strongly, yet somewhat loosely, attached to each other by shorter links of rope. Sometimes, if a hole be cut in the butt of one tree, the young

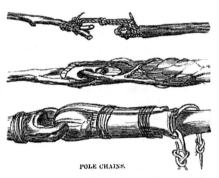

POLE CHAINS.

branches of another will be found pliant enough to pass through it, and weave around the stem and the few forks that may be left on it for that purpose.

Bamboo may be partially cut away nearly up to a joint, leaving long strips on either side, which being doubled back on themselves form excellent links; or they may be split up and spliced together like the strands of a rope; and, from the great number of very small, long, and pliant branches growing from every joint, bamboo offers great facility for the attachment of other fastenings at every foot of its own length.

The cables having been stretched across and securely fastened, the next requisite is the construction of the roadway. If bamboo is the material, the large stems may be cut into lengths of Cane and twig roadway. about 5ft., and split into four, giving pieces of, perhaps, from 4in. in width; these should be laid with the convex side upwards, projecting about 1ft. beyond the cables on each side, and securely lashed to them—the small shoots already mentioned will very materially assist this process. If smaller bamboo is about to be used, it can be split into three or four parts, or put in place without splitting. Small ropes should be provided as hand rails or safety lines, and these must be confined to the sides of the bridge by upright stancheons about 3ft.

CABLE AND TWIG BRIDGE.

or 4ft. high, and placed tolerably close together. Twig ropes stretch very unequally in use.

Rattans and creepers are often of very great length, and pieces 100yds. long, and not above 1½in. in thickness, may be disentangled in the forest. These can be utilised in a variety of ways. Sometimes a roadway is made of short pieces of wood suspended at either end from the cables, but in this case the amount of small line required is greater; and, what is of more importance, the safety of the traveller depends at every step on the fastening of the piece he treads on, while in the former case, even if the fastening were insecure, the cable would support his weight. Besides this, in order that they may not swing apart, every piece must be lashed to its neighbour; and it seems more safe and economical to build the roadway on the cables, and stretch lighter ones above them for safety lines.

If the ravine is not very broad, a tree, such as the stem of a tall palm, which will often be 60ft. high, and 1ft. in thickness; or a bamboo, which will be sometimes 80ft. or 90ft., may be raised, and secured by stays and guys in a vertical position; or, still better, two may be lashed together as shear legs and then raised. If the ground is good this need not be done at the very edge of the cliff, for when once the shears are nearly upright, smooth planks may be put under the butts of the spars, and they may be pushed or hauled in any direction.

Bridge shears, to construct.

If men can find a passage to the other side, and carry over some of the stays and guys there, the work will be much facilitated. If not, make another pair of shears exactly like the first, and lay them horizontally on the ground, with their butts resting against and fastened to those of the upright ones; let the stays come to the head of these, slack them a little till the uprights incline forward 20° or 30° over the gulf, then keep all fast, and allow the horizontal shears to rise as the others are lowered, keeping a check upon them all the while, until the first are laid fairly across.

If the gulf is wide, this operation might be carried on from both sides till the shears meet, and could be secured together in the middle, as in our illustration; and the roadway could then be constructed between them.

BRIDGE SHEARS.

When vessels first went to the island of Ichaboe for guano, it was customary to require every new comer to bring two or three stout spars for the purpose of extending the landing jetty; and as each had the benefit of the spars left by former vessels, Guano stages at Ichaboe. so each was expected to leave her own for the use of those who followed.

Owing to the irregularity of the rocky bottom, thickly covered with seaweed, the depth of water, and the distance from shore at which the surf began to break, all the ordinary methods of constructing a jetty were impracticable, especially when the object of each captain was to load his vessel as quickly and easily as possible, and to get away without expending the labour of his crew on works more than sufficient for his own service. Besides this, even had holes been bored, piles driven, and a staging laid down upon them, the platform, if permanently spiked down, would inevitably have been torn up by the surf in even a moderate gale; or, if loosely laid, would have been liable to such constant derangement as to be practically useless. It was necessary, therefore, that the base, while strong enough to support the traffic, should present little or no surface for the waves to act upon, and that the roadway should be so elevated that breakers could not touch it. Even under these conditions, it was found that the first structures were washed away, and other forms had to be adopted; these could only be built on the north and east sides of the island; they were not less than 200ft. or 300ft. in length, and seldom or never in a straight line.

A heavy bower anchor, sometimes weighted by several lengths of chain frapped round it, was laid down well outside the surf, with one or two fifteen fathom lengths of chain, and to the end of this a stout hawser was bent on and carried to the shore, passing over and lashed to the intersection of a pair of stout poles set up as shears, and with its shore end leading to another anchor or secure fastening, to which, when the structure was completed, it could be tightly set up by means of tackles.

The first pair of shears having been erected, it was comparatively easy to erect others, and often as many as a dozen or sixteen pairs were fixed, the hawser passing over and serving as a ridge rope to them all. At about 12ft. above high water smaller spars were lashed fore and aft, so as to connect all the shear legs on either side through the whole length of the jetty, and others were laid across and well secured by cleats and lashings between each pair of legs, with some at shorter intervals, on which the roadway was constructed of planks and spars, sometimes nailed, but more generally securely lashed. At the end of this staging was a small platform, slung by tackles to the outermost pair of shears, and capable of being raised or lowered, so that boats might lie alongside it either at high or low water.

GUANO STAGE AND FLYING RAILWAY AT ICHABOE.

Other vessels, not so well provided with spars as to entitle them to share in the accommodation of these stages, adopted a kind of flying

The flying railway. railway, such as is used on the rocky coast of the Cape Verdes for the shipment of salt. A stout spar, 40ft. or 50ft. long, or sometimes, if the vessel was totally unprovided, her own mainboom was taken ashore. Smaller spars. were set up as shears, and by these the large one was erected, and stayed in a perpendicular position as a derrick. The heaviest bower anchor, with several fathoms of chain, was laid outside the surf, in thirty or forty fathoms of water. A stout hawser was bent on to the end of the chain, carried to the derrick head, and hitched round it or otherwise secured; and the shore end was extended inland toward another anchor, to which it was hauled taut by a powerful tackle. Another tackle served to raise the guano bags to the derrick head, and on the hawser travelled a large snatch or natch block (so called because one of its sides is notched to admit any part of a line, the end of which cannot conveniently be reeved through). A man, seated on a kind of cross-tree, would pass the hook of the travelling block into the slings of the bags when they were hoisted, and would detach the hook of the tackle, and the bags were eased down to the boat lying out, where the hawser nearly reached the sea by a stout line passing through a single block at the derrick head. Generally, the travelling block alone had to be brought back; but if provisions or other stores were to be landed, they were hooked on before it returned. Passengers would be landed or embarked in the same manner; sometimes in a stout basket, or in a cask cut into the fashion of an arm-chair; but more generally, in disdain of such luxuries, in the loops of a double bowline—the bolder spirits glorying in being let go by the run, and gliding down the hawser just as the Russians do in their sledges on artificial ice hills.

It will often happen that in the erection of some makeshift contrivance, or the laying out of a ground plan for future operations some rough and ready mode of levelling will be needed.

The Dutch African farmers use a very simple and effective level in laying out water furrows for the irrigation of their farms, and, when it Levelling. is understood that even on very favourable ground these furrows are often two miles long, it will be seen that some little engineering is required. They take a table, the longer the better, and having tested its surface by the eye, and by lines stretched across, they place on each end a large basin filled to the brim with water. When these are perfectly full without overflowing, the sight is taken over them at a staff set up upon the next station, and the height of the mark on this, less the height of the table and basin, gives the difference of level.

We had a tube of tin 4ft. long and 1in. diameter, with two pieces of glass tube bent upward, passing through corks in either end, so that, by using water coloured with charcoal, or mud, we could at once observe the true level. A long bamboo or reed, closed at the ends, but open in all its intermediate length, will do just as well, and there is no necessity that it should be straight. Smaller pieces of reed, 3in. or 4in. long, should be set up in each end, and the bore of these must be

SOUTH-AFRICAN LEVELLING TABLE.

large enough to allow the water to flow freely to its natural level. The top of these may be notched for sights like those of a rifle, or sliding

DEODAR BEAM BRIDGE.

sights may be fitted on the side of them. This instrument may be used for taking vertical angles by fixing the eyesight upon a pivot, marking the place of the foresight on the staff, when the level has been taken; then pouring away the water, sighting the top of the object, marking the elevation upon the staff, and then either drawing the obtained angle on paper, or taking the difference between the base and perpendicular, and then working out the result by the rule of three.

One of the bridges over the Sutlej is formed of lengthy deodar cedar Deodar bridges. beams, supported at either end by piers formed of very strong timbers wedged for half their length in the solid rock, the next timbers overlapping those on which they rest by 2ft. or 3ft., these in turn being overlapped by others, till the space between is so much diminished, that it can be spanned by the long deodar beams.

The Jhula, or rope bridge, has a kind of seat slung to it capable of being hauled to and fro by lines to either bank, and the live stock, as well as the baggage of passengers, is secured to this and sent across. Other bridges are made of ropes of birch twigs, two of which are stretched across from rude piers, upon the banks. and Rope Bridges from these hangs, cradle like, a continuous hurdle of the same frail material serving as a footway, and attached to the ropes by a sort of open basket work, a couple of smaller ropes stretched

INDIAN ROPE BRIDGE.

beneath helping to support the roadway. This apparently, by its own weight and the unequal stretching of its parts, soon gets out of order, and the passage is a somewhat hazardous feat (see illustration, p. 298).

Sometimes the rivers are crossed on deris, or skins of bullocks, which are thus prepared: One cut is made along one hind leg, the skin is then turned forward and stripped off uncut, Deris, to make. except at the hocks and knees; it is buried a few days to facilitate the removal of the hair; it is then again turned inside out, and the openings of the eyes, mouth, &c., sewn up; it is then turned back again, and the incision stitched together with thongs of raw hide; the open ends of the limbs are tied, except one, which is left as a tube to inflate the skin; the thin tar of the deodar, or other pines, is poured in and shaken about till the flesh side is well charged with it, and the outside is tanned with an infusion of pomegranate husks.

A double cord is fastened round the inflated skin, across which the waterman lies on his chest, holding the string with his left hand and working a short paddle with the right, assisting himself also with his feet. The passenger, with as much baggage as he can carry, sits astride on the ferryman's back, with his knees on the skin. When

PLANK ARCH.

heavy goods are to be carried, two skins are brought together, each man laying hold of a projecting leg of the other skin, and a frame —often of a "charpai," or Indian bedstead — is laid upon their backs to receive the load. Horses or mules are made to swim, the ferryman leading them by the halter. The appearance of the inflated skin when carried by the waterman, is most ludicrous (see p. 295) ; but when the air is let out it packs very conveniently. It is exceedingly serviceable, costs about 3s., and weighs about 16lb.

Very neat and effective bridges may be made on the rafter principle, which our engraving at p. 268 will sufficiently illustrate. The roadway,

Rafter, plank, and slab bridges. either horizontal, as in Fig. 1, or with more or less rise in the centre, as in Fig. 3, being supported by the king-posts, a tolerably broad river may be spanned by a bridge supported on latticed-worked sides, like a number of XXXX's set up without intervening spaces; but this would require skilled workmanship and secure fastening. Arches of great strength may be made of thin planks laid one upon another; a dozen inch planks would thus give an arched beam 1ft. in thickness, and when properly

CHINESE SLAB AND TRESTLE BRIDGE.

clamped, or bound together, exceedingly strong. This beam may be easily lengthened, no joining or scarfing of the individual planks is required, their ends may simply butt against each other ; but care must be taken that no two joints come even nearly together, or much of the strength will be thrown away.

Many Chinese bridges are constructed with slabs of stone, set up much in the same manner as those at Stonehenge. A number of bridges of this description, formed entirely of granite, are to be seen on the Cornish moors.

An Indian army was once sent to act against an enemy accustomed to a colder clime. A broad river checked the advance of the Indians, who had to remain day after day shivering from cold which their enemies bore with impunity; but their leader observed that ice was forming on the river, and, though the strong current kept the centre clear he found a place some miles below the hostile camp where it had nearly united. By pushing forward poles and faggots into the water he made a nucleus on which fresh ice was formed, and before morning he had sufficiently bridged the river to allow of the passage of a few men who held their position till the rest could cross.

In fording deep and rapid streams, the tendency of the body to float greatly diminishes the power to resist the force of the current. We have seen a short and compactly built man, struggling against this difficulty, when a couple of tall aborigines came to his assistance, and with mistaken zeal put their hands under his   Hints on arms to hold him up, till he explained that he   fording rivers. wanted them rather to press upon his shoulders and keep him down. A detachment of our troops found themselves before a ford where the stream was deep and strong, and while they hesitated, the tall guide picked up a heavy stone, placed it on his head, and walked safely through. It is to be remembered, however, that the ford which is safe for the first man is not always so for the last. An ancient general attempted the passage of a river, but the trampling of the men and horses loosened the sand, the stream swept it away, reinforcements were unable to come up, the advance was beaten, and in attempting to recross the river, numbers were drowned, owing to the increase in the depth of water.

In most countries native paths will lead to the practicable fords, and very frequently villages will be established near them, so that information and guides may generally be obtained. In the Cape colony, people who live near the drifts or fords of large rivers frequently keep spans or teams of powerful oxen for the sole purpose of drawing the waggons of travellers across, and these are generally led by some stout young fellow on a horse that is also well accustomed to the locality. It will often happen in the course of exploration that the traveller will have to find the shallow places for himself. Reefs, or edges of strata, running across the river are, of course, obvious enough, but to find moderate shallows in a river of more even depth is not quite so easy; the best way, therefore, is to follow the windings, bearing in mind generally it is better to seek up the river than down where fresh tributaries increase it. In all the hollows where the stream impinges strongly upon the banks they are generally very steep, with considerable depth of water, while the points will be found to slope downwards with shoals extending from them, and there is generally an eddy or return current on the upper side; therefore, if a point can be found, with another somewhat below it on the other side, a ford may reasonably be looked for, especially if the width between the points seems greater than usual. A ford seldom leads straight across a river, and there is little use in looking for one in a hollow or under a steep bank.

Mr. Percival, who has travelled much in Abyssinia, tells us that he used what he calls portable inclines to facilitate the passage of his long and heavily-laden mule trains over difficult places, especially such as the perpendicular edges of stratified rock 2ft. or 3ft. in thickness, which to laden mules would be as impassable as precipices of a thousand times the height. To

Abbyssinian mule platforms.

PORTABLE INCLINES USED IN ABYSSINIA.

obviate this difficulty, he employed one or more mules in carrying roughly-made platforms of stout poles about 10ft. long, with others lashed across them, ladder fashion, so as to present a surface of about 10ft. by 2ft. It would be the duty of the drivers of these mules to have, at least, one of them well to the front in anticipation of any difficulty; the platform would then be laid down, the train would walk over it and pass on, leaving it in the rear to be loaded up again and brought on, while one of the other platform mules would pass to the front in order to be ready for the next difficulty.

The length of these would depend on the height of ledge of rock to be mounted. Suppose the strata were 3ft. in thickness, then a platform of 4ft. 6in. would present a surface lying at an angle of 45°, while one of 7ft. 6in. would lie at 22° ; this, for short distances, would not be at all a difficult incline either to descend or to climb, and platforms of 10ft. would give plenty of spare end to rest on the supporting edges, and would not be very inconvenient in carriage. Mr. Percival says he has made them of wattled or hurdle work from 12ft. or 15ft. up to 24ft. in length, and yet so light that one mule has carried two of them; and in following what are called the torrent roads, at the bottom of deep ravines, these would come into requisition at every few hundred yards.

Besides the modes of crossing rivers or ravines before described, there are various methods of passing over comparatively narrow impediments to the onward journey. A chance tree, storm-felled across the stream or gully, not Natural bridges. unfrequently affords the requisite footway without the expenditure of labour. There are, however, localities in which old hollow logs, cast in this manner across water, are to be looked on with some degree of suspicion, as the following incident of travel will serve to show : An old friend of ours chanced one day to arrive much

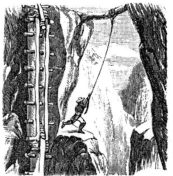

MINERS' SWING AND LADDER.

fatigued at the brink of a tropical stream, which had one of these natural bridges thrown by some storm across it. Before passing over, he lit his fire, cooked his food, and indulged in a quiet smoke ; happening to cast his eye along the fallen tree trunk, he perceived something of rather sinister appearance, in slow motion, on its surface. On looking more closely, he saw a huge python, half in and half out of a hole in the log, apparently enjoying the rays of the mid-day sun. The bark of the tree near to the bank, on which our friend was sitting, was worn quite smooth by the passage of numerous animals, and there is no doubt that this formidable toll collector had long enjoyed the monopoly of his tree bridge. Our friend selected another crossing place less carefully guarded. Small streams, or the narrow channels of swamps, may be Leaping poles. easily and expeditiously crossed by the aid of the leaping pole. Tall bamboos or tough, straight, well-grown poles are suitable for the purpose. In soft fen ground, it is a good plan to shoe the bottom of the pole with a piece of flat, strong wood, formed somewhat after the manner of a half ball, with a hole in the middle for the reception of the end of the pole.

In exploring the cliffs at the edges of ravines, the metal seeker not unfrequently swings himself from ledge to ledge by the aid of a rope attached above, as shown in the engraving on page 307. The cliff climbers, who search for the eggs of sea-fowl, roam about at times in much the same manner.

In descending from points of danger, where a leap for life affords the only hope of escape, advantage may be taken of the contrivance

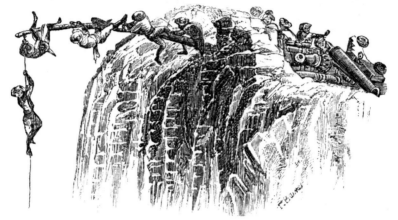

INDIAN ESCAPE POLE.

which was used by the rebels at Kotah, in India, during the mutiny. They, on being pushed hard by our troops, who had gained possession of the approaches to their fortified works, within the town, bolted like rabbits in a warren, and made for an embrasure, or rather casement, in one of the bastions of the outer wall; from this they thrust out a strong, but flexible bamboo pole, from the end of which a rope depended. The inner end of the bamboo was secured by heavy weights being placed on it. The fugitives worked their way out by clinging under the pole, until they in turn reached the rope at the end, when they slid down to the end, and then dropped off into the dry ditch. Judging from the immense height of the bastion, and the rocky nature of the ground, we should have had but faint hopes of escape with life; but there is little doubt that many who braved the peril of the fall escaped more or less injured. We had no

Makeshift ladders. means at hand of measuring the bamboo, but should judge it roughly at 40ft. The above illustration will serve to show the manner in which it was made use of. Not far from the bastion just referred to we found a number of Indian scaling ladders. They were much in appearance like large bamboo hurdles. The canes composing them were bound at their intersections with strips of twisted cane. They were, for their size, remarkably light; and the nature of the material of which they were constructed, and the way in which they were put together, made them immensely strong. A number of men abreast might have ascended them easily. There are many forms of makeshift ladders, amongst which, perhaps the following are the most noteworthy. The ordinary rope ladder is too well known to need more than a passing comment. The rope and batten ladder is perhaps not quite so well known, but is far more easy to mount and dismount; its form

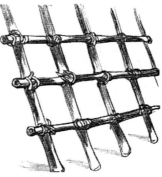

INDIAN SCALING LADDER.

is shown at A in the accompanying illustration. Two strong chains, and a set of suitable sized bars, form a very useful kind of ladder, much in use among miners; its mode of arrangement is shown at B in the annexed illustration. In South America and some other countries, the notched log ladder is much used both in mining and surface operations. It is, as its name implies, a log notched deeply to re- ceive the feet and hands of the climbers. Another form of log ladder is made by boring a row of auger holes at equal distances, say 2ft. apart, and then driving

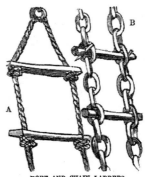

ROPE AND CHAIN LADDERS.

long stout treenails through them, so that each end of the treenail may project beyond the side of the log, for a hand and foot hold. Long forked branches may have their lateral shoots cut off at convenient distances apart, so as to form a footway of short prongs. A row of spikes or treenails may be driven into the side of a cliff, a wall, or the trunk of a tree to climb up by. The natives of many wild countries adopt this method, about which we shall have more to say when the subject of tree-climbing is under consideration.

PEG, BRANCH, AND LOG LADDERS.

There are times when the principle of the common step-ladder might be advantageously remembered; and a traveller who expected to have much climbing might have one of those in which a groove is run in the inside of each standard, and the rungs, working on pivots, are shut up into it, the whole forming a light and compact pole, which a man might easily carry on his shoulder. It would, however, be cheaper and better to purchase this at home than to make it abroad. A rope and batten ladder is more easily made. The rope is double, an eye is turned in to the bight, holes are bored in the ends of the steps or rungs, the ends of the rope are passed through, and double knots turned on to keep each step in place. A light ladder, either of this kind or that previously described, with a coil of rope to fling over the lower branches, would enable a botanist or collector of birds or insects to climb many trees otherwise inaccessible.

In case of fire in a town, if anything—say the end of a sofa or part of a bed frame—could be projected only 1ft. or 2ft. from a window, and weighted by a chest of drawers on its inner end, it would form what persons unskilled in climbing so much require—a clear point of departure; and the blankets, sheets, and coverlets torn into strips of not less than 4in. or 6in. wide, and twisted into a two-stranded rope, could be fastened to this and used—first, to lower the more helpless persons into the street, and, finally, for the active to glide down by. It would be too much to expect, as has been proposed, that every house should have a coil of rope, but it is well to remember that if there be only a ball of string it may serve to haul up stronger lines, brought by volunteers from without. If infants are to be lowered, it is better to put them in a bag than to tie a rope round their bodies; a couple of pillow cases would be strong enough, and there would be no fear of suffocation during the minute or two of their descent. A man may tie a child on his back or descend with it in his arms, but it is much safer to lower it separately. If flames are bursting from the windows beneath, perhaps the rope may be taken to the next lower story of the opposite house so as to avoid the danger of burning the rope or scorching those who descend. Of regular fire-escapes we need say nothing, as where they are provided, competent persons, very frequently seamen, are appointed to work them; but it is well to bear in mind that, as the property of flame and heated air is to ascend, a man creeping close to the floor may often traverse in safety a chamber the upper part of which is impracticable. A towel or piece of sheeting dipped in water and tied round the mouth and nose will prevent heated smoke and particles of burning matter from entering the air passages, and thus enable a person to struggle for life in situations where suffocation would be inevitable without some such expedient for its preservation.

Fire-escapes.

In some parts of the world, the operation of landing from a boat, or embarking from the quays or jetties built out into the sea, is rendered both difficult and dangerous by the great range imparted to the boat by the roll of the Landing derrick. swell, which in the Eastern seas is at times very great. In such situations, it is a good plan to have a stout post set in the masonry, or in a hole made in the rock, and to the top of this post a swivel crutch, which holds the trunnions of a long projecting arm, like that of an Egyptian well lever, to the small end of which a rope and cross-bar are securely fastened. To the short, heavy end, several ropes are attached, by which when the person to be landed has either grasped the cross-bar, or seated himself on it, the contrivance is at once raised aloft, and turned steadily but rapidly

LANDING BY SWINGING DERRICK.

inward, when by easing off, the man is allowed to drop easily to his feet on solid ground. There used to be such a contrivance as this at St. Helena, by the aid of which we have often landed. The illustration above will serve to show how the apparatus is managed and constructed.

A barrel, stoutly lashed with rope, fitted with a seat, and cut away at the side, so as to admit of the traveller sitting in it, as in a chair, is used for ladies or invalids, who are slung in it at the end of the arm, and hauled in as above described.

Sometimes it is necessary to construct bridges of boats; and these are often works of great magnitude, requiring a considerable amount of material, especially when an army with artillery Bridges of boats. and baggage waggons has to cross. Whether large or small, the method of proceeding must be nearly the same. First, a number of stout beams must be collected, sufficient to make a double line across the river, with their ends overlapping each other by more than the breadth of the boats that are to support them. The boats should be brought to the shore and moored a little above the site of the intended bridge. If anchors are procurable, they should be laid at regular intervals across the river; a buoy should be attached to the end of each cable, and a small line should lead from the farthest to each nearer one in succession, till they are all connected with the shore. A substantial frame of beams should be constructed at the edge of the bank, and a boat brought alongside it riding by the first cable, and secured by a temporary mooring to the shore. Two beams must be launched across her near the head and stern, and firmly lashed to the thwarts and stringers. The boat must now be swung out to the full extent of the beams; the second cable must be laid hold of, and the first cast off and hauled to shore for the next boat, which is dropped down stream under the

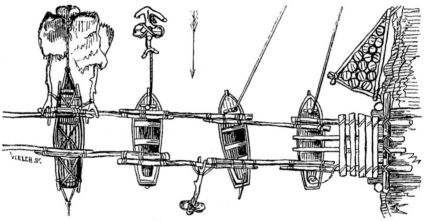

EXPEDIENTS FOR BOAT BRIDGES.

shore ends of the beams, which are laid upon her gunwales and made fast there; while two others are pushed from the shore and fastened to her as the first pair were to the first boat. Intermediate beams, if requisite, can be laid, and planking lashed or pinned upon them so as to complete that part of the platform. Then other beams and planking, sufficient for a similar platform, should be brought on board, for the purpose of finishing the bridge when this pair of boats reaches the other shore. The outermost boat should now pick up the third cable, and pass the second to the inner one; while the first cable should be taken by a third boat, which will drop down between the others and the shore, to receive her portion of the platform; and so on in succession until the bridge, completed as it goes on, extends so nearly to the other shore that the loose material carried by the first pair of boats serves to complete the connection.

Anchors may be extemporised from forked branches of trees—the harder and heavier the better. These should have stones or iron lashed to them, in order to give weight. Several forks should be left on the main stem, and pointed to insure their holding. If charred in the fire, so much the better, as their durability and strength are much increased by the process. If there is but one fork, care must be taken so to balance the anchor with the stone below and the cable above, or a stock lashed across, that this fork or arm shall be sure to take the ground. The bridge may be also shored against the stream by branches, with their forks taking the beams, while their lower ends, weighted by stones, rest against the bed of the river. Stones are of no use as anchors, as they lose so much of their specific gravity when immersed; but if a heavy stone can be dropped beyond a cleft in the rock, as in our sketch, it will hold well.

If no anchors or substitutes can be had, the cables may be made fast to a stout tree as far up the stream as possible; and being brought in upon the inner bow of each boat, she will take the stream upon that side and be forced outward. The rudder, if she has one, will assist in this, but it is not material, as she can be kept at the proper angle by making the foremost beam a little longer that the after one.

If the bridge is constructed so low down the river as to be within the ebb and flow of the tide, anchors are indispensable, and each boat must be moored head and stern, as shown in one of the examples in our illustration; or, if there be but one cable to hold her against the ebb, shores may be set so as to counteract the influence of the flood, unless a great rise and fall, or violent rush at the turn of the tide, should render it unsafe to use them. If boats cannot be had, two or three large casks, placed end to end and firmly lashed to poles laid parallel to their length, may be used at each junction of the beams; or if a number of small casks can be obtained, they may be collected within a triangular frame of poles; but in any case each float must be sufficiently buoyant to keep the bridge at least 3ft. clear of the water, if there is any current; if there is none, the platform may even touch the water and be partially sustained by it. In our sketch we have omited all but a small portion of the planking, in order to show more clearly the manner of connecting the framework.

In some parts of India and China very heavy weights are carried on an ingeniously constructed framework of bamboo. A stout pole is crossed at its ends by two lighter ones, and Carrying, rolling, and each of these again by two others, each of parbuckling heavy spars. which is again crossed by smaller ones 2in. or 3in. in diameter and 6ft. or 8ft. long; the sixteen ends of these are raised on the shoulders of as many men; the weight is slung to the centre of the larger beam, and borne with ease and comfort on the elastic frame. In our illustration (p. 314), two gangs of coolies are represented carrying a tree. For rolling, the tree should be cleared of projecting stumps as much as

possible; long skids should be placed under it, and if the ends from
which the tree is to be rolled can be elevated by wedges or otherwise,

BAMBOO CARRYING FRAME AND PARBUCKLING LOG.

so as to make an inclined plane for it to roll down so much the better;
at all events, get the thick end under the tree and let the thin end
be in the direction that you wish to roll it. Parbuckling is effected
by making fast the end of a line to a stump or other holdfast in the
required direction, then bringing the end of the line under the log,
and taking one or more clear turns, bringing the end back over it and
hauling on. A few hands judiciously using handspikes or levers will
greatly assist this operation.

CHAPTER VI.

TIMBER AND ITS UTILISATION.

WE have before stated that timber should never, except in cases of emergency, be felled with the sap in it; still, during the vicissitudes of rough travel, it will frequently happen that, in order to execute repairs imperatively needed, the Extraction of sap. trees must be cut down, hewn into form, and made use of at once. When this is done, the object will be to get rid of the sap which fills all the minute pores and tubes of the wood, as quickly as possible. To do this, a trench, proportioned in length and depth to the quantity and size of the timber to be treated, must be dug in the earth. Lay in the logs, after denuding them of their lateral branches, fill the trench with water, and let them soak in it whilst you build a strong hard wood fire. When this is throughly ignited throw a number of large heavy stones into it, and as they become red hot withdraw them with twisted sticks, and throw them into the trench until the water boils actively. Continue to do this until there are a number of heated stones in the already boiling sludge; throw then a thick layer of clay, turf, and earth, over the whole mass, and leave it to steam and stew for the night. A large log, intended for the axle of a waggon or other heavy work, may be, with advantage subjected to a second application of the same process, when it will be found much more tough and durable than if converted with the raw sap in it.

Before proceeding to fell a growing tree for immediate use, it is well to search carefully about for a dead storm cast trunk of the kind required, which will, as a rule, be found in tolerable condition. When a depôt is formed, or a point Seasoning wood. selected as a rendezvous, it is advisable to fell a few trees, and let them lay in store, so to speak, until they are wanted. Cutting a deep notch round the whole circumference of a tree, and letting it stand until required for use, much improves the quality of the wood. When practicable, and time will allow, it is well to leave logs of timber intended for seasoning to soak in rivers, lakes, or arms of the sea; but it is wise, at the same time, to ascertain, by the examination of pieces of wood which have fallen accidentally into the water, whether any of the creatures addicted to timber boring are found in that locality. The rivers flowing into the Black Sea abound with the *Teredo navalis*, or ship worm, to such an extent that floating logs very shortly become so perforated as to be perfectly useless except for firewood. Much of the timber we obtained in that part of the world was defective on account of the depredations of this pest, whose range, unfortunately, is a pretty wide one; and his works, and those of other borers, are therefore to be jealously looked for in the neighbourhood of a proposed salt or brackish water timber pond. In countries where hot springs are met with, they may be utilised for timber seasoning and other purposes. Sticks or poles intended for bending into ox bows, or other curved forms, should be placed either in boiling water or the hot embers of the camp fire until thoroughly heated through. They may then, after being properly shaped, be tied in the required form with cords, and hung in the air to dry. Several long crooked sticks may be straightened at once by forcing them side by side into the hollow of a large bamboo cane from which all the knots, except that at one end, have been removed. When a sufficient number of sticks are arranged in the cane, place it mouth upwards, and fill it to the brim with boiling water. When the first charge is cold add a second, and so on until the sticks have been about an hour in their hot bath. They can now be forced separately into smaller bamboos without water, or lashed between battens of stiff wood until cold, when such small irregularities and curves as remain may be removed by heating the part requiring treatment over the fire and carefully straightening it over the knee. Nearly all the spear handles, whether of cane or forest wood, found among wild tribes are straightened and rendered fit for use by the agency of fire. Strong and perfectly straight tubes for blow-pipes, &c., are formed by inserting a small cane into the hollow of a larger one and turning it round till any deviation from the straight line in one counteracts that of the other.

The elegant curve given to many of the bows found among the Northern Indians is gained by first heating them in the camp fire, and then, after bending them carefully to the desired shape, keeping the curves in position by the aid of thongs. We have one of these bows now, which was even charred in the course of making, but has never lost its contour or elasticity. The bending of ships' planks is effected by a process very similar in principle. In the absence of a properly constructed steaming chamber, the planks of a makeshift vessel may be efficiently steamed in the following manner. A long hollow log should be set horizontally on trestles of convenient height, one end must be stopped with a plug, and Steaming log. the other have a tight wooden stopper and cross-bar fitted to it. When the required number of planks are thrust down the log, steam is admitted through a bamboo, or hollow tube of wood, from a large covered cauldron placed on a fire beneath the log. All the joints of the bamboo should be luted fast with clay, and kept tight until the planks are sufficiently steamed for bending, when they are dragged out with wooden tongs, and put in place on the vessel. The full page illustration shows the mode of using a steaming log.

Wood which does not require straightening is rendered much more hard and durable than it would otherwise be by the action of carefully applied fire-heat. The clubs and grubbing Hardening wood. sticks of natives are generally fortified in this way. Spear, arrow, and blow-pipe darts have their points so hardened by the action of heat, that they more closely resemble the texture of bone than aught else, and perforate almost as readily as sharpened iron. We have seen the tough, dense scales of a large fish penetrated with the greatest facility by a spear prepared in this way. Flat strips or laths of bamboo cut to a fine edge, and fire-hardened, are used by many of the inhabitants of the islands of the Eastern seas as substitutes for knives; some of these truly makeshift blades are as keen as surgical instruments, and are at times used in the performance of minor operations of surgery.

Many of the trees of tropical countries will be found to possess heart wood of great strength and density, whilst the outside or "sap" is light coloured, weak, and next to useless. In such cases, all the outside layer of timber should be cut away with the axe or adze, Hard wood. and the central core alone made use of. In selecting poles or sticks for purposes where toughness and durability are matters of importance always, when practicable, take young seedling trees. Next in quality to these are the shoots which spring up from the underground roots of large trees. When either of these kinds are intended to be put aside to season, they should be pulled up by the roots rather than cut; the earth may be beaten out from among the fibres by striking the roots of the sticks together; they can then be hung in an airy place to dry; late in the autumn or in the winter are the best seasons for rooting up saplings. In countries where Larch trees. the larch fir grows abundantly, a number of tall young trees will be found from some cause to have died as they stand, to have withered and become perfectly dry. These will be found extremely tough and well seasoned.

Bamboos must be selected according to the purpose they are intended for. The female bamboo, as it is called, is remarkable for the largeness of the cavities placed between the internodes; this quality renders it buoyant, light, and well adapted for splitting up into planks. We have seen a very large bamboo slit from end to end by making one long cut in the side. The cane is heated and carefully opened. The knots are then all smoothed off, when the hollow shell is laid between boards on which heavy stones are placed, until it is pressed perfectly flat, and becomes a bamboo board. The knots of large female bamboos make excellent pails or water vessels.

Bamboos.

A joint of bamboo cut longitudinally in half, and supported on feet formed from another joint of the same cane, after the manner of a pen tray, makes a most convenient receptacle for pins, steel pens, pencils, sail needles, and a host of other matters which are required to lay parallel to each other.

Water pipes, for irrigation, can be made from a train of canes with their ends thrust into each other, and secured by transverse pegs, as at Fig. 1 in our illustration. All long bamboos, intended for

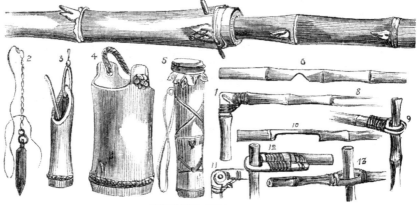

BAMBOO PIPES, BUCKETS, ETC.

pipes or tubes, must have their internodes removed. This we used to do as follows; We prepared some short pieces of round bar iron of a size just to fit the bore of the canes easily. We then pointed one end of the iron chunk and sloped the upper end, by hammering on the anvil, to a wedge form. Through the centre of the upper edge we punched a hole, through which we passed a wire long enough to reach the entire length of the cane to be treated. The chunk was then heated red hot in the fire and dropped down, like a bucket in a well, on the first knot, through which it would rapidly burn. It was then lowered away until it reached the second knot, and so on until all were entirely removed. When the chunk became cooled by contact with the wood, it was reheated and entered again. Fig. 2 shows the form of the knot chunk, &c. Excellent tar buckets (Fig. 3) or water pails (Fig. 4) are to be made from the ends of large cane joints. Boxes for wheel grease (Fig. 5), drinking cups, boxes, and a whole host of other receptacles for various matters, solid and fluid, are made from the same material. The mode of cutting and bending bamboos is shown by Figs. from 6 to 13. In Eastern countries one occasionally meets with specimens of the female bamboo of such gigantic proportions and huge growth that no little wonder is excited as to the mode of cultivation had recourse to in their production. We were for a long time quite at a loss for a solution of the mystery, but at length discovered that among the stools or root clumps of the canes one of promising appearance was by the natives selected for treatment. This was dug up and carefully replanted in a favourable locality. All the shoots which sprout up save one are cut away. This is allowed to grow up until it has reached a fair average size. It is then cut off to within about 6in. of the ground, leaving a hollow projecting stump. Into the bore of the cane thus left, a mixture of sulphur and stable litter is tightly rammed, just as you would charge a hole for blasting or would load a gun. For a period of three years every shoot which shows above the ground is cut away. The best shoot of the fourth year is allowed to grow to its full altitude and bulk, which at times is truly prodigious, leading to the false conclusion that some cane of peculiar species was the subject of wonder and investigation. From the lesser members of the bamboo family waterwheels, bows, arrows, spear heads, paper, bow strings, pens, baskets, brooms, brushes, shoulder poles, buckets, masts, spars for boats, &c., are made. The male bamboo differs from the female in having scarcely any cavity running through it. Canes of this description are peculiarly well adapted for the handles of hog spears, waggon whip handles, and a multitude of other purposes where great strength and elasticity are required.

The cocoa-nut palm is a tree which, on the score of usefulness, is perhaps second to none. On the uses of its fruit, leaves, gum, fibre, and sap we shall have more to say further on in our work. The wood is extensively used for   Cocoa-nut palm. cane building. It is hewn into form by the small sharp adzes of the islanders. Clamps are left on the inside and bored through. Dowels of hard wood are inserted in the edges, and the planks are sewn together with rattan or fibre of the cocoa-nut husk, while the timbers are bound to the clamps by lashings of the same material, as shown in the full page illustration. Much of the coir, or cocoa fibre, used in the manufacture of this and other descriptions of twine, and for caulking seams and crevices in the canoes when finished, is obtained by the natives of the islands which dot the Eastern seas and Pacific Ocean from the underground burrows of the great cocoa-nut-eating crab (*Birgus latro*), whose subterraneous workings are at certain seasons abundantly stored with this useful material, which is sometimes hooked out with long flexible sticks armed with a species of barb, and at others procured by digging out the crab, nest and all. Canoe paddles and clubs are often made from the stalk of the cocoa palm.

A great number of useful and almost indispensable articles called into daily use by the traveller and explorer can be made from wood. Swivels of one kind or another are in constant demand, as the

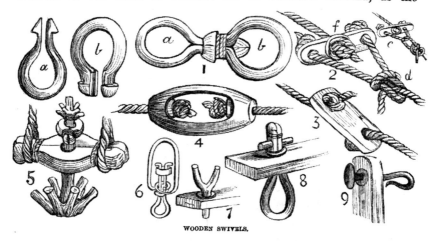

WOODEN SWIVELS.

ropes used for tethering animals would without their aid soon become masses of hopeless entanglement. A very neat and useful form is shown in Fig. 1; it consists Wooden swivels. of two bars of flexible wood, bent by steaming or otherwise into the requisite curve. The parts which form the neck of *a* are thinned off, but the ends are left of their full thickness; the neck of *b* is also left thick, and in each of its parts a groove is cut, forming a hollow through which *a* passes; *b* is then closed by a lashing, and the swivel is ready for use. Fig. 2 is very effective, and easily made. A bit of wood has three holes bored in it; a short piece of rope is passed through the end holes, and double knots turned upon its ends. This forms a "bridle;" and if it is requisite to attach a longer line, this should not be looped through so that one cord may saw upon the other, as at *c*, but properly hitched, as shown at *d*. The other line is passed through the central hole; and it will work more easily and wear out less quickly if a small ring or washer (*f*) of hard wood or sole leather is put on before the knot is turned upon its end. Fig. 3 is a plain form of swivel, and easily made, but is apt to chafe the rope. Fig. 4 is a very neat and useful form. A longitudinal hole is bored in a block of wood, two larger ones are bored across it, and with a knife or chisel these are cut into one large opening; the ends of the lines are passed in towards the centre, washers are put on, the knots are made, and the swivel is complete. Fig. 5 is a useful pattern. The swivel is made of the joint of a fir tree, and any number of lines may be hooked on to it. The collar is made of two parts, lashed together and suspended from each end; the washer is also in two parts, like the collar. Fig. 6 is easily made with two pieces of wire. Fig. 7 would form either a crutch for a rowing or sculling oar, or a swivel rest for a gun or telescope, &c. Fig. 8 is a rod of flexible wood, with the two ends passed through the collar and fore-locked, leaving the loop to turn freely. Fig. 9 is simply a broad-headed nail passed through a piece of wood, and with its point bent into a hook; a washer of iron saves wear and tear. This is very similar to the swivels used by rope makers.

The common flail swivel is excellent for many purposes. Sometimes it is made with two pieces of stout hide or sole leather, shaped like Fig. 1. One of these is turned so that the narrow part in the middle forms a loop; while the broad ends are nailed, tightly stitched, or lashed to the thick or swinging arm of the flail (Fig. 3); the other piece, being linked through this loop, is also bent till the broad ends meet; and their edges are then securely stitched together so as to form a collar, which works freely on the handle (Fig. 2), at the end of which is a knob to prevent the collar slipping off.

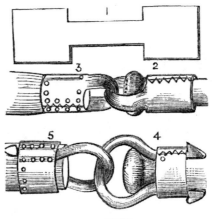

FLAIL SWIVELS.

Occasionally two flexible rods (withies) are bent for this purpose: one is firmly fastened by a leather band nailed or lashed to the extremity of the swinging arm (Fig. 5); the other has small knobs left on its ends to prevent the leather collar slipping off, and this works freely on the handle (Fig. 4). Either of these arrangements may

Y

be thrown out of gear by taking hold of the knob and drawing the thin end of the handle out of the collar. A slice of bullock's horn, shaped as Fig. 1, after softening it in hot water, makes an excellent collar.

Every traveller ought to carry with him the means of measuring feet and inches, and as instruments for that purpose are so cheap and portable there is hardly any excuse for being without something of the kind. We have a little waistcoat-pocket ivory rule, folding into lengths of 3in., and occupying no more room than a small penknife, and with this, even if an elephant were killed, we could mark off 5ft. or more upon a stem of grass, and use it as a measuring rod, with the little rule ready for the fractional parts. We had at one time half-a-dozen rules (sold at a penny each), 3ft. in length, and folding on pivot joints into lengths of 6in., and they were quite correct enough for common carpentry. Tape lines for 6ft. or 12ft. may be had in cases not larger than a Geneva watch. Chesterman's patent, shutting with a spring, is a good form. And even if a traveller should (as he may often be obliged to do) disburden himself of every incumbrance, he ought to have inches marked upon something he is sure to carry with him, say upon the ramrod of his gun, or perhaps on the rib of the gun itself; but let this be done neatly by a skilled workman before leaving home, for we should esteem the companion of the chase too highly to let it be recklessly disfigured. The inside of the waist-belt may be marked also in inches. It is at all times well to know the length of the different joints of the limbs. Suppose the nail-joint of the forefinger be 1in., the next joint will be 1¼in., the next 2in., and from the knuckle to the wrist 4in.; in this case the finger is bent, so that each joint may be measured separately, though when held straight the distance from the tip of the forefinger to the wrist would be only 7in. The span with thumb and forefinger would be 8in., and with the thumb and any of the other three 9in., or equal to the length of the foot; from the wrist to the elbow would be 10in., and from elbow to forefinger 17in., and from collar-bone to forefinger 2ft. 8in., height to the middle of the kneecap 18in. From the elbow to the forefinger is usually called a cubit, but it is seldom strictly so, a cubit being 18in. In like manner the full stretch of the extended arms is called a fathom, but it is generally somewhat less, a fathom being 6ft.; and in paying Africans with calico, we found it best to let every man measure off his own fathom, even though he protruded his chest and threw back his arms to the utmost, he generally took a trifle less, and was much better pleased than if we had measured it strictly with a rule. If a man stands with his back to a flat wall, and extends his arms, his fathom will be nearly equal to his own height; but if he tries

Extemporary measurements.

to measure the girth of a tree by placing his breast against it, and as it were embracing it, he will find his fathom many inches short, and on an average perhaps not more than 5ft. Ths Dutch farmers at the Cape clench both fists, making the extended thumbs meet, and they call the whole 1ft., when it is some-times nearer 15in.; and an elephant measured in this manner would be reported unduly small were it not that they also measure from the edge of the foot round the curve of the shoulder to the wither instead of taking a straight line, so that one error nearly balances the other. This is a very useful measure but every man should grasp a foot rule, as in our sketch, and ascertain for himself how much his thumbs over-lap in doing so.

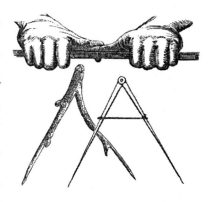

FIST MEASURE AND PACING STICK.

The step is commonly supposed to be 3ft., and the pace 5ft., but this is a most uncertain mode of measurement; a man may step 3ft., mea-suring from the heel of one foot to the toe of the other, but even if he does so two steps must be less than 6ft. by the length of his own foot, and very few men can take with any correctness a hundred con-secutive steps or paces. Besides which, so many travellers confound the terms step and pace that it is impossible to tell which they mean; it is much better, therefore, to use the word yards, and to measure them by a military pace stick; this may be two light sticks like a walking-cane sawed down the middle and riveted at the head like a pair of com-passes; then if, at 1ft. from the joint, a stick of 1ft. in length be fast-ened across the opened legs they will form an equilateral triangle, and the points will be 3ft. apart; with these, used like a pair of compasses, a man may measure off 100yds. almost as fast as he could walk it, and would be certain of his distance. A forked branch cut on the spot and trimmed, so that the ends are 3ft. apart, answers the same purpose.

For measuring a base for rough triangulation, a fishing line of 100ft. is easily carried; three measurements will give 100yds., and six will give as many fathoms. 120 fathoms is a cable's length, a common and useful unit in maritime surveying. To measure successive lengths let your line have a little stray end beyond the marks, and as the hanks are usually sold in lengths of 120ft., an over-hand knot may be turned, 10ft. fron each end, to mark the 100ft. Stick a perfectly smooth peg in the ground, without projecting head or catch of any kind, make a loop in the end of your line, and put it over the peg, carry out the 100ft. and put in another peg, then jerk the line upward, and you will cause a wave to run along it which will lift it off the end of the first peg (Fig. 1); but, as a permanent loop might catch thorns or projecting branches, it is well to make it with a hitch (Fig. 2), so that it may shake out as it comes off the peg, and leave only a free end to be hauled in. Several hitches, or a sheepshank (Fig. 3), might be used for the purpose, but probably none would answer better than the signal halyard hitch (Fig. 4), and with this the end may be made fast to any convenient tree or bush that stands fairly in the line you wish to measure. Pass the end twice round the branch or peg, then, taking the end and a small bight of the measuring part, hitch them as if you were going to tie a reef knot, pull the first hitch tight, but do not complete the knot by making the second hitch; this will hold quite fast enough and a slight jerk will be sufficient to set it free when you wish to haul in the end. Hitch it to another branch, and so in succession you may measure any number of lengths you wish, taking care always to keep the several pegs or points of fastening in a straight line.

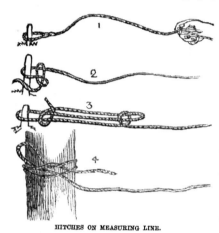

HITCHES ON MEASURING LINE.

A measuring line should merely be straight upon the ground, and never be subjected to any tension; still less should it be lifted up and then stretched to a straight line in the air; slopsellers know this when they ask sailors to hold up a length of serge while it is being measured, but any experienced hand meets this by insisting that his cloth be laid fairly on the deck and measured there.

The first step in diminishing the labour of dragging a heavy body along the ground is to put rollers underneath it, and the use of these

To make or build wheels.

is exemplified in the earliest Assyrian monuments; but these are left behind as the mass moves onward, and have to be constantly carried forward and replaced beneath. The next step is to connect them with the mass, or with the carriage supporting it, by axles, forming either integral parts of the rollers and turning with them, or by fixed axles, on which the rollers or wheels revolve. It is probable that many of the ancient vehicles were supported on axles revolving with the wheels; but we now only retain this form in that of the wheelbarrow, and the simplest way of making this, where timber is cheap and plentiful, is to cut a log of sufficient length, then to saw or chop down the ends so as to leave a disc of sufficient size and thickness in the centre, with two arms projecting from it to form its axle, as shown in Figs. 2 and 3. The barrow itself may upon occasion be made of a forked tree, of which the single part is thick enough to have a space cut in it to receive the wheel, while the two branches serve as the handles, and minor ones from them perhaps answer the purpose of legs; otherwise a rough frame, as shown in our sketch, may be built, and pegged or treenailed together.

In Mexico, Chili, Tartary, and elsewhere, rough discs of timber (Fig. 1) are sawed or chopped off from large trees. A hole is made in the centre to receive the axle. These wheels answer well enough for countries

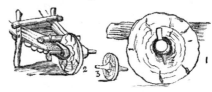

SOLID LOG WHEELS.

where time is of no value, mercy to draught oxen unthought of, and where the inhabitants would rather hear a dry wheel grate on its axle tree than take the trouble to grease it. "Evil spirits dread a creaking wheel," say they, and so the primitive contrivance is allowed to revolve noisily. A wheel of this kind might be made much more efficient by leaving a nave or boss in the centre, sheathed with hard wood or raw hide, and by binding it with the latter material let into a groove cut round the circumference in place of a tire; an endless band cut out of the hide of a rhinoceros, hippopotamus, elephant, or giraffe, put on wet, and allowed to shrink and dry before it was much used, would be almost everlasting.

A very neat and serviceable barrow wheel may be thus built: Take a piece of deal 4in. wide, 3in. thick, and 14in. long; set a pair of compasses to a radius of 8in.; and, fixing the centre leg 4in. from the block, describe on it the segment of a circle; draw this on both sides, and cut the block truly to the outline; then saw it down into six thicknesses of somewhat less than ½in.; lay three of these together, so that their chords form an equilateral triangle, each angle being 60°, and their segments will complete the circumference of a true circle. Then take the other three, and lay them on so that the centre of each shall cover the ends of each pair of the lower series; then bore holes and screw or nail them together (inch copper nails, with rooves for clenching them, are the best for this purpose), and you will have a wheel ¾in. thick, and 16in. diameter. Take a 1in. bar of wood 3in. broad, half check it into the opposite triangles where there is but one thickness of wood, strengthen it by bars from the other angles, bore a hole in the

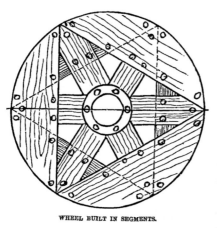

WHEEL BUILT IN SEGMENTS.

centre, and insert an axle of hard wood or iron. If you have a piece of iron hoop, reduce it, and rivet the ends together, so that it forms a tire that will just go on ; punch half a dozen holes in at intervals, heat it, put it on quickly, hammer it into place, and cool it with water ; then put nails or screws through the holes, to keep it from working off, or tire it as before with an endless band of raw hide ; or bore holes through it 1in. or 2in. apart all round, at about 1in. from the edge, and lace thongs of raw hide through these and round the edge, so as to preserve it from splitting, or being worn by contact with the ground.

To build a waggon wheel, clear a smooth place upon the floor, levelled with ant-hill clay or preferably smooth planked. Take a ½in. straight-edged batten of rather more than 5ft. in length and 3in. or 4in. in width ; clench or screw a cross piece on this, so as to form a boss in the centre, as in the figure annexed ; and through this, at

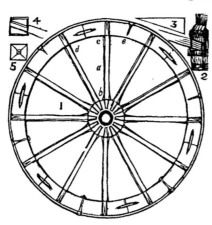

THE CONSTRUCTION OF A WAGGON WHEEL.

the edge of the batten bore a hole, with a bradawl, which being also bored into the floor forms a pivot for it to work on. At 1in. from the centre, bore a hole, through which a pencil or a pointed scoring iron can be passed, to draw the first circle for the bore of the nave. At 4½in. bore another, to mark the circumference of the nave. If a front wheel is required, bore two holes at 15in. and 18in. for the inner and outer crcumference of the felloes, or make them at

2ft. 2½in. and 2ft. 6in. for a hind wheel. Having drawn these circles, decide upon the number of spokes you intend to use, which will most

likely be eight or ten for a fore wheel and twelve or fourteen
for a hinder, such as is shown in our example (Fig. 1). Divide
360, the number of degrees in a circle, by the number of spokes,
thus—360° divided by 8 is 45°; in like manner, 10 spokes
would form an angle of 36°, 12 of 30°, and 16 of 22½°. To
obtain these angles, strike a circle on a good-sized sheet of writing or
cartridge paper; fold it across the centre, exactly in half, open it and
fold it in half the other way, taking care that the two parts of the previous fold perfectly coincide with each other; you will thus have angles
of 90°, which may be called north, south, east, and west. Fold it
again between every two of these, and you will obtain angles of 45°;
these again divided will give angles of 22½°; and the next subdivision
would give the thirty-two points of the compass, equal to 11¼° each.
To obtain angles of 10°, divide each angle of 90° into three parts, and
subdivide each of them into three. The strong lines in our next figure
indicate angles of 22½° for a sixteen spoke wheel, and the faint lines
angles of 10°. Our diagram of the wheel was drawn with a bit of
card cut to the exact size shown
in our figure, pivoted on one pin,
while the point of an H H pencil
was passed through other pin-
holes to draw the circumference.
If two of these lines should come
very close together, it will be
seen that the pin-holes are not
pierced in the same radial line,

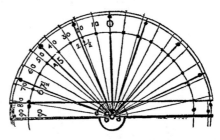

or they would break one into the other; but by placing them a little
on either side concentric circles can be drawn as closely as requisite.

Now, cut a piece of thin board or stiff paper to the angles at which
the spokes are to be set—in this instance 22½°—and with the aid of
your straight-edge draw a line across, through the centre, to both sides
of the circumference of your wheel; draw another across this at right
angles, and test the lines by trying whether each quarter will contain
four times the mould you have cut to the angle of 22½°; then draw
two other lines of 45°, and subdivide each space into the required
angles of 22½°.

Suppose your spokes are to be 1in. thick, withdraw the bradawl
that has served you as a pivot and bore two holes, each ½in. from the
central line, and pivoting the batten on each of these in succession, you
will be able to draw the lines showing the thickness of your spokes, *a*,
the original line still indicating the direction of their centre. Then
divide the circumference of your felloe into eight segments of 45°,

and draw short lines across it as at *d* (p. 326), to indicate the length of the felloe pieces, each of which must contain one pair of spokes, while its ends come fairly in the centre of the space between two others. Take a thin piece of board and cut a mould for the felloe pieces, marking on it the lines for the dowel holes, *d*, and those for the insertion of the spokes, *c*. Then in like manner cut a board with a circumference of 9in. as a mould for the nave, and on it draw the lines which mark the mortices for the insertion of the spokes, *b*. The nave should be turned of some good solid even-grained wood, not too hard; elm is well calculated for the purpose. It is generally 9in. or 10in. long, and it should have a hole 1in. in diameter through its centre. A narrow pit, 3ft. in depth, is dug, and two stout beams, 9in. apart, laid along its edges; a 1in. rod of iron is passed through the hole in the nave, which, with its iron bands already driven on, is placed between

the beams, supported by the ends of the rod which rest upon them (stout trestles, 3ft. high, are sometimes used instead of the pit). In one of the beams at the back of the nave is a stout upright, with a line marked upon it as a guide in boring the holes truly.

To turn a nave to the proper form without the assistance of a turning lathe, the following makeshift contrivance will be found useful

Naves, to turn. and efficient. Fit up four strong planks, or a strong stool, of form shown in the accompanying illustration. Cut out two upright checks, which must be fitted by mortices to the upper surface of the stool. Then make a ⊤ rest and fit in the centre of the stool, in one of a train of square holes cut behind the line of the checks. The block of wood intended to form the nave must have an ordinary auger hole bored through its true centre, and in this must be firmly wedged an iron bar, with a crank or handle bent at one end; this bar rests on bearings prepared for it in the cheeks, one bearing is formed by boring a hole just large enough to let the plain end of the bar through, and the other by sawing out a deep notch for the handle end to drop into, when it is prevented from becoming displaced by a pin passed in above it. The man about to officiate as turner sits astride on the stool, presses a long-handled gouge or chisel by the action of his shoulder firmly down on the rest, with its cutting edge against the nave log, which is turned steadily round by an assistant who has charge of the handle; the whole operation being conducted much on the principle of tool grinding, only the motion of the log is always toward the man, who manages the chisel. The rest is advanced as the log decreases in diameter.

If the wheel is to have what is called a dish, cut a small piece of wood (Fig. 3, p. 326) to the angle at which the spokes are to project forward; and, having marked off all the mortices, which will be ¾in. wide by 1½in. long, take a brace and ¾in. bit, or a ¾in. screw auger, and bore two holes in the space marked for each mortice, as in Fig. 2, taking care to centre most accurately the spot at which the point of your bit or auger, is inserted and to keep its true direction by the aid of the upright line and the small angled board. The mortices will then be finished with a ¾in. mortice chisel and mallet. The holes in the felloe (Fig. 4) will be bored at the same angle with a 1in. auger; for as the spoke will be 1½in. from back to front, there will be shoulder enough in those directions without weakening it by cutting a shoulder on the sides. Of course, the shoulders, both at the felloe and at the nave, will be cut to the same angle at which the holes are bored. The tenon should be less than 3in. in length, so that it may allow of the subsequent boring of a 3in. hole in the nave to receive the bush or iron sheathing in which the axle turns; and in like manner the ends inserted in the felloes should be less than 3in. long, so that they may not receive any pressure from the tire. Fig. 5 shows the centreing of the felloe ends to bore the dowel holes. Now, resting the nave on its iron rod upon the beams of the pit or trestles, drive in the first spoke, testing it by the upright line and by your angled board. Then, boring a hole in your upright, drive in a peg and cut it off at such a length that the first spoke may just touch it in passing. Drive in all the other spokes so that they also touch the end of the peg, and then in the end of each spoke make a cut 1in. deep with a fine tenon saw, to receive a wedge of hard wood when the wheel is built. Then in one end of each felloe drive a dowel (*d*) rather stiffly, but so that it does not bottom in the hole; leave half its length projecting. Take a screw clamp and compress two of the spokes together till their ends will enter the holes in one felloe piece; drive it about ¾in. on, and slack off the clamp. If you have not a clamp, pass three or four turns of rope or thong round the two spokes, and twist them tightly with a hammer handle or other lever. Do the same with the next pair, and fit on the next felloe piece, taking care that it receives fairly the dowel of the first. Proceed in this manner all round, then look carefully to the fair insertion of all the spoke ends and dowels, and, being satisfied of this, keep the wheel turning slowly, and strike the felloe pieces homeward by smart blows of a mallet as each spoke passes you. When they are all fairly home, drive in the wedges to the spoke ends, trim off the felloe as neatly as you wish, insert the bush in the nave, and have the wheel tired in the manner described at pp. 170, 171.

A ship's wheel differs from that of a waggon in being, not a roller moving freely on its axle and supporting the carriage and its load, but To make a rather a series of levers arranged as spokes, connected steering wheel. and supported by the felloe for the purpose of turning the axle and gathering in or slacking off on either side the ropes or chains by which the tiller is moved; the spokes, therefore, project

6in. or 8in. beyond the circumference of the felloe, and are smoothed and rounded off so as to be easily and conveniently grasped by the steersman's hand. The diameter of the felloe should not be less than 30in., or it will not give sufficient leverage; nor more than 4ft., or a man cannot command it easily. Neither the nave nor the felloe are made solid, but are built up in the following manner: The lines of circumference are traced, and the angles of the spokes set off in the manner already described. A disc of hard wood 9in. in circumference, about 2in. thick and with a hole 3in. square in its centre, is laid upon the floor. The spokes are arranged on this, and screwed or clenched firmly to it; the interstices are then filled up, and another disc of similar size is screwed or clenched over all to form the front. The bush, or axle box, which of course is square, is fitted in, and an ornamental boss, generally covered with brass is screwed over to conceal it.

The felloe pieces are 3in. or 4in. broad, and 1in. thick : the back pieces are laid so that their centres come upon the spokes and their ends between ; the next set, exactly as thick as the spokes, are laid in the intervals ; and the front pieces are laid so that their ends meet upon the spokes, where they are generally confined by an ornamental lozenge, a cross, or an oval of brass, screwed down upon them. The axle is supported in a true fore and aft line by a couple of stancheons, with bushes for it to work in ; and on some part of it, behind the wheel, is fixed the drum, over which the tiller chains or hide ropes are passed with two or three turns, so that as one is gathered in by a turn of the wheel, the other may be slacked off.

A windlass may be of any size, from that of the old cross-bow, to one fitted to weigh the anchor of a vessel, although in large ships the capstan is thought to afford the best and steadiest means of applying the continuous exertions of   *Windlass.* the men. A windlass may be roughly formed by setting up a couple of forked logs, or still better, if possible, choosing two forked trees firmly rooted in the proper place, and laying across them another log, thinned off as much as possible where it rests in the forks, to reduce the friction without too much impairing the strength. The central part ought to have paul notches cut in it, and a heavy paul log may be hinged or pivoted to a stout staple, nearly level with the ground, so that its end, acting as a "paul," catches the paul notches and prevents the windlass giving way to the strain of the cable while the men are shifting their handspikes. The barrel of the windlass ought to be chopped or adzed down to an octagonal form (expressively though erroneously called 8-square), and holes should be morticed right through in each face so that each man, without change of position, should have eight opportunities of inserting his handspike. A Spanish windlass may be extemporised with the boat's oars. Two of them are lashed together as sheers with legs of unequal length, the longer leg being in the direction of the strain. A pair are set up in each side of the boat and lashed to the thwarts, care being taken to put some piece of wood or other dunnage under the ends, so that they may not hurt the planking. Another oar is now laid across with its loom resting in the forks ; a grummet strop or a short piece of rope is made fast to the middle of each of the boat's stretchers ; if the end is frayed out, so much the better. The end is applied to the loom of the oar that represents the windlass, and the stretcher is turned round and round it until the rope tightens so much as to make it an efficient handspike. It should then be "stopped" in position with a bit of yarn. If there is a davit in the boat, the buoy rope is carried over the sheave, three or four turns are passed over the "wind-lass oar" and the end is carried forward and held by one of the boat's crew, who gathers in all he can and loses none as the

SPANISH WINDLASS.

men heave round. When the boat's stern is hove down as low in the water as is prudent, all the men go in the bow, and sometimes jump there, to jerk the anchor from the ground.

GUNNER'S CAPSTAN.

The gunner's capstan is made by sinking one end of a waggon or gun axle in the ground, placing a wheel on it upside down, and lashing handspikes to the spokes to act as capstan bars. The rope to be hove on is passed round the nave of the wheel below the line of the spokes, as shown in the annexed illustration.

In many countries where navigation is not very far advanced, wooden anchors are commonly used. We have seen and sketched these on the coast of Java, and elswhere. In tropical countries the hard heavy wood that sinks of its own weight is Anchors. peculiarly suited for this. A forked tree of suitable size is chosen, and sometimes, but not always, the fork or fluke of the anchor is strengthened by a cross lashing to the shank. A heavy stone, as long as possible in proportion to its thickness,

THE TREATMENT OF TIMBER BY STEAM AND SAW.

is lashed across underneath the shank, serving the purpose of a stock. A loop for the attachment of the cable is made above it, so that the anchor, when cleared for letting go, may hang in the position shown in Fig. 1, and may take the ground fluke downward. A many-forked tree of heavy wood, with stones lashed on (Fig. 2) for additional weight, is more certain to hold, but does not stow so snugly when not in use. This, in a lighter form, may be used as a creeper for dragging over the bottom to recover a lost cable, &c. Canoes, in shallow sluggish waters, are often moored by one or more of their poles stuck into the mud. A stone lashed to one of these and a guy carried aft, as in Fig. 3, will give addi-

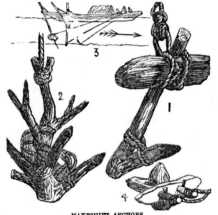

MAKESHIFT ANCHORS.

tional security; or a couple of poles may be put over the sides and crossed under the bottom, the lower ends being guyed in the same manner, but this would be dangerous in a strong tide-way. If the boat is dropping down with the tide, a pole over the stern about a foot longer than her draught of water, will take the ground, and either pre-vent her running ashore or at least give warning before she does so. Where heavy wood cannot be obtained, a couple of holes may be bored in a slab of sandstone (Fig. 4), the ends of a forked branch thrust through and fore-locked, another stone being jammed into the fork at right angles with the first. We have often seen anchors of this de-scription in use among Indians.

A pump, or nave auger, may be advantageously worked with what are called "slinger sticks." Set the log upright, either in a hole in the ground, by shoring it, or by a combination of both methods. Above it rig a stage, on the forks of trees, with a firm

BORING WITH SLINGER STICKS.

socket for the stock or shaft of your auger to work in. Then fit a waggon wheel on the top of it, *lash* an upright pin to one of the

felloes (do not spoil a *good* wheel by boring holes in it). The sticks
Working in have broad, flat ends, with holes to work upon the pivot,
timber. and crutch handles for the men to take hold of. In some
parts of the Indian Archipelago even gun barrels are bored out in
nearly similar fashion, only two boys walk slowly round with a kind of
capstan bar, the drill being weighted with a basket of stones.

We have seen Africans, in Portuguese service, working a common
handsaw very efficiently by fixing a cross handle to the end of the
Saws and blade; then two men would sit opposite each other, and,
drills. holding the log between the soles of the feet, as shown in
the full page illustration, would work the saw between them. For
rough work this serves well enough. In such case let them have a saw
with teeth widely set, and pretty much their own way; but if you want
anything well done do it yourself. Saws for natives need not have much
temper, and the teeth should be set very wide, so as to do a great deal
of what carpenters call "sawing wood." The Germans are very fond
of using frame saws, like that shown in the same illustration—a long,
narrow strip of soft steel, stretched tightly in a heavy rectangular
frame of wood. Such a saw could be extemporised with a few feet of
iron hooping, with teeth filed on it. It would do for soft wood, but on
hard wood would wear out quickly; nevertheless, it might last long
enough to do the required work. We had three small web-saws,
assorted sizes; they are very handy to carry; frames (like that in our full
page illustration—"Boat building at Logier Hill") are easily made when
wanted, and they should not be neglected if weight or bulk in carriage

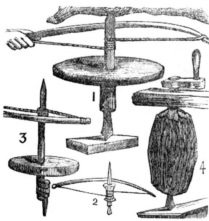

is objectionable. Stock and bow
drills may be easily made, as in
Fig. 1. The arm of a tree will
afford a socket above, and the
wood or iron to be bored must
be firmly fixed below; a good
sized disc of heavy wood, the
sheave, say, of an old block, or a
piece sawed off a hard tree, acts
as a fly wheel. For smaller work
a cotton reel (Fig. 2) does well
for the bow strings to work on;
in this case the stock ought to
be of iron, purchased at home.

STOCKS AND DRILLS.

The Bowditch Islanders lash
their drill on alongside the stock (Fig. 3), but we can hardly sanction
this plan, though it might exceptionally prove useful. If weight and

not rapid motion is desired, make the drill stock of a heavy log (Fig. 4), with the pivot going up through the upper socket, and fit a crank on it.

We have had at times not actually to make casks *ab initio*, but what comes to very nearly the same thing, to pick out the material of old ones " shaken out," when we abandoned a camp, to tie them in bundles, and carry them as best we could till they were again required. Sometimes it is impossible to gather all the individual parts of one cask, and heads and staves must be taken as they come. In this case, pick out two heads of the same size, or pieces which will make two. Measure their diameter, and as the circumference is, for practical purposes, three times as much, measure across the end of the staves on the inside of the chine groove, until their united widths fully equal three times the diameter. If you have another cask a little larger, set up the staves inside it ; or if you have one somewhat smaller, arrange them outside, and put on temporarily a larger hoop, or lash them with a turn or two of rope. Then take the hoops which you have selected for the cask, and get the larger ones over the end, drive them down tolerably tight, nearly to the centre. Then, taking one of the heads, bore a couple of gimlets into it to hold it by, or screw it on a clamp, across the grain, so as to hold all its pieces fair and level. Let this down edgewise into the belly of the cask, then, drawing it up, enter one edge of it into the chine groove, and, slacking the hoops if necessary, lift it till it fits in all round. If you find any difficulty in this, take a knife blade, or thin piece of hoop iron, pass it through one of the interstices of the staves under the head, and lift it till it enters the groove. If this is done at the four quarters, it will be impossible for the head to fall down inside. Drive the lower hoops down, and when the staves begin to close up, take out the knife or hoop iron and tighten the hoops with the hammer and driver. Then turn up the cask, and if you wish to close it at once, do the same with the other end, if not, drive the hoops on leaving it open, and slack them up when you want to put the head in. Put knives or thin iron between the staves, as before, to keep the head from slipping down, and withdraw them before you tighten up. If you have not another cask to set up the staves in or upon, take one of the hoops and support it as a horizontal ring by tying it to small trees or posts, or set up the head itself on a pole, breast high for the staves to lean against, or dig a circular trench a few inches deep in the ground to set the staves in. Remember that if iron hoops are worn or rusted or bent much, and have to be straightened out, they are very easily broken or burst by driving too tightly.

Cooper's work

Of course they can be mended by punching holes and riveting a piece in; but they require good punches and a matrix, for which a

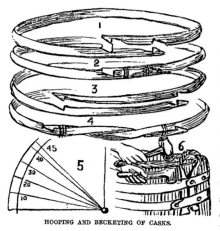

HOOPING AND BECKETING OF CASKS.

piece of hardened wood may be substituted, and some skill and patience. Always heat both the iron and rivets, and do not punch holes or clench rivets cold. Wooden hoops are generally withies or saplings, split down the middle, and left with one flat side and one round. The ends are thinned a little, and notches cut on the upper edge of one and the lower of the other. These are made to catch each other, either with a short overlap, as in Fig. 1, in which case the two parts lie parallel with each other, or with a long joint (Fig. 2), in which each takes a half turn round the other, between the notches. The joint is then served either with slips of osier or split rattan, or other substitute for cord.

If it is necessary to make a cask, the pieces forming the discs used for the heads should be dowelled together, with a bit of pith of reed, or other caulking material, between them, and the circumference must be thinned off to an obtuse edge. The staves, to look neat, ought to be nicely rounded as segments of a circle, and the ends should be narrower than the centre if belly is to be given to the casks; but if it is not essential that the cask should be perfectly round, the staves may be of flat plank. It is, however, indispensable that their edges should be cut to the proper angle, or they will not fit closely nor support each other when hooped up; the diagram we give will facilitate this. If their are to be 20 staves in a cask their edges must be cut at an angle of 18°, thus 360 divided by 20 is 18, and the angle of any other number may be found by dividing 360 by the number of staves. The chine groove may be cut with a saw, and it is better that the staves should be always a little narrower towards the ends than in the middle, so that the hoops may tighten in being driven on.

To becket a cask, slacken off one or more of the hoops, take a strip of raw hide, slip one end under, twist the middle a little, then turn it, Water casks, slip the other end under, nick them that they may not to embark. draw out, and tighten up the hoop. A kind-hearted American, captain of the "Mechanic," of Boston, who filled our water casks when we were on scant allowance, off the coast of Australia, taught us this expedient. In towing a number of casks from shore to the vessel becket them in this manner at both ends, and on two sides; then put them end to end, and pass a rope on each side through all the beckets. If there are two boats let one tow ahead of the other, so as to leave but one wake; let the bunghole be *downward*, for if the cask leak, the salt water, being heaviest, will not run up into the fresh, nor will the fresh run down into the salt; whereas if the bung is up, the fresh water may splash out and the water of the sea run in and spoil the remaining contents.

Hoops may be made by taking thin strips of any flexible wood, three or four times as long as the circumference of the required hoop, coiling them as it were, and then binding Bent wood.
or clenching them together. These are very strong and flexible (Fig.

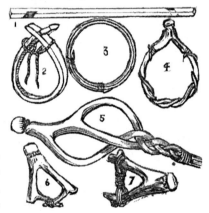

3). Jib stay hanks (Figs. 1 and 2) are made of any tough wood, in bars 14in. or 16in. long, 1in. wide, and a little more than ½in. thick at one edge and somewhat less at the other. These are notched about 2in. from the ends, so that when they are bent the ends may cross each other and afford a hold for the lashing that attaches them to the leach of the sail. They are not fastened as the sailor opens them to put them on the stay, and the lashing to the leach rope fastens them sufficiently. Hanks may be made of the fork of a branch (Figs. 4, 6 and 7), and if a double hank is required, a branch with two forks (Fig. 5) will serve the purpose.

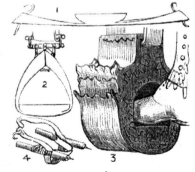

In South America stirrups are very neatly made by taking a bar of tough wood (Fig. 1), 1ft. or 14in. long, notching it so as to leave in the centre a piece of the full thickness, thinning down from them to the notch on each side till the wood can be safely turned up so that the ends meet and form the bow of the stirrup (Fig. 2). The ends are cut to the proper bevel, and fastened by a thong in hole bored through them. A couple of horizontal bars, 2in. long,

z

fastened above, form a slip for the stirrup leather to pass through.
This is a very neat arrangement, but its only fault is its extreme

Stirrups. lightness, as, when the horse is in rapid motion, the foot
cannot readily find the stirrup if it should be lost for
a moment. In this respect, the block of wood, sometimes richly
carved and ornamented, used by the Chilians (Fig. 3), is, notwithstanding its clumsy appearance, far superior. Three bars, so
lashed as to form an equilateral triangle of at least 5in. inner
measurement, will make a good stirrup. The fork of a branch, with
a cross piece lashed on it, or suspended so that one of its arms
forms the tread or bottom piece, a thong of hide making the other
side of the triangle, will answer if sufficiently heavy. The hide of
the hippopotamus, rhinoceros, or giraffe, when sufficiently dried, may
be cut into stirrups, and left to harden. Sometimes the block which
forms the stirrup is cut with a projecting spike to form a spur; but
the Mexican wooden spurs, consisting of two sticks a little thicker
than a pencil, 4in. long, armed with small iron points, and provided with straps as in Fig. 4, are about the neatest and most easily
extemporised form we know.

Never, if you can by any possibility avoid doing so, ride with
rope loop stirrups, as they are both inconvenient and highly dangerous. We on our last expedition to the northern forests, extemporised a capital form of stirrup by first twisting a long flexible

Birch twig birch stick by placing one end on the ground under foot,
stirrups. communicating the requisite torsion by hand, and then
forming a small compact, strong coiled hoop from it. Two of these

hoops, attached to a stout double thong passing
over the pad on the horse's back answered admirably, admitting of the free passage in and out of
the foot, without binding or cramping it. A rope
loop stirrup renders sudden dismounting in case of
accident or emergency next to impossible, whereas
the tough wooden hoop is shaken free in an
instant, and is capacious enough to admit a clay or
mud coated boot, no small advantage in rough
travel. Long tough sticks of any kind, will serve
to make these stirrups from. The annexed illustration will serve to
show the exact manner, in which they are made, and mounted for use.

Among the native tribes of South Africa, where iron, owing to the

Makeshift small scale on which they smelt it, is very scarce
axes or adzes. and valuable, considerable ingenuity is shown in the
mounting of an axe blade. This is generally a triangular piece

of iron, with one of its sides thinned down and ground to a rounded edge, and the other two tapered to a spike. It is well known that weight is an essential quality in all chopping instruments, and the deficiency of iron has therefore to be made up with wood. A stout branch, with another projecting from it at an angle of from 70° to 80°, is so cut as to leave a block of the larger limb attached like a mallet head to the smaller one, as in the uppermost figure of our illustration below. The spike of the axe head is made red hot, a hole is bored through the knob in the direction of the grain, and the axe is ready for use, and has besides the advantage of being

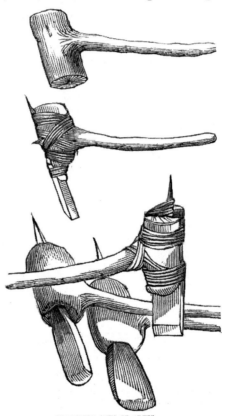

convertible into an adze by simply taking out the iron and inserting it again athwart the hole instead of keeping it parallel with the handle; the two lower figures will give a sufficiently good idea of this. We have seen these tools very efficiently wielded by honey hunters and by native woodsmen and carpenters, who, when tired of work, convert the axe handle into a pipe by taking out the iron, partially stopping the middle of the hole with a few green leaves, putting the tobacco into one end, and applying their broad lips to the other.

The other two figures represent the manner in which a broad chisel may be converted into a serviceable axe or adze, by smoothing off and channelling the front of the knob, and firmly lashing the chisel to it

MAKESHIFT AXES OR ADZES.

with raw hide either fore and aft or athwartships as required. A plane iron is often made to answer the same purpose. The hoes used by the women in Africa are made in nearly the same manner as the axes, but larger; sometimes they are flat, thin, and oval; sometimes chisel or adze shape; and sometimes a gouge-like form is given to the blade, but in all cases a spike is left at the top for insertion into the heavy knob of the handle. At times this knob is cut where two branches project from it, so as to form a double handled hoe, an example of which is shown in our engraving of a Bechuana hut on p. 249.

It may not be amiss here to give an example of the manner of making a piece of wattle work for a door, a window-shutter, a table, Hurdle or a bedstead, or any other purpose. As many stakes as wattle work. are required are planted firmly in the ground, either in a trench or, which is better, in holes separately made with a "grau-wing" stick for the purpose. Rattans, osier, twigs, reeds, or grass, are then wattled in in the manner shown in the sketch, their ends being

WATTLED WORK.

either cut off, if they are not flexible enough to bend well, or returned round the outermost stake, and wattled in again if they are. In doing this, care must be taken not to draw the outermost stake unduly together; and to prevent this it is a good plan to cut a strong stick, with a fork at one end and a notch like gaff jaws in the other, and set it between the stakes to keep them apart, removing it when it is necessary to put fresh wattles over the top, and replacing it when they are to be forced down. Baskets, crates, or gabions of any size, may be made by setting up squares or circles of stakes, and removing them when wattled; or houses may be built by fixing them more permanently and using them as the walls.

We have often admired the simplicity of the equipment of a Javanese ship carpenter; the ponderous maul or heavy axe and adze of our workmen is unknown to him; all his tools, axe, adze, maul, hammer, and augers, are made so as to fit successively on one handle about 2ft. in length (see p. 46), and are carried in a canvas haversack slung upon his shoulder. We have seen perhaps a hundred Javanese workman squatting about the decks and sides of our little schooner busy as bees, and tapping away like so many woodpeckers, where one-fourth the number of English carpenters could not have worked without injuring each other.

The attention of the traveller is too seldom directed to blocks and tackle. These useful and unpretending economisers of labour are thought to belong to a ship, and therefore to be out of place on an inland journey. Nevertheless, we have found that the possession of eight or ten blocks of different sizes and two or three coils of rope to suit them, has often done us most essential ser- Blocks or pulleys. vice; and as a traveller may unexpectedly find them necessary, where perhaps nothing but rope of hide or native vegetable fibre can be obtained, we subjoin directions for making the simplest forms, which we believe will meet most of the probable requirements :

To make a single block, take a piece of good sound wood of medium density, and of a kind that will not easily split. Elm is much used at home : oak will do very well; so will also the stinkwood of Africa, and others of like quality in other countries. Let it be, for instance, 7in. long, 4in. wide, and 3in. thick ; suppose it is to carry a rope of 1in. in diameter, properly called a 3in. rope, all ropes being measured by their circumference. Gauge along each of the narrow sides two parallel lines 1in. apart, and 1in. from each edge, and draw lines across at 1in. from each end ;

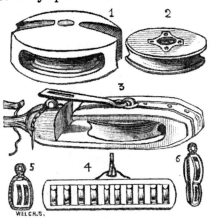

SINGLE AND COMPOUND BLOCKS.

then, taking a brace and an inch centre-bit, insert the centre so that its cutter shall just come within the cross-line at either end ; bore the holes half through, and between them bore two other holes with the same bit, thus taking out nearly all the wood between the lines; reverse the block, and bore in like manner from the other side; take a chisel and mallet and clean away all the intermediate parts, and you will have a sheave hole 5in. long and 1in. wide. Clean it up with a file or rasp. Then, drawing a longitudinal line along the centre of each of the broader sides, mark it at 3in. from one end and 4in. from the other on each side, and, placing the centre of the bit on these marks, bore through each side for the pin-hole.

Then for the sheave select a log of the hardest wood conveniently obtainable ; *lignum vitæ* is generally used, but many kinds of acacia would answer very well. See that it is large enough to cut away all the sap wood, and leave a heart 4in. in diameter; trim this to a circular form, saw off a disc 1in. thick, fix it in a lathe, and with a gouge or half round rasp or file sink a hollow all round the edge. If you have not a lathe, saw the disc not quite off, and, while it is still attached to the log, make the hollow on the edge and saw it off when finished; bore an inch hole in the centre, place it in the shell, drive a pivot of hard wood right through, and you will find that at one end of the block the sheave very nearly fills the hole, while at the other a vacancy of about an inch is left to reeve the rope through.

Then, with a gouge or half round rasp, sink hollows in the outside of the shell along the centre line towards each end, and across the ends, to receive the strop; round off the corners and edges as neatly as you wish, and you will have a servicable block like Fig. 1 (p. 341). Sometimes iron pivots are used, but these are a trifle smaller than the wooden ones; ¾in. iron would do, but then an iron socket ought to be let into the sheave, as in Fig. 2. Some sheaves have small iron rollers let into them to run round on the pivot, and so diminish the friction; but a traveller need not work to such a nicety as this.

The natch-block has already been two or three times mentioned, and perhaps this is a good opportunity to show its form, which is given

The natch-block.
in Fig. 3. The shell is longer and stouter than that of a common block, and in one side of it is cut the "natch" from which it takes its name; it is iron bound, but part of the strop is fashioned into a hasp which is opened when the bight of a rope is to be passed into the natch and shut down upon its staple and forelocked to keep the rope from coming out should the strain be suddenly released.

Fig. 4 is a very useful kind of block for signalling; it has ten or more sheaves side by side, and as many lines running over them; in

Signal block.
fact it ought to have as many sheaves as there are flags. It is kept in the signal locker with the halyards always rove, and each flag bent on to its own line. When required for use one end of the peak down-haul is bent on to the cleat in the centre, as shown in the figure, and it is hoisted to the peak end; the flags required are then sent up, care being taken to hoist each to such a height that they may read properly one under the other in the required order. These being done with are hauled down and others sent up, and much confusion and loss of time is saved by thus avoiding the necessity of bending on and unbending the several flags from one pair of halyards.

We give also figures of two useful forms of double block. No. 5, on which the sheaves are side by side, is called a sister block. No. 6,

Double block.
in which they are one above the other, is a fiddle block. Notice that in this form the lowermost sheave is the smallest, and thus the rope passing over it is not jammed by the one that passes over the upper.

In the manufacture of a number of wooden articles, such as the
sheaves of blocks, bowls, round balls, &c., the aid of a makeshift
Makeshift lathes. lathe will be required. There are several forms of
lathe made use of in different countries. No. 1 in
the annexed illustration is the best we know of for the use of the
traveller or explorer. To make a contrivance of this kind proceed as

MAKESHIFT LATHES.

follows: Prepare three squared posts, bore an auger hole through the
top of each at about 5in. from its head; to these holes fit a spindle
made of some hard tough wood, in such a way that it will just easily
play round in the holes without shaking about; cut a slice from a log
about 7in. in diameter; trim it until it is quite round; cut a tolerably
deep groove round the edge, and bore a hole in the centre for the
spindle to come through. Now, from a piece of pointed iron rod or bar
make a pivot pin, as shown passing through the head of the post
which stands alone; fit this in the hole so tightly that the driving of a
single wedge prevents it from sliding forward or back. All the posts
must be firmly fixed in the ground at an even depth, and at the relative
distances shown in the engraving. In the end of the spindle opposite
the pivot pin three sharp iron spikes, made from nail points, must be
driven; these hold the work in its place when revolving. This it is
made to do by the action of the spring overhead, which is usually made
from a tough elastic pole or bamboo cane. The end of the spring is
fitted with a long strip of hide or a rope, which, passing once round the
grooved slice of log, is attached to the end of the treadle. This is made
from a naturally-forked branch, with a bit of plank lashed fast to it
for a foot board. The chisel rest is made by driving a post into the
ground in front of the work, making a saw-cut in its head, and then
driving a bit of thin board or a piece of broad hoop iron into it, in the

form of the letter T. The spindle is prevented from moving too far back by having pins driven through it before and behind the tail post.

The lathe represented at Fig. 2 is common throughout the East. It is by the use of this contrivance that we have seen the long and beautifully straight pipe tubes, for which Stamboul is so justly celebrated, made. We have also seen the turners of Poone, in India, making their wonderful nests of almost air-tight boxes by the aid of the bow-lathe (Fig. 2). It is erected much on the principle of Fig. 1; but is usually placed so close to the ground that no one but an Asiatic could work conveniently at it.

Few border stores will be found without a Newcastle grinding stone, and very few expeditions of any magnitude omit including one or more Grinding stones, in their list of useful matters. There are several modes to mount. had recourse to for setting up a grinding stone, but we usually adopt one of the plans shown in the accompaning illustration.

Fig. 1 represents a natural fork set up in a slanting direction, and then treenailed against the trunk of a tree. To mount the stone, a straight bar of wood or iron, squared in the centre, must be wedged tightly in the square hole of the stone. If the axle is of wood, the two ends must be rounded, in order that they may revolve freely in the notches cut for their reception in the support. A wooden winch handle must then be fitted to one of

GRINDING STONES.

them. If the axle is to be of iron, it should be first heated in the fire to a red heat; the form of the handle bent in it by hammering; the centre squared, and roughened at the edges by the use of a cold chisel; and the two bearing or revolving surfaces made round by the use of the hammer and file. Wooden pins or iron staples will serve to keep the axles from rising out of the notches and becoming displaced. A suspended bullock's horn, with a hole in the small end, through which a wisp of tow or moss is loosely pulled, makes a very good water drip, to prevent the tools from losing their temper when being ground. Some prefer putting a wooden trough, to contain water, under the stone. This is a mere matter of taste.

The foresters and settlers amongst the great pine and birch forests of the far north, make use of a most efficient and ingenious arrangement for turning the large, massive, grinding stones, made use of in sharpening their axes and other cutting tools. The stone is mounted on a long axis or spindle, as shown in the annexed Lapmark illustration. Two stout notched posts support the grinding stone. weight of the stone, whilst a heavy wooden cross, to which a double hooked brake staff is linked, serves to act as a fly wheel. The motive power being communicated by a boy, who merely throws his weight, by the aid

of his hands on the staff, as it rises and falls with the revolution of the cross and wheel. An immense saving of labour is effected in this way—a small seat is usually erected, for the person engaged in grinding to sit on. The stones are kept covered when not in use, in order to keep the frost from splitting them.

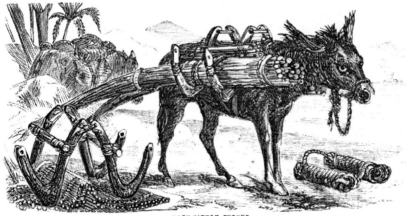

PACK-SADDLE CROOKS.

A vast deal of trouble may be saved when various useful articles are being made from wood, by a judicious selection of such branches as nature has already fashioned to the hand of the bush The use of carpenter. The above illustration will serve to give an forked sticks. example of this; it represents a set of pack saddle crooks. To make these, it is only necessary to cut with the axe four stout hooks and two straight bars; bore or burn a hole through the upper end of each hook, lash them together in pairs with strips of raw hide or rope, and lash on the side bars as shown in the engraving. The hooks are then ready to be placed on the pack-saddle, to which they are secured by a girth, which is attached at each end, to the side bars of the hooks. We have found these contrivances most useful for carrying dead game packs, or bundles of poles.

A very useful description of makeshift hand-barrow can be made
from four forked branches arranged as shown in the following illustra-
Hand barrow.   tion, and lashed together with strips of raw hide.   We
first saw these contrivances in use on the borders of
the Mena country, where the natives used them for the purpose of

MAKESHIFT HAND-BARROW.

carrying a peculiar description of clay, which was collected among the
ravines between the hills, and used for the manufacture of pottery.
These barrows, from their lightness, elasticity, and great strength,
answer admirably.

Whilst in Lapland, we saw in use a very ingenious contrivance for
Lapland kettle   carrying open vessels containing water, or other
carrier.   liquids.   It consisted of a long stout pole, slotted
at the end for the introduction of a small wooden truck or wheel,

mounted with three or more
hooks, made from reindeer antler
prongs, and furnished at the
side with a short lateral hand-
grip like that of a scythe.   The
annexed illustration will serve to
show the manner in which the
carrier is used; by its aid, the
apparently   difficult   feat   of
carrying three pails of water
at once is performed with ease and safety.

Excellent camp tables and stools can be made by selecting such
branches or tree trunks as have grown in either three
or four prong form, as shown in the engravings (Figs.   Camp furniture.
1 and 2 representing a table and stool).   The tops are made from slices

cut from convenient-sized logs. The table top is supported and strengthened by having natural grown knee pieces treenailed to the sides of the main upright or pillar. A small stool is best made by cutting away the top of the pillar until it is made to fit a large auger

CAMP TABLE AND STOOL.

hole bored in the centre of the seat, when driven in, the pillar head is split with a chisel, and then wedged tight. Should a larger table leaf be required than an ordinary log slice will afford, one may be built up by boring holes in the edges of boards, and treenailing them together as shown in Fig. 3.

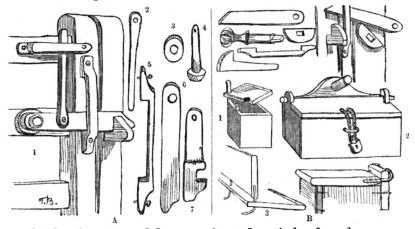

Latches for gates and doors can be made entirely of wood, as represented in the illustration A, in which, Fig. 1 shows the latch in use, and Figs. 2 to 7 the form to which each Gate latches. part must be cut before being put together. The illustration B represents another form of wooden door latch well adapted for cupboard fastenings, and three makeshift modes of forming box hinges.

Fig. 1 is the swivel hinge ; Fig. 2 the salt-box hinge ; and Fig. 3 the claw hinge. Their mode of construction will be at once understood on reference to the illustration B.

NATIVE PLOUGH.

The knee-like bends and forks so often found to exist in the branches of trees are often taken advantage of in *Agricultural implements, &c.* the manufacture of makeshift ploughs. The preceeding and following illustration represent a native and settler's makeshift plough.

SETTLER'S PLOUGH.

Many useful agricultural and other implements can be made by

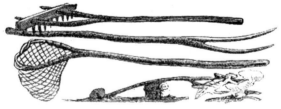

the use of forked sticks, some of which are shown in the above illustration.

A strong fork, with treenails driven through holes bored in its ends, makes a very convenient yoke for carrying pails of water or other heavy weights, as shown in the accompanying illustration.

It not unfrequently happens that pigs, when the settler is fortunate enough to have any, are apt to cause much mischief among the young canes or maize plants. To prevent them from doing so, prepare a good number of "hogs' cravats" from stout forked sticks, as shown above, put them on, and a fence of very moderate strength will keep the pilferers out effectually.

Many descriptions of trees will be found on which the branches grow in a species of crown at each joint of the trunk. The holly and some kinds of pines are familiar examples, and are commonly found in this country. From a piece of the main stem of a young tree of a suitable size, a contrivance called a "supple jack" can be made by cutting off the radiating branches to a convenient length, removing all the bark, and then pointing each projecting spine like a skewer.

When the jack is hung up by its small end it forms a most convenient contrivance from which to suspend dead game, fish, or odds and ends.

To hang a bird to the jack pass one of the pointed hooks up through the angular space between the lower mandible, and bring it out at the beak. A fish is best suspended by entering the hook at one of the gill covers, and bringing it out of the mouth; hares or rabbits by passing one hind leg through a space formed by cutting a slit behind the back tendon of the other. The legs thus form a loop to slip over one of the hooks of the jack. The foregoing illustration shows the jack in use. Saddle rests, wall and tent pole hooks, &c., can be made from knee,

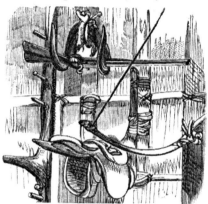

elbow, or hooked branches of trees. They can be attached to any fixed point either by the use of treenails or lashing, as shown in the preceding illustration.

The maple and some other kinds of trees are not unfrequently found with large projecting excrescences growing on their trunks; these, when carefully chopped off with the axe, will be found to have a hard, dense crust or shell next the bark, whilst the main body of the wood is soft and easily scooped out. From these abnormal growths excellent bowls may be made. Some of them are sufficiently large to admit of vessels capable of containing from eight to ten gallons being made from them. Very excellent platters or shallow trays can be obtained from the same source.

CHAPTER VII.

SLEDGES AND SLEDGE TRAVELLING.

THE use of the sledge in some of its various forms is general throughout the greater portion of the known world. The northern regions may, however, be fairly considered the great field for the performance of sledging operations. Men, animals of various kinds, and the wind are all at times made available as means of applying either traction power or propulsion to the sledge; and as the build and rig of ships and boats are found to vary according to the seas they are sailed over, and the requirements of those who sail in them, so will sledges differ in form, size, capacity, weight, and the material from which they are constructed according to the nature of the climate and country they are used in. The far north, and in regions where long and rigid winters lock the earth, the rivers, lakes, and even at times the sea itself, in ice, and covers the whole with a thick mantle of snow, such travelling would be next to impossible, without the aid of the sledge, which, although apparently simple in design, requires much care and judgment to construct successfully.

Dr. Kane, the Arctic explorer, thus writes on this subject:—

"The dimensions and structure of the sledge are of vital importance, almost imperceptible differences cause an increase of friction equal to the draught of another man or dog. The Dimensions of curvature of the runners must be determined experi- sledges. mentally. The 'Faith' was even preferable to the excellent model of Captain McClintock; the dimensions of both are as under:

McCLINTOCK'S.	Ft.	In.	'THE FAITH.'	Ft.	In.
Length of runners	13	0	Length of runners	13	0
Height of ditto	0	11½	Height of ditto	0	8
Horizontal width of all parts	0	2¾	Horizontal width of rail	0	2¼
			Base of runners	0	3¼
			Other parts	0	2
Thickness of all parts	0	1¼	Thickness of all parts	0	1¼
Length resting on a plane surface	5	0	Length resting on a plane surface	6	0
Cross-bars, six in number, making a width of	3	0	Cross-bars, five in number, making a width of	3	8

" The shoeing of large English sledges was burnished $\frac{1}{8}$in. iron, ours was annealed $\frac{3}{16}$ in. steel, as light as possible to admit slightly countersunk rivets. Sealskin lashings, applied wet, were used for the cross-bars, the wood was hickory and oak, not the Canada elm used by the Lancaster Sound parties. A sledge like this, with a canvas cover on which to place and confine the cargo, would load from 150lb. to 200lb. per man. The 'Faith' has carried 1600lb."

When manual labour is brought to bear on the sledge it is usually

Sledges, to draw. applied through the medium of traction, propulsion or the two combined. The men who propel a sledge simply push behind, whilst those who draw do so by the aid of track

ropes and shoulder bands, which latter contrivances are called "rue ruddies," and are used as shown in the illustration.

The track lines are best made from twisted horsehair, but in the absence of that material Manilla rope is the next best. Each man of the tracking party should be provided with his own track line and rue ruddy, for which he should be held responsible. The sledge to be drawn is fitted at its front end with a species of bridle loop, to which all the lines are attached by rings, in such a way that as the sway or motion of the sledge inclines to either side, the rings travel forward or back on the bridle.

It is well, however, to attach one line on each side without a ring to the sledge runner outside the attachment of the bridle, in order that when the sledge has to be turned, or its line of direction suddenly changed, the power of one man on each side may be brought directly to bear. The sliding lines must be so adjusted with regard to length

that the whole party of trackers may use their full powers without coming in contact with each other. The longest lines may be from 16ft. to 20ft. from ring to end.

The rue ruddy is a broad band of double canvas or skin with

The rue ruddy. the edges sewn in, and the bearing joints padded and stuffed with hair. A loop is formed at the point at which the track rope is attached, through this the toggle of the line is passed. When an extra man is attached to a line, a spare toggle is attached to it by a timber hitch, as shown in the illustration on page 352.

A short mast and small square sail can be used with great advantage when the wind is fair.

In passing sledges or boats across frozen lakes, rivers, or arms of the sea, considerable assistance may be at times derived, from the traction executed by tolerably large kites, which can be easily constructed by lashing two light tough sticks together in cross form, and then covering them as a square, with light, dark, or other suitable material. A string from each lower corner of the kite should be caused to meet at a small bag of sand or other weight, which will keep the kite steady in the air. *Kite "haul" for sledges or boats.*

The dog sledge is a most valuable and important accessory to northern travel, and without its assistance the Esquimaux hunter and Arctic explorer would be at times almost helpless. The form of the dog sledge, and the manner of harnessing the dogs, varies according to the customs of the countries in which it is used and the period of the year when its aid is required. We shall *Dog sledge and harness.*

therefore, confine ourselves to a description of such as are most likely to be of value to the European traveller, leaving him to select the form of harness best suited to his particular tastes. Dog harness is usually made from strips of sealskin sewn together with threads formed from sinew. Some drivers make use of one trace, others prefer two. The most common plan is to lead two traces, so to speak, into one, as shown in the above illustration. Many drivers of great experience work their dogs abreast when the single trace arrangement is adopted. Others use a leader, harnessed ahead of the other dogs.

Dr Hayes, the Arctic explorer, thus writes regarding his dogs : " We harness them each with a single trace, and these traces are of a length to suit the fancy of the driver, the longer the better, for they are then not so easy tangled. The draught of the outside dogs is more direct, and if the team comes on thin ice and breaks through, your chances of escape from immersion are in proportion to their distance from you. The traces are all of the same length, and hence the dogs run side by side, and, when properly harnessed, their heads are in a line. My traces are so measured that the shoulders of the dogs are just 20ft. from the foremost part of the runners.''

With a twelve-dog team, harnessed in this manner, a high rate of speed may be gained. Six measured miles have been run over a
Speed and tolerably good surface in twenty-eight minutes. The
the whip. direction and speed of the team are regulated partly by the voice, but mainly by the whip ; and, as this instrument is so important and difficult to handle, we cannot resist giving the reader the benefit of the experience of Dr. Kane, than whom few have had greater experience in dog-sledge management. He thus describes the whip he used for his teams. " The whip is 6yds. long, and the handle but 16in., a short lever by which to throw out such a length of seal hide. Learn to do it, however, with a masterly sweep, or else make

HELPING THE DOGS.

up your mind to forego driving a sledge, for the dogs are guided solely by the lash ; and you must be able, not only to hit any particular dog out of the team of twelve, but to accompany the feat also with a resounding crack. After this, you find that to get your lash back involves another difficulty, for it is apt to entangle itself among the dogs and lines, or to fasten itself cunningly round bits of ice so as to drag you head over heels into the snow. The secret by which this complicated set of requirements is fulfilled consists in properly describing an arc from the shoulder, with a stiff elbow, giving the jerk to the whip handle from the hand and wrist alone. The lash trails behind as you travel, and when thrown forward is allowed to extend itself, without an effort to bring it back. You wait patiently, after giving the projectile impulse until it unwinds its slow length, reaches the end of its tether, and cracks to tell you that it is at its journey's end. Such a crack on the ear or forefoot of an unfortunate dog is signalised by a howl quite unmistakable in its import. The mere labour of using this whip is such that the Esquimaux travel in couples, one sledge after the other. The hinder dogs follow mechanically and thus require no whip, and the drivers change about so as to rest each other."

Many of the Esquimaux sledges are most ingeniously constructed—some being formed of light slabs of bone, lashed together with sinew and shod with runners composed of highly- Esquimaux sledges polished walrus ivory. Should the surface of the and expedients. runners become roughened from any cause, the Esquimaux fills his

SMOOTHING ROUGH RUNNERS.

mouth with water, and then, by contracting his cheeks as in the act of blowing a trumpet, forces the water in a strong jet over the face of the runner. A coat of thin ice instantly forms, and becomes frozen firmly to the bone, producing a coating like that of glass. The above illustration will serve to show how this operation is conducted.

To estimate the speed at which a sledge is travelling, a log must be used. This is constructed as follows : A wooden reel and spindle, such as shown in the engraving on page 356, must be made; Sledge log round this the log line is coiled, leaving a free end for to make. the log or weight, which may consist of a piece of scrap iron or a stone, to be attached to. About 20yds. from the log a bit of red rag should be knotted to the line ; then at every 50ft. knot in a bit of seal hide. When about to use the log line, cast the weight well clear of the sledge, let the reel give off the line freely until the red rag is free. Directly that is off the coil, turn your half-minute glass up, and let the sand run, and when it is all down, stop the reel. It will be then seen,

A A 2

by the following calculation, what the speed has been. As 120 times half a minute make one hour, and 120 times 50ft. make very nearly a geographical mile, so many bits of hide will run clear of the revolving reel as the sledge travels miles in the hour.

When fitting up your sledge equipment procure some large-sized marrow bones, and saw them up into a number of tolerably stout rings; then, from other bones of solid texture, make toggles to accompany the rings. These contrivances, shown in the following illustration, are invaluable for attaching leather straps to each other. A simple slit in the end of each strap admits of the toggle being passed through them, when its notched form prevents it from coming out again. Knots in dog harness tend to endless hitches and entanglements; and buckles, from being composed of metal, would be stolen to a certainty. Three modes of attaching strips of hide to each other are shown below. Fig. 1 and 2 illustrate how the bone rings before described can be made use of. Fig. 3 shows two loops twisted over each other. A good-sized bladder, or skin bag, forms a convenient receptacle for both rings and toggles, of which make plenty.

Sledge equipment.

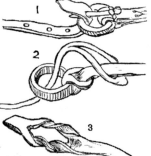

When about to pitch camp, or whilst resting, drive the spears into the ice to secure the dogs to by short neck ropes. Most sledge dogs are trained to lie down when the whip handle is passed lightly along their backs. Never heedlessly quit your sledge whilst on the march, unless you have fast hold of the upstanders, or without first bringing it to an anchor. This can be done by thrusting a seal spear or lance down into the snow between the first two transverse bars of the sledge bottom. Should you neglect these precautions, you stand a good chance of seeing your runaway team go rattling off in the far distance, leaving you to follow as you best may. To check the speed of your sledge when you are on it, plant your heels on the snow

Camping.

and sit fast. It will be generally found that in every team there will be one master dog, who, by the use of a sharp set of teeth and a strong will, contrives to keep all the rest in subjection, The habits of and not unfrequently quells disorder among the quarrel- sledge dogs. some pack by dashing in among them at the height of their constant skirmishes, and sending them head over heels to the right and left, thereby aiding his master in maintaining due discipline. Frozen or dried fish, and the offal of such animals as may be captured in the chase, are used as dog food. The Esquimaux usually feed Food for the their dogs but once in two days; it is better, however, to dogs. feed every day, but not until the work is finished, the journey ended, and the camp pitched. No dog works well on a full stomach. Great care should be exercised in the feeding of your dogs in order that all may share alike, as some are so desperately artful and cunning, that they do all in their power to delude their master into a belief that, instead of having had their full allowance, it is yet to come.

No northern traveller ever willingly allows his dogs to eat any portion of the liver of the polar bear, as it is pronounced by all the Esquimaux to be most unwholesome and injurious to dogs; they, therefore, either bury the bear's liver under the ice, or, if practicable, cast it into the sea. No sledge or portion of the sledge equipment in the construction or repair of which thongs or tendons have been used should be left in reach of the dogs during the night, or they will be pretty sure to reduce the whole to a wreck before morning. With such makeshifts sledges as have their runners made from rolls of frozen hide this precaution is especially necessary.

The following hints on the subject of sledges, given by Dr. Kane, are most valuable, being the result of no ordinary experience. To encounter broken ice in the midst of darkness, Hints on sledges. and at a temperature destructive to life, everything depends upon your sledge; should it break down, you might as well break your own leg—there is no hope for you. Our sledge, then, is made of well-seasoned oak, dovetailed into a runner shod with iron; no metal is used besides except the screws and rivets which confine the sledge to its runners. In this intense cold, iron snaps like glass, and no immovable or rigidly fastened wood-work would stand for a moment the fierce concussions of a drive. Everything is put together with lashings of sealskin, and the whole fabric is the skeleton framework of a sledge as flexible as a lady's work-basket, and weighing only 40lb. On this we fasten a sacking bottom of canvas, tightly stretched, like its namesake of the four-post bedstead, around the margin. We call this ticking the apron and cover; the apron being a flap of 16in. high surrounding the cover, and either hanging loose at its sides, like a valance, or laced up down the middle. Into this apron and cover you pack your cargo—the less the better—and then lace and lash the whole securely together.

The following rules to be observed on the march or during a halt are valuable and practical to a degree. " Keep the blood in motion

Rules for the march. without loitering on the march; and for the halt raise a snow house, or, if the snow lie scant or impracticable, ensconce yourself in a burrow, or under the hospitable lee of an inclined hummock-slab. The outside fat of your walrus sustains your little moss fire : its frozen slices give you bread; its frozen blubber gives you butter; its scrag ends make the soup. The snow supplies you with water, and when you are ambitious of coffee there is a bagful stowed away in your boot. Spread out your bear bag, your only heavy movable, and stuff your reindeer bag inside, hang your boots up outside, take a blade of bone and scrape off all the ice from your furs. Now crawl in, the whole party of you, feet foremost, draw the top of your dormitory close, heading to leeward."

When about to start on a sledge journey, a certain number of useful matters will be required in addition to those already mentioned.

Useful odds and ends. A few green or blue gauze or tarlatan veils, to protect the eyes from the glare of the snow, will be found of the greatest value. In the absence of these, sledge men not uncommonly collect a quantity of the deposit of black found in the sconces of the lamps. This they mix with grease, and with it black the eyelids and upper part of the face. This expedient, although not equal to a veil, is far better than nothing. We have made use of green glass spectacles, but found them next to useless, as the glasses soon became coated with ice, formed from the condensed vapour given off with the breath. Never travel without a small pocket mirror ; by its aid you can discover at once whether your nose or ears are becoming frost bitten, and can act accordingly. Directions for the treatment of frost bite will be given further on in our work. Never go without your possible sack, which should contain lots of hide strips, of all lengths and sizes, awls, needles, cord, leather, knife, whetstone, and any number of bone rings and toggles. A large fine-toothed rasp is of great service in fashioning bone ; take one, or more; one handle will serve for all, and the sharp, tang ends serve to bore holes with. Few men have managed to reduce their sledge equipment to more simple elements than the doctor. He says, " My plans for sledging, simple as I once thought them, and simple, certainly, as compared with those of the English parties, have completely changed. Give me an 8lb. reindeer

SLEDGING OVER ROUGH ICE.

fur bag to sleep in, an Esquimaux lamp, with a lump of moss, a sheet-iron snow melter, or a copper soup pot, with a tin cylinder to slip over and defend it from the wind, a good *pièce de résistance* of raw walrus beef, and I want nothing more for a long journey if the thermometer will keep itself as high as minus 30°. Give me a bearskin bag, and coffee to boot, and with the clothes on my back I am ready for minus 60°, but no wind." During long journeys over rough and uneven ice the paws of the dogs are liable to become worn and Dogs' boots. sore. It is well, therefore, before encountering such hindrances to travel, to protect them with mocassins. These are made by rounding a piece of soft hide, with the hair side in, and then cutting all round its edge a number of small slits; through these a strip of hide is passed. The dogs' paw is placed in the centre of the round. On the string being drawn home, the foot will be fitted as shown in the annexed illustration. Tolerably well-fed dogs will rarely eat these protections off, as they seem to know perfectly well what 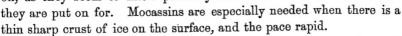 they are put on for. Mocassins are especially needed when there is a thin sharp crust of ice on the surface, and the pace rapid.

When the snow is soft, the form of sledge known as a "tobogun" is very useful, not only as a dog sledge, but as a convenient means of carrying packs, traps, or dead game; when used for The tobogun these purposes, the hunter, who usually travels on snow sledge. shoes, draws it after him by a track line. The tobogun is made by either bending up the end of a tough plank by steam, or cutting the desired form of wood out of the solid with the axe.

There is another kind of sledge somewhat on the tobogun principle, known as an ice board. This is made from exceedingly tough, elastic wood. It is turned up at the bow end like the toe of a Ice boards. skate, and usually measures about 1ft. wide by 8ft. long. It is made thus in order that it may freely pass along the narrow Indian trails across the lakes. This board, although tough and flexible enough to pass over the inequalities of the uneven way without breaking, is stiffened at the upturned prow by a piece of wood, which, being fastened inside the curve preserves its bent form. Several cross bars, disposed at intervals in the line of the sledge, serve to add to its strength. The bridle or drawing point of the sledge is formed of hide, and is secured to the beak or stiffener. The team of dogs used in drawing this kind of conveyance is harnessed to two stiff tough poles, which project to the front. The load is so packed as to admit of its being divided equally throughout the entire length of the board to which it is secured, by passing two hide ropes along its side from end to end. These side cords are attached by lashing to the cross bars, and form a series of points of attachment for the lashings which pass forward and back, and from side to side over the load. After being hauled up as tight as possible, there should be rope enough for two tail pieces to trail behind; these are useful to seize on when going down a slope, if the sledge requires turning, or in event of the dogs taking it into their heads to bolt on a steep incline, the sledge, load and all, is turned on its side, and allowed to drag to the bottom, where it is set right, and proceeds as before.

The common runner dog sledge is better adapted for travelling over tolerably hard snow, and the mode of harnessing the dogs is shown Common in the annexed engraving. The bearing points, chest dog sledge. band, and collar piece of the harness, should be made of thin soft hide, sewn double like an old fashioned shot belt, and then

stuffed with hair-wool, pounded bark, fibre, or moss. A seal should be always drawn head first, as it travels thus with less than one half the traction power. When the ground is hard, or in the absence of snow, The travail dogs are frequently used to draw a contrivance known as sledge. a " travail "; this is made by attaching two long tough sticks, slightly turned up at the hind ends, to the neck collar of the dog. The small ends of the sticks should rest nearest the head of the

dog; by some dog drivers these are made to just cross each other over the dog's neck, where they are bound to each other by a lashing of hide; others prefer attaching each stick in a line with the body of the dog, as in the above illustration. The travail sticks are padded at their points of contact, and kept asunder before and behind the load by cross bars of different lengths, the shortest being next the dog's hind legs. Horses are frequently equipped precisely in the same manner, as will be seen on reference to the engraving representing Indian lodges. A horse of fair average power will carry a travail load of about 212lb, twenty-five miles per day, and a good dog will draw 75lb. in the same way over prairie land.

Such dogs as are not employed in pulling very often carry packs on their backs,. as shown in the annexed illustration; these should be at all times very light, and the girths and breast strap wide enough to prevent undue pressure. We have

Dog packs.

seen the Tartars pack their dogs by placing a broad band of sheepskin with the wool inside round the dog, fasten it with loops and toggles, fit on a breast strap of the same material in the same way, and then secure the load to the girth by passing thongs through a set of bone rings sewn in for the purpose. The thongs pass across the load, and go through the rings on the opposite side, and thus secure the pack, without compressing the dog, as shown in the accompanying illustration.

When horses are used for sledge drawing it is no uncommon practice to attach them to a conveyance formed by mounting a common carriage body on runners. We have seen the Russians use a most convenient and durable sledge body; it was formed of strong wicker work, strengthened by stringers of light wood, bound with lashings of raw hide. The runners were faced with steel, and the horses, three in number, worked abreast; that in the centre having a sort of arch or hoop over his neck. Bells should

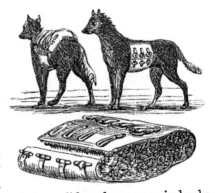

be used on all sledge teams, as the sledge glides along so noiselessly that collisions would be frequent without the cheerful warning note of the bells, which can be heard at a

Horse sledges.

great distance in the clear frosty air. It is not our intention here to enter on the subject of sledges, as used by the sledge clubs for amusement or display, as they are not within our province. Field artillery can be easily worked on the surface of frozen lakes and rivers, by attaching runners instead of wheels to the guns and waggons. The recoil of guns, when fired

Field artillery sledges.

from sledge runners, is often considerable, and many modes are adopted to govern it. The best makeshift plan we know is to prepare two long thick straw mats for each gun sledge, and before laying the gun, raise the breech ends of the runners by handspike power, to a sufficient height to admit of the mats being drawn well under them, when the handspike may be withdrawn, and the runners allowed to rest on the mats. A species of rough basket work formed from pine branches will answer the same purpose.

The reindeer is a most valuable animal for sledge drawing, and, from the immense number of animals of this description kept in a state of partial domestication in the north (it has been roughly computed that in Lapland alone there are 100,000), extensive use is made of them as beasts of burden, some being used as pack animals, and others worked on the snow in

The reindeer sledge.

the form of sledge (represented in the above illustration) known as the *kerres.*

The mode of harnessing the deer is peculiar, the bridle loop, formed of tendons, being under the front of the sledge; this arrangement gives lifting power. Then a single trace, attached to this bridle, passes between the deer's hind legs, and is attached to the collar (which is well padded with hair), after passing through a loop in the back band, where it meets under the chest. The guiding rein is single near the sledge, where the driver holds it, but double near its termination; one part is fastened to the collar, whilst the other is secured to the deer's head. This rein is used much as our ploughmen use a plough rein; it is composed of strips of plaited hide, and, by a dexterous turn of the wrist and elbow, can be made to do the duty of a whip, and, although little control can be exercised over a wayward animal, a tractable one will perform journeys of surpassing length in a wonderful short space of time ; from seven to eight miles an hour over tolerably good ground may be considered average travelling. It is recorded, however, that an officer charged with important dispatches once travelled from Umea, which is situated in the Gulf of Bothnia, to the city of Stockholm in forty-eight hours with one deer (the distance is little short of 500 miles) ; but the life of the deer was sacrificed in the performance of the journey. The weight of a deer's load will depend much on the nature of the work he is engaged on ; when employed in bringing in dead game, produce, &c., at a slow pace, he can easily draw 3cwt., but when equipped for a rapid journey the weight drawn should not amount to more than from 230lb. to 245lb. English. Sledge deer not unfrequently perform some curious and inconvenient freaks with their drivers. Should they from any cause consider themselves unfairly dealt with or harshly used, they immediately turn back on the conductor, who, to save himself, at once turns over the sledge and gets under it. The deer now tries to make use of his horns, but finds them of little avail against the mummy-like clothing of his skin-clad master, who usually settles the matter by the production of a lump of salt, which, when licked by the eager tongue of the irritated and cantankerous deer, acts like a charm in restoring order and a good understanding, when on he goes again as fresh and willingly as ever. In some parts of Siberia reindeer are regularly ridden, just as horses are in England and bullocks in Africa and the East.

Summer sledges of various forms are common to the whole world. We shall only deal with the most noteworthy and valuable to the settler or explorer. The most common of these, Summer sledges. known as a *wishing bone* sledge, is made from a curved and forked branch cut off to the required length, a deep notch

is cut at the point of the angle at the union of the fork to fasten the horses to, transverse pieces are trenailed across the prongs, the tail ends are slightly rounded up like the runners of a sledge, and the head is also curved in an upward direction with the axe, as seen in the above illustration. Sledges of this kind are very useful for the conveyance of rough heavy substances, such as building stones or mineral ores, packed in skin bags. Another usual form of farmer's or emigrant's sledge is also shown in the following illustration.

Auger holes are bored through the ends of the runners, through which

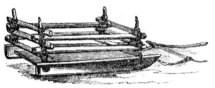

a strong wooden bar is passed, to this the traces are fastened.

The description of snow shoes used by the natives of different countries and localities vary just as much as the sledges. We can, therefore, only deal with the general principles of their construction and use. The "racquet" or snow shoe of the Canadians Snow shoes. varies in length with the degree of supporting power of the snow. The form of the snow shoe is shown in the accompanying illustration. The frame or outside rim of the shoe is made from tough, light wood; ash is much used for the purpose. The

network is often made from strips of moose skin, deer skin, or some other untanned hide. There are two modes by which the network is secured to the frame. One is to bore a train of gimlet holes at proper distances apart all round the frame, and with thin strips of hide or tendon passed

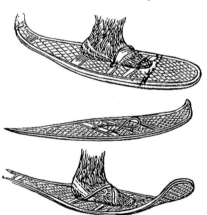

alternately backward and forward through them, the side loops of the racquet work are taken up and tied fast to the frame. The other method consists in winding a long thin thong round the frame, and so binding the interlacing to it. The annexed illustration shows some other forms of the snow shoe.

The snow shoe is not strapped to the foot like the skate, but is fastened in two ways. First, there is an arrangement of strap through which the foot is thrust without the aid of the hands; the length and attachment of the thong being proportioned to the foot of the wearer; then there is an orifice left in the middle of the network in the centre line of the shoe, but nearer to the toe than the heel; into this hole the front part of the foot is thrust, much as one would put on an old heelless slipper.

In the adjustment of the shoe fastenings, the ball of the great toe is made to rest on what the Indians call the "bimikibison," or walking strap. This is secured by its ends to the frame of the shoe, and by its sides by means of short straps to the front cross bar. In addition to these, a small loop is attached to the walking strap of just sufficient length to allow the toe to pass through, but narrow enough to keep back the ball of the foot, which acts as a sort of stopper, and by its pressure lifts and pushes the shoe upwards and forwards. In order to prevent the foot from working its way backwards, a strap or sling, the "adiman," passes round the back of the heel. With this arrangement the foot works, so to speak, like a scale beam, the bearing part being the ball joint of the great toe; and as either end of the beam tilts up or down, so the shoe is dragged on or becomes a resting spot until its fellow passes skimmingly forward, leaving a well-marked pair of grooves behind the traveller.

Makeshift snow shoes are often made in the forest from light, tough boards. These are hewn into the rough form of a fish—broad before and narrow behind. The toe hole, or "eye" of the shoe, is cut as in the more perfect shoe, and an indentation is hewn out of the solid to admit of the foot always dropping into its proper position. These are generally used over very soft snow or swampy unsafe ground. The curved snow shoes shown in the illustration on p. 364 are at times over 6ft. long, and are used on open ground; the shorter kinds being better adapted for walking the forest, where roots and other impediments to travel abound.

Such boots as are worn for ordinary travelling, are utterly useless to the snow-shoe runner, who could not perform his work in them. Here, again, customs vary with countries. The Snow-shoe boots. Esquimaux, after covering his feet well with birds' skins, encases them in coverings of sealskins, chewed pliant and soft by his loving spouse; over these he draws a pair of fur boots, made from the skins of bears' legs, with the feet left on. The mocassin is

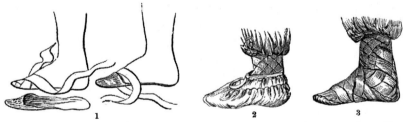

the form of foot gear best adapted for the use of the European traveller, and to put it on properly requires some little practice and management. The following directions will at any rate show the form and nature of the materials best calculated to insure comfort in walking and prevent frostbite. First make a pair of thick flannel *cap* socks, as shown in Fig. 1 (page 365). These are merely flannel soles or socks with a toe cap sewn to them. These are put on just as you would put on slippers, over the crossed ends of the long flannel bandages which fold evenly under the toes on each side, and lap over each other. The long ends are now brought round the foot, over the sole, round the heel, and are wound evenly and spirally over and under each other until brought well up under the calf of the leg. Here they are fastened off by passing the free ends two or three times under the coil. The mocassin may now be fastened on over this arrangement, as shown in Figs. 2 and 3, when a good thick pair of blanket leggings makes all complete for a tramp.

Unlike the snow shoes, the *skidor* of Lapland and Norway have no *racquet* work, but are merely long, narrow, upturned runners, to which the feet of the *skid löpare* or traveller are strapped. A peculiar staff, with a projecting rim round it, is carried to aid in propelling, guiding, &c., when ascending

Norwegian skidor.

or descending uneven surfaces. The annexed illustration will serve to give some idea of the way in which the skidor are used, but an immense deal of practice is required to make even a tolerably good *skid löpare*. We have seen skidor measuring over 7ft. in length.

The annexed engraving represents an excellent form of " boot mocassin" in common use throughout Lapland and the north of Sweden and Finland. As a foot and leg covering for those who tramp through wet forests over fallen logs and slippery

The Lapland boot.

boulders, we have found it unequalled, being flexible, waterproof, and easy to wear. It is entirely composed of tanned reindeer skin. The sole is formed from one piece of stout tough leather, and is continued into the sharp pointed and turned up toe. The lines in the illustration represents the position of the seams. Soft fine marsh hay is used inside the boot as a sort of sock, and the top of the leg or "mouth" of the boot is made so as to be closed under the knee by the aid of a long leather thong, which is passed through a number of small slits made in the leather, and then secured.

In some localities the shin bones of animals are used as aids in passing over frozen surfaces. One is securely strapped under the sole of each boot and made to act somewhat after the manner of a small sledge runner. On the use of skates we should have little to say, as the art of plain, straightforward Skates and their substitutes.

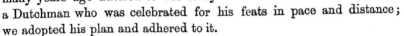

skating is too general to need more than a passing remark. We show in the accompanying illustration the mode of fastening which we have found most reliable for use on rough ice, and for hard work. We were many years ago advised to use it by a Dutchman who was celebrated for his feats in pace and distance; we adopted his plan and adhered to it.

CHAPTER VIII.

BOOTS, SHOES, AND SANDALS.

WE have already advised the traveller to include in his outfit a good store of English made boots and shoes—suited to the work he is likely to engage in—in warm countries such as Africa or India. We prefer shoes, and like them as light as is consistent with durability; but, for wear in the jungle or by the river side, we have never found any foot gear to equal moderately stout, but flexible, laced shooting boots and saumber-skin gaiters. The chief defects of a shoe is, that if it is too low, or ill made, so as to open at the sides, it may admit dirt or small stones, and that it does not protect the ankle or shin in walking through sharp grasses, such as the spear grass of India (the seeds of which are like the heads of Liliputian arrows), the *Triodia spinifex* of Australia, or the low "haak doorns" of Africa.

Medical and military writers recommend shoes either without or with only very low heels, and say that the so-called military heels give 2in. of additional height at the expense of all other good qualities; and this will at once be evident if we consider that the proper use of the foot in springing, walking, or running, depends upon its being able to move from a perfectly horizontal position, till the line of the sole from toe to heel forms an angle of 45° or 50° with the ground. If then, by the interposition of a block of leather, we prevent the heel coming within 15° or 20° of the horizontal line, we diminish the power of the foot just as much as we should the power of a bow, when, knowing that the archer could draw at 36in. we were to insist that the bow should be made with a curve of 18in., instead of being, as it ought, very nearly straight.

The so-called support to the ankle is not only unnecessary but positively injurious. Opera dancers do not usually perform in boots, but shoes as light as possible. Men, in the constant habit of wearing tight or heavy boots, are not likely to have good legs, and none march better than Highlanders in their kilts and shoes; or natives of wild countries, who only put on sandals when the expected march is so long that the hard skin of the foot would wear through faster than the natural growth could replace it. We suppose that it will be sufficiently definite to consider boots as having the upper leathers sufficiently high to cover the ankle, or as much of the leg or thigh as may be requisite. Shoes, as covering a part, or the whole of the foot up to, but not above, the ankle, and sandals as being merely soles fastened on by laces or thongs, but not covering or inclosing the foot. The form we have found most useful is that called the Oxonian (Fig. 1), coming just high enough to cover

1   2

the whole instep without interfering with the action of the joint, and fitting closely round beneath the ankle. Fig. 2 represents the Irish brogue, a good serviceable foot covering. Elastic sides do not stand hard wear in tropical heat, and therefore we use a front lacing. We object to bluchers, because after some wear the flaps of the quarters become loose, and bits of rotten stick or stiff grasses frequently are forced in in walking. Most countries have some form of shoe easily made from materials obtainable upon the spot, and in Africa the "velschoen" of untanned leather is the general wear.

African boots.

Sometimes these are very clumsily made, the naked foot is planted on the piece of leather intended for the sole, and the

outline is marked out with the point of a knife, the blade being held so far clear as to obviate all danger of cutting the foot, a plan which certainly has the merit of making the shoe sufficiently roomy. The thinner hide intended for the front is then laid on over the instep, and the edges, being brought down, are cut even with those of the sole; and, both being bored with an awl, are stitched through and through with leather thongs, the quarters are then fitted on in the same manner, and the only reason that the stitches do not wear out is that the sole is so much wider than the foot, that no weight comes upon the part in which the seam is made. A couple of holes in the front of the quarters receive another thong which serves as a tie, and this, being the only part that is in anyway tight, must considerably gall the instep.

The hides of the giraffe, the eland, or the buffalo are used for soles, and a piece large enough for a pair may generally be purchased for eighteenpence. These are simply dried, and a native must be hired to beat and soften them, working grease into them as he does so till they become so soft and supple that, though they are not waterproof in the sense of absolutely repelling the liquid, they may be wetted through and dried again without becoming hard. Sometimes a native will do this for a knife (value ninepence or a shilling) and the grease; but a sharp look-out must be kept upon the latter, or he will rub it into his own skin instead of that which he is employed to soften. An African can no more be trusted with fat than many of our own countrymen with ardent spirits.

For the upper leather the hide of many of the larger antelopes will do, but that of the "koodoo" is most universally esteemed, being somewhat thicker than stout calf, and very soft and durable; that of the wildebeeste is too hard and stout, and those of the springbok and smaller antelopes too thin. The skin is also subjected to a long preliminary rubbing and working in the hands of the natives, grease being occasionally smeared on.

The preparation of a good-sized skin—such as that of a koodoo, or of an ox, if it is to be softened so as to be fit for purposes where lightness and pliability are required—is performed as follows. If the hair is to be removed, the skin is wrapped up with the hair inward, fresh cattle dung having been previously spread over it to keep it moist, and if the party be not on a journey, it is buried for a day or two, to "sweat" the hair off; but if the hair is to be retained, the preliminary process is dispensed with. If the thickness of the hide is to be reduced, it is then pegged out tightly upon the ground, with the hair side downward, and the flesh, and as much of the inner side of the skin as requisite, removed by scraping with the small, broad-edged, soft iron blades set like adzes, across the handle, and used very much in the manner of the scrapers, which so much disgust passengers on long voyages when used upon the deck above their berths. The hide having been still kept damp and soft by being covered with cattle dung, or moist clay, is next taken in hand by half a dozen or more natives, who, sitting around it and grasping each their handful of the edge, compress and rub it in every possible direction, ever and anon driving all their hands together towards the centre, and then simultaneously falling back, stretching the skin to the utmost. Grease has to be applied occasionally, and the skin, when put away for the night, must be carefully rolled up and kept under moist earth till morning.

Most of the native tribes also have some species of mimosa, generally a small variety, the bark and young roots of which they pound as fine as possible in their wooden mortars, and, by rubbing in the powder during the dressing of the skin, they partially tan it, and impart to it a reddish brown colour.

Before proceeding to make or repair boots or shoes, shoemakers' wax will be required. It is a good plan to take a hornfull out from England. The wax horn may be made from the horn of a common cow; fill it with softened wax Shoemakers' Wax. until nearly full, put in a wooden bottom, secure it in its place by driving in three or four wire pins, and all is made secure. When the wax is required for use, saw off the small end of the horn far enough down to reach the contents. Apply heat to the exterior until the wax runs out in sufficient quantity on a greased stone; take up as much as is needed for use, work it into a ball, and put it to swim in a little water. If you have to make your own wax proceed as follows: Take 4oz. of resin, grind it to a fine powder between two stones, ¼oz. of beeswax chopped up small, and 2oz. of common pitch; mix these substances with the resin, and place the whole in a small native chatty pot. Then put the pot in a bed of hot wood ashes, and with a long flat-pointed stick work and stir the mass about until thoroughly melted; then add ¾oz. of good clean fat, and keep the whole in a state of solution for about a quarter of an hour or twenty minutes. Grease the bottom of a calabash or bowl, half fill it with cold water; take your pot off the fire with a twisted stick, and pour the molten materials into the water. When cold enough to handle, grease your hands, and work the wax about; pull it out into long strips, double these back on themselves, and so proceed until all the materials are well amalgamated; then work it out into a long stick or rod, take a greased knife, and divide it up into pieces large enough to make convenient-sized balls for use. These are best kept floating in water until wanted.

In making a pair of shoes the mode usually adopted is that previously described, and, by dint of patience and careful fitting, some persons will make them very neatly and effectively in this manner; but, after all, there is always an uncertainty as to their fitting properly, and we found it much better to take the trouble in the first instance of making a pair of lasts. For this purpose it is best to take the length of the foot, its extreme breadth and Lasts. height at the instep, and cut two logs of tolerably hard even-grained wood (we used the sweet gum), rather larger, and square them up to these dimensions—say, length 10in., breadth, 3in., and height 4in., more or less. Then, placing the foot upon a piece of soft ground, trace its outline, and then, holding a board vertically against the inner side, trace off on this the profile, and, removing the foot, trace also the outline of the print it has made upon the ground. The inner side and the bottom of each block ought to be nicely and truly squared up, even though, from scantiness of wood or other causes, the other sides should not be so. Take all the measurements for breadth from the straight line made by the edge of the board upon the ground, and measure them from the inside edge, right and left, upon the bottom of the blocks; draw the outline, and inside it draw also the actual tread of the foot, measured in the same manner from the impression on the ground. Then measuring from the bottom of the board, transfer the profile. of the foot to the inside surface of each block, and with axe or saw cut them to the outline of the heel and instep, taking care not to attempt to round them till you have also cut them to the outline of the breadth; then, having ascertained that all your measurements are true, and that both lasts are of similar size and form, begin to round.them as nearly as possible to the natural form of the foot, lowering them more on the outer side toward the small toes than on the inner, where the line of the instep extends from the ankle to the great toe; then, having ascertained the arch of the foot, commence rounding away the edges of the sole from the inner line, observing that in the waist of the foot the tread runs very nearly along the outer edge, leaving nearly all the hollow to be cut away on the inner side. Let the sole rise from the ground a little also under the toes, as their pressure downward will make the shoe fit better, and it will be less

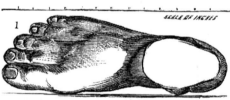

liable to catch small impediments when walking.

Bear in mind that in the natural foot the great toe is as nearly as possible parallel to the straight line drawn along the inside of the foot, and if it is forced from this position by ill-cut shoes, such as some years ago were inappropriately called "straights," or by the wearing of high heels, not only is the beauty of the foot sacrificed, but its elasticity, its strength, and usefulness are materially diminished. In

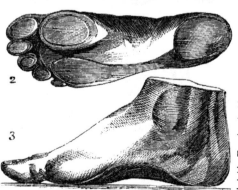

Figs. 1, 2, and 3 we have represented the natural form of the foot, distinguishing by the flat shadow the part that actually touches the ground, and by a

lighter outline along the hollow, that which may be considered as the average limit of the sole. These are one-fourth the natural size, and, by using inches for the quarter inches in our drawings, the enlarged outlines will be a sufficient guide in cutting the lasts, the average proportions of feet being very nearly the same, though of course dimensions will vary. In Fig. 1 of the next illustration we give the forms of sole that may be used. If the ground is bad, and it is necessary to defend the foot against thorns, sharp stones, &c., the outer lines may be adopted; but on tolerably fair ground, it is only the actual tread that requires protection from the sole. However, as the foot is constant in its size, the smaller the sole is the larger must be the upper leather. Of this last we have represented two forms. They are both shown, folded and stitched, so as to be ready for lasting; but the smaller figures within show the form of each part before it is parted.

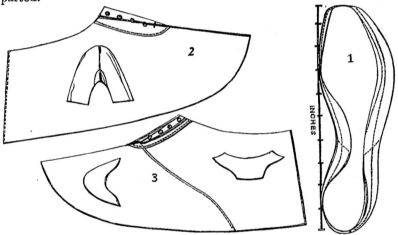

In Fig. 2 the whole upper is cut out from one piece, folded in the centre of the front, and stitched at the heel. The edges should not be cut off too close to the seam (otherwise neatness will be gained at the expense of strength), and they should always be outside; for, if they be turned in, it would be very difficult to flatten them so perfectly as not to gall the heel. The front is split 2½in. or 3in. down the instep, and a piece of stout leather, with its edges thinned down, is stitched on and pierced with holes to receive the lacing. It is split not quite through, but about ½in. is left to strengthen the front of the shoe, and prevent the thinner leather tearing. The edges in which the holes are pierced are, of course, left the full thickness. A tongue of soft leather ought to be stitched in, that the lacing may not gall the instep, but the edges of this must be carefully thinned down, and no knots or ends of thread should be left inside. The ends may be fastened off very neatly without knots by merely taking one or two stitches backward along the already finished seam, and even if the fastening should show outside, it will still be better than that after a long march the instep should be found chafed and bleeding, and a sore established which will be very difficult to heal.

In Fig. 3 the front is in one piece and the quarter in another, and this is a convenient arrangement when, though you may have plenty of leather, it is not of sufficient size to cut the upper in a single piece. Generally, the edge of the quarter is laid over that of the front, and stitched, leaving the upper part loose as a flap or ear to receive the tie or lacing. In this case, the centre of the front is left long enough to come up as a tongue to defend the instep, but this method has the disadvantage of leaving a space on either side the foot, opening forward as in the case of bluchers, and liable to receive in walking broken sticks, reeds, or grass stems, which are often forced in with considerable violence. We, therefore, prefer to stitch the front edge over that of the quarter, inserting a tongue as neatly as possible, and stitching on, as before, edgings of stiff leather to receive the lacing, taking care, also, that all edges inside the shoe are trimmed off to nothing, and that no fastenings off are made inside.

All these should be sewn with saddler's seams "—that is, the two parts should be laid together, and holes being pierced with a fine straight awl, the two threads should be passed through from right and left simultaneously, and drawn tight with an equally firm pull on either hand. The seam will thus show no difference on either of the sides; but, if a section were made, it would present the appearance of a chain, as in Fig. 5 of the engraving on p. 376, each link inclosing the thickness of leather left between the holes. Although the threads should be tightened with a firm hand, they should not be hauled upon so as unduly to contract the leather, and so make the seam grip the foot like a cord when the shoe is finished.

The dorsal sinews of the springbok, or the domestic goat, separated into fibre of the proper size, will answer very well for this purpose, the points, being cut sharp, wetted, and twisted a little, will be quite rigid enough to pass through the holes previously bored; but while we have a stock of good whity-grey thread, we prefer to use it double and well waxed, in a couple of stout tailor's needles, always, however, boring the holes with a fine awl to insure regularity.

A pair of clamps are necessary to hold the work, as both hands are employed in sewing. They may be made of two staves of a powder barrel, or an American flour cask, or any other light elastic boards that can be made to curve inward, and grip with a fair edge with tolerable firmness. These are held between the knees, so that the work may be in a convenient position for eye and

Clamps.

hand. If barrel staves cannot be had, two small bits of plank, with fair edges, may be fitted in the smith's vice. A young sapling, 2in. or 3in. thick, may be cut off about 30in. from its root, and the stump slit down with a sharp axe, the edges being trimmed off thin and fair: or the boat nippers described at p. 113 may be pressed into service.

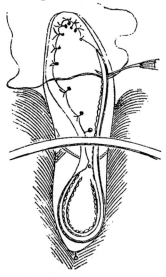

The orthodox material for sewing on the sole is, of course, the waxed thread, made by taking from three to six or eight thicknesses of the flax sold in balls for that purpose, twisting them loosely together, and waxing them with the mixture before described. The ends of the thread are thinned to a fine point, and, a bristle being split part of its length, the fine end of the thread is laid between the parts, and then rolled several times round both of them; and the fastening is made by opening

Thread.

the strands of the thread, and passing the perfect end of the bristle through them. It is much more easy to do this than to describe it, and in five minutes practice almost anyone ought to be able to learn it. We prefer, however, fine "reimpjies," or thongs, rather less than ⅛in. broad, cut from the skin of a steinbok, and nicely rubbed up, stretched, and smoothed. The points of these cut sharp, wetted a little, twisted, and allowed to dry, will be quite fine and hard enough to be passed through the awl holes; but we have upon occasion taken a bit of fine brass rabbit wire, and passing it through a hole in the end of the thong, as far as the middle, have doubled the two ends together, and twisted them into one, to obtain a more rigid point.

Of the several methods of stitching, the simplest, as has been mentioned, is to lay the edges of the sole and upper leather together, and stitch them through and through (Fig. 1, p. 376). In this case, however, either the thread appears outside, and is ex-

Stitching.

posed to be chafed upon the ground, or the sole itself must be cut so as to let the stitches in, and sometimes a cut is made in the edge of the sole, as in Fig. 2, but this has by no means a neat and finished appearance.

Some of the Dutch farmers use what is called the "binnen naaid," or

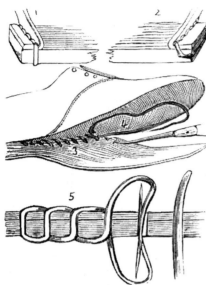

inside seam. This is made by turning the edge of the upper leather (Fig. 4) in upon the sole (Fig. 3), and sewing it with a kind of back-stitch, which will be better understood by reference to the figure than by description. It must be begun in the waist of the foot and worked round the front to the other side. The heel is finished last of all, as, when the shoe is once closed, the fore parts of it could not be reached. This seam is very neat, but a last cannot be used in making it. The plan we adopted is that used by shoemakers for pumps or single soled shoes, and we believe this to be the easiest, the neatest, and, at the same time, the most durable. The sole (Fig. 1) is cut with the heel toward the thickest part (if there be any difference) of the leather, and if greater thickness is required, another piece (Fig. 2) should be cut to the shape of the heel and thinned

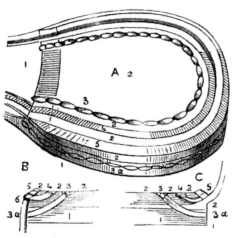

away to nothing in front, as it must be placed on the inside of the true sole, and a thick edge would of course give pain to the foot. A small groove or channel (Fig. 3), just deep enough to bury the stitches, should be cut about ½in. from the edge upon the upper surface, and a similar one (Fig. 3a) in the edge of the true sole; then, the holes being pierced with a curved awl, the two parts should be firmly sewn together. Fig. 4 represents the channel cut all round the sole and heel for stitching on the upper leather, and Fig. 5 the bevelled edge against which the upper leather is laid. B is a sectional view, with all the parts similarly numbered, the upper leather being stitched on; and C another with the upper stitched and turned into its proper position when the shoe is finished. The sole, with its inside uppermost, must then be laid upon its proper last, and tacked to it with nails or pegs that will easily draw out when no longer required, and care must be taken that the waist fits well down into the hollow of the last. The edge must then be bevelled off, at an angle of 45° all round, reducing its apparent thickness by about one-half. In very fine work the edge is thinned down almost to nothing in the waist, but is left nearly of its full thickness in the heel. The object of this, however, is to present an inclined surface for the upper leather to rest against and be stitched to.

The upper is then turned inside out, and placed upon the last; its height at the heel, at the sides, and on the instep, is measured, and these points are first secured by small tacks, driven about half in, so that they can be withdrawn when no longer wanted. The edges are then drawn tightly over the edges of the sole, and tacked to it, beginning at the toe and proceeding equally along the sides as far as the beginning of the heel. The last is then taken, with the sole upward, between the knees, where it may be confined by a strap long enough to pass round the feet; holes are pierced with a sharp curved awl, through the upper leather, and the bevelled edge of the sole, to the channel previously cut. The thread or thong of steinbok hide, being pointed at both ends, is drawn as far as its middle through the first hole, the two ends are passed simultaneously from right and left through each successive one, and the seam, commencing from the fore part of the heel on one side, goes forward round the toe, until it comes as far back on the other side. In commencing the sewing of the heel, if an inner thickening piece has been put on, care must be taken that in front, where it is yet thin, the stitches take up also a portion of the thickness of the true sole, and do not depend only on the inner heel, until they have passed the end of the seam that connects the two thicknesses together. If the stitches of the connecting seam have been set far enough into the substance of the leather, there will be no danger of cutting them in boring the holes for sewing on the upper.

In fastening off, take two stitches back upon the seam, and a hole may be bored through one part of the thong to pass the end of the other through, but no knots must be made; inside they would gall the feet, and outside they would look clumsy and unworkmanlike. Our sketch will sufficiently illustrate the foregoing description. Fig. 1A is the sole; Fig. 4, the channel and stitching; Fig. 4a, the stitching seen through the upper leather, and D the last; B shows the relative position of the parts when the shoe is taken off the last, and turned

ready for use. No inner sole or lining is needed, for the leather itself
is softened sufficiently in the native process. We generally preferred

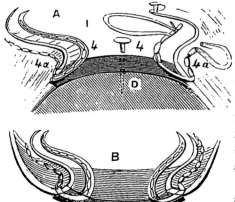

to turn the outer side, or that
from which the hair had been
stripped, inward, as it was
smoother to the foot; and
besides this, if left outside,
would soon have looked shabby
from contact with grass or
thorns, whereas the inner or
fleshy side would suffer no
change of appearance by casual
abrasion.

The shoe first finished
should be kept in a cool moist
place, and not suffered to dry
till both are done, when they should be taken off the lasts, turned right
side outward, and each put upon the last on which the other was made,
and allowed to dry, a very little fat being rubbed upon them, that it
may be absorbed as the water dries out, to prevent their becoming
hard.

In one pair of shoes thus made, with soles of buffalo hide and
koodoo uppers, we have performed three journeys of eighty miles
each, with quite enough intermediate walking to make up the 300.

It may be thought that we have insisted too much on the lightness
and pliability of foot gear, but it must be remembered that we now
speak of what, under particular conditions, we have found useful. A
change of circumstances might render large and heavy boots an absolute necessity. The American Indian wears the lightest possible
mocassin ; the South African, when he comes near his game, takes off
his sandals, that he may step as noiselessly as a cat. The European
hunter will do well to follow their example as closely as he can, and,
whatever the form of the foot-gear he adopts may be, let it be light
and flexible enough to walk, jump, climb, or run with facility.

The principle of the mocassin appears to be that in almost
universal use among all the Esquimaux and North American Indians,
Mocassins.   the leading difference in form of construction being that
the former usually carry the upper leather up over the
leg to form a species of boot, whilst the latter covers the foot only
with the mocassin. Unlike the shoes we have described, the Indian
mocassin has far more sole than upper leather, as the so-called sole
extends up over the sides, front, and heel, to be united with the border

leather and front flap by a gathering seam. When about to undertake a journey over very hard or rough ground, a sort of supplementary sole of green hide, with the hair left 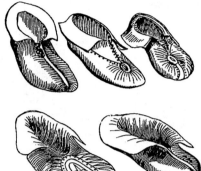 on the outside, is not unfrequently put on. The leather used in the manufacture of the best and softest description of mocassins require an immense deal of rubbing, dressing, and manipulation; that used by the Esquimaux tribes is chewed by the women until beautifully soft and pliant. Different tribes of Indians adopt different styles or fashions in the cut and finish of their foot gear, as shown in the illustration annexed, which represents the mocassins of distinct tribes; thus it is by no means difficult to detect attempted imposition by closely investigating the foot coverings of a spy or secret enemy.

Various makeshift foot coverings are used by different nations. Some of the bushmen and half-civilised Hottentots, when they have killed an animal of suitable size, such as a buffalo, quagga, or Makeshift any of the larger antelopes, will cut the skin all round foot coverings. above and below the hough, and, having stripped it off, will draw it upon their own foot, so that the heel comes where the hough of the  animal used to be; the toe is then closed with a few stitches, a slit for a small tie or lacing is made on the instep, and, by walking in it before it dries or hardens, it is trodden into the shape of the foot. We have chosen the quagga skin for our illustration because the stripes help to identify the parts used for the hough-skin shoe; but it is, perhaps, the least eligible for the purpose, as it dries so hard and rigid that it must be very unpleasant wear. The North American Indians use the hough-skin of the moose in the same manner.

The peasantry and brigands of Calabria and many other portions of the South of Europe, wear a very simple and useful kind of makeshift shoe. A piece of soft hide is cut to several sizes larger than the foot, a number of points or corners are allowed to remain along the edges, the foot, after being well swathed in bandages, is placed on the piece of hide, which is then gathered up round the foot by looping and knotting a long strip of cotton cloth or tape forward and back to

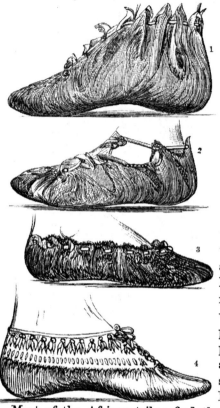

the corners of the hide until all is secure and compact, as shown in the illustration annexed (Fig. 2).

The old Highland caterans shod themselves in much the same manner. We have seen the Crim-Tartars make excellent winter foot coverings from sheepskin, with the wool inwards (Fig. 1). This was cut much after the Calabrian plan, but the corners, after having slits made in them, were looped to short flat leather straps, which when crossed forward and back over the front, were laced together with a long narrow thong of sheepskin, which served to hold a wider piece of wool-covered skin in place, as a sort of gaiter. They also make a summer shoe from soft tanned hide, as shown in Figs. 3 and 4.

Most of the African tribes find the skin of their sole sufficiently hard for their ordinary and daily walks, but when they expect to make long marches they invariably use some sort of artificial protection; and there is no surer sign on the frontier of the Cape Colony that the Kafirs intend to make war than to see among them a general preparation of velschoens or sandals; and often the cattle farmers on the frontier have been thus forewarned, while the Government authorities, deceived by plausible excuses, have imagined there was every prospect of a continued peace.

Various forms of sandal are in use among different tribes, but those used by the Bechuana (Fig. 1, next page) may be taken as a sufficiently useful type. The leather is sometimes rendered slightly pliable by being pounded and beaten, but very often not. The foot is planted on it, and the outline drawn, the sole being cut somewhat larger than this.

Two slits are made, one on each side the hollow of the foot, and the two ends of a piece of hide are passed up through them, as shown in Fig. 2 ; and in each end of this are cut two slits, as seen in Figs. 1, 2, 3, for the two parts of a thong of dressed hide to pass through.

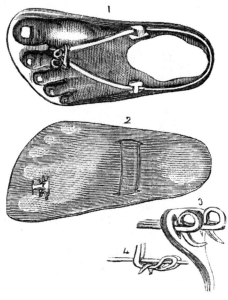

The ends of this are passed through another piece which goes down between the great toe and the next, then passes through the sole, and is fastened sometimes by being returned through two other holes, and the divided ends passed through a hole bored "in their own parts," as in Fig. 4, and sometimes by being simply returned only once in the manner shown in Fig. 3, which represents the very

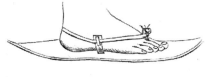

simple arrangement for tightening the side straps; in fact, a thong of hide, with several holes bored in it for its own end to pass through, may be lengthened or shortened up as conveniently as a strap and buckle, the sandal being put on or off simply by drawing the loop of the thong over the heel in the same manner as a low shoe.

The Damaras wear sandals with the toe and heel pointed, and elongated 2in. or 3in. beyond the foot, like a small snow shoe; this saves the toes from contact with small thorns, and they often strap on greaves of stiff hide to protect the shins.

In Timor, we purchased two or three pairs of palm leaf sandals, very nicely woven ; these last are very well for a few hours' walking, and, being very cheap, may be renewed as often as requisite. On some of the pilgrim roads in India, the poorer travellers seldom provide sandals for themselves, but pick up those that are thrown away half worn by the more luxurious.

Small rope, not more than ½in. in diameter, makes a good sole, and by thinning one end, and beginning by bending this just before  the hollow of the foot, then coiling it six or seven times round, and finishing off on the inside of the foot, so as to leave the front two turns wider than the heel, a very fairly shaped sole may be made ; this may be fitted either with thongs as a sandal, or as a slipper with a canvas upper. The Malays wear a wooden sole, the heel and tread of which are about 2in. thick; it is held to the foot simply by a peg, with a knob or button on the top, which is taken between the great toe and the next, and thus held on or dropped off at pleasure; this is, in fact, much the same that is worn by the Turks, Japanese, and Persians, only that they use a leather strap instead of a button.

Sabots are, at times, extremely useful ; they can be made from any light soft wood, such as withy, willow, poplar, or cotton wood (*Populus tremuloides*). Cut two blocks from a log with the axe, fashion them roughly into the form of a high shoe, and then, with a mallet and sharp gouge, proceed to hollow them out to the requisite capacity and thinness, when the outsides may be finished off with the spokeshave. Socks formed of sheepskin, with the wool on, add much to the comfort of the wearer. The Russian soldiers, before Sebastopol, made excellent socks or false soles from plaited straw ; these were worn inside their long boots, and served to preserve the feet from damp; no stockings were worn with them. An excellent description of sabot was forwarded to us during the Crimean war for use in camp; the sole was of light wood, the upper leather was like that of a high shoe, and the lining of thick felt. The leather and wood were connected round the edges by the use of a row of small flat headed tacks, much like those used in making a pair of bellows. No description of foot gear we have ever seen equals these felt-lined sabots for use during tent life. In Chinese Tartary a sort of boot composed of thick felt is worn over both stocking and shoe. When camping in or travelling through tropical countries, never omit turning your boots or shoes upside down, and rapping the soles sharply before venturing to put them on, as scorpions, centipedes, and other unwelcome intruders, are particularly fond of taking shelter in such convenient retreats. We have found it an excellent plan, when boots or shoes of native leather get thoroughly water soaked, to fill them tightly with any kind of grain ; the moisture is absorbed rapidly by it, and the leather is prevented from shrinking by the expansion of the seed.

Sabots and socks.

It is well to keep a good-sized pot or canister of dubbin for your English boots and shoes. This is best made as follows :—Take of oil, obtained by boiling ox feet, half a pint ; beeswax, Dubbin, to make. 1oz. ; spirits of turpentine, 1oz. ; Burgundy pitch, ½oz. ; resin, ½oz. Mix all the ingredients, except the spirits of turpentine, together in a chatty, and melt them over the embers of the camp fire until thoroughly dissolved ; then remove the pot from the fire, pour in the spirits of turpentine, and stir the whole with a piece of lath until cold. To apply the dubbin properly, the boot or shoe must be held to the fire until warm, when every part of it, sole, heel, and upper, may receive a thorough dressing over, and subsequent rubbing. This not only preserves the leather from the effects of hot sun and wet ground, but prevents the white ants, cockroaches, and other devouring insects from eating it.

One of our naval friends, who was an ardent naturalist, had a pair of French wooden shoes, which he found a great protection while wading among sharp rocks in search of specimens, where india-rubber boots would have been cut and become leaky. A perfectly waterproof boot or garment of any kind is an excellent thing, but an imperfect one is worse than useless ; and for wading after specimens or working in the water, if it is not convenient to be naked, a pair of wooden clogs, with a flannel shirt and drawers, and a straw hat or Tam o' Shanter bonnet, is as good an equipment as any.

We have before spoken of india-rubber wading boots, which, to be of value, should be of first-class quality and finish. India-rubber boots, It will sometimes happen that, notwithstanding all to mend. the precautions you may take to guard them from injury, that sharp-pointed sticks, thorns, &c., will make holes in them large enough to admit water. In order to enable you to repair these injuries when they occur, it will be well to purchase from the maker of the boots a good supply of sheet india-rubber. Get also from a chemist a bottle of coal-tar naphtha fitted with a glass stopper. When about to mend your boots, take a sharp knife or pair of scissors, and snip or cut up about 2oz. of the india-rubber sheet. The cut pieces should not be larger than good-sized buck-shot. Put these into a wide-mouthed bottle, such as is used for gum ; now pour in enough naphtha to cover the rubber ; put in the cork, and let the mixture stand for a few hours to soak ; then shake the bottle, turn it upside down, and rattle it from side to side ; repeat this process from time to time until the rubber is thoroughly dissolved in the naphtha, which it will be in about three days. Should it become sticky and thick, pour in a little more naphtha and shake it about until of a convenient consistency for use. Now cut a patch from the sheet rubber, large enough to extend well beyond the margin of the hole; give both the patch and the surface to which it is to be applied a good coating of the rubber varnish; lay on the patch; press it well home; place a flat board in the boot under the patch, and another board on the outside over it, so as to nip both patch and boot between them; lay a heavy stone or other weight on the outside board, and let the whole arrangement remain until the varnish is dry and the union between the parts complete. If the hole is in the leg of your boot, turn it inside out until the injured spot is reached and the patch is seen through the hole. Proceed now with the inside exactly as you did with the outside, when the mend will be complete. If the hole is in the foot of the boot, use only the single patch attached to the outside.

When the sole of a shoe has once been soaked with salt water, it always retains dampness, and cannot again be worn with comfort or pleasure. India-rubber shoes cannot be worn in warm countries either alone or over the ordinary shoes, unless they are cut low and open, and even then the lengthened use of them is inconvenient and painful.

Sore feet. It not unfrequently happens that the feet of those not thoroughly accustomed to hard tramping will become blistered. When the eggs of either poultry or wild birds are to be obtained, it is a good plan to break one or two, according to their size, into each shoe before starting in the morning; or, if you have any spirit, put a little in a cup or dish, place a lump of tallow on a flat stick, and hold a hot brand over it until the fat melts and runs

into the spirit. The ointment thus prepared may now be taken from the spirit and applied thickly to the sore surfaces and bottoms of the stockings. When large bladders form, take one of your needles and draw a piece of soft worsted or woollen thread, obtained by unravelling a bit of old shirt, directly through the bladders. This acts as a seton, and causes the fluid to freely discharge itself.

Whilst in Germany we were shown a very portable and simple form of strap boot jack, which can be packed up and stowed away in a very small space. The contrivance consists of a small The German boot jack. endless band of leather, with a long slit made in it. The boot to be drawn off is placed in the slit in the manner shown in the above illustration, whilst the loop of the strap is pulled on by the other booted or unbooted foot. This contrivance is especially useful for drawing off long riding, wading, or sea boots, when their legs do not admit of the free passage out of the foot.

CHAPTER IX.

WAGGONS AND OTHER WHEELED VEHICLES.

THE wheeled carriages made use of in different parts of the world are even more various in their design and construction than the sledges before described ; and, as a general rule, it will be found, when the test of actual use is brought to bear, that the description of contrivance (or at least a modification of it) in use among the civilised and semi-civilised inhabitants of a country or colony will be best adapted for such work as may have to be performed in it by the traveller or explorer. It is, however, difficult to overcome home prejudices, and, as an almost invariable rule, the British emigrant, on his arrival at the Cape of Good Hope or Australia, commences by denouncing the colonial waggon as clumsy, unworkmanlike, and inefficient, and usually threatens to effect immense improvements, and just as invariably, if he has to make a journey of any distance into the interior, he adopts, if he be a sensible man, the vehicle which, by the experience of many, has been found the best for the work it has to do. On the well-made roads near Cape Town or Port Elizabeth, or on the broad plains of the Orange River Free State, imported carriages from England, or vehicles upon their model by colonial builders, may be used with safety and advantage ; and even some of those wondrous combinations of strength and lightness imported from America, under the names of spider or skeleton carriages, are found to do good service ; but when really hard work comes on, and densely wooded kloofs or rugged mountain passes, with rough stretches of road over hill-side or valley, with fords in which stones of several hundredweight seem to lose their gravitation and become the mere playthings of the torrent, the ponderous Cape waggon will be at once appreciated, as all its parts are so strongly put together that the strain of twelve or twenty oxen cannot draw them asunder, and yet fitted so loosely that they will give and bend to every inequality of the road. The Cape waggon is found to hold its position against all rivals as the vehicle best adapted to the wants of a travelling or exploring party, and the

c c

exigencies of the transport service and general carrying trade of the country.

We have already, at pp. 52 and 53, given an example of a Cape waggon with side tents; at p. 114, we have shown how the tent frame or other material of a waggon might be converted into a boat; at p. 123, we have indicated the manner in which the waggon chests might be made available as a raft ; at pp. 188—192 will be found diagrams and instructions for repairing axles, fore tongs, dissel-booms, strengthening wheels when the spokes are shaken loose, tightening up the tires by driving wedges between them and the felloes, or making and putting in new spokes without taking the wheel to pieces; at pp. 170—172 are remarks on tiring of wheels and prolonging the efficiency of strained bolts by shifting them so as to freshen the nip; at p. 263 waggon camps are described; and the method of building wheels is given at pp. 324—330.

It is therefore, now only necessary to give a general view of a full-sized "kap-tented" travelling waggon, with diagrams of such parts as have not hitherto come under notice. Such a waggon is represented in Fig. 1, and the buik plank, or floor (*a*), will sometimes be 17ft. or more in length, though in moderate-sized vehicles it does not exceed 13ft., or thereabouts. The sides are generally of yellow wood (⅜in. plank), *b*, secured to a substantial ladder-like frame, the longer pieces of which (*c*) are called "leer boomen," or ladder trees. The sides and bottom are not fastened together, nor are they fastened to the understell or carriage, but the bottom plank is simply laid upon the schammels (*d*) and secured from moving by cleats (*e*), which grip the after one. The fore and hinder axles are connected by a stout beam, called the "lang wagen" (*f*), working freely on a pivot passing through the aftermost jaws of the fore tong (*g*), and strengthened by a bar of iron (*h*), called the iron "lang wagen." The dissel-boom works like a carriage pole in the foremost jaws of the "fore tong." In this tong, also immediately behind the axle, is a stout ring-bolt (*i*), to which are attached the drag chains, and they, with the reim schoen and the tar bucket, are looped up to hooks, fixed at the attachment of the after tongs (*j*) with the lang wagen. To the back of the after axle is suspended a kind of framework, called the "trap" (*k*), for the reception of pots, kettles, and general lumber. Into the ends of the schammels are set rungs, or stancheons (*l*), which confine and support the waggon sides. Fig. 2 shows the arrangement of the carriage, clear of the wheels and top hamper. All the parts are distinguished by the same letters. Fig. 3 shows how the buik plank (*a*) is laid upon the after schammel (*d*), and kept from shifting by the

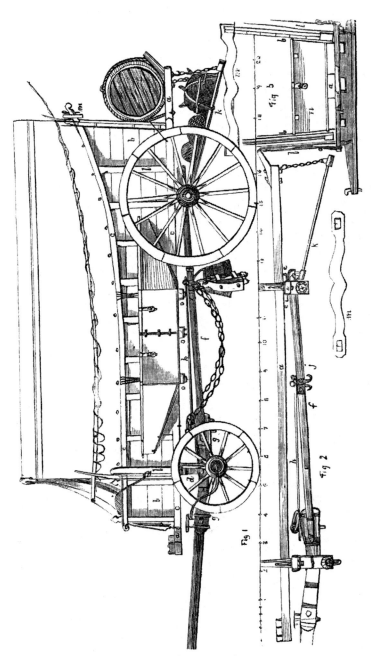

CAPE WAGGON (WITH DIAGRAMS).

clamps (e) ; it will be seen that there is room enough between it and the rungs (l) for the sides (b), and these are kept apart at the after part by the after bar (m), as well as by the after chest (n), and in front by the fore chest only, leaving, in the present instance, a space available for stowage of rather more than 11ft. long, 3ft. wide, and 3ft. in height; though frequently the cargo is piled much higher. The kapel, or bed, an oblong frame (o, p. 188), with a netting of raw hide thongs, is then either slung above the cargo to the stancheons of the tent, or laid upon spars placed across the waggon with their ends resting on the top rail or leer boom (c). The tent frame should be first covered with reed matting, similar to a cheese mat, and often obtainable from the Hottentots. Above this should be the under sail, which is very often painted to render it waterproof, though for durability we prefer to have it of stout unpainted No. 1 canvas, and above this is drawn on the upper sail. In the case of a kap-tent, this is sometimes in three or more pieces: first, the roof; then the sides, which are tacked on under a neat border at its edges ; and, lastly, the fore and after klaps or curtains. Sometimes, however, the whole of these parts are made in one. The central breadths of canvas are left 5ft. or 6ft. longer at each end, so as to serve for the fore and after curtains, and the sides are stitched to the roof, so that the whole may be put on or taken off in one piece. The edges are then either buttoned to brass studs along the leer boom, or tied down with thongs of koodoo hide, stitched on for the purpose. A couple of bamboos or forked sticks are lashed to the foremost and aftermost stancheons of the tent frame, to serve as "nicks" in which to lay the waggon whip, which is a well-selected straight-grown "vaderlandsche" (male bamboo), from 10ft. to 15ft. in length, with a lash of about 20ft., as thick in the middle as the little finger, and with a "voorslag," or lash of koodoo hide, about 4ft. or 5ft. more. This, in the hands of a practised driver, is a most formidable weapon. Any particular ox in the long team of twelve or fourteen may be gently filliped in any part, or have the whip cracked next to his ear as a reminder, or if he shows stubbornness or obstinacy, a cloud of hair may be cut from his sides from hip to shoulder, or each successive stroke of the long voorslag may be made to draw blood, until he goes to his duty.

The side chests are supported on stout bars (o), which cross beneath the bottom of the waggon, projecting 1ft. or 16in. beyond its sides, and these, besides being bolted to the bottom planks, are generally lashed tightly to the top rail by reims of raw hide (p), which serve to keep the bottom from bending too much with the weight of the cargo, and help still further to bind the waggon together. On open colonial roads, the side chests are generally rectangular, but we have seen them on the waggons of elephant hunters, brought to a sharp point forward, because, in passing through a thickly wooded country, trees or stumps would knock off in passing the corners of a rectangular chest.   We think, for economy of room, a long chest, tapered at both ends, as shown in our sketch, might be adopted ; and if there were a probability of the waggon chests being required for a boat, as described at p. 123, this might be made in two lengths, as we have shown it, so that the ends would serve for the respective ends of the boat or raft.   They would be secured either by bolts and nuts, or by lashings of hide to the cross-bars and to the stancheons of the waggon sides. Padlocks and hasps are generally used, but a very stout branch may tear them off.   Rim locks would be better, were it not that the same cause might disarrange the set of the lid, and prevent its fitting pro-

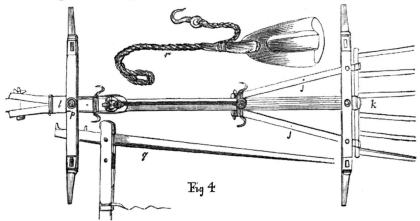

Fig 4.

perly.   A couple of stout knees and chocks should be screwed or bolted on to the after part of the floor for the water cask to rest in, and this should be securely lashed, and never allowed to stand or travel without at least a day's water in it, both to keep it from shrinking and leakage, and also as a safeguard against any unexpected emergency or failure of supply.

Fig. 4 is a plan of as much as is necessary to show of the " under stell," or carriage.   The same letters are attached to the parts: The junction of the two bars (*j*) of the after tong with the " lang wagen " is shown more distinctly.   *p* is the head of the schammel bolt or perch bolt, which passes down through the schammel and axle, allowing the latter to turn freely.   The top of the schammel is seen partly hiding the arms of the axle, underneath it ; in its ends are the mortices for the rungs.   *q* is the lifter, composed of two parts—the " legter voet, " or upright, with two mortices, corresponding to the height of the fore and after axles—and the "legter hout" or lever, which is passed through the required mortice and forelocked by an iron pin. The shorter end is generally armed with one or more iron studs, to keep it from slipping; the longer end is tapered and rounded just so as to be easily grasped. Sometimes, when iron reim shoes are not to be had, or are worn out, a log of wood is roughly shaped and slightly hollowed (r) to receive the tire of the wheel, and, instead of chain, is attached to the foretong by a stout hide rope. A short end is also left near the reim schoen, to hook round the felloe of the wheel.

For rough work, such as carrying stones or packages of unhandy form or dimensions, a "buik waggon" is very convenient. In this the regular lang wagen is released from the fore tong, and either replaced by a rough beam of any required length, or the beam is simply lashed under the original lang wagen, and its end is trimmed down so as to be inserted into the jaws of the fore tong; but as the bolt might probably split and draw out from the unprotected wood, the drag chains should be led aft from the ring bolt, and hooked on as tightly as possible to the after axle, a turn or two being taken, if they are too long, round both the lang wagen and the pole by which it is lengthened. They may be set up tight by using reims of raw hide as lanyards.

The sides consist of a couple of stout planks set on edge—a couple of 21ft. deals for instance. Cross-bars are lashed under these at intervals, to keep the bottom from sagging.

A durable and convenient form of waggon can be extemporised in any wild country where wood and raw hides are procurable by proceed-
Extemporary ing as follows : First from dead, but sound, trees,
waggon. or seasoned wood (see "Wood, to season"), fashion the
pieces for your waggon bed frame, as shown in the illustration on p. 391. Both the fore and hind axle trees are composed of two pieces of wood matched so as to lay evenly on each other. On the surface of contact of each piece half holes are cut for the admission of the pole (A), prong piece (B), and cross prong ends (C). The perch bolt (D) should be an iron pin, but may be a hard wood treenail. Either lashings of raw hide or treenails may be used for securing the upper and lower axle pieces to each other. The lower piece of wood, or axle bar should be composed of some hard dense, yet tough wood, as the axles have to be formed from it. The butt end of the prong piece (E) is so adjusted as to travel forward and backward on the pole, thus lengthening or shortening the body of the waggon. There are two methods by which the regulation of the prong piece is effected. One is to have a train of holes

in the pole and one hole in the butt end of the prong piece for a pin to pass through, which being driven down through one of the holes in the pole holds it at that length. We, however, prefer hollowing out the lower surface of the prong-piece butt with a gouge until it fits on the pole after the manner of a hollow slide or rider. This we lash fast to the pole with a long strip of raw hide, taking several turns both before and behind the joint. The prong piece must be cut from a natural fork of suitable size and length. The butt end should be left at least 18in. long, in order that sufficient bearing surface may be left to rest on the pole under the hide lashing. By adopting this mode of regulating the movements of the prong, a pole of moderate and convenient size may be used without fear of breakage. A very stout pole is required for the pin plan, as the auger holes bored through it tend greatly to decrease its strength. The four

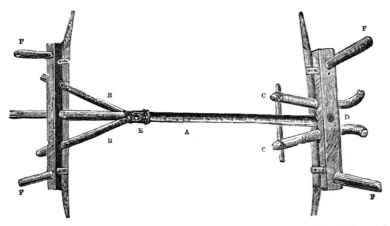

upright posts (F, F, F, F) are fitted into four square holes chiselled out in the upper axle piece for the purpose of receiving them; and they serve to secure the planks, hurdles, wattle work, or poles forming the sides of the waggon.

Directions for building and fitting wheels have been given in a former portion of our work; and we need therefore only repeat that slices cut from suitable-sized log ends form very fair makeshift wheels (see p. 325); but care should be taken, if native carts are used in the region where the makeshift waggon is building, to ascertain the gauge at which their wheels are set and regulate yours accordingly, or the wheel tracks on these trails will not match with yours, and so cause strains and breakages. The adjustment of the contrivance just described will entirely depend on the purpose for which it is from time to time required. For the conveyance of the packs and baggage of a large party it may be drawn out to its full length, as shown in the illustration below, leaving only pole enough for the attachment of draught animals. By bringing the prong piece farther back a short four-wheeled waggon can be formed, and by slipping the fore axle and prong over the end of the pole you leave the perch and hinder axle to be used as a two-wheeled cart, whilst an extra pole fitted to the first axle and prong makes a second pair-wheeled cart just as handy as the other. Should there be but two available draught animals for the two carts, shafts can be used instead of poles. These are easily made by lashing on poles with raw hide, or cutting wide prong-shaped branches which spread out wide at the butt, which must be left long enough to fit into the pole hole of the axle piece, when, if cut with a good curve, these shafts will some-what resemble those of a Hansom cab. Acting somewhat on this principle, the Californian teamsters make use at times of a sort of train waggon, which, with a powerful mule team, is, over favourable ground, worked entire; but when the vicissitudes of travel require it, they work each separate compartment of the waggon just as we should an ordinary cart.

About the year 1842, we were accustomed to see the primitive wine waggon of the Cape Colony toiling over the dreary waste of shifting sands known as the Cape Flats. Its wheels were large and broad, the hinder ones being often 7ft. in diameter. The fore and after carriages were connected by a long fir pole, and the sides and bottom were formed of six or eight trees of the same kind, so arranged as to form a convenient bed for two or three beakers of wine. At the hinder end would be a tent and sides of wattled work, or perhaps the sides of an ordinary waggon, with the tent attached, would be fitted temporarily

Cape wine waggon.

on, so as to form a place of shelter for the owner and his family. It was generally drawn by twenty or twenty-two oxen.

The illustration on p. 392 represents one of these wine waggons; and, as it may so happen that the lot of the settler may be cast in regions resembling the district we have just spoken of, it may be well that he should know how to construct a conveyance of this kind, as the fore part of the waggon affords ample space for stowing away barrels or bales. As will be seen, on reference to the illustration, the length of the waggon can, like that before described, be regulated according to the requirements of the owner.

The illustration below represents a vehicle in which we performed some very rough travelling through Central India. Its cover, or tent, was composed of painted cotton cloth stretched over bamboo hoops and nailed to the framework. On the bottom, or bed, of our conveyance we placed a stout mattress

Indian gharrie.

stuffed with cotton. Our rifles, guns, water barrel, and revolvers hung in pouches against the inside of the waggon tent. The door was at the rear. The windows had curtains fitted to them. The bullock teams varied in strength from one pair to three, according to the character of the country travelled through. Conveyances much like this in construction, and of admirable quality, are manufactured at Ahmednugger, in the Bombay Presidency. When travelling in this vehicle our heavy baggage followed in two hackeries, or country carts, each drawn by two pairs of bullocks. These hackeries, like the arobas of the Tartars, merely consist of an axle, a pair of rough strong wheels, a pole, and number of odd poles, sticks, and pieces of board bound together with hide. Our men were much puzzled in Crim-Tartary when we overtook, on the only road leading from passes perfectly impracticable for wheeled carriages, several of the bullock arobas of the country laden with bales of skins and bags of grain. The Tartars had simply taken their arobas to pieces by casting off the hide lashings, packed the bullocks, themselves, and their wolfish-looking dogs, with the divided loads and waggon gear, marched over the passes, and then put the whole affair in travelling trim again. Much like these in construction is the single ox cart of Red River. In this the ox is harnessed very much as a horse would be, working between a pair of ordinary shafts. Each driver conducts his own train, which may consist of a dozen carts. The oxen are driven with a long-handled, heavy-thonged whip, which is a sort of compromise between the whip of a Cape waggoner and that of an Australian stock-man. Each of these primitive carts is capable of transporting about 9cwt. of buffalo flesh and hides from the hunting grounds to the depôt of the hunters.

Horse and mule waggons and carts vary so much in construction according to the nature of the country they are used in, and to the
<small>Horse and mule waggons.</small> purpose for which they are intended, that it would be impossible to describe one-tenth of their number. The mode of harnessing, too, differs in almost every country. Whilst we, in England, usually content ourselves with a team harnessed in pairs, the Russians not unfrequently work three and four a-breast. The Spanish and Portuguese race, in their devious wanderings about the world, have taken the enormously high wheel of the Peninsula with them, and delight to see a big-booted postilion, black or white, acting as pilot to the lumbering old-world conveyance they journey in. Scarcely any two artillery services in the world correspond in their draught arrangement—some making use of the pole, whilst others, England amongst the number, use the shafts. Our province being to deal more particularly with vehicles calculated to bear the rough usage and vicissitudes of travel, we naturally turn to vastly extensive countries —where long journeys over hill, plain, and valley are commonly performed—for the best form of waggon to do it with. Experience in these matters is always the best guide. The constant demand almost invariably brings about the required supply. We have no long waggon journeys in England; and, as neither the artillery or military train waggon of this country, nor the "equipage militaire" of France, is in accordance with our notions of what travellers' mule waggons should be, we go a little farther a-field, and select the Wilson waggon of the United States of America, the subject of the full-page illustration. The American mode of harnessing is also shown. All these waggons have wheel friction breaks fitted to them, as had all the Sardinian waggons used during the Crimean war.

The annexed illustration represents one of those truly excellent conveyances, the cariole. The body or fore-part of the arrangement is made two-seated, like that of a very strong The Swedish Cariole. roomy gig, but behind that extends a stout and tolerably deep open wooden tray or hind box, large enough for a man

to sit in. The wheels and shafts are stout and substantial, and the splash board low. Carioles are built with and without springs. For rough forest travel and on rugged ill-kept tracts, it is better to dispense with such a piece of mechanism and trust to the strength of the tough wood and iron of the framework. For the use of a couple of travelling sportsmen and their attendant, it would be difficult if not impossible to select a more useful vehicle, as it is comfortable to sit in, capacious, and if built in Sweden by a Swedish builder and of Swedish materials, breakage from ordinary causes need never be feared. Good carioles are built at John Copping, pronounced "Yen Choppin." The mode of

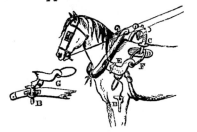

harnessing a horse to a conveyance of this kind differs materially from that commonly adopted, and is represented in the illustration annexed. Each shaft has a narrow slot cut through it for the passage of the "tug ring," (A) which is screwed in its place by the pin (B), the drawing out of which instantly detaches the horse from the cariole. A bow with a back-pad at each end extends over the spine of the horse. From the crown of the arch the crupper strap extends. A distance of 4 in. is allowed between the back of the pad (D) and projection of the loin marked (C), (E) is made of strong wood, and has a smooth hole made in its curved and rounded end, for the free play of the stout leather link (F), (G) shows the manner in which the shaft and "tug ring" are pinned.

In travelling over rough passes and steep acclivities great attention should be paid to the application of proper break power to the wheels. The use of the skid and common drag-chain are too well Wheel drags. known to need comment here, only that it may not be amiss to remark, *en passant*, that, conducting your waggon down the edge of a steep hollow, or ravine, you must have your shoe placed on the wheel *away* from the drop side. Never use your drag-chain when you can

safely do without it, as, by confining the wheel in one position during
the descent of steep pitches, the portion of the tire in contact with the
ground will be seriously ground and cut up. All comparatively light
carts and waggons should have the lever friction breaks before mentioned attached to them. These contrivances are simple in construction,
powerful in action, and, by allowing a certain amount of retarded
action to the wheel, many advantages are gained. The detail of
the break arrangement varies greatly in the different countries in
which it is used; but the illustration below will serve to show the
principle on which it is constructed. The roller (A) has two stout pieces
of hide rope wound round it. These are attached to the break-bar (B),
which slides forward and back under the staples (C). By depressing
the end of the lever (D) and hooking down its end, the friction blocks
(E) are drawn against the surfaces of the wheel tires and retained there

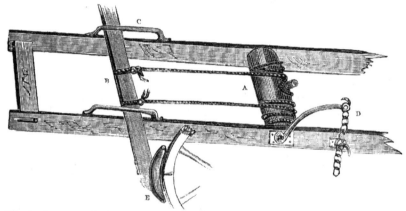

with just as much force as is thought requisite. The movements of a
waggon train furnished with these contrivances are not retarded and
rendered irregular by the constant and harrassing stoppages consequent on the leading waggoners skidding and unskidding. On the
crest of a steep descent being reached, all the teamster has to do is to
heave down his lever to the required pitch, and hook on without
stopping his team. On getting near the bottom he unhooks, and is
prepared to move smartly up on the rise before him, all the other
waggons following his example. In this way there is no check. In
going down dangerously-steep inclines it is a good plan to attach a
short bushy tree of good weight, root ends forwards, by a strong rope
or chain to the hind axle.

A very effective makeshift break can be made by cutting a tough,
stout pole, long enough to extend some distance beyond the diameter
of the wheel to be dragged. Lash the ends of the pole to the frame-

THE WILSON MULE WAGGON (UNITED STATES OF AMERICA).

work of the waggon, so as to nip the wheel, as shown in the accompanying illustration. Almost any amount of nipping power may be gained by tightening the lashings. A large exploring party, or troops on the march, can also, when requisite, make use of drag ropes, by which to ease a load down a difficult place. When it is desirable to completely lock a pair of wheels cut down a young tree of suitable size, trim off branches, and cut it to a length sufficient to pass directly across the bottom of the waggon, through the spokes of each of the wheels to be locked, and extend a couple of feet

Makeshift break.

or so beyond the nave of each wheel a few turns of rope round both the tree and the felloe of the wheel prevents the arrangement from slipping. This is a very good plan to adopt when a waggon has to be stopped for any time in the middle of a very steep incline. The two wheels on one side of a short-bodied carriage may be locked by applying a rope or chain, as shown in the above illustration. By treating both sides alike all four wheels would be locked, as when waggons are drawn up to resist attacking Indians, only that chain must be used in order to prevent the locking from being cut free, and the waggon being started out of its place.

If one wheel of a four wheeled carriage gets broken on a journey, or when some distance out of camp, and there is no spare wheel to replace it, make the two fore wheels good, leaving the deficiency with the hind axle; then cut down *Substitute for wheels.* a tree about 8in. or 9in. in diameter, cut a deep notch in its large end, lay this on the axle directly inside the fore wheel on the side towards the absent hind wheel; measure the length of the tree, and see that it is long enough to trail on the ground

sledge-runner fashion, behind the carriage, round up the ground end, like the toe of a skate, with your axe; cut another notch on its upper surface for the end of the axle from which the broken wheel came to rest in. Now lash both the front and hind axles in their places firmly, as shown in the illustration on p. 397, and you will be at least able to get to a convenient place to effect a perfect repair; and here we would advise the reader never to despair of making a successful mend in almost any case of breakages among wheeled carriages, provided wood, a few tools, and raw hide can be obtained. A raw hide band, properly fitted on wet, and allowed to dry gradually, is little less reliable than good wrought iron, and far more so than bad.

Every wheeled carriage used in exploring or travelling long journeys should have its own grease box secured in a convenient situation; just

Waggon equipment.

above and before the near fore wheel is a good place. The form of the common Indian bamboo grease box is shown at p. 318, illustration No. 3. A good-sized ox-horn makes a convenient grease box. A mixture of Stockholm tar, 6lb., and fat, 1lb., makes a good grease. If a little common plumbago can be got to put into it, so much the better. In countries where native vegetable oils are abundant, they may be used, instead of fat, to mix with the tar. Bear in mind that keeping the wheels well greased is a duty of no common importance. In hot countries it is an excellent plan to work the naves of the wheels over with strong twine, just as boys work balls in some parts of England. The twine-work affords a hold-fast for a thick layer of wet cowdung, or clay, which should be renewed whenever the waggons are stationary for the day or night. We never omit this custom when it can be by any possibility adhered to. By keeping the nave moist the spokes of the wheel remain tight. It is a good plan to well water the ground under each wheel when encamping on very dry ground. The treatment of injured wheels will be found at p. 191. When any of the iron work of your waggon becomes bent from an upset, or other accident, never attempt to straighten it cold. Light a fire, heat it to a red heat, hammer it back to its proper form, and then let it cool gradually before putting it in its place. Plunging it suddenly in cold water is apt to render the metal brittle. In the purchase of all iron fittings for either waggon work or horse equipment, about which we shall have more to say as our work proceeds, insist on seeing it, without paint or varnish, bare from the forge, as you can then see that there are no hollows, cracks, or defects in it. It is wonderful what a number of shortcomings a good thick coat of coal-tar will cover when laid on over the hot metal. Avoid malleable cast iron as you would a broken limb. It cannot be bent without the danger of nipping off short. When broken, it cannot be welded or faggoted up. It is not reliable in any way, and is a mere delusion and snare to the unwary; and yet, incredible as it may appear, not only the greater portion of the cheap horse equipment iron sent to the colonies is made from it, but we have ourselves seen more than one attempt made by unscrupulous contractors to introduce it in Government work, where wrought metal had been specially insisted on and agreed for. An experienced man will generally detect the nature of the material at once, but the inexperienced requires some rough and ready way of judging the quality of that which he is about to purchase. Buckles, D's, rings, hooks, &c., will not unfrequently show the mark of the mould in which they were cast. If there is no such mark, take one of the suspected objects in the tongs, put it on an anvil, and with a light hammer knock it about a little to see if it breaks up; as a further test put it in the forge fire, heat it to a bright red heat, cut and open out the object to its full length, and then proceed, with your hammer, to draw out the end, as if you were going to make a long sharp nail from it. If the suspected metal is wrought iron it readily takes the spike form, but if malleable it will give under the hammer and break up. Too much care cannot be exercised in the selection of all matters of iron intended to meet the vicissitudes of rough travel. The iron of Sweden, Russia, and India is excellent when it is obtained of native manufacture. Its admirable purity and toughness partly depends on the quality of the ore from which it is obtained, but mainly from the absence of sulphur in its composition. This arises from charcoal being used as a fuel for smelting instead of the coal made use of in this country, which, from its containing considerable quantities of sulphuret of iron (the mundic of the miners), is but ill-adapted for the production of iron of high quality. Thoroughly good iron is convertible and reconvertible into an endless number of objects of usefulness. Thus the links of an old chain makes excellent staples; these, when broken, can be worked up into nails and pieces of these, when filed up, are used to make goad points and many other things. Every waggon should have its "odd and end" box for small matters in iron, such as linch-pins, S hooks, D.'s, spikes, union links, &c., &c. All these are worth their weight in gold in a wild country, and must, therefore, be kept carefully out of the reach of natives.

The settler in the vicinity of a frontier beyond which native tribes, who may become hostile at any time, reside, will not unfrequently find it useful to know how field artillery and the waggons belonging to it are handled in cases of breakage. Well-organised labour will perform more in a few minutes than would double the amount of force in hours expended in ill-directed efforts. Works exclusively on artillery matters rarely reach the hands of any save

Field artillery.   officers in that branch of the service. We, therefore, give the following directions for the management of disabled field artillery, furnished by General Lefroy, R.A., F.R.S., in his handbook of " Field Artillery Service."

CASE I.—GUN WITHOUT A WAGGON—CARRIAGE DISABLED.

(1.) Dismount the gun.

(2.) Nos. 2 and 3 put a handspike in the muzzle, and raise it. Nos. 4 and 5 take a prolonge or drag rope, pass it in the rear of one trunnion and in front of the other, and sling the gun securely to the limber hook ; then pass the long end of the rope between the boxes to the front.   Nos. 6 and 7 steady the wheels.   Nos. 8 and 9 raise and hold up the shafts whilst 4 and 5 sling the gun. As soon as the gun is slung, 8 and 9 haul down the shafts, and hold them about the same height they would be if a horse was hooked in them.   Nos. 6 and 7 then take the long end of the rope left by 4 and 5, and bring it down at the end of the box frame, close to the boxes under the breach of the gun about the vent astragal, as between the frame and footboard, according to the length of the gun, so that the rope will have no tendency to slip off the carriage.   When 6 has done this and handed the end of the rope to the other side to 7, and put the first part of a reef knot on it, 1 gives the word " Bear down the muzzle," when 2 and 3 bear down.   Nos. 6 and 7 take a turn round the breech, bring the end of the rope up at the end of the box frame, and secure it.   Nos. 8 and 9 now let down the shafts and leave them.

(3.) The trail is now thrown round, and the carriage is dismounted and turned over.

(4.) *To lift the carriage.*—Nos. 8 and 9 place themselves at the breast, 6 and 7 at the axletree arms, 4 and 5 at the cheeks of the carriage, close to the axletree, 2 and 3 at the trail, 1 in the shafts. At the word " Lift" the numbers all lift, and carry the carriage to the rear of the limber, and rest the breast on the rear of the boxes, as far on as the front cap square bolts.   Nos. 8 and 9 then mount on the footboard, and, taking hold of the breast chains, the whole of the numbers lift again, and, moving forward, continue to lift until the elevating screw box rests on the rear of the limber boxes.

(5.) No. 1, who has been in the shafts during the operation, gives the proper directions for balancing the carriage.

(6.) *Placing the wheels.*—Nos. 4 and 5 put on the washers and linch-pins ; the numbers on each side will put on the wheels " dish down;" and the four lowest numbers will lash in rear, and the four highest numbers in front. Nos. 2 and 3 will then secure the trail to the handspike in the muzzle by the locking chain.

(7.) *Lashing the carriage.*—Nos. 4 and 5 use the box lashings 6 and 7 the drag rope and breast chains. The side-arms are laid on the top of the boxes close to or between the box guard irons and the carriage.

Case II.—A Gun with a Waggon—Carriage disabled.

(1.) The gun and carriage are dismounted, and the gun is slung as in the first case.

(2.) The waggon and gun carriage are so placed that the rear of the waggon will be close to and in front of the carriage; or, in other words, the gun carriage will be brought to the rear of the waggon, and placed with the trail to the waggon before it is dismounted.

(3.) The carriage is then turned upside down, as in the first case.

(4.) At the words "Prepare to lift," 2 and 3 place themselves at the breast, 4 and 5 at the axletree arms, 6 and 7 at the cheeks, and 8 and 9 at the trail. At the word "Lift," the carriage is lifted, and the trail rested on the footboard. Nos. 8 and 9 then jump up and seize the trail handles, and at the next heave bring the trail on the rear box. Then, lifting and moving forward, they bring the trail eye near to the limber boxes, but not to touch them. In this position the cap square bolts will injure the lids of the boxes, but by placing a piece of wood about 3in. or 4in. thick on the boxes it will raise the carriage clear.

(5.) *To unlash the waggon boxes and place the wheels.*—Nos. 2, 4, 3, and 5 unlash the rear boxes; 6, 8, 7, and 9 the front boxes. Then the two extreme numbers and the two centre ones will each take one of the box lashings (or 2, 9, 5, and 6) and lay them conveniently to where they are needed.

(6.) *Placing the wheels.*—The four numbers on each side then lift the gun wheels, "dish inwards," inside the rear wheels of the waggon, and rest them on the axletrees. Nos. 2 and 3 lash the wheels together at the rear. Nos. 4, 6, 5, and 7 lash to the box handles. Nos. 8 and 9 lash together in front, and then fix the trail to the perch.

(7.) The spare side-arms to be put in their proper places on the gun carriage, and the other alongside the gun.

Case III.—A Gun Axletree Arm broken.

(1.) The gun is slung under the limber, as in Cases I. and II., and the carriage is limbered up. Here it may be remarked that a piece of chain would answer best for slinging the gun, because a rope sling takes up so much room that the trail eye is sometimes prevented from being keyed; besides a rope may get chafed.

(2.) *To take off the disabled gun.*—No. 2 takes a handspike and passes it under the axletree close to the wheel. It is manned at the other end by 8.

(3.) Nos. 4 and 6 stand ready to take off the wheel; 3, 5, 7, and 9 take hold of the highest part of the opposite wheel, and place their feet against the lowest part, to ease 2 and 8. At the word "Take off the wheel," 2 and 8 lift; the numbers on the opposite side pull over; 4 and 6 take the wheel off the axletree, but hold it in such a position that the axletree will pass between the spokes, where it is to rest, and they remain to keep the wheel steady.

(4.) Nos. 2 and 8 then take a stout spar, about 12ft. or 14ft. long, and pass it under the axletree and secure it to a piece of wood in the trunnion holes to the cheeks of the carriage.

(5.) The numbers on the opposite side place the wheel, "dish side up," on the limber boxes; and all the numbers assist to secure it— 2, 3, 4, and 5 in rear, 6, 7, 8, and 9 in front.

Case IV.—A Gun and Waggon—The Gun Limber disabled.

(1.) This case can only occur when a gun and its waggon are by themselves; for if two or more guns and waggons are acting together, a waggon limber would be taken for the gun, and then the case would be as No. 6.

(2.) *Unlimber and run the gun in rear of waggon.*—At this word 2 and 3 bear down the muzzle; 4 and 5 man the wheels; 6, 7, 8, and 9 man the trail; and the gun is run in rear of the waggon, with the trail eye under the rear axletree. Nos 8 and 9 pass the locking chain through the trail eye. If it will not pass through, it must be brought up at the side; but it is better through the eye or handspike ring.

(3.) *Limber up.*—Nos. 2 and 3 bear down the muzzle; 4 and 5 man the wheels; 6 and 7 raise the trail. One of the next numbers passes the lock chain of the gun over the axletree of the waggon, from rear to front, across to 8, who will pass it over the axletree from front to rear, and, assisted by 9, will take a turn under the neck of the trail plate and round the returns. It is then secured by its own hook.

(4.) *To remove and place the limber boxes.*—The limber will be lashed to the side of the waggon body by the numbers on that side on which the limber stands. No. 1 in the shafts; 2 and 4 unlash; 6 and 8 untie the boxes, and slip them a little to the rear. The limber will then be lashed close to the waggon wheel in the centre of the limber, in line with the axletree of the waggon. No. 1 then lets down the shaft-prop. Nos. 2 and 4 mount on the waggon, and 6 and 8 on the footboard of the limber. Nos. 2 and 6 lift one box on the top of the waggon wheel, whence they will be assisted by 3 and 5 to place it on the rear box of the waggon body. Nos. 4 and 8 will then lift on the other box, and, assisted by 7 and 9, place it on the front box of the waggon body, the locks front and rear.

(5.) *Dismount the limber.*—The limber is now moved forward a little. Nos. 6 and 7 hold up the splinter bar. Nos. 8 and 9 take out the shafts and lay them down; then relieve 6 and 7 at the splinter bar, who will take hold of the front part of the wheels, and 4 and 5 the rear part, 6 and 2 attending to the linchpins and washers. Nos. 2 and 3 take hold of the rear of the limber, and at the word " Take off the wheels," 2, 8, 3 and 9 lift, and 4, 6, 5 and 7 take the wheels off. Then the whole is laid on the ground.

(6 and 7.) The waggon boxes are unlashed and the wheels placed, as in Case II.

(8.) The limber body is now turned upside down and placed on the top of the boxes of the waggon limber, axletree to the rear by the whole of the numbers, and secured behind by both of the limber box lashings, and in front of the splinter bar and pitchells by the prolonges or fitting ropes. Nos. 2, 3, 4, and 5 lashing behind, and 6, 7, 8, and 9 in front. The small box of spare linchpins and washers to be laid on the disabled limber by 8.

(9.) The shafts are then placed, one on each side, between the disabled limber boxes and the guard irons of the waggon body, point to the rear, and secured by the pocket straps.

Case V.—Waggon Limber disabled.

This case is so similar to Case IV. that the details would be a repetition, except when the word " trail " is used in that use the word " perch " in this. The waggon body being secured the same as the gun.

In South Africa, the oxen draw from the neck, or, rather, the yoke is laid upon the neck, and is prevented from slipping backward by the hump, which, when the ox presses forward, is ~~Yoking or harnessing~~ pushed strongly against it. The form of the ~~draught oxen.~~ yoke and its furniture is shown on p. 189. The yoke is about 6ft. in length, and 3in. thick. In its centre is a strong staple, through which are passed several turns of reim or hide thong, to lace it to a corresponding ring on the " dissel-boom " (K), or on the " trek touw " (8). Near each end are two mortices, 3in. long, ¾in. wide, and about 1ft. apart, through which to pass the "jeuk skeis," or yoke keys, which

D D 2

keep it in place on the neck of the ox. The ends should be rounded so as not to chafe the animal. A knobbed head, more or less ornamented, keeps them from slipping through the mortices, and on the outside edge of each key are cut two notches, to receive the throat strap, which is simply a double thong of softened hide, so twisted as to leave a loop at each end. This is hitched to the upper or lower notches to tighten or loosen it, and it may be more nicely adjusted by twisting or untwisting it till it attains the required length. The strap will readily be recognised on p. 189.

When the oxen are to be "inspanned," the span or team is driven to the waggon, and the nooses of the reims or raw hide halters are thrown over the horn and tighened on the forehead. The oxen are then arranged in pairs, and held by one or more assistants, as seen near waggon No. 9, on p. 263. The driver then leads out the fore oxen, lifts the yoke over the neck of the farthest, hitches the throat strap into the nicks, and then, holding up the yoke with one hand,

CAPE OX TEAM.

with the other he draws forward the other ox, and induces him to walk to his proper place under the yoke. The " voor looper," or boy that leads them, then holds the reims of the fore oxen so as to keep the "trek touw" tolerably tight, while the other oxen are yoked, as seen before waggon No. 2, on p. 263. In outspanning the order is reversed, the fore oxen being left to keep the trek rope tight till the very last. An ox requires fully 8ft. to pull in ; therefore, a trek touw for twelve oxen must be fully 40ft. long, as the two after oxen will be yoked to the dissel-boom, and require no rope. Our accompanying sketch of Cape oxen in their yokes will sufficiently show the arrangements. A Cape waggon is supposed to be loaded with about 2000lb. of cargo, but 3000lb. is not uncommon, and we have seen a waggon with 4000lb. start as lightly as could be wished, though when it came on bad roads it was too heavy for the oxen. The trek touw is usually of hide rope, but hunters sometimes use chain and sometimes hempen rope, either of which defy the teeth of jackals and hyænas. Chain may, perhaps, gall the sides of the oxen, but we have seen it used on long journeys without bad effect. Hemp is apt to rot, from exposure to alternate wet and excessive dryness, but we have seen it do good service. With a hempen rope get a sailor to splice in all the rings before you leave the coast. A Hottentot will do well with a hide rope, but not with one composed of hemp.

In Australia, two-wheeled drays, somewhat like the Scotch cart, are used. They will sometimes carry 3000lb. of wool over bad roads.

They are very handy, but strain the necks of the pole oxen rather. Sometimes, only two oxen are used, as in our sketch—sometimes, six or more. The yoke lies upon the neck, like the African, but is fastened by iron bows passed up through the yoke and keyed above it, so that, when once an ox is yoked, nothing on earth can free him till the bow is removed. The long bamboo whip in Africa is unknown in Australia. The handle is short, the lash long and heavy, and is often terminated by a bit of silk, to produce a more effective crack.

In many parts of Spain, the yoke is simply laid across the

THE SWING OX GOAD.

foreheads of the two oxen, and lashed fast to the base of their horns. his is not only a source of great discomfort to the animals, but is an absolute waste of their muscular power; for, strong as the neck of an ox undoubtedly is, that part of the spinal column which forms it cannot with impunity bear the continued heavy strain or the occasional concussions which might without injury be received upon the shoulder.

In some parts of the world the yoke is laid across the back of the head, and is lashed fast to the roots of the horns. This plan is followed by some of the Hispano-Americans, who make use of an enormously long goad, hung in a sling, to drive the cattle with. In addition to the point of the weapon a sharp " dropper," or bob, is hung on in such a way that, by lowering the shaft of the goad, it may fall end downwards on the bullocks working too close to be attacked by the point. The preceding illustration will serve to show the nature of this contrivance and the mode of fastening on the yoke.

GERMAN OX HARNESS.

Some of the Germans adopt a much better plan. They take a broad band of stout leather, so stuffed and padded as to form a cushion, and fit this upon the hump of the ox, as shown in our sketch. In each end of this are stout rings, to which the traces are attached, and there is a slight collar and a belly band to keep it from slipping in its place, but the whole strain comes upon the part best able to support it, *i.e.*, the shoulder hump; and this simple gear has the advantage of being applicable to one or any number, while the yokes can only be used for pairs of oxen. Remember that the prudent as well as the merciful man is merciful to his beast; and if you want an animal to work for you, take especial care that he is not galled nor incommoded by superfluous or ill-fitting gear, nor fretted and irritated by unnecessary chastisement, inflicted in such a manner that he cannot understand it. If it is necessary to flog him, take care to do it in such a manner that he can escape the punishment only by going to his work, and discontinue it so soon as he really does so.

Little good could result from our describing the various modes by which bullocks are harnessed in different parts of the world, as the explorer will, in great measure, have to be guided in the selection of the way in which he intends to work his teams by the description of animal with which he is about to deal. Humped cattle draw efficiently by either the German plan, before described, or the yoke and pin plan shown in the annexed illustration (A), because a much larger amount of pressure comes on the anterior point of the hump, or bearing point of the yoke piece, than in any other direction, the pin merely keeping the neck of the bullock in the proper position, and regulating the line of draught; whilst humpless cattle require, in lieu of a collar, either a neck bow, as shown at B, or some other mode of adjustment, by which neck and shoulder power can be brought to bear. The Indian, African, and Eastern cattle work according to

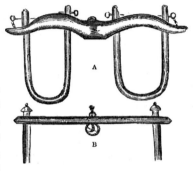

the former rule, whilst the English and Australian draw by the latter. The Australian ox bow, as we have before stated, is usually composed of iron, bent into the required form; whilst that in general use throughout the western counties of England is made from a pole of tough wood, commonly elm, moulded to the requisite shape by the aid of heat. The yoke should be made from some tough light timber, and the neck bows of some wood not liable to splinter.

CHAPTER X.

HARNESS AND PACK ANIMALS.

WHETHER mules or horses are selected for waggon and cart draught too much attention cannot be paid to the arrangement and fitting of the harness they are intended to work in; and, although the pattern will vary somewhat not only in every country, but in every province the traveller passes through, the leading principles remain much the same, and whether the traces are of rope, chain, or leather, the office they perform remains unaltered. Collars, let the pattern be what it will, require especial care in fitting, as nothing tends more effectually to disable a harness animal (mule or horse) than a collar carelessly or injudiciously applied. Every animal in the team should have its own, and on first selecting the collar for fitting, so put it on that the collar strap can be buckled up to the last hole in the tongue strap. When you have done this there should be room enough at the bottom of the collar in front of the animal's chest to pass the open hand, when laid flat, freely forward and back between the inside of the collar and the animal's neck. When new collars are found to fit uneasily, and chafe in particular places, it is a common expedient among mule teamsters to lay the ill-fitting collar in water, and allow it to soak for the night; it is then taken out wet and fitted to the animal's neck, to which it at once adapts itself. Much trouble is often experienced on long and toilsome expeditions from loss of condition and leanness of the animals causing the saddles and collars to fit badly, and, consequently, cause severe sores. Take, therefore, plenty of curled hair stuffing with you, in order that deficiencies in the padding may be from time to time made good. When a collar is too large to be adapted to a thin neck by stuffing, it will be well to cut a portion out of its centre at once, which can be done by first measuring the excess of space roughly, then take the collar off the animal; lay it on a board or table, and cut out evenly as much as is thought requisite; and if on testing the collar it is found still too large, cut out a little more from each side of the incision until the collar takes its proper bearing, but take care that a proper medium is observed regarding the position of the lower end, or bow, of the collar. If it hangs too far down the movements of the muscles of the shoulder are interfered with. If it presses too far upwards the windpipe becomes unduly pressed on. Some persons use what are called "crown pads" for the top, or ridge, of the neck, under where the narrow portion or crown of the collar rests. These are sometimes made from sheepskin with the wool on, but it will be better to get some moderately stout but smooth and soft leather. Cut this into pad pieces, each of which may be 13in. long and 8in. wide. Make a cut at each end of the pieces about 2½in. from the end of the pad, extending it to about an inch from the centre. Then turn your pad, and cut from the opposite side until only the inch of sound leather remains between the two cuts. Treat the other end of the pad in the same way, and it will be fit for use.

A very tolerable makeshift collar and pair of hames may be made as follows; Collect a good quantity of reed, either wheat or marsh reed; cut off all the heads, or tops, leaving nothing but the clear shafts of the plant. Make these up in a bundle, and place them to soak in water for one night. Measure the horse's or mule's neck for size of intended collar with a piece of cord; lay this on the ground in the form and of the size of the collar; then close to the string, as it is placed on an even spot, drive in a double row of long pegs at about 6in. apart; then proceed to lay in your reeds between the two walls of pegs, so disposing the reeds that too many ends do not appear at any one place; continue to lay in reeds, working them round the ends of the oval and thumping them well down in their places, until sufficient substance has been gained for the fore part of the collar; then, with fine twine, proceed to bind the reeds firmly together by lashing them spirally. Now make a second reed collar just as you did the first, only let it be larger and more bulky; and, with a packing needle and twine, sew the two collars together, one on the other—that first made on the top. Now try the united collars on the animal, the large collar being next the shoulder. See that there is plenty of space below the windpipe in front of the chest when it is made to fit at both top and bottom. Line the inside of the bearing or large collar with soft pliant leather laid over a layer of soft moss, fine cocoa fibre, fur of animals, or anything else you can get calculated for stuffing purposes. A piece of hide laid on and sewn wet will cover the outsides of both collars; but whilst it is drying the hames should be fastened in the groove formed by stitching the two collars together.

The hames are made as follows: Get two well-seasoned pieces of tough strong wood; cut them to the shape of the curve and length of the collar, and fashion them as shown in the annexed illustration. A is the trace hame-tug, formed of a loop and several turns of raw hide; B

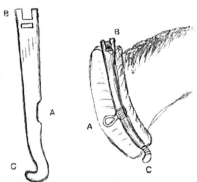

is the hame strap fork, below which an oblong square hole is cut for the strip of hide forming the hame strap to pass through; C is the lower end of the hame cut into hook form, to admit of its being securely lashed with hide strips to its fellow on the opposite side.

Breast straps may be used in lieu of a collar and hames.

When starting on an expedition take plenty of harness leather with you. Raw hide and strips of sinew are admirable for repairs, but good tanned and curried leather is needed for the harness itself.

The illustration below represents a very useful and plain set of mule harness, and also the way in which a long rope or lasso is used for securing a refractory mule to the side of a waggon whilst the harness is being put on. Some mules are so dangerously skilful in the

use of their fore and hind feet, that even an accomplished prizefighter might view their feats in the art of attack with envy. To guard against the effects of this objectionable skill, we proceed as follows: Throw the running noose end of your lasso over the mule's head, and let it settle well over his neck; then edge him quietly away until he is standing stem and stern with the waggon on the near or left-hand side; then, keeping well before your mule, pass the free end of the lasso between the upper spokes of the near fore wheel; draw out your end by walking backwards with it, keeping up a steady strain until you walk iu a wide circle well outside the range of mules' heels; slip dexterously behind the wheel and tail of the waggon, keeping your lasso tight all the while; then pass your lasso end, from without, inwards between the spokes of the near hind wheel; haul taunt and belay. There are very few mules that cannot be successfully handled in this way. The guide as to the proper height of the lasso is given by the point of the elbow and the line of the stifle joint. If the mule is a small one, choose lower spokes in the wheel than for a tall, long-legged animal.

The adaptation of hames to collars is almost as important as the fitting of the collars to the animals. Hames are sometimes made of wood fitted with iron work, but they are far better when made from good tough wrought iron. Here we again say, beware of " malleable cast." During the rough work of a campaign hames are constantly getting broken, particularly at the union of the ring point and the blade of the hame. The old pattern used by our horse artillery and field batteries was especially objectionable, as the point of union (shown in the above illustration at

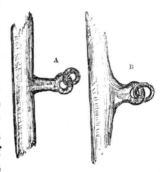

A) was so unmechanically effected that incessant trouble and constant breakage was the result. We have submitted to the Horse Guards authorities that which we believe to be a far more durable and efficient pattern (as shown at B). The hames now in use are certainly better than they were at the commencement of the Crimean war; but those which we used during our long forced marches in India during the mutiny were very far from being perfect.

We, some time since, invented and patented a very simple contrivance, by which a fallen or disabled horse or mule could be instantly freed from the tension of the traces without cutting or unbuckling. The latter operation, by-the-by, it is next to impossible to perform from the strain on the trace. By the use of our slip

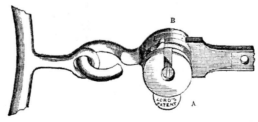

(represented in the accompanying illustration) the trace can be released by turning up the pendulum (A) until it matches with the slot (B), when it drops out to the front, and forms a cross handle, like that of a corkscrew, to draw the lock pin by. The instant the pin is drawn as far as it can be pulled out, the trace is detached from the ring of the hame. The lock pin cannot be lost, as it can only be drawn out to a certain distance—in fact, just far enough to free the trace from its hold.

Much mischief is done to team animals by having bits of insufficient substance and solidity. See that they are of sufficient diameter to prevent cutting, and that they are long enough from cheek to cheek to prevent pressure on the angles of the mouth and lips. See also that the bit is so attached to the headstall that the corners of the mouth are not drawn up by it. Let the throat latch be long enough to see plenty of daylight under, or, by drawing on the headstall, the poll of the head may be severely rubbed and a poll evil established. The nature of this injury will be fully dealt with under the head of " Veterinary Surgery." If bearing reins are used at all, see that they are slack. A good store of anti-friction pads will be found of the greatest value on the march to keep such portions of the harness as are found to rub the skin of any animal in the team from doing furthur mischief. These are made of very soft pliant leather, stuffed with soft curled hair. Seven inches long by 4½in. wide, and 2½in. thick, will be found a convenient size. They are secured between the strap causing irritation and the skin by bits of thong fastened to their backs for the purpose. Galls from saddles or collars are not unfrequently caused by some hard and uneven point of bearing. When this is the case, take a long sharp-pointed instrument, pass it through the leather or woollen, and, by working it about and pushing in every direction, force the stuffing back until a cavity much larger than the gall is formed ; thump the covering over and into the cavity well with the round end of a tool handle until it fits the injured spot without pressure. Never allow teamsters or drivers to tie knots in straps of any kind with a view to shortening them. Insist on more holes being punched for the buckle tongue, or the cutting of the strap to the proper length. Knotted straps and serious galls go hand in hand. In adjusting your traces to the swingle trees, see that there is length enough given them when slack for the swingle tree to reach just sufficiently far down the back of the hind leg to cross half-way between the point of the hock and the hollow of the heel. As the trace is tightened, there will then be enough space for the animal to move his legs freely in. Watch him as he walks off, and see that nothing touches him behind at full stride. There are more kickers made by ill-adjusted swingle trees than any other cause. The weaker the animal is, the more liable he is to get his hind legs battered by the bar, as he lacks spirit and energy to keep well clear of it. The bar is, however, his enemy from that time, and it is difficult to make him forget past sorrows.

Waggon chains of one sort and another often snap when it is highly inconvenient to repair them. Keep, therefore, in your "odd and end" box a good number of union links, made as shown in the Chains and above illustration. They are forged rather flat, stouter in links. proportion than the chain they are intended to unite, in order to guard

them against opening. A leather thong or tie, with a toggle end is passed through the slots at the two ends of the union, in order that the links may not come out when the chain is slack. The looped ends of ropes are conveniently attached to chains, or chains to standing rings, by 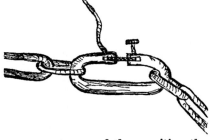 these union links. The illustration represents one of them uniting the ends of two chains.

Pack animals are of the greatest service and value to the explorer, as they travel easily through tracts of country which are impassable for wheeled carriages of all descriptions. Horses, ponies, Pack animals. mules, donkeys, oxen, elephants, camels, dromedaries, lamas, goats, and dogs are all, more or less, used as pack animals in different countries; and no two can be found in which the pack saddle and its gear will exactly correspond. The nature of the ground to be passed over and the description of load to be carried; will in great measure call for some special arrangement in the form and adjustment of the gear. For the use of a well-organised exploring or hunting party provided with horses or mules, we know of no pack saddle equal to that described and figured at pp. 30 and 31. Saddles of this description although admirably adapted for carrying the well-made and evenly formed bags of the explorer, would not answer to the requirements of the professional packer, who carries objects of every imaginable shape, from a bundle of pick-heads, or a case of bottled ale, to a barrel of powder. For the safe transport of such matters as these no saddle is better than the Hispano-American pack saddle.

No people in the world understand the management and packing of mules as well as the Spaniards and their descendants. The foundation of the Spanish pack saddle may be said to be the "aparejo," which is, so to speak, a framework for the back of the mule composed entirely of hide. Its form is represented at A in our illustration entitled "Horse Equipments." Each side flap of the aparejo is composed of a double layer of hide, with space sufficient between the layers to introduce an efficient stuffing of hay, dry moss, fibre, or other stuffing material. The cushions or side pads, when stuffed, should be about 3ft. 8in. long by 2ft. 8in. wide. Each flap and side cushion will thus constitute one side of the saddle body. These, when stitched together at the top, will form a sort of hollow ridge within which the backbone will rest free from pressure and friction. The aparejos of the Andalusian muleteers who, with their mules, accompanied us from Spain to the Crimea had layers of small twigs disposed between the stuffing of the panels and the covering of hide, so that the "riata," or rope used in securing the load, was prevented from cutting grooves in the padding.

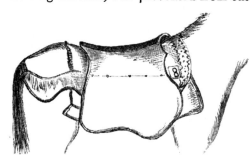

Each of these aparejos weighed, when new and dry, 35lb. On the inside of each cushion leather a hole is left, through which the material constituting the stuffing can at any time be got at. The careful packer will constantly avail himself of this orifice, in order that such portions of stuffing as may become shifted and worked up into hard lumps by the movements consequent on travel may be redistributed and evenly disposed of. The above illustration represents this aparejo when placed on the back of the mule.

Next the skin of the animal is placed a piece of soft well-washed canvas, 4ft. 6in. square; on this is then laid three layers of thick woollen blanket; on these layers, the true saddle cloth—the "corona" of the packers. This is made of stout woollen cloth, with fringed, worked, and ornamental borders. The corners of each of these cloths bear on them the letter or number of the mule to which it belongs. When removed from the mule, it is placed with the saddle gear on or under the aparejo, so that every mule can be at once fitted with his own trappings.

To secure the aparejo, and the cloths beneath it, to the mule's back, a wide girth, called a "synch," is used. This may be composed either of hide, grass, cloth, or common sail canvas doubled. Its edges should be sewn in a broad hem. The width may be about 13in., and the length not sufficiently great to go round the mule's body, over the aparejo and cloths under it. One end of this girth has a ring sewn into

[GROUP OF HARNESS.

it, and the other a bent stick of natural growth, as shewn at B in full-page illustration of "Horse Equipments." To tighten the synch by drawing the two ends together, a long strip of well-greased thong is used. This is passed several times through both ring and wooden eye, after one end has been made fast. By powerful and continuous hauling on the free end, the ring and eye are at length drawn close enough together below the saddle to make all secure. A loop is then formed in the free end, and the bow pulled under the forward and back lashings of the thong. When the synch is to be relaxed, it is only necessary to pull on the free end to set all free.

Two ropes are used for lashing on the load. One is called the "riata," and should be of pliant, evenly-spun $2\frac{1}{2}$-in. rope, 70yds. long; the second, or sling rope, is best made of stout patent Pack ropes sash line. Forty feet will be found long enough for a and saddles. sling rope. No written directions or pictorial illustration will give the least idea how to lash fast the heterogeneous objects constituting a general pack load; nothing but experience and ingenuity in the handling of rope will ever teach the traveller how to form the intricate spider-web-like lashing, interlacing, and cross binding, which by a professional Spanish or Mexican packer are woven until as tense as a harp string.

The Hudson's Bay Company and many traders and explorers in North-West America make use of the so-called cross-tree saddle for transporting their peltries and stores. One of these is Cross-tree shown at C in our full page illustration representing saddles. "Horse Equipments." The girth for that description of saddle has two sets of holes made in it, so that the ends may be laced together by the use of a strip of hide, represented at D.

A good number of narrow flat battens of tough wood and bundles of twigs will be found very useful for placing between the load ropes and load, as in the case of bags containing soft sub- Tightening stances, or articles likely to be crushed in, a groove is harness. at once formed by the tension of the strained rope, and without some interposing medium no little mischief is done. When a rope is found loose from any cause, it can be tightened by thrusting a short curved stick into the loop formed by the slack part, when, by twisting the lever round and round, the required tension is soon gained. When packing a mule or adjusting a disarranged pack it is well to partially blindfold the animal. This is done by the Spaniards by the use of a contrivance called a "tapajo" represented at E in the full-page illustration of "Horse Equipments." The hind strap of this is placed behind the ears, just as the head strap of a halter would be. The leather part hangs before the mule's eyes, whilst the fringe-like tails hang down at the sides. When not on a mule's head, the tapajo is used instead of a whip by placing the forefinger through the ring in its middle.

In travelling through a country tolerably free from large animals of prey·or hostile natives, it will not be requisite to hobble a large train
Bell mules. of mules during the night, as they will not stray far from the hobbled bell mare. This animal leads the march by day and keeps the " mulada " together at night. A gelding not uncommonly takes the place of the mare as the bearer of the bell. White or grey animals should be selected to perform this duty. Never, on any account, allow a stud mule to accompany your band; he rarely thrives, is always ready for a fight, and is as bad as an enraged wild beast when fairly roused. It is not wise to work mules hard until after three years old—four, five, and six are better ages to buy at.

Examining a strange or ill-tempered mule's teeth with a view to ascertaining his age is at times rather a risky operation. To do this,
Hints to put on a blind, get a halter put on the mule's head;
mule buyers. stand well in against the near fore-shoulder, pass the right hand gently up the neck patting the animal as it goes until you are enabled to take a steady firm grip of the root of the ear with your right hand; then, with your left, seize quickly, but tightly, on the upper lip and nose. Do this quickly and resolutely, guarding against a blow from the fore-foot, and you will probably get a glance of the front teeth, or incisors, and see if the corner tooth is temporary or permanent.

Another piece of important information will be gained at the same time, and that is whether the dentition of the upper jaw is free from deformity. It sometimes happens that both mules and horses are what is called overhung or parrot-beaked, which simply means that the upper row of front teeth projects so far beyond the lower that the two rows can by no effort of the animal be brought in contact. This defect is often overlooked, but when present is a fruitful source of loss of condition and consequent weakness, as food, easily gathered by animals with naturally-formed rows of teeth, is all but lost to the unfortunate possessor of a parrot-mouth. See, too, that the tongue is perfect.

Mules for packing purposes should not be too large or high on their legs. Some of those which accompanied us from Andalusia to the East were 16 hands and over; whilst the great majority of the trains we worked in Central India were very little larger than common donkeys, and certainly less than a great many we have seen in Egypt.

The experience of the last American war has shown that the

Hispano - Mexican mules are a most hardy and valuable strain. Speaking of these animals, the superintendent of the Government mule corral at Washington says:—" There is in Old as well as New Mexico a class of Mules that are known to us as Spanish-Mexican mules. These mules are not large, but for endurance they are very superior, and, in my opinion, cannot be excelled. I am not saying too much when I assert that I have seen nothing in the United States that could compare with them. They can apparently stand any amount of starvation and abuse. I have had these Spanish mules in a train of twenty-five six-mule teams, and starting from Fort Leavenworth, Kansas, on Colonel (since General) Sumner's expedition in 1857, have travelled to Walnut Creek, on the Santa Fé route, a distance of 300 miles in nine days, and this in the month of August. The usual effects of hard driving, I noticed, showed but very little on them. I noticed, also, along the march, that with a halt of less than three hours, feeding on grass that was only tolerably thick, they will fill up better and look in better condition for resuming the march than one of our American mules that have rested five hours and had the same forage. The breed, of course, has something to do with this; but the animal is smaller, more compact than our mules, and, of course, it takes less to fill him up. It stands to reason that a mule with a body half as large as a hogshead cannot satisfy his hunger in the time it would take a small one. This is the secret of small mules outlasting large ones on the prairies. It takes a large one so long to find enough to eat when grass is scanty that he has not time enough for rest or recuperation. I often found them leaving camp in the morning quite as hungry and discouraged as they were when we halted the previous evening. With the small mule it is different. He gets enough to eat quickly, and has time to rest and refresh himself. The Spanish or Mexican mules, however, are better as pack animals than for a team, They are vicious, hard to break, and two-thirds of them kick."

These observations of the superintendent are highly practical, and well worth bearing in mind in the purchase of pack mules. We are of opinion, however, that there are other qualities to be found in small well-formed animals, apart from the comparatively small amount of food required to support them.

Activity, endurance, and muscular power do not, so far as our experience has enabled us to judge, increase in the ratio of size; and the great majority of noteworthy and remarkably clever performances under saddle or pack related by hunters and explorers have been achieved by animals of comparatively small size. We do not think that even the English hunter will be found an exception to the rule.

Often have we devoutly wished that it might be our good fortune to possess a 16-hand horse with going and staying qualities, equal in proportion, size for size, to those of a sturdy, but very tiny cob we were once 'cute enough to select from a drove fresh from the wilds of Bulgaria. We conceive that a well-formed mule—that is to say with clear bright eyes, hocks not inclined to give in like those of a cow, stout muscular haunches, a short back, and dark small compact feet—should, for average service, be about 14 hands high, and weigh about 8cwt. Avoid all spotted, dappled, or white mules. These are, among the packers, known as "painted" or calico mules, and are by no means as hardy as those of dark uniform colours. Mares are always to be preferred to horse mules. They are more tractable, and follow the bell mare better on the march.

About 140lb. is as much as a mule of average power can travel well with from day to day. Never start a mule train without looking care-
Hints on   fully at each mule as he passes; and if you see one
mule equipment. of them raising his lips and twitching his mouth and nose, depend upon it he is getting galled, and requires looking to. Particular care should be taken that the halter heads fit easily across the back of the head, and that, in putting the halter on, the ears of the mules are not injured or roughly handled. Nothing makes a mule so shy and disposed to be vicious as sore ears. The halters used for pack mules are just such as we use in this country. We, however, prefer leather head collars with ropes attached to them.

There are many ways of preventing horses and mules from straying from the spot at which they are intended to remain. The Indian

Hobbling cattle. method of picketing
horses by the use of
head and heel ropes is by far the best
and most convenient we have ever had
recourse to. The heel hobbles—the subject of the accompanying illustration—
are best made of stout tanned leather;
the inside surface should be lined, and
have a slight stuffing of curled hair put
in to prevent friction; one hobble end
terminates in a leather loop; the other,
in a leather toggle. The heel ropes
themselves should be made from soft
flexible rope (cotton is often spun into

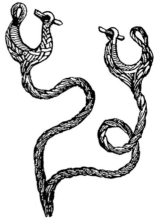

heel ropes); the strands are opened and untwisted to a short distance,
n order that they may be securely stitched fast to each hobble. At

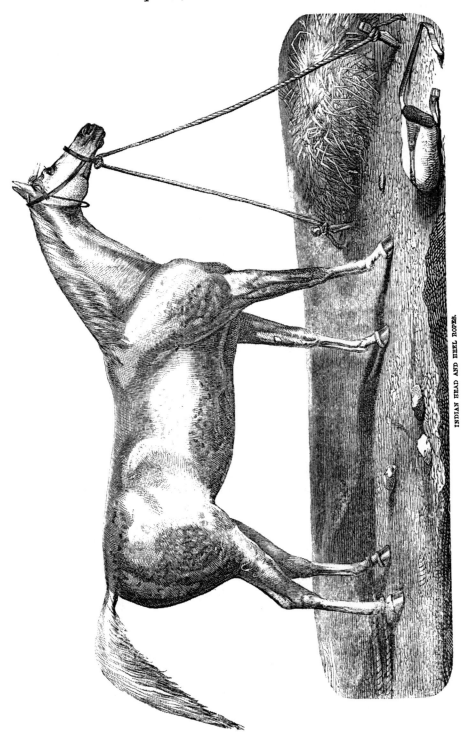

INDIAN HEAD AND HEEL ROPES.

about 6ft. from the hobbles the two heel ropes are spliced together and form one tail rope, which is secured round a peg driven into the earth. Two ropes attached to the head collar are also secured to pegs, as shown in the illustration on p. 419. When on the march each horse

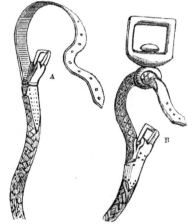

should carry his own head and heel ropes secured in a leather wrapper behind the saddle.

Head ropes may be conveniently fastened to the head collar by having a strap and buckle like that represented at A in the next illustration attached to the end of each rope, if the other end is finished as shown at B. One head rope left on when the horse is equipped for marching forms a convenient head-collar rope, which can be coiled up and secured as shown at p. 32.

The Cape hunters usually secure their horses during a temporary halt by the use of the knee halter. The manner of adjusting this is shown at A in the following illustration. In Australia, the hook hobbles, figured at p. 29, are adjusted as at B in the illustration below.

It is a common practice in the army to stretch a long rope between a number of posts, and then secure the horses to it at intervals by fastening the ends of the head collar chains. We have seen mule trains in India fastened in a similar manner to a long cord stretched out on the ground. Although space is economised by the adoption of these plans, they lead to an endless number of serious accidents from kicks, bites, and stake wounds from the splintered posts. The addition in weight to the present scale of military horse equipment may be, perhaps, urged as a reason why the head and heel ropes of India have not been universally adopted by the troops of this country. The result of our experience is that the very slight addition which is made to the burden by the strapping on of a pair of light strong head and heel ropes to the rear of the saddle is a mere mite in the balance when compared with the constantly recurring and serious evils we have just referred to.

If you are without hobbles, your horse or mule may be prevented from straying far by fastening the fore and hind leg on the same side together with a piece of rope or a couple of leather belts.   Horses, The two fore feet may be hobbled together in much the   to tie up. same manner, allowing just a short scope for the animal to move one foot before the other.   In countries where the lasso is used either in the form of hide lasso or hair cabresto (the manufacture of which will be treated of further on in our work), a horse or mule may be secured by first putting the noose end over the head and adjusting the neck loop just to fit the small of the neck easily, and then with the free or trail end taking a single hitch knot through the loop. This prevents the noose from running up and strangling the animal should it become suddenly alarmed and hang back. Mustangs, however, very rarely hang on a lasso after once experiencing its powers. Never trust the security of your riding animal, when either hunting or scouting, to either the regulation head-collar chain or headstall-rope, as, should a sudden alarm from any cause arise, your steed will in all probability give a sudden snort, tuck his haunches well under him, get his fore legs well to the front, give his head a violent shake, with one effort send all your head gear to the four winds, and go scampering away perhaps for ever. Lassoes are not so easily broken. If halting among trees or bushes fasten the trail end to a flexible branch; if there are no bushes, and you have a peg, fasten the lasso to it. If out on the prairies without a peg, dig a deep hole in the earth with your knife; tie a large knot in the end of the lasso, force it to the bottom of the hole, and then stamp the earth and turf well in over it. On sandy desert ground the lasso end may be secured to any odd article, such as a bag or blanket, which may be then deeply buried in the sand. An ox may be conveniently secured by passing two or three turns of a rope round the roots of the horns and then making a knot in front. All ropes long enough to admit of the animal walking and feeding in a moderately large circle should have one of the forms of wooden swivel before described attached to it in order to prevent twisting and entanglement.

Should a party of Iceland horsemen wish to halt for a short time, they place their horses with their heads together, and heels forming the outer border of the circle; the bridles are then looped and knotted together. Horses secured in this way cannot stray because no two animals pull in the same direction. This plan will only answer with very quiet animals. The entire horses of the East would fight desperately if thus brought in contact.

Large bands of horses may be driven or led in strings fastened head and tail, or marched on what is called a waggon line. This is Horses, to lead. a long strong rope fastened at each end to a cart or waggon, sufficient distance being maintained between each vehicle to keep the rope moderately tight. The halters of the horses to be led are fastened at convenient intervals along the line of the rope, and as the waggons travel so the horses march in a line. If there are many stores to be transported at the same time, put them in the rear waggon, as the line of marching horses aid greatly in drawing the load. An arrangement of this kind is very convenient when a stampede from Indians is to be dreaded.

Horses may be conveniently embarked by the use of the sling shown in the illustration below. The belly-band is made of very stout Embarking horses. sail canvas, mounted on two straight strong bars of wood. The ropes, which should be of thoroughly reliable $4\frac{1}{2}$in. or 5in. rope, after passing round under the edges of

the belly-band, are securely fastened to the ends of the bars, and each terminates in a loop. Four strong rope loops are secured to the edges of the band for the breast and breech ropes to pass through. One man holds the horse's head steady by the halter, and, if requisite, adjusts a blind; two men, one on each side, pass the rope loops through each other; whilst others bring round the breast and breech ropes, haul them up tight and double knot them. At the word "hook on," the hook of a fall working from a derrick is passed through the upper loop and stopped with a piece of small stuff. At a given signal the men on board at the tail of the fall, walk smartly away with it, and the horse moves rapidly aloft guided by two guy ropes until directly over the hatchway, which should be well padded with bags of straw. At the signal to lower away, the horse is lowered steadily to the hold or lower deck, where a deep bed of straw is spread, and men wait to cast loose and conduct it to the stall allotted for its reception.

In regularly-fitted horse transports, boxes are not unfrequently fitted for the horses to walk into before being lowered in them. Sometimes, when near the shore, horses are allowed to swim to land.

The management of horses on board ship will be treated of under the head "Veterinary Surgery."

Horses and ponies for packing should be of sturdy short-legged, cobby breed. A full-sized horse's pack for moderately fast and continuous travelling should not weigh more than about 120lb. A lively well-formed ox will carry about the same burden. Donkeys will carry from 50lb. to 60lb., according to size and condition. A pair of strong cane or wicker panniers, with lids made to hinge and lock, and covered with stout waterproofed — Pack animals and packs.

duck, will be found very useful for putting in articles for immediate use. Cooking utensils, food for the day, and a change of dry garments, are conveniently stowed away in these receptacles. Beware how you pack a number of rattling, clattering pots, pans, and kettles loosely on a timid ox's back. Should sudden alarm seize him, it will most probably lead to such a scene as is represented in the illustration on the preceding page.

CHAPTER XI.

CAMELS.

CAMELS and dromedaries are frequently most valuable to the traveller ; and, although generally associated with the torrid zone and its belongings, we see no reason why the camel should not be successfully acclimatised in many countries in which it is now practically unknown to the packer and traveller. " Camel Land " has been said to embrace the Canaries, Morocco, Algiers, Tunis, Tripoli, the Great Desert, Egypt, Africa, Arabia, Turkey in Asia, Persia, Cabool, Beloochistan, Hindoostan, Burmah, Thibet, Mongolia, Tartary in Asia, the Crimea, and a comparatively small tract of country in the neighbourhood of Constantinople. The camel has been kept and rendered available for general use on the estates of the Grand Duke of Tuscany, at Pisa, for very nearly two centuries. Australia and America are, we conceive, particularly well calculated for the utilisation of the labours of the camel. The opinion commonly entertained that the camel can only flourish in tropical lands is most erroneous. The ordinary geographical range of this animal may be roughly stated as being between 15° and 52° of north latitude, and 15° of longitude west of Greenwich to about 128° east of it. We have had opportunities of working camels of the Bactrian, Arabian, and Saundney breeds, under more than common vicissitudes of both climate and labour; we have ridden, muffled up in fur helmet and gloves, through the deep snow, where the woolly-coated Bactrians, crouching behind a sheltering rock, discussed their meal of coarse steepe hay contentedly, and were hardy to a degree; we have seen the burden camels of Egypt, under huge loads, trooping across the dry deserts of that land as if they were in their element; we have performed over 3000 miles of packing with Indian camels, and have taken part in most severe forced marches with Saundneys, carrying two men (an Englishman and a native), a heavy saddle, two sets of arms, accoutrements, and ammunition, over difficult tracts of country bordering on the sandy desert regions of Central India. .

Although we have seen the camel harnessed much after the manner
of an ox, and used in draught, it will rarely be found of much service

Harnessing   to the explorer when used in harness; as pack animals,
camels.   camels are invaluable.   A good form of camel pack saddle
is given at ꜰ in our full-page illustration of "Horse Equipments";
and the following diagrams will serve to show how ordinary camel riding
saddles may be made.   Any strong tough wood will answer for the
uprights and side pieces; the lashings are of raw hide; the cushions,

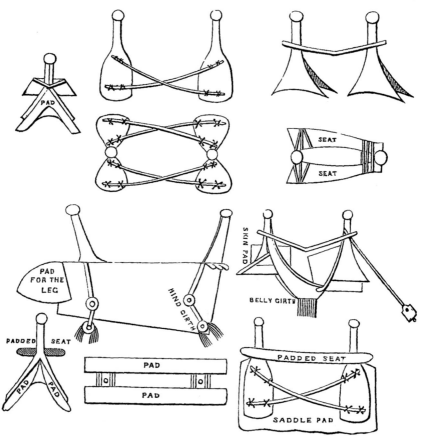

or pads, of leather, stuffed with wool or curled hair; the girths are
of spun goats' hair; and the breast strap is a wide band of plaited
thongs.   Some idea may be formed of the courage, power, and speed
of the camel when we state that, before the opening of the Suez
Railway, the mails were transported on camels' backs twice per month
across the Desert between Grand Cairo and the head of the Red Sea, a
distance of eighty-four miles, without halting, in about eighteen hours.

The weight of each camel-load (four mail boxes, &c.) was about 300lb.

Few matters of animal nomenclature have led to more confusion and misunderstanding than the terms "camel" and "dromedary;" and this has mainly arisen from the distinction laid down by Buffon, who states that the camel has two humps, whilst the dromedary has only one. If this point of distinction were correct, there would be no camels in Egypt, and one would have to travel to Tartary and some remote parts of Asia to find them; and the dromedary, and that only, would be found in Turkey, Arabia, Grand Cairo, Africa, and India. Amongst the Arabs and Egyptians the word "gimel" is applied to all the members of the genus—the term "dromedary" never being made use of. An animal used exclusively for riding purposes is called a "hagine." It will, therefore, be convenient to follow their example, and call a baggage animal of this family a "camel," and that used for riding purposes a "hagine." Our space will not admit of our entering on the subject of camel breeding, or the various crosses of breeds found in different parts of the world, as, like those of the horse, they would fill a volume.

The following directions to purchasers of these animals are given by Linant Bey, engineer-in-chief of dykes and bridges to the Viceroy of Egypt, and were translated for the information of the President of the United States of America.

A dromedary should not be too tall, nor its legs too long, which would give it a gaunt appearance; nor should the chest be too wide nor too heavy.

The fore-legs should not touch the callosity upon the breast. The two rowels or mullets (*molettes*) of the fore-feet should be far from touching each other when the animal walks.

The belly should be round, without being puffy; and the hump should not be too big.

The neck should be rather wide than narrow, the head well set on, the eye large, and the lips closed.

In walking the animal should show suppleness in the neck, and have a wavy movement of the head. The more suppleness there is in this motion the easier will be the gait.

To be highly esteemed a dromedary should not cry when touched; and, when bridled, haltered, or saddled, it should give utterance only to a low grumbling.

A dromedary should not be taken that has been seriously hurt near the shoulders, where the saddle rests, though it does not indicate disease, but proceeds only from the little care the Arabs give to keeping their saddles in repair. In a female this is less objectionable; for, in giving birth, if her wounds have caused any disease, it is almost always cured. Fine cautery marks on either side of the callosity, on the breast, or on the belly near the navel, indicate always internal, incurable disorders.

The hind-legs should not be too angular, but rather straight. The hump should not be too much to the front; rather to the rear is better, as then the saddle is more easily adjusted. The hair should not be too short, as then the animal is more easily injured.

The feet should be small, the nails and the hair round them black rather than white.

Fawn-coloured dromedaries are more highly prized than those entirely white.

When mounted, the dromedary should instantly and quickly rise and start off.

When the dromedary moves, it should be with such spirit that the rider is obliged to hold him in; this supports both. To urge him on kick him on the shoulder with the foot. It is very difficult to find a dromedary uniting in itself all these requisite qualities, and very rarely can such an one, especially if it is a female, be purchased; for the Arabs love their fine-blooded dromedaries as much as they do their horses, and it is only as presents, or else at enormous prices, that the choicest animals can be obtained.

A first-rate Nomanieh is worth in Cairo from five hundred to six hundred dollars; but those ordinarily met with there sell from one hundred to two hundred dollars.

The Bichariehs sell for less; good ones—that is to say, such as are for sale—may be had for from sixty to one hundred dollars.

At nearly for the same prices as for the Bicharieh can be purchased also the other breeds of the Mahazi, Cawarah, and Ababdi. I will remark here that the Bicharieh dromedaries do not carry as heavy burdens as the Nomanieh. These last carry a saddle called "gabit," fitted with pads, and with saddle-bags termed "krourque," that hang down on both sides of the saddle and carry the baggage, provisions, &c., of the rider and of the dromedary.

The Bicharieh carries a wooden saddle, laid over two small pads, which are not fastened to it. This saddle is called "kyarpah," "maraloup," &c., &c., according to its shape. Saddle-bags cannot be carried over it, on account of its form; but behind it a small sack of hide called "bila," in which a little luggage can be packed, may be attached after the manner of a valise or portmanteau.

Often, in expeditions, a servant or follower rides behind upon the dromedaries of the two breeds. Both riders carry their arms.

In a word, the Nomanieh generally carries from 200lb. to 230lb.; the Bicharieh, 180lb. At the utmost their burdens are 300lb. and 350lb. A dromedary, well equipped, well ridden, and in good condition, can easily make in a day over suitable ground, level and a little sandy, about ninety miles, that is, between morning and evening; but it cannot keep on at that rate. It can make fifty miles a day for fifteen or twenty days, and for a long journey can be counted upon for that. I have myself travelled upon one ninety miles in eleven hours, and gone twelve miles in forty minutes.

The carrying power of the camel will depend in great measure on the stock they came of and the climate in which they are employed,

Camels and the Central Asiatic camel being, as a rule, more vigorous their loads. and enduring than that of either Africa or India. The loads of camels will vary greatly with the nature of the work they are employed to perform. Where very short distances under burden have to be travelled, as for instance from the depots of a town to a camp in the immediate vicinity, a powerful and healthy camel can carry from 1100lb. to 1200lb.; for the march, or when produce or baggage has to be carried any distance, from 300lb. to 400lb. will be found quite heavy enough to admit of regular and continuous performance of carrying duty. We always roughly estimate our weight of stores and equipments at seven camels to the ton; for slow ordinary travelling of about twenty miles per day of from eight to ten hours in duration; for more rapid movements the loads should be proportionately lightened.

The following table of camel burdens made use of in various parts of the world may prove useful to the traveller in many lands:

COUNTRY.	WEIGHT.	DESCRIPTION OF ANIMALS.
Algeria, Morocco, Tunis, Tripoli,	From 300lb. to 400lb.	Ordinary camels of the country.
Egypt,	From 350lb. to 550lb.	Camels of the country.
Syria, Asia Minor, Turkey in Asia, Persia and Tartary,	From 500lb. to 600lb.	Large-sized bull camels (*loks*, as they are called) and hybrids (or *booghdee*).
Beloochistan, Cabool, Hindoostan, Thibet, Birmah, Mongolia	From 300lb. to 400lb.	Ordinary breeds.
Crim-Tartary and the borders of Southern Russia,	From 300lb. to 500lb.	Bactrian.

The age of a camel, like those of a horse or mule, may be judged of by the teeth. It remains without incisor teeth until the termination of the third year of its life, when it has two; at five years old, it will have four; at six years old six incisors; and at eight there will be a full complement—canines and molars. *Hints on camels.*

The condition of the hump is a good index of the general well-doing of the animal, as that structure is the first to fail or diminish from want or overwork.

The food of camels may be said to be found everywhere on the earth's surface where vegetation, of even the most scanty and unattractive character, is to be found. All is food that comes to tooth with the camel, and when low trees have been scarce, we have often sent a native armed with our hatchet or billhook to climb into a large peepul, neem, or baubul thorn tree, and chop down a cartload or two of branches.

The Arabs generally maintain that the camel should not drink more frequently than once in every three days, although in dry hot weather we have known them drink much more frequently without being apparently the worse for the indulgence. We have on many occasions endeavoured to ascertain the quantity of water taken at each period of thirst-quenching, and the result of our investigations have led us to the conclusion that about five gallons should be allowed as a drink to each camel, when he takes in water on the march. The stomachs of the camel, like those of other ruminating animals, are constructed so as to admit of a store of both food and water being laid up in them to meet the demand when other sources of supply fail.

In cases of extreme necessity, and when the preservation of human life depends on the obtainment of water, the supply to be found in the stomach of the camel should not be overlooked or forgotten.

During the Algerian campaign the French made some investigations in order to find out the quantity of water a dead camel's stomach would contain, and the result was that about 15 pints was the average arrived at. This water, although green and turbid, had no offensive smell. It is asserted by the Arabs that water of this character requires three days to clear itself. People, however, dying of thirst, are not very nice.

In a case of emergency, we should simply pass the water through our pocket filter, which will be described under the head " Water, and the sap of Plants," and drink it at once.

The regular purchase, collection, embarkation, and transport of camels has rarely been so carefully and successfully conducted as by the officers appointed by the Government of the United States of America, and the report forwarded to Congress by the officer in charge of the embarkation department will not fail to be of interest and value. He says:

Camels, to embark.

In the first place, the ship is anchored as close as possible to the place of embarkation to save time. The camel boat with the car in it is rowed on shore, and a force of about ten men sent to get the camels in. There is also sent on shore in the boat a good tackle (not very large), a camel harness complete, spare plank, hammer and nails, and about 50 fathoms of 2in. rope, all of which will be of use.

It is requisite to select a place for the boat where she will lie with her bow on a level with the wharf. If this cannot be done, and it is necessary to "beach" her, then a strong bridge made of stout plank, and about 8ft. wide, will have to be constructed, strong enough to bear not only the camel's weight, but to stand his struggling. The bow of the boat being secured firmly to the wharf or bridge, the harness is placed on the camel, which is led up as close as it will go. If it will walk right into the car, one end of which is placed on the gunwale of the boat, so much the better (in no instance did we find them willing to go without force), but if it will not go in then hook on the tackle to the breast strap of the harness on the camel; let the men keep a steady pull upon it, and the camel will go in without a hurt, no matter how much he may resist. Four men guide the camel, and keep it in the centre of the planks, and one man leads it by the halter into the car, through which the tackle is led, one block being hooked to the other end of the boat. After the camel is in it is made to lie down, the knees tied round with ropes, a rope across the neck and made fast to the knees. and two or three ropes across the back to keep it down. It is then hoisted on to the camel deck without fright or excitement of any kind.

The accompanying illustration will serve to show how the ropes and tackle are arranged for the purpose of urging a reluctant camel onward.

EMBARKATION TACKLE.

When the camels were all on board the report goes on as follows :—

Having taken in all the camels, two days we occupied in fitting to each one its proper harness (for almost every one of them differed in size and form), marking their numbers on the harness, and fitting out each one with brush and currycomb— all of which is necessary to be done before going to sea. Hayracks, made of large open network, were fitted amidships, extending the whole length of the camel deck. Large bags filled with hay were also placed against the ship's sides for their haunches

PREPARED FOR ROUGH WEATHER.

to rest against, and two ropes fitted for securing to the harness on each camel. The above engraving will show the manner in which the camels were secured when a gale of wind or a heavy sea prevailed.

To enable the camel guard to efficiently watch their charge at night, four large lanterns with reflectors were put up, and lighted every evening at sunset; and, in case of accidents from fire, two large water tubs were kept always full.

The American camel journal kept on board the United States ship *Supply* is so thoroughly practical and useful, that we insert a specimen of its form of construction for the guidance of travellers who may have to perform a voyage with camels newly purchased for an expedition or campaign.

Camel journal.

CAMEL JOURNAL.

DATE.	HAY.	WATER.	OATS.	PEAS.	MEAL.	MEDICINES.	REMARKS.
18 .	Bales.	Galls.	Bags.	Galls.	lb.	lb.	
Jan. 21	280lb.	30	2	—	—	¼ sulphur	Received on board 6 camels (2 of them males). Washed them and secured them in their stalls. Put sulphur in their water.
,, 22	220lb.	40	1	—	—.	—	Fitted the harness when required, and rubbed the camels well with curry-combs and brushes. Named the camels and lettered the harness.
,, 23	1 bale	40	1	—	—	—	Refilled the netting with hay, as also the fenders for their behinds. Went round the camels with sulphur oint-ment, and applied it on all suspicious-looking places. Ceased to issue oats. Littered with hay.

The treatment of camels when suffering from disease or accident will be given under the head "Veterinary Surgery."

CHAPTER XII.

CATTLE MARKING.

In all large and imperfectly settled countries the use of a private mark, or brand, is most important, not only as a means by which animals can be identified and recovered when lost, but as the evidence of legal transfer and of particular breed or strain of stock. Animals are most commonly marked with either some conspicuous and tenacious pigment, by slits or cuts of definite form made in the ear, or by initials or some symbol branded with a heated iron on some part of the body. Sheep may be both ear-marked and lettered with either red or black paint. The lettering is easily and expeditiously effected by the use of the cover or bottom of an old biscuit tin. Lay your sheet of tin on the table, and with the point of your knife sketch out the outline of the letter or letters you have determined on as your mark, taking care that they are of conspicuous size; then with a mallet and chisel cut out the letters. You will then have a sort of stencilling sheet; cut it to a convenient size, nail a piece of wood to it for a handle, and your marker is complete. Place it against your sheep, paint over the outside of the plate with a large paint-brush, and your mark is made in an instant. Your sacks, bags, and boxes can be marked in the same manner with the same contrivance. A herd of cattle can be temporarily marked by a newly-arrived settler in a quarter of an hour or twenty minutes, as follows: Procure a waggon whip handle or a long pole; then lash to its end a round ball of either hide, with the hair on, or a bit of old blanket, fixing on your ball to the stick just as the striker of a drum-stick is made. Dip this in a pot of paint or tar, and then put it adroitly against the haunch or shoulder of the animal to be marked. Give it a sudden sharp twist round, and there will be instantly formed a round ball-like spot. With a lot of timid newly-purchased cattle, with which you are anxious to move off at once, the above plan will be found a good one.

The cutting of marks in the ear seems to be the more primitive and, perhaps, the easier, as involving less need of tools or apparatus;

F F

but it is difficult to give sufficient variety to enable many farmers to have each a distinctive mark. One slit, or more, in the right or left ear, a "swallow-tail" in one and a slit in the other, or a hole punched with a wad cutter, are among the most common ; but all are liable to be torn off by dogs or wild animals ; and the hole in the ear is especially objectionable, as the creature itself is almost sure to tear it through by scratching with his hinder foot. Moreover, almost all are liable to be altered should the marked property fall into dishonest hands ; and most farmers, and, it may be said, all traders, now employ the branding iron—fashioned to represent either their own

 initials or some arbitrary sign, as a cross, a square, a triangle, a circle or any segment of it, a star of any particular number of rays, the figure formed by crossing two triangles (as here shown).

In America, and some other countries, it is requisite, on the purchase of animals—horses and mules especially—that the traveller should not only get a receipt for his purchase money, but get indorsed on it by the seller his acknowledgment of the new owner's counterbrand, in manner as follows : "Received of Capt. ——, the sum of —— dollars, in payment for a brown mare mule. Seller's brand, O. B. ; buyer's brand, W. Signature, &c." The new brand should be placed under the old one, and unless these precautions are taken the new purchaser stands a very excellent chance of having his recently-acquired stock seized on at some frontier post, and detained until the legality of the transfer has been ascertained. It is sometimes agreed on that the owner shall renounce all claim to an animal by reversing his own brand above that originally made by him, thus, $\frac{\Xi-\chi}{A-B}$.

There are tales, however, of certain dwellers at a distance from the law who have acquired considerable skill in altering the marks of any stray cattle that may fall into their hands, and this is an operation requiring no little skill, for should the mark be old, an iron made too hot will burn the addition in so deeply that it will for a long time display an air of freshness not in accordance with the original. Some initials are very easy of alteration ; thus, C may be converted into O, or Q, or G ; I may be made at least into thirteen letters without increasing its size,

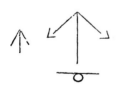 which, when it is used in combination with others, is a point of considerable importance, and into several more if a slight increase may be ventured on. P may become B or R, and L or F may be changed to E. It may be well for us to point out to those who have charge of Government stock, or are likely to have stolen animals offered them for sale, that the

thief not unfrequently thinks fit to adopt an anchor as his brand, as, if it is of proper size, the broad arrow, by the addition of the stock and flukes, makes a very respectable one. We have heard of an unscrupulous colonist who branded all his cattle with a frying pan, and had *no particular place* on which to apply it; thus, no matter what the brand on a stray horse or ox might be, he had nothing to do but to clap the red hot disk above it, and his own mark speedily and effectually obliterated every other.

It is a good plan to have a small iron and to brand cattle upon the horns, as it is impossible to efface the mark by any process that would not betray itself. This iron may also be used for branding small articles—such as tent poles, yokes, waggon-gear, or anything in the traveller's possession—not only as a precaution against theft, but as a means of affording an indication of his fate should he perish, as many a poor fellow has done in a gallant but fruitless effort to explore an unknown country.

Any man with a few tools and a moderate share of ingenuity can make his own branding iron from a suitable-sized chunk of soft iron. File it to the right form, give it an even face; then with a pencil sketch the letter, or mark, on the iron, only taking care to reverse the object as you would in drawing on wood. When your pencil lines are complete, scratch them in with a sharp hard point. Rub a little gunpowder and grease into them in order that they may show conspicuously, and then, with a hammer and small cold chisel, proceed to chip away the superfluous iron until the pattern stands boldly and sharply out. Heat it and try the print on a board, and, if requisite, trim and file again until it is to your satisfaction. A large drill is of great service in making branding irons, which, when finished.

can be attached to handles either by leaving a piece of metal on the back of the chunk long enough to weld the hand iron to, or a screw may be made at the back to hold it in its place. Some persons make chunk, hand iron, and all from one piece of metal; others form the letters, &c., from narrow strips of iron, bending them to the required figure, and then riveting them fast to a sort of frame. We, however, consider the solid chunk form of iron by far the best and most durable. A clear charcoal or wood fire is best for heating the brand in. It should be heated just hot enough to singe rather than burn into the skin; so long as the roots of the hair are destroyed the burning may be considered effective. As we have before stated, the particular strain, or breed, of certain animals may be known by the peculiar way in which they are branded. The Arabs have a great number of private marks, which few, save themselves, understand. Horses and dromedaries are marked in an entirely different manner. There is also a distinction drawn by them between large and small horses. The former are known as "Aneezah" Arabs, and, if of high caste, usually bear the peculiar mark of the tribe by which they are reared. All Arab horses under 14 hands are called "Nedjdi." These, when found by any tribe to possess more than ordinary purity of breed and excellence, are marked with an extremely narrow crescent, like a new moon, with the horns a little more than an inch apart. In the illustration on p. 435 we give a few examples of dromedary branding, as showing the particular class of animal indicated by it. 1. Amadabieh. 2 shows the general mark of a Bicharieh tribe, which will be seen to exist on all the other examples. The additions show the private brand of each small community, or division of the tribe, thus: 3. Amitirah; 4. Mahomed-Ouzabieh; 5. Menacir; 6. Achabab; 7. Cawarah; 8. Mahazi; 9. Valgat.

CHAPTER XIII.

WATER, AND THE SAP OF PLANTS.

THE whole success of an expedition and the preservation of the lives of those composing it have not unfrequently depended on the obtainment of this precious fluid ; and, as its importance to the traveller is vital, so the sources from which it is to be obtained are numerous. Rivers, lakes, springs, and rain pools are the most common and obvious, needing no comment here. Showers of rain often yield a Locality for considerable quantity, which may be caught in sails or   water. sheets spread for the purpose, selecting those which are free from the perspiration of men or animals. Deep clefts among rocks and ravines often contain a great deal, and the cliffs by the sea-shore, although there are no rivulets to be discovered, frequently contain cracks and crevices, through which water runs and loses itself in the sand.

The beds of apparently dried-up watercourses should be always explored carefully, as high up as possible, and the stones at the bottom of the deepest pools lifted out, and their resting places examined. A piece of woollen cloth, a sponge, or a bunch of soft moss, will much facilitate the withdrawal of chance finds in such places. Spots of low ground, on which reeds, rushes, or other water plants are found, should be carefully examined, and their depths probed with a strong sharp-pointed stick.

The tracks of wild animals are often valuable guides to water ; but careful examination is needed lest the searcher should take the back track, and go from, instead of towards, it. A sharp lookout overhead towards evening will often be rewarded by a sight of the flocks of wild-fowl or other birds winging their way towards the drinking places. Baggage animals and dogs at times show extraordinary instinct in finding pools and springs where they are least expected to exist. We have also seen Indians apparently guided by some singular faculty to their neighbourhood. In most countries some particular kind of tree will be met with generally associated with the presence of water, and growing near it.

Should moisture be discovered a hole should be at once dug by loosening the earth and gravel with the stick, and then clearing out the hole with the hand, a small "well" as deep as the arm is long, may be very rapidly made in this manner : Well hardening the point of the digging stick in the fire will add much to its efficiency, and is much better than a mere pointing with a sharp instrument. Where the soil is of a loose character and the sides of the well likely to fall in, a long bundle of reeds or rushes should be bound together and thrust down. Holes of this kind may be long preserved as drinking places by making up a round ball of slender twigs just sufficiently large to fit the hole, ramming it firmly to the bottom, then placing a bamboo

or other hollow tube long enough to reach a couple of feet or so above the surface, and then filling in the hole with earth and pressing the whole well down. The water is thus preserved from evaporation, and can be sucked freely through the tube. At times it will be found to flow up the tube and run over, or a second tube may be put in to blow through, when the water can be caught in any convenient vessel by boring a hole through a bit of bark for the upper end of the tube to fit into, thus forming a shoot for it to run off through, as in the above illustration.

When horses or cattle have to be watered from a pool or "well" of any size, and the water is any distance below the surface, the old expedient of the lever and post, so common all through Egypt and most Eastern countries, will be found an exceedingly useful one. (See the following full-page illustration.) When travelling through Central India, where the wells are often very large and deep, we used to find our small brass "lota pot," which was carried strapped fast to the front of the saddle, with a long coil of whipcord stowed away in it to lower and raise by, of great service.

Drinking troughs for cattle are conveniently made from hollow tree trunks, sheets of bark with the ends nipped up, or by digging a trench in the ground and placing a piece of canvas or an indiarubber ground sheet in it. In watering cattle from contrivances of this kind two separate herds should be formed consisting of those which have to drink and those which have drunk, letting them up one at a time, and keeping back the rest. Much confusion and irregularity are thus avoided, and you are sure that each animal has had its share.

We can only give a few general hints on searching for water. Perhaps the surest way is if there are natives in the country to make friends of them, not by hurriedly and lavishly forcing upon them presents—costly, it may be, to the giver, but Water, to find. valueless to them—but by quietly waiting to see what they value, and giving it in moderate quantities, as if the donor knew its worth as well as they. Half a stick of tobacco, a short pipe, a sixpenny knife, or cotton handkerchief, blue spotted with white, or a few strings of beads of the kind they value—generally white, red, blue, or black opaque seed beads —will gain their good will better than useless tinsel or gewgaws of ten times the cost; while a Dutch brass-barrelled tinder-box, with flint and steel, value 1s. or 1s. 6d., becomes far in the interior an article of such value that it ought not to be given except as a reward for real service. Extravagant liberality will only be attributed to fear, more especially if haste accompanies it; therefore, it is wise to spend a little time before making even the preliminary offer of a pipeful of tobacco, and more before giving the real present and making known what is desired in return. But in reality the traveller will save time, and when he does ask for water the native will bring him a supply, or point out where to obtain it; whereas, were he to open the negotiations by hurriedly demanding information, the natives would become suspicious of his motive, and would in the first instance tell him a lie in order to throw him off the scent and gain time to discover his supposed intentions.

In the absence of native guides, converging footpaths of men or animals will probably lead to a pool. Most antelopes drink every day, but this is not the case with the gemsbok or the eland, the last of which never drinks, or, if he ever does, the instances are quite exceptional.

As before stated, the flight of birds morning and evening should also be watched, but this, however, is not always an infallible sign, as we have seen cockatoos drinking water so black that we could not use it; but when, as we have also seen, even the parrots desert an island before sunset it becomes tolerably certain that no water will be found upon it.

Depressions on the ground should be followed, and additional freshness of vegetation carefully sought for. An iron ramrod may be thrust into the ground when there is any chance of dampness below the surface, and the traveller should make himself acquainted with the peculiar plants of the country which grow near the water. The pandanus, or screw pine of Australia, is one of these.

In savage countries the labour of seeking and digging for water falls principally on the women, who usually make use of a fire-hardened grubbing stick for working a hole in the ground. The stick is loaded with a perforated stone of several pounds weight to give additional force to each stroke, and as the soil is loosened it is cleared out by the insertion of the hand and arm, using the bent fingers as a scoop. Use is also made of a stick split to about 12in. or 15in. from the end, and this, when worked down into soft soil, catches and brings up a quantity in the cleft, and this being shaken out upon one side the stick is again clear and fit to bring up more. A bamboo cane, with the end split up into several filaments, is used for the same purpose by the natives of India.

Where only salt or saline water is to be obtained recourse may be had to distillation, which may serve, as it has done in many well-authenticated cases, to at least save the lives of the human beings and dogs of a party. Little hope could, however, be entertained of being enabled by this means to supply the wants of cattle or horses.

A "still" may be very easily made from any vessel which will stand fire, such as one of the copper water barrels hereafter

Makeshift still. described, or even a common cooking pot and a gun barrel (single or double), a hollow bamboo with the knots removed, or, in fact, any hollow tube. If a pot

is used, a stout heavy wooden cover must be fitted to it, through which two holes are to be cut—one at the side for the barrel or tube, and the other a bung-hole at the top, which must have a stopper fitted securely to it, and is used to introduce the water as it becomes exhausted. This saves the trouble of removing the cover, and thus disturbing the other arrangements. The annexed illustration will serve to explain the nature of a contrivance of this kind.

The boat-shaped box resting on the forked sticks is made of bark, pinned at the ends with wooden pins. This is filled with a couple of woollen blankets or a quantity of moss, or even seaweed. The barrel passes directly through the centre, and is kept cold by constantly throwing cold water over it. The fresh water runs out through the hole from which the nipple is unscrewed, and is caught in any suitable vessel; and the waste salt water through holes bored in the bark for the purpose. Many modifications of this plan might, of course, be had recourse to, but this will be found about as convenient as any. Barrels, or hooped vessels of any kind, are about the very worst that can be taken into a wild country, as the hoops come off as the wood shrinks, causing leaks and endless trouble.

For carrying water on the backs of animals a pair of thin sheet copper flasks (20in. long, 12in. broad, and 8in. thick) will be found exceedingly convenient. These should have broad and Copper strong loops soldered on to pass leather straps and water flasks. lashings through, and in using water it should be taken alternately to preserve an even balance. The bung-holes should be at the ends, and have a stout raised ring round them, through which a hole is drilled; through this a pin is run, passing through a corresponding hole in the wooden stopper, thus keeping it secure. These flasks, when made, should be thoroughly tinned inside. They are useful for a number of purposes. Water can be boiled in them as well as carried. They can, on an emergency, be converted into a "still," as before stated, and when corked up air-tight are a great support to a raft. One at each end of an outrigger pole renders the upsetting of a canoe or float log next to impossible. No knocking about hurts them, and should at any time a leak be discovered, a bit of solder puts the matter to rights at once.

Next in value to flasks, perhaps, come leather mussacks, of the description used in the East. They can be made of any size, and, when injured or pricked, as they sometimes are by sharp Water skins sticks or thirsty niggers, they are readily repaired for and pails. the time by pinching up a piece of leather at the orifice and passing a sharp-pointed stick through, over which a clove hitch (see "Knots and Hitches") may be secured. A patch may be sewn on when there is time to do it, just as a cobbler mends a shoe. But bear in mind that, instead of the ordinary thread or hempen cord used in mending or making leather utensils or articles in this country, a dry carefully-cut leather thong should be used instead, as when once in place it swells from the action of the water on it, and completely fills the holes through which it has been passed, thereby preventing leakage.

In Mongolia they use a very useful pail or bucket for carrying water. It has a head fixed into it much like that of an ordinary barrel, and there are two openings or bung-holes; one tolerably large on one side, just below the edge of the head, and another through the head itself. In these orifices wooden plugs or stoppers are fitted, and, when water is to be poured out, the stopper in the head is just eased like the vent peg of a cask, so that air may be admitted; when the stopper is taken out the larger hole freely discharges the water, which would not run without the vent-peg arrangement.

During the year 1865, when we had entered the Victoria River, North Australia, and the *Tom Tough* was still drifting, in daily danger of breaking up upon the sand-banks, we had become tired of carrying water overland from distant pools to supply 140 sheep; and, considering that if our inflatable boat (p. 42) would hold air to float upon the water she would also hold fresh water to float in salt, we determined to seek supplies farther up the river; and putting the four sections into the schooner's gig, we sailed or pulled alternately thirty or forty miles up the river, till the entire cessation of the mangroves and the appearance of the pandanus, or screw pine, upon the banks and islands showed that we were above the influence of the tide and in a stream of permanently fresh water.

We halted at Palm Island, and, choosing a place where the water was a little more than knee deep, we threw the inflatable sections over-

Canoe board, and, fixing the bellows in the valves, held
water transport. them beneath the surface and pumped water into them, just as we would have pumped air had we required them for boats. We did not quite fill them with water, but forced in a little air to give them buoyancy, and, at the same time, to preserve their shape. In towing them, however, the pressure of the water caused the foremost ends to assume a wedge-like form, while the water and air, being forced aft, carried all the buoyancy thither, and they went down head-foremost. We remedied this by cutting a long spar and lashing them to it, making fast also an indiarubber mattress to the parts most liable to go down.

Tedious enough was our voyage down the river. To make anything like speed with such a drag astern of the boat was impossible, either with oars or sails; and during the heat of the day we found the cement of the bags beginning to soften and give way. They had been warranted to stand 170°; but, testing them by the thermometer, the internal heat was only 120°. We gathered up the defective part, knotted it with a bit of twine, and laced the bag along the gunwale of our boat—keeping her in trim by lacing its fellow on the other side—leaving only one pair to be towed astern. The extensive shallows, where for half a mile on a stretch the river percolated through rather than flowed over broad banks of angularly-broken stones, caused us considerable labour and anxiety lest some sharper point than usual should pierce our bags and deprive us of the fruit of all our toil. We found, however, that they yielded kindly to the varying pressure; and we rolled them, one by one, over the successive reaches—working for

hours together through the night, and frequently in pools in which we saw alligators, and sometimes sharks of considerable size.

Our week's work, however, toilsome as it was, resulted in a supply of 600 or 800 gallons of fresh water, tasting somewhat of indiarubber, but still available for the sheep. This supply we could have obtained in no other manner.

Water-bags for ship use may be made of stout No. 1 canvas. They should be of oblong form, about 2ft. long by 18in. wide. They should be in two thicknesses — the inside or lining being kept perfectly clean, and the outer one previously oiled with good boiled linseed oil and allowed to dry before it is made up, so as to keep the inner canvas as free from taint as possible. Generally the canvas is wetted with salt water, and then hung up till it is wind dry, or just so damp that no water will drip from it. It is then considered to be capable of absorbing just so much oil as will suffice to render it waterproof without clogging it or making it unpleasant to handle when it is dry. A sufficiently stout rope should be stitched round the seam of the bag; beckets or loops should be left in it at the four corners for convenience of handling; and a wooden tube or stopper should be inserted, and firmly seized in with small cord at one corner. *Ships' water-bags.*

These bags are most convenient when a supply of water is needed on any emergency, especially if the landing be difficult or dangerous, or the inhabitants hostile. They occupy no room in the boat while empty. The oarsman may pull in unencumbered through the surf; or, if it is necessary to fight, the riflemen may use their weapons. When the landing is effected each carrier may seize his bag, sling it over his shoulder with a lanyard, and experience no hindrance until he actually fills it, when, of course, the weight of the water will become a burden. The bags will lie flat in the boat's bottom, accommodating their form to that of the space they occupy. If it is necessary to carry sail they serve as ballast; and even were the boat to fill, they would not sink her, but, as fresh water is of somewhat less specific gravity than salt, would, if secured by bottom boards laid over them and beneath the thwarts, help to keep her up; and on this account they would form the most eligible ballast for boats on separate service, and even for pleasure boats on excursions, where they might not be in actual need of a large supply of fresh water.

Cattle horns serve in South Africa for powder-flasks or water vessels, some, especially among the Bechuana tribes, being 13ft. from tip to tip, and capable of containing several gallons each; while the Hottentots use them to hold honey beer, and the Abyssinians for "tedge" or mead. A calabash, or gourd is used by most of the natives of South Africa, as well as many other countries, as a water

Calabashes, horns, and egg-shells.

vessel. It is light, water-tight, not very easily broken, and even if an unfortunate fracture should take place the natives repair it by boring holes on either side the crack, pointing them diagonally towards each other, so that, by giving a slight turn to the point of the sinew used for thread, they either pass it through the next hole or bring it so near that it may be caught, crochet fashion, by a fine thorn or a crook-pointed needle. The leakage is stopped by a little grease and clay rubbed into the holes. A calabash with a long neck may be cut so as to form a spoon or ladle. Others of smaller size are used as snuff-boxes, or receptacles for many trifles; and in some parts of Turkey calabashes are used for powder flasks. An ostrich's egg-shell with a net worked tightly round it makes a good water-bottle.

The bladders, or paunches, of slain animals are very generally used as water vessels. If an animal has drunk recently

Bladders and paunches.

water may be found in its stomach. We have quenched our thirst with the milk of a blesbok doe as she lay dead, though not yet cold, upon the plain.

We have often seen our followers, when a buffalo or other animal has been killed, take out the paunch, shake out its contents, and hasten with it to the nearest stream, where, with barely a preparatory rinsing, they will fill it with water quite clean enough for their idea of culinary operation; and, calling on the nearest native resident, would invite him to bring his pots with him and assist in cooking the banquet.

Sometimes the paunch scraped thin is suspended by thongs passed through like purse strings. Occasionally two mimosa thorns, which are not unfrequently 4in. or 5in. long, or a couple of skewers, are thrust through and the cord tightened round under them. If a small hole should be found, it may be stopped by putting a somewhat larger pebble upon the place, gathering the skin around it, and then tying the neck firmly with a cord; or the edges may be skewered together with a thorn, and the neck bound tightly with cord.

When a rhinoceros has fallen we have seen the Damara women carefully extract the long intestines, distend them with air, and bring them home coiled round their bodies, to be used thereafter as water vessels.

The Kafirs on the frontier of the Cape Colony plait baskets of so fine a texture that they employ them for holding milk and even water;

Waterproof baskets.

but it is better that they should become saturated with the first before they are used for the latter, as, though they swell while wet and are perfectly tight, pure water would dry out with the heat from the fibre of an empty basket, and the consequent shrinking of the texture would make it leaky.

We have seen most elegant and serviceable baskets made in Timor of the leaves of the fan palm. The ends of all the spreading leaflets are gathered together in a point, and a cord of twisted fibre is passed as a handle from this point to the stump of the footstalk. A pair of these baskets, holding two or three gallons each, are slung to the ends of a bamboo, and the bearer taking this across his shoulder carries water, or sometimes palm juice, about the town. The latter refreshing beverage is sold at a doit per cup; the cup itself being made of a smaller palm leaf, and also purchasable for a doit or two.

At Walvisch Bay, in South-West Africa, where rain falls perhaps once in two years, and the river runs with fresh water once in ten, there is a small water hole called Sand Fountain. This is about four miles from the landing place, and the water was, and perhaps still is, brought by two or more Hottentots dragging a cask fitted up like a garden roller, with the pivots set firmly into stout cross-pieces nailed or screwed upon each end of the cask.

Shafts of wood, with holes bored in them to fit upon the pivots, may be used as means of traction, or, if more convenient, ropes with thimbles or grummets turned in the ends for the same purpose; but in this case the trek ropes should be kept apart by a horizontal bar that they may not chafe upon the chine of the cask. It will also be advantageous to fit on felloe-pieces, near each end, so as to form a substitute for wheels, on which the cask may travel, and this will save a great deal of wear and tear should the country be rough or stony.

A larger cask mounted on the after wheels of a waggon, and fitted with chocks on a frame lying on the axle is useful.

Filtering bags can be made of woollen or other cloth. An excellent and convenient camp filter is thus made: Take a wooden box or barrel, long and deep. Bore a number of holes in the Camp filter. bottom, fasten in a blanket bag, and then place a layer of grass, small twigs, or moss on the bottom, over the holes; then a layer of sand; then a thick bed of coarse lumps of charcoal; then fresh layers of grass or moss, until the box or barrel is about half filled. Then fashion a false head or cover, making it just large enough to move up and down the cask or box freely; burn or bore a number of holes in it, and, when fitted in, press it firmly down on the arrangement below, and drive a few nails in above to keep it from rising. When this contrivance is partially sunk in a pond or lake the water will ascend to the upper compartment above the false head, from which it can be dipped or drawn for use.

Another useful barrel filter can be made by knocking both the heads out of a small cask, boring it full of gimlet holes, placing it

on a thick layer of charcoal and pebbles in a larger cask, also bored full of holes, and then filling in all the space between the outer and inner barrels with the mixture, as shown in the above illustration.

The following is an expedient easily extemporised and frequently used in damp soils, where water is scarce. A quantity of grass is tied up in a wisp, or plaited into a bag; two reeds are inserted in this—one as a suction tube, and the other to admit air; and the apparatus is buried wherever a sufficiency of moisture is likely to permeate the soil.

The illustration below shows a very common expedient. Suppose the waters of a river to be excessively turbid: a well may be dug in the bank at any convenient distance, and the water that collects in it will at least be much clearer than that of the river. Of course none of these modes will correct chemical impurity.

We have heard it said that even sea-water by filtration through a considerable mass of sand will lose much of its saltness and become drinkable, and, that by digging wells at some distance from the margin of the beach, it may be obtained with a very small amount of brackishness. We

Hints on springs.

should like to hear a well-authenticated instance of this, in which there could be no doubt that the sea-water had been thus purified, and that the diggers had not in fact struck upon a stratum moistened by the inland drainage, and rendered more or less brackish by meeting with the sea-water.

We have known a remarkable instance of the discovery of a spring of fresh water in the immediate vicinity of the salt. In 1855, while attached to the North-Australian Expedition, we had great difficulty in supplying the sheep carried by our schooner, *Tom Tough*, with water. We made one trip up the Victoria River, with indiarubber bags—and this we purpose to notice more fully under its proper heading—and searched the country on either side the river in all directions. We found many little pools in shady hollows of rock, or of alluvial soil, marking the course the rivulets would take in the rainy season, and many of them decked with waterlilies. But these were too distant to be of service to us, and we again examined the country in our vicinity. In one cleft of rock we found a pint or two of water, and with a long twig and the broken shell of a gouty stem fruit we drew up enough to allay our thirst; but after traversing the arid ridges for hours we were returning unsuccessfully, when, passing at half-tide along the muddy margin of the river where a bold projecting headland forbade us any other path, Mr. Gregory noticed a little water collected in a hollow of the mud around a boulder. We thought at first it was only the drainage of the retiring tide, but on tasting it, we coincided in his opinion that it was not salt water. We set to work with our hands and cleared away the mud and brackish slime till, having reached a stratum too hard for our fingers' ends, we rested, and soon had the satisfaction of seeing a small threadlike streamlet of clear water forcing its way through the muddy sediment. In a few minutes nearly half a pint of fresh water had collected, and having satisfied ourselves of the value of our discovery, we returned to our schooner, and putting a couple of puncheons in the long boat, waited till the turn of the next tide, and dropped down with the ebb to the headland. Our well was not yet uncovered, but we began to work as soon as the water fell below our knees, greatly to the astonishment of our Dutch sailor, who could hardly

find terms strong enough to express it. "Allamagtig," said he over and over again, "have I lived so long in this world that I must come to dig for fresh water underneath the salt!" We made a fire on the uncovered boulder to give us light, at no small risk of injury from the splitting off of heated fragments; and removing as many large stones as we could, cleared  out a spring of perfectly pure fresh water, abundant enough to fill both our puncheons before the tide again rose high enough to cover it. Nor was this a transient phenomenon, for the next year, before we left the river, we again cleared out the "Gregory" well, and filled all the casks of our vessel for her voyage. The sketch represents very nearly the locality in question; the high-water level is shown in the upper horizontal line, and the half-tide by the lower one, and that of the well is observable between them.

A makeshift filter can be made as follows: A small reed is inserted into a walnut shell, or any other receptacle of about the same size, pierced with small holes, and packed, not too tightly, with hemp, cotton, coir sponge, or other porous material; it is then placed in the shell of a cocoa nut, an ostrich's egg, or tin pannikin of any kind, and the interval between the two moderately packed with charcoal made either from wood or, still better, bones, with any fibrous material, and a mixture of sand or gravel. This is plunged beneath the water, and the tube being taken into the mouth, a little suction does all the rest. The shank or wing bone of a crane, a stork, or albatross, may be used as a tube in the same manner.

The Bushmen of South Africa always carry one or more suction reeds in the quiver with their arrows, and, whenever the water is surrounded by banks so steep that the lips cannot conveniently reach the surface, lie down and suck the water through the tube. When there is only damp soil they dig a hole, and, wrapping up the end of the reed in a tuft of grass, they bury it, and suck the water that filters through. But as the Bushwoman fills the ostrich's egg-shells, to be carried away for home consumption, she takes another reed, or often merely a bit of grass or straw, as a conductor, and spirts the water along it from the other side of her mouth into the shell. The orifice is then plugged with a wisp of grass; and, a dozen or more of the shells being packed in a net, she takes them on her back and marches, perhaps, many a mile to deposit them wherever the men require water.

Sometimes the Bushmen take a good handful of grass, and lash it very tightly up at the taper end, leaving the butt spreading and at Grass filters. liberty; in fact, they tie it on an exactly opposite principle to that on which a broom or birch rod is made. They dip the large end into the muddy pool, and then allow the water to drip from the taper end into their mouths if they have no other vessel at hand to receive it. Often, when the mud is composed mainly of vegetable matter, and is too light to separate and fall to the bottom of a pannikin as sediment, this is about the best way of clearing it.

Many plants, like the aloe in South Africa, or others whose leaves point upward, and have a cup-shaped cavity at their junction with the stalk, retain a considerable quantity of water after rains; and some seem to have the power of imbibing moisture from the air, even though no rain falls.

Rain-water is collected at sea by spreading the ship's awnings, and hanging buckets under them by means of sail hooks; these, of course, depress that part of the canvas to which they are hooked on; the water flows towards it, and runs down the lanyard into the bucket.

In situations where a good supply of reeds is to be obtained a tolerably effective contrivance for water clearing may be made as follows: Cut enough reeds to form a bundle as large as a six-gallon barrel; lay them evenly, with their heads one way and their cut ends the other. Now cut three long slender poles or rods; form them into hoops by lashing their ends with cord, raw hide, or a few creepers, and then secure them round the bundle of reeds, as shown in the following illustration. The reed cylinder, if properly made, should be firm, compact, and capable of standing alone like a cask. It should now have a bowl-shaped depression cut in its centre, and be placed in the foul water, and secured there by driving a stout rough pole down through the centre of the depression. The bottom of the reed cylinder may or may not touch the bottom. In deep water it remains hung, or, rather, impaled on the pole in such a way that about 6in. of the cut ends of the reeds are above the surface. The water will quickly fill the depression, out of which it may be dipped with a cup or other vessel.

The Indian water-carriers spread a piece of thick native cloth over the mouth of an earthen chatty pot, and then pour the tank water on

it until the vessel is full, when the contents are transferred to the leather "mussac," or water-bag. We have often had recourse to this expedient on a small scale, and made use of our brass lota pot, with a double silk handkerchief spread over its mouth, to strain off impurities.

Turbid water is cleared to some extent by placing a piece of common alum in it. A lump the size of a common nutmeg will be found sufficient to throw down a heavy sediment from a pailful of foul water. In India a species of nut or seed is made use of in the same way, and appears to act much in the same manner, although from different chemical affinities. In speaking of this water-clearing nut, the late Sir Emerson Tennent, in

Clearing nut.

his admirable work on Ceylon, says: "To correct the impurity of the tank water when intended for their own use, the natives employ a horny seed (the production of a species of 'strychnos') about the size of a coffee bean, called by the Tamils 'tettan kotta,' and by the Singhalese 'ingini' (*Strychnos potatorum*). This they rub round the inside of the unglazed earthen chatty in which the muddy water is held till about one-half the seed is ground off, which, mingling with the water, forms with it a delicate mucilage. In the course of a few minutes the impure particles, being seized by this, descend, and, on their subsidence, form an apparently viscid sediment at the bottom, whilst the clear fluid remains at the top ; and, although not altogether bright, is sufficiently pure for ordinary purposes. The curious and valuable plant *S. potatorum*, or the 'clearing nut bush,' is abundant in the woods and mountains of the East Indies. It bears a shining fruit, which becomes black as it ripens. The trivial name is derived from the use which is made of the seeds, which, when dried, are sold by the native dealers in the bazaars expressly for the purpose of purifying turbid water." This plant (*Strychnos St. Ignatii*, or St. Ignatius's bean) is a climbing shrub without tendrils, bearing long drooping white flowers, which have the perfume of jasmine. The species is identical with the *Ignatia amara* of Linnæus. It is a native of Cochin-China and the Philippines, as well as of India proper.

We, a short time since, invented and patented a small portable filter, which can be carried either in the breast pocket or holster. Its mode of use will be understood on reference to the illustration. Place the end of the tube (A) firmly in the pipe (B) ; fix the cover securely on the cup, and then thrust it with the

Patent filter.

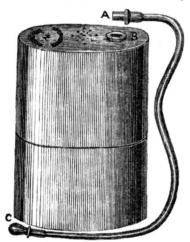

hand beneath the surface of the foul water. Hold the mouthpiece (C) between the lips, and draw the air by sucking from the interior of the flask until the water flows freely into the mouth. If a draught of water is required for immediate use, the cover may be now removed, when the cup will be found full. If a larger quantity of water is needed, one or more flasks may be placed in an erect position in a tub or pail of water, set in action as before directed, and allowed to run until the water in the tub has reached the level of the flasks, which will not require holding under water when once filled by exhausting the air contained in them. To renew or cleanse the packing, which may consist of sponge, woollen cloth, flannel, wild cotton, or fine moss, unscrew the cover of the packing box within the cover, when it can be easily withdrawn and replaced. The tube, when not

INDIAN WELL.

in use, is carried, coiled up, within the flask, which, on an emergency, may be made use of for boiling water, tea, soup, eggs, or meat.

We have now applied the same principle to stoppers for bottles, or any other vessels, so that a common beer or soda-water bottle can be instantly converted into a syphon filter, as shown in the annexed illustration.

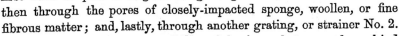

By the use of our invention we effectually get rid of the ova and larvæ of water insects, and the thousand and one living and dead impurities which are so abundant in the lakes, streams, and ponds of tropical countries. To get into the water contained in the flask or bottle, they would first have to pass through metal grating No. 1; then through the pores of closely-impacted sponge, woollen, or fine fibrous matter; and, lastly, through another grating, or strainer No. 2.

There is scarcely any possibility of foreign substances of any kind passing through the stuffing box, so that water, unless chemically tainted or poisoned by mineral solutions, can be rendered fit for use in two or three minutes by the use of either the metal flask or stopper.

We extemporised a camp filter in the Crimea by knocking out the bottom of a common claret bottle, turning it large end upwards, fastening a piece of doubled rag over the orifice intended for the cork, stuffing the neck tightly with sponge and sand in alternate layers, hanging it up with twine over another bottle, and then filling it with the by-no-means clear fluid brought to the tents by the water carriers.

Ice, even when taken from a very dirty puddle, is comparatively pure, as in freezing most of the impurities are set free.

Very impure water from stagnant pools should, before use, be boiled in the camp-kettle with a good netful of charcoal. This process not only tends much to purify it, but kills all water insects, their ova, and the legions of animalculæ which inhabit the pools of the tropics.

In some parts of the world, Central India for example, the water in certain wells, although perfectly bright and clear, is so highly charged with saline matter as to be perfectly undrinkable.

The accompanying full-page illustration represents one of the modes by which ox-power is, in the East, brought to bear on water raising. The greater number of the extensive tracts Water raising. of irrigated land devoted to the growth of the opium poppy, the cotton plant, and the various native grains are watered by its aid. The form of the water-bag, or bucket, differs somewhat in

G G 2

particular localities. By some makers it is formed from tanned hides fastened to an iron frame ; by others, the hides are merely tanned (according to directions given further on), spread open at the top, and tapered off to a long narrow open bag at the end. To explain the use of this contrivance, we will suppose that the bag is at the bottom of the well, at the end of the well rope and point guard, which latter cord is fastened to the taper end or delivery mouth of the bag. Now this guide being shorter than the main well rope, on which all the strain falls, draws up the tapered point like a doubled coat-sleeve above the level of the bag's mouth. At a signal (usually a shrill yell) from the well boy, the well-trained ox walks away down an inclined plane, hauling on the main well rope, which works over a smooth round stick fitted above the well, whilst the point guide rope works over another fitted at the side. Now it will be seen that as the great leather sack, with its doubled-up sleeve bottom, reaches the mouth of the well, the point guide will draw the cuff of the sleeve out over the round stick, which will then be considerably lower than the mouth of the bag, or bucket; all the water will then gush out through the sleeve, which will be as the small end of an enormous funnel. The water thus poured out is usually received in a sort of pond made from pieces of matting filled with earth. A large hollow tree trunk is then fitted to one side, or the end, for the water to flow through into the main canal of the system of irrigation.

In Tartary, water is raised in much the same manner ; but a man on horseback makes the line fast to his girth or saddle, and gallops from the well up to a mark previously made at a proper distance from the well, and which should be a trifle more than the actual depth from which the water is to be raised.

In almost all countries, from the earliest times to the present, levers, heavily weighted on the shorter arm, and with a bucket attached to the longer, have been used for raising water from deep wells. The pictorial records of Ancient Egypt attest the antiquity of this method. The shadoof of modern Egypt is the same, and we have seen it used both in that country and on the remotest mission stations in Southern Africa. The mode of applying it will be seen by a glance at our full-page engraving. The water raised by the shadoof is commonly used for irrigation. We, however, found it very valuable during the Crimean war for raising water for both men and horses. When used among the crops, the water is received sometimes in a reservoir with embankments, guarded by matting, and at others, into troughs which lead direct to the main irrigating channel, from which smaller furrows lead off to every part of the field. These are stopped with lumps of clay or earth, and when the water is required in any direction, the irrigator removes the obstruction by thrusting his toes beneath and lifting it out of the way.

In Egypt, India, and other countries, wheels and machines, more or less elaborate, are used for lifting water. There must be, for this purpose, at least one vertical wheel of sufficient diameter to carry an endless band, on which are fastened a series of buckets, in such a manner that they will retain very nearly their perpendicular position, until they surmount the highest portion of the circumference of the wheel, and will then "tip" and discharge the water into a trough or reservoir. These buckets may be wooden bowls, earthen chatty pots,

bags of leather or canvas, joints of bamboo, or anything that is moderately water-tight; but, of course, the less leakage there is the better. The band should run round a similar wheel the axle of which is nearly level with the water, so that the band is kept tight and the buckets forced beneath the surface; but this may be dispensed with if the band and upper wheel are sufficiently rough, or if there be studs or points to catch the full buckets and prevent their slipping. The wheel may be turned either by a crank, by manual labour, or oxen or other animals may be employed. In this latter case there may be another larger wheel or drum upon the same axle, and several turns of rope being taken over it, the ox may be driven away, unwinding it as he goes; or an endless screw, sloping at an angle of 45°, may be cut upon the axle, while a similar one working in it is cut upon a vertical shaft. Or cogged wheels of the same angle (as shown in our figure) may be used; the vertical pillar will then be turned by an ox yoked to a cross-bar and walking round it in a circular path; but it will be necessary that the discharging trough should pass beneath a little bridge in this path, and that the communication with the water to be drawn up should either be by a well within the circle, or by a channel to the river passing under a similar bridge. The stancheons of the frame which supports the vertical bar must stand outside and well clear of the path.

We give, also, an example of a box pump. Four deals or boards, of any length or breadth, are nailed together, but their lower ends for about a foot or more should be left a little wider than the rest of the length; two wheels of nearly equal diameter should be fixed, one with part of its circumference below the water, and the other somewhat higher than it is requisite to raise it; an endless band of canvas or other material must pass round both wheels, and one side of it through the trough. On this band must be fastened by one edge a number of boards or floats of such size as nearly to fill the inner diameter of the trough, without being so tight as to stick in any part of it; a hole should be bored in the centre of each, and a small line run through and knotted, so as to keep the floats always at right angles to the band. There should

be a spout near the top of the trough, to lead the water off in any required direction. Fig. 2 on the same illustration shows part of an endless band, with pockets or bags stitched on it; these may be of almost any stout material of tolerably close fibre—No. 1 canvas would answer very well. They would discharge the water over the wheel into a reservoir, and no tube, as in Fig. 1, would be needed.

We give, also, an example of wheels driven by water power over and undershot. In the first the water is conveyed by a pipe or trough, and allowed to fall upon the wheel into buckets or receptacles formed in its periphery by fixing boards across between the two rims, at such angles as are indi-cated by the dotted lines, which may be taken to represent the heads of the nails driven into their edges; and thus they will retain water until, by the revolu-tion of the wheel, they have sunk so far as to be below the level of the axle, when they allow the water to escape, and come up light and empty on the other side.

Some of these wheels are as much as 30ft. or more in diameter; indeed, the larger they are, the greater is the leverage obtained from a given amount of water; and, the wheel once set in motion, the power thus gained may be applied by connecting gear to any mechanical purpose.

The "undershot" simply has boards or floats fixed across it with their edges coinciding with the lines of the spokes. Indeed, if a paddle steamer were anchored in a tideway, and her wheels disconnected and allowed to revolve with the force of the tide, they would furnish a good example of the undershot wheel; and the paddle of a wrecked steamer would be better than anything a colonist with scant appliances could make for the purpose.

Still, with a few tools and a moderate share of ingenuity very fair makeshift water-wheels may be constructed in situations where they may be found most valuable. We have, when among the Tartars, seen them erect a small wooden hut over a narrow rapid mountain stream, leave a sort of trap in the floor, fix in some rough forked tree trunks and beams, and on them mount a little water-wheel made of hewn planks and bars treenailed together on the double-cross system, like that adopted in building up the wheel A in the illustration on p. 454, which is supposed to be erected for mining pumps, and is fed by a two-plank shoot. The Tartar wheels were invariably undershot, like that at B, and were used for setting in motion the trip hammers used in fulling their coarse native woollen.

In the beautiful valley of the Kowie River, a few miles below Grahamstown, we saw a rather ingenious application of wind power to a horizontal wheel. The principle will be best shown by calling to the reader's memory the well known nautical toy which consists of four or more cutters, or fore and aft rigged vessels, sailing in a circle on a mast-head or flag-staff. In the fore and aft sails the foremost leach, or edge, is attached by rings, or otherwise, to the mast or stay of the respective sail, and is stretched tight, while the after leach is left more or less free, according as the sheet is hauled in or eased off. In consequence of this, when the vessel is before the wind the sails fill, but as their surface catches it obliquely they do not exert their full force till the vessel receives the wind upon her quarter. When the wind is " a-beam," or blowing across her at right angles, the sails are still helping her forward, and continue to do so, even when her head comes up so near as just not to shake the wind out of them. When this happens, the sails lose their power, as they present only their foremost edge to the wind, and not a broad surface like those of a square-rigged ship when she is taken aback. (We will therefore suppose four cutters, *a, b, c, d.*) The cutter *a* is before the wind, *b* has the wind somewhat on the quarter, while *c*, having " come up " several points, is now nearly head to wind with her sails shaking, and *d* has taken the wind on the other tack. Thus, there are always three vessels whose sails are helping them round in one direction, while the fourth, for the moment that she is in the "wind's eye," is powerless to resist them.

This power can be applied to a large horizontal wheel. There should be two wheels, one 18in. or 2ft. above the other; they are made as light as possible, and each has a smaller rim or felloe, say 18in., within the other. The sails are in this instance flat boards, with a dowel left on each end for a hinge. These dowels work in holes in the upper and lower spokes, midway between the inner and outer felloes. It will be seen that the sails marked will receive the wind on one side until, coming so far before it that they "jibe," they assume the position of those which receive it on the other. When they come up to the wind on the other side the wheel they present their hinged edge to the wind, and shift like the sails of cutter *c*, but without shaking. The best angle for them to make is $22\frac{1}{2}°$ on either side the central line, and this is also the angle at which the sails of a windmill should present their surfaces.

The explorer, or settler, will not unfrequently have to sink wells for the obtainment of water for himself and his animals. It will often

Well sinking.   happen that Nature has commenced the formation of a well, which merely requires the labours of man to complete. The crowbar and pick will, in such cases very quickly enable the traveller to deepen it sufficiently to meet his temporary needs. Where a long-continued residence is intended, and a regular and continuous supply of water is required, apart from that obtained from rivers or lakes, wells of greater or less depth, according to the nature of the ground and water supply, must be undertaken.

The Indians manage to construct walled wells of great depth in loose sandy soil in the following ingenious manner: They first mark a circle, the size of the intended well, on the earth. They then dig a groove, or trench, of the width of the intended thickness of the lining wall of the well, much as our masons sink a foundation for a house. They now proceed to build a circle of masonry in the groove, and carry it up to a few feet in height above the surface. Other men now get inside the wall, and with short-handled hoes and fire-hardened sticks, dig away the sand from beneath the foundation of the wall round the entire circle. As the sand is loosened and dug out, it is taken up in cane baskets and thrown outside. As the wall sinks into the earth by being undermined, it is constantly added to by building above until the required depth is reached.

The Chinese sink very narrow and deep wells by the use of a kind of jumper, or boring bit. This is hung suspended from the end of a long bamboo spring beam, which is constantly worked up and down, thus causing the bit to constantly drop and pick, so to speak, on one spot. The bit is hollow, and when it becomes full of sludge produced by its incessant tapping, it is withdrawn from the hole, cleared out, and entered again. A little water added from time to time much assists the operation, and tends to keep the bit from becoming heated. As it will be seen this method, although very useful as a makeshift, is tedious to a degree.

Much fear was entertained at the commencement of the Abyssinian war that there would be a great scarcity of water in consequence of the comparatively limited number of wells and indifferent quality of the water to be found in that portion of the country over which our troops had to march shortly after their arrival; and there is little doubt but that serious inconvenience, if no worse, would have been experienced, had not a contrivance, known as the "American tube well-borer," the invention of Mr. Norton, been brought to the notice of the Government authorities. The wells formed by these deeply-penetrating sets of tubes were found to supply |water freely and expeditiously in that country. How far the perforated end of the tube would be effective, if driven through clay, we have had no means of ascertaining ; but we are of opinion that for reaching deeply-buried water-yielding deposits of ordinary character the tube-borer will be found most valuable. Its action is simplicity itself.

The foregoing illustration represents the contrivance fixed on the ground and ready for use. B, B, B are the legs of a triangle. C is the striking point for the monkey (D), which is raised by the pulley ropes (E, E) until it reaches the head of the triangle when it is allowed to fall on C, which is secured to the joint of tube F, which, having a sharp arrow headlike point, readily enters the earth. Joint after joint are added, like those of a fishing rod, until the required depth has been reached, when a small pump is attached, as in the annexed cut, which shows the position of the set of tubes in the earth after the water-yielding bed, or deposit, has been penetrated. When very large quantities of water are needed, as for the use of troops, troop horses, and baggage animals, several tubes can be driven in at one spot and coupled together at the top, when one pump can be made to draw from all.

The weight of such an arrangement as that represented would be by no means great, and the cost a mere trifle when compared with the costly process of Artesian well boring as usually carried out. Should it be decided on to abandon a well, the tubes can be drawn up and driven elsewhere.

With regard to the quantity of water which tube wells of a certain diameter of bore are capable of bringing to the surface, Mr Norton informs us that some of his $1\frac{1}{4}$in. wells yield as much as 900 gallons of water per hour, whilst some of the large bores have poured forth as much as 10,000 gallons per hour. It is, however, necessary that there should be a spring in the place where the well is driven.

The modes by which water can be raised from common pit or shaft wells are numerous. Some of them we have described ; others, such as the old-fashioned bucket and rope, are too well known to need description.

The miner's pump will be found described at p. 233. A very useful and effective pump may be readily made by boring an auger hole through a tree-trunk, mounting it with a brake-piece and handle as at A in the annexed illustration; fixing on a valved sucker and plunger, as represented at B. c represents a barrel pump. This is made by fixing a short square wooden box in the bottom of a large strong cask in such a manner that a large bung-hole may be bored where the centre of the box comes. (The accompanying engraving will serve to show the nature of the arrangement.) Then outside the hole attach a long tube made of stout sail canvas. Wind a stiff rope into a spiral, round a spar or pole, which can be withdrawn when the coil is complete, and attach it here and there with stitches of twine. This spiral coil will keep the tube from collapsing when in use. Then in your square upright box fix a valved sucker, made as shown at D, and another valve in the bottom of the box, as at E. A brake and handle may be fitted to the side of the barrel,

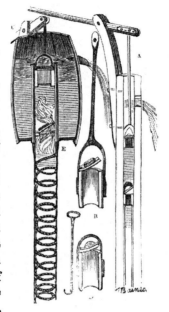

and a hard wood or iron plunger attached, when the pump will be ready for use. As the water flows out over the rim of the box it is caught in the barrel, to which a spout of leather, tin, or bark may be attached.

There are numerous trees and plants to be found in various parts of the world which yield, in addition to their fruits, large quantities of sap and other products, which often prove of inestimable value to the traveller. It would be next to impossible to separate arbitrarily the fruit-yielding members of the vegetable world from those which furnish juice or sap only. We shall therefore in this work treat of the most valuable and noteworthy, dealing with them as they happen to come under notice. Even in the most desert parts of South Africa the traveller ought not to despair of finding means to quench his thirst, even though water may not be obtainable. In some parts he may, perhaps, catch sight of small antelopes pawing the hard red soil, or may at least come on places that have been so scratched; and though in many instances this may have been done only to clean the hoofs, he will find that in others holes of several inches in depth have been made for the purpose of obtaining succulent roots looking very like small turnips. Sometimes these may be found partially eaten, or left behind entire, when the timid animal has been startled from his repast. The form of these roots should be carefully noted, together with that of their leaves, as the traveller can only discover the whereabouts of other roots by external indications, and cannot be guided—as the antelope probably is—by the scent of moisture beneath the ground.

The natives of nearly every separate district know of some peculiar root that is, perhaps, confined to their own locality; and it is always well to encourage them to bring a supply, not only of the root, but of its leaves, and to ask them to point out the plant, so that its appearance may be observed before it is disturbed. Some of these are small tubers, about the size of a pigeon's egg, on a long underground stem; others are much larger; and we have seen one of the kind called " marquæ," which measured in its longest circumference 3½ft., and 2½ft. in its shortest. The " marquæ," or " markhwæ," is properly of a flattened spherical figure, with an indication of tap-root below and a small conical protuberance above, from which the slender stem springs up. Its seeds are strung upon a skein of fibres in long round tapering pods, 4in. to 6in. long, and thicker than a goose-quill. The taste and appearance, when cut, would be something like that of a very fibrous watery turnip; but when thirst-quenching plants are sought for, we believe that the more tasteless they are the better. The smaller roots are more agreeable than those of larger size; and we have frequently found that the mastication of even a small portion of such a root affords more relief than the drinking of any quantity of water.

In certain countries, where rain seldom falls and the night dews are heavy, a very considerable quantity of water may be obtained from the grass and low bushes before sunrise, by shaking them over some wide shallow vessel; or a piece of waterproof cloth stretched across the prong end of a wide-forked stick. When properly put together an implement of this kind is not unlike a large dustpan. Sponges, or soft porous cloths, absorb a large quantity of water when brought in contact with wet plants or moist surfaces of any kind. They can be squeezed out as fast as they become charged with water.

After a long journey, when the throat is parched, the skin of the lips dried and cracking for want of moisture, the teeth fouled, and the tongue, with all its papillæ, dry and hard as the teeth of a rasp, rattling against them, there is no immediate relief in drinking water.

We have at times halted in a melon patch, and have selected and cut into slices the tasteless melons for our horses. The Hottentots and Bushmen collect these in quantities, and with a stick mash up the inside until it becomes a pulp; and, as the water exudes from the broken cells, they obtain perhaps a mouthful from each melon.

In some parts of the Kalahari Desert it is noticed that there are individual elephants, rhinoceroses, or other animals, that never drink water, having attached themselves to a locality in which they find melons and succulent roots as substitutes. Indeed, we believe that at least one tribe of Namaqua Hottentots live very comfortably in an absolutely waterless country, subsisting chiefly on the milk of their cattle, which in turn quench their thirst solely by eating water melons.

The beautiful "traveller's tree" of Madagascar collects and retains through almost the driest seasons a welcome store of water. Its ample leaves point upwards to the heavens; and all the rain, dew, or atmospheric moisture from their broad surfaces, is conducted down until it lodges in the hollow formed just above the junction of the midrib with the stem. The natives pierce the leaf-stalk with a spear; the water gushes out, and is caught in a vessel held under to receive it. So unfailing is the supply from these trees, that where one of them is seen no native will trouble himself to walk even a short distance to a river. The most valuable property, however, of this tree is that it may be tapped again and again without vital injury. It is most likely that the orifice will close, and the wounded leaf will again collect water; or, at most, the injured leaf will die off, leaving the others in full vitality. It is different with the collection of palm juice, in which the tree itself is materially injured and often completely destroyed.

On the low lands at the Delta of the Zambesi, where the various species of mangroves have fulfilled their office in winning from the dominion of the ocean the broad sand-banks annually deposited by the river, an abundant growth of the Doum palm and wild date begins to occupy the new formed land. The natives seek those that have grown to not more than a man's height, and, cutting off all the leaf-stalks with the exception of the merest sprout in the centre to continue the vitality, make a deep incision where the leaves should be, stick in a bit of folded leaf as a spout, and hang an earthen pot under it by a strip of leaf, sheltered in from the sun by a kind of basket, loosely but ingeniously woven from another leaf in the manner shown in our sketch on p. 461.

In connection with the subject of water we may here appropriately notice the expedients used by many nations for the separation of juices from the fruit containing them, or for expressing from grain or fibrous substances the water in which they have been washed or steeped, and which may either be collected as holding in solution some nutritious matter, or thrown away as carrying off something distasteful or even poisonous.

In Kafirland the stem of a species of Zamia is laid for several days in a running stream, and we have generally seen it pointed in the direction of the current so that the moisture with which it is surcharged might drain gradually from the lower end, carrying with it the acrid or unpleasant juices, while the impact of the stream from above would force more water into its pores and continue to dislodge all that it was desirable to remove, leaving the farinaceous matter between the fibres.

Another plant, commonly known by the appropriately descriptive name of elephant's foot (*Testudinaria* of Burchell, or *Tamus elephantopus*), is used as an article of food by the Hottentots, and on this account is often called Hottentot's bread. We have not actually seen the preparation of it, but believe that very little is required beyond cutting out the internal pith, which resembles the inside of a turnip, and baking it on the embers. The remarkable lump which rests upon the surface of the ground bears in general shape and colour, some resemblance to the foot of an elephant, and averages nearly the same size; but we have seen some nearly 3ft. in diameter. It is covered with rough angular projections, reminding one of the scales on the shell of a tortoise.

On the Zambesi, near Logier Hill, we have seen the native women frequently washing a kind of cassava, cut into discs across the grain so thin as to leave the fibre as short as possible. These were put into the closely-woven baskets of the country, which, being about half immersed, were worked with a rotatory motion similar to that of gold washing— removing some acrid juice, and leaving what little nutriment might be contained in the fibre.

In many countries great and long-continued pressure is employed.

Some vegetable substances contain, in addition to their nutritious properties, juices so acrid as to destroy almost every other fibre that might be used to contain them; and therefore, as in South America, particular kinds of palms or other trees are valued because pressure bags can be woven of them that will resist this action. These bags are of various shapes; but a very favourite one is that of a long double cone, loosely woven with the slips, which represent the threads, crossing each other in a long lozenge-like form, so that when the bag is filled it shortens up and greatly enlarges its central diameter; but when it is hung by one end to a tree, and a considerable weight is attached to the other, its elongation contracts its diameter and squeezes out the juices of whatever is placed inside it.

We have seen various forms of these bags, which were in use amongst the ancient Egyptians for expressing the remainder of the juice after the grapes had already been trodden in the wine-press. Both the ancient and modern contrivances appear to have been matted bags of elongated form, and with a very stout eye or loop at either end; and the chief difference is in their size. The upper one is worked by two men, who, inserting staves into the loops at the ends, twist them opposite ways; while the lower is worked by five—four of whom having twisted it as tightly as they can, haul the staves apart, while the fifth, throwing himself between the upper ends, forces them apart still farther. The effect in each case is the flow of a copious stream of second quality wine, which pours from the twisted bag into the receptacle placed for it.

There is a plant, which much resembles the " bachelor's pillow " of our hothouses, found growing in Mexico and some other countries. When it is rooted in the earth it is more like a vegetable hedgehog than aught else, being covered with long pointed thorns, like those of the cactus. Hunters and travellers often collect these unpromising-looking productions for the sake of the water they contain. When freed from their attachment to the ground, they are taken on a forked stick, which is held in the left hand, whilst the thorn-covered rind is sliced off with a hunting knife held in the right. The pulp, thus laid bare, affords enough moisture to quench the thirst of either man or horse.

The agave (*Agave Americana*) yields a very large quantity of sap. To obtain this, the crown is cut off, and a deep hole scooped out in the substance of the plant. This, in a short time, fills with fluid, which, when collected, fermented, and properly prepared, is the celebrated " pulque " of the Mexicans.

Large-sized bamboo canes not unfrequently hold bottled-up between their internodes a considerable quantity of water, the presence of which can be detected by giving the canes, one after another, a sharp sudden shake, when the imprisoned fluid gives out a hollow, gurgling sound easily recognised, to obtain the cane water, it is only necessary to tap the joint or cut down the cane. This juice is not only an agreeable and refreshing drink, but is by the natives believed to be particularly wholesome and sanitary in its effects on the constitution.

It is somewhat curious that the silicious element found covering the outside of the cane like a hard varnish should be held in solution by this fluid; but that it is so there can be no doubt, as, when the liquid or sap, is allowed to remain for any length of time in the tubular cavity of the cane, it either becomes absorbed altogether, or leaves a hard concrete substance far more like a mineral than a vegetable substance; possessing, in fact, all the attributes of an earth product. It is not acted on by any of the ordinary acids; it remains unaltered by fire; and forms, with the alkalies, a clear glass, just as flint would. This curious substance is the celebrated "tabascheer," which is renowned throughout the East for its marvellously curative qualities; and it is not improbable that this, like many other Oriental productions, may contain virtues little dreamed of by the medical practitioner at home.

In some of the forests of the tropics a large description of pitcher plant is found. The natural cups found on it not only contain a considerable quantity of water, but have the disadvantage of being natural traps for insects and all sorts of small creeping things, which, attracted by the moisture, fall in, and are drowned. Sometimes, however, a pitcher is found with perfectly clear and deliciously cool water in it, which well repays the thirsty searcher.

In many nations, the palm trees peculiar to them supply an almost inexhaustible variety of the necessaries or the conveniences and luxuries of life, from timber for house or ship building to fine cloth for wearing apparel, as well as many articles of food and refreshing, or often intoxicating, drinks.

Nearly all the palms contain what is called a cabbage, or in other words a mass of young vegetable matter, in taste nearly resembling the heart of a cabbage stalk, and both in Australia and Africa we have occasionally availed ourselves of this. We do not advise it, except in cases of necessity, because the cutting of it out even from a young tree involves considerable labour, and it is always with some regret that a man feels himself obliged to destroy a noble tree, perhaps 40ft. or 50ft. in height to obtain hardly vegetable matter enough to serve him for a single meal.

At Coepang, in Timor, we have seen the leaves of the fan palm converted into buckets or pails by simply drawing the points or leaflets together and securing them; while the lesser leaves or fronds were in the same manner made into exquisite little drinking cups, capable of containing one " doit's " worth of palm juice, which, when perfectly fresh, is most delicious and refreshing.

The large leaves of the palm may be used for the collection of dew or occasional showers. The water casks of one of the Dutch gunboats were set out upon the beach near her anchorage, and the stems of three or four palm leaves inserted in each bung-hole to conduct thither all the moisture that might fall upon their broad surface.

The tall palm tree is usually climbed by the aid of a loop of loosely-twisted rope, or a hoop of any sufficiently strong and flexible material large enough to encircle the tree and the body of the climber, allowing him to lean back in it at such an   *Palms, to climb.* angle that the pressure of his feet against the trunk is sufficient to support him. Short steps are taken upward, and the rope is jerked up skilfully a little at a time; but great care must be taken duly to proportion these motions, for if the feet be too high, the head and shoulders will project so far that the power of the arms will not suffice to bear the strain, while if they are too low they will not be pressed with sufficient force against the tree, and will slip downward.

The northern limits of the palms are—in Europe 43°, in Asia 34°, and in America 34° of latitude; the southern are—in Africa 34°, in New Zealand 38°, and in America 36°. The known species amount at present nearly to 600, but it is supposed that at least from 1000 to 1200 will be found. The stems of some do not rise above the ground, while others are 200ft. high; some are no thicker than a goose-quill, while others are as large as a hogshead; some are climbing plants, with long flexible stems; some are covered with fibrous network, and some have spines or thorns 8in. or 10in. long, that may be used for needles or arrows. Some of the leaves are 50ft. long and 8ft. wide— these are composed of numerous leaflets on a strong midrib; some are undivided, and yet are 30ft. long and 5ft. wide; and others again are fan-shaped. The fruits are generally small, the cocoa-nut being the largest of the family; the kernel is often too hard to be eaten, and the covering fibrous or woody; but in some the seeds are covered with a pulpy or farinaceous mass that offers sweet and nutritious food; one species on the Zambesi reminded us of gingerbread.

The cocoa-nut, especially in its green and immature state, is a most agreeable fruit, and the water, or milk as we call it, is then most cooling and refreshing; when it more nearly approaches to ripeness

H H

the kernel may be scraped or pounded up in its own liquor, and it then forms a very efficient substitute for milk in a cup of tea. A large amount of oil and other valuable products may be obtained from the tree and its fruit.

Each young nut, when in the true milk stage of its growth, will yield about a pint of fluid, cool, and of slightly acid taste. The younger nuts contain a soft, rich substance, not unlike blanc-mange, which can be easily scooped out. From the juices of these immature nuts the natives manufacture an indelible black dye. Toddy, cocoa-nut wine, arrack, or rack as it is sometimes called, is made from the sap of the cocoa palm. In favourable seasons the plumes of cocoa-nut blossom are shot out from amidst the fronds of the tree crown about every six weeks. Immediately on the appearance of the new flower spathe the toddy maker ascends the tree after the manner before described, or, as on the Malabar coast, by cutting a train of notches in the tree trunk. On arriving at the cluster of young fronds and the sheath containing the blossom, he binds the whole together with twine. He then makes a puncture in the stalk of the spathe with his toddy knife, raps the part well with the handle, and then hangs a chatty pot to receive the juice as it drains out during the night. Before sunrise he reascends the tree, lowers the full pot, which may contain from two to six pints, and replaces it with an empty one. Immediately on obtainment this juice is extremely cool and sweet to the taste. In the course of a very few hours fermentation sets in, and it becomes slighty acid. In twenty-four hours it becomes quite sour. Before too great a change takes place, however, the toddy man properly treats his brew by the aid of the true vinous fermentation, and then distils it in a rough, makeshift still, which among some of the Easterns is extemporised from a hollow stone, rock, or piece of hollow tree trunk, which forms the head of the still, with a long hollow cane for a tube, and piece of bark, and some coir saturated with cold water for a condenser, almost any pot or jar will, with a little ingenuity, form a tolerably efficient still.

Excellent vinegar is made as follows from the palm juice: After collection, the toddy or sap is placed in earthen pots and covered down for about four weeks. At the end of that time the fluid is strained and returned to the pots, with a few pods of capsicum, a piece of the fruit of the gamboge tree, and a pod from the Indian horseradish (*Hypertanthera moringa*) are thrown into each pot of fluid, which is then allowed to remain at rest for five weeks, when excellent vinegar, well adapted for the use of the settler, is the result.

If, instead of toddy or vinegar, sugar is required, it can be readily made from the palm sap, which, for this purpose, is treated before fermentation. It is, on being drawn from the tree, boiled in a suitable pot or other vessel until it becomes thick and stringy; a little lime is added; rough crystallisation takes place, and "jaggery," or palm sugar, is the result. Cocoa-nut oil is valuable for a great number of purposes. It is obtained from the ripe or mature nut in a variety of ways. The natives of many of the islands of the Eastern seas cut the kernels of the nuts in pieces, boil them with water in a large kettle; collect such oil as rises to the top with a sea-shell mounted on the end of a stick; then pound the boiled nut in a mortar made from a piece of hollow log, with a wooden pestle; reboil the paste thus formed; skim again, and so on. The mills used for the expression of this and other oils, and the crushing of sugar-canes, we shall describe as our work proceeds. The shell of the cocoa-nut makes excellent cups and bottles. To extract the kernel to form the latter, the natives bore out one of the eyes, pour out the milk, fill the nut with sea-water, and bury it in the sand exposed to the sun's rays. In a short time decomposition is set up, and all the contents of the shell can be easily shaken out at the eyehole.

The fibrous husk from time immemorial has supplied the native craft of India, as well as our vessels trading there, with a cheap and generally useful kind of rope, called coir, which possesses the valuable property of being so light as to be of much less specific gravity than water, and which is, therefore, much used for buoy ropes, life lines, warps, and cables, and the ropes for the upper edges of fishing nets. Hats, bags, baskets, sandals, and many other things, are made from it; its leaves form the covering of huts, and its leaf-stalk forms their framework, and serve any purpose for which light elastic wands are required.

The date palm, both wild and cultivated, furnishes fruit more or less delicious according to the species from which it is taken. The Arab and his horse, and camel too, upon emergency, will live upon it; and without it the deserts, to which it is indigenous, would be uninhabitable.

Sago is the produce of a palm, which in the East yields the food of thousands; it is the pithy centre of the stem, requiring scarcely any preparation to fit it for food, and a single tree sometimes yields 600lb. weight. Those which furnish the so-called cane for chair bottoms are a species of calamus; they hang on trees by long hooked spines, and are sometimes 600ft. or 1000ft. long. These are often used as stays or standing rigging among native vessels, and sometimes we believe as cables. When split into smaller sections and twisted they form tolerable, but not perfectly flexible, ropes; and

H H 2

slips of them, as is well known, are commonly used by the Chinese for tying up various packages. The helmet which we wore through the Indian campaign was composed of this material closely woven.

Many varieties of palms all over the world yield a sugary sap from their yet unopened spathes or from their stems, and this, when partly fermented, is the palm wine of Africa, and, as we have shown, the toddy of the East Indies; while similar beverages are obtained by the South Americans from the *Mauritia oinifera* and others.

A nation at the mouth of the Orinoco River live almost entirely on a palm (probably *Mauritia flexuosa*) ; they build their houses elevated on the trunks, and live upon the fruit, sap, and such fish as the waters around them may afford.

Resins and wax are produced by some species. The fruits of a calamus, in the Eastern Archipelago, are covered with a red resinous substance, which, in common with the produce of other trees, is the dragon's blood of commerce, and is used as a colour, a varnish, and in tooth powder.

The *Ceroxylon andicola*, a lofty palm growing in the Andes of Bogota, secretes in its stem a resinous wax, used for making candles. In the north of Brazil, the Carnauba (*Copernicia cerifer*) has the underside of its leaves covered with pure white wax, with no admixture of resin.

Thatch for houses, awnings for boats, and even the upper streaks of large canoes, umbrellas, hats, baskets, water buckets, cordage, and numberless other things, are made of palm leaves. In Cuba the *Chamærops argentica*, and in Sicily the *Chamærops humilis*, is used for making hats and other fine work. In India the place of the papyrus was supplied by palm leaves, on whose hard and glossy surfaces Pali and Sanscrit characters were inscribed with a metal point; the leaves of *Corypha talieri*, strung together, form the Hindoo volume. The fruit of *Areca catechu* is the betel nut, the favourite stimulant of the Eastern people, which they chew with lime. The fibre of the Piassaba palm is made into cheap and durable cables on the Amazon, and is introduced into England in the form of brooms, &c.

Although the settler or explorer who directs his steps to North America has no palms to supply him with food, drink, and clothing, he will find other members of the vegetable kingdom ready to his hand.

Maple sugar is of vast importance to the settler in the backwoods, as it serves not only as a substitute for cane sugar, but is not unfrequently used instead of salt. It is obtained by treating the sap of the *Acer saccharinum*, or sugar maple. The range of this valuable tree is very extensive. It is met with, in greater or less abundance, from the neighbourhood of St. Jean in Upper Canada to Virginia. It abounds in Nova Scotia, New Brunswick, Vermont, and New Hampshire, some of the trees being found to reach 80ft. in height. Sugar-making may begin early in the month of April, or, in fact, directly the sap begins to rise. Frosty nights, followed by warm, genial days, are the most favourable for the process of sap drawing, which is proceeded with as follows: One or more auger holes, up to four, are made, at a convenient distance from the ground, in the trunk of each tree to be treated. Into each of these holes a little hollow shoot or tube of bark is thrust, which conveys the sap as it flows into vessels placed for its reception. Each tree will produce from 15gals. to 20gals. of sap, and 5gals. of sap will yield about 1lb. of sugar. When the vessels under the spouts are nearly full the sap should be ladled from them into pails and carried to a shed, in which a large barrel, with the upper head removed, has been set up as a reservoir. In this it is allowed to remain at rest until all foreign substances have settled to the bottom. It is now quickly drawn off and conveyed to the boiler, which, in the absence of a proper arrangement, may be a large camp kettle, in which it is heated steadily until evaporated down to the consistence of treacle, when it is again removed and placed in an open vessel to cool. When cold, it is strained through a flannel bag into a second boiler, where it is again heated, clarified with eggs, a little bullock's blood, or new milk. The boiling is now continued until a little of the syrup, taken on the point of a clean chip and held in the air, shows a disposition to assume a crystalline appearance, when the heating process is stopped and the charge withdrawn from the pot.

It is now in the candy state, and is cast into a variety of quaint forms by the use of small moulds prepared for the purpose. If granulated sugar is required, a small barrel is set up at a moderate distance from the ground; the upper head is removed, and the lower one bored full of gimlet holes. On the charge of candy being thrown into this, all the fluid portions drain away in a state of thin molasses through the holes into a tub or box placed below the barrel, in which the sugar is soon found fit for use.

Gum sugar is made by throwing the candy when hot from the pot out on the snow. This treatment has the property of checking crystallisation and converting the sugar into a tough material much used for chewing.

A settler's family in a good maple district can, by the use of proper sized boilers, &c., make upwards of 700lb. of good serviceable sugar in one favourable season.

Manna is a substance well worth the attention of the explorer, as it is, curiously enough, produced by trees and shrubs of totally different orders in different geographical ranges.

Manna, to prepare.

The Arabs and Persians obtain a kind, known as " Guzunjbeen," from a species of tamarisk called the " Guz bush." The description known on the Arabian coast, and in the district surrounding Mount Sinai, by the name of " Toofra," is also procured from the tamarisk thickets, where it drains from the ends of the thorns, and falls on the dry leaves, small twigs, and sticks which have fallen to the ground; it there congeals into hard masses, and is in that condition gathered for use. It is by the Arabs consumed as a substitute for honey, and is eaten on bread or other food. The " camel thorn " of India and Syria is manna yielding, producing the description known in the East as " Al haj." The so-called Beiruk honey is in reality a kind of manna which is yielded by a low stunted tree, not unlike a dwarf aspen, which is known as the " Ghrab bush." In the Uzbec country manna is obtained from a small tree whose trunk is divided into knots by a series of annular rings. In Arabia, the " Ashur" is the manna-bearing plant. In Mesopotamia, it flows from a species of oak, and is most abundant on such trees as have the largest share of gall nuts. A medicinal and highly valued manna is obtained in some districts in Persia from a peculiar willow, which grows in moist ground. A kind of larch furnishes the *Manna Brigantica*, and in the Lebanon district it flows from the cedars. In Europe, the ash is the manna bearer, and three kinds are found to produce it more or less abundantly. The two most commonly treated for its obtainment are *Fraxinus rotundifolia* and *Ornus Europœa*. To obtain the manna from these trees incisions are made in the bark with a knife; the first cut is made near the ground, and the others at 2in. or 3in. apart, the cuts being 1in. long and ½in. deep. These cuts are made at the rate of one per day, mounting upward, cut by cut, in each row. Immediately below these perpendicular cuts ⊥-shaped incisions are made in such a way that each cross cut may receive and hold fast the end of a leaf gathered from the tree, which serves to conduct the sap away from the trunk and allow of its dropping into Indian fig leaves placed on the ground for its reception. The Indian fig leaf, cultivated for the purpose, has the peculiar property of drying with its edges curled up, rendering it extremely useful as a sap receiver. August is the month usually selected for tapping the manna trees, and dry warm weather is most favourable for the operation, as rain dissolves and destroys the congealing mass of produce. The manna collected from the bark by scraping, after having run in long tears down the trunk, is considered very inferior to that caught in the fig leaves, and is, consequently, sold at a much lower price.

A great number of fruit, berry, and nut bearing trees and bushes are be found on various portions of the North-American territories. Further south, the productions assume a more tropical character. Here we are merely dealing with some of the forest stores of the north and north-west. The following is but a brief list, as our space is limited:

The "pagessaveg" of the Indians, *Prunes sauvages* of the French-Canadians, or "wild plum" of the trappers, is usually collected American late in the month of October. It grows abundantly on wild fruits. the river sides and lake shores. The Indians either dry or boil it with maple sugar, when it is converted into a sort of cake by boiling and stirring the fruit about in the kettle until the mass is thick enough for treatment, when it is thrown from the pot and spread out to about an inch deep in a flat layer on a piece of birch bark, when it is exposed to the sun until it becomes quite tough and tenacious. It is then rolled up like soft leather, placed in a birch bark box, and buried in the earth until wanted. During the winter season, when dried meat is in use, large pieces of this preparation are cut off with a knife and boiled with it.

The "sand cherry" of the trappers, or "la cerise à grappe" of the Canadians, grows abundantly about the borders of sugar-maple groves, on the edges of old clearings, and about the borders of the prairies. It is fit to gather in the month of August. The Indians gather large quantities, crush them between flat heavy stones, stir the mass well together with deer fat, and then boil it in a kettle until it becomes a thick tenacious cake or paste, when it is, like the wild plum cake, buried until required.

The small red forest crab apples can be thoroughly prepared by drying, when they are both wholesome and nutritious.

The "wortleberry" of the trappers, or "bellois" of the Canadians, is extremely abundant in a great number of localities. To prepare the fruit a thick close basket-work tray, or hurdle of white cedar, is used. This, when covered with a layer of ripe berries, is suspended over a slow steady wood fire until dry, when they are packed away in bark boxes. They are either mixed with dough to form cake, or boiled with meat or fish.

The "mashkigimin" of the Indians, "les ottakas" of the Canadians, the "cranberry" of the trappers: this fruit, although commonly known among trappers and English settlers as the cranberry, is much larger than the European variety. Swampy ground is most congenial to its growth. It is fit to gather as early as the month of October, but remains on the bushes even after being thickly buried by snow in the winter season. Immense quantities of these berries are annually gathered by the Indians, not only for their own use, but as a branch of trade with the United States traders, who readily purchase them for preserving. For Indian use, they require no treatment, as they do not readily decay; but by settlers they are usually boiled in syrup, or preserved in maple sugar.

Wild hazel nuts are found in great abundance. These are best kept by first packing, and then burying them in an earthen jar or bark box.

"Swan potatoes" are found growing on the shallow margins of rivers, lakes, and streams. These, when dug from the soft ooze and washed clean, are strung on a long thin strip of white cedar wood, and hung up over the fire to dry. They are boiled for use, when they become plump and palatable.

Wild raspberries, strawberries, &c., are to be met with in many parts of America.

Butter nuts, hickory nuts, and pinons, or cone nuts, are all, more or less, deserving of the attention of the hunter or explorer.

In some islands of the Indian Archipelago nature has so bountifully provided for the wants of the human race that it seems as if a remnant
Sago-making. of Paradise yet lingered upon earth, and man had never been sentenced to eat his bread in the sweat of his brow. At all events, the inhabitants of these islands are relieved from that necessity, and to all appearance they are little better for it. The

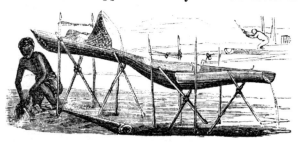

man who, by chopping down a tree and washing its pith for a week or two, can provide himself with a substitute for bread for a whole year is not likely to be, nor is he really equal either in physical strength, activity, or intelligence, to him who must earn his food by cultivation of the soil, by chasing wild animals in their forest haunts, or by launching his little craft upon the waters, and ensnaring or doing battle with the denizens of the ocean.

Our sketch represents the principal processes of sago-making. The palm which yields the sago is cut down; a slab is chopped off from the upper side of the trunk, leaving the pith which occupied the large internal hollow exposed; this is beaten out in fragments, rather than chopped, by a club of heavy wood, in the end of which a sharp angular fragment of quartz or other stone is set. The pith is then washed in a trough composed of the swelling portions of the leaf stems, where they embrace the trunk on which they grow, just as the jaws of a cutter's gaff go round the mast. Two of these are placed with their broad ends together, supported by stakes and cross-bars, so as to form a long trough widest in the middle, and out of level. A third is set with its narrow end meeting that of the next piece, whilst the wide end rises at a slight elevation. Across this is placed a screen of fibrous cloth, supported by another stick, elastic enough to keep it always tolerably tight without undue strain, and a mass of the pith being placed behind this is washed by water poured repeatedly upon it and allowed to percolate through and run off till all the superfluous matter is washed away, and the sago alone is left.

The different members of the banana and plantain family, too, lend their aid in furnishing a larger quantity by far of life-supporting elements than the finest description of wheat grown on the same area of ground. Whether eaten in a ripe state as a fruit, or boiled green as a vegetable (when it is not a bad substitute for the potato), this production is both palatable and wholesome. A good store food is made by cutting the fruit into slices, hanging it up to dry, and, when required for use, boiling it into a pulp.

Plantain flour is made by thoroughly drying the fruit, and then grinding it in one of the native mills hereafter described. Then the root of the Taro (*Calandium esculentum*), that of the sweet potato (*Battata convolvulans*), and the roots of certain edible ferns (*Pteris esculenta* amongst the number), are valuable as yielding food. Many of these productions furnish drink as well. The plantains before referred to yield a very palatable cider, which is made as follows: A deep hole is dug in the earth, and a number of plantains stripped from the main stem are thrown in; straw and earth are cast on, and the plantains are allowed to remain at rest for eight days. The peel is then stripped off, and the pulp is placed in a large open trough with water, where it is thoroughly washed and mixed with it. At the end of two days the cider may be strained off for use.

Whisky may be made from sweet potatoes in the following manner: Dig up as many of the tubers as you may find it convenient to treat; boil them until quite soft; place them in large jars, or other vessels, with about their own bulk of water; stir this mixture well about, and then to each jar add a little "merissa" barm (obtained from native beer-brewing), which may be placed on a small bundle of cocoa-fibre or cotton. When fermentation has taken place, erect your still, which may be of the kind described and figured at page 410; or a large native pot may be mounted on a hollowed-out ant-hill to serve as the still boiler; a smaller pot inverted and placed on the open mouth of this forms the still head or dome. When the lower pot is charged with the fermented "wash," the upper pot is luted fast with clay. A small hole is bored near its top for the reception of the end of any hollow tube you can get; this is also secured with clay. The condensing process is carried out by keeping the tube cold with cloths or mats and cold water. The depending end of the tube should discharge itself into any convenient vessel partly sunk beneath the surface of cold water. A native pot, or a common tea-kettle, will make a good receiver; and an ordinary pail, or tub, a convenient water tank in which to place it. By the use of such a contrivance as this, half-a-dozen bottles of very good spirits may be made in one day's distilling.

The Mongols make their milk-spirit—known as "kumis"—in the following manner: A large quantity of milk of any kind (mare's milk

Milk-spirit.   is considered best) is first turned sour, and then allowed to ferment. It is then poured into a large iron camp-kettle or pot; one of the wooden bowls or dishes in use among the Tartars is now fitted closely into the mouth of the kettle or boiler, and luted fast round the edges with wet cow-dung or clay; an elbow-shaped, hollow branch of a tree, or a curved tube, is now fitted into a hole in the convex surface of the bowl, and more cow-dung or clay is applied. Into the mouth of this bent pipe a wooden tube is fixed, which is kept cold by the constant contact of a wet sheepskin. As the pot boils the spirit passes over, and is collected for use in some suitable vessel placed as a receiver. This is also kept cold by the aid of sheep-skins and water.

CHAPTER XIV.

CAMP COOKERY.

AFTER the obtainment of food, the art of preparing it in its most nutritious, wholesome, and palatable form ranks next in importance. It is well, when travelling with a large party, to ascertain the qualifications of a couple of steady men, and regularly appoint them to the cooking department, taking care that exemption from guards, with a few other privileges, may make the office of cook one to be rather envied ; and, in order that his operations may be successfully conducted, he should fully understand the art of fire-making.

The natives of Australia, the Bushmen of South Africa, and the tribes along the whole course of the Zambesi, as well as many other wild nations, kindle fire by the friction of two pieces of wood against each other; there are of course varieties Fire, to make. of method, but the principal, that of whirling the point of a moderately hard stick in a hollow, cut in one of a somewhat softer character, is very generally the same. The Bushmen carry these fire-sticks in the quiver with their arrows ; and when they need fire, two men sit opposite each other, and one, laying his sandal on the ground, places on it the fire-stick, perhaps as thick as the little finger, and holds it between the soles of his feet, or between his toes, which for many purposes can be used by the natives with little less effect than the fingers. In the end of this stick a small notch is cut, and in this is placed the pointed end of another stick, about the thickness and nearly the length of a common ramrod. One man, taking this between the palms of his hands, rubs them so as to communicate to it a rapid whirling motion, keeping at the same time a gentle, steady, downward pressure. In a few seconds, this causes his hands to reach the bottom, and his companion therefore sits ready to clap his hands to the top and continue the motion till they also come down, and he in turn is relieved by the first. Very shortly fine wood dust is produced, and soon after the end of the whirling stick and the hollow in which it turns become charred, and smoke rises from the little heap of dust.

A small nest of very carefully prepared dry grass or fibrous bark, rubbed very fine, has already been provided, and in our illustration a third man is applying this to the smouldering wood-dust, some ignited particles of which he will try to catch on the nest of fibre, the whole will then be enveloped in coarser material, and whirled rapidly round, at arm's length, until it bursts into a blaze.

Where two or three men assist each other in this manner, a couple of minutes suffices to obtain fire ; but if one man attempts it alone, he cannot keep up a continuous friction, for he loses speed and heat every time he has to shift his hand from the bottom to the top of the whirling rod, and, even when he has produced the first ignition, he is more liable to lose the spark than a third man who would watch his oppor-

OBTAINING FIRE BY THE AID OF THE WHIRLING ROD.

tunity for catching it while the other two were keeping up the heat by the vigorous motion of the whirling rod. Among many tribes the producing of fire in this manner is a thing of daily occurrence.

The inhabitants of some of the Pacific Islands obtain fire by placing a piece of bamboo, which has been previously split in half, convex side upwards, on the ground ; a small cut is then made in it as a sort of holding point for the end of a flat piece of bamboo, held somewhat after the manner of a chisel, to work on. The flat piece, on being driven by the hands rapidly forward and back on the surface, or back of the long hollow piece of cane joint, rapidly works a hole through it ; the wood dust, formed by the friction, falling through the orifice soon begins to smoke, smoulder, and burn, when it is placed in a tuft of dry fibre, like an egg in a nest. A small creeper or vine is now fastened to the nest, which is then rapidly whirled round the head until it flames.

There is a very convenient and portable means of carrying fire, sold under the name of a " strike-a-light," or " chucknuck;" it is formed from a brass tube of 1in. calibre and 3in. in length, which has a cap and a sliding bottom to it; it is filled with tinder, made as usual by setting fire to a piece of rag and extinguishing it as soon as it has ceased to blaze; it contains also a gun flint or bit of agate, and its chain passes through an oval of steel or case-hardened iron. When fire is required, the cap is taken off, and the box held in the left hand, with the flint so held against its edge that any sparks struck from it by the steel, which is taken in the right, must fall upon the tinder. When it is done with, the flint is put in again, the cap put on, and the movable bottom is pushed up so as to leave no vacant space, but to exclude all the air, and to extinguish the burning tinder. These tinder-boxes are highly prized; and one of them, value one shilling or so, is by no means a despicable present to a native in the remote interior. The shank bone of any small animal is easily converted into a chucknuck tube.

Slow match and tinder are important matters to the explorer. Loose cotton, or almost any other vegetable fibre twisted into a cord, and then soaked in water in which a little saltpetre or gunpowder has been dissolved, will serve for a slow match. The large puff-balls, or devil's snuff-boxes as they are called by hunters, found growing about the borders of the forest, form excellent punk or tinder. After being gathered they should be hung on a string to dry, then cut into thin slices, and beaten on a board with a stick until all the powder or snuff is driven off, when it will be fit for use, either as tinder or to smoke wild bees from their holes. The soft, partially-decayed wood found in dry dead logs or hollow trees makes a very good description of tinder.

In default of a tinder-box, most persons carry a pocket-knife, and a gun flint. If a bit of rag, with a little dry gunpowder bruised into it, is rolled up tightly, and held with the flint in the left hand so that the sparks may fall on the end of the roll, it is very likely to take fire.

Many stones, as quartz, agate, jasper, iron pyrites, &c., will give forth a spark, so that if the traveller has a knife, a bit of steel, or case-hardened iron about him, he need not despair if he can only find a stone.

The Malays not unfrequently obtain a spark by striking a piece of broken china ware sharply against the hard flinty surface of a well developed bamboo joint.

Lucifer, congreve, or vesta matches are now so common, that few travellers think of carrying anything else ; yet it is not safe to trust to them alone, as a little accidental damp may spoil the whole stock. If they ignite by simple friction there is danger of accident; if they "ignite only on the box," a supply of friction tablets should be carried, for the box will soon go to pieces with rough usage.

The trappers of North-West America make use of the German matches, such as are packed in round wooden boxes being preferred. The composition ends of these are dipped in a varnish composed of shellac and a little methylated spirit, which, when dry, as it will be in about half-an-hour, renders them perfectly damp-proof.

In countries where the sun shines continuously, a burning glass, such as the lens of a telescope or a Stanhope microscope, will obtain fire at any time during the day.

A man armed with a gun or pistol has always the means of obtaining fire. If it be a flint lock, he need not even draw the charge, but, throwing out the priming on some dry surface, he may plug up the touch-hole with a bit of wet clay, wet or greasy rag, string, or wood ; in fact any of these materials, even though dry, if rammed in tightly, become incombustible. The end of a bit of packthread wetted, or of raw hide reimpjie, is better than any, because the remainder can be used to pull it out with. The priming can then be rubbed on a bit of rag—dry or slightly moistened—a corner of it stuck into the pan, the gun full cocked and the trigger pulled, when most likely the sparks will be found to have ignited the tinder. With a percussion gun the charge, if it be loaded, must be drawn or fired away so as to leave the barrel empty, then a little powder must be put in, and a bit of dry rag, with powder rubbed upon it, rammed loosely into the barrel; the gun should be fired with its muzzle downwards or towards a rock or stump, that the rag may not be blown too far away.

The fire being obtained by any of these means, and secured by being communicated to a small collection of inflammable material, the next process is to build up and ignite the fuel that is to serve the traveller for warmth or culinary purposes. This will, of course, have been already collected. Prudent cooks generally tie a dry thorn branch behind their waggon on leaving their outspan, so as to have it ready as soon as they again halt ; or, if fuel be scarce, they keep a bright look-out upon the way for dry sticks or the dung of tame or wild animals. Such fuel should be broken up, and the sticks roughly assorted into sizes. A small elevation will be chosen or made on a dry patch of ground, and the fire being laid on a little faggot of small sticks, others are carefully piled round it, pointing upwards, at an angle of

45° or more towards the centre—just as if a conical roof or a church steeple were to be built—and round these the larger ones are arranged in the same manner, and in successive sizes. (See Fig. 2, p. 489.) Thus, the property of heated air being to ascend, the flame is led naturally up along the twigs, and through the interstices, and when sticks as thick as the thumb are well kindled, others may be piled on with less attention to regularity. If the intention is to make a transient blaze as large as possible, perhaps for a night signal, dry thorn branches of the mimosa, with their large thorns and loose twigs, thrown on as lightly as possible, will answer excellently. We have seen in the Karroo veldt of South Africa a bush or shrub of which the leaves blaze up with almost a resinous flash, but of which the stem is almost incombustible. This would serve well for such a signal; but when wanted for the purposes of cooking, the fire requires constant replenishing, and from the repeated calls for fresh supplies, the shrub has acquired the expressive name of the " Bring on bush."

A species of " prolea," locally called " Waggon bush," is also highly in request, as its resinous blossoms maintain a more steady heat.

If the fire is required as a day signal, large quantities of green wood, leaves, &c., should be heaped on to make as much smoke as possible; and *vice versâ*, if concealment is desired—green wood should be avoided, and only small quantities of dry wood used.

We have often, during a night halt among the date-palm jungles, selected a tree at a convenient distance from its fellows, to form a sort of gigantic torch. The dry fronds give off in burning sufficient heat to make the whole crown of the tree inflammable; this, in turn, ignites the trunk, which burns for some time, and gives a most brilliant light.

The lighting of a fire in a hot dry climate is a matter of comparative ease when compared with the obtainment of one in the damp woods of a cold inclement region. An experienced campaigner will generally contrive to carry with him a few pieces of dry resinous wood, known as " kindling chips," with which to start his fire. In the absence of these, look out sharply for a dead tree or hollow log, and from the lee side of it, if rain is falling, chop out a good supply of wood as a foundation for your fire. If you cannot find a dead tree or log, select the dry side of a living one; chop off the bark with your axe, and then from the exposed timber remove some long thin chips. Now, under the shelter formed by spreading your blanket or coat, proceed with your hunting knife to cut these chips into long, thin, narrow shavings, much like those used in making Bavarian toy brooms. When a good quantity of these has been prepared, gather a bundle of the very finest and most slender brushwood you can find. The largest stick should not be stouter than wheat straws; cut these up into foot lengths; place your bunch of shavings on as dry a spot as you can find. If there are stones to be obtained, place one on each side of it. Now, with your small sticks, build a sort of cone loosely over the shavings, each stick being arranged end upwards, just as hop poles are stored for the winter; lay over and outside these a few stouter sticks and bits of bark. When your cone is complete introduce your fire to the centre of the cone's base. A tube of bark or hollow reed, a piece of curled up dry hide, or a gun-barrel with the nipple taken out, serves for a blowpipe to gently urge on the fire with. We—as stated in the early portion of this work—endeavour, if possible, to have a small pair of bellows as part of our travelling kit. It is well, however, to know how to manage without them. Small quantities of gunpowder cautiously sprinkled in will aid considerably in setting up the first flame of a sluggish fire. The greatest care must, however, be exercised in order to guard against accidents from explosion.

We in our early days narrowly escaped the loss of a hand by strewing a little powder from the flask on some damp moss, which we were endeavouring to coax into a fire. The instant the grains of powder reached the fire they ignited, communicated with the contents of the flask, and, fortunately, blew the brass top from the copper body, without bursting the metal. On another occasion, nearly a half-charge of powder exploded in the left hand, whilst we were strewing in the powder with the right finger and thumb in a manner which we are to this day utterly at a loss to account for. When making use of gunpowder as a fire stimulant, we now invariably pour the quantity about to be used on a leaf or a piece of bark, and place the flask in a place of perfect safety, some distance from the fire, which, when once fairly established, may be treated with more boldness, and supplied with sticks of larger size. If you intend camping down for the night with your party, the first thing to do, after seeing that your fire is burning strongly, is to collect a good and sufficient store of fuel to last through the night and well up into the morning. One of the elements of fitness in the locality for camping purposes will be the close vicinity of proper firewood; and here we must caution the inexperienced against the choice of soft wood trees for a true camp fire. Pines, and other members of the coniferæ, are very ill adapted to the purpose. Ash, maple, beech, birch, and other hard woods are the sorts to be sought for. Trees of about 1ft. to 14in. in diameter are the best for the purpose. When felled with the axe, they should be cut into logs of about 12ft. in length, and all the branches chopped up short to feed the fire with. Prepare two strong heavy stakes of about 5ft. in length, sharpen the points and drive them into the earth just behind your fire, in such a way that they may stand at about 6ft. apart. Cut a notch in the rear of each near the top for the support or back stake to key into. Now place three of your fire logs one on the other, as if you were building a log wall. This forms your fire-back; now take two shorter logs and fix them at the ends as log rests, and on these lay another long fire log, when the arrangement will be complete. A fire of this kind, when once thoroughly established, will burn during the longest night, form a perfect wall of fire, and cause little trouble, as all the feeding fuel is cast in between the front log on the log rests and the fire-back. A pot, to be boiled on a fire of this kind, is conveniently suspended from a stout green pole, so placed as to rest above the fire-back, whilst its point is forced into the ground behind.

To keep a small fire steadily burning, let three logs as large as possible be laid end to end, diverging at an angle of 60° from each other (as in Fig. 1, p. 489), push their burning ends occasionally together, and they will last many hours, with but little attention. The natives of Australia take dry logs, 6ft. or more in length, and laying them down 3ft. or 4ft. apart, set them on fire in several places. Letting shorter logs meet them from the outside, and laying good-sized pebbles around them, they then stretch themselves on the ground and sleep between the two lines of fire, and when the wood is consumed the stones continue for some time to radiate the heat they have previously absorbed. Many tribes of American Indians have their own especial fashion of fire-building, so that a deserted camp fire will not unfrequently reveal the identity of the tribe by whom it was made.

However tempting a smooth peat rock may look as a convenient spot for a fire to be established on, first take the precaution to spread a tolerably thick layer of sand, earth, or clay as a fire Caution as to bed, or in all probability the rock on becoming heated camp fire. will expand with some violence, and scatter far and wide the embers and such food, &c., as may be in the course of cooking, besides endangering the lives of those who may be in the neighbourhood of the blow up.

In South Africa, when the flats are swamped with heavy showers, and it would seem almost impossible to kindle the scanty fuel that can be obtained, the ant-hills with which the plain is covered prove the greatest imaginable boon to the traveller. One of these hills, 3ft. or 4ft. high, is selected, its top cut flat off, and a hole dug like an oven in its side. In this the fire is kindled, the flame rushes up through

I I

the galleries, the clay becomes red hot, and the kettle or frying-pan soon begins to feel its influence. But this is not all, for the galleries are most likely full of vegetable matter as well as of ants' eggs and larvæ, and these help to increase the flame. Of course it is cruel, but the traveller and his followers must have food. By the exercise of a little ingenuity, hollows can be cut in it for convenience of baking bread, &c. Most farmers build a clay oven at some little distance from their houses to avoid the necessity of having a fire actually under their roof. In the Zuur veldt, in Tartary and Central India, where fuel is scarce, we have seen the cattle-dung collected and piled along the tops of all the walls and other inclosures to dry.

When camping down for any length of time a stack of logs and split hard wood should be formed. Straight logs are easily split by wedges, but stump ends, which form excellent fuel, are so tough that they require blowing open with gunpowder. To do this, we bore an auger hole into the substance of the stump, pour in our charge of powder, and then screw into the hole a tapered iron plug, on which a very deep

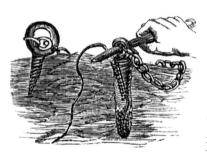

rough screw thread has been cut. This plug has a ring made in its upper end to admit of the passage of an iron pin used in screwing it in, and the ring to a bit of old ox chain, the other end of which is secured to the log under treatment by a large staple, or a screw bolt, in order to prevent the plug from being blown away and lost. The annexed illustration represents a section of the stump; and it will be seen, on examination, that the plug has a hole running longitudinally through it for a slow-match to go through. The inside end of this match is allowed to remain long enough to reach the powder in the bottom of the hole, and that at the outside of sufficient length to enable you, after lighting it, to get behind a tree, or in some other safe place, until the explosion takes place, and the flying splinters and fragments settle. In the absence of one of these iron blasting plugs, a hard wood treenail may be used to stop the auger hole, and the vent may be bored with a gimlet.

In dealing with many of the food, drink, and oil yielding products with which we shall have to deal, mills or crushing contrivances, more or less complicated, will be required. The most simple and primitive of these is formed by placing the substance to be treated between two stones, and grinding it by working them forward and back with the hands. The tortillas or thin pancakes of Spanish America are made from flour prepared by the aid of a contrivance of this kind. The maize or Indian corn used in their manufacture is first steeped in water to soften it. Handfuls of the prepared grain are then thinly scattered over the surface of the lower or bed stone. The top stone is then brought into play until the whole is reduced to a species of paste. This, when flattened out between the palms of the hands, and rapidly baked over the fire, forms a description of bread in general use throughout Mexico and other countries where the Spanish races have formed settlements. Most of the Eastern races and tribes make use of

Makeshift mills.

the ancient quern or hand-mill to crush their grain. This primitive mill, the subject of the annexed illustration, is, with trifling modifications of arrange-ment, almost world wide. A bed stone, slightly con-vex, is capped by a running stone somewhat concave. A hole in the centre admits of the grain being poured in with the left hand, whilst a second hole out of centre receives the end of the handle used in causing the upper stone to revolve on the lower. As the grain is re-duced to powder it falls out on a cloth placed to receive it, and by repeatedly passing between the stones a meal of sufficient fineness for practical purposes is formed. When two or more persons work at a mill of this description, supplementary handles are attached to the upright turning stick by strips of raw hide. The "chupatees" or "aps" of India are usually made from meal ground in mills of this description. Chupatees, like tortillas, are not unlike pancakes, and form a most important element of an Indian hunter's diet. Our native followers always contrived to bear with them in some way or another the pair of stones necessary to form a quern, and a piece of sheet iron to bake the aps on, so that, wherever grain of any kind was procurable, we were at least sure of bread. When a sufficient quantity of meal has been ground out, it is, by the aid of a little water and much manipulation, converted into dough or "attar." This is divided into balls, each ball being sufficient to form one chupatee. The balls are then one by one taken between the palms of the hands and dexterously slapped and patted until quite round and as thin as an ordinary pancake, and then adroitly transferred to the piece of sheet iron which rests on a small fire close at hand. A little ghee, or native butter is then added. The aps, when baked brown, are taken off the plate, and eaten hot or stored away for future use.

When attached to the expedition sent into the jungle for the capture of the Nahwab of Banda, we saw our native hunters and followers, when particularly short of grain, gather the seed of a thin wiry grass called "nardoo" for meal making purposes. This nardoo must not, however, be confounded with the Australian seed of the same name, as that grows on a plant not unlike our English wood sorrel, the "hare-bell," or a long-stemmed clover; whilst that of India is a true cereal, with a head furnished with many grains, like very diminutive barley.

In Africa and many other countries the pestle and mortar are extensively made use of for grain and seed crushing. A hard wood log is easily hollowed out by the aid of fire and cutting tools, and a pestle is extemporised from any suitable piece of heavy wood.

A powerful and simple description of mill is made by making a round and somewhat tapering hole in a large slab of sandstone or grit.

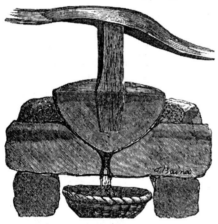

In this a conical block of stone is fitted in such a manner as to admit of its being turned round by a cross-handle, as shown in the annexed illustration. The corn or other grain to be crushed is thrown into a groove which surrounds the hole in the bed stone.

A generally useful oil or sugar-cane mill is in general use throughout India and Ceylon. Its main bed or cylinder is formed from a solid block of hard stone, which is hewn out until of the form of an upturned mortar; in the bore or barrel is fixed, at an angle, a piece of hard, heavy, and massive baubul thorn tree, which acts as a pestle or crusher; to this is attached, by lashings of raw hide, a head bar, which serves to guide its movements and direction. This head bar is in turn connected with the travelling bar, which runs round the cylinder much as the jaws of a boom might be made to run round a mast. The illustration on p. 485 will serve to show the manner in which the arrangements are made. One or more bullocks are made use of to turn the pestle of the mill; and such liquid as may be forced out of the substance under treatment runs through an orifice, like the vent of a cannon, into a cane tube, which conducts it into a pot sunk in the earth. The greater portion of the native cane sugar made in the East is manufactured by the aid of this description of mill.

Whilst at Tette, in Africa, we had an opportunity of seeing the process of cane sugar making carried out by the native cultivators, which is conducted as follows: Early in the morning a quantity of canes, minus their tops, were brought in, and a couple of men, armed with thin double-edged soft iron knives, 2ft. long and 3in. wide, caught up the canes in their left hands and chopped off pieces about 2ft. long, letting them fall in heaps, whence they were taken by others, who dressed off any knots or young shoots that might impede their progress through the mill. As soon as this was completed, the parts of the machine, which are always taken asunder and cleaned

after a day's work, were set up, the whole consisting of eight pieces of wood—first, the trough, or canoe as the natives call it (an oblong block 5ft. long, 2ft. 6in. wide, with a hollow 3in. deep to catch the juice, and three circular holes or sockets in the centre, cut not quite through, to receive the lower ends of the rollers); secondly, two posts, one at either end of the trough, with their upper ends tenoned to carry another log with corresponding sockets for the upper end of the rollers; thirdly, three vertical rollers, 4ft. long and 8in. diameter, their upper parts being cut into the form of a long screw, the worm of the centre one running in the usual direction, and those of the two others in the opposite. The head of the central roller projects above the framework, and is squared so as to fit into a mortice in the middle of a long beam, the two ends of which are used as levers, and, when turned, the deep-cut worm, acting on those of the other rollers, causes them to revolve in the opposite direction. A heap of cane was laid by the mill; and, while eight or ten men ran round with the lever bar, a native, squatting on the receiving side, fed the canes by handfuls between the centre and the right-hand roller; while another, catching them as they came out (as shown in the illustration below), sent them back again between the centre and the opposite roller on his own right. This was repeated till the canes were crushed dry and the trough filled.

The juice was baled out with a calabash; and when it became shallow was scooped up by the hand, strained through a basket into two large copper pans 30in. wide and 8in. deep, and boiled on open wood fires, a couple of women stirring it till sufficiently evaporated. The pans were then placed on small heaps of soft earth, and the stirring continued till the whole mass assumed the consistency

of dough or toffy, and eventually crystallised into a fine bright yellowish brown sugar, leaving no treacle, molasses, or refuse of any kind.

The green cane chewed to express the juice is pleasant and nutritious; the fresh sap is a most luxurious draught; the syrup, thickened by boiling, but not yet crystallised, is of a bright golden colour, and better in taste than what we call treacle; the pap or toffy is by no means bad.

Next morning, as the friction of the rollers had worn the outer side of the sockets, and thus increased the space between them, a native carpenter let in pieces of hard wood across the grain of the beam, and in them cut hollows to the proper outline of the sockets. This is frequently necessary; and, if it is too long delayed, the rollers separate so much that the thread of the centre screw catches the edge instead of the hollow of the others, and is liable to break both. A set of rollers will last from one to three seasons, according to the amount of work required. The penellas, or earthen sugar jars, are made by women.

A shallow wooden dish, of about 14in. internal diameter, is chosen, and in this the clay, previously kneaded into a long roll, is so coiled as to make a circular wall; this is next pressed and patted Sugar pots, into a compact mass, with a smooth surface; it is then to make. built upon, tapering into a kind of pear shape towards the top, which is 4in. in diameter, and is finished in a smooth edge (a woman will do this in about ten minutes); it is then gently lifted from the dish and set aside to dry. Next day it is turned up, and the wide part, which has previously been the base, is gradually built upon with fresh clay, till it arches over so as to leave a very small aperture; the fingers of the left hand are introduced to support the work, while the hole is being diminished by applications of fresh clay until it becomes so small that the last finger has to be withdrawn, and it is finally closed by the dexterous application of a small piece, quite moist, dabbed on with correct aim, and slightly smoothed off at the edges by gentle application of the fingers. A hemispherical cap is then made for the finished panella, which appears beside it. The jars are then baked to a dull red. From 15lb. to 20lb. of sugar is put in each, making the gross weight from 27lb. to 29lb., a pad of grass to give a flattened base is laced to each jar with strips of palm leaf, a couple of loops or beckets are left to lift it by, and each jar is sold for about three fathoms of calico.

In cooking an " as-koekie," or ash cake, a fire is made upon a smooth flat piece of ground, and when this is well heated, and there are plenty of glowing embers, the fire is swept away; the cake, Cakes, to bake. generally of meal or of seconds flour and water, with a pinch of salt in it, is laid upon it, the ashes are then strewed over the cake, and the embers raked over all, fresh wood being heaped over if necessary, and it is left for two or four hours, according to its size and the intensity of the fire. The Australian damper is made in the same manner, except that the finest flour is used and kneaded with as little water as possible; in fact the flour is merely damped sufficiently to make it adhere, and then by dint of hard kneading is converted into a solid mass, the object being to have no moisture in it that would cause it to become mouldy if kept or carried for several days upon a journey. As this article of breadstuff, is such a general favourite with old bushmen, it may not be amiss to give full directions for its preparation. The size of the damper of course depends on the numerical strength of the party for which it is about being prepared. The first thing to do is to obtain a flat, broad, dried sheepskin, or slab of bark, large enough to constitute a kneading-board; on this pour from your flour sack enough flour for use; sprinkle in some salt; work a wide basin-shaped hole in the middle of the flour, keeping the right hand moving round it whilst water is thrown in, a little at a time, from any convenient vessel held in the left. Continue to do this until a thick, strong, adhesive dough is formed; work this well about on the board with dry flour until a large pudding-shaped ball is formed; strew your board with fresh flour, dust over your ball with a little, and proceed to press and flatten it out until a round, even, pancake-shaped mass is formed—about 2½in. in thickness will be found a convenient substance. This may be ascertained by cutting a notch in a sharp stick at 2½in. from the joint, and thrusting it through here and there, working away in the meantime until the thickness is uniform. The red hot embers of your camp fire, which should be good, clear, and well-burned, must now be scooped aside with a shovel, flat-pointed stick, or a sheet of green bark, leaving a clear even surface of hearth. Now, deftly taking the damper in the palms and outspread fingers of your two hands, drop it evenly and lightly on the heated ground, making all flat and compact with your hands, and then with your shovel or makeshift spade rake back the heated embers over your damper until it is deeply buried in them, and in between one and two hours, depending on the weight of the batch, it will be cooked to a turn, be of a light rich brown, and a feast for a king. Hungry men not unfrequently satisfy their hunger by making dough nuts, or " beggars on the coals " as they are called, whilst the damper is cooking. These are merely small lumps of dough hastily twisted off and cast on the embers to grill. The dried yeast powders prepared by some good makers are well worth taking on an expedition, when very superior bread can be made by their aid. We have made good bread with and without them, by placing the loaf under an upturned copper or iron cooking pot, heaping on the ashes until the baking process was completed, and then dusting the loaf well with a bunch of fresh green twigs. We made an excellent oven in the Crimea from an old powder canister. This we buried in a horizontal direction in the bank at the back of the cook house. Clay was well rammed in round it, and after it had been sufficiently heated by a charge of vine roots and aught else we could obtain, it was swept out, the bread, pies, or tarts (for we even arrived at that stage of the baker's art at last) were put in, the copper cover of the canister was luted fast with wet clay, and the baking proved most satisfactory. A small iron-hooped barrel makes an excellent oven. Lay it on its bilge in a deep groove, scooped in a convenient bank, cover it with a complete and thick coating of strong clay, leaving one head, the outer one, open; then fill in the earth above the cask, and well stamp it down; now lay a few stones in the cask, and light a fire on them, letting it smoulder the whole of one day and a night, in order that the clay may dry. Now remove the stones, and light a strong fire of dry wood in it. This will burn out all the staves, and leave the clay oven fit for use. A large flat stone and some clay makes a good oven stopper.

If a light cake for present use is required, and the ashes adhering to the outer surface are thought objectionable, a frying-pan, of which the handle had been broken off, may be inverted over it, or a plate of iron may be supported upon four stones, and the fire piled over all as before. (See Fig. 3.) The three-legged iron pot, or Meg Merrilies (Fig. 4), forms an excellent oven ; light bread may be baked in it, or joints may be roasted, or pastry made to suit the most fastidious taste. A fire must be made underneath it, and a sufficient quantity of clear glowing embers raked out and piled upon the iron cover, which ought not to be lifted until the moment when the contents are judged to be properly cooked.

But it is when the larger animals of the wilderness fall before the hunter's rifle that the resources of the African *chef de cuisine* are really called into requisition. Suppose an elephant has been laid low, and, after an extemporised supper of steaks, or "car- Flesh meat. bonatjies," the party determine to have a foot for breakfast, the fire, which has already partially dried the ground, is swept away, or perhaps a new spot is chosen, and a hole 30in. in width and depth is made, a fire is lighted in this, and a quantity of dry wood thrown on and allowed to burn until the sides of the hole and the earth immediately surrounding it are thoroughly heated ; the fire is then raked out, the foot, generally a fore one, which has been amputated at what may be called the wrist-joint, and answering to the knee of the horse, is placed in its natural position in it (Fig. 5), the ashes are shovelled in, the hot embers above them, the hot earth over all, and a roaring fire is lighted on the top and left to burn all night. In the morning this is cleared off, the foot is dug out, the upper parts soiled by the contract of the ashes are cut away, and the rich gelatine and other morsels are left to be dug out by the stout keen pointed knives of the expectant hunters, the tough skin serving all the purposes of a dish. Very frequently a piece of the trunk is put in at the same time, and this is generally left as a stand-by, to be eaten cold, when it looks and tastes almost like coarse tongue; the foot, on the contrary, being best while still warm. The hump of the white rhinoceros, treated in nearly the same manner, is in reality a most delicious morsel, the rich juices accumulating in the dish formed by the thick skin, while the upper part and adhering ashes is cut off and thrown away; but, if proper care has been taken, another flap of skin slightly larger will have been cut out and skewered, as in Fig. 6, for a dish cover, and this will not only prevent the annoyance caused by dirt and ashes, but will prevent the absorption of the juices which would otherwise take place.

A mode of cooking a dish of hippopotamus, discovered by Sir Samuel Baker, is well worth bearing in mind. Speaking of it, he says: " I tried boiling the fat flesh and skin together, the result being that the skin assumed the appearance of the green fat of the turtle, but is far superior. A piece of the head thus boiled, and then soused in vinegar, with chopped onions and cayenne pepper and salt, throws brawn completely into the shade." The rump steak from an eland is also a delicacy hardly to be surpassed. The side of the rump, skin and all, with as much flesh as can be dug out with it, is cut off; the edges of the skin are then gathered together and skewered like a pudding bag (see Fig. 7), and it is then put into the heated hole, or a fire is built around and over it upon the surface, the advantage being that the juices have no chance of escape and the meat is most deliciously cooked; in fact, if the quantity be insufficient, all the inner portions of the skin may be pared away and eaten, leaving only the scorched cuticle. The gipsies' method of rolling up a fowl in a ball of clay, putting it into the fire till it becomes red hot, and then breaking it open, with all the feathers scorched, so as to be no longer recognisable, and the fowl itself deliciously cooked, is well known. Fish when dressed in this way are delicious.

In some countries the natives appear to have a taste for boiling and stewing their food, although at the same time they do not possess vessels of iron, or even of clay, that will bear the action of the fire; nevertheless, their case is not hopeless. We have frequently seen the cooking holes of the Australians—generally beside some rivulet, where fish and fresh water mussels were easily to be obtained, and even an alligator might occasionally be killed. A hole (see Fig. 8, p. 489), 2ft. in diameter and 1ft. in depth, is dug in the ground, and the inside nicely clayed; the fish or flesh, carefully wrapped in grass or in the leaves of the pandanus, is put in and the hole filled with water. In the meantime large stones have been heated at a fire not far off, and these are dropped one after another into the water, being removed by means of crooked sticks as they cool to make room for others more thoroughly hot; then, when the water boils, or is as nearly boiling as it is possible for hot stones to make it, the hole is covered with grass; earth is heaped on it, and the food is left to steam until it is considered sufficiently cooked. Should the mess be large, and require longer boiling, a fire may be lighted above the cooking hole, less for the purpose of imparting fresh heat than for that of preventing the loss of the heat already produced below it. The New Zealanders, Sandwich Islanders, and some of the Indian tribes of North-West America, cook most of their food in this

Makeshift furnace.

manner. In the Pacific Islands a pig, with the potatoes, yams, or other vegetables, is nicely wrapped in several folds of mat or native cloth and left to stew all night; and we have heard it said that flesh may be boiled by this process in a sufficiently water-tight basket. Salmon and other fish are commonly boiled by Indians in birch bark by the aid of hot stones.

While coasting along the shores of North Australia we were often at a loss for something like a warm meal; fortunately, we had as a compensation a case of gin with us, and, as long as it lasted, we thankfully availed ourselves of it as a means of restoring the animal heat after we had been chilled and wearied by a night of exposure and incessant labour. When the weather moderated a little, we took a 6lb. preserved beef tin (see the above engraving), cut out the top of it, and then, after making a number of triangular cuts in the sides about half-way down, we turned the tongues inwards so as to make at the same time supports for the piece of tin we had cut out from the top, and holes by which the air could enter freely ; the upper edge we cut into vandykes, turning alternately one point inward and one a little out, so as to make a firm rest and secure hold for another tin of the same size, which we used as a boiler. We set the whole on the bottom of our upturned baling tub, and lighted our fire upon the false bottom with coir, or fibre of cocoa-nut husk, steeped in cocoa-nut oil, and with chips of deal cut off the trail of our little carronade. In this manner we not only made tea and coffee, but warmed up our preserved meat, and fried our salt pork

During this voyage we fell in with one of the very few so-called "edible" things we have been unable to eat, and this was the "trepang" (*bêche de mer*, or sea-slug) ; this, with the scanty boiling or roasting we could afford it, was about as tender and well tasted as the sole of a shoe well saturated with sea-water; but after having been parboiled and dried by the Malay collectors, sold by them for 15*l.* per ton to the Chinese, and subjected to the elaborate culinary operations of that people, we have no doubt that, with sufficient condiment, it produces a soup quite worthy of the praises they bestow upon it.

When we were left with a couple of Krooboys in the pinnance of H.M.S. *Hermes,* on the Zambesi, we took an empty preserved potato

box, composed of sheet iron, between 16in. and 18in. square, and cutting out the top as in the case before described, we made half-way up the sides a series of triangular cuts, turned the points inward as supports, and let the top sheet previously punched full of holes down upon them; above this we cut a good-sized hole for the admission of fresh fuel, and another below for access to the ashes accumulating there. This proved a first-rate portable furnace ; it was large enough to accommodate the coffee kettle and a moderate-sized stew pot or frying-pan. The bottom being made with a flange riveted to the sides, as shown by the rivet heads in the sketch, was sunk nearly 1in. within the edges, and therefore left just that amount of vacant space between it and the boat's thwarts or other plank that it might be set upon, thus preventing any danger of burning the plank should even the falling embers heat the iron before they died out. For additional security, we put a couple of chocks under to raise it; but there was no necessity for securing it by cleats or lashings; still we have drawn them to show how they might be applied, if requisite. A piece of the iron wire netting, now commonly sold for fencing, if neatly turned up at the sides, would make a very efficient fire-basket; and, if the meshes prove too large, a couple of pieces so cut or folded that they cover each other unequally would reduce the size of the apertures to something less than half. This might be slung by wires (as in Fig. 1), set upon legs, or supported according to convenience. The form of the old cresset, which may be well enough imitated with a few bits of iron hoop (Fig. 2), with or without rivets, is worth bearing in mind. Light may be obtained by sticking a pole into the ground, splitting the top of it, and sticking in the cleft a slip of red pine or other resinous wood; the burning

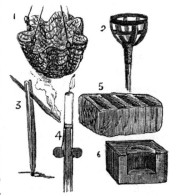

may be accelerated by depressing the lighted end (as in Fig. 3), or retarded by raising it.

When wood is scarce, almost any animal substance may be used as fuel; the dung of all graminivorous animals, the dried flesh, cartilage, fat and bones, will all burn. Dr. Livingstone once burnt the dried bones of an elephant in the furnace of the little steamer *Ma Robert;* and in trying down the blubber of a whale, the scraps from which no more oil can be extracted are used as fuel to melt the rest. Arctic explorers constantly burn bones to obtain heat. Parties away from a vessel on boat service frequently have blue lights or rockets with them. A blue light is usually provided with a percussion cap, so that it bears its own means of ignition; but, if there should be no need to burn it, the sulphur may be removed and used in small quantities to tip the ends of bits of paper, wood, or any light combustible matter to serve as matches.

Fuel.

A candle may be saved from guttering by being placed in a tube large enough to contain it with a small aperture to let the wick come through; if a spiral spring is at hand to force the candle gradually up, so much the better; if not, have the tube long enough to allow a stick of the same size to be inserted under the butt of the candle, then weight the tube heavily (see Fig. 4, p. 555), and it will of itself press downwards as the candle burns away.

Fig. 5 is a clay mould used by the natives of some of the islands of the Eastern Archipelago for cooking sago; it is heated nearly red hot, the sago paste is ladled into the hollows shown in it, and, when cooked, taken out in the form of very palatable biscuits. In South Africa we made very excellent fritters by mixing a stout batter of meal or flour with a little sugar; then setting a pot of sheep's-tail fat upon the fire, we kept it boiling, and taking up a spoonful of the batter dropped it into the boiling fat. When a South Sea whaler is trying out blubber, the men take biscuits, saturate them thoroughly with water, tie them in a cloth to which a line is made fast, and throw them into the boiling oil. They also tie up fish in a cloth and throw them into the pot, secured in the same manner.

Commander E. Belcher says that farmers throw a bag of flour into the

Hints on food. water to keep it cool; the outer layer only forms paste half an inch in thickness. The Americans whalers put their flour casks into salt water to prevent weevils getting in; the outer paste dries as hard as a flint, and resists their attacks. And lastly, speaking from his own experience, he says the flour balls washed ashore from a wreck, dirty-looking and studded with sand, gravel, and pebbles till they seem almost like plum puddings, were most carefully gathered up and preserved; they were broken when required, and the dry flour inside made into cakes; this, with a little rum from the wreck and a scanty supply of salmon purchased from the natives, supported him and his crew for ten days; even the flour which had been reached by salt water was not quite spoiled, if the gravel and sand could be extracted.

What we rather absurdly reject as the offal of the animal contains in reality some of its tenderest and best parts, and the natives who follow a white man for the game he kills are well aware of this; and they know that he has a prejudice in favour of cleanliness, which to them seems groundless. However, they do not fail to take advantage of it, and, in cutting up an animal, generally contrive to break up the interior in such a manner that, without actually spoiling the tit bits, they give them a very unsightly appearance. If the traveller is content with the solid flesh, of course he can let them do as they like; if not, he must look out in time. It is quite well to know that the marrow-bones slightly warmed afford most delicious food; the marrow of the ox is good, that of the buffalo is better, but that of the koodoo is the *ne plus ultra*. The bones of the quagga—at least, so far our experience goes—afford no marrow; indeed, there is no hollow for it, the inside being a cellular structure filled with oil. The flesh, also, being rather rank, persons of very delicate taste do not relish it. The wild Hottentots, however, not only eat it, but use the name "quagga" as the general term for food. We have frequently eaten it, and can safely say that it only requires a good appetite to make it palatable enough. The head of this or any other animal is best cooked in its skin—a good fire being made round it and earth heaped over the embers all night.

The skin of most animals will afford nutriment—of course, the thicker it is the better; that of the hippopotamus, which varies in different parts from half an inch to two inches, is very good. It may be roasted, or broiled, or boiled down to a soft jelly, or even to a soup or gelatine, and in all these various forms it is good. We have saved large slabs of the hide after killing a hippopotamus; and after the flesh was gone the skin served us well, the Damaras washing it and pounding it between a couple of stones till it was tender enough to eat. When that was done, however, and we had to come down upon the hides of buffaloes shot three months before, and at that time dried so hard in the sun that we had to cut them up with a hand-saw, we found that, even after a couple of days' soaking in the pool and two days more of boiling, nothing but the simple fact that we had nothing else would have induced us to eat them. The quagga skin is even harder; but our native followers cut it out piecemeal from under a Dutch lad who was using it as a bed till they barely left him enough to lie upon. We had used the hide of a black rhinoceros to make side chests for the waggon, and these, though much harder than the hardest wood we know, were taken off, roasted, pounded between stones, and eaten. Meat that had been cut into small pieces and exposed to the heat of the sun, so as partially to dry without allowing it to become tainted, may be eaten without further cooking.

In Tartary it is said to be common for a rider to cut a thin steak of beef and lay it under his saddle before he sets out on his journey, and after some hours he finds that the combined effects of constant pressure and warmth have, if not cooked it, at least rendered it palatable enough to be eaten.

In Norway, the stew-pot, after having stood for some time upon the fire, is taken off and wrapped in a thick covering of felt, which, being a bad conductor, prevents the escape of the heat, and forces it to expend itself on the continued cooking of the meat. A very neat arrangement of this kind was recently exhibited at the Polytechnic under the name of the Norwegian cooking stove. It consists of a small wooden box, thickly lined with felt, in which there is just room to deposit a stew-pan. After it has been brought to boiling heat upon the fire, it is then shut close, and in three or four hours the dinner is thoroughly cooked. We should think this, in waggon travelling in Africa, for soldiers on the march, or on board fishing boats or small vessels, would be a very desirable acquisition.

In Australia we constantly ate our ration of salt pork uncooked; and, even when recently taken from the cask, it was very good in this manner with a little lime-juice and sugar. *Per contra*, however, the pork, with the bone cut out, and packed in canvas bags for carriage by pack horses, soon became dried by the sun; the fat all melted out of it, and was used to grease our boots or harness; and the once juicy, succulent, full-sized four-pound piece of pork became, after a few months' carriage, a semi-fossilised bit of non-descript matter, not much bigger than our fist, and weighing just three-quarters of a pound.

It may be of interest here to give the scale of rations on which we travelled, and on which, though we could certainly have consumed more, we lived and worked for several months without finding our health or strength in any way impaired:

Salt pork, per diem, 1lb. (nom.)	Sugar, 3oz.
Flour, 1lb.	Tobacco, $\frac{1}{4}$oz.
Coffee, roasted and ground, $\frac{3}{4}$oz.	Soap, $\frac{1}{4}$oz.
Or tea, $\frac{1}{4}$oz.	

In camp, if we killed a sheep, the allowance was $1\frac{1}{4}$lb. of flesh meat instead of salt; a pint pannikin was also used as holding an equivalent to 1lb. of flour. But on the journey we were never able to issue a full pound, because drying it in the sun diminished its weight; and, beside this, as we carried two $\frac{1}{2}$lb. tins of gunpowder in each 50lb. bag of flour, their weight, as well as that of the double canvas bag, had to be deducted, leaving a net weight of very little over 48lb. In serving the weekly rations, our plan was to weigh every man's bag of flour against our own, and, if he thought his was in any way deficient, to give him the option of changing; also, when the pork was laid out, to let every man choose his ration, and to take that which remained for ourselves; and we found, as we believe will generally be the case, that the men, seeing that they were fairly treated, did not abuse the confidence we placed in them.

In times of scarcity, it may be well in killing a sheep to follow the example of the Tartars, who are perhaps the most dexterous sheep butchers in the world. When they kill a sheep nothing is wasted; even the blood is most carefully preserved for use. Instead of cutting the throat of the animal in the usual way, they pass a long slender knife in by the side of the breast-bone in such a way that all the large vessels above the heart

Sheep killing.

are instantly severed. All the blood therein contained is poured out into the cavity of the chest without the escape of any. When requisite, it is ladled or scooped out, and placed in some convenient vessel. To skin the animal, the knife is first run along the whole abdominal line, from the top of the throat under the chin to the inside of the root of the tail, lines are then cut up each leg to the hoof, and the skin is dexterously stripped back from each side until nothing but a mere line of adhesion is left from the top of the tail, along the middle of the back, and up the neck. The sheep is now turned on its back, and the skin spread evenly out, like a mat, under it. The process of division into convenient joints now takes place, each piece being arranged in order on the skin, whilst the offal is secured in a wide basket. When all the joints have been duly cut out, the skin is taken by two men, one before to grasp the skins of the fore-legs and the other those of the hind, just as a hand-barrow is carried; and in this way the meat is carried to the tents for use.

Once, in Australia, after having emptied a 50lb. bag of sugar, we rinsed out the bag with half a pint of water, making a strong syrup, which we poured into a small iron bucket; then, rinsing it again with another half-pint, we obtained *Economy in food.* a like quantity, somewhat less sweet; and this we repeated till the bag was washed clean, and we had about three pints of sweetened water in our bucket. We then drew from the store half a ration of sago for four persons—*i.e.*, ½lb. each—boiled it in the syrup, and thus produced a mess which everyone who tasted it declared to be delicious.

One of our party devoted a spare hour to fishing, and, with hook and line, caught a large water tortoise and some fish; and shot a bird. The first of these when killed—*i.e.*, so far as the division of the jugular would kill it—was laid upon its back upon the embers, served up in its own shell, and was a most palatable addition to our meal.

The large lizards of Australia, sometimes from 4ft. to nearly 6ft. long, are most excellent and delicate food, but the proper method is to roast them in the skin; and we have known the most intense anxiety felt lest we should require the skin of a particularly fine one as a specimen of natural history. This was somewhat calmed by the assurance that we only wished to sketch it, but the operation was most jealously watched, and when we had completed our picture, we divided the body into quarters and the tail into four junks, for the four members of the party; and these dainties, carefully spread upon forked branches cut for the purpose, were set up above the embers of an ample fire, raked out into glowing heaps under each junk or quarter. In about twenty minutes they were thoroughly cooked, and proved, indeed, a delicacy, the flesh being white as chicken, and the taste reminding us rather of turkey than anything else.

The various cockatoos, parrots, wood-pigeons, storks, and cranes are all good. The dawn or rose-breasted cockatoo (*Cacatoa eos*), the white variety with the sulphur-coloured crest, or the black cockatoo, each form a very tolerable, though not an ample, meal for one man. Various species of hawks or kites, though not so delicate, may also be eaten; and in Australia, where carrion is not so plentiful as in Africa, and the hawks feed principally upon insects or small fish, their flesh, though dark in colour and tough, is by no means bad. We have eaten the white-headed African fish eagle and the large horned owl, which, though somewhat tough and rank, were better than going upon scanty fare.

We first ate the flesh of a snake at Graham's Town, South Africa. A friend had brought us a puff-adder as a specimen; and, when we had skinned it, the flesh looked so white and firm that we cut out a junk, about six inches long, and as thick as our wrist, and desired the Kafir girl, who acted as cook, to fry it. An acquaintance who partook of it acknowledged that it was good, and that only the thought of eating snake prevented his enjoying it more fully.

The Australian blacks eat snakes of every kind, as well as any small animals they can catch; and we have often seen fellows whose sole apparel consisted of a snake girded round their waist, with two or three rats hitched by their tails to it. We were taught the orthodox way of cooking them by a first-rate fellow, John Fahey, an Irishman, who had been nearly fourteen years among the blacks. He first let the flame expend itself, and then spread out the embers, on these he coiled up the snake until the scales were slightly scorched; then taking it by the tail, he drew it repeatedly through his hand, brushing the crisp scales off towards the head, and again coiled it on the embers till it was thoroughly cooked; then opening it and throwing away the offal he picked out the tit bits and offered them to us, and afterwards divided the body.

The flesh of the alligator while young, and not more than 6ft. in length, is very good; but when larger, it becomes very strong, and acquires a musky flavour. We once killed an alligator of 11ft. on the Horseshoe flats, near Curiosity Peak, Victoria River, North Australia. The smell was to a degree rank; yet when we took the carcase to the vessel next morning, and the second overseer cleaned the skin and skeleton, we found that excellent cutlets were to be obtained from the muscular portion of the tail; and after breakfast, when the prejudices of the crew had given way, claimants were found for the flesh as fast as it could be stripped from the bones. Considerable seasoning was required, but still it was better than salt junk.

In South Africa, just when the white ants are about to swarm and take the half-hour's flight which is allowed them before their wings drop off, the natives collect with torches; the ants, being attracted by the light, assemble and are swept up by basketfuls. After being scorched, they· are kept in mat bags, holding two or three gallons each, and are really delicious food. They are pleasant to the taste, and very nutritious ; for if one be left on a sheet of note-paper when the sun is shining brightly on it oil enough will exude to make a spot a couple of inches in diameter. The chief convenience of these is that they require no cooking, but any quantity may be carried in a bag, and a handful taken out and eaten when wanted.

White Ants.

The vast clouds of locusts, which in some countries both darken the air and devastate the land, are eaten greedily by nearly everything possessing life—men, animals, birds, fish, and insects, all join in the locust feast. The provident savage lays by a store merely smoke dried, to consume at his leisure with such tuberous roots or other under-ground productions as his sable spouse, armed with her sharp pointed grubbing stick, can procure for him.

The inhabitants of many of the islands of the Eastern Archipelago consume certain insects as food, wherever they can procure them. Mr Wallace, who resided some time among the Dyaks, says : " Every day boys were to be seen walking along the roads, and by the hedges and ditches, catching dragon flies with birdlime. They carry a slender stick, with a few twigs at the end, well anointed, so that the least touch captures the insect, whose wings are pulled off before it is consigned to a small basket. The dragon flies are so abundant at the time of the rice flowering, that thousands are soon caught in this way. The bodies are fried in oil, with onions and preserved shrimps, or sometimes alone, and are considered a great delicacy." In Borneo, Celebes, and many other islands, the larvæ of bees and wasps are eaten either alive as pulled out of the cells, or fried like the dragon flies. In the Moluccas the grubs of the palm beetles (*Calandra*) are regularly brought to market in bamboos and sold for food ; and many of the great horned Lamellicorn beetles are slightly roasted on the embers, and eaten whenever met with. In many districts where the cocoanut palm grows abundantly, the curved and tightly rolled up immature fronds are perforated by the workings and burrowings of the " Tucuma " or " Grugru," the larvæ of *Oryctes rhinoceros*. These are large plump grubs, with black hard heads, and are esteemed a great luxury, being either fried in cocoanut oil, or seized by the head, dipped in a little lime juice and disposed of without further preparation.

The nests of the white ants are often broken by the natives in search of the eggs, and even of the insects, for scarcity of animal food compels them to eat anything, and the grubs that lurk under the bark of the gum trees are accounted delicious fare. John Fahey was

K K 2

an adept in searching them out; and in fact, when we first made our camp, girdled several trees in order that they might die, and that grubs might accumulate under the bark. The grubs are eaten fresh, raw and living, just as they are taken from the tree.

In most countries there will be some vegetable product or other available for food. In Australia we have cut out what may be called the cabbage from the roots of the pandanus leaves, and found it, when boiled, almost as good as a very inferior turnip. The seeds from the large globular fruit were also worth looking for, because in the pencil of fibre by which they are attached to the base is contained a quantity of sweet and farinaceous matter; this we found also was highly relished by the small fish and fresh water tortoises in the rivulets, and we frequently baited our hooks with them.

In Africa, if we were accompanied by a Damara on a shooting trip, and were unsuccessful, we returned hungry, but if we took a Makalaka, he would be sure to dig up roots or gather wild fruit, or vegetables of some kind or other; and perhaps catch a lizard or other small creature, or occasionally discover a bees' nest in a hollow tree. Once when we were much exhausted with long continued want of food, the man who accompanied us saw a few of the small African bees around the branch of a tree, he forthwith climbed it, and chopping off a piece of bark, bruised up the ends with the head of his axe, till he had formed a kind of trough, which he set his assistants to hold, and chopped away till he had sufficiently enlarged the hole to allow him to extract the honeycomb.

The roots of the lotus or blue water-lily are very good, and have a taste, when roasted, something between that of a chesnut and a potato.

Lotus roots are obtained from the bottoms of some of the Eastern lakes and rivers by making use of a very long and soft leather sack. Into this the lotus gatherer gets until the top of the sack is on a level with his neck. He then walks, or rather hobbles, into the water, wades by short steps out to the lotus beds; and when he feels the roots beneath his feet, he digs and works with his toes and heels until they are detached from their hold on the bottom, and float on the surface, from which they are readily raked and collected for use.

The Bushmen wade in the shallow pools and pluck them up by hand, but in the deeper rivers the canoe men have long poles with a hook at the end for detaching the roots. In these pools, also, they frequently capture the "matamaetlie" or edible frog, which is sometimes nearly as large as a chicken. The Bushmen grip them by the nape of the neck, strike them across the thighs and across the spine to disable them, and then, placing their lips to the vent blow till they force the stomach and all the entrails out at the mouth. The flesh of these frogs is exceedingly good, more like chicken than anything else, and we often found a good-sized one make us a very satisfying meal.

The seed of the lotus is extensively used as food throughout the East; the Chinese esteem it highly, and prepare it in a great number of ways. Sir Samuel Baker, in speaking of lotus seed, Lotus seed. says: "All the tribes of the White Nile have their harvest of lotus seed; there are two species of water-lily, the large white flower, and the small variety. The seed pod of the white lotus is like an unblown artichoke, containing a number of light red grains, equal in size to mustard seed, but shaped like those of the poppy, and similar to them in flavour, being sweet and nutty. The ripe pods are collected, and strung upon sharp pointed reeds, about 4ft. in length. When thus threaded they are formed into large bundles, and carried from the river to the villages, where they are dried in the sun and stored for use. The seed is ground into flour, and made into a kind of porridge."

Rice is so well known as a food grain that little need be said of it further than that a wild kind is found growing in many of the swamps of America; the grain from this is Rice, to boil. beaten off with sticks into canoes which are propelled through the shallow water in which the rice stalks grow. Some skill is required in cooking rice, in order that each grain may be separate. Our native Indian cook used to proceed as follows: The rice was first thoroughly washed in a large jar of clean cold water, two washings being generally required to remove all stain. The water was then strained off, and the clean rice drained quite dry. A cooking pot full of water was then placed on a brisk fire, and allowed to boil actively; when in full ebullition the rice was cast in, the fire stirred, and the boiling continued actively for about sixteen minutes, when the pot was lifted off, placed on one side, and a pint lota pot of cold water thrown suddenly into it; the sudden chill thus communicated divides every grain from its fellow, and, when strained dry, rice prepared in this manner is truly excellent and attractive.

Ostriches' eggs have often been treated of, and every traveller speaks of them according to his particular experience. Probably, when a party of half-a-dozen men have plenty of bread and every other necessary for a good meal, they will find that one egg is quite enough for them; while a stout fellow, destitute of everything but a keen appetite, would find an ostrich's egg not more than enough to satisfy himself. The capacity of a good-sized one is about $2\frac{1}{2}$ pints, the taste is rich, and sometimes a trifle strong; in fact, we could never eat much of one unless it were mixed with flour and made into a cake. The readiest way of cooking them is to break one end of the shell, set the other end into the embers on the ground, and so cook and serve the contents in their own shell. We prefer, however, to start the egg into an earthen pot, and add nearly an equal quantity of flour or meal, making cakes or fritters, seasoned or not according to taste.

Indeed, we should think that, if eggs in plenty could be obtained, this would be a very economical and effective way of provisioning a
Various foods. small party for a journey where everything must be carried, and where the means of carriage was scant or perhaps altogether wanting; but, in this case, the eggs would have to be mixed with as much flour as they would take up, and the cakes baked as dry as possible without burning any part of them. A nautical friend has told us of a plan adopted on surveying expeditions, when boats are sent for several days from the ship. A rough grater is made by punching holes in a sheet of tin, and a junk of salt meat grated down tolerably fine; the meat powder is then mixed with flour with very little water, rolled up into small balls or cakes, and dried in the galley. When wanted, a portion is broken off, kneaded with a little water, enveloped in a crust of flour and water, tied up in a cloth, and boiled in the boat's copper as a meat pudding.

The North Australian expedition was abundantly supplied with preserved fresh meat, but the tins in which it was packed could not conveniently be carried in bags on pack horses, and therefore, in preparation for an extensive inland journey, estimating the quantity required, we took out of store equal weights of preserved beef and flour; then taking the contents of a 1lb. tin of beef and 6lb. of flour, we kneaded them together, divided the mass into forty-eight parts of ¼lb. each, and baked them in an oven built of clay and the schooner's pig ballast for the purpose. Nearly 3lb. weight were lost by the evaporation of the moisture in the process of baking, so that the forty-eight cakes representing 12lb. of meat and flour, and forming six days' rations for one man, could be carried at a weight of 6lb.; the rations of sugar and other groceries making the total weight only about 10½lb. or at most 11lb. As long as the biscuits remain whole four of them were considered equivalent to 1lb.; but when they were broken up into dust a pannikin about three-quarters full was reckoned an equivalent. In either case, the best way of using it was to mix it with water and warm it up as a thick soup. This compound has been adopted by other travellers in Australia, and found to answer the purpose exceedingly well.

We should think that where fresh and really good fruit is plentiful it might be treated with flour nearly in the same manner, and would form a very agreeable variation in the diet. Dried fruit may be had in many countries, such as Cape Colony, where dried peaches, raisins, &c., are constantly in the market; and these stewed with the meat are not to be despised; but in some form or other vegetable matter, as acid as possible, is absolutely necessary; for no one who has not been compelled to live for weeks together upon meat alone can imagine how utterly disgusting the smell and taste of even the freshest and most savoury joints become when unvaried by any vegetable, to say nothing of the injury to health that such a diet must cause. In Australia we have gathered the young shoots of the wild vine and made what our cook called rhubarb tarts of them; and when these failed, a small succulent herb called "portulac," or more popularly "potluck," which could be eaten as a salad, supplied their place. In Africa we have found unspeakable relief from a bundle of dry tamarinds brought from a distant tribe; and when recrossing the desert during the rainy season, we found abundant supplies of wild grapes growing luxuriantly along our path. No matter that they were not ripe; the more tart and sour they were the better; and by the time we had got well within the desert border, and were beginning to find that the intense sourness, which had already served its purpose as a corrective, was beginning to set our teeth on edge, we also began to find riper clusters on the bushes as we advanced; they were, of course, not equal to the cultivated varieties, but were by no means a bad substitute.

We also gathered daily large quantities of the beer berry, or "ovúmbapoov," about the size of a cranberry, but nearly filled with a hard stone or kernel; these were of a pleasant, sweetish, acid taste, and could be eaten as we gathered them and walked along, or when we halted could be pounded with water in a "halwe stamp block," or modern mortar, into a very pleasant pulp; the only drawback was the small quantity of food in proportion to the amount of kernel, and the difficulty of getting rid of the latter. Sometimes we would collect a quantity, pour boiling water upon them, let it stand to extract the juices, and then put it aside to ferment. The liquor thus obtained was not unpleasant, it was somewhat between inferior beer and second-rate cider. Once we boiled the juice down to a thick syrup, which was so sweet that a spoonful of it served instead of sugar to our tea, but the quantity produced was so small in proportion to the trouble that we never repeated the process. Many other fruits, roots, and vegetables might be named; but if the traveller makes friends of the natives they will find whatever the country produces for him, and they will never refuse to share what they pick up either with him or with his hungry comrades. Indeed, their language supplies no title of contempt equivalent to that of "the man who eats alone," or who saves anything for the morrow.

We cannot omit, however, to mention the fruit of the Baobab or "Adansonia," which, both in Africa and in Australia, we have found extremely valuable. The tree will at once be known by its enormous size. We have generally seen young, well-conditioned trees 30ft. in circumference, while others have been 50ft. or 60ft., and the largest we know of was actually 101ft.; its height, however, is by no means proportionate, it being seldom more than 60ft., or at most 70ft. or 80ft. The fruit is generally about the size of an ostrich's egg, though we have seen it much larger; the rind is about as thick as the egg shell, and easily broken; the interior is occupied by seeds imbedded in a pleasant sub-acid pulp, of a white colour, which when dry resembles cream of tartar, and has caused the Dutch Africans to bestow upon it the name of "krem tart boom," or cream-of-tartar tree. This pulp the bushmen pound up with a little water, and sometimes mix with it a little meal of grass seeds, to thicken it, or by adding more water make a very pleasant drink.

In Australia we found even the soft wood so succulent that we could cut out a junk with the axe, and chew it for the moisture it contained like a wet sponge; while the fruit of the Gouty-stemmed tree (*Adansonia Gregorii*), when boiled up with a little sugar, acted as a powerful anti-scorbutic among the sailors of our little schooner, completely curing the disease, and leaving only the unavoidable weakness, from which, with the advantage of better food, they gradually recovered. Millet of various kinds, known under the general denomination of Kafir corn, can be purchased from most of the Kafir and Bechuana tribes. It may be eaten boiled with meat, but should be previously husked in a wooden mortar, and would be better and more digestible if it were also bruised. We have ground it to a kind of rough meal in a coffee-mill, but found that it would not knead up into cakes without a little European or colonial flour to bind it. Sometimes the native women bruise it to meal in their wooden mortars, and in times of scarcity gather the seeds of several wild grasses, which they treat in the same manner.

This meal will not make bread in our sense of the word, but it will make a very good mess, something between bread and pap or porridge, called "maassa." An earthen pot with water is set upon the fire, and when the water boils a little meal is dropped in and stirred, more and more is then gradually added and stirred until the mess thickens, and is served up like a very dense paste. A very little soup or meat gravy makes it agreeable enough.

Maize or Indian corn is very extensively grown in Africa, and most other warm countries, and nothing can be more delicious than the young ears, either boiled or roasted in their sheath, the leaves of which everyone strips off for himself . when it comes to table, spreading a little butter on the ear according to taste; it is perfect etiquette in this case to take the ear up in both hands just as you would pick a bone, and bite the grains off; indeed, the young corn cannot be properly eaten in any other manner.

Maize grains, when in the milk stage, can be preserved for future use in the following manner: The heads are first cut from the stalk, the covering of leaves and the tassel are then stripped off, and all the grains broken from the cob or core with the fingers into a shallow basket; a wide pit is then dug in the earth, and red hot stones and embers are cast in until the bottom and sides of the pit are thoroughly heated. All the stones and ashes are then removed, and all dust brushed away with green branches. A quantity of maize leaves are now brought and made use of to line the pit, and form a sort of nest for the reception of the maize, which is covered with a thick layer of leaves and left until baked. The grain subjected to this process, instead of becoming parched and dry, remains sweet, and when boiled with meat much resembles green peas.

The ground nut, such as is brought from Sierra Leone, is obtainable in many parts. It may be eaten raw, but is better slightly roasted. The Portuguese make a very nice confect of it, and it contains so much essential oil that one nut will burn with a clear flame, like a wax candle, for fully a minute. This oil makes it one of the best substitutes for coffee we know of. Slightly roasted and ground, and infused in the ordinary manner, it is exceedingly good. Most of the indigenous grains and grasses are also used, but some of them only act as a kind of vegetable charcoal to give a toast-and-water like colour to the morning beverage. We have frequently tried the beans of various species of mimosa, and have found them valuable in exact proportion to the quantity of essential oil contained in them. The dwarf shrubs, carrying generally the largest beans, were the best, and we should think the diminutive tree, scarcely 18in. high, and bearing a pod more than a foot long, called "Eland's boontjia," would be best of all. At other times we have used burnt pumpkin, but this produced rather a kind of vegetable soup.

Tea is one of the most valuable and important stores carried by the explorer or' traveller, and an ample supply should always be taken. We prefer the Australian method of tea-making to any other; and, whether with our brass

Uses of tea.

lota pot or tin quart mug and pint cup, proceed in the same manner to brew it. We first pour as much water as we think requisite in the pot, put it on the fire, and raise it to the boiling point; then take it off and add tea in proportion to the number to be brewed for, covering down the vessel with an inverted tea bowl until the tea has drawn; it is then fit for use. By adopting this plan the tea for the early morning's start need not be made the night before; a few chips, sticks, dead leaves, or a lamp will serve to give heat enough to boil a well-blackened pot; and a very few minutes will suffice, while the packs are being arranged, to prepare a bowl of warm tea, which, with a little bread or native cake, will serve as a stand-by until the regular breakfast hour. For a very long time it was our custom when in India to strike tent at two A.M., and march at three, in order to avoid the heat; but we never omitted our bowl of tea.

Among the natives of Chinese Tartary extensive use is made of brick tea, not only as an article of diet, but as a medium of currency and exchange.

This curious preparation is commonly made use of by travellers and the lower orders throughout the length and breadth of Tartary, Tibet, and the Kirghis steppes. The bricks vary in size according to the particular district in which they are made; but to be of convenient and saleable character they should be about 1ft. long, 6in. wide, and from 1in. to 1½in. thick. To make tea bricks, all the late shoots, imperfectly-formed leaves, and immature buds to be found in the tea plantations, after the tea harvest is over, are collected; they are then subjected to the action of water until soft and pliable, bullock's blood is then added, the mass is then thoroughly mixed and incorporated, and, when of a tough, firm consistence, it is divided into portions of convenient size, which are pressed into brick moulds prepared for them. When turned from the moulds the bricks are laid on hurdles, and subjected to heat until dry. They are then fit for the market, to which the finished commodity is usually carried in sheepskin bags. When required for use, the portion to be consumed is broken from the brick with the head of a hatchet, or a heavy stone; the fragments thus detached are broken up small between two flat stones, and then rubbed between the palms of the hands until fine enough for preparation.

There are several ways of preparing brick tea for consumption. One is to place the rough powder in a pot or kettle with water, and boil it until a red decoction is formed, a little salt is then thrown in, which causes a slight effervescence to be set up; when this ceases, and the liquid becomes tranquil, and of dark colour, milk is added. If it is desired to make the tea thus prepared more than commonly attractive to the visitor, butter is added. Sometimes a mixture, called "Imitanka," is made from it; this is formed by adding a quantity of clotted cream which has become sour to the boiled tea water, and when it has boiled a short time, adding salt and a bowlful of millet seed flour. The whole mixture is then boiled for about three-quarters of an hour, and is ready for the table, or rather floor of the tent, on which it is usual to sit. Barley meal and suet added to the tea water makes a kind of gruel, or stirabout, which is much relished by the wandering Tartars, and appears to agree vastly well with them. Brick tea is not only used as we have described, but is common among Tartar dealers, and those who attend the fairs held for the purpose of sale and exchange, as a medium of currency, just as the beaver skin and the Dentalium shell are by the Indians of North-West America.

Almost every country has its own peculiar method of preserving animal food for future use. The salting of meat, and the consequent deterioration of its nourishing properties, must be well known to all who have made long voyages, unless, indeed, they have always sailed in first-class ships, where the appearance of salt junk upon the cabin table is quite exceptional. Where it can conveniently be carried, we think that boiled fresh beef, preserved in air-tight tin canisters, is by far the best, as being in effect equal to fresh killed meat cooked in the same manner. We have seen considerable quantities of this meat used after being carried by land and sea about the world for years, and we do not remember that we have ever opened a tin which was not in good order, and perfectly fit for food. And we should also think that in many places where immense herds of cattle almost encumber the land they live upon, this method of transporting their flesh to a better market would be well worthy the attention of their owners. There are many variations in the method of preserving, but we believe the simplest and most effective to be as under. Kill the animal by a rifle shot behind the ear or otherwise, skin it, and hoist it by block and tackle to a convenient tree, then commencing at the hind-legs, which are of course uppermost, strip off all the flesh from the bones, leaving the skeleton still hanging, cut the flesh into pieces as nearly 6lb. in weight as possible, put them into a cauldron with very little water, and boil them well. Have a number of cylindrical 6lb. tins, and set them ready in a trough of boiling water, kept hot by a steam pipe or other available means; put a piece of beef in each tin, with liquor enough nearly to fill it, and then solder on the top, which should have a hole in it; when all the tins of meat are thus far advanced, pour in at the small hole liquor enough to fill the tin, clean round the edges of the hole, and close it with a drop of hot solder, so as to seal the tin hermetically; then remove them from the water, dry the outsides, paint them with any coarse colour, mixed with boiled oil, and they are ready for exportation to any part of the world.

Where meat in this form cannot be carried, perhaps the next best method is to cut it into strips or flakes, and dry it thoroughly in the sun, with, or more frequently without, a little salt upon the surface. Meat by this process loses some of its nutritious quality, but it is so conveniently kept and carried, and so little liable to damage, that there is scarcely a country in the world having sun-enough for the purpose where it is not adopted. In North-America the flesh of the buffalo, or bison, and in South America that of the domestic, or rather half-wild, ox, is used; and Sir F. Head, in his rough notes of the pampas, remarks that a man can live longer on dried beef and water than he can on any other unvaried diet.

The trappers and traders of North West America make extensive use of a kind of prepared food known as "pemmican," and very large quantities of it are manufactured on the buffalo range. It is thus made. Buffalo flesh is cut with the hunting knife into convenient flakes and flat steaks or layers. These are either hung in the sun or near a slow fire until dry, when the dried meat is ground between two stones until sufficiently fine. A bag is then made of buffalo hide, with the hair side out, and the preserved flesh, after having been thoroughly mixed with hot fat, is well rammed and pressed in. The bag is then securely stitched up, and the pemmican allowed to cool and harden. When required for use, it is cut from the mass like hard sausage meat, and either eaten cold, or, when mixed with flour or meal, a sort of thick porridge, called by the trappers "robiboo," is made from it.

In many of the Australian islands and New Zealand vast quantities of seal-fowl (the sooty petrel or mutton bird, especially) are captured for food by the sailors and natives. These birds visit the islands annually in vast flocks, arriving generally about the latter end of November, for the purpose of depositing their eggs, of which each hen bird lays one

Food,
to preserve. or two, about the size of ordinary goose eggs, and some-what similar in flavour. The cock bird takes charge of the nest during the day and the hen by night, taking in turn the duty of going to sea for food. Perfect warrens, like those of rabbits, are formed by these birds, who burrow in the soft ground for a distance of 2ft. or 3ft., and there form their nests. Some of the islands are so thickly and completely honeycombed by these feathered miners as to render walking a very unsafe proceeding.

The collection of the eggs and young birds from the depths of the holes is a task usually assigned to the native women, who not uncommonly find a snake coiled up where the young petrel should be. When a large catch is determined on for preservation and the obtainment of feathers, a number of bird hunters assemble and construct a sort of hedge or fence a short distance from the beach, and just before daybreak, when the birds, about to proceed to sea to feed, are out of their retreats, a sudden rush is made by the whole assembled party of birdcatchers who, with the most hideous yells and cries, drive the throngs of waddling, flapping victims, who cannot rise from the ground to fly, towards the centre of the fatal barrier, where a deep pit has been prepared for their reception. Into this they are forced, layer on layer, until they literally suffocate each other in their vain endeavours to escape from the treacherous pitfall. The feathers, when plucked from the birds, are worth about 3*d.* per pound, and it requires the joint plumage of about twenty to produce that quantity. Thirty bags of feathers, constituting the cargoes of two trading boats, were obtained by the sacrifice of 18,000 birds. A portion of the birds are preserved by dry smoking, and are extensively made use of. Some of the New Zealand tribes, by whom this bird is called the " Titi," have recourse to a most ingenious and effective method of preservation for it, and some other articles of food. The petrels, after having been carefully plucked, have all their bones removed. They are then cooked over the fire in large shallow dishes or platters, made from the bark of the " Totara " tree, and when sufficiently done are placed in the natural bottles or flasks formed of a species of seaweed, like a huge variety of the bladder-wrack (*Fucus vesiculosus*) of our own coasts. The heated fat from the birds is then poured in, and the sea-bottle securely tied up. Provisions treated in this manner remain perfectly good for a very long time, being completely excluded from both air and moisture. The Indians of Vancouver Island make use of seaweed bottles, made like those just described, to store up fish oil in.

In Africa, the flesh of the ox and of all the game animals—from the antelope and buffalo to the giraffe, and the rhinoceros, the hippopotamus, and elephant—is used under the general name of "biltong." The scene, when one of the larger animals has been shot, and is found perhaps next morning by the hunter's native followers, is exciting enough. In the case of an elephant which has lain till ten or eleven o'clock, when the heat of the sun will have begun to form gases in the stomach, and to distend the carcase till a man may tread upon it as he would on an unyielding rock, the man, whose

Hints on large game.

duty it is to make the first incision, approaches cautiously, taking care, if possible, not to come to leeward, and especially to see that his retreat is clear; then reaching forward at the full length of his arm, he drives his spear into the abdomen, leaping backward at the same time to avoid the gaseous and liquid discharge which ensues. The rest wait until the carcase has collapsed, and the stench is somewhat dissipated, and then rush in and commence the cutting up. The thick skin is torn in broad planks from the sides, groups of men mount upon the ribs, and, squatting there upon their hams, use their assegais in cutting down through the flesh; others, having effected a breach in the thinnest part of the abdomen, enter and tear out the internal dainties, and then assegais in hand, begin to cut the flesh from the inside of the ribs—an operation, it will readily be believed, involving no small risk to those who happen to be sitting just above them, and who not unfrequently receive a hint that the human skin is by no means invulnerable. The surrounding bushes now begin to be covered with blanket-like flaps of skin and meat, by membranes and sheets of the internal fat, and, from every fire arises the savoury odour of some tit bit, being hastily grilled to appease the appetite while the pot, which has been filled with the first cuttings of the flesh, is being boiled. Long, straight poles are next cut, and laid across like rails from fork to fork of other trees, and on these the flesh, cut into strips from 3ft. to 16ft. long, and about two fingers thick, is hung to dry, care being taken not to hang it so closely as to prevent the air passing freely between the pieces. Two or three days will generally be enough to dry the meat, which is then taken down, and either tied up in bundles if to be carried by men, or stowed as loosely as possible in the waggon, being opened and spread out at every halt for the first few days to guard against the possibility of putrefaction; further cooking is not abso-lutely necessary. The biltong may be bruised up with a yoke skei, or the head of an axe, and eaten raw, or it may be broiled and bruised as before, or if boiled it may be put into a native mortar and pounded with pestle or a yoke skei until the fibres are thoroughly separated, and much trouble is saved in the way of mastication. With the addition of a little cinnamon or other spice, dried peaches, shreds of dried onions, or any little thing to vary the taste, this is by no means a bad dish for hungry men.

In all cases, however, it is well to make a proportion of the meat carry itself; and here the traveller will be called upon to exercise great caution. It will never do to purchase at random a number of animals of various species, because, in the first place, the different kinds will not herd together, and, therefore, each will require separate attendants; and, secondly, because the country to be explored may be unfavourable to the existence of some of them. In North Australia we took no cattle, because we had reason to think that plants poisonous to them abounded there. Of our flock of sheep we took none beyond the standing camp, and even of them we lost more than three-fourths by the disasters of the sea and river voyage before they were landed. If men would make up their minds to eat horseflesh, we believe it would be more economical, and would give less trouble to the exploring party, who might purchase at the outset a considerable additional number of horses, young of course, but at least sufficiently docile to carry a pack and travel with the others; and when the burden of one of these had been eaten off, to shoot him, and convert as much of his flesh as could not be eaten in the first two days into biltong.

In many of the later expeditions camels have been used more or less successfully, and their flesh has also served as food to the explorers on emergencies.

In South Africa oxen are so generally used that no one thinks of undertaking a journey of any extent without them, and not less as a matter of course, his vehicle is the ox waggon; horses, as many as the traveller can afford, also accompany him; but, if he is really a hunter, these are seldom or never ridden until their energies are required for active service, but leisurely driven on by a Hottentot lad, and carefully tended, so as to husband their strength and keep them in good condition till they are really wanted. Sheep and goats need not be taken because most of the native tribes are so essentially pastoral that these animals may be cheaply purchased from them; and young lads, willing to drive them, may be hired for a trifling reward, in addition to their food.

Nevertheless, all these animals are liable to casualties on the road: the goats or sheep may die from feeding on the beans that fall from the kameel doorn and various acacias; the stud may be thinned off by the annual horse sickness, even though the traveller may have taken the precaution to buy, at a higher price, what are called salted horses— *i.e.,* such as have once had the sickness—for it is well known that if a horse takes the sickness in a district where it prevails in a mild form, which is generally the case in such as have been for a considerable time colonised, it will not protect him in the remote wilderness where the disease still maintains its unmitigated strength. It is, therefore, always advisable to ask not only whether the horse has had the sickness, but where he passed through the ordeal. We have known as much as 100*l.* given by a hunter for a horse up to his weight and warranted to be salted, with the proviso, however, that if the horse died of sickness during the first season his price was to be reduced by 60*l*.

In all cases of extreme scarcity of food, we strongly advise the traveller to leave no stone unturned which may yield aliment of some kind to help him on his way before he sacrifices his riding horse or mule. Where a number of animals accompany an expedition, a few may perhaps be parted with from time to time; but we earnestly advise the solitary hunter or explorer to exercise every faculty he possesses for food finding before he makes up his mind to destroy his four-footed friend. Different regions not only furnish different food-yielding products but possess climates which necessitate the use of appropriate kinds of aliment. Food may be viewed in the light of fuel, and man as a lamp. The more intense the cold and severe the exertion the greater will be the expenditure of elements rich in carbon, such as oil, fat, blubber, flesh, &c. Arctic travellers and those who dwell in the regions of ice and snow find themselves compelled to follow very closely the customs of the Esquimaux in their diet scale. Dr. Kane, the Arctic traveller, says : " Our journeys have taught us the wisdom of the Esquimaux appetite, and there are few among us who do not relish a slice of raw blubber, or a chunk of frozen walrus beef. The liver of a walrus (Awuktanuk) eaten with little slices of his fat, of a verity is a delicious morsel. Fire would ruin the curt pithy expression of vitality which belongs to its uncooked pieces. Charles Lamb's roast pig was nothing to Awuktanuk. I wonder that raw beef is not eaten at home. Deprived of extraneous fibre, it is neither indigestible nor difficult to masticate. With acids and condiments it makes a salad which an educated palate cannot help relishing; and as a powerful and condensed heat-making and antiscorbutic food it has no rival. I make this last broad assertion after carefully testing it truth. The natives of South Greenland prepare themselves for a long journey in the cold by a course of frozen seal. At Upernavik they do the same with the narwhal, which is thought more heat making than the seal, while the bear, to use their own expression, is 'stronger travel' than all. In the far north, where the explorer has to carefully husband such food as good fortune may cast in his way, no portion of an animal is wasted." The Doctor, when speaking of the value of every part of a beast, says : " The skin makes the basis of soup, and the claws can be boiled to a jelly; lungs, larynx, stomach, and entrails are all available." Starvation is far less to be feared by an experienced traveller in tropical climates than among the ice of the polar regions, as, in the first place, the large quantities of animal food consumed to sustain vital heat are not needed; and, in the

Hints on food gathering.

next, the vegetable and insect world far more abundantly contribute their aid in furnishing his larder. Here again the explorer will do well to follow, in cases of necessity, the example set by the natives, who not unfrequently manage to sustain life in regions which to the unpractised eye would present nothing but hopeless barrenness. The inhabitants of very extensive tracts of country, extending through the Presidio del Norte, in Mexico, subsist for months together on the large bulbous roots of the Maguay (*Agave Mexicana*), which grows in the dry arid soil of these regions. These roots vary in size from the diameter of a 4lb. loaf to that of a two-gallon jar, and are not unlike a huge onion in external appearance. When intended for food they are simply dug up and roasted in hot ashes, when they become palatable and wholesome. It is from these roots that the Mexicans prepare their celebrated "Mescal," or aguardiente, a spirit stronger than the best whisky. To prepare this, a pit is dug in the ground to about the depth of 3ft. and about 10ft. in diameter; a complete layer of stones is then made on the bottom and round the sides of the pit, which is then filled with billets of wood and branches of bushes; these are then ignited, and the fire is suffered to burn until the stone lining and borders of the pit are strongly heated; a quantity of freshly-gathered grass is then thrown in and formed into a sort of lining for the stones, and on this the bulbs of the maguay are cast until the pit is nearly full, when a quantity of grass is thrown over the top layer, and the baking or roasting process is suffered to go on until the roots are thoroughly cooked. Large leather sacks are then brought to receive the roots. Water is thrown in until a sort of gruel is formed, which ferments for about a week, and is then distilled in a rough makeshift still, when the liquor is fit for consumption. This is the plant which produces the pulque, which we have before described. The fibres of the leaves make excellent ropes and twine; the young and immature leaves, when doubled up in the hand, make an excellent substitute for soap; and the fresh crisp sprouts are good for cattle food. The region of the Gila and the Sonora district also produce the "Petahaya," the great candelabra cereus. This curious plant grows in the form of either a fluted column or gigantic candelabrum; the stem is not unfrequently from 2ft. to 3ft. in diameter, and grows to a height of from 40ft. to 50ft. Mr. T. R. Bartlett, in his exploration of the Gila, made extensive use of the fruit of this plant. He thus describes it: "The plant probably blooms late in May or early in June, and the fruit is matured in July and August. The flowers, borne on the summits of the branches, are 3in. in diameter, and about the same in length. The petals are stiff and curling, and of a cream-white colour; the stamens are yellow and very numerous. The fruit is about the size and shape of an egg, sometimes rather longer than the true egg shape, having a few small scales without spines. The colour of the fruit is green, tinged with red when fully ripe. It consists of an outer coat or skin filled with red pulp, inclosing numerous small black seeds. The fruit when mature bursts at the top, and exposes the pulp, which at this time is rather mawkish to the taste; but a few days' exposure to the sun dries it to about one-third its original bulk, and the whole mass drops out of the skin. In this state it has the consistency of the pulp of a dried fig, and the saccharine matter being concentrated by drying, it somewhat resembles that fruit in taste. The Pimo and other Indians collect the pulp and roll it into balls, in which state it probably keeps the whole year, as it was offered to our party which passed through in January. They also boil the pulp in water and evaporate it to the consistence of molasses, after which it is preserved in earthen jars."

Insects, as well as fruit and fruit products, contribute largely in some parts of the world to the subsistence of the natives.

Wild honey not unfrequently proves an acceptable addition to the explorer's larder. To obtain this the movements of wild bees should be carefully watched. Sometimes they may be seen high overhead flying in a direct and steady double stream; one throng bending its way heavily laden to the hive or colony, and the other departing on a fresh expedition. In some parts of the world—India, for example—the wild bees usually construct their combs either beneath the shelter afforded by the bifurcation of the large branches of a timber tree or the stems of the palm fronds as they shoot from the main trunk. In America, Africa, and some other countries they generally seek the protection afforded by a hollow and partially decayed tree trunk. To find the stores of a swarm of wild bees, cast your eye sharply overhead and note the general line of flight. Catch a bee and tie a thin filament of down, wild cotton, or white floss silk to his leg and let him fly; he will generally wing his flight homewards, and can be followed. If there is any uncertainty about the line of direction in which the bees fly, which may proceed from other swarms being in the neighbourhood, catch two bees at different points, plume them, and carefully note the point at which their line of flight joins. When you have to track a long bee flight, it is a good plan to dress a piece of bark with honey, in order that it may act as a lure to the bees. As they take in a store and fly away with it, note their flight, taking the line followed by the greatest number; advance your bark a couple of hundred yards in the line; take a fresh departure, and so on until the bee tree is discovered. The honey guide of Africa (*Cuculos indicator*) will, by his restlessness and efforts to attract attention, not unfrequently conduct the traveller to the bees' nest; but when following this feathered conductor be on the alert and keep both barrels of your rifle at full cock, as he sometimes brings you face to face with a creature far more formidable than a honey bee. To take possession of the honey few Europeans like to venture on the bold course followed by many natives, as from some cause or another, which we are utterly at a loss to explain, a naked black fellow will invade the stronghold of the bees and carry off the honeycomb in their very midst, with little or no preparation. When bees are in a hollow tree the best plan is to fell it with the axe, light a long line of damp brushwood to leeward, make as much smoke as you can, and during the panic caused by the general crash, split up the log, chop the bee hole large enough to be practicable, and get the honeycomb out as fast as you can into some convenient vessel.

In New Caledonia we find the large spider there found (*Aranea edulis*) greedily partaken of. It is simply roasted over the fire when required for use. There is another curious description of food made use of by the natives of the lake borders in the neighbourhood of Chalco and Texococo; this is made from the eggs of a species of boat fly (*Notonecta*) and two or three insects of similar habits. The insects deposit their eggs by myriads on the stalks of the reeds growing in and about the margin of the lakes. The natives, when going on an egg-hunting expedition, provide themselves with cloths and sticks. The reeds, when bent to the edge of the spread cloth, are beaten and shaken, when the eggs drop off into the sheet placed for their reception. After being spread on other sheets, and thoroughly dried in the sun, they are treated just as if they were grains of corn. Flour is made from them by grinding; this is regularly packed in suitable bags, marked as to weight, &c., and sold in the native markets.

In laying in the stores of an expedition about to start from any large city it is well to obtain, if possible, a good supply of compressed vegetables, as they can be made available when nature furnishes no green food. The space occupied by this useful preparation is so small that a very large quantity can be stowed away in a very small compass. It has been computed that 3ft. of cubic space will contain 16,000 full allowances. In pastoral countries there is usually little difficulty in obtaining milk; and in regions destitute of domesticated cattle the explorer can generally manage to get on without it. Goats yield a great deal of excellent milk, and trot along freely with animals on a march. When it is desirable to carry milk for any distance for the use of children or sick people, it may be preserved as follows : Take a tin canister, a bottle, or a large ox horn, with a bottom and mouth made in it; fill the vessel with milk; put it in the camp kettle, and let it boil steadily for three quarters of an hour. Now, if your vessel is a canister, solder down the cover; if a bottle or horn drive in the stopper and wax it down with melted beeswax. The milk will then keep well. In some countries preserved toad-stools are extensively made use of as an article of food; but here we must give the traveller a caution regarding the mushroom or *Agaricus* family when viewed in the light of aliment, as, strange to say, varieties which are found perfectly wholesome in one country are not so in another. Thus, for instance, we find some of the most poisonous toad-stools found in England (*A. virosus* and *A. muscarius*) amongst the number eaten with impunity in some parts of Tartary and Russia. There may be said to be only three kinds of true edible Agarici found in Great Britain. *A. campestris*, the common meadow and garden mushroom, remarkable for its pleasant odour and the colour of its gills; *A. pratensis*, or the fairy-ring mushroom (which is found growing in the green rings or circles in our grass lands, attributed by the superstitious to supernatural agency); and *A. Georgii* which in some respects resembles *A. campestris*, but has lighter coloured gills and less flavour. When driven by necessity to seek mushroom food, either in this country or out of it, bear the following rules in mind: Avoid every one you see with its cap or head thin in substance as compared to the thickness of the plates or gills—with the upright or stalk attached to one side of the crown—with the plates or gills all of the same length—yielding a juice like thin milk; and, if you find any with a sort of band composed of a substance like the webs of spiders surrounding the upright, have nothing to do with them. We have seen whole strings of dried *A. muscarius* suspended to dry from the rafters of Tartar huts. These you may eat safely in Tartary, but not out of it. Fish roe, like mushrooms, when intended for food, requires care in selection. The large barbel, found in many of the large rivers and lakes abroad, yield at times a very considerable quantity of roe or spawn. This we have known on several occasions to prove very unwholesome, if not absolutely poisonous. Herring spawn is collected on some coasts in vast quantities by the natives, who place long lines of bushes at low-water mark for the ova to collect on. Salmon roe is also eaten to a great extent by many Indian tribes. We have seen great quantities of sturgeon spawn collected for conversion into "caviare." To prepare the spawn large bags, with their ends sewn up, are made; a slit is then made in the side, just large enough to put the hand through; into this the roe and a good quantity of strong "bay salt" brine are introduced and the hole is then secured with a wooden skewer. When the brine has nearly all soaked out through the bag, a pair hand sticks are fastened to its ends; these are seized by two men and twisted round until the bag resembles a thick rope. Roe pickled and pressed in this way will keep a long time, and is very nutritious. The eggs of poultry or seafowl can in some countries be collected in considerable quantities and laid in as a store. Eggs boiled hard in a strong solution of salt keep well. They may also be preserved by first breaking them into boiling water, with a little salt dissolved in it, just as you would prepare poached eggs; boil for three or four minutes, and then take them out of the water; place them to drain, and when dry heat them on a thin iron sheet over the fire until deprived of moisture; they are then fit to pack away. To preserve native butter, first melt, then strain it through a cloth, boil it steadily in a camp kettle, skim off all the froth with a large shell, set in a stick, until no more rises; then pour it whilst hot into leather bags or earthen jars to settle. Do not omit the straining process, or you will find more hairs in your butter than are agreeable. A search among the rocks, pools, and over the ledges on the seacoast will generally repay the food hunter. Shell fish, small crustaceas, and in some localities edible seaweeds, may be found; both lavar weed and cara-green moss will help to furnish out a meal. When shooting seafowl to help to fill the larder do not pick them; open the skin across the vent, taking care not to cut through into the abdominal cavity; turn back the skin with your knife, cut off the projection or oil gland, known as the parson's nose, and then strip the skin forward, cutting off the legs at the knee-joints, wings at the pinions, and the head half way up the neck; now remove the entrails from your bird, wash it well in the sea, and if you have an onion or two for stuffing cut them up and put them in the bird, which may be sewn or skewered up, and then roasted. A sea bird makes a good grill if split down the back, pegged open with a stick, well peppered and salted, and then broiled over the embers. Captain Bligh found that by keeping seafowl in a hencoop and feeding them with grain that they become fat and of good flavour.

Snails form nutritious and wholesome food, as do the Unios and Adontas (popularly known as fresh-water mussels). These shells are to be found in most lakes and rivers. Fish of one kind or another will generally repay those who search for them.

CHAPTER XV.

FISH AND AMPHIBIOUS ANIMALS.

THE sea, estuaries, rivers, lakes, brooks, and ponds often yield an acceptable supply of food to the explorer, who usually adopts the most effective means of securing his prey, without troubling his head much as to whether the mode of capture is strictly sportsmanlike or not. The inhabitants of little known waters are not, as a rule, particularly shy in taking a bait; but some investigation will at times be needed to discover what description of fish are procurable before a successful plan for capturing them can be put in force. Sea fish are generally to be taken with small fish, pieces of fish, fish entrails; shellfish, such as mussels, clams, limpets, cockles, &c.; small strips of salt pork rind, the lug worms from the sand, and the rag worms from beneath stones and drift wood. Artificial baits, too, are often used with much advantage. The bowl of a common pewter spoon, mounted with a pair or three strong hooks, tied back to back, is an extremely killing lure for most predatory fish in both fresh and salt water. To mount and prepare one of these, it will be requisite to cut off the handle of the spoon close to the bowl. Drill a small hole just inside the point from which the stem has been taken off, and another at the small end. Loop through the hole at the large end a piece of strong fine line, about 4ft. long, and to this attach a swivel; then loop on 3ft. more line of the same description to the first swivel, and to the end of this attach a second swivel. A loop fastened to the end ring of this serves to attach the trace and spoon to the main line. Gut or gimp may be used, instead of ordinary line, when it is desirable to fish "fine." The hooks, either in the form of a "triangle" or simple pair, must be of size proportioned to the description of fish they are intended to catch; and, when securely attached to a 3-in. piece of very strong double gut, should be fastened to the hole in the small end of the spoon. When used with a rod the spoon is spun with, after the manner of any other spinning bait; but when used from a boat or canoe a lead of sufficient weight must be attached to the trace, in order to keep it some considerable distance below the surface, when, as the boat is urged onwards, its rapid revolutions and glittering, flickering play prove most fatally attractive. Many of the pearl-shell baits used by the South Sea Islanders are much the same in principle, only that the hooks they use are usually of shell, wood, or bone. Boneta and albecore are at times taken in considerable numbers by making use of a rude imitation of the flying fish; and the form of this contrivance (represented at Fig. 4 in the accompanying illustration) will show that one need not despair of catching fish because he has no fish hook. A

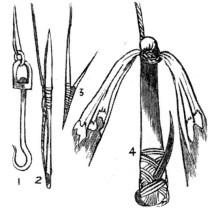

Makeshift hooks.

piece of oak or other hard wood, about 7in. long, is procured. This is cut slightly tapering towards the tail, like the body of a fish. About 1in. from the tail a hole is bored, and through this a strong sharp nail, such as carpenters use, is driven obliquely. A few turns of twine round the wood and nail serve to prevent shifting or splitting. The "head" end of the stick has a notch cut round it to fasten the line to, and secure a couple of strips of white rag in, so that the free ends may represent the wings or fins of the fish. This affair, when finished and attached to a strong line, is cast into the sea, and kept leaping from wave to wave, when it is greedily seized by the pursuing boneta or albecore, who discovers when too late that, instead of securing a rich and palatable flying fish, he has swallowed a nail instead. The Esquimaux make an excellent substitute for a fish hook by scraping a strip of whalebone round and fine, and then binding on a piece of hard, finely-pointed bone at an acute angle, with a strip of sinew or split ground willow, as shown at Fig. 3. A sail needle may be made to do duty for a hook by attaching it to the line, as shown at Fig. 2.

The albatross can be conveniently taken when following a ship at sea by the use of a baited sailmaker's hook. The point holds in the curved portion of the bird's beak, whilst the swivel at its looped end prevents the line from twisting and becoming entangled. Fig. 1, above, represents the manner in which this hook is formed.

The shanks of horse-nails make very good fish hooks. These, when filed down to the proper thickness, must be laid, one by one, in a narrow groove made in a piece of hard wood, and the barb struck up with a chisel or the sloped edge of a knife. One

Fish hooks.

smart, well-directed blow on the instrument usually effects this. The point is now to be filed up sharp, the wire gently heated in the fire, and twisted with pliers—or, in the absence of these, a split stick—into proper hook form, when it is to be subjected to the case-hardening process. (See " Case-hardening.") Hooks of any size may be made in this way, merely taking care to use good tough iron for the purpose.

Stout, large sized needles may be used straight for the capture of eels and some other kinds of fish. When so used, the line is firmly secured by waxed thread or silk to the centre of the needle, which is baited by drawing a large worm or other bait over both needle and line, which, when so prepared, lie in a line with each other. On the fish swallowing the bait and the line being drawn tight, the needle at once becomes fixed across the throat, and thus holds the captive until dragged to the shore. The needle is then easily withdrawn by pressing back one end with a bit of stick.

A very efficient but rough description of fish hook is made by the Laps from a piece of sheet brass. On this they first sketch the form of the intended hook, without the hole in its end for the reception of the line or point of the barb. They then, with a common knife and a file, proceed to cut away the metal until the general contour of the hook has been arrived at. The ring is then bored with the sharp end of the file, and the barb cut out and point finished. The bait is usually a small fish, which is run on the hook until its mouth holds the base of the ring; the point is brought out close to the tail, which is tied fast to the hook by two or three turns of strong thread. The line is usually as stout as common whipcord and is knotted to the ring, a lead sinker as large as a sparrow's egg attached about 4in. from the bait. A long birch pole is used for a

Lap fish hooks.

rod, and the most rapid runs below the cataracts fished in. A 4lb. or 5lb. trout or grayling is when hooked hauled bodily out at once, and cast over head, high and dry, in a manner calculated to astonish the fisherman whose experiences had been confined to British waters.

We strongly advise the traveller to include in his list of stores a liberal supply of fish hooks of various sizes, for both sea and river fish, together with some strong brass swivels, a few hanks of stout gut, and fishing lines for river and sea fishing. The former should be of the kind known as prepared salmon line, and the latter hemp or cotton sea line. The sea line should be all "barked" before use; any tanner will subject them to that process for a mere trifle. Lines so treated are infinitely more durable than those used in a raw state. It will sometimes happen that when separated from your stores, short of food, and with very few appliances about you, a catch of fish proves highly acceptable, and tackle of some kind has to be extemporised. We have had on many occasions to do this. Rods can be made very easily from tough sticks or bamboo canes. Fishing lines should never be put away wet, as they will soon decay, and become weak and

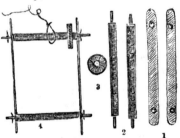

unreliable. The most portable and convenient form of hand reel we have ever used is made as follows: Two pieces of well-seasoned wood are cut flat, like stout rounded-ended paper knives. Two holes are burned or bored in each, as at 1 in the annexed illustration; then two round bars are cut with points and shoulders, as at 2. A cork bung is then fashioned and bored in the centre, as at 3; the hole in this admits one of the round bars, and serves to stick the points of the hooks in. No. 4 represents the frame or reel put together, and shows the position of the bung and the loop of the line. The ends or shoulder pieces of the round bars are secured by small pins driven through them. Reels of this description afford free ventilation to the lines coiled on them. They can be taken asunder in an instant, and will pack in a very small space.

We made an excellent outfit for fly-fishing in the Crimea as follows: We selected a set of straight tough dog-wood sticks from the fascines for the joints of our rod; these were feruled with tubes made from preserved-meat tins cut and soldered. The rings were made from|wire buttons with the thread coverings cut off; the line from hair pulled from the horses' tails, twisted or laid up by the aid of a set of quill sticks, the use of which will be described as our work proceeds. The winch was made from a large-sized cotton reel mounted on a frame of forage hoop iron, and the handle from a piece of a broken Russian ramrod. We were often asked by envious fellow campaigners where we had picked up such an excellent fly-rod and fittings. Our having made it from the limited means at our disposal was never even suspected by them.

The following adventure will serve to illustrate the manner in which a little ingenuity will often procure a dinner. Our little party A dinner extemporised. encamped one morning, after a very long fatiguing night march in Bengal, under the shelter of an immense banyan tree which grew on the banks of a deep reed-fringed lake. A small native village, situated at no great distance, had been pillaged and deserted some time before, and a miserable pariah dog or two wandering disconsolately about between the huts, and a few inquisitive-looking crows perched on the roofs, were the only living creatures to be discovered. No land of Canaan was this; commons of the very shortest kind stared us unpleasantly in the face. Still we had some bags of grain of the country, and a little "ghee" or native butter. An old corn mill, of the "quern" pattern before described, was foraged out from some forgotten nook or corner, and set to work preparing flour. A needle from the doctor's instrument case, when heated in the fire and bent to a proper form, made a very tolerable hook; a skein of his suture silk, a line; a bamboo cane, pulled from the roof of a hut, a rod; a bit of bark, with a stick through it made a float; a few shot split with a knife, sinkers; and some beetle larvæ, which were routed out of a decayed log, formed a very toothsome bait. The lake was clearly our larder, and to it we betook ourselves with as little delay as possible, the long cane over one shoulder, a double-barrelled gun over the other, and a leather bucket swung over the arm in lieu of a fishing creel. No Waltonian enticements in the shape of ground bait were needed here; the bait was hardly out of sight before the float vanished, and then, on the "haul devil, pull baker" principle, out our floundering victims came amongst the sedges and reeds. A shrill blast on our railway whistle not only brought one of the sable camp followers to carry the welcome capture to the cook, but roused six or eight large grey wild ducks, which had lain like so many water rails amongst the tall reeds, and sent them with outstretched necks and whistling wing wheeling round the lake, when by dropping under a hollow bank and keeping well down, we lulled suspicion, and the flock came cutting the air right overhead. Now is our time, and, pitching the heavy double well before them, we let drive in rapid succession the two charges of big shot. Three thumping ducks came like clods to the earth; a few feathers drift off on the wind far in the rear of the survivors, who do not linger on the wing; and little did we care where their flight might lead them —our hunter's dinner had been earned, and in less than two hours from its obtainment was duly cooked, eaten, and its merits discussed.

A very effective contrivance for taking caymans or alligators was made use of by Waterton's followers in British Guiana. The annexed illustration represents a modification of it. Two or more tough fire-hardened sticks are notched at the large end like the end of a tent peg, and barbed at the point like a straightened fish hook. The notched ends are bound fast with raw hide lashings to a stout rope, which has been served for about 6ft. or 7ft. with stout wire. When this contrivance is to be used, the barbed tines and rope are thickly wound round with the entrails of some animal, and then suspended just above the water by supporting the rope on an upright crutch, which is so adjusted as to give way on the bait being taken. When the whole mass has been pouched by the alligator, and the rope is hauled on, the tines open, catch across the gullet, and act as a hook. We have heard of alligators being destroyed by inclosing a canister of powder, with the wires of a galvanic battery attached to it, in the offal of any animal; this, when fitted with a line and float, was cast into the water, and, on a bite being perceived, the connection of the circuit was made, when the alligator was shattered by the force of the explosion which followed.

Alligators, to catch.

Alligators are incorrigible pests to the fisherman, waiting until the fish is securely hooked, and then carrying it off line and all. The following plan is the best we know to baffle the greedy marauders. Strong flexible sticks, like small fishing rods, are to be cut, taking care to select such as have lateral branches some distance down. One of these is to be cut to about 2in. from the main stem, and a notch made in its end for a button on the line to catch in, as shown in the illustration on p. 524. This, when freed by the biting of the fish, allows the rod to spring smartly up, and swing the fish high enough to be beyond the reach of the prowling pirate.

Alligators, to baffle.

A variety of fish may be taken in ponds and lakes by the use of inflated bladders, of which several can be used at once. They are thus prepared. The bladder, after being well filled with air by blowing into it through a quill or bit of cane, must have its neck securely tied up with twine, and to this fasten-

Liggers and trimmers.

ing a piece of stick the size of the little finger must be attached, so that it forms a sort of stem-like appendage to the bladder. The line, with the baited hook attached, is now to be knotted fast to the centre of the stem, and then wound on it just as thread is wound on a reel. The lower end of the stick or stem must now have

FISH SPRING.

a slit made in it. The line, when pulled into this, should have just a sufficient length to hang freely in the water. The bladder is now to be taken to the windward side of the pond or lake, and cast adrift. On the bait being seized by the fish, the line is jerked from the slit. The bladder, revolving on its own axis, allows the coil to unwind from the stem, and from its extreme buoyancy soon tires out the largest captive, whose position it serves to indicate to the fisherman, who gathers up his prizes at his leasure from his canoe or reed boat. Bundles of rushes, large corks, empty bottles, and a number of other things, can be used as substitutes for the bladders. Contrivances of this kind are commonly called "trimmers" or "liggers." Large turnips are often used by poachers to mount lines on for the capture of pike in preserves, as, unless rather experienced hands, the keepers do not suspect the dangerous destructive character of these floating roots.

On the Vaal River, in South Africa, we caught barbel up to 27lb. weight by thus using an empty powder canister; but it was anchored in mid stream by a stone not heavy enough to prevent a large fish from dragging it. This was left all night, and if in the morning it was missed from its place, a black boy was sent up or down to discover it. Our canoe was then launched, and the prize secured. If barbel were fished for, the hook was allowed nearly to reach the bottom; if otherwise, it was kept but a little below the surface. Frogs were generally used as bait. If the fisherman is not occupied as we were by other work, and can spare the time, or does not possess a canoe, he may make fast a sufficiently strong hauling line, and so bring his capture to the

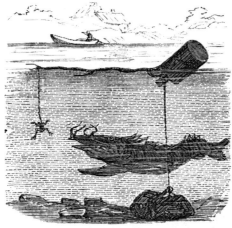

BARBEL LINE.

shore whenever he wishes. The method of arranging this contrivance is shown in the preceding illustration.

"The otter" is another contrivance with which great numbers of fish are often taken, and thus it is made: Procure a piece of very light strong wood, and from it fashion a board 22in. long, 9in. wide, and 2in. thick. Trim the ends to a sharp edge, and round them off in boat form. Then, on that portion which would correspond with the keel of a boat, fasten a long strip of lead of the same thickness as the board, and so adjust its weight that, when your board with its lead keel on is placed in water, about 1in. only of the upper edge appears above the surface. Two holes are then to be bored at each end, and through these two separate strings are to be passed, and the end so knotted as to prevent them from pulling through the holes. The loops thus formed must be just long enough to come in contact in the centre of the board. Four knots will thus be on one side of the board, and the loops the other. A 4in. piece of very strong, stiff brass wire must now be used to connect the two loops, and on this a stout ring must be placed so that it may travel forward and back on the wire. To this ring the main line on which the hooks are fastened is to be attached by a loop and swivel. To work the otter, it will be necessary to launch it in the water, and walk away along the bank until it runs out with the line, which is coiled on a wooden frame or reel and carried in the

Otters, to make.

hand. The otter travels backward or forward according to the direction in which the string or line is pulled, and that is in principle much like a paper kite, the loops performing the part of the " belly-band."

Ground lines often well repay the trouble bestowed on setting them. They are best made of strong, fine hempen line. A heavy Ground lines, to manage. rifle ball or other suitable weight must be fastened to one end, and a pointed peg to the other. A number of hooks on twisted horsehair traces are to be looped on, at equal distances apart, at the end nearest the sinker. The line when duly baited and pegged fast to the bank is to be taken on a long

fork-ended stick, so that the end has a swing of about 8ft. or 9ft. With this the baits and sinker can be cast a very long distance out ; and when it is requisite to take up the line to re-bait or take off fish, the fork is again made use of to draw it over, and thus keep the hooks clear of the bank. When using a night line, it is a good plan to fasten the shore end to a tough branch twisted in the form shown in the annexed illustration, as by the play it affords when the fish makes a sudden rush the line is saved from being broken.

Wide pools in rivers and the stretches of sea beach frequented by fish at the rising of the tide are conveniently fished by the use of a "traveller." This is simply a double line with one half only mounted Traveller, to make. with hooks. It is thus used : At dead low water a heavy stone is procured, and round it is placed a piece of strong cord, to the end of which is fastened a link of chain, the bow of an old key, a slice from the end of a marrow bone, or a common curtain ring ; and through this one end of the double line is passed, and brought back to the standing place of the fisherman. As the tide flows and approaches the shore, that half of the line without hooks is drawn in, which, of course, causes the drawing out of that half provided with them. A small cross stick knotted to the centre of the line prevents the first hook from passing through the ring and causing entanglements. As fish are caught, or the bait requires renewing, the line is hauled out and pulled back again to its old position without the trouble of casting. By this method a much larger space can be covered by the tackle than could be commanded by the ordinary method.

The harpoon arrow is at times a very effective means of securing fish, especially when they are basking on the surface of the water or among the weeds. The arrow-head is made from
a large-sized sea-fish hook, heated in the fire and *Harpoon arrow.*
straightened. This when cut to the right length is secured to the shaft of the arrow with waxed thread. A small loop is also fastened on, to attach the harpoon line by. This should be composed of very fine strong line ; and when about to be used it is coiled carefully away in a small wooden bowl or calabash. The bow should be rather short, and of considerable power. A little practice at floating corks or other light substances will soon serve to teach the method of discharging the harpoon and adjusting the line.

Basket traps of different forms of construction, are much used by Indians for the taking of fish. Some are simple in the extreme, and much resemble a lady's crinoline. With it the native *Basket* wades about in the wide shallow lakes, keeping the bell- *fish traps.* shaped mouth downwards, and frequently striking the bottom with it. When a fish happens to become inclosed, it immediately darts off and endeavours to escape ; but its head coming in contact with the side of the basket, the shock is at once felt by the wader, who thrusts his bare arm down through the small or upper opening of his contrivance, and so secures his victim, who, when a strip of vine or ground cane has been passed through his gills, is allowed to trail after his captor. On the Zambesi the women wade in the clear shallow water with a funnel-shaped basket, the smaller end of which is prolonged by a pole or handle. When a fish is seen, the wide lower end of the basket is at once darted down upon him, and he is captured at leisure.

Wicker cages of trumpet form, constructed much on the principle of the ordinary eel basket, appear common amongst the aborigines of nearly every part of the world. Some we once discovered when hunting in the Bheel country were of most elegant form, and woven entirely from the finely-split fibres of single bamboo joints, the knot being left entirely at one end, to form a ring through which the bait is introduced. By some tribes of North America Indians long rods are used to form these, just as we employ willows. Some traps made in this way are very large. Huge baskets are often suspended and secured beneath waterfalls in the run of the salmon, which on missing their leap fall back into these traps. When a sufficient number have been inclosed, the Indians, armed with short clubs, enter the baskets and despatch the ill-fated fish, which are then cast out on the rocks to the dusky ladies of the tribe, who are waiting to receive them. On the Zambesi, the Bō-tlét-lē River near Lake Ngami, and in North Australia, the natives are very ingenious in the construction of dams or weirs, and creels or trap baskets are skilfully placed at the outlets. Some of these are of stiff reeds or osiers; others, of rushes so flexible as to be merely a bag or net. Long semicircular pounds are, by the natives of some countries, constructed of sticks and twigs between high and low water marks. The fish, getting embayed within these, are left high and dry as the tide falls, and are gathered up before the return of the waves.

Dams and fishing weirs are built across streams by the inhabitants of most countries. At these the fish are either entrapped in hutches

Dams, weirs, and spears. furnished with bars, on the eel basket or sparrow-cage principle, shot with arrows, scooped up in hoop nets, or speared with hand spears of various forms. Some of these are perfectly simple in construction whilst others are remark-

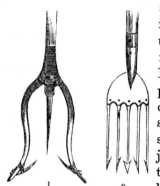

ably ingenious and curious. The annexed illustration (Fig. 1) represents one much used by the inhabitants of northern regions for the capture of the salmon. By the Esquimaux these implements are made principally of horn. The handles are of drift wood, neatly bound together with strips of tendon. The centre spikes are of sharpened bone, whilst the barbs in the jaws of the spear are usually made from two common iron nails, obtained by burning chance fragments of wreck. Fig. 2 represents the trout spear of the trappers. The tines are of steel, set in an iron head-piece.

Many of the natives of Africa and Australia are very skilful in the construction of dams and weirs. We have seen in some rivers the smaller channels effectually blocked against the passage of fish, which have at first been gently led—by very slight obstructions, and then forced by impassable barriers, narrowing like a funnel as they went on—to take the desired course, at the end of which creels or basket traps, sometimes of soft rushes, or in other cases of twigs or cane, have been set to receive them; while in sluggish waters, such as the Bō-tlét-lē River at Lake Ngami, long zigzag fences of reeds are set up, inclosing a considerable space, and narrowing gradually to several funnel-shaped outlets, at each of which one or more creels are set, belonging to various families. Openings are left in the lines for the ordinary passage of canoes; but when a " take" is to be made these are carefully closed, and the canoes in deep water, with a promiscuous medley of waders in the shallows, form an extended line, gradually closing in and driving the fish towards the traps. Most of the creels are pointed at the farther end, so that the fish wedging themselves in cannot escape, and in all the mouth is armed with a set of elastic reeds like the wires of a mouse-trap, allowing free ingress, but opposing any return. Fig. 1 shows a Zambesian creel of this class.

Fig. 2 is ingeniously made of a pole of bamboo, as before mentioned, which is carefully split in the direction of its fibre, in any number of thin rods or strips, care being taken to leave the last joint or internode intact, so that they all remain connected like branches springing from one root; they are then opened out, bent into the proper form, and either laced together with smaller cross pieces of cord or fine rattan, or the strips themselves are often inter-

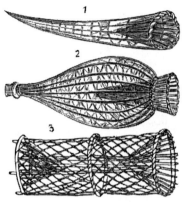

woven or plaited so as to form a most elaborate piece of artistic basket work. Fig. 3 is a creel or trap extemporised with three iron hoops, four poles to keep them at a proper distance apart, and sufficient spunyarn to form a net round them; there is an entrance at each end, and, as these are also formed of yarn, their ends must be kept in form and position by lines stretched tightly between them.

Fishing lines can be made of a variety of materials. Prepared seaweed of a particular description is extensively used by some of the coast Indians of North-West America. Wild hemp is also made use of by them; narrow strips of hide are in use for some kinds of fishing amongst the Esquimaux; whilst yucca, aloe, and pineapple fibres are made available in tropical countries. The inner bark of trees and the hair of animals, horses especially, are materials well adapted for the purpose. To twist this into traces for fastening hooks to, in the absence of silkworm gut, a common pocket knife can be conveniently used, as shown at Fig. 1 in the illustration on p. 530. When a hair line of many strands, of considerable length and free from knots, is required, recourse may be had to " quill sticks," as they are called (Fig. 2). These are made as follows : Three pieces of deal, or any other light wood, are to be cut to the size of

Fishing lines, to make.

common penholders, and to 4in. in length; one end of each is to be very slightly tapered, and have a half-inch piece of quill fitted to it like a "float cap." Supposing a twelve-hair line is wanted, that number of hairs from an "entire horse's" tail are knotted together at one end, and then all the free ends at the other are to be cut to uneven lengths; four are then placed in each quill, and a stick put in to hold them fast. The knotted end is then secured to a fixed point by a pin, and the

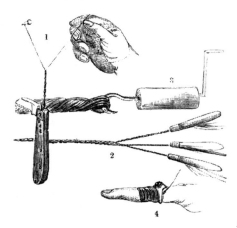

sticks laid side by side in the left hand. The right hand stick is now taken up by the forefinger and thumb of the right hand, the proper twist given to the united strands, and the stick passed over the other two, so that it may lay the third in the row. The next stick is now taken up, twisted, and passed on in the same way, drawing out the hairs from under the cap as the strand shortens until a hair is free of the cap, when another is inserted in its stead, taking care to keep all the lengths uneven. To taper the line, drop a hair from time to time until the line is long enough, when the protruding ends are nipped off. The line will then be fit for use. The above engraving will explain the arrangement of the sticks, quills, &c., and the way in which the horsehairs are inserted. Many descriptions of fibre admit of being twisted in the same manner. Fig. 3 shows the manner in which wires are twisted by the aid of a winch handle and hollow stick; Fig. 4, the way in which a ring can be taken from the finger by the aid of a bit of twisted line. The finger is bound above the ring, and the free end used to draw off the ring, like the worm of a screw.

Very strong serviceable lines can be made from almost any of the endless number of vegetable fibres to be obtained by soaking the stems of plants, or the inner bark of trees, and then "laying them up," as it it called, which is done by forming the number of strands intended for twisting by dividing a small hank of fibres equally, and then, after imparting the required degree of twist to the strand nearest to the right hand, passing it over the other to the extreme left, and so on, laying in fresh fibres as they are needed. The Indians often twist their lines on the thigh under the hand, as shown in the annexed illustration. The surplus twist may be taken out of all lines by fastening one end to a tree or other fixed point, and then, after having taken a turn round a piece of smooth stick, walking backwards until all the line has been passed under a moderate strain round the stick. In such countries as produce silk yielding caterpillars, excellent lines may be made from the cocoons, and then twisted into thread. "Silkworm gut" can also be obtained wherever silk-spinning worms are met with. Silkworm gut, To make it, a number of the caterpillars are to be col-   to make. lected just prior to their time of spinning. These are to be placed in a pot or other convenient vessel, containing a mixture of vinegar and

water in equal quantities ; they are then to be covered down and allowed to stand about twelve hours. A worm may be then taken out, opened, and tested as to its fitness for drawing. If, on pulling the yellowish green coils which will be found within it to their full extent and extreme length, they break from softness of texture, the worms must be allowed to remain in

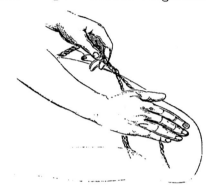

the vessel some time longer, temperature having much to do with the condition of the pickled insects. When the coils are found to be tough, and stand stretching fully out, one end of the strand must be placed in a slit made in the end of a thin board or sheet of bark prepared for the purpose. The strand is now to be drawn and evenly stretched to the other end of the board, in which corresponding slits have been made, when the extremity of the gut is secured in one of them. When all the worms have been thus treated, the stretching board is to be placed in the sun, in order that the gut may dry, which it usually will in about twelve hours. It will now be found that a considerable quantity of yellow substance will remain adhering to the gut. This must be removed, and in order to do so dissolve a piece of common soap about the size of a musket ball in a gallon of rain water. Place this with the gut in it in a boiler, and boil it for ten minutes, when the gut must be turned out on a cloth to drain. Before cooling each strand must be lightly and smartly drawn through a pledget of cotton held between the finger and thumb, which will at once strip off the yellow coating ; but great care must be taken not to press the softened strand hard enough to render it flat or curled. As fast as the strands are run through the cotton they must be replaced on the board, and again dried in the sun, after which they can be selected as to size, quality, length, &c., and packed up in hanks by twisting cotton or any other kind of thread round them.

Nets of various forms have been in general use from periods of the most remote antiquity, and, so far as we know, no aboriginal people have yet been discovered who were ignorant of their use. The material and form of construction are found to vary with the region in which they are had recourse to, and the character of prey sought to be captured. Perhaps the most primitive form is that of the common hoop or landing net, so generally used on our coasts for catching shrimps. A forked pole, a net bag, and a little twine, are all that is required to construct one of these of efficient pattern. The two sticks constituting the fork are bent round towards each other, the two ends overlapped, and then lashed together. The net bag is then fastened on. A great number of modifications of this description of net are used, some worked by hand, and others raised from the water by mechanical contrivances. The following illustration represents a fishing raft and lever net as used by the natives of Ceylon and some

Fishing nets.

FISHING RAFT WITH LEVER NETS.

other islands of the Eastern seas. Some of the Chinese fishermen construct engines much on the same principle; only, instead of raising the net by a rope and lever, a long plank is made use of. This runs along the centre of the fishing boat, and on it sits the fisherman waiting for the shoal to pass over the radius of his trap, when with a sudden backward movement he throws his whole weight on the extreme end of the balance-board on which he has been crouching, and thus raises the nets with a smart upward jerk. The trammel is another form of net of much value to the voyager and explorer. It simply consists of two nets—one coarse in the mesh, and the other comparatively fine—leaded at the bottom and corked at the top, and so moored with heavy stones that they may hang curtain-like in the water across the run of the stream or tide. The fish in their nocturnal wanderings dart against the first net, which is forced through the large meshes of the second forming a sort of purse in which the fish are secured. Many others become entangled by the twine of the meshes, which in their efforts to escape gets under the gill covers and so holds them fast. Incredible quantities of fish are at times taken in nets of this kind. They are especially valuable on account of the ease with which they can be set and taken up, two men being sufficient for the performance of either operation. When a promising spot has been selected, the first anchor stone is cast over, together with a buoy line and large cork. The foot line, net and cork line then follow, being cast evenly over by one man, whilst the other either rows or

sculls slowly ahead. When all the net has been thus allowed to run out, the other end is secured by an anchor stone and indicated by a float. The spoils are secured in two ways. One is to raise the first anchor stone by the buoy line, and then gather in the net fold after fold, with all it may contain, in the bottom of the boat. The other is to raise one of the stones, pass it over the boat and allow it to sink again to the bottom, thus leaving the foot line and leads in the hands of the boatmen, who proceed to draw the boat along by it, clearing the net of fish, weeds, or entanglements as they go, and allowing the net to sink again as they proceed, until the whole length has been overhauled and re-set.

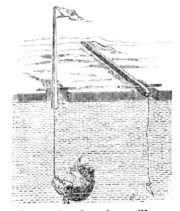

A trammel net may be used under the ice by cutting two holes through it at a convenient distance apart. A pole is then passed from one to the other, as shown in the above illustration. The net is suspended from a set of rings which run freely on the pole, and ropes are rove so as to haul the net forward or back to either of the holes, at which the fish are taken out. When clear, the net is set again. Great numbers of fish may at times be taken by fishing with the hook through holes made in the ice. A contrivance known as a "tip up" is often used. The illustration on p. 533 will serve to show the nature of the arrangement. A hole is "Tip-up," bored in a piece of flat stick; through this a cross-pin to make. is driven, leaving it long enough at the ends to rest across the hole in the ice. The line, hook, and bait are attached to one end of the flat stick, and a bit of coloured rag to the other. When the fish has taken the bait, the flag end of the stick tips up, and the little pendant flutters aloft and signals "fish caught

here." A number of tip-ups may be set at once, and are easily watched. When fishing with a common line at an ice hole it is well to rig up a little wigwam or break wind. Strips of cow's udder make excellent baits for use under the ice. Seals may be speared in their blow holes by waiting patiently over them. The form of the excavation in the ice made by the animal is shown in the annexed illustration; an examination of it will show that it is requisite that the harpoon or spear should be very carefully, yet powerfully, thrust down or the seal will probably escape.

The trunk or bow net is extremely useful for catching fish in comparatively narrow streams. These are long tunnel-shaped network bags, flared out widely at one end, and tapered to a pocket form at the other. Hoops of suitable size are made use of to keep the tube properly distended, and a mousetrap-like arrangement of meshes and twine prevents such fish as may enter from going back again. The purse end of the net is made to untie like a bag, and has a piece of rope and a stone fastened to it, so that the wide end of the net is always down stream and in the run of the fish, which is upwards. The larger description of nets, such as seines, drift nets, trawls, dredges, &c., do not strictly come within the province of this work; still all vessels, and even large boats proceeding on surveying or exploring expeditions, should be furnished with both lines and nets. A small ground seine,

Cornish pattern, and a light trammel, such as are made and sold by the French, will occupy but little space, and pay well for taking. A few pieces of spare net, and a good supply of twine, are matters by no means to be overlooked.

When engaged in fishing from a boat on rocky ground, it not unfrequently happens that the grapnel or creeper, if simply secured to the end of the painter, and lowered away, will, on an attempt to haul it up again being made, resist every effort and remain firmly fixed among the rocks. To prevent this pass the painter down the shank of the creeper, and take a turn with it over one of the claws just at the back of its bend; now bring your painter up the shank again, and with a piece of common twine tie it fast to the head ring, as shown in the accompanying illustration. Should the creeper get fast, the string will give way on being hauled on, causing the claws or  flukes to be upset, when they are at once set free, and the creeper can be weighed.

Crayfish and some other crustaceans can be taken readily in some situations by stretching pieces of net over hoops of casks, and then, when suspended by cords weighted with stones, and baited with any offal, these contrivances are lowered down to the haunts of the fish. Crayfish are met with in incredible numbers on some portions of the coast of South America and the adjacent islands, that of Juan Fernandez yielding them, as well as other fish, in vast numbers.

In Table Bay crawfish are caught in great numbers in baskets made of rough netting of rope yarn, stretched upon an iron hoop, and baited with bits of fish or offal (as in Fig. 1), 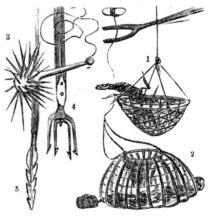 let down nearly to the bottom, and hauled up as soon as the "krief" is seen or felt tugging at the bait. The crawfish constitutes the food of a great proportion of the Malay or Mahometan population. Fig. 2 is a crab pot. Fig. 3 is a peculiar

Crustaceans, to catch.

Fishing implements, &c.

kind of mace, with spikes as long and as sharp as possible, used by the Malay lads in Table Bay. We do not at present remember the name by which it is locally known; but it is thrown in the manner of a lobstick into the midst of the shoals of small fish that frequent the bay, and seldom fails to secure one or more of them.

The haunts of fish will be found to vary considerably, particular species abounding in situations where other inhabitants of the same

Hints on the haunts of fish.

waters are but rarely met with; and, although no absolute set of rules can be laid down for the discovery of the fish of either rivers, lakes, or the sea, still there are conditions favourable to their congregation. Thus the mouths of streams discharging themselves into the sea are usually good fishing pitches, as are the waters covering reefs and beds of sunken rocks, which crop out and raise their crests above the ordinary sea bottom. On sand and gravel stretches flat fish of most kinds are to be successfully sought for; whilst a rugged, rock-strewed bottom, broken up into deep crevices and yawning weed-fringed gulfs, is a favourite resort of the larger crustacea. Nearly all sea fish are most disposed to feed as the tide rises. In tidal rivers many species of fish come down in force to the coming flood; whilst others run up from the sea—mullet, bass, and many others do this. Tributary streams and rivulets discharging themselves into lakes, rivers, or ponds, usually supply a considerable quantity of food suitable for fish, and form gravel beds on which spawn can be deposited. The mouths of such streams are much frequented by all kinds of fish. The deep well-like spots amongst the beds of water plants, and the still deeps beneath the shade of overhanging trees, are favourite spots with most of the soft mouthed fish, such as carp, and many others of similar habits and tastes.

In some localities the seeds and blossoms of certain plants overhanging the water, and occasionally falling in, act as a lure to

Hints on baits.

considerable numbers of fish. In North Australia the large globular fruit of the water pandanus yields seeds round which is a sweet, well-tasted farinaceous pulp, which may not only be eaten by the fish, but by the traveller as well. This substance is an excellent bait for both fish and water turtle. The latter are best caught by a short, strong hook, which need not be barbed, as it is not expected to pierce through, but only to catch in, the horny bill, and to bear the heavy back strain as the creature resists the attempt to heave him in. A short stiff pin bent into a hook will do for the small kinds, or a sail maker's hook for the larger. Ship-biscuit dust, cast by the handful into the water and allowed to sink gradually, will frequently attract large shoals of many kinds of fish.

The fish inhabiting ponds and water holes are at times destroyed by some tribes of Indians by the use of juices of the euphorbia, or the Indian milk bush. The juicy branches of either of these are crushed between stones until a sort of pulp has been formed. This is cast into the water, and soon poisons the fish, which float helplessly about, and are soon collected. A powder made from the *Cocculus Indicus,* when mixed with dough, is also used for this purpose. Small pellets of the paste are broken off and thrown to the fish, who soon become intoxicated, and swim round in a circle at the surface, when they are taken up with a small hand net, or a piece of cloth stretched on a forked stick. Lime is often made use of to destroy fish, but dire necessity can alone justify the use of either of these latter modes of fish capture, as they lead to wholesale and indiscrimate slaughter. Pools, wells, and water holes are often completely drained of their contents by thirsty men and equally thirsty cattle. Search should always be made under stones and in sly corners, for both fish and water tortoises, which will frequently repay the trouble of looking for. Some chains of ponds in Australia, and water holes in other countries contain enormous eels. These should be well looked after, as they make a most palatable and nutritious meal. The largest are to be taken with night lines, the lesser ones in the eel baskets, before described.

When mackerel fishing off the island of St. Helena, we provided ourselves with a good supply of biscuit dust, which, when sprinkled broadcast in the sea, brought immense numbers of the small-sized brilliant mackerel usually taken there round our boat. The bait we used was a narrow strip of very white pork rind. The hook was a very small one, and the tackle as fine as that usually used for trout fishing. There is no limit to the quantity to be thus taken when the fish are off the island. We on one occasion had great sport amongst the bream at the Cape de Verds by having recourse to the same expedient. We often attract numbers of sea fish to the neighbourhood of our boat or canoe by placing bran, biscuit dust, or pulverised crab shells, with all the fish offal we can collect, in a piece of old fishing net, and then lower the mass, with a good-sized stone in it, by a stout cord until within about 6ft. of the bottom and directly under the boat, when the cord is made fast. Bait with fish entrails or strips of fish, and use a lead sinker.

When about to fish the waters of little-known lands, it will at times be requisite to employ baits gathered about the immediate neighbourhood of the scene of operations, and the naturalist-sportsman will usually discover some kind suited to his purpose. Some species of ground nuts when roasted over the fire make a very attractive bait for some members of the carp family, amongst which is the " Roheta," or sacred carp of India.   Grasshoppers, locusts, mantis, beetles of various kinds, and the larvæ found feeding amongst the leaves or burrowing in the decayed logs, are all good in their way.   Small fish, frogs, and young birds are excellent for trolling with, or for baiting night lines.   Earthworms, slugs, snails, and pieces of meat from any animal or bird which may be shot, are all available.   Pieces of beef are in high repute as baits on many rivers of South America and amongst the Falkland group. Artificial flies of the rudest style of manufacture often prove as destructive as the most elaborately finished specimens.   Feathers and coloured fur or wool secured to a hook, in the shape of a rough hairy worm, form a very killing bait for both sea and river fish.   It is hard to say what these anomalous-looking contrivances are taken for.   Flies they in no way resemble.   Still they are greedily snapped at by the fish, and that is the main point after all.   The Indians of the lakes and Pacific coast of America make use of a very singular feather contrivance, with which they attract the fish within their reach. A shuttlecock-like affair is constructed and loosely attached to the end of a long rod or pole, which is thrust far down in the clear deep water.   The shuttlecock is then detached by a sudden jerk, and comes spinning and gyrating towards the surface.   The fish on seeing it make a rush and endeavour to effect a capture, but are transfixed by the ready spear of the Indian sportsman.

Fish spearing by the aid of fire has been practised in all parts of the world from the very earliest ages.   Canoes or boats of light draught of water may be used.   Pine knots, or any other resinous or fatty fuel, is usually made use of.   A species of grate or fire pan is fixed so as to project beyond the bow, and the spearman stands ready with his weapon—such as is represented at Fig. 2, page 528—and strikes the fish when he sees him.   Torches of reed or vegetable fibre bound together are often carried along the banks of rivers, or out on the wide sand shallows of certain seas, to effect the same object.   Great numbers of turbot and small sturgeon are speared in this manner by the Tartars inhabiting the Russian shores of the Black Sea.   Fig. 4, p. 535, is a set of grains for striking dolphins or small fish.   The smaller pair of prongs screw on and off, or turn on a pivot, so that they can be laid flat with the others, and stow in less room.   The line is made fast round the neck of the iron close by the barbs, and the end of the staff is heavily loaded with lead, so that when a fish is struck the weight turns up the points, and prevents any chance of its escape.   Along the shallow beach of Walvisch Bay we used frequently to wade with a harpoon, striking sting-rays, flat sharks,

Fish spearing.

fiddle or angel fish, or occasionally a more dainty sole in the shallow water. We found in striking the smaller fish that the great barb of the common harpoon would frequently either drive them out of its path with a superficial wound, or would cut through their sides without securing them ; and we therefore took as a substitute a soft iron Kafir assegai, or spear (Fig. 5, p. 535), and, fitting it into a bamboo shaft, cut several barbs in each of its edges with a fine tenon saw, which caused it to hold all it penetrated.

The few Hottentots who maintain themselves in the vicinity of the bay do so partly by assisting in the fishery or in discharging the cargoes of vessels, and also in a great measure by spearing sand sharks and sting-rays in the shallows of the lagoon. For this purpose they use either sticks pointed and hardened in the fire, or the sharp straight horns of the gemsbok (*Oryx capensis*) set like a pike-head upon a stick ; and, because they have to wade a great distance in the shallow waters, and it would be inconvenient to go ashore with every fish they kill, they set up a tripod of sticks near them, and on this they hang their prizes until they have accumulated enough to be worth carrying ashore to the women, whose task it is to clean and dry them for winter use.

The spear or javelin—launched from the hand, projected from a bow, dropped from a height above head, or in some cases fired from a gun, and yet secured to a line—seems to be known in some form or other to most nations, whether civilised or barbarous.

The elaborate combinations of mechanical skill and scientific knowledge supplied to our whalers, and intended in some cases to be fired from swivels or shoulder guns, sometimes to destroy the creature in whose body they are buried by their explosive power, and sometimes to paralyse the vital energies by chemical compounds or by powerful poisons, are beyond the province of this work, and we shall take, therefore, as our type of this species of weapon the harpoon in its most simple and, as we believe, it most generally effective form, as used by whalers in every ocean that has yet been traversed. The weapon itself consists of two parts, the iron and the shaft, so fitted as to remain firmly united till the blow is struck, and then, when the strain comes upon the line, to separate from each other, so that there may be no danger of the barb being torn from its hold by the weight or leverage of the staff when violently swayed by the struggles of the whale.

The head of the harpoon is triangular, or perhaps more nearly heart-shaped, the point representing the apex, and the barbs the two sides of the base. Its size is about 3½in. each way, or as large as the palm of a moderately-sized hand, and its thickness where it joins the shank nearly three-quarters of an inch, and from this it rounds off gradually, rather than tapers, to the edges.   There are various opinions as to the metal of which it should be made; same prefer iron so soft that the back of a sailor's jack knife will scrape it to an edge, somewhat rough and anything but permanent, but yet sufficiently keen to cut through the skin and blubber into the flesh of the whale; others say soft steel which may be sharpened by a file; and some insist on having it edged with steel of the finest quality, and ground and set to as fine an edge as a razor.   Each has its advantages.   The fine keen edge of the last will be more certain to enter, and will pierce more deeply, but, if once blunted, it cannot be so readily sharpened by the simple appliances at the command of the sailor.   It should be guarded from blunting by being kept in a leather sheath of such form that the edges cannot come in contact with any portion of the sheath, and at the same time cannot damage it by cutting the seams.   It is well partially to fill this sheath with grease or tallow, in which the edge of the harpoon may be embedded, and so kept perfectly secure from rust.

Of the material of the shank there can be but one opinion.   It should be of $\frac{1}{2}$-inch iron of the best possible quality, smooth, even, free from flaws, tough of fibre, and so pliable as to admit of being coiled round its own staff, uncoiled, and straightened again without breaking.   It should be from 20in. to 2ft. in length, and should terminate in a conical socket to receive the shaft.   The shaft should be of ash, hickory, or other strong and even-grained wood, 3in. in diameter, and generally about 5ft. long; though in one of full size it would be 6ft., and the iron part 3ft., making a total length of 9ft.   A lanyard about 3ft. in length, and of $2\frac{1}{2}$in. rope, is attached to the shank by simply taking two turns of it tightly round the iron, and then returning and seizing the end down upon itself.   The lanyard is "stopped" to the staff with spunyarn so tightly as to keep the point of the wood firmly pressed down into the iron socket under all ordinary circumstances, and in its farther end is spliced an eye, into which, when required for service, the line is hitched, the regular whale line being $2\frac{1}{2}$in. in circumference and 200 fathoms long; and when the whale is struck, and the line checked as the wounded animal darts away, the increased tension draws the staff from its socket, and it remains fast by the "stops" already mentioned to the lanyard, secure from being lost, and incapable by its leverage of loosening the hold of the barbed iron upon the flesh.

Many of the less frequented bays and harbours in our colonial possessions are frequented by whales and cetaceans of various kinds;

and we have seen exciting chases even within the limits of the anchorage in Table Bay. The peculiar construction of the whale boat is well known. She is generally from 25ft. to 30ft. in length, 6ft. or 7ft. in breadth, and 2½ft. or 3ft. deep, rising with a graceful sheer till the stem and stern would be from 4ft. to 5ft. high. She generally pulls five oars, the boat-steerer taking the bow, while the boat-header steers with a long oar or sweep, confined by a grummet to the stern-post. A tub, with the whale line coiled in it, is placed in the stern sheets; the harpoons, each properly sheathed, are hung in beckets in the bows, and near them are the lances. These are half-inch iron rods, 5ft. or 6ft. long, with one end flattened out to the shape and dimensions of the bowl of a large table-spoon, only that the narrow end is attached to the shank, while the broad one is forward, and is sharpened as a cutting edge. The other end of the iron has also a conical socket, in which a shaft of wood similar to that of the harpoon is fitted, making a weapon about 14ft. in length, to which is attached a lanyard of perhaps 20ft. to prevent its loss. The blades are also sheathed like those of the harpoons, not only to preserve their edge, but to prevent their accidentally cutting any of the crew; a broad-bladed knife is also kept handy in its sheath for the purpose of cutting the line should it be necessary.

Generally the whalers keep a man on watch upon some commanding height, or agree with the keeper of some signal station to hoist a private signal when a whale is in sight, and sometimes even to turn the advantage of his elevated position to account by signalising to the men in the boat the movements of the whale.

The end of the line is taken from its tub, led forward over the thwarts between the rowers, and bent on to the eye of the harpoon lanyard. As the boat approaches the fish the boat steerer lays in his oar and stands up, harpoon in hand, watching the most favourable moment to drive it with all his force, through skin and blubber, deep into the solid flesh, the boat sometimes actually touching the whale before the harpoon is launched. The oarsmen back the boat off as quickly as possible out of the reach of the sweeping tail, and the whale generally dives, then darts forward at full speed, sometimes below and sometimes at the surface of the water. The boat steerer now makes his way aft, and takes the steering oar, while the header goes forward and takes charge of the line. While the whale is strong it is allowed to run out, checked only by one turn round the bollard, while the boat is towed with almost alarming swiftness through the water; but as soon as he becomes weakened, or slackens his speed, another turn is taken, and the line checked as much as possible, or even hauled in, if it is safe to do so, water being freely used to keep the rope from burning when the line is running on the strain.

As soon as possible the boat is hauled close up to the whale, the long lances are thrust into his side, still further weakening him with wounds and loss of blood, until some vital organ is reached, and the condensed breath blown from his nostrils is crimsoned with his blood. Then the boat backs off till the death struggle is over, and the carcase of their mighty victim being taken in tow, is beached upon some convenient spot for cutting it up and trying down the blubber.

Of course the whale is towed head first, as in that position the involuntary action of the fins, moved by the ripple of the sea, helps the boatmen; while, were they to attempt to tow him by the tail, the same action would not only neutralise all their efforts, but would most probably tow them in the opposite direction.

Few sailing vessels bound upon long voyages go to sea without a harpoon, a dolphin grains, and a shark hook; and the former is called into requisition whenever a shoal of porpoises are seen keeping way with the vessel, ever and anon letting her pass them, and then darting ahead to recover their position in advance. A rope, generally the end of the fore bow line, passes through its own block at the bowsprit end, is then bent on to the lanyard of the grains. One of the crew goes out on the martingale guys, and, having made a line fast about waist high to the martingale or dolphin striker, to give him a little additional support, stands watching the movement of the porpoises beneath. At length one comes directly under him, keeps the same course as the ship, and perhaps, for a moment, the same speed. He launches the grains, and, if his aim has been true, the porpoise is transfixed. The men at the inner part of the bowline haul on, and raise the victim clear of the water. The harpooner seizes the end of a rope previously laid near him, and passing it round the harpoon line quickly ties in it a running bowline knot. This he passes over the head of the porpoise, and tightens it at the juncture of the body with the tail; and not till then does he consider his prize secure. Of course in this case the sport, the trial of skill, the opportunity for displaying quickness of eye and skill in the management of the weapon, is the chief inducement; yet the capture is not without its value. The flesh of the warm-blooded porpoise is in reality fresh meat, and is sold as such among the lower classes in many foreign ports. Several gallons of oil may be obtained from one of moderate size, and the skin furnishes good tough leather for making thongs, or covering any portion of the rigging that needs

HIPPOPOTAMUS TRAP.

serving with raw hide. Long narrow strips of the fish, when carefully cut out with a sharp knife, make a kind of porpoise biltong; this, when thoroughly aired by laying it in the sun, makes a fair kind of food. A kind of rissole is also made from the solid portion of the fish; these are cut into mincemeat, formed into balls of suitable size, and then fried. Steaks are also to be extemporised from the best cuts.

The hippopotamus harpoon of the Zambesi differs considerably from that just described. The iron is only 6in. or 8in. long, with a small barb at one end and a spike in the other, to stick loosely into a staff of light wood 2in. thick and about 5ft. long. The iron has a kind of knob or thickening in the centre to serve as a catch for the line, which is knotted round it. The line is about the thickness of a small lead line. It is very neatly and firmly twisted by hand from the fibres of plants and shrubs bordering the river, and is coiled tightly and evenly round the staff of the harpoon from end to end, so as to increase its thickness, and make it as large as can conveniently be grasped in the hand. The end of the line is securely stopped to the staff, which is secured from splitting by being bound round with small cord, with a kind of Turk's-head knot turned upon the end that receives the iron.

The hippopotami live in families or small herds of from half a dozen to twenty each, basking upon the sandbanks in the tropic sun, bathing in the depths and raising their clumsy-looking equine heads above the surface to look out, or taking nightly walks for miles into the country to crop the herbage of some favourite spot. Taking advantage of the prowling habits of the animal, the natives construct in his path or run, a harpoon trap or drop. The full-page illustration will serve to show the manner in which this contrivance is arranged. The instant the ground cord is detached from its hold by the advancing foot of the hippopotamus, the heavy beam holding the barbed iron drops with tremendous force, and fixes the spear-head deeply in the flesh beneath the tough skin of the victim, who rarely escapes with his life. A general hippopotamus hunt is not unfrequently undertaken, which is conducted as follows: The natives, having decided which herd they intend to attack, muster about half a dozen canoes, each carrying two men—a harpooner and a paddler; they close gradually and cautiously round the herd, and deliberately select their victim; closer and closer they draw in, till, as the semicircle of canoes narrows round them, the animals exhibit first curiosity and then alarm, and extreme caution is necessary to avoid so terrifying them as to make them break the line and take to flight instead of gazing at the advancing boats. When the animals dive, the canoes come on; when they rise or appear much alarmed, they stop, or approach but slowly. At length a fortunate harpooner finds himself near an animal; the hippopotamus dives, the canoe perhaps gains another length and is close upon him; when he again rises, the harpooner stands erect and next to naked, like a magnificent statue, in the bow, his upraised right hand grasping the harpoon, and his left a paddle, every muscle of his body as rigid and immovable as if he were in reality of bronze. The hippopotamus eyes him suspiciously; he seems to know that danger threatens him; but, like a cunning fencer, he waits the moment of the blow, and will not expose himself by prematurely attempting to avoid it. His instinct, however, is no match for the cunning of his enemies; the harpooner makes a feint of striking with the paddle; the animal starts aside to avoid the expected blow; and as he does so the hunter delivers the harpoon with all his force. The small barb penetrates the tough thick skin, and no power can draw it out again; the line uncoils; the light staff, sometime even with a bladder attached, floats behind to mark his track; the wounded animal finds no rest; other harpoons are delivered; and as he becomes wearied with exertion, pain, terror, and irritation, opportunities are found to thrust at him with broad-bladed spears until he sinks beneath his wounds and dies.

The harpoon of Lake Ngami and the Bō-tlét-lē River differs from that of the Zambesi, and more nearly resembles our own, except that, as iron is scarce and valuable, the head is still a mere spike, barbed at one end and pointed at the other, for insertion in a heavy beam of mimosa or kameel-doorn. The iron draws from the staff as soon as the barb pierces the thick hide, and the animal springs forward in its efforts to escape; but it is attached to the staff, not by a long line like the Zambesian, but by a short skein of twenty or thirty small cords of mimosa bark loosely twisted together, firmly seized or lashed to the iron at one end and to the staff at the other, and slightly stopped to it in the middle, still further to prevent any risk of fouling. The staff is of wood too heavy to float; a hole is bored in the upper end, and a short loop of strong rope woven or twisted into it, and to this loop is bent on the end of a stout rope of twisted palm leaves, which serves as the harpoon line, and is kept in the canoe, paid out or hauled in again like ours, and has beside the advantage of being so light that, even were the hunter to let go the end, it would float upon the surface, and eventually lead to the discovery of the animal. In consequence of this arrangement the chase of the hippopotamus nearly resembles that of the whale, differing chiefly in the fact that it is carried on in a fresh-water river or a shallow lake, instead of the sea. When hippopotamus hunting on Lake Ngami the canoes approach with the same caution as those on the Zambesi, until the harpooner finds an opportunity to strike ; then, when the wounded animal darts away, the canoe men hold on to the line, slacking it out when they are obliged, and gathering in as much as possible at every opportunity, and endeavouring to haul alongside as soon as they notice the first symptoms of fatigue, and use the formidable spear they carry for this especial service. This is, however, a task of difficulty and danger, for the irritated animal may turn and crush a tolerably large canoe in his tremendous jaws, and has been known, although not carnivorous, completely to sever the body of a man ; more frequently, however, as the natives dexterously avoid his charge, he champs the staff of the harpoon, and endeavours to bite through the skein which connects it with the iron in his side. Were this a single rope he would soon liberate himself, but the small cords become entangled between his teeth, and, though he may cut through a few of them, others are sure to remain strong enough to hold him. Many canoes join in the chase, annoy him on every side, bewilder and weary him, and drive him at length into shallow water, where the hunters, carrying the line ashore, catch a turn round the nearest tree, yielding a little if his strength appears yet sufficient to tear out the barb, but always gathering it in as the assailants, some in canoes and others wading in the shallows, drive him nearer and nearer to the shore, inflicting wound after wound with their broad-bladed spears, till, spouting blood from his nostrils like a whale in its mortal agony, he ceases to resist, and becomes the prize of the hunters.

The carcase of an animal like this is indeed a valuable acquisition ; the flesh of even a moderate-sized one is at least equal to that of three oxen, even after allowing for the wasteful manner in which wild flesh is generally consumed. His hide, 2in. in thickness on the neck and withers, is excellent as food, or profitable as an article of barter with the colonists, who make the great " agter zamboos," or whips for the after oxen of their waggon teams ; while the tusks, which will frequently weigh 6lb. or 7lb. each, and sometimes more, are, or used recently to be, worth about 18s. per pound in London, though, since the introduction of mineral compositions for dental purposes, we believe the value of the " Zeekoë " ivory has much declined.

The natives of Australia use spears of considerable length, varying from 10ft. to 12ft., and are also remarkable for the great distance to which they can throw them, attaining in some instances, we have been assured, to a distance of 270 yards, a range for which they are indebted to the use of the womera or throwing stick, an instrument that assumes different forms among various tribes, though its principle is the same in all. Those we had an opportunity of seeing in North Australia were rather narrow boards, 3in. wide, and little more than ½in. thick, so cut as to be conveniently grasped, and tapering from the handle till they were barely ¾in. wide at the point, on which a little reverted piece of bone about the size of a cock's spur was affixed with gum and lashings of vegetable fibre, and the point of this just fitted a corresponding indentation in the end of the spear shaft.

The womera is about 30in, in length, and is held in the right hand, the forefinger of which sometimes grasps the spear also, to steady it until the moment before it is thrown, while the left hand supports the centre of the shaft, prevents the weight from depressing the point, and steadies and directs the aim.

The advantage gained by the use of the womera will be readily understood by anyone who will remember that the length of stroke is an important element in estimating the power of a steam engine. Suppose the length of a man's arm, from collar-bone to fist, to be 3ft., and the chord of the arc through which he is able to swing his body in the act of throwing 4ft., we shall have 10ft. as the length of his stroke; and if we add to this double the length of the womera, or 5ft., we shall find that he is able to apply propelling force to the weapon while it is passing through 15ft. of space, an advantage which naturally exhibits its corresponding effect in the increase of range. The spear point is generally charred to harden it.

The boomerang, a weapon whose apparently mysterious property of coming back to the hand that has thrown it, must be now well understood in England. It is a thin blade of wood, curved either sabre-like in the segment of a circle, or bent in the centre at an obtuse angle. But its peculiar property is that, owing to a slight twist or change in the plane of surface on either side the centre, it becomes in reality a segment of one turn in the flange of a screw of exceedingly small pitch, and if its length were indefinitely increased it would assume the form of the spiral springs used in candle lamps, or in the well known toy of Jack-in-the-box; and supposing a small segment of one turn cut from the wire of such a spring and flattened, without altering either its circumferential or its spiral curve, we should have an exact representation of the boomerang. Little more need be said of this weapon, as no one but a native could ever hope to use it effectively.

A very simple form of harpoon is used for spearing turtle by some Australians we fell in with near the Goulburn Islands. They had evidently been alongside European ships, and it was probable from this source that they had acquired the essential part *Turtle spears.* of their harpoon—an iron spike about 6in. long, and pointed at both ends. To this was fastened a small line, which was also stopped to the staff—a light pole about 8ft. long—the remainder of the line being held loosely coiled in the hand. Sometimes the Australians use their paddle as a spear by having the blade end sharpened, barbed, and hardened.

CHAPTER XVI.

POISONED WEAPONS, ARROWS, SPEARS, &c.

THE arrows of the South African Bushmen are worthy of notice, not only for the ingenuity displayed in making formidable weapons from such apparently insignificant materials, but for the deadly poison with which in many cases they are imbued. A crooked stick, a few reeds, bits of bone, and the dorsal sinews of any antelope, are all the materials required in the formation of the weapons. The poisoning is sometimes a more elaborate affair. Among the southern tribes, some of whom still maintain an existence as hunters and occasional marauders on the borders of the colony, the juices of the bulbs of various species of amaryllis and hæmanthus, mixed sometimes with serpent poison, and aided by the adhesive acrid juice of the euphorbium, are boiled down in the hollow of a stone to the tough viscous consistency of birdlime, and sparingly smeared upon the arrow heads. Farther to the north the process is much more simple. The Bushmen of the Kalihari Desert, and the regions in the vicinity of Lake Ngami, use the entrails of a grub called 'kaa or ngwa, an almost inarticulate sound, which it is impossible to write so as to enable the English reader to pronounce it with anything like correctness. Both forms of spelling are attempts to indicate a click of the tongue against the teeth, followed by a slight nasal ringing, and ending in the broad sound of the vowel " a." The grub is of a creamy white, and is soft, with the exception of its head; and when full-sized seldom much exceeds three-quarters of an inch in length. It lives chiefly, perhaps almost exclusively, upon the leaf of a tree called " Maruru papeerie," which varies from the size of a small low-growing shrub to that of a moderately-sized tree, upwards of 20ft. high, or 12in or 14in. in thickness. It is covered with thorns, and its wood in the vicinity of Lake Ngami was soft and of a very even texture; but toward the Zambesi it seemed harder. When we first saw the grub it was feeding on these leaves, and we were rather puzzled by a loose ragged mantle or envelope of green matter, which seemed to be peeling off

(marginal note:) Poisoned arrows.

like a skin in process of being cast. It lay in loose rolls, mostly parallel to the muscular rings upon the body, and was gradually forced forward, so as to form a hood or shield above the head, where it dried and broke off as it accumulated, and was replaced by fresh matter. Our highest magnifying power was the microscope of a sextant; but this at length enabled us to decide that the green matter was merely excrement issuing not only in the usual manner, but also from pores ranged along the whole length of the body. As the grub attains its full size, this matter issues more sparingly, and is of a browner colour. The grub drops to the ground, buries itself to the depth of a couple of feet, and forms its cocoon of a thin shell of earth, cemented by glutinous juices around its body. This is quite hard enough to bear handling, even rather roughly, so long as it retains its perfect form, and we brought several specimens to England; but if it is once broken, the slightest touch is enough to complete its destruction.

In applying this poison to their arrows, the Bushmen collect a number of the cocoons, which they lay near them on a skin, a leaf, or on a sandal; they break one of these, and, taking out the grub, hold it between the thumb and forefinger, and squeeze the entrails, or rather the internal juices, in small drops upon the arrow head, which is then carefully laid upon any extemporised rest to dry in the sun, much as an artist lays his brushes on something that will keep the hair from contact with anything capable of giving or receiving damage from the colour with which they are charged. They take the greatest possible care not to let these juices come in contact with any cut or sore, or abrasion of the skin, for they would in such case produce the same excruciating agony that is inflicted upon a wounded animal ; and it is said that a man with a wound, however slight, so infected, would become a maniac, and would probably destroy himself in the extremity of his pain. It is, however, believed that fat rubbed plentifully on the wound, and taken internally in sufficient quantities, would prove an antidote ; but this is a medicine by no means likely to be always at hand among persons living a nomadic life, and but occasionally supplied with animal food, like the Bushman. Fortunately for them they possess another remedy, growing plentifully and naturally in most parts of their country. We were aware that they knew of this ; and a friend, who had been personally acquainted with the chief for a considerable time, had long attempted to induce him to reveal its name, but he was unwilling to do so, till in a conversation with another member of his tribe he mentioned its name; and our friend, who perfectly understood the Bechuana and some of the other native languages, asked him at the next opportunity if the remedy in question were not the "Kàla haétlwe," and thus surprised him into the confession that white men knew everything, and that further attempts at concealment were useless. The word kala signifies friend, but we are not aware of the meaning of the concluding syllables. The "Kàla haétlwe" is a small, soft-stemmed plant; the flower is yellow, star-shaped, and has five petals; the stamens are numerous, and the calyx is divided into two sepals. The root is something between a bulb and a tuber—rough and brown outside—and, when cut, is seen marked with concentric lines of light reddish brown and purple. The leaves are 2½in. in length, and ¼in. wide. The mid-rib of the leaf projects on the under surface, and forms a depression on the upper. There are, however, two other plants which bear the same name, and are used for the same purpose. One of them has a broader leaf and larger flower, and tastes like sorrel; and the third has a waved or wrinkled leaf. The root or bulb is chewed and laid on the wound, and is followed by plentiful applications of fat.

The natives use an arrow with a bone head dotted over with the ngwa or 'kaa poison, and loosely inserted into the shaft. This is a slender reed, seldom more than ⅜in. thick. It is bound with sinew at the end to keep the head from splitting it, and is also bound for the same purpose near the notch. In fastening this sinew no knots or hitches are used, but the end is frayed out very fine, chewed soft, and, while still soft, is firmly pressed down upon the rest, where its glutinous properties cause it firmly to adhere.

The preparation of the wourari poison is usually conducted by natives, from whom it is best obtained. This substance may be at times of service to the explorer. The sumpitans of the Dyaks and Borneans should also be noticed. Mr. Bates says that salt is put on the tongue of the coati as a restorative from the stupor induced by the wourari poison. We have often heard of poisoned bullets, and once saw an experiment tried. A hole was bored in a revolver bullet and filled with the juices of the 'kaa or ngwa—the Bushman's poison grub; this was fired into the rump of an ox; the animal showed little or no sign of acute pain, but seemed to be dull and stupefied for some hours. At length it seemed as if it were likely to recover, and, partly because the flesh was really wanted for food, and partly to end an experiment which seemed likely to lead to no useful result, the poor creature was shot dead. Probably the fire might have neutralised or destroyed the active principle of the poison.

We have heard of some native tribes who prepare arrow poison by first making a hollow nest in the liver of a dead animal. They then fill this with living centipedes, scorpions, tarantulas, and other poisonous creatures. These they irritate by striking the liver with a stick, when the virus of the united assemblage of venom bearers is poured out and at once absorbed by the liver, which is rubbed over the weapon to be treated. The Chinese plunge their arrows in a putrid carcase in order to poison them. The Malays keep their poison preparations strictly secret. Poisoned weapons retain their destructive qualities for years, and should therefore be handled with extreme caution.

The Bushman makes use of a simple and effectual method of sheathing his arrows, so as to render any accidents impossible. When not intended for use the point is reversed and enters the socket in the shaft.

They make use of a very ingenious expedient for tightening the bowstring. A small knob of hardened sinew is firmly lashed to one end of the bow, the string made of the dorsal sinews of the springbok or other antelope, slightly twisted, has a loop at one end, which is hitched on to the end of the bow; the other is brought up and passed between the knob and the wood, several turns are taken loosely round the latter. When required for use the bow is bent by holding it with the hand and knee, with the action represented in the beautiful statue of Cupid, and then with the other hand turning the coil of sinew around the end of the bow until the string is sufficiently tightened.

They also adopt a very simple plan of preserving an ostrich feather. The Bushmen, it may be after weeks or months of patient stalking, kills an ostrich. He knows the feathers are valuable, and that from a white trader he may obtain for them tobacco, clasp knives, tinder boxes, or other articles of value to himself, but he also knows that he must keep them clean and unbroken. He therefore inserts the quill first into a reed, and taps it on the ground till the whole feather has vanished, and he can carry it about in his quiver.

The simple apparatus by which the Bushmen obtain fire is shown at page 476. It consists of two sticks of moderately close-grained but not very hard wood. One of these, which may be called the fire stick, is somewhat thicker than the little finger, and may be of any length, generally about 1ft. or 18in., and in this small notches are cut with the point of an assegai, at about 1in. apart, for the reception of the end of the other, or the whirling stick. This is about the size and length of the ramrod of a common fowling piece, and both are carried in the quiver, with their arrows, sucking reeds, and rushes, for the manufacture of bracelets, &c.

A square of paper folded diagonally across, may be used as a "feather" for a blowpipe arrow. Wild cotton is also used to make the arrow fit the tube.

A cross-bow of peculiar construction is used by the Chinese; the action of the trigger is sufficiently simple to need no explanation, and the chief peculiarity consists in the fact of its having a kind of reservoir above the barrel, in which half a dozen or more arrows or bolts lie one upon the other; this is connected with the barrel only at the foremost end, the string passing beneath it, and the lowermost arrow resting on the string until the bow is bent; then the string being pulled back allows one arrow to drop into its place in the barrel, from which, of course, a sufficient length of the upper part has been cut away to admit of the arrow falling in. When the trigger is pulled, the string drives the lower arrow out from beneath the others; the next arrow then rests on the string, and, when that is again drawn back, drops like the first into the barrel; and so on until all are exhausted, and it becomes necessary to replenish the reservoir.

The pellet bow, the subject of the illustration below, is an instrument with which many tribes make excellent practice with small pellets

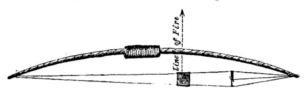

of hardened clay. For the inexperienced, a padded glove is necessary for the protection of the left thumb, and there is also a peculiar knack in so holding the bow that that arm shall be the merest trifle out of the line of flight of the pellet.

Many semi-barbarous nations are perfectly aware of the advantage to be gained by rifling their arrows, and this is done sometimes by having rather large barbs, and giving them a pitch or turn on opposite sides, or by putting on the feathers spirally.

In using the arrow for the capture of tortoises on the South American rivers, the archers like to shoot at such a distance that they may give their arrow a good elevation, and allow it to fall more perpendicularly on the back of the tortoise, as it has then a better chance of ⸱ penetrating the shell. It has no barb, as,if its broad point once pierces, there is not much fear of its being dragged out.

A thorn wreath is used by the Uganda and other nations in Central Africa, and is described by Captain Speke. The thorns all point to the centre, and yield just enough to allow an antelope or other animal to put his foot through, when their points are sure to enter the leg, and prevent its coming off. A log is made fast to it, heavy enough to impede the motions of the animal, but not sufficiently so to tear the wreath off from his leg and allow him to get away. Young branches of many kinds of mimosa in South Africa, which have thorns 5in. or 6in. long, would answer well for this. The ancient Romans and Greek made use of this contrivance in deer hunting.

We remember seeing, several years ago, the foot of a Vaal rheebok encumbered with a joint of the spine of a horse or ox. The poor creature had literally put its foot in it some time before, and had worn the painful appendage till the skin beneath was destroyed and the tendons weakened, which led to its being eventually caught.

Europeans are very rarely reduced to such a state of destitution as to be entirely without some tool or weapon of iron or steel, even if it is merely an old jack knife; yet such cases may, and sometimes do, happen. We remember read- *The manufacture of stone weapons.* ing with great interest the tale of two seamen who, during many weeks' sojourn on a small island, possessed absolutely nothing but one knife, which served them to cut up the sea birds they managed to catch, till at length this, having been wrapped in a bloody cloth and carefully stowed away in a crevice of the rocks, was found by some bird, dragged from its hiding place, and irrecoverably lost; then they with great labour beat out and ground down upon the rocks an old spike nail. Under such circumstances, the ability to produce a cutting edge from a flint or other pebble of sufficient hardness would have stood them in good stead; and even, if we remember how often edged tools are spared by using a piece of glass as a scraper, we shall be ready to acknowledge that a keen-edged fragment of flint, obsidian, or agate may advantageously be used in the same manner. Perhaps it may be thought absurd to give directions for the breaking of glass for this purpose, yet, simple as the matter seems, a hint may not be thrown away : Take the back of a knife, or the smooth straight edge of any piece of iron fixed with tolerable firmness for a moment, then, taking the piece of glass in both hands, rest its edge midway between them on the edge of the iron ; let the upper edge of the glass lean from you, and push it gently along the iron, so as slightly to indent the edge of the glass ; then, reversing its position so as to make it lean towards you, draw it smartly along the iron, and you will find it separated by a clean fracture directly across, forming a line more or less curved, and leaving one edge of the glass much sharper than the other. By a little practice, and by pressing a little more with one hand than the other, almost any curvature that the work to be done may require may be achieved.

In North Australia we had reason to believe that many of the tribes through whose country we passed were utterly ignorant of the use of iron. Fragments of jasper and other stones were found in several localities, where they had evidently been used for cutting up or skinning animals.

The following explanation of the progress of stone-implement making was given us by a fellow traveller, and our own examination of the fragments on the spot confirmed his statement :—The operator, squatting down before a block large and solid enough to be used as an anvil, selects a pebble as nearly oval as possible, and about the size of an ostrich egg or a cocoanut. One end of this he strikes on the large block, so as to detach a fragment, which leaves a flattened base; then, taking it vertically in his hands, he strikes the edge of this base upon the anvil, detaching in succession two ovate chips as nearly as possible equal in form and size; and this, if cleverly done, leaves a sharp and well-defined central rib, with a slightly hollowed facet on either side· The next blow should, if successful, split off another piece, small at the base, spreading slightly as it goes upwards, and finally tapering to a keen point, with the rib previously formed running truly along the centre; and this chip constitutes the spear head, which is fastened to the shaft with gum and lashings of bark or vegetable fibre. If this is well done, at least three chips must have been made in the production of one head ; but if, as is most likely, the failures greatly outnumber the successes, the proportion of chips must be greatly increased. Sometimes, when a pebble is found well suited for the work, facets are struck off on all sides, and spear heads are formed as long as the cleavage of the "core" remains sufficiently perfect. Some of these, when about half worked out, present so great a resemblance to a common beer glass with facets on it, that we hardly know how to convey a better idea of the peculiar form. The stone tomahawks discovered were generally of trap or greenstone. They were first chipped out into a long wedge-like form, and then with great labour ground up to a uniform rounded edge upon other stones, and with gum and lashings securely fixed into a branch, part of which is generally made to bend round them as a handle. Blacksmiths in this country secure their cold chisels much in the same manner.

CHAPTER XVII.

TRACKING, HUNTING, AND TRAPPING.

MOST readers of works on travel must be familiar with the apparently wonderful power possessed by savages of following the tracks of men or animals, and yet this is in reality only a habit of closely observing effects, and referring them to their natural causes. On the roads of a populous country, passengers, animals, and vehicles succeed each other so rapidly that no continuous spoor of any one of them remains; but it is otherwise in the desert and the wilderness. There it is impossible for man or beast to efface the track that he has made. In countries such as Kafirland, where cattle thefts are common, no evidence is required but the trace of the stolen animals entering a village, and the headman is considered responsible until he shows where the same track has gone out again. Kafirs have been known to sweep out the spoor with branches where they were about entering a river; but such a ruse, though it might prevent a farmer making oath to the exact place at which they crossed, would never actually deceive him, or prevent his finding the track on the other side.

Sometimes a number of men will tread in each other's footsteps, or they will walk backward for short distances, or will put on their shoes heel formost; but a practised eye will soon detect the deceit, and be aroused to double vigilance. It may be thought that a man passing barefooted over a hard rock would leave no trace; and yet the fine dust of the road he left, caked by perspiration, has been sufficient to betray him. Sometimes, in a grassy country, the track is best seen by looking out ahead, when it appears as a continuous line, showing where the grass has been turned, although it is almost invisible at a short distance; and this is sometimes the case on plains of coarse sand or shingle. Very frequently, though no actual footprint may remain, stones or pebbles will have been turned so as to lie with that side uppermost which has for a long time rested on the ground, and an eye accustomed to observation detects this at once, and will sometimes see, by the condition of the upturned side, whether it has been moved so recently as not yet to be perfectly dried. If a shower has fallen, it will at once be seen whether the tracks were made before the rain, during it, or afterwards; in the same manner the morning or evening dew upon the tracks will furnish a test of time, as will the grass withering, if crushed in the heat of the day or partially restored if bent while the dew was on it.

If there has been wind, it may be known whether the tracks were made during its continuance, by the position of the grass, or by the sand or dust drifted from it; and if the wind has changed at a remembered time it may be possible to tell exactly the point at which the track and change took place. If periodical or alternate winds blow, as, for instance, the land and sea breezes near the coast, it will be easy to tell during which of them the track was made.

Sleeping places, or halts for rest, for food, drink, or other purposes, should be carefully sought for. The condition of the grass cropped by an animal, and the fragments dropped from its mouth, must be examined, as also its dung, the comparative moisture or dryness of which is an unfailing index to the time that has elapsed since it was dropped.

If there are two or more tracks, and the time when one was made is known, that of the other may be inferred by looking sharply for any place where they cross, and ascertain which overlies the other. We have been followed for many miles at night by a lion, but though we knew by the panic spreading among the oxen that something was disturbing them, we were not aware of the fact till our Hottentot went back next morning and reported the track of " a great man lion, step for step upon our horse's spoor."

Not only can the period of time at which tracks are made be very closely estimated, but various circumstances connected with the track will not unfrequently afford most important information. As, for instance, where the tracks of naked feet are investigated, it will generally be found that savages in walking turn their toes in, whilst Europeans turn theirs out; if the track is left by shod men, the description of foot gear will often tell a tale. A mocassin print with the toes turned out would indicate that a white man in Indian gear had passed. The army pattern boot or shoe, the native sandal, worn by aborigines of some countries, the shooting boot, and the light buckskin shoe, all leave their well-marked and distinctive tracks. The particular manner in which a boot or shoe sole has been nailed or repaired will enable an experienced tracker to follow its print unerringly amongst fifty others; large or small, narrow or wide, the track will in almost all cases retain its individuality, except when cunning Europeans put on other men's boots for the purpose of crime.

The nature of a footprint will, by its comparative depth and form, show whether the person who made it carried a burden, or was in light marching order; or if in a hurry, or travelling leisurely; whether travelling willingly, or led as a captive; whether sober or intoxicated. In following horse tracks, the pace at which the animal or animals were going can be judged by the impressions left on the ground. A stray horse walking leisurely away, feeding as it goes, will usually leave an irregular but well marked track, causing but little disturbance of the surface of the ground; a sudden fright caused by the appearance of a wild animal or an attempt at capture will be shown by a scattering of earth, sand, or gravel, and probably by the casting out of the pellets which collect in the hollows of the feet. A frightened horse starting without a rider will usually leave the deep and disturbed tracks caused by ill-directed speed at the very commencement of the run, which will in most cases prove rather erratic. Had the same horse been galloped away by a rider, the man's track might be found, or if not, the first sixteen or twenty hoof strokes will vary in distance, depth, &c., from those farther on, where the animal had been caused to strike into his regular stride. Most hunters can identify the track of their own horse. A defect in either hoof, a broken shoe, and the mode of shoeing, are all matters to be well looked to. The horses of wild tribes, from not being shod, are to be distinguished from those belonging to Europeans, who either shoe all "round," or leave the hind feet bare and only shoe the fore hoofs. Mule tracks are not of the same form as those of the wider and rounder footed horse, and can be instantly recognised. Tracking on snow is usually followed with much greater rapidity than when prosecuted on the uncovered ground; still no little experience is needed to successfully follow up partly obliterated and wholly filled up footsteps. The impressions left in snow by different animals require some study before the inexperienced hunter can with certainty distinguish one from another. The art of tracking can no more be taught without the aid of the forest and the plain to demonstrate in, than can a skilful cricketer be made without allowing him to play the game. The hints which are here given are merely intended to form a sort of groundwork, on which the experienced hunter must himself build. In traversing the woods and wilds let nothing escape the eye, and never allow the slightest deviation from the common order of things to pass without close scrutiny and the application to the case of a system of inductive reasoning. No living creature acts voluntarily without aim; and, although at times much mystery surrounds the doings of some furred or feathered inhabitants of the wilderness, depend on it a little close scrutiny will not fail to show both plan and purpose in that which at first appeared an enigma. The stranger to the wilds would feel no little compassion for the poor crippled lapwing plover, who, crying plaintively, totters on and struggles to escape from the hunter, until at length, on a good space of ground being travelled over in fruitless pursuit, the cunning bird wheels away aloft with a mocking whistle, and shortly rejoins her brood of mouse-like little ones among the moss hags. We once saw a hyena near a camp take a piece of old dry goat's hide in his mouth and perform a number of strange and uncouth movements, as if either lame or drunk; a second, however, crouched, partly concealed by some euphorbium bushes and stones. Their object was to lure away our dogs whilst they themselves remained at a safe distance, when the pair would have made short work of some of them. In tracking wounded game look out sharply for even the most minute blood specks or flakes of foam, these, where found, are great helps over hard ground. Dead or dying animals are discovered in an incredibly short space of time by birds of prey; and when they are seen curling and wheeling over any particular spot you may rest assured that food is the attraction. Nothing requires greater care and circumspection than the approach of the hunter to the lurking place of any animal capable of doing mischief when suffering from the effects of a wound. We have known even antelopes to use their horns freely when unable to escape. No large beast of prey should be approached, although apparently dead, until all doubt on the subject is removed by either a shot through the head or a pelting with stones.

Within the colonies, of course, roads are regularly made, but in the wild country beyond, and less important places within the boundary, the so-called roads are merely foot or bridle paths or waggon tracks. We have heard a farmer say, "I have made a new road round the mountain to-day," and we understood by this merely that he had driven his waggon by a fresh route, leaving others to follow his track if they thought it better than the old one. Sometimes the waggon is not employed upon this work, but the track having been first carefully estimated by the eye a thorn tree is cut down, dragged along it by the oxen, and the road is made. A waggon track across the country seems practically indelible, the wheels are almost sure to crush the side of an ant-hill here and there, and even if the insects repair the damage the new work will always show. If it passes during the rains, the clay kneaded by the feet of the oxen, or furrowed by the wheels, is baked so hard by the succeeding hot weather that ordinary vegetation for many seasons will not efface the marks. If in the dry season grasses are crushed down, the stumps of a tuft will show for a long time the passage of the wheels. More especially is this the case if a fire sweeps over the plain immediately after, or if the waggon passes during or after a prairie fire. We have known a fellow traveller recognise in this manner the tracks his waggon had made seven years before. The lines of charred stumps crushed short down remaining to indicate the passage of the wheels, though all other impression had been obliterated by the rank annual growth of grass, fully 12ft. in height.

Often when waggons have passed for the first time across a grassy plain, the vegetation they have crushed down will be partially replaced or mingled with other kinds, either indigenous, and only waiting for this opportunity to spring up, or growing from undigested seeds from other localities deposited in the droppings of the oxen; or even it may be exactly the same vegetation simply rendered more luxuriant by being thus manured. We have seen a broad grassy plain looking like an immense corn field, but right across it the road was marked by a broad band of yellow flowers contrasting with the deep green around.

In many countries the prevailing winds leave unfailing indices of the direction of the points of the compass. Thus all the unsheltered trees on the road from Cape Town lean towards the north-west or north-north-west; and on the sub-tropical Points of the compass. plains of South Africa and Australia we frequently noticed that the continued winds from the south-east had laid the grass towards the opposite point. The rising or setting sun is a useful guide, so is the moon, and also the stars; but the traveller must acquire for himself the habit of observing where any of the heavenly bodies are likely to be at a given time, by day or night, and this while he is upon known paths, and not in actual need of them, and then his knowledge will serve him if by accident he should loose the road. If the declination is the same as the latitude of the place, the sun will be vertical at noon, and therefore of no service as a guide for nearly a quarter of an hour, but by extemporising a plumb line, and observing whether its shadow shortens or lengthens, it may soon be found whether the sun is east or west of the meridian. In using stars select, if possible, those that are far north or south, and as low as possible; or, if the pole be far above the horizon—as it must be in all places far removed from the equator—take the star that is nearest to it, and that consequently revolves with the least possible change of position. In the north the constellation of the Great Bear will serve, but if the pole star can be seen, it is, of course, the best—the two stars called the Pointers will guide the eye to it. And in the south, when the southern cross is vertical, either above or below the pole, it is due south; and this may be ascertained by trying when the two stars of the longer beam coincide with a plumbline, but at any time the position of the pole may be estimated by remembering that it is half-way between the lower star of the cross and the little Magellan cloud.

In travelling with a waggon from almost any civilised colony, it will generally be found that traders and hunters have penetrated so far, that for perhaps 1500 or 2000 miles there is nothing to be done but to let the waggon driver follow their tracks, which will generally be in every respect the best that could be selected, while the traveller hunts or explores on either side the path, or gains experience as to the slope a waggon can climb, descend, or travel on without capsizing; the average size of trees under the branches of which it can pass, and the density of the grove in which it can continue a gently meandering course between the trees without the absolute necessity of cutting a road, which, of course, he avoids if possible by making even a considerable *détour* for the labour is excessive and severe.

The professional hunters in South Africa, and indeed most of the amateurs who are ardent in the pursuit of game, not only follow the wild animals by day, but as they become shy, or few in number, lie

Hunting.   in wait for them at the waters at which they come to drink by night; for the less dangerous animals they merely throw up a circular wall of loose stones, 2ft. or 3ft. high, to hide the hunter from the view of the approaching animals; and not unfrequently an experienced hand will even watch in these for the lion, the rhinoceros, or the elephant, trusting for security to a quick eye and ear, and to skill in handling the two or three spare guns which are kept ready loaded within easy reach.

With the larger animals it is, however, more advisable to dig a pit about 10ft. long, 3ft. deep, and 30in. wide, and to roof in 5ft. or 6ft. to the central part of this with stout logs, that an elephant would not break were he to tread on them in passing over; the ends are left open, and a bank of earth is left in each, large enough for the hunter to sit upon, with nothing but his head showing above the edge of the "scherm." Generally two men lie in each pit, one watching whilst the other sleeps. The pit should be made in a spot carefully chosen to leeward of the path by which the elephants or other animals are likely to come, and great care must be taken to cover any signs of human work about it. The cut ends of the logs placed across it must especially be hidden, and if chips have been made in the vicinity, they ought to be removed, and everything reduced as nearly as possible to its natural appearance and condition. Most hunters carry a pick and one or two spades for this and similar purposes, but we have found a worn-out adze exceedingly handy and much liked by native servants. The work should be commenced early in the day, so that it may be finished by a little after noon, and left to recover its natural quiet, and the air to purify itself from the taint of man, for even though the elephant may not be so early on the watch, smaller animals, disregarded by the hunter, are sure to be about him, and any alarm among them will most assuredly spread itself, until a general sense

SOUTH AFRICAN "SCHERM," OR RIFLE PIT.

of danger pervades the wilderness; and if this extends to the keen senses of the elephants, they will not approach till they have assured themselves by every possible precaution that all is safe.

We have seen the path marked for a considerable distance by the serpentine track of the extended proboscis, sometimes actually touching the ground, and at others moving so closely in contact that the breathing would disturb the dust, as the leader of the herd deliberately tested the scent for every inch of the way. And the change of elephantine tactics since rifle pits were introduced sufficiently proves that what we call instinct is in reality an intelligence capable of receiving new ideas and guiding its possessors in meeting novel dangers. A few years since, when all the elephants had to fear was the pitfall of the Bushmen, with its sharpened stakes at the bottom, they would come fearlessly on, trusting to their leader, as with extended trunk as above mentioned, would literally feel the ground inch by inch, and, having once detected a frail deceitful covering that masked the pitfall, would toss aside the sticks and grass, and the whole herd would follow in contemptuous security along the very edge of the now undreaded snare. Far differently do they now act; if they but suspect the presence of a pit they will not approach until, by making a careful circuit far to leeward, they have assured themselves that their chief enemy man, and especially the white man, has not recently been near the water.

If a taint remains upon the air they act with the extremest caution; for hours they will remain motionless, waiting till their keen senses detect the recently tainted breeze, or their huge expanded ears catch the crackling of a twig or the slightest sound made by the incautious hunter. If their fears preponderate, they may not only refrain from drinking, but even desert the locality, and travel 50 or 100 miles during the night to another water, but thirst may overcome their prudence, and they may approach and enter the water ; the hunter must then, in perfect quietude, make himself acquainted with the individuals of the herd, selecting the male that carries the heaviest ivory, and wait patiently until he comes near enough and exposes his shoulder, then, aiming upwards, at the lower part of the after lobe of the huge ear, he reckons either to cripple the animal by breaking its shoulder bone, or to kill it by sending his bullet to the heart ; then, judging at once the effect of his shot, he catches up his spare gun and either fires again at the same elephant or selects another, and endeavours to cripple him also.

If two hunters are together, they can agree beforehand whether they shall fire together at the word given by one, or whether one man shall fire both guns. In the latter case at the word, or rather at the sign signifying " be ready," both set the hair trigger of their rifles, and the man who is to fire being assured that his comrade is prepared, waits a favourable moment and fires ; the other does not consciously pull the trigger, but, with his gun carefully aligned upon the vital part and his forefinger hardly touching the trigger, waits patiently till either the concussion of the air or the slight nervous action induced by the report of his friend's gun causes his finger to contract upon the trigger, and his gun is fired.

In elephant shooting it is always well that two men should be together, for though it is not probable, it is at the same time possible than an elephant may attack the scherm. An attack of this kind occurred to the brothers Green, the well-known African travellers and hunters; the enraged elephant began tearing off the beams and earth that roofed the scherm, and in a few moments more would have dragged forth his victim, when the brother fired with deliberate aim and killed the enraged animal. We have already said that the favourite place for the death shot is behind the lobe of the ear, just where it overlaps the shoulder, but if the shot can penetrate about 1ft. below any part of the spine it may cut the large blood vessels there; or if fired from behind, and striking about 1ft. below the insertion of the tail, it may pass through to the vital organs in the chest, and prove fatal.

If an elephant is walking or running in such a manner that the death spot (" dood plek ") behind the shoulder is exposed the shot should be delivered, if possible, so as to strike when his leg is thrown forward and the thinnest part of the skin is tightly stretched; if the leg is back-ward, the skin will hang in loose yielding folds, and the shot will most likely fail to enter. African hunters seldom fire at the head of an elephant unless he is charging and they must check him—he seldom fails to swerve from his course on receiving the bullet—but this rule is not infallible; we have hit an elephant as fairly as possible in the fore-head without effecting this.

Another rule is to run from the elephant the moment you have fired, and then look round to see if he is giving chase; if he is, you can increase your speed, if not, you can easily stop and get another shot; but if you wait for him to charge before you run you give him the chance of diminishing the distance very materially before you can get up the requisite speed. Wahlberg, the eminent Swedish naturalist, held that a man ought to stand like a rock, and the elephant would be sure to swerve before he reached him; sometimes the boldest course is the safest, but in his case at length it failed, the elephant came right on, and the career of the brave naturalist was closed for ever.

Sir Samuel Baker, although he has personally killed African elephants by shots in their head, found that he could by no means depend upon being able to do so, and remarks that the man who stands to meet the charge of an elephant by a shot in the head cannot feel the proper amount of confidence that his shot will be effective; indeed, the proba-bility is that it will decidedly fail to kill.

Captain Faulkner, who volunteered to accompany Mr. E. D. Young in his search for Dr. Livingstone, told us that he determined to prove experimentally whether an African elephant could be killed by a head shot, and that he, by walking close up to them, killed several in that manner. It must, however, be remembered that he travelled in a new district, where never white hunter had been before, and that the elephants there were ignorant of their danger, and not prepared to meet or avoid it like those frequenting the old hunting grounds.

In hunting the elephant the favourite shot of the hunter in India is that in the head; but in Africa this is seldom successful. It is related in the early history of Natal that a party of sailors (Lieut. Farewell's, we think), were challenged to go out with the Zulus to kill an elephant, chiefly with the desire that their defective weapons or want of skill would render them objects of ridicule to the natives. Neither their courage nor their good fortune, however, failed them; they formed front as the elephant came on, fired at the head, and killed it.

In Africa, as we have before stated, the " dood plek," or death spot, of all the animals of the chase is considered to be behind or in the shoulder; and in the case of the elephant this is marked by the posterior and lower edge of the ear, which is so large that in a male 10ft. 9in. high at the shoulder the ear measured 5ft. 3in. in depth and 3ft. 9in. from front to rear. The African elephant is much larger than the Indian, which does not average more than 10ft.; while one shot by a friend measured 11ft. 8in. at the shoulder, and probably between 12ft. and 13ft. at the highest part of the back. Mr. Petherick also tells of one 12ft. 4in. at the shoulder, with a pair of tusks weighing 140lb.; and of another of 15ft. at the shoulder, whose pair weighed 100lb.

In general a bull's tusk will weigh from 50lb. to 90lb., and a cow's not more than 30lb. The largest we have ever seen weighed 153lb. and the other 163lb.—100lb. Dutch being equal to 108lb. English.

The native methods of killing the elephant seem to alarm the survivors but little, and would probably never drive them from the country; but since the introduction of firearms they have gradually been forced so far towards the interior that it is difficult to believe that herds of them had once browsed on the slopes of Table Mountain. A few are left in the dense forests of the Kuysna, where they may not be shot without special permission, and some in the Addo and Sundays River Bush, between Algoa Bay and Grahamstown, and it will be long ere they are thoroughly extirpated from the country to the northward of Natal; but in the district of Lake Ngami they are becoming scarce, and the hunters from Walvisch Bay have to go yearly much farther to the northward, and follow them to new districts. Under these circumstances the waggons of the hunters have to be fitted out for the season's journey like ships for a long voyage. Groceries and meal must be purchased before starting. If bread should be desired, corn may in general be bought for beads, and flesh will be supplied by spare cattle, sheep, or goats, driven with the waggons, or by the hunter's rifle. Of working oxen there must be a sufficient number to replace those that die from the deadly sting of the tsetse, or other causes; that the stud should also be numerous enough to allow for the ravages of the horse sickness, for exhaustion, and for casualties in the field. A " salted " horse—*i.e.*, one that has recovered from the sickness, and is, therefore, supposed not to be liable to it again—is worth any money; but this depends much on the locality, for if a horse that has passed the ordeal in a district where the sickness is in a mild form be taken to one where it is more severe he is liable again to disease and death.

The Western negroes are very ingenious and clever in hunting elephants. The herds are watched for weeks, their haunts are ascertained, their paths carefully traced, and the possibility of catching them in, or driving them to, the thickest parts of the forest debated on; then the bush vines, monkey ropes, lianas, or bindweed are cut, so as not quite to fall, but to hang loosely from the branches. Some of the paths are blocked by trees felled across them; others are left open as entrances and others as escapes; and in these last, where two stout trees, with conveniently forked branches, narrow the pass between them, a heavy beam, pierced with several holes, into which spear-heads are inserted and tightly wedged, is raised, so as to hang as high as possible directly across the path; a stout rope at each end of the beam is looped over the short thick end of a pole, which rests on a forked branch, and of which the longer end is held down by another rope attached to a peg stuck into the ground at the foot of the tree, the immense leverage afforded by the longer arm making it easy for a small strain to keep it down, and the shorter end pointed up, so that the loop cannot slip off. When all is ready another line, about 16in. from the ground, is stretched from peg to peg across the path.

The forest is then surrounded, the elephants disturbed with loud noises, driven from their favourite haunts, and forced to take refuge in the thickest forest; and here men, previously stationed in the trees, cut the remaining bush vines, and let the tangle fall like a boarding netting among and around the elephants; spears and assegais are also hurled down on them at every opportunity. This is, however, a service of great danger, for the persecuted animal, with his far-reaching trunk, may seize the nearest hunter and dash him to jelly against a tree, or trample him to death. But while thus engaged, the others cut and let fall more tangle, and drive down upon him their broad-bladed spears until he sinks exhausted; while others that break away are driven with loud shouts into the openings that gradually narrow as the paths approach the beam falls (contrivances much like those used in the capture of the hippopotamus), where at the next step the elephant must trip the horizontal line, draw out or break the pegs, release the lever ends of the long triggers, and the next moment, with wounded body and disabled spine, lie writhing in the power of his enemies, some of whom, if they approach too closely his powerful wide-sweeping trunk, may yet, however, pay dearly for their victory.

The Cape farmer, whether English or Dutch, is seldom so spirit-less as not to enjoy the hunting of his own lions, and the avenging with his own hand the depredations on his cattle. With game more worthy of his lead, the Dutch colonist works more methodically; and though in general he exhibits but little of the dash and recklessness characteristic of the British officer, he lacks not courage or 'determination when occasion calls it forth.

When it becomes known that a lion has established himself in the vicinity, and his depredations become annoying to the cattle owners, his "spoor" or trail is taken up and followed as far as prudent towards his lair; this ascertained, a council is held as to the best means of dislodging him and bringing him into position to receive the fire of the hunters. If there be natural shelter so much the better; if not, the horses are fastened together in line, and held by the after riders or Hottentot servants, are backed down so near as to afford the marksman an opportunity of a fair shot; one or more, who can be implicitly relied on for certainty of aim and steadiness of hand in the moment of peril, are chosen to reserve their fire in case the rest should miss, and the others are told off to fire in regular order. The marksman, edging a little clear of the shelter of the horses, sits down, rests his elbows on his knees, and, grasping his ramrod as an additional support, takes as deliberate an aim as circumstances permit at the lion, aiming to hit him, if possible, in the breast; for it is seldom that the animal, when thus bearded in his den, refuses to face his foe, or expose his shoulders to the deadly missile. Possibly, he lies with head extended forward, so that it would be useless to fire at the sloping skull; and it is likely also that the fore-paws so cover the chest that there is the chance, by breaking one of them, of somewhat crippling, but at the same time provoking him to a headlong charge, in the fury of which even the loss of a fore-paw would be unheeded, and would diminish but little his power of doing mischief. Suppose him irritated by a painful wound, with a roar like thunder he bounds forward, and the inexperienced hands, if any such there be, discharge their guns as he comes on; but there are always some cool-headed fellows who know that within about five and twenty yards he will stop and gather his energies for a final spring. Deliberate as the Dutchman is, he knows when time is precious; the heavy roer is steadily aligned, and, if the aim be true, the monarch of the forest falls dead upon the spot, or, collecting his last energies, springs upon the horses. Now is the time for the reserve. At a glance he takes in the exigencies of the situation, he steps aside for a clear view, his bullet crushes through skull or shoulder, and the fierce animal falls helpless to the ground.

The restless steeds are brought again to quietude, the visitors

Lion hunting.

gather round the prostrate foe, examine the perforations, and adjudge to each the merit of his respective shot.

Of the method adopted by English hunters, so many illustrative anecdotes are before the public, that in our limited range it is difficult to select one that shall be new and, at the same time, sufficiently striking to arrest attention. Generally, if the country is tolerably open, two or three gentlemen, with their native servants, and perhaps a few dogs, to distract the attention of the lion, will ride up, and one, checking his horse as he passes, will fire from the saddle, starting forward if the lion springs, and trusting to his comrades to relieve him.

Among the Bushmen the lion is not much hunted; in fact, some of them seem to look upon him as an involuntary benefactor, who, after he has killed his prey, will certainly let some remain for them, and may, perhaps, be scared from his repast, so as to leave them all. Sometimes, perhaps, they venture, if annoyed by one of men-eating propensities, to track him to his lair, and as he lies in dreamy enjoyment after a full meal, to lodge a poisoned arrow in his side.

But in general they prefer to enlist the white man in their cause, partly because they know his weapon to be more instantaneously effective, and partly because they are sure he will reward them for showing him the sport. The feat of Gordon Cumming delivering a village from the persecution of a pair of man-eaters, by killing them both with two shots from his double-barrel gun was still talked of by the natives when we were in the Sovereignty. The general introduction of firearms among the half-castes and the native tribes has rendered obsolete many of their customs, and it is now rare even in Africa to see some of the weapons they formerly used; such, for instance, as the long spears with which the Kafirs attacked the hippopotamus or elephant. But a lion hunt on fair and open ground, by a tribe of savage warriors, must have been an exciting scene. With them the preparatory tracking up and gathering of information essential to the English hunter are needless; the haunts and habits of the lion they intend to hunt have long been too familiar to them. The hunters with their naked bodies fresh anointed, and lithe and well-turned limbs, assemble around with light assegais or javelins, and with long sticks tufted with black ostrich feathers. A few feints and false attacks are made, and the lion is drawn or driven from his covers to the open plain. Now the fight begins. Encircled by the active warriors the lion stands at bay, perplexed and baffled by their rapid change of place, and perhaps somewhat confused by shouts from every quarter. At length the irritated beast exposes himself to the attack. Some bold warrior rushes past and darts his assegai, escaping if he can, while the manœuvre is repeated by the next. Not all are thus successful. The wounded animal charges furiously, but in the moment of extreme peril the native strikes his plumed staff into the ground, and, before even the quick eye of the lion can detect the cheat, darts off in another direction, driving home, perhaps, another assegai as he passes. Many, perhaps, are wounded; but unless he does it at a stroke the lion has no time to kill, for he is already bristling like a porcupine with spears, and one moment of inaction would expose him to the fatal shower that would pour in upon him from every side. His fate sooner or later is sealed; whatever way he charges his foes elude him; wound after wound exhausts his strength, till, bleeding and helpless, he sinks upon the ground, and his skin and paws are borne in triumph to the chief; while the women of the kraal, with clapping of hands and extemporary songs of triumph, welcome and congratulate the victors.

The elephant, unfortunately for his love of ease and indolence, or perhaps rather quiet and undisturbed enjoyment, is endowed with many qualities which offer peculiar temptations to his apparently contemptible, yet in reality formidable, enemies. To savage tribes the amount of flesh acquired by the destruction of an elephant is a sufficient inducement for a small tribe to labour in digging pitfalls, or unite in the attempt to weary out and irritate him almost to death by numberless light javelins, till some one, bolder or more fortunate than the rest, is able to approach and drive the larger spear with skill and strength sufficient to give a deadly wound. To the ardent sportsman, who is also a clever artist and lover of nature, the mere act of engaging with and conquering single-handed this gigantic animal, affords an almost delirious excitement.

But beyond all other considerations, the paramount inducement to traders, hunters, and even to natives among whom white men have already penetrated, is that, like the greatest of marine animals, the whale, he carries about him that which may be made profitable in a commercial point of view, and thus repay the hunter for the labour of destroying him. Of course, in the case of the elephant this inducement is the ivory, with which in Africa both males and females are provided; while in India the hunters find the females without tusks, and the males so frequently so that profit from this source rarely enters into the sportsman's calculations, nevertheless, great numbers are annually killed in Ceylon and other parts of the Indian Empire. It requires a knowledge of the immense damage a single elephant is capable of doing among the cane or grain fields of the natives to induce those who cannot enter into the enthusiasm of the sportsman, to return a verdict of justifiable elephanticide.

Tigers, panthers, leopards, pumas, &c., are taken in various ways. The former animals, as we have before stated, are captured in large cage traps fitted with drop doors and trigger levers, which are thrown out of gear when the animal seizes a bait suspended from them. . The Malays are very skilful in setting traps of this description. The systems adopted in shooting the large animals of prey just mentioned in the jungles of the far East are too well known to need description here. They may be said mainly to consist in shooting from a howdah placed on an elephant's back; shooting on foot, aided by beaters; watching a live or dead bait from a "meechaum" or scaffolding erected in a tree; or shooting at night from the rifle pit, after the manner already described. To hunt antelopes by the aid of tamed leopards, or to take deer with the bearcoot, or hunting eagle, it is necessary to secure the services of a regular staff of native hunters, keepers, and trackers—in fact a retinue which few mere travellers could support. Sword hunting, as practised by the inhabitants of the Abyssinian borders, is a pursuit requiring more than ordinary skill and adroitness—in short, almost a lifetime may be passed in fruitlessly endeavouring to successfully imitate the feats of the "Aggageers." There are, however, many weapons and hunting appliances used in wild countries which the traveller will do well to familiarise himself with. The spear, the bow and arrow, the sling, the lasso, the bolas, the sumpitan or blow pipe, and the club, may, as makeshifts, stand him in good stead. A knowledge of the use of the boomerang would be extremely valuable; but we have never known a white man who could throw it even passably well. The spear, as cast from the womera, or throwing stick, is another weapon marvellously accurate, long-ranged, and deadly in the hands of the black fellow, but resolves itself into a mere sharp pointed stick when the European attempts to use it. It is much the same with the Kafir assegai. Very few Englishmen learn to use it well, whilst the natives hurl it with astonishing force and precision. There are calls, too, which are successfully used by the natives of many countries for attracting game to the lurking place of the sportsman. The birch bark calling trumpet of the American and Canadian moose hunter is an example of these; but practice alone will enable the traveller to use it successfully.

The natives of South Africa excel in the construction of pitfalls, and there is scarcely a tribe, with the exception of the   Pitfalls. pastoral Kafirs on the frontier, or the half-castes, who possess firearms, that does not more or less supply itself with wild flesh in this manner.

The tools used in sinking pitfalls resemble chisels, perhaps a hand breadth broad, and 8in. or 1ft. long; these are set in stout handles 6ft. or more in length, and used in a manner that may be understood after a glance at the beautiful group of Michael overthrowing Satan. The pits will be 10ft. or 12ft. long, 2ft. or 3ft. wide, and more than 8ft. deep, but they taper wedge-like towards the bottom, which is only a few inches wide, the intention being that an antelope or other animal shall jam his body immovably between the sides before he can touch the bottom with his feet. About the centre the pit is crossed by a wall of the hard soil, reaching about half-way to the top, and left standing for the purpose of catching any animal that, having once fallen in, is able to spring forward, and of holding him helplessly suspended by the belly.

The top is carefully covered with small sticks, over which reeds or grass are laid, and earth dusted over the whole as naturally as possible. A little water is then sprinkled over all to equalise the surface. Of course this has to be very artistically done to deceive the timid game; therefore there is no wonder that a mounted hunter, or even a traveller on foot, should occasionally fall in. Sometimes, to insure the capture of the animal, a small hole, also carefully covered, is made just before one end of the pit, and the creature stumbling in this leaps forward and precipitates itself into the true snare.

We have on three occasions fallen into such pits (unprovided with the little hole last mentioned, which might have proved a warning to a man, who, if possible, would instinctively step forward), and once had considerable difficulty in getting out, because, owing to the wedge-shaped form, our hips were tightly jammed between the sides, while our feet could not reach the bottom; but, by vigorously sticking our elbows into the sides above, we at length extricated our lower extremities.

A fellow hunter had a more dangerous adventure than this; for the one that he fell into had three stakes, that would certainly have impaled an antelope, fixed upright in it; but fortunately a man goes straight down feet foremost, and seldom or never falls lengthwise. These pits for single animals, however, are but petty affairs compared with the extensive hopo or tellekello fences, built for the purpose of inclosing large herds of game, that are either driven during the day by extended lines of men from all quarters into the wide entrance, or suddenly find themselves forced into it when they come by night to drink at the water; in either case the space between the fences narrows rapidly, funnelwise, the fences themselves being made stronger in proportion to the diminution of the space between them, until this becomes little more than a narrow lane, and the fences assume the proportions of palisades, high and strong enough to prevent the escape even of the large animals that crowd into it. At the end of this passage is a low fence, partially concealing from view the yawning pit beyond, the apparent size of which is diminished by beams and poles so laid as to cover a considerable portion of each side, and thus rendering it impossible for any animal attempting to spring out to make his escape.

We have often seen these fences; but the Bushmen will very seldom get up a drive when white hunters are in the vicinity, preferring, very naturally, to eat game which, with very little trouble to themselves, has been shot by the European or the colonist, rather than to assemble their tribe and be on watch all night at the tellekello.

On occasions such as we have referred to, the widest opening of the fences is kept as near as possible to the pool or river where the wild game comes to drink, without encroaching so far as to interfere with their free access to the water. The Bushmen dig holes outside the fence, make in them large fires of hard wood, and cover the still glowing embers with dry earth, which absorbs a great amount of heat, and gives it out gradually during the night to those who come to sleep, or at least to lie down and watch beside it. In addition to this, they fashion a number of torches of some dry light wood, preferring that of a dead baobab; and at night, when the herds come down to quench their thirst, they draw their cordon round in rear of them, light their torches, and, waving them in the air, rush forward with wild gesti-culations and loud outcries. Sometimes the larger animals, such as the black rhinoceros, or others, instead of submitting to be driven, will endeavour to break through the fence, but the active Bushmen swarm along the outside, and meet every attempt by waving their blazing torches, or throwing them in the faces of the animals; at length the herd crowded together comes to the narrowing neck of the funnel. The height and strength of the palisade forbids all hope of escape; the natives, wild with delight, are shouting and pressing on their rear, they rush thundering on to the narrowest part, the slight fence which hides the pit from view is easily leaped, others follow, blindly pushed on by the crowd in the rear, until at length the pit is filled with perhaps one or two hundred animals, writhing, struggling, and suffocating, and moreover bruised and stunned by the hoofs of those which rush madly on, seeking to escape over them. The Bushmen now assemble near the pass, and stab with their assegais as many as they can, but these are few in comparison; and when the pit is once filled, the escape of the majority of those that remain is tolerably certain.

The most serious impediment which stands in the African hunter's road to success is the tsetse fly, which haunts the forests and the banks of streams in many parts of southern and subtropical Africa. Horses and dogs are also liable to be fatally affected; but men, mules, and donkeys, as well as sheep or goats and wild animals, are not injured. When cattle are "bitten" by "the fly," as this dreaded pest is called, *par eminence*, they begin to lose condition, the coat ceases to be sleek and glossy, and in a period, proportioned to the severity or number of the bites, generally from twelve hours to a fortnight or three weeks, or even a month, the animals die.

Tsetse fly.

If the tsetse infested district is not large, it is much better to make the circuit of it, or to pass through it in the night. We have seen a horse thus taken through the belt on the shores of the Zambesi as a present for Tekalatu. He would be towed by a canoe across the broad river, and hurried on to a place of security before the morning. The fly, as may be supposed from these remarks, is very local. One of the Transvaal republicans told us that a mimosa tree, with bright yellow bark (probably the sweet gum), was one tolerably certain indication of its habitat; but it is best to inquire of the natives what are its particular limits, and especially to learn whether the tribes in advance keep cattle or dogs, and if they do not, to ask why so. Have they possessed cattle, and been plundered of them, or can they not keep them because of the proximity of the fly? If this is the case, the oxen must be kept beyond the bounds; but mules or donkeys may be used with safety.

The boundaries of this pest are well defined; and we have heard the Dutch colonist speak of "De Kant van de Vleigen," or the "edge of the flies," with as much precision as a municipal officer in defining the boundary of his parish. Frequently one side of a waggon road will be spoken of as infested, while the other is safe; and sometimes the hunters speak of riding up to the "edge of the fly," and going in on foot to shoot game. Whether the rather more than half-reasoning elephants know that the fly kills horses or not, we cannot undertake to say; but they certainly connect the idea of comparative security with the "fly country," just as an Australian horse knows that the stockyard is the only place in which he is never flogged, and retreats to it whenever he hears the cracking of the dreaded stock whip.

That the fly is local there can be no doubt; and the only chance, so far as we have heard, of this pest being found out of its proper district, is that a herd of buffaloes or other game may be chased to some distance, and carry the fly with them; but if they remain long the insect will leave them and return to its proper range.

The fly, a little more than half an inch long and more slender in proportion than a common house fly (the illustrations given below, Figs. 1 and 2, give the true size and an enlarged view of the insect), hovers steadily over the devoted cattle with a peculiarly rapid motion of the wings. To speak either of its bite or its sting would convey an erroneous idea; it seems to pierce the skin, and dilute the blood it wishes to drink by the injection of a fluid, just as the mosquito does; the surplus liquid mingles fatally with the blood. We believe neither goats nor sheep are injured by the virus. The piercing apparatus must be of considerable length, as the insect will penetrate a pilot coat and full suit of under-clothing; the puncture leaves no

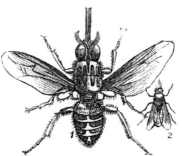

subsequent pain like that of a mosquito, but is startling enough at the moment. The description of the fly may be thus summed up: The abdomen is marked with transverse stripes of yellow and dark chesnut, fading towards the back, and imparting the appearance of a longitudinal stripe of yellow down the centre of the back. The belly is a livid white; dusky glassy-brown wings folding over each other; eyes, brownish purple. It has six long legs. Its proboscis is about one-sixth of an inch long. It has tufts of hair on the body, which are dingiest about the mouth, on the back, and near the tail. It is keen of smell, quick of sight, and its flight is rapid and straight.

It is said that a peculiar breed of dogs, known as the "Moscoba," or Bàylyè dogs, remain exempt from injury, from having from time immemorial been reared in the fly district, and escaped a cow-milk diet *as the natives say*. It has no injurious effect upon game whatsoever.

The Cape Colony, the Free State, Kafirland, Natal, and most of the Transvaal Republic, as well as Namaqua and Damara land—the Kalihari Desert and the desert between the Bō-tlét-lē and Zambesi rivers—may be regarded (speaking generally) as clear of the fly, but the hunters on the various tributaries of the Limpopo suffered very heavy losses; and Mr. Coqui and party, who travelled from Origstadt to Delagoa Bay, lost all their cattle, we believe, from the tsetse, not far from the last-named place. When travellers first began to find their way to Lake Ngami many, for want of local knowledge, lost sometimes half their cattle. At Tette, and the other Portuguese possessions on the Zambesi, very few cattle and no horses are kept, but Senhor Pascol possessed a few donkeys. The natives in the vicinity have no cattle. We do not remember that we saw the tsetse there, but possibly this may have originally prevented their introduction, and the fly may have died out in places where the wild animals have been destroyed. When we travelled from Walwisch Bay, we fell in with no fly all the way to Lake Ngami, but turning thence to the northwest we feared to push too far to the northward, as the banks of the Teoughe, and probably the woods some distance from it, were known to be infested.

From the lake eastward we travelled in comparative safety along the Bō-tlét-lē River, and turned north over the elevated riverless plain towards the Zambesi. In the valley of that great river system we first felt ourselves in actual proximity to the fly. At Dākā, the cattle grazed in safety; but a servant, who was sent to outspan, ten or twenty miles to the west, had to return because he had got into an infested locality; and when we started with one waggon only to visit the Falls, we found that patches of mimosa and other forests on the banks of the Matietsie River were also frequented by these little pests.

We tried to save the oxen by rushing them past whenever the edge of the bush approached too closely to the river; but an accidental delay exposed the cattle to the fatal influence of the tsetse. At the Anyati, or Buffalo River, we had to leave the waggon and cattle as the long bed or sand hill covered with mopani and other trees, between it and the Falls, was known to be infested.

Mr. Baldwin also on his way to the Victoria Falls, from Natal, left his waggons in Moselekatses country, on account of the fly in the intervening districts, and made his way on foot. A fellow traveller of ours had a safe camp for several months with cattle at Boana; and at Logier Hill on the Zambesi (lat. 18° 4′ 58″ S.; long. approx. 26° 38′ E.) we do not remember to have seen any, though we resided there from September to the following February, in 1862-63.

In the parts about Chobè the fly is found near rivers only, in or near rich soils, and marshy spots—generally in mimosa or mopan forests. It sometimes shifts its position, and has been known to leave a spot which has been greatly hunted with guns—probably because the game had diminished or left.

The following are the first symptoms in oxen of being bitten: A swelling under the throat, which, if lanced, emits a yellowish fluid; the hair stands on end or reversed; they become debilitated, and though the herbage is ever so luxuriant, refuse to fill themselves, and become very thin; their eyes water, and at length, when their end is approaching, a continual rattling in the throat or chest may be heard a few paces off. Sometimes one out of the number recovers, but very rarely, and only when it has no work to perform after being bitten. Horses generally swell about the eyes, nostrils, and testacles, where, probably, the bites are most numerous; the hair becomes reversed, and pining gradually away, they die. Both cattle and horses live from a fortnight to six months after being bitten, but generally all die shortly after the first rain falls.

After death the heart of an ox is encased in a yellowish and glutinous substance, which might be mistaken for fat. The flesh is full of little bladders of water, and the blood is half water at heart, which, on cooling, becomes congealed into a yellow glutinous substance. The vitals are of a livid colour.

We do not believe that the flesh is rendered unfit for food if the animal be killed in the early stages, but when the poison has made much progress in the blood, and the creature becomes much out of condition, it must of course be greatly deteriorated. We do not know of any remedy, and no certain preventive; it would be a great boon to travellers if any composition, disgusting to the insect, innoxious to the animal, and easy of carriage and application, could be discovered. We have heard a hunter propose to tar his horse, and then ride "into the fly," and shoot elephants; and it is supposed that the anointing of cattle with their own excrement mixed with milk will save them from being bitten, but both these expedients, beside being annoying to the animals, would be liable to lose their efficacy in a short time.

The vang-stock is generally used to slip the noose over the hind leg of an ox unwilling to be caught. If a turn can be got round the other leg so much the better; another noose is thrown over his horns; men catch him by the tail, others seize him by the horns, using them as levers, and, with all his members thus pushed and hauled in contrary directions, down he must go. If he is meant Catching cattle. for a waggon ox the yoke is put upon his neck, and once fast in the middle of a dozen well-drilled yokefellows his struggles are unavailing, and he soon begins to feel the necessity of taking kindly to his work.

If he is wanted for a pack ox, a hole is bored through the cartilage of the nose, and a small stick 4in. or 6in. long, with a fork at one end like a Y pushed through; this serves as a bit, to which his halter is made fast; a long reim is passed very tightly, with many turns, round his body, some old skins are tied upon his back, and he is forced to stand or walk with these for several hours. Next day heavier packages are put on, and he is thus exercised till he is well accustomed to carry a load. The Kafirs very frequently tie packages upon the horns of their oxen. For riding oxen, those that seem of a less gregarious or dependent temper, and go most freely alone, are selected, as they give less trouble to the rider. Many of the most highly valued have loose, pendent horns, swinging, like locks of hair, with every motion of the head. We believe this is malformation, and is produced by beating and breaking the core of the horn while still young. In riding, the reim is carried from the nose-bit over the forehead, and thus the nose can be jerked up into the air at the rider's pleasure, or the animal guided by a gentle pull from side to side. Among completely uncivilised Kafirs or Hottentots the ox is ridden with only a few skins lashed on his back, but after communication with Europeans they generally impro-

Riding oxen.   vise some sort of saddle, perhaps a couple of pads connected by strips of skin, or a piece of skin with the ends turned up towards the middle and stitched, so as to form two bags, which may be filled either with grass or with any soft articles that have to be carried. We have ridden oxen very comfort-ably with an English saddle, and have used spurs, which are well enough for gentle admonition, but the sambok, or hide whip, must be at hand as a more convincing argument.

The armament of a hunter is expensive. A couple of hundred pounds may very easily be spent upon his rifles, without subjecting him to the imputation of extravagance. He must have his good, stout, plain

Hunting fit-out.   gun (smooth-bored) for general purposes—double-barrel, of eleven gauge; then his rifles, carrying bullets of from 2oz. to 6oz. each; and most probably one or more smooth bores, of still heavier metal, for night shooting at close quarters, when extreme accuracy of aim is not of much importance, and where the shock to the nervous system by the concussion of a large round bullet which bruises the parts around, instead of merely penetrating them like the sharp pointed cylindro-conical, is much more likely to bring down the animal before he has had time to wander very far from the place where he was shot.

Powder is required in large quantities, for, besides being always liable to waste or injury from damp, the loading of guns, with from 6drs. to 10drs. to a charge, the number of shots fired for practice at ant-hills, ineffectively in the chase, or shot away by native servants, counts for something. A liberal stock of shot of various sizes, caps, wadding, and gun requisites should be laid in. Of course there must be a proportionate amount of mercury, tin, or type metal, to harden the bullets, till they can just be indented between the teeth, when they are supposed to be hard enough, without losing too much of their weight.

When engaged in hunting in the forests during the day, the hunter will not unfrequently find it convenient to set either gun or bow traps for the purpose of destroying mischievous and roving night prowlers. Almost any old gun or musket, provided that it will go off when the trigger is pulled, and will not burst from the effects of a good heavy charge, will answer the purpose. The most convenient form of gun trap we have ever used is formed by lashing a piece of horn, bone, or polished wood, to the back of the trigger guard with waxed thread, as shown in the annexed illustration. The trigger string is then brought back, passed through  behind it, and led forward through the ramrod hoops. The gun, when heavily loaded, is lashed fast to some tree or post at a convenient height from the ground. A stout forked stick placed in the ground, about 18in. from the muzzle, will, according to its length, serve to regulate the line of fire to the height of the animal the trap is intended for. The trap is baited either by attaching a piece of meat of suitable size to the end of the trigger string in such a way that, as the food is seized and dragged away, the trigger

Spring guns.

may be drawn, and the gun exploded. Where jackals or other small animals of prey are abundant, they are very apt to spring your trap

P P

and waste your ammunition. In order to prevent them from doing so, it is well to form a sort of pass or road up to a large bait staked to the earth with crook posts or pegs, and then carry your trigger line at a slight strain high enough for a jackal to go under it, but low enough to be struck on the advance of a larger animal. The outer end must now be tied fast to a tree or post, as shown in the engraving on the preceding

page. Some hunters we have known adjust their trigger lines on the lever principle, as shown in the accompanying illustration. The plan is a good one for drawing a trigger with a heavy pull; but we prefer our own plan, because it is always available. The bit of horn need never be taken from the guard when once properly secured there. A very good porcupine trap is made from the barrel of an old cavalry pistol, stapled to a block of wood, and exploded by the fall of a piece of old spring. A little bone peg or setting pin rests on the top of the barrel, and supports the spring until the string which is fastened to the middle of the setting pin is drawn. The least pull on the string

PORCUPINE TRAP.

causes the lower end of the pin to slip off the barrel, and allows the spring to fly sharply down on the crown of the nipple.

Bow and arrow traps are in use in many parts of the world. The Arrow traps. Chinese and Tartars are very clever at constructing them. Very large and powerful cross-bows, charged with poisoned arrows, and set much after the manner of a gun-trap, are often used for the destruction of tigers and other animals.

Large and very strong bamboo bows, charged with a number of arrows placed in a row, are set with a line stretched across the run of the animals in such a manner that a set of trigger sticks, shown in the illustration below, may be acted on when the line is drawn on.

There is an arrow trap, the "Elg-Led," used for the destruction of elk in the forests of northern Europe. No bow is used in the construction of this engine. The hunter, when about to set an elg-led, seeks for a regularly used elk track. On each side of this, when found, he plants a post about 4ft. in height, like the posts of a gate. At about 6ft. from one of the posts he plants another in the same line, and on the tops of the two uprights he fixes by pins a fir-pole chopped flat, just as a hand rail of a bridge is made. He then cuts a long tough spring pole, and lashes its large end fast to two more uprights in such a way that, when forcibly bent back like a spring, its small end may sweep the whole length of the hand-rail, as we will call it. On

the top of this hand-rail a deep grove is cut, and in it rests a heavy-headed arrow. When the spring pole is drawn back to its full extent, it is held in place by a hard wood pin, set at a slope in a notch cut in the top of the hand-rail. To the bottom or heel of this pin is attached one end of a stout copper wire, whilst the other end is carried across the elk track and made fast to the other gate post. Brushwood skil-fully disposed on either side of the track keeps the elk in the direct road, whilst fresh young branches and "elk food lichen" scattered freely here and there serve to so attract the attention of the advancing animal that the first intimation he receives of anything being amiss is the passage of the massive steel pointed shaft through his body. We were first shown how to set an elg-led by an old Norse skipper, who as a warning informed us that the best cow he ever possessed, or was ever likely to possess again, was found dead within ten yards of the first elg-led he ever constructed. The northern Siberians destroy bears by the use of a very similar contrivance. Whilst on the subject of traps of this kind, it may not be amiss to caution our readers against placing any of them in situations where either domestic animals or human beings are likely to stray. When you set gun or bow traps near camp, warn all your followers that you have done so. In setting a gun trap be sure that the cocking of the gun and putting on the cap are the last two operations performed. In the case of arrow traps never lay in your arrow until every detail of your arrangements have been completed. Never cross in front of a set trap, or you may pay dearly for doing so.

In situations where it is not convenient or profitable to construct arrow traps, deer are often taken in considerable numbers by first

Deer Traps.

forming a rough fence of tree trunks and branches, and then making openings just large enough for the animals to pass through at intervals. In these pass ways nooses of strong cord are suspended in such a way that, as the deer endeavours to force its way through, the slip knot tightens round his neck and holds him fast until dispatched. Tough, elastic young trees are not unfrequenly made to do duty as deer traps, by bending them down until their tops are a few feet from the earth; a running loop of strong cord is then made fast to the extreme end of the natural spring, which is held down by a line, peg, and trigger arrangement set in the deer path. As the animal, in straying onward, catches his leg in the line, the trigger sets the bow free, the noose runs home, and the captive swings aloft. Some of the jungle tribes of India make use of an ingenious hook arrangement for deer and antelope catching, which is thus prepared: A pebble from the river bed, a stout, sharp, hook-shaped thorn and a short piece of twisted hide or grass rope are used to make the trap. The pebble has a hole made in one of its ends, through this one end of the rope is looped, whilst the other .end is securely lashed to the thick end of the hooked thorn, as shown in the annexed illustration. This contrivance

is baited by placing a small round jungle fruit, of which deer are very fond, on the hook, which is, with its cord and pebble, laid in the path which the animals follow in going to and from water. On the bait being taken into the mouth, the hook quickly becomes embedded in the loose skin below the tongue. The deer, being unable to get rid of it, strikes impatiently upwards with one of its fore-feet, stamping furiously, like an enraged sheep; in doing this, the cleft between the two hoof-tips, being open, receives the cord, the pebble runs up to the back of the pastern, into the hollow of the heel, holds fast there, and so compels the deluded beast to caper about on three legs, when a well-directed arrow soon settles the matter. On the American Continent a sport known as fire-hunting is much followed. This mode of hunting is prosecuted at night. The hunter provides himself with a rifle, an old frying-pan, fastened to the end of a pole, and a good supply of resinous pine knots. These he ignites in the pan, and as the bright flame leaps up, he watches carefully for the gleam from the eyes of the deer amongst the dark shadows of the forest. When the two glowing orbs are perceived a ball is directed immediately between them. Canoes are not unfrequently used in fire-hunting, when the deer are lily-root hunting on the borders of lakes and rivers. Salt-licks or saline incrustations are powerful attractions to deer, who will travel long distances at night to indulge their fondness for salt, when they can be often shot in great numbers by the aid of fire kindled near the lick. Trappers and squatters at times manufacture artificial salt-licks by boring a great number of augur-holes in prostrate tree trunks; these, when tightly rammed with salt, seldom fail to attract such deer as may be in the vicinity. Care must, however, be taken that domestic cattle are not shot at the lick in mistake, as the salt is much relished by them.

When a deer is killed by the hunter at some distance from camp, he either protects it from the attacks of animals or birds of prey until it can be conveniently removed, or proceeds to prepare it for packing at once on his horse, pony, or mule. In countries where there are no vultures, animals of medium size may be kept in safety by attaching them to a springpole, or "riser." This is made by bending down a tough, elastic young tree until the crown fork is reached; trim this in such a way with your hunting knife that a sort of hooked crutch is formed. Now lock the hind legs of your animal together by making a slit behind one back tendon, and running the opposite leg through until the hough joint prevents its return; place the loop thus formed over your hook-crutch, and then let the tree spring back to its original erect position, and your game will be safe from ground pilferers. The pole will be too small for bears to climb. Birds and wild cats are scared away by attaching a few bits of coloured rag, or a fluttering pocket handkerchief, to the prong. Large red deer or moose can be cut up before suspension. When large animals have to be left whole and unskinned in the woods, lay them longways against the side of a fallen log; cover them with thorn bushes, and then proceed to cut some long thin wands, or small branches; strip the bark from them, in order that the white stick may show. Plant the ends in the earth, and bend the upper portions of the rods over the thorn bushes, amongst which they can be wattled. Few wolves will face this arrangement, as it looks too much like a trap to be safely ventured on. To prepare a deer for packing on a horse which has to carry the hunter as well, proceed as follows:—First make an incision directly behind the back of the head above what is called the pithing spot, or joint between the *atlas* and *dentata* of anatomists; cut round the neck until the muscles, &c., are all divided; then twist the head round, using the antlers as a pair of levers; divide the attachment between the two bones just mentioned, and the head is separated from the neck. Cut the neck from the body just at the last neck joint, which lays in front of and above the shoulders. Cut off all the feet at the pastern joints. Now pass your knife directly in through the front line of the breast bone, and cut forward and back until the brisket is completely divided. Then in the same line carry your cut straight down the centre of the belly until the point of your knife rests on the root of the tail. Feel for the arch bone of the pelvis, skin back the tissues from it, place your knife on its centre with the heel of the blade close to the border of the bone. If the knife is a powerful one, and in good order, a little dexterity in its use will suffice to divide the arch at once. When this has been done, return to the brisket, force open the cut made in it, insert the two hands, and pull right and left until you can bring your knee to bear in flattening out the two sides by the giving way of the heads of the ribs. Take the two thighs and spread them open in the same manner. When this is done seek for the end of the windpipe; when found make a hole through it and pass in a short stick for a cross handle to hold on by, pull it upwards and backwards, cutting away right and left above it such adhesions as will be found, turn out all the intestines by freeing them in the same manner, taking care not to puncture them during the operation. If the work has been properly done nothing but the kidneys will remain in the body of the deer, which can be easily lashed fast to the Ds behind the saddle. The liver and heart can be made a separate package of, as they are well worth taking home.

A great number of forms of the fall-trap, as it is called, are to be found in different parts of the world, and trappers of fur-bearing Fall and other traps. animals avail themselves extensively of the use of engines of this description. From the largest bear to the tiny ermine the drop or deadfall produces death, just as we see the common slide-door cage successfully used in taking alive either the royal Bengal tiger or the pilfering kitchen mouse. Dead-fall traps are especially valuable to the northern trapper, who, with axe, knife, and rifle, penetrates vast solitudes in search of furs. The materials for his traps cost him merely the trouble of cutting in the surrounding forest; but no little ingenuity, forethought, and deep calculation are needed to so arrange the tree-trunks, pegs, sticks, and baits, as to successfully impose on creatures so richly endowed with instinct as the fur-coated inhabitants of the wilds.

The martin trap is a contrivance much used for taking small animals of the weasel tribe, is generally useful, and is made as follows : When

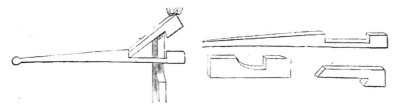

FIGURE OF FOUR TRAPS, SET AND DIVIDED,

you have reason to suspect the presence of the animals you are in search of, either from having seen their tracks or noted their move-ments, proceed to build your pound wall, as it is called. This is a horse-shoe or half-tower arrangement, about 4ft. in height, built up with heavy stones and pieces of hard compact turf. Through the centre of the back of your half tower pass a stout, rounded, smooth stick, about the size of a common broom handle, sharpen the end which comes to the front, and ad-just it so that, when the wall is completed, it may project at about 2ft. 6in. from the ground, and 4in. within the line of the two side walls. Now, with your axe, fell a good heavy straight young log, long enough to lay well across

BEAR TRAP.

the front of your pound when brought up almost in contact with the stones forming the ends. Now, with your knife, make your "figure of four," the principle of which is shown in the above illustration. When this is completed make your loop-line. This is a stout strand of twisted cedar bark, with a smoothly-tied loop at one end. This loop is run on the projecting stick in the centre of the pound, and pushed back until the loop touches the back wall. The other end of the line

SQUIRREL TRAP.

is made fast, about 4in. from the ground to the bait, which must be perfectly fresh, clean, sweet, and uncontaminated, to be of any use. Any small pieces of bird or squirrel will do. When the bait is attached, the figure of four is brought into use. The main stem or king-post rests on the sharpened end of the centre projecting stick which holds the loop and bait, whilst the drop log rests on the crown point at a slant. Immediately on the animal taking the bait, he walks backward with it, draws the loop along the stick until it draws the king post away, when down drops the fall log across his back and instantly kills

PLANK FALL-TRAP.

him, without injuring his skin. In the North of Europe a variety of modifications of the "figure of four" are used for destroying bears, gluttons, and other animals. The woodcuts given on this and previous page will serve to explain the nature of three of them.

A very efficient trap for mice or other small rodents is made as follows : One flat slate or board is placed on another of about equal size pegged at the heel end to keep it from slipping backward, and then supported between two posts united by a stout thread on which a perforated bean is strung after the manner of a bead. The animal, in attempting to carry off the bean, nips through the supporting thread, when the upper stone or board instantly falls and crushes the pilferer to death.

Great numbers of foxes are taken by the Swedish hunters by the use of a contrivance known as a " tana." This is usually made from the stump end of a small tree, chopped with the axe to a sloping or wedge-like form. Two cuts are then made, one on each side the centre or highest point, on which the bait, usually a cat's head, or any piece of offal, is fixed. In performing a series of leaps to get at the bait, the fox gets one of his fore-paws in a slit, as shown in the annexed illustration, when he remains a prisoner until dispatched by the hunter.

The fox hook is another contrivance for the capture of foxes and wolves. The following illustration shows the hook when set and before baiting. The body or slip of the contrivance is made by pinning two hard wood sheaves or trucks to a block-piece of any tough wood; a tough young tree is bent down to form the spring; a loop, or bellying of the line, which must be of strong cord, is placed between the trucks, and a small wedge inserted to keep it there.

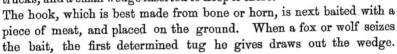

The hook, which is best made from bone or horn, is next baited with a piece of meat, and placed on the ground. When a fox or wolf seizes the bait, the first determined tug he gives draws out the wedge.

The block-piece, with its trucks, remains attached to a stump, whilst the pole-spring flies violently up, and carries with it the prowler, who hangs like some fur-jacketed and odd-looking fish. Assafœtida, when rubbed against stumps and logs, is said to attract wolves.

The following contrivance is commonly used in the far northern forests for the capture of foxes and other small prowling animals. It is made by heavily weighting the butt end of a young pine tree or pole, which is so placed in the fork of a tree as to be capable of moving freely and smartly upward by the action of the weight at its large end when the small end or point is set free; to the point or light end is attached the trap, which consists of a strong noose of flexible copper wire, two thongs of reindeer skin or other leather, a wooden "hook pin" and a "slip stick." A, in the accompanying illustration, represents the point of the pole with one end of a thong secured to it. The other end, after passing through a hole burned with hot wire in the slip stick at about two inches and a half from its half rounded end, is carried along its under surface, and after taking two or three turns round the notched end of the stick, firmly knotted to the inner end of the twisted wire noose. The hook pin B, after being firmly driven into the earth, has a short "bridle" thong or loop of leather slipped over its head; under this the half rounded end of the slip stick passes in such a way that its under side shall rest on the head of the hook pin, whilst the bridle loop keeps it from being drawn upward by the tension caused by the

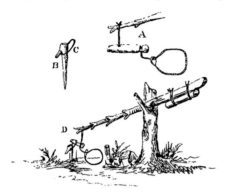

weighted pole. D shows the complete trap set in the run of the animal. On the noose tightening round the neck the slip stick is drawn on one side, slips off the head of the hook pin, the pole flys up, and the captive dangles in the air.

The professional trapper, who derives his livelihood from the sale of the skins which good fortune and skill combined may cast in his way, avails himself largely of the use of the steel trap or gin for the capture of animals of all kinds and descriptions; and in no country in the world has the manufacture and use of this valuable contrivance reached such perfection as in the United States of America.

The steel traps manufactured at Oneida, on the Newhouse principle, are admirable, and range from the "0" size, adapted for musk-rat, to No. 7, or "the great bear tamer," represented in the annexed illustration.

When large traps, such as that just described, are used, there will not unfrequently be some risk and danger in setting them. Mr. Newhouse, the maker of the Oneida trap, gives the following hints on the subject in his valuable work on American trapping: "All that is necessary to be carried into the woods to do this is four strong leathern straps furnished with buckles. When you wish to set a trap, cut four levers of a size and length proportioned to the size of the trap, take two of them; make a loop of one of the straps and slip it over one end of each, then bring the trap spring between them, press them together, and adjust a loop over the other ends of the levers. Serve the other spring in the same way. Now spread the jaws, adjust the dog and pan, loosen the levers, and your trap is set. The traps weigh only a few ounces, and are easily carried." He also gives us a valuable hint or two on the use of so-called "sliding-poles," which are contrivances much used by trappers, and astutely remarks as follows : "Animals of aquatic habits, when caught in traps, invariably plunge at once into deep water, and it is the object of the trapper, availing himself of this plunge, to drown his captive as soon as possible, in order to avoid his violence, and keep him out of the reach of other animals. The weight of the trap and chain is usually sufficient for this purpose in the case of the musk rat. But in taking the larger amphibious animals, such as the beaver, the trapper uses a contrivance which is called the 'sliding pole.' It is prepared in the following manner : Cut a pole 10ft. or 12ft. long, leaving branches enough on the small end to prevent the ring of the chain from slipping off ; place this pole near where you set your trap in an inclined position' with its small end reaching into the deepest part of the stream, and its large end secured at the bank by a hook driven into the ground ; slip the ring of your chain on to this, and see that it is free to traverse down the length of the pole. When the animal is taken, it plunges desperately into the region towards which the pole leads. The ring slides down to the end of the pole at the bottom of the stream, and, with a short chain, prevents the victim from rising to the surface or returning to the shore."

Whilst on the subject of steel traps, it may be well to observe that the bait, whatever it may be, should never be placed on the plate of the trap. Hang it up on a stick ; strew it round about ; lay it before or behind the trap in a run, or set the trap without bait, but do not bait the trap itself, as doing so with wild forest animals is next to useless. Do not secure your trap chain to a fixed object, as the animal will probably get free. When setting your traps, cut clogs for them ; these clogs are merely short lengths of pole, of weight and size proportioned to the size of the trap. Do not fasten the clog so that it may drag crosswise, or it will become fixed amongst the undergrowth. To make it travel end-on place the ring of the chain over the end of the clog, which should be large enough to fit it moderately tight, then with your tomahawk (which should always be at your side whilst trapping) split the clog end, insert a stout flat wedge, and drive it home ; this will effectually keep the ring on and prevent crossing. Traps should be rendered perfectly sweet before setting by putting them in the camp fire and heating them up to a point just below that which would tend to injure the springs. Boiling hot water and wood ashes are sometimes used for the same purpose. Sheepskin gloves with the wool on may be used to handle the traps with in order that no taint from the trapper may remain about them. Many baits are prepared by trappers for luring animals to the trap. The much-lauded beaver medicine, or castor·bait, is a white creamy secretion found in the neighbourhood of a set of glands near the scrotum of the male beaver. Foxes are often attracted by laying down some earth taken from a fox den, or by scattering small pieces of fried meat dressed with honey about the neighbourhood of the traps. Mr. Newhouse strongly recommends as a fox bait the following preparation : Obtain from the female of the dog-fox, or wolf, the matrix in the season of coition, and preserve it in a quart of alcohol tightly corked ; leave a small portion of this preparation on something near the trap, and then, putting some of it on the bottoms of your boots from time to time, strike large circles in two different directions leading round the trap. A very attractive baiting oil for mink and other fish-eating animals may be made by cutting any kind of fish into small pieces, leaving them in an unstoppered bottle, and allowing them to be exposed to the sun and air ; putrefaction soon takes place, and a thick strong oil is formed, the smell of which is a great attraction.

Musk rats, which abound in many of the shallow lakes and river bottoms of America, are either speared through the walls of their winter houses by trappers who travel over the ice in pursuit of them, or captured in steel traps of the description already spoken of. A musk rat spear is made by mounting a smooth polished rod of highly-tempered steel in a 3ft. or 4ft. handle, just as a chisel is fitted. The blade or tine should be about a yard long and a little under half an inch in diameter. The point should be as sharp as a needle. In using this instrument, the hunter looks out sharply for a spot of white or hoar frost on the dome of the musk rat house ; through this he plunges his spear, knowing that the sleeping family is beneath it. The heat given off by the animals causes a partial thaw, which leads to the tell-tale white incrustation. On the rats being transfixed, a hole is cut with a tomahawk through which to take them out, when a steel trap is set for the capture of such fugitives as may have escaped the pointed steel.

The explorer's larder will not unfrequently depend for a supply on such feathered game, large or small, as good fortune may place at his

Catching birds. disposal. In many regions animals of the chase, properly so called do not exist; in others, they are so thinly scattered over a large extent of county that their capture is at the best precarious and uncertain. Few routes, however, which the traveller could select on the face of the habitable globe will be found destitute of feathered inhabitants of some

kind. We know of no bird which could not, under the pressure
of hunger, be turned to account. Vultures are, perhaps, the most
repulsive feathered creatures in creation, and yet instances are not
wanting in which starving men have fed on them. Our space will not
admit of our entering on a description of the various and complex
net arrangements made use of in the capture of wildfowl in decoys
by the continental sportsman. We shall deal only with such contrivances as may be turned out of hand by the exercise of a little
ingenuity and the use of simple tools and common appliances. Ostrich
catching—the ostrich being the largest known bird—perhaps deserves
the first place in our list.

A variety of methods are adopted for the capture of the ostrich and
emu by the natives of the countries in which they are found. The

Arabs and Cabiles of Algeria organise regular ostrich hunts, for which
the horses are systematically trained by having their food gradually
decreased in bulk, and being ridden long distances daily in the full heat
of the sun. The ostriches, when found, are headed towards an ambus-
cade of mounted hunters, who, when the birds approach within the
required distance, dash out from their concealment, and literally ride
down the game, which, when thoroughly exhausted, is knocked on the
head with short heavy sticks. The Bushmen of Africa lie carefully
concealed, with their bows and arrows, at a convenient distance from
the nests of the birds or the edge of a vley or pool to which they
come to drink. Stalking is an art the Bushman excels in; and,
with a piece of ostrich skin on his back, a stick roughly hewn into the
form of the neck and head of the bird, together with his short bow, in
the left hand, and a supply of arrows in his head band (as shown
in the above woodcut), the cunning hunter creeps up wind towards
the feeding flock, and not unfrequently succeeds in shooting down

more than one before the alarm is given. The Australian native, when emu hunting, provides himself with a leaf-covered branch large enough to effectually conceal him as he advances step by step up wind towards the birds as they stalk forward and back on the plain in search of food. When within range the native fits the hollow end of his long fire-hardened spear into the tooth of his womera, or throwing stick, and sends it whistling on its mission of death. In South America the ostrich is hunted by mounted men, who capture it by the aid of the bolas, which consists of three rounded pebbles sewn up in raw hide cases and attached to strips of hide, which are united in the centre. In the use of this contrivance the balls are made to whirl rapidly round the head of the hunter as he gallops towards his prey, and diverge to the full extent of their thong attachments. When sufficiently close to the object of pursuit, the whole affair is launched forth with extraordinary force and precision, entangling the legs, wings, or neck of the bird, and not unfrequently inflicting a heavy stunning blow or two as well. In districts where wheeled vehicles are employed by either settlers or natives, ostriches or emus may be successfully approached by concealing yourself in one of them as they go creaking and jolting slowly in a line with the flock. By a little management the bullock team may be so guided as to edge down until at very close quarters, when a heavy charge of buckshot under the wing, or a well-directed bullet through the body, seldom fails in bringing the game to bag. We have successfully approached bustards in this manner, both in India and Tartary. Before commencing your stalk, it is well to arrange some straw or reed in the cart, waggon, or hackery in such a manner that it shall afford concealment without preventing you, when within shot, from instantly starting, gun in hand, to a kneeling posture, which we have found the best attitude to shoot in when subjected to the irregular motion of a vehicle with wheels out of circle, and travelling over a plain without roads. For this description of shooting, a strong hard-shooting gun is needed. One of the kind described at page 8 of this work will be found well adapted for this purpose, and is identical in size of bore— viz., 11—weight, &c., with one we always use. When about to commence bustard shooting, it will be well, if you have no Eley's wire cartridges, which are of the greatest value for all large fowl, to prepare some from old kid-glove fingers, or oiled silk, as directed at pp. 206 and 207. It is seldom, even when shooting with heavy charges of powder and cartridges, that standing or running shots at bustards prove fatal. We have found it the best plan to continue the approach steadily, until the bird, becoming alarmed, makes a short rapid run, as it almost invariably will, and then spreads its wide wings for flight. Then fire well to the front, and below the wing, and the chances are greatly in favour of the sportsman.

Wild turkeys are approached by the aid of a call made from a hollow bone. Some skill and experience are needed both to make the call and use it when made. Some hunters succeed in imitating the cluck, or " yelp" as it is called, without the aid of the bone; but to do this it is necessary to study the exact pitch and intonation of the bird's voice, which can only be done by listening to it. Great numbers of wild turkeys are taken in " cribbets," or pens, which are made much on the same principle as the bird trap shown at the front of our full-page illustration, only that, instead of sticks of ordinary size, poles are made use of. The following directions for making a wild turkey pen or trap are given by Audubon, and are thoroughly practical and to the purpose : " Young trees of four or five inches in diameter are cut down and divided into pieces of the length of twelve or fourteen feet. Two of these are laid on the ground parallel to each other, at a distance of ten or twelve feet. Two other pieces are laid across the ends of these at right angles to them, and in this manner successive layers are added until the fabric is raised to the height of four feet. It is then covered with similar pieces of wood placed three or four inches apart, and loaded with one or two heavy logs to render the whole firm. This done, a trench about eighteen inches in depth and width is cut under one side of the cage, into which it opens slantingly and rather abruptly. It is continued on its outside to some distance, so as gradually to attain the level of the surrounding ground. Over the part of this trench within the pen, and close to the wall, some sticks are placed so as to form a kind of bridge about a foot in breadth. The trap being now finished, the owner places a quantity of Indian corn in its centre as well as in the trench, and as he walks off drops here and there a few grains in the woods, sometimes to the distance of a mile. This is repeated at every visit to the trap after the turkeys have found it. Sometimes two trenches are cut, in which case the trenches enter on opposite sides of the trap, and are both strewn with corn. No sooner has a turkey observed the train of corn than it communicates the circumstance to the flock by a cluck, when all of them come up, and, searching for the grains scattered about, at length come upon the trench, which they follow, squeezing themselves one after another through the passage under the bridge. In this manner the whole flock sometimes enters, but more commonly six or seven only, as they are alarmed by the least noise, even the cracking of a tree in frosty weather. Those within, having gorged themselves, raise their heads and try to press their way through the top or sides of the pen, passing and repassing on the bridge, but never for a moment looking down or attempting to escape through the passage by which they enter. Thus they remain until the owner of the trap, arriving, closes the trench, and secures his captives." Great numbers of both capercailzie and blackcock are taken in the forests of northern Europe by the aid of traps and snares. The former differ in form of construction with the district in which they are used. Deadfalls are in common use. They are either made in such a way as to allow one long heavy pole to fall on the bird, or seven or eight stout poles are battened together as they would be to form a door. A hole is cut in the upper end large enough for the main post or setting stick to pass up through as the flap of the trap falls. The figure-of-four form of release is that usually made use of. The illustrations at page 663 will serve to show the arrangement when put together and the mode of notching the separate portions. Birch or beech wood makes excellent figure-of-four traps. Cowberries and other forest fruits are used as baits to strew in and about the traps. A very ingenious form of pen trap is also much used in the North for blackcock capture; it is called the " orre tratt," and is thus constructed: A young pine of about 12ft. high is selected as the centre pole; all the branches are removed, and the top of a well-grown young spruce fir tree lashed in a reversed position to the pole about 4ft. from the ground; a crutch or fork is now fastened with cord to the head of the pole; within about 1ft. of the top in this crutch is lashed the tip stick, which is so tied as to act as a scale-beam or the *see-saw* used by boys; a bunch of wheat or other corn in the ear is secured to the extreme end of the main pole. When these arrangements have been made, a number of larch poles with the bark on are driven in round the main pole in funnel form, much as young trees are defended from the attacks of deer or rabbits in this country. The top of the funnel should be about 4ft., and the bottom about 20in. across. A few tough sticks or vines wattled in here and there give firmness and compactness to the structure. When this is complete, plant a few poles, with bunches of partly threshed oat or barley reed tied to their tops in such a way that a good foothold may be afforded to birds on cross branches left for the purpose, which should be near enough to the tip stick of the main pole for a blackcock to hop easily off when attracted by the bunch of wheat ears. The instant he settles on the tip stick it gives way, and allows him to drop down into the pen on the fir-branch frill in the centre, which instantly gives way under his weight, and lets him down to the bottom. Should he attempt to rise, the

TRAPS FOR SMALL GAME.

barb-like pine branches keep him down. The tip stick, having fallen back to its original position, is ready for a fresh victim, who quickly descends to join his fellow in the bottom of the pen, which has been known to become well filled during a short winter's day.

Snares may be made of annealed brass or copper wire, or of several strands of twisted horsehair. Twisted copper or brass wire makes excellent snares, but it must be very soft and pliable. Iron wire, when used as a makeshift for the two former descriptions of material, should be annealed before use : this process, which adds greatly to the pliability and tenacity of iron wire, is conducted as follows : Double your wire into a hank or bundle of convenient size ; twist a loose rope made of dried grass or straw round it in all directions until the coil is completely covered ; ignite the straw or hay band, and let it burn to ashes ; let your wire cool gradually, and you will find it almost as pliant as a thong. The snoods, or "grains" as they are called, are best made from stout white horsehair, twisted by the aid of a half-opened pocket knife, as at Fig. 1, page 530. Immense numbers of these are made in some districts for the capture of snipes and woodcocks, and are used in a kind of trap known as a "springle." As a ground trap for birds, it is, perhaps, the most remunerative that can be set; its form, when adjusted for use, is shown at the front of the full page illustration,.

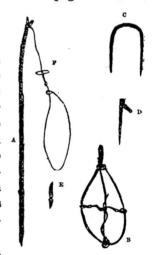

"Traps for Small Game." Common hazel is the best material to make all the wood-work of a springle from. The annexed illustration shows the arrangement in a divided form. The parts consist of the riser A, the "sweik" B, the bow C, the hookpost D, and the button E. The riser line—a piece of stout twisted twine—the grains, and the button in place are shown at F. The riser should be planted so as to lay well back, in order that it may exer-cise its full power when in action. When setting this description of trap for snipes or woodcocks no bait is used. A conve-nient spot is chosen on the ground in which they bore for food ; and a roading is then made with small bent twigs, as in the illustration on next page, in ex-tended V form. The sweik is set directly across the narrow pass, formed by the convergence of the two twig walls or edges. No woodcock or snipe will ever pass out over the barrier formed by the bent twigs. Feeding and running onward, they merely touch their beaks against the border hedge, work their way up the gradually

narrowing passage, until the sweik, with its surrounding of grains or snare, is reached, when the head or feet of the bird, pressing down the former, releases the button from its hold on the notch. The riser flies up, and the neck, or some other portion of the body of the bird, is caught within the noose, which holds the game firmly against the bow, until strangled or taken out by the trapper. We have seen hundreds of springles set along the lines formed by the wheels of a waggon across an open stretch of plain or moorland. Water settling in these forms a sort of water road for snipes to run in. Two or three twigs on each side are all that will be needed at each trap, in such a favourable trapping ground as this. On an open flat or marsh meadow, 14ft. or 15ft. of twig roading will not be too much for each side or limb of the double or single V arrangement. Springles set for birds requiring a bait, such as fieldfares, blackbirds, missel thrushes, redwings, &c., should have their sweiks placed over shallow oval pits; hawthorn, paracanthus or cotoneaster berries, rotten apples, or ears of unthrashed wheat or barley make good baits for springles. Vast numbers of migratory birds of the thrush tribe are taken for the market on the Continent and in the north of Europe by the use of various forms of the " dona." This is a trap made by either bending into half-hoop form a stick

either growing or inserted in an auger hole bored in a tree. The string used to bend the bow, and form a head line for the hair nooses or snares, is usually made of bast obtained from the lime or linden tree; twine, or any other cord-like material, will answer the same purpose. Several forms of this kind of trap will be seen suspended from the trees in the full-page illustration, representing " Traps for Small Game." A very excellent form of spring bow trap is made by bending a strong pliant hazel or other stick into the form shown in the annexed illustration. Bore a hole through one end with a red-hot wire; draw the snare or grains through the hole until the two ends of the bow closely approach each other, then force the end of the treadfork (A), which must be cut to a truncated conical form, into the hole (B), until the grains is held by it in such a way that the force of the bow cannot draw it through the hole, and yet pressure on the tread-fork will displace it, and set the grains free to be drawn through the hole, unless the bird which has stepped on the fork is caught; in which case it is held, as shown in the full-page illustration. Larks, quails, finches, &c., are readily taken in snares, hung either from bows or stretched lines adjusted so as to hang just above the ground; several of these arrangements are shown in the full-page illustration. Chaff or grain should be scattered about traps of this kind, which answer best when snow is on the ground. A great number of both birds and small animals are to be taken in "crib-bets:" these are pyramidal-shaped pens, or cages, built up by placing round, straight sticks, with the bark on, one on the other, just as a log house is built, only that cribbet sticks are not notched as logs are for building. When the cribbet is built to the required size and height for the description of game to be caught in it, a string at each corner, brought to the apex of the trap, gathered together in a knot, and made tight by twisting round a stick placed in the loop, makes all firm and compact. A piece of bent vine or briar serves to set the trap, which is arranged as shown in the full-page illustration.

Wild geese, ducks, widgeon, teal, water rails, coots, &c., &c., are taken readily by traps properly set for them. On the coasts of Finland and Lapland great numbers of wild geese are taken by forming a little fence or hurdle (which stands about breast high to a goose), on projecting points or spits of land which stretch out into the bays or harbours. Unbarked sticks, about the size of a common walking stick, are thrust firmly into the ground, at about 10ft. or 12ft. apart, and then at every third or fourth stick a second is placed at about a foot from the other, forming, so to speak, a pair of gate posts, and in such a manner as to form an irregular line, completely surrounding the sea-line of the spit. A string or wire is now stretched tightly from stick to stick, only omitting the spaces left between the pairs of posts. These are left unfenced, and are each provided with a running noose, made of twisted hair or wire, which is secured to one of the posts. When the arrangement is complete, barn refuse is scattered inside the fence. The geese, coming in from the sea to feed, breast the fence, until an opening, formed by one of the gates, is found. This is quickly entered, and the noose, running in round the neck of the intruder, holds him fast. A sort of trap raft frame is much used for duck catching during winter in the north. Some short pieces of board serve to form the side and end floats of the raft. An upright post is set at each corner,

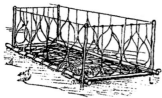

and a top line is stretched round the heads of the side and end posts, as shown in the annexed illustration. Hair and wire nooses are set all round the duck raft, which is usually floated in a hole made in the ice; a quantity of water plants, pulled up by the roots, are thrown within the barriers. The ducks or other fowl, in endeavouring to force their way through the loops, are hung by the neck, and strangled.

Wooden frames are also mounted with wire snares and cross strings, as shown in the illustration below, and prepared for sinking, by the aid of stones, through holes in the ice, until they are about 3ft. or 5ft. beneath the surface. The ducks congregate in these holes, and in diving after food become entangled in the snares, and are drowned. The frames are hauled up once or twice during the day, for the purpose of removing the dead birds. Small-sized fish hooks, fastened to stout line or twine, and baited with bits of unio, pond mussel, or other fresh-water molluscs, removed from the shell, make

good traps for ducks. Herons, storks, egrets, and other wader birds, can be caught by hooks baited with small fish. Sea-fowl are caught in considerable numbers by baiting ordinary fishing hooks and lines with bits of pork rind or fish offal.

Ducks and other wildfowl are captured by the natives of Australia by the aid of a long rod or wand, to which a fine strong noose of twisted bark is attached. Furnished with this contrivance, the native proceeds to make for himself a head dress or crown of river weeds, and then, wand in hand, swims and wades out to where the unsuspecting fowl are feeding and disporting themselves; here, with the rod resting on the surface of the water, and pushed forward, duck after duck is first noosed by the neck, and then drawn under the surface to the duck-catcher, who quickly attaches the victims to his belt by slip-loops fastened to it for the purpose. Both the Chinese and Indians take wildfowl on ponds or lakes by the aid of a gourd shell placed on the head. A few real gourds or pumpkins are first launched well to windward, and allowed to float amongst the birds in order to allay suspicion. The fowler then, with his gourd-shell cap (in which two small peep-holes are cut) on his head and neck, enters the water at some spot where a clump of reeds or rushes can be found as a concealment, and then swiftly swims or wades, as the depth of the water may render necessary, out amongst the birds. Here he proceeds to draw as many as he requires down by the feet, securing his game just as the Australians fasten theirs. The shooting or trapping of wildfowl by the white hunter or explorer is often much facilitated by the use of false or decoy birds. These may be either solid blocks of carved wood, painted so as to imitate the plumage of real birds (the heads and necks of these should be made to take off) stuffed skins mounted on wooden or bark floats, sheet metal, or gutta-percha models; many of these are beautifully made, but are rather costly and troublesome to carry. We prefer, when making use of a few decoys, to employ duck, goose, or widgeon skins stuffed with bark chips, and balanced with lead attached to a loop fastened to the breast. Bits of lead pipe make good weights. Each decoy bird should have an anchor weight and cable string attached to it, so that it may remain in its proper place until picked up from the canoe by the aid of a long forked pole. Ambushes are often made use of in marshes, on the borders of lakes, or the banks of tidal rivers, for the purpose of concealing the sportsman from the quick eyes of the passing fowl. A good sized cask sunk in the ooze, and then well furnished with straw, makes a good lurking place. On flats, where the tide flows, it is a good plan to plant four stout posts in a square. Bore sets of auger holes up each post in such a way that four stout iron or hard wood pins may be passed completely through the holes in the posts, and project about six inches towards the interior of the square. On these projecting ends a light platform or stage of boards is fixed for the sportsman to stand on; a few bundles of marsh reeds, fastened to the frame, are so spread out as to form an effectual screen. A narrow board to sit on is supported on two bars run through each pair of end posts. When shooting ducks on the marshes of Southern Russia we used to form a sort of screen by cutting a bundle of marsh reeds, fastening their tops together with a piece of twine, spreading the lower ends out like a large extinguisher or the hat of a beehive, and then placing the whole arrangement on the head. When seated thus arrayed on a good thick pile of reeds, with your legs encased in well-greased boots, and your gun placed well under cover, the ducks, geese, widgeon, and other fowl, come fearlessly by on whistling wing, and are knocked over and bagged accordingly. A contrivance, known as the "crinoline stalker," may be used with advantage in approaching many descriptions of wildfowl; this contrivance is made from four bars of wood nailed together in a square, as a picture frame is made. At each corner a leg is placed, about knee high. A string serves to sling the arrangement over the shoulders of the sportsman, just as a falconer's hawk stand used to be carried. A number of short lengths of cord or ropeyarn attached to the frame serve as lashings for bundles of reeds or long green branches, so that, when the stalker is adjusted properly, the sportsman walks as though in a very large and high topped crinoline. When he wishes to remain stationary, he drops his frame so that the legs may rest on the ground. He can then sit down on the hind bar and remain well concealed. The gun is usually carried slung until required for use, in order that the hands may be free to manage the crinoline.

Calls of different kinds are generally made use of to attract deer, Calls. wildfowl, rails, plover, and partridges. The moose deer is called with a trumpet formed from birch bark. Duck and goose calls vary in form with the locality in which they are used. The natural windpipe and larynx, freshly stripped from the bird, are, in the hands of a skilled performer, the best that can be devised. Landrails can be brought close to the sportsman by the use of a small thin flat bone (beef-rib bone is as good as any), cut into teeth, like those of a saw. Over these a thin flat strip of bone is drawn sharply and repeatedly until the answering bird is within shot. Partridge calls are made by stretching a bit of stout parchment or moistened vellum over the mouth of a common bottle neck, broken off short. When the stretched membrane is dry, a small pin hole is made in its centre, and through this a knotted horsehair is passed, until the knot is drawn against the inside of the drum-head. A little powdered resin is placed on the fingers, and the hair is drawn sharply through in such a way that the voice of the real bird is closely imitated.

Woodpigeon, plover, and weasel calls can be purchased for a small sum from any respectable gunmaker, and are far better than most amateurs could hope to make. They occupy a small space, and can be easily stowed away in the gun case. Much might be said on the subject of wildfowl punts, sunk flats, fowling canoes, &c., but a consideration of such appliances can be scarcely entered on in this work.

The use of birdlime may be often had recourse to for the capture Birdlime. of a great variety of birds, particularly such as assemble in large flocks about the neighbourhood of springs or water holes. The most expeditious and best mode of preparing birdlime is to place about a pint of linseed oil in an earthen pot or other vessel, which should be set upright in the hot ashes of the camp fire, and boiled slowly and steadily until reduced to about a third in quantity, when, instead of oil, birdlime will be left in the vessel. The inner bark of the holly, some kinds of elm, a parasitical plant like a mistletoe which grows from a mango tree, the straight upright shoots of the common elder, and several creepers or vine-like plants found in tropical countries, produce birdlime. To prepare it, the bark, after being scraped free from the outer shell, must be boiled in rain-water for at least ten hours; throw it then in a mass out on a cloth to drain; dig a pit in the earth in a cool place, put a flat stone in the bottom of the pit, throw your bark in on the stone, letting it rest as a pile or heap. Now place another flat stone on the top of the pile, throw in grass round the edges to keep any earth from getting in, fill up your pit with earth so as to leave a slight depression in the middle; throw a little water into this every other day for three weeks, when the bark will have become stringy and tough. Lay it now little by little between two rough stones, and grind it into a paste. Work the paste with clean hands in a clear running stream, until all impurities and foreign substances are washed away, and then place it in a clean earthen pot, covered with a tile or flat stone for a week, when the lime will be fit for use. When intended for the capture of small birds, it should be smeared on sets of twigs or branches, so set that the birds may settle easily on them. When used for crow catching, it is placed in a thick coat on the inside of paper cones, which are made as though intended for silk-worms to spin in; each cone is baited by placing a piece of raw meat in its narrow end, and then thrusting a thorn or sharp splinter of wood through both it and the paper. The crow, in attempting to get at the bait, thrusts its head into the cone, which remains fixed on like an extinguisher. Birds thus caught either flap about helplessly or keep mounting in the air until, becoming exhausted, they fall to the earth, and are easily taken. On some of the islands of the Pacific vast quantities of dragon flies are taken for food by boys, who, armed with long wands tipped with birdlime, lightly touch the insect, which is at once secured, and placed in a basket carried suspended from the shoulders.

We have always a great aversion to the use of poison as an agent for the destruction of animal life; and it is only in cases of absolute necessity that recourse should be had to it. The skins of *Poison.* fur-bearing animals so destroyed are very inferior to those obtained in the usual way. The flesh of birds and animals poisoned by strychnine (the agent commonly made use of by hunters and travellers for poisoning purposes) is so intensely poisonous, that any creature partaking of it is almost sure to perish. It is, therefore, the best plan, when it is considered advisable to rid the vicinity of the camp of the presence of furred or feathered carnivora, to destroy some suffering or worn-out baggage mule or horse with strychnine, and then place its remains in a position in which access to them is easy; but see that your own dogs are secured, or they, with all the magpies, crows, vultures, wolves, wild dogs, &c., &c., in the district, will stand a fair chance of being destroyed.

We remember hearing of two settlers in Australia who, finding that their crops were seriously damaged by cocatoos, tried all in their power to shoot them, but to no purpose. They at length prepared a quantity of corn with strychnine, and spread it about the clearings. The cocatoos eagerly devoured the grain, fell dead in the forest, and were in due time devoured by the " dingoes," or native wild dogs, who in turn fell beneath the powers of the potent vomic nut. It is best to take such strychnine as may be required from England. Apothecaries' Hall is the best place to obtain it from. The best way to pack it for travelling is in a stout glass-stoppered bottle, which has had a strong tin case or jacket soldered over it. The tin cover or cap fitting over all should have a skull conspicuously marked on it. (See " Box markings.") Too much caution cannot be used in handling or dealing with this most deadly and fearful poison.

CHAPTER XVIII.

PALANQUINS, STRETCHERS, AMBULANCES, ETC.

In many countries where it is difficult to keep riding or draught horses, or where the want of roads precludes the use of wheeled carriages, those who can afford to ride are borne upon the shoulders of men in conveyances more or less simple or elaborate; and not only do these vary much in different countries, but the mode of shouldering, and even the step of the bearers is as various as the fashion of the vehicle. The peculiar short trot of the palkee bearers differs from the elastic spring of the Zambesians when they carry in single file, and that again from their swinging walk or run when they carry in pairs—each man embracing his comrade, while the pole rests on the right shoulder of one and on the left of the other; while they walk on separate paths, about 3ft. apart, each man leaning inward, at an angle of 15 degrees or 20 degrees towards his comrade, just as the horse and rider lean inward in a circus.

The machila, or masheela, is simply a couch, slung by chains or leather thongs to a pole of female bamboo of the largest possible diameter, so that it may bear easily on the shoulders of the men, and not cut them, as a smaller pole would. Generally an awning of chintz or calico, spread on yards like a boat's awning, with curtains on either side, is attached to the bamboo; but sometimes, when the masheela is intended to be more strictly a private carriage, a sloping roof or pent-house of reeds is slung saddle-wise over the pole, completely screening the occupant from the public eye, while a small window on each side affords sufficient facility of observation from the interior.

When it is actually necessary to carry a sick or disabled man, a hammock may be extemporised, by rolling a small stone into each corner of a blanket, and thus forming a knob, or projection, which will prevent the slipping of the cords or thongs with which it is made fast to the pole. We saw a young Dutch lad, under the influence of fever, carried by a couple of Zambesian natives in a skin hammock, two corners of which were fastened to a short cross-pole, or yard, at the head, while the other end was gathered up and tied altogether to the main or bearing pole.

The pressure of this pole on one shoulder was partially relieved by a stick held lever-wise over the other, so as to take a portion of its weight, as shown in our illustration; and, in connection with this, we may well remember the carrying stick of hawkers and packmen :—Smooth, round, and just thick enough to be grasped with

comfort in the hand ; then spreading to nearly 3in. in breadth as it curves gently over the shoulder, and again turning more decidedly upwards, to form a hook for the pack to hang upon. Almost anyone with ordinary ingenuity and a little patience could find out the most convenient form for himself.

Fig. 1, in the series of sketches on p. 603, is a hammock, either of canvas, like a seaman's, or of ornamental grass rope, like those of South America, Sierra Leone, or other places, where considerable taste is often shown in weaving in the different lace-like patterns of the borders or in arranging the various colours. The ends are spread by two sticks or stretchers, about 2ft. long; these may either be stitched or woven into the material, or simply kept in place by having the ends of the clews knotted round them. It is slung to a pole of female bamboo, which should be as light and of as large diameter as possible.

Fig. 2 is a cot, a most luxuriant arrangement, which may be made up to any degree of simplicity or completeness. The bottom consists of one breadth of stout canvas, fully 6ft. in length, or more if for a very tall man. A piece about 1ft. in depth is then strongly seamed on to each end, and a similar piece along each side; and the upper edges of these should be turned down, and sewn into pipes capable of containing poles or stretchers of about 1½in. in diameter. These pieces should not be stitched together at the edges, which meet when they are turned up, but should have eyelet holes and lacings, so that when not in use, or when laid down as the foundation for a bed, or taken apart to be washed, the canvas may lie like a flat sheet. The eyelet holes for the clews should be so made that each clew may encircle the stretcher in its canvas pipe and tie round it. The ends of the stretchers should have holes bored in them, so that they may be firmly, but not too stiffly, lashed together with small cord; and those at the bottom may either be secured in the same manner, or a regular frame of joiner's work may be made

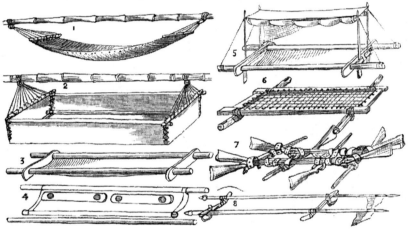

to fit it, and a web of stout sacking or of cords tightly interlaced, as in Fig. 6, may be substituted.

Fig. 3 is the common military stretcher, which may be thus made: Take 6ft. of 30in. wide stout canvas, draw a line with chalk or charcoal 6in. from each side and parallel to it, or fold and crease the canvas along a thread; turn each edge down to one of these marks, and stitch it so as to make a pipe of 6in. in circumference, into which a pole, somewhat smaller or a little less than 2in. in diameter, will slip easily in and out; these poles should be at least 8ft. or a trifle more to leave sufficient ends for the bearers. Then take two boards, 5in. broad, 1in. thick, and a little over 2ft. long; bore or cut in each two holes large enough to let the ends of the poles pass through; and with the nearest parts of their circumference, just 18in. apart, put them together, as shown in Fig. 3 ; when not in use, lay the boards in, as in Fig. 4, and roll them upon the stretcher; in this figure one of the poles is shown withdrawn from the side pipe. In active service one of these is usually carried by a soldier in the rear of his company; and if a comrade is wounded, four men carry him on the stretcher, while four more carry their muskets, and act, if necessary, as a relief. The wounded man's blanket and great coat serve for his pillow, and those of his comrades, if necessary, are used to cover or support him in any position his injury may require. A plot of ground, as smooth and as much sheltered from shot as possible, is selected. The sufferer is laid down, the poles are withdrawn from the pipes on each side, so that there may be no impediment to medical examination ; and when the wound is dressed, the poles are once more inserted, and the man borne to the temporary or permanent hospital.

Fig. 5 shows a little addition we improvised in Damara land. We screwed clamps of wood upon the end pieces, and in them inserted other poles, the lower ends of which were short, and stout enough to serve as legs, and converted the stretcher into a low bedstead, while the upper supported a small awning, and were steadied by stays leading to the ends of the bearing poles. This was constructed for the purpose of bringing home a friend who had been wounded, at a distance; and during our journey towards the spot we used it nightly, and found it a most comfortable bed; it rolled up like the military stretcher, and the clamps of the awning poles increased its bulk very slightly.

Fig. 6 is the "kadel," or bed frame, usually slung in a Cape waggon, with two of the yokes, or more, if necessary, lashed under it as bearers.

Fig. 7 shows how the muskets of a small party may be used to carry a wounded comrade. The belts serve as lashings, and overcoats or blankets as bedding; or if grass, or small branches are available, a quantity may be cut, and a tolerably soft couch made of them. Of course it is quite possible that eight muskets could not be spared; in this case two only might be laid side by side, with three across them—one to support the head and shoulders, one under the hips, and the third under the knees, the belts passing as much as possible under the other portions of the body.

Fig. 8 indicates the use of lances and swords for the same purpose; the sketch is purposely made in the simplest possible form, in order to show more clearly the principle of construction. If more lances or swords are at hand, the possessors of them will see at any moment

how to suit the comfort of the wounded man better than any details
we could give would teach them.

The form of stretcher indicated in the accompanying engraving is
worthy of remembrance : it resembles two short ladders, hinged side
by side, and is furnished with
stout straps, being often used
with more regard to the security
of the prisoner than to his comfort.

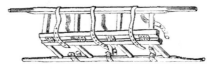

In some countries a couple of horses or donkeys are harnessed
between the ends of two long poles or shafts, on the centre of which
the load is supported, as shown in the annexed illustration. This
arrangement might, under favourable circumstances, be made available
for the carriage of a wounded man, or in a case of great emergency
the ends of a blanket might be knotted together; and, two men
being laid in the bights, the
central part might be laid across
the back of a horse, with one
man hanging on each side, and
secured with the best means
available at the moment. Among
civilised nations it would, perhaps, be better to leave the
wounded to the mercy of a victo-

rious enemy than to risk the extinction of life by such rough means ;
but in fighting savages no living man ought, under any circumstances, to be left in their power, and a soldier had better die under
the rough, though kindly, efforts of his comrades to remove him than
become a prisoner—to be kept alive as long as he is capable of enduring torture.

The Kaffirs, and we suppose most other savages, carry off not only
their wounded, but also the dead, not from any motives of humanity,
but simply to deprive the enemy of a trophy. Among some tribes a
quantity of reeds are cut and made into a bundle, with the corpse
inside ; this is firmly lashed to a long pole, and is easily carried upon
men's shoulders. When our late friend, C. J. Anderson, was wounded
in his gallant and self-sacrificing attempt to free the Damaras from
their Namaqua oppressors, we had to adopt a somewhat more
elaborate arrangement. The fact that a limb had been shattered
rendered it impossible that he could lie with comfort upon the
yielding canvas of the stretcher (Fig. 5 of the group given on
page 603) ; and, therefore, when it was found necessary to remove

him, we sent to Objimbengue for planks, and with them made a level and unyielding surface, supported by cross battens, notched at each end, so as to lie securely on the bearing poles. On each side we raised one breadth of about 9in., making them work upon claw hinges of brass wire, so that they could either be turned down or entirely removed at pleasure; on these sides we screwed uprights or stanchions, with notches in their edges, so that crossbars could be laid in them (as may be seen in our full-page illustration), and raised or lowered from notch to notch as needful. One of these crossbars was near the head of the stretcher, so that he could occasionally rest his shoulders, by taking hold of it by partially lifting himself from his bed; and two others were nearer to the foot, for the purpose of slightly supporting and steadying a box, with falling sides, in which, for further security, we encased the shattered leg. When we halted to dress the wound the crossbars were first removed, the sides let down or taken away, the sides of the small box containing the limb also removed; while the awning was left spread, and occasionally blankets were stretched from trees to shield it from the direct action of the sun. When the dressing was completed everything was easily restored to its place, and a few points and lanyards, knotted in their proper places, made all fast again. The same engraving also shows a rude but not an uncomfortable form of litter, extemporised for a wounded Damara, from a forked branch with the smaller twigs lopped off where they were in the way,

or interwoven where they would serve to fill up a gap in the bed; other boughs and cross pieces were added, and a few skins, karosses, or blankets, converted it into a very comfortable couch.

Sometimes a man, though unable to walk, can sit and practically support himself; in this case two men may lay their muskets together, end for end, and hold them across between them for him to sit on, with his arms upon their shoulders; and even if they have no weapons at hand they may make him a very comfortable seat by joining their hands and arms, as shown in the above illustration.

Thus, the two bearers stand side by side, and half facing each

VARIOUS MODES OF CARRYING THE SICK OR WOUNDED

other, No. 1 grasps his own right wrist with his left hand; No. 2 does the same; No. 1 then grasps the left wrist of No. 2 with his disengaged right hand, and this brings the right hand of No. 2 into the proper position to catch the left wrist of No. 1. In this easily extemporised chair they can bear a tolerably heavy man without undue strain on the muscles of their own arms; and when they become weary two others can at once take their places, or they may gain a little relief by interchanging the position of their right and left hands; while nothing can be more comfortable to a disabled man than the easy chair thus formed for him. Fig. 4. shows how a short pole can be used to form a seat-rest for carrying.

The mode of carrying used in mountainous countries by a chair strapped on the back of a porter, and still further secured by a band passing round his forehead, as shown at Fig. 5, might occasionally be found useful. The principle of the sedan, or of the electioneering chair, fastened on two fore and aft shoulder-poles, in a manner which any sailor could effect with a few bits of cord, should also be borne in mind, to be used or not, according to the necessity of the case.

In our illustration on p. 608, Fig. 1 represents the cross bandages applied to an injured head; and here we may remark, once for all, that in bandaging, as in knotting or lashing, simplicity   Bandages and is the essence of security. Let as many turns   medical appliances. of the bandages be used as are absolutely necessary to cover and secure the dressing of the wounds; all in addition are not only superfluous, but detrimental.

Fig. 2 (p. 608) shows the support for a dislocated shoulder or broken collar-bone : a roll or pad of calico is placed under the armpit, and secured by a bandage over the opposite shoulder; another bandage is then passed in figures-of-8 fashion round the arm and the body, in order to confine the arm close to the side. The arm of this figure, with the palm of the hand placed against the breast, as at Fig. 3 (p. 608), shows the position in which the limb should be placed in cases of fracture of the bones or other injury; the hand then lying between the prone and supine positions, and the bones and muscles assuming, without constraint, their natural relative position towards each other. This figure also shows the manner of applying a bandage to a taper limb. If the bandage were wound spirally round, one edge would be unduly tight while the other would be slack; therefore, at every turn round the limb a turn more or less decided is taken in the bandage, which thus accommodates itself easily and exactly to the shape of the limb.

In the next figure is shown another form of head bandage (Fig. 4), one part of which forms a loop, while the next, passing through it, is turned upwards at right angles over the head, and this is repeated until the whole, or as much of the scalp as is necessary, is covered. This is a very convenient form when, from any other injury, it is not advisable to pass a cross bandage under the chin.

Fig. 5 is the strapping or bandage for a broken jaw. It is made of

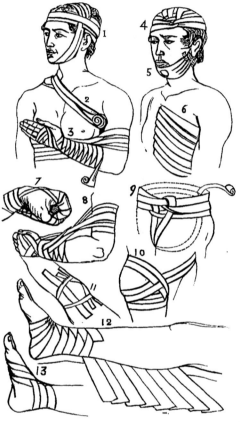

sticking plaster, a hole is cut for the chin, and the ends are cut in swallow tails, to allow them to take the shape of the face they are laid on.

Fig. 6 is the bandage for a broken rib. If the body is at rest, the bones will assume their natural place, but the expansion and contraction of the whole chest in breathing disturbs and disunites them. Sometimes, therefore, the whole chest is tightly bandaged; but as it will answer the purpose just as well if the injured side is prevented from expanding, strips of adhesive plaster may be cut sufficiently long to reach from the sternum to the spine, and so to confine the wounded side and leave the other free.

If the back of the hand should be injured, it may be necessary to place a ball of calico or other soft substance in the palm of the hand, then closing the fingers upon it to bind the fist firmly down, as in Fig. 7.

If it is required to keep the elbow bent, a bandage may be applied, as in Fig. 8; this may be in case of cuts in the bend of the arm or similar injuries.

Figs. 8, 9, and 10 are T and cross bandages in case of injuries in the groin.

Fig. 11 is in case of a broken knee-cap. The limb must be supported with the foot as high as possible, so that there be no possibility of the muscles drawing asunder the parts of the patella, which must farther be drawn together by bands of sticking plaister, crossed over to prevent the broken edges rising out of their place.

Fig. 12 is a many tailed bandage. It may be made of several slips of calico stitched upon one, crossing them all in the centre; or, if the sore be of such a nature that it may be necessary to remove one or two without displacing the others, it is better simply to lay them on a flat sheet of calico or a small pillow made for the purpose, and gently introduced beneath the limb.

In the figure the bands nearest the knee are laid first on the pillow, the others overlap them as they go down, then that which is nearest to the toes is first lapped round the foot, and the others follow in succession to the knee; the last band alone needs fastening, and this is perhaps the neatest and most secure bandage known.

Fig. 13 is a cross, or figure-of-8 bandage, exceedingly useful when applied to the turn of a joint, as in the sketch.

Fig. 1, in the group of illustrations on p. 610, is in case of injury to the radius close to the wrist joint. It may be necessary to have a crooked splint and bend the hand on it, as shown in the figure. We believe it will more frequently be found advisable to place the palm of the hand to the splint; but this must be left Splints, &c. in a great measure to the judgment and daily experience of the operator and his patient.

Fig. 2 is a splint in case of fracture of the bones of the lower arm. There will also be a short splint on the inner side, and the arm must be supported by a sling.

Fig. 3 is an angled splint for injuries near the joint. It may be carried ready made of gutta percha, or may be extemporised with the best materials at hand.

Figs. 4 and 5 of the following illustrations are splints for the inner and outer bend of the arm; the outer may support the arm nearly to the wrist; the inner should be shorter; others should be ready made in gutta percha.

Figs. 6 and 7 are substitutes for them, extemporised from the smooth bark of a young tree, as near the size of the arm as possible. Fig. 8 is a piece of bark so cut as to allow of its being bent to the form of No. 6. Figs. 9 and 10 are inner and outer splints for the leg, usually made of gutta percha, and of course made right and left. Sometimes a fully sufficient hollow is left for the ankle, and sometimes a hole is cut entirely through.

Fig 11 is a leg with a cradle of bark supporting the thigh, the calf, and the sole of the foot, and with a splint or shield of the same covering the instep and the shin.

Fig. 12 is a leg which has been broken, bandaged and supported in the best position to avoid any derangement of the parts by unequal tension of the muscles. Of course splints would have to be secured above these bandages.

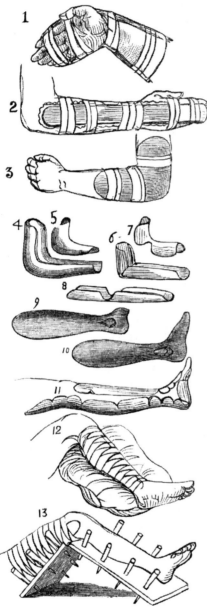

Fig. 13 is a jointed rest, sometimes used in fractures of the thigh to give ease to the limb when there is not much fear of muscular action disarranging it. The pegs at the side draw out for convenience of dressing, and serve at other times to keep in position the pads or cushion which are placed under the limb.

Fig. 14 is the full-length splint for a broken thigh. The limb is bandaged, the splint secured at the ankle and hip, and the over-all bandage partially passed on. We have had to wear a splint bound over all with starched bandages from toe to armpit. Sir Samuel Baker mentions one of the Agageers who broke his thigh, and whom he bound up in this manner like a mummy with strips of bark and calico, stiffened with gum, and who, after lying on his back a few weeks, was able to rise and join in the chase as energetically as before. Fig. 15 shows the extension of the leg without a splint, by folding a long strap of sticking plaister up each side of the calf, making a line fast in the bight, leading it over a sheave or roller, and attaching a weight, say of 6lb. or 8lb., to the other end.

Fig. 16 is a sheet, or long towel, or piece of cloth, with two half hitches made in the middle, and passed over the ankle for the purpose of extending the limb; care must be taken that ends on which the pull is made come out on the inner side, abreast of the hollow of the foot.

These last two expedients are useful in case of fracture in a strong and muscular limb; for, by keeping up a continued strain, they weary out the muscles, and cause them to relax, when the bone may be set with less difficulty. We once assisted Dr. Kirk to set the thumb of a Zambesian negro. We had no appliances at hand, but had to sit behind him, embracing and holding him back, while Dr. Kirk grasped and hauled upon the thumb. The involuntary contraction of his muscles was for a long time more than a match for us; but at length we succeeded in wearing him out, and slipping the thumb into its socket.

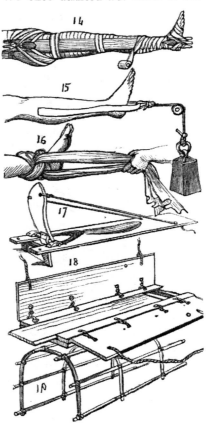

Fig. 17 is a foot-rest we made for our friend Anderson. It is simply a piece of board about 27in. or 30in. long, hollow where the calf of the leg comes, and cut completely through where the heel would otherwise rest. A piece of thin board is then cut nearly to the shape of the foot, and is fixed by a pivot joint across this space; a couple of strings leading from holes in the board support it at any angle that is most comfortable for the foot, which is bound to it; and a small bracket beneath the end of the principal board raises it so far that the heel cannot chafe or press upon the mattress, which, however slight may be the contact, becomes, when endured for hours without a change of position, more painful to a helpless man than one in health, and free from constraint, can readily believe.

Fig. 18 is a box-splint, with sliding bottom and falling sides, which we also made on the same occasion. Its use was to serve as an external case and protection for the wounded limb.

When all the dressings were on, the hinges were merely pieces of cord, passed figure-of-8 fashion through the holes, and the lanyards were strong enough to suspend the whole perfectly clear of the bed when it was necessary to change the linen.

Fig. 19 (p. 611) is a light awning frame to support the weight of the bed clothing, which might otherwise press painfully upon the toe. The last three articles were made at Barmen, a remote mission station in South-West Africa, with no more tools than a traveller usually carries with him, and therefore we presume that they are by no means beyond the power of others who may be similarly situated.

The annexed illustration represents the mode of setting a dislocated shoulder. A man takes off his boot, sitting beside the

patient, places his foot under the armpit, then taking hold of the wrist he pulls it steadily towards him, until the muscles relax and the bone slips into its place. A pad must then be secured under the armpit and the arm bound firmly to the side.

Sometimes it is necessary to stop the too copious flow of blood from a wound; and for this purpose the torniquet (Fig. 1), as shown in the annexed illustration, must be extemporised; a handkerchief may be rolled up with a stone in it, or an overhand knot may be turned in the thickest part, or any means adopted to insure pressure on the injured blood-vessel; each end of the handkerchief must be then returned upon itself, so as to form a bight, through both loops so formed a short stick must be passed and twisted tightly, until the compression stops the flow of blood; if an artery is cut, the blood gushes forth in regular pulsations, bright and red; if only veins are injured, the flow, however copious, is steady, and the colour is darker.

Many of the South African Kaffir and Bechuana tribes have a very ingenious method of cupping. They take the end of an ox-horn, about the size of a small wine-glass (Fig. 2), and perforate the smaller end with a small hole communicating with the internal cavity; they scarify the part to be operated on with a group of perhaps half a dozen cuts, half an inch long and a quarter of an inch deep, made with an assegai or rough-edged iron knife; the large end of the horn is then placed over the wounds, the operator sucks with all his might, and as soon as he has produced a partial vacuum dexterously plugs the little hole with a bit of wax, and allows the horn to remain until the blood drawn from the wounds so far fills the cavity that there ceases to be a vacuum, and the horn drops off. The clot of blood, about as large as a florin and half an inch thick, is then cleared out and thrown aside, a fresh operation is then performed, and others in succession, till the whole surface of the limb, generally the inside of the thigh or arm, is covered with groups of little scars, and blood enough has been extracted.

TAILOR'S WORK.

Although it is in every respect better and more economical for a traveller to take full supplies from home so as to be able to devote all his time to the real objects of his journey, yet it is quite possible that these may fail, and that he may have to trust to his own ingenuity to replace them. A cotton or woollen shirt, worn over all, and belted round the waist, is in cold weather a very simple, and not inconvenient or unsightly, addition to the clothing. We have taken a navy serge frock, and folding in and stitching a slight gore down the back, and turning up the skirts inside towards the waist, and stitching them there, have made a very neat and comfortable hip jacket for walking or riding, without cutting it in any part, except down the front, where a couple of buttons, in addition to those already attached, were quite sufficient to confine it. A cotton shirt may be treated in this manner for a lighter blouse or jacket; and for those who wish something more stylish in appearance we give a diagram, which we think will sufficiently explain itself. We have, in cases of need, cut out a pair of trousers, and stitched them while sitting on the waggon box during the morning journey, so as to have them ready to put on at the next station; and we have done this without intermitting our usual observations for course and distance and notes of the route. These may be made in two pieces, one for each leg—2½yds. or 3yds., according to stature, being enough for a pair. The duck, or other material, is folded along the centre through its whole length, and it may then be folded in half, but should not be cut until the measurements are taken; if the stuff is scant, the diagonal line of each part at the waist may cross into the other half, and thus it may be found sufficient. The duck, of which trousers are usually made, is 27in. in width, and in general this is found to be enough, with little or nothing to spare; if stuff is plentiful and time of any importance, the trousers may be made in two pieces, each of which forms one leg and half the body; there is no difference except in the front, the buttons being sewn on the right side, while the corresponding holes are on the left. Presuming the length from above

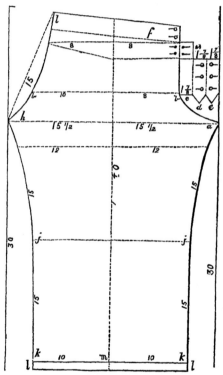

the hip to the heel to be 40in., 2¼yds., or 81in., with care in supplementing one part by the pieces cut out of the other, will just serve; but we will suppose that we have 2½yds. or 90in., and are not compelled to such an exercise of ingenuity. Each half will now be 45in. long, of which mark or crease off 1in. at the end, *l l*, for the hem at the bottom; from this line *k k*, measure 40in. along the edge, 41in. along the centre, and 42in. along the other edge; draw a diagonal line through these points, and draw another 2in. beyond and parallel to it; this will be sufficient to turn down for the waistband, and will occupy the remainder of the 45in. of stuff. In duck or canvas, where both sides are alike, some inches might be saved by cutting it diagonally across the centre; but in drill moleskin, or anything that has a right and wrong side, this will not be the case, so that it had better be left out of the question. The inner seam of the leg will be 30in., measured from *k k* to the points *a* and *h*, where the duck will remain of its full breadth; take the girth of the waist at the point *l*, and, finding it 32in., divide it by four, and mark off 8in. on each side the central line; then take that of the hips along the line *b b*, and finding it 36in., divide it by four, as before, but instead of marking off 9in. on each the centre, mark 8in. before and 10in. behind it; then on the edge intended for the front draw a curved line from *a* to the point *b,* and continue it in a straight line upward; then draw the outlines of the piece that is to be folded into the parts *c, d,* and *e,* each of which is to be 1¼in. wide, and cut round the outline, which is strongly marked in the diagram, folding and creasing sharply, but not cutting the material along the dotted lines. Cut the back of the trousers from the point *h* with a slight curve, touching the end of the measured lines *b* and *j.* We should then commence by turning down the parts, *c, d,* and *e,* working button-holes in them as in the diagram, and stitching them firmly, but very neatly, in their places, and remembering that we are working on the left half of the garment. We should then take the right half, fold in the parts, *c, d,* and *e,* as before, and stitch them, omitting the button-holes. We should then take the two parts, and laying them together at *a,* stitch them as far as *b ;* · then laying together the point *h,* stitch up the back seam; next bringing *a* and *h* together, stitch down each leg, turn down the waistband and stitch it, making button-holes as at *f,* in the diagram, and fixing buttons to match, turning up and seaming the bottoms of the legs. Making eyelet holes for a lacing at the back of the waistband braces we usually make no provision for; but if the wearer desires, buttons may be affixed for them in their proper place.

We give also the outlines of a plain and useful jacket, which may be made in six pieces, of which three only are drawn: Fig. 1, half the back; Fig. 2, half the front; Fig. 3, one Jacket sleeve; the others of course are exact duplicates of to cut out. them. Our drawing is made on a scale of 1-12in. to 1in. Fig. 1 is half the back, the first measurement for which is taken from the collar, so far down the centre as just to clear the saddle—say, for instance, 24in.; the next is the girth of the chest —say one quarter; say 8½in. is allowed for the half back, and a little more, or 9½in. for the half front. The rectangular figures, 1 and 2, should be first drawn to these measurements, and this will much facilitate all future operations. In like manner, if the circumference of the neck for collar be 12in., the proportions will be for the half back 2½in. and for the half front 3½in. From the collar down to the line across the shoulders will be about 6in., and from the collar to the line of chest measurement 9in. The first of these lines drawn on the parallelogram will give the point from which to draw the diagonal line for the shoulder seam, and the second the bottom of the oval that is to be cut out for the armhole; the edges are hollowed about ½in. for the waist. The diagram, we hope, will be sufficiently clear to indicate the few remaining measurements.

From the front of the collar on Fig 2, down to the line of the shoulders will be about 5in., and from the collar end of the shoulder seam to the same line will be fully 7in.; the oval for the armhole will be 6in. deep and 4½in. across, of which 1in. is to be cut into the half back and 3½in. into the half front. About 4in. beyond the front line of the diagram may be allowed on each half of the front for overlapping, and on this the buttons will be placed according to taste.

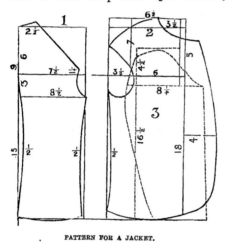

PATTERN FOR A JACKET.

The dotted lines of Fig. 3 represent the sleeve, the measure for which will be from centre of back to armhole; 7½in. from armhole to elbow; when the arm is raised and bent inwards, 10½in. from elbow to wrist; 10½in. the circumference of the arm—loosely taken, will probably be 10in.; and the wrist 9in.; but more may be allowed, according to the wearer's fancy. A straight line, 21in. in length, must now be drawn, and at 4½in. from the top it must be crossed by another of 10in., 8¼in. of which must project in front, and 1¾in. behind; on these lines the curve which marks the insertion of the sleeve must be drawn, beginning from the longer end of the cross line, and sweeping round by the top; down again to the shorter, then continuing downward for the convex seam till it crosses the first line, about 8in. from the bottom, and farther on the base line, about 2½in. in front of it; 9in. more forward must be allowed for the width at the wrist, and a straight line drawn from this point to the longer arm of the cross will give the inner seam.

In stitching the parts together, we should commence with the shoulder seam, from the armhole upward; then with the side seam, from the arm downward; then, folding the sleeve piece, we should stitch the inner seam from the wrist upwards; and, placing the termination of this seam on the fore part of the armhole, 1½in. or 2in. below the shoulder line, stitch the sleeve in; then, commencing at the collar, would make the back seam, and, this done, would trim off all inequalities of the edges; then turn down, and hem them, and finish, more or less, according to taste or convenience.

DISTINCTIVE BOX MARKINGS.

When a traveller has to employ (as is most generally the case in wild countries) servants who cannot read, it is as well to mark his boxes with some rudely-drawn pictorial sign, which should, if possible, have some relation to the contents; though this is not a matter of absolute necessity, so long as the owner himself knows what is in each and what distinguishing mark is placed upon it. We give a few specimens, which will sufficiently illustrate our meaning; and any

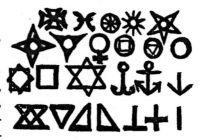

number may be devised if necessary, such objects being chosen as are most likely to be familiar to the servants employed: thus, on maritime or fishing stations, different vessels, cutters, luggers, schooners, brigs, barques, or ships, or parts of vessels, as guns, anchors, capstans, windlasses, various knots, as the reef-knot, bowline, &c., remarkable and at the same time familiar forms of fish, or implements used in catching them, as hooks, large and small hand-leads, harpoons, grains, nets, &c., would be appropriate; while in hunting or pastoral countries

various animals—the ox, the horse, the sheep or goat, the elephant, the camel, the giraffe, the lion, and many others—would naturally be chosen. One box might bear the figure of a man, another of a woman; the tool chest might have a saw or an axe; a powder horn would indicate the box containing gunpowder; while others, holding round or conical bullets, cartridges, or small shot, might be marked with their peculiar sign; clothing might be indicated by a jacket and trousers.

The medicine chest should be marked with the figure of a snake, signifying poison; and it would be well if all chests, bottles, or cases containing either poison or medicines, which might be hurtful if wrongly used, were marked with a death's head, a snake, or crossed bones, or some other unmistakable warning.

DEMEANOUR TOWARDS COMPANIONS OR NATIVES AND WHITE SERVANTS,
HINTS ON TRAVEL, ETC.

Everything during a journey beyond the limits of civilisation depends upon the good feeling and harmony among the party, and nothing short of unavoidable necessity should be suffered to interfere with this; there are, of course, cases in which human nature can stand no farther provocation, but it should be remembered that forbearance is seldom repented of, while hasty resentment, even if expressed only in words, may lay the foundation of ill-feeling, which becomes all the more bitter because the parties cannot separate from each other. At the same time, even forbearance should be exercised in a kindly spirit, for even an outspoken quarrel is better than the habit of "nursing the wrath to keep it warm;" the first may admit of explanation, or the parties to it, if reconciliation does not follow, may agree to dismiss the subject and work together till the close of the journey; and, if both be honourable, each will disdain to do less than his duty, or to throw an unfair share of labour or privation upon the other. But in the second case no such explanation is possible; the person who feels himself the subject of displeasure has no chance of learning what is the nature of his offence, and goes on unconsciously, perhaps repeating it, till, like an overcharged thunder-cloud, the storm bursts, and the restoration of peace which, in the first instance, would have been easy, becomes impossible.

The choice of servants must be very much guided by the habits and disposition of the traveller himself; but if he can, as ought to be the case, dispense with many of the luxuries of civilised life, then we should consider it best for him to engage people accustomed to the duties they are required to perform from among the servants of the colonists or white residents, who know and can answer for their character and ability.

Many travellers who start for the Cape Colony like to have a white man as an overseer, and he generally acts also as cook and personal servant. Such men as these are to be found in most of the frontier towns, and one who is really competent to the work in hand is invaluable; but care must be exercised in the selection, for, however inexperienced the traveller may be, he had better command his own attendants than submit to the intervention of a man who is unfit to manage them. In the first case, they will at least look upon him as the "master," who hires, who pays, and feeds them, and for whom they feel bound to work; in the latter, they have no hesitation in saying to an incompetent overseer, "You are not our master, but only a servant like ourselves, and we care nothing for you." More especially is this the case if they find him ignorant of the management of oxen, an inefficient hunter, or too much dependent upon guides for indications of his way in the bush. Nor is this to be wondered at; the discipline of a ship may be carried on, though the captain be incompetent, if his first lieutenant be a thorough seaman; but if that officer is not up to his duty, even a first-rate captain can hardly atone for the deficiency.

If a man who, in his youth, has been a soldier or a sailor, enters the service of a traveller, he possesses many advantages over ordinary servants. The soldier ought to have learned something of the value of discipline and order, and to be able to combine respect for himself with obedience to his employers; while the sailor must have learned, during his probation, a thousand shifts and expedients; and, above all, have acquired a habit of self-reliance in difficulty and danger that cannot be too highly valued. Efficient men, however, must be *sought* out and well paid; it is of little use to expect them to flock to the intending traveller and ask employment; they are not of the class who generally hang about large towns, but are more likely to be found on the very borders of civilisation. Moreover, they are not too plentiful; they would be more likely to ask, as was the case in Australia, have you a good character from your last servant? and inquiry should be made in time among other travellers as to the character and reliability of such persons as they have reason to think fit for the charge.

Within a colony, in case of a dispute with a servant, an appeal to the magistrate is possible; though if, as is sometimes the case, the nearest justice should live from thirty to fifty miles away—not always convenient—the master perhaps inquires of his native herdsman respecting the fate of a missing ox or two or three sheep; and, the replies not being satisfactory, hints his suspicion that they have been killed and eaten; the herdsman indignantly denies it, shortens his knobkeerie in his right hand, and gathers his kaross, or blanket, over his left arm, as a Spaniard does his cloak. If the master be of quick temper, he closes with and disarms him, or perhaps gets knocked down. If otherwise, he takes the more prudent alternative of riding to the magistrate. If he does the first, the native, whose time is of no value to him, starts off at once to the magistrate, and obtains a summons against his master for assault. If he chooses the latter, his herdsman probably takes advantage of his absence to add as many more cattle as he can to the missing list, and before he can be legally summoned is far away from the power of the law, seeking refuge among remote tribes.

Under these circumstances, it is not to be wondered at that occasionally the colonists took the law into their own hands; and of their manner of proceeding the following incident, related to us by a friend, may serve as a fair example. A native servant having transgressed in this manner, the people of the farm were assembled, and he was put upon his trial; the evidence was against him, and he was asked, "Will you be taken before the magistrate? Will you receive forty lashes at the waggon wheel, or will you be shot? "They generally," said our informant, "choose to take the flogging offhand." "But how," said we, "if some cunning fellow should choose to be shot?" "Oh," said he, "that is not very likely; but a man once did so, and he was allowed to run a hundred yards, when a bullet was fired past him, but sufficiently near to let him hear the singing of it.

It was not very far from the locality where this event happened that a flock-master began to find a steadily-increasing mortality among his sheep, the very healthiest of which, without any apparent cause, sickened, and in a short time died. Now, when merino or other wool-bearing rams are imported at a cost of 120*l.* each, it behoves a man to look well after the good condition of their progeny, but no symptom of disease marked the approaching deaths; the shepherds asked for the carcasses, and, finding these, he proposed to serve them out as rations, but they refused, and insisted that sheep should be killed for them as usual. "Very good," said he, "dig a pit and throw in the carcasses, and I will kill for you." Next morning he found the pit had been opened and its contents abstracted. When sheep were again brought in dead he threw quicklime into the pit with them; the mortality began to diminish, and a post-mortem examination resulted in the discovery that a very fine mimosa thorn, specimens of which may be had of all sizes, from that of a sewing-needle to 5in. or 6in. in length, had been thrust under the shoulder, and left to work its way to the heart of the animal.

Unless, in case of gross and insolent disobedience, which it is necessary to chastise with a strong hand upon the spot, some form of trial and examination of evidence for and against the culprit ought always to precede the punishment; and this course, so far as we have seen, is generally adopted by English travellers, a love of fair play being, we are fain to hope, in spite of occasional excesses, inherent among us.

With native servants, very much must depend upon the custom

of the country in which they are hired. Among some of the superior tribes, if men are well chosen, they may be left to perform their own duty in their own way; an occasional expression of approval from the master, and half an hour's chat with them now and then, to show that, though he trusts them, he is not careless of his own interests nor unmindful of theirs, being nearly all that is required; while the power of withholding a good character or making a deduction from their pay at the end of the journey is enough to restrain any irregularity they might be tempted to. Sometimes they may be hired from the chiefs, who then transfers to the master, for the time being, his authority over them, and looks to him for the safe return of his men at the end of the stipulated time. In this case the traveller becomes *pro tempore* their chief, and may exercise his power in summary punishment of a culprit, or may reserve his right to appeal to the actual chief on his return. In other cases, as with Lascars or other natives of India, a gang may be hired with their own Serang, or Tindal, to whom all orders respecting them should be given, and from whom they will submit to any amount of punishment, though they would resent it as an insult, only to be atoned with blood, if inflicted by a white man. The Kroomen of the coast near Sierra Leone, who are usually employed on board our men-of-war, are generally engaged in this manner.

In some places it is almost impossible to avoid the employment of slave labour in some form or other; for even though the master do not, as of course no Englishman with proper feeling will, retain a man in compulsory bondage, or sell him for profit when his term of servitude is expired, it is in some countries impossible to hire a free labourer; and to give a man his liberty immediately after he has been purchased from his chief, or master, would only deprive the hirer or purchaser of all benefit during the expected period of service. This is particularly the case in some of the countries bordering upon the upper branches of the Nile. A well-known traveller in that region was once taxed with slave trading; he indignantly denied the charge. He had bought men of their chief, as everyone who required servants was obliged to do; but he challenged proof that he had ever detained one in bondage or sold him again when his service was completed.

In South Africa the English travellers, or traders, very properly refuse to have anything to do with the purchase of slaves, though men and boys will come to them desiring to be bought. A friend of ours had an offer of this kind made while we were together; but, though it would have been very advantageous to have a couple of lads who, in a short time, would have been well qualified to act as interpreters, he declined the offer.

On a previous occasion, however, when a boy had begged hard that he would buy him he refused, but told the lad to go and make the best bargain he could for his own liberty; the price was handed over to him, he ransomed himself, and joyfully returned to enter the service of his new master.

Frequently a white man picks up some miserable, neglected child, lets it sit by his fire, and huddle among his servants, getting a share of their food; and if he be, as he ought, a kind-hearted fellow, an occasional pat upon the woolly head and a tit bit from himself. When its condition is improved, he perhaps sets it to some trifling work; but no sooner is it supposed to have become useful than down come the parents or brothers, or some imposters who represent themselves as such, and threaten to take the child away unless they are properly paid for allowing him to keep it.

In Damara land especially such cases were common; and we became quite accustomed to hear the native servant girls telling each other, as a matter of very little importance, that such a one had "thrown her child into the fire that morning." Not that the statement was to be taken literally; but rather that the mother had just abandoned it, and the poor creature had crawled towards the fire for warmth, and so scorched itself.

There were also some natives who had a great facility for establishing a relationship with these unfortunates; and two or three had gained quite a reputation for their skill in discovering some genealogical affinity with anyone that had become the pet of a European supposed to be able to afford to pay for the luxury of keeping it.

In the Portuguese settlements on the Lower Zambesi a modified form of slavery exists, totally distinct from, and unconnected with, the slave trade, and rendered much more endurable by the fact that the slaves, or, more properly, serfs or bondsmen, are subjects of the Crown, and may not be removed from the colony, an ordinance, however, respecting which something may be said on both sides; for, if it prevents subjects being sold as slaves into foreign bondage, it is sometimes assigned as a reason for not legally marrying a native woman, that if a man were to do so, he could not take her from the country, and, not being allowed to leave her, would thus pass upon himself a sentence of confinement there for life.

With regard to the question of servitude under the Crown, the position of a slave seems to be that he cannot change his master, and his master cannot discharge or sell him, except under certain restrictions.

The following valuable hints on travel were communicated by Captain Stuart, the Australian explorer, to Mr. A. Gregory, on his taking command of the expedition before referred to in this work, and in which we took part. In order to render the directions as concise as possible, we have, in repeating them, avoided the repetition of the leader's name, &c. In other respects we give the directions, words of advice, and hints, in Captain Stuart's own words. In communicating them, he says :—

I would recommend the leader to come to a strict understanding with his men before he engages them to conform to the terms of the agreement I have drawn up, and which is a copy of that which I made the men sign who accompanied me on my central expedition. It is the only means, when at a distance from home, to keep the men in order and subjection. I found it most efficacious on one occasion ; when, one of the men having misconducted himself, I struck his name off the pay list, reduced his supply of provisions, and only reinstated him at the earnest solicitation of his comrades and on their guarantee that he should not offend again.

The commanding officer should have his camp always compact. His sheep in the centre of it, and the drays flanking the sheepfold with the tents at the angles. I would caution him never to be without a guard. Let him give his men to understand that he will never dispense with the guard. I never did but on one occasion, which might well have been excused, and on that one occasion I was robbed. Mr. Gregory may rest assured that his safety at all times, whether in the presence of natives or not, depends on this necessary vigilance.

I have been peculiarly fortunate in my intercourse with the natives. I believe the reason of this is that I have always put myself in their position, and deemed the alarm and vehemence they have exhibited at the approach of men and beasts they had never seen before as only natural. Instead of approaching nearer, I have given them time to recover from their amazement before I have separated myself from my men, and walked singly and unarmed towards them, and sat quietly down on the ground, until they have lowered their spears and appeared pacified. One of the natives is sure to advance and sit down as I had done, and so, by gradual approaches, we at length sat down side by side. But it is long before the native raises his eyes to look at you. I have always respected their customs in this respect, and am happy to say that I never failed. Treat the natives kindly, and they will so treat you. On no account did I allow my men to have any intercourse either with the men or women. This I interdicted under the severest penalties. The leader should not remain too long in one spot. He will understand that familiarity subdues fear.

I would recommend him to have a respectable and responsible storekeeper, who should have a tent with the overseer of stock. The provisions should be weighed out weekly to the men, and stock taken once a month, and a return of what has been issued and what remains given by the storekeeper to him. Such regularity inspires confidence.

If the commander should follow a river into the desert, he will most probably find it assume a chain of ponds, and ultimately disappear in a vast plain. I would beg of him in such case not to move on his party until he has ascertained that there is water in front of him. He can have no idea how soon he can place himself in jeopardy.

The following general rules for the treatment of Indians, given by Dr. Brown, may also be useful in reference to other tribes, though a traveller's behaviour to a barbarous or savage people must, to a great extent, depend on circumstances—his position in the tribe and the customs of the nation, which ought never to be wantonly outraged. These rules were partially drawn up for me at an early date of my residence among the North-West American Indians by a gentleman whom to mention would be to name, perhaps, the most celebrated of all the *eeries* of the fur trade. I afterwards added and amended them by my own experience.

1. Never pass an Indian village in the night if you suspect any mischief. They will be sure to find you out, and then, like all bullies, seeing that you are afraid of them, will act upon that knowledge.
2. If you suspect mischief, camp outside at a distance, and pass in daylight; you can then see better what you are about.
3. If you come to a village where you think there is likely to be an attack made on you, go into the chief's lodge, and, if possible, into one where there are a number of women and children. If their sense of hospitality does not prevent them from molesting you, they know that when white men are attacked bullets fly about, and some may strike the women and children. It is an axiom that no man likes to put his head down a gun-barrel.
4. Trust to an Indian's *honour*, and you are tolerably safe—you and your goods; but not to his *honesty*, for he will steal the ears off your head, unless you are very skilful in making a *cache*. If in a neighbourhood where there are Indians, you had far better leave your goods in their charge until you come back; you will generally find them safe; but if they find your *cache*—their honesty being doubted, and having no honourable scruples—they will be sure to clean it out.
5. Never appear to be afraid of them.
6. Never give them one cent less or one cent more than you bargained for—*as a right*. If you do, they will think it only yielding to them, and then imagine you have cheated them at first. You may give a small present if you like. It is a custom the Hudson's Bay Company have introduced of giving after a trade has been completed a small "potlatch," or gift, of their free accord, according to the value of the goods traded. Those Indians who have traded with the Hudson's Bay Company expect it.
7. In making presents, take into consideration their wants; only make presents where you may expect a return; they do that with you; and goodness of heart is only thrown away. Never calculate on this last weakness.
8. In making presents for conciliatory purposes, always make them to the head people; never mind the smaller tribes' men. Be sure, however, that it *is* the chief you are making presents to, and not some forward and impudent fellow, who is usually the first to accost you at the outskirts of a village. The chief generally retires on his dignity, and wants to be sought out. Secure the head man's regard, and you need not mind the favour of the smaller ones; but even if you had abundance of goods to distribute, you would be sure to create red blood and heart burnings by one man's present being better than another, or supposed to be, &c.
9. I have generally adopted the practice, when I had not much to give, of giving it to the children. If you win the children, you win the mother, and of course the father. A little present goes a long way with the children. If you give it to the mother, you often excite the father's jealousy, and frustrate your purpose. Always remember, in addition, that a savage values a man's generosity, &c., according to the size of his presents, and act accordingly.

10. Never allow the natives to eat with you as your equal. As a rule, play the great man with them.

11. If a savage is travelling with you, give him food whenever he wants it. Food given when he wishes it is of ten times more value than when he gets it when he does not need it, or is not hungry. Consult his wishes in this respect.

12. Never attempt to gain anything by force; always by persuasion, argument, and *presents*.

13. Notwithstanding all you will be told about the value of a medical knowledge in travelling among savages, I have generally found it of very little benefit, and frequently, when put in practice, of real detriment. An Indian will never come to you unless when at death's door and he has lost confidence in his own sorcerers. You may give him some medicine, and perhaps in nine cases out of ten the patient dies, as he would have done anyhow. Their professional jealousy is raised, and you are accused by the "medicine men" of killing the person; and the worst of the matter is, it is often believed by the credulous people. If the man recovers, it is rarely that you get the credit of it. It is the medicine men who have done it. With surgery it is somewhat different. If the operation is one not involving any very serious consequences if unsuccessful, by all means perform it. They then *see* the working of your superior knowledge before their eyes.

14. Be just and firm, patient and equanimous with them. Display no anger or violent and passionate gestures, and never be very prone to notice insults.

15. Never say you will do a thing and not do it. Never threaten to do anything unless you intend to do it.

16. No people notice the weakness and moral shortcomings of a man quicker than savages; therefore beware, especially *in re fœminâ*.

17. Try by all means to learn the customs and social etiquette of the people; for nothing raises you more in their estimation than this knowledge, or enables you to see when you are slighted.

18. If you are attacked, and at the *last extremity* have to fire, take to the bush. An Indian does not like to venture in. He knows there is a man there and a gun, and that somebody may be shot, and that somebody may be himself.

19. If you have a watch at night, never stand near the fire; for then you are only giving the man a chance to fire at you.

20. Always, and above everything, remember that the hearts of all mankind are the same, and that all the difference between one and another is merely the overlay caused by etiquette, custom, and education; at heart they are the same.

There are many arts which might be mentioned as useful in treating with Indians; but, as these depend upon a knowledge of the particular tribal customs, these *general* rules must suffice.

CHAPTER XIX.

ON SKETCHING AND PAINTING UNDER THE ORDINARY DIFFICULTIES OF TRAVEL.

FOR artists making a tour of the Lake Districts, the Highlands of Scotland, or the mountain districts of Wales, every possible convenience is supplied by the colourmen of London. The explorer-artist must, however, have recourse to many shifts and expedients.

The talented author of " A Painter's Camp in the Islands " actually fitted out a little studio on wheels, the front of which was a large sheet of clear plate glass, so that, whatever might be the weather, he would be able to paint upon the spot, and with all the truthful reality that working in the presence of nature only can impart. And when such luxurious appliances can be obtained, and are used, moreover, to so good a purpose, far be it from us to say a word against them. In fact, we would advise every one who determines, as he ought, to make his sketches as perfect and truthful a realisation as possible of the country they illustrate, to provide every convenience he can afford or carry for the successful prosecution of his work; regarding them, however, simply as means towards that end, and casting them aside unhesitatingly when, from the labour of transportation, they become hindrances instead of helps to him.

We will suppose, first, that the intending traveller wishes to take sketches in pencil or in water colours, as occasion may serve, of the objects of interest that he meets with, he should be provided, as we have said, with folding sketch-books of folio and quarto sizes, with drawing paper, white and tinted, cut to their respective sizes. He will be able to form a tolerable estimate of the number of sketches he is likely to make in a day, and had better not encumber his folio with more than a good allowance of paper for the work he expects to do. Suppose he reckons six or eight sketches, and, allowing margin enough, takes a dozen sheets—three white, and two each of the pearl, the warm and cool grey, and the drab paper, putting away at the close of the day his finished sketches in a case specially provided for them, and replenishing his folio from that in which he keeps his store.

The preservation of his folio and its contents from injury by rain, by the dash of sea water, or by other causes, is of the first importance, and for this purpose he should have a haversack of good stout canvas —*i.e.*, sail cloth—for each; this may be slung by a leather strap and buckles, but we prefer that the shoulder strap should be of double canvas 2½in. wide, and that the end, which comes forward over the right shoulder, when the sketch book is carried on the left side should pass through a loop at the corner of the haversack, and doubling back upon itself be provided with points or other means of fastening it at the required length. If buckles, hooks and eyes, or other such expedients are used, let them be not of iron or steel, but of plated or well-tinned material, so that no rust or oxide of metal shall gather on and rot the canvas.

Let the part which would then hang next the body of the wearer be of double canvas so stitched with two vertical seams that it may form three pockets, one large enough for the box of water colours in front, one in the rear for the japanned or plated water bottle, and the central sub-divided, so as to carry a few spare pencils, a memorandum book, to which, if the traveller cares about mapping his route, may be added, a 6in. scale, protractor, and dividers; in which case he will do well to add a sheet or two of the squared mapping paper to the contents of his folio, and two or three sheets of foolscap, with a leaf of semi-carbonic paper and a H H H pencil for his journal. A third thickness of canvas will at once form the pocket for the folio and the front of the haversack; and we would advise that the double strip, already spoken of as forming the sling, should be sufficiently long to form also the sides and bottom of the haversack.

The octavo, 11in. by 7½in. folio, will be found very convenient and handy on boat expeditions, horse or foot journeys, hunting trips, or when the artist has to carry everything himself, and must diminish weight and incumbrance as much as possible. In the Australian exploring trips we were not able to carry any other, and this hangs easily from the quarter of the saddle on the near side. In Kafirland, we slung the sketch-book itself (covered with skin to keep off the occasional rain) by short straps and buckles to our waist belt; and one long strap, passing over the shoulder to the belt in front, remained always fast, so that if a sudden movement, either of our own troops or of the enemy, necessitated it, we could at once throw the sketch-book over our shoulder, and advance or retreat as requisite.

We would advise, however, that the imperial, 15in. by 11in., folio should be carried if possible, as it gives so much more space for detail in landscape or other subjects than can be gained upon the smaller scale. With the large book the twenty-four tube colour box can be carried, with the smaller a twelve tube must be taken; and in either case weight may be economised on short trips by carrying only the lid that forms the palette with the little divisions that should always be found along its edge charged with patches of colour; in this case a slip of tin or copper must be fitted as a temporary cover to the box left at home.

We do not advise the solid sketch-block for hard service; first, because it exposes to risk an unnecessarily large quantity of paper, and next, because, with rough usage, the sheets may become loose, and cease to be a block. The folio with japanned tin frame, for confining the sheet actually in use, is the best. It should be made of strong, light, saddlers' leather, rather than of the flimsy materials; which serve well enough for lady students a mile or two from home. The mill-board surfaces may be varnished with boiled linseed oil, and allowed to dry thoroughly. Do not have them covered with paper pasted on, but with the plain surface of the milled board. We found it very convenient to mark a scale of inches along the sides of our frame, and have a movable slip of thin brass fastened upon it by simply bending the ends round, so as to enable us to draw a truly horizontal line at any height, and this would be especially useful in mapping, or the horizon in sea-views.

If a sketching-stool can be carried, it will be found a great convenience, as, when the artist has to sit upon the ground, to say nothing of possible unpleasantness from storms or dampness, the eye is lowered so much that often the grass in the foreground will hide the greater part of the landscape. The triangular stool, which folds up into a stick but little larger than a policeman's truncheon, is the most convenient form. One of the legs may be longer, with a couple of cross-bars, on which to rest the sketch book; or such a convenience may be made with a couple of thumb-screws to slip on when required.

In sketching a landscape it is of great importance to decide, first, what you intend to make the principle object, and how much in the way of accessory you can include beside it. About sixty degrees, or the sixth-part of a circle, is all that can be seen horizontally, without moving the head, and about forty vertically, and this may be roughly estimated by holding up the hands like blinkers on each side of the face, and observing where they shut off the view. Photographers have a little frame made specially for this purpose, and the artist may, by opening the frame of his folio, and holding it nearly at arm's length, see how much of the landscape it includes. It must also be remembered that no one looking at a landscape can see the spot he stands on; and, therefore, if it is desired that this spot shall be the foreground, he must retire, say ten or fifteen yards, so as to bring it within the limit of his vision. In practice, however—when, for instance, he is looking over the edge of a cliff—this might deprive him of the sight of some of the most beautiful portions of the view, and it might be better to remain on the edge, leaving a sufficient blank at the bottom of the paper, and then retiring to sketch the foreground choosing such a position as should make its characteristic features enhance the beauty of the view. It conduces very greatly to correctness if the bearings of distant hills are taken by compass and noted in pencil on the upper margin of the sketch, while nearer features are similarly noted at the bottom—if the estimated distance in miles is added, this enhances greatly the value of the sketch, as it becomes then a geographical record, in addition to its merit as a work of art. Holding up the paper steadily at nearly arm's length, and making on its upper edge the apparent horizontal distances, and on its side the heights, assists the drawing very much; and the pencil may be held up and the distances gauged on it by the thumb-nail, and measured on the paper. Two knots on the ends of a bit of string, one held on the pencil, and the other between the teeth, will ensure the measurements being all taken at the same distance from the eye, which is of great importance. The angle formed by the side of a mountain may be estimated by making the pencil coincide with it, and then bringing it down on the paper. The perspective of receding lines may be found in the same manner; but care must be taken to hold the pencil in the plane of the picture, and not let it point away from the observer; the limits being thus ascertained, the forms may be slightly indicated, and then, after a steady and searching gaze at the object, firmly, but not heavily, drawn. When once the paper is indented by the pressure of the pencil, the line can never be entirely erased; and the surface, once injured, can never be restored. No line should be made at random; be the touches few or many, each should definitely represent some form. The merest outline accurately sketched upon the spot is preferable to any amount of indefinite filling up, which the artist had better leave to his own imagination, assisted by memory and a faithful sketch, when he finishes his picture.

In a pencil sketch, little notes, indicating the nature of the soil, the foliage, the colour or condition of the water or the clouds, may be neatly written in, in such a manner that, unless on close inspection, they blend into the forms of the objects, and rather assist the drawing than detract from its appearance : for instance, the word rocks may run alongside the shadow of a fissure, and their kind or colour— red, grey, basalt, or sandstone, &c.—grass, sandy plain, water, dark clouds, cumuli or light cirri, accidental or cast shadows, or gleams of light, are all worthy of notice ; while the direction of a river may be indicated by a small arrow-head. It may also be enough if several objects of a kind are together, as a crowd of men, a herd of animals, or a flotilla of small vessels, to draw one or more carefully and simply indicate the position of the rest. If there is time, a few touches of colour on the principal parts—say the grey of distant hills and the stronger tints of the nearer ones in flat washes. If a sketch is to be finished in colour on the spot, the outlines should be made as before, with the greatest care ; but no time should be wasted in attempting to shade or finish with the pencil. If the paper is of a light pearl or a warm grey tint, so that Chinese white will tell upon it, it will be less dazzling to the eye when reflecting the rays of a vertical sun ; but it must be remembered that all tinted grounds impart their own character to the work, and, if strict fidelity is sought, nothing but pure white paper, with a sufficient grain or texture to take the colour well, and to give that slight broken uncertainty of touch which is of so much advantage in foliage or rough surfaces, and yet sufficiently fine to admit of the most delicate manipulation where it is required. The right side of the paper is that on which the maker's name, pressed into its texture, is properly seen ; and, if the sheet is cut, each piece that does not include some portion of this should be marked with an " R " on the right side, to prevent mistake. The pencil sketch being completed, wet the paper all over with your largest brush filled with pure water—this somewhat softens, while it fixes the pencil lines, and disposes the paper to receive colour more readily. Take up with the half-dried brush any drops of water that may hang under the edge of your sketching frame, which should, of course, be perfectly clean. Determine now what parts of your picture are to be white, or of pure and unmixed blue, and then, with the large brush, pass a very faint tint of pale orange over all the rest.

The three primitive colours, red, blue, and yellow, in their greatest obtainable purity, should now be placed on the pallette, which ought to be clean, and if possible unencumbered by other colours. Suppose you have Indian yellow, carmine, and cobalt. With a little diluted cobalt wash in the clear blue spaces in the sky, carrying a tint downward on any part of the ground in which grey is to predominate, so as to impart depth of colour as speedily as possible, and reduce the distracting effect of the white paper as seen in opposition to the parts you are painting; if the lights on the clouds are to be pure white, form a grey with a little cobalt and carmine and paint their shadow sides, then with a clean half dry brush soften the harshness of the edges, and reduce them to the form you wish, bearing in mind that the more correctly and evenly you can lay the edge of the original wash, and the less it wants re-touching the better for your picture. If the sky is to be cloudless, turn the picture bottom up, take a very faint wash of cobalt and carmine, and lay it along the horizon, letting the lower edge hang full and wet, so as to give you time to work on it before it dries, and yet not so full as to run down in a drip, and so produce unequal lines across the sky; then take up a little pure cobalt and wash in another line of colour a little deeper than the first, the wet edge of which will run imperceptibly into your second line, and thus in succession keep working in lines of deeper blue, until by an imperceptive gradation you reach the zenith. If sunset or sunrise is to be represented, keep a pure white space for the sun, round this lay a wash of Indian yellow, round this another of carmine, and beyond this another of cobalt with a little carmine in it, keeping the picture still reversed, so that in graduating the tints the most brilliant colours may run into those that are less so—as the yellow into the red and the red into the blue, rather than that the colder colours should run into the warm, and thus impair their purity. The sun may then be tinted as required, remembering always that the source of light must be brighter than the atmosphere through which it shines—though, if the sun be setting in a bank of cloud or haze, great effect may be gained by painting it of a deep and lurid red; while its clear and nearly white light shines on the light clouds in the zenith above the influence of the haze.

Calm water will reflect the colour of the sky according to the angle at which it is viewed; if you look down on it, it will reflect the dark blue of the zenith, but at the same time, if it be transparent, it will also transmit the broken colours of the ground beneath, and thus many beautiful effects are produced—the yellow sand of the tropics imparting a brilliant green to the shallow sea, while rocks or sea-weed will give rich tones of brown. If the spectator is low down, the water will reflect the colour of the horizon, and its own local colour will be lost or much diminished; the reflection of objects on its banks will also appear more perfectly in proportion to its stillness; but never fall into the error of making the reflection an inverted facsimile of the real object—it is in reality an image as seen from the level of the water at a point midway between the spectator and the object. Get a good photograph showing a reflection, or lay a looking-glass horizontally and place an object on it, and you will see at once what we mean.

. The distant hills may either melt into the soft tints of the sky, partaking of roseate light and faint sky shadow, or may rise cold and dark against a clear horizon, or may be shown in full light against a heavy storm cloud; in any case, the tone of colour proper to their respective distances must be preserved, and in this respect there can be no better rule than to copy those that nature herself presents. Objects in the middle distance will be more strongly coloured; and if any particular object be selected as the subject of the landscape, the attention should be directed to this, and the remainder made subservient to it, by having somewhat less finish bestowed upon them. Fix the eye steadily upon the chosen object, and observe how all detail becomes indistinct towards the limits of the vision, and then in like manner, having worked up the detail around the centre of interest, let the colours become a little fainter, and the work less definite toward the corners of your sketch. In foliage, take the lightest tint, say Indian yellow and French blue, or Prussian blue toward the foreground where intense green is required, and lay in the masses, keeping the forms large and broad, and blending a little more blue with the parts that are to represent the farthest side of the tree; then, when this is dry, take a darker tint and somewhat more minutely represent the forms of those portions that take the middle tint or local colour ; and lastly, take a third for the deeper shadow, strengthening this with touches of rich warm brown or cool grey as you wish the masses to advance or to retire. Even pure crimson may be used with advantage as a shadow to cool clear green in the foreground ; in like manner the proper shadow for a yellow sandhill on a beach is not a deeper yellow, but a cool purplish grey, composed of the complementary colours blue and red.

To give some idea of the work that may be done with three well-chosen colours, we append the following list, which might be much enlarged :—

Primaries......
- Yellow and red produce orange.
- Yellow and blue, green.
- Red and blue, purple.

Secondaries...
- Orange and green, citrine.
- Orange and purple, russet.
- Purple and green, olive.

When the eye is fatigued by looking at one of the brilliant primary colours it seems to relieve itself by seeing the secondary colour which is complementary to it : thus if we have looked at red—say at a red light—for some time, and turn the eye away we shall see a green one of the same size and form, being seen in fact by that portion of the eye only that has been fatigued by the strong impression of the red. If we have looked at a yellow light we shall behold a purple image, because this is composed of the other two colours; blue and red is complementary to yellow. Blue, being a cool colour, does not so much fatigue the eye ; hence, though by the foregoing rule we ought to see its image in bright orange, in practice we rarely do so. From these facts we learn that, whenever one of the primary colours is used in a picture, the complementary colour formed of the other two ought to be placed not very far from it, so as agreeably to relieve the eye. In most cases the landscape actually being copied will afford sufficient facility for this ; sometimes it will not ; but these instances are exceptional, and probably will occur in the snow wastes of the north, in the solitude of the ocean, or in the sandy deserts of the tropics, where drear monotony or wild and terrific grandeur constitute the charm of the picture, and fidelity rather than pleasing composition must be the artist's aim.

We subjoin also a few combinations of colour which will be found useful in landscape painting :

Aerial tints for skies, clouds, and distance : for very delicate preparatory wash, cadmium yellow and rose madder ; strong ditto, Indian yellow and carmine ; neutral ditto, yellow ochre and brown madder ; still darker and less aerial, light red, Venetian red, or Indian red. Cobalt for delicate blue skies ; French ultramarine for stronger. Cobalt and rose madder for delicate cloud tints. For golden sunsets: aureolin, gamboge, lemon yellow, cadmium yellow, Indian yellow, yellow ochre—to be used according to the brilliancy or depth of colour required, and to be contrasted by cool greys composed of cobalt and rose madder, or French ultramarine. Crimson sunsets : rose madder, carmine, crimson lake, Indian red, purple madder, contrasted with cool grey ; and sometimes greenish tones formed by adding a little yellow to the blue and red.

In dark storm clouds, French blue or indigo, with light red, Venetian red, or Indian red, or purple madder. Indigo and Prussian blue require great caution in their use. With any of the before-mentioned yellow, they form rich greens for sea tints or foliage ; with raw sienna or burnt sienna, they give very deep greens for stormy seas or heavy forest trees. Light red and Prussian blue give a greenish grey.

Light red with cobalt or ultramarine give greys somewhat less aerial for middle distance, mountains, &c. Indian red, with the same blues, gives a more opaque grey. Sepia and French blue make a cool grey; raw and burnt sienna are good colours for autumnal foliage, stems of trees where grey is not required, rocks, Dutch galliots, and many other foreground objects; brown madder and vandyke brown afford great depth for foreground shadows. For native complexions, raw sienna with a little of the burnt will give the colour of a Hottentot. A Kafir requires burnt sienna in the half tints, vandyke brown in the shadows, and a cool grey like the reflection of the sky in the lights—this is best produced by a little Chinese white and cobalt laid on thin over the brown. There may be a little blue put into the back of the hair to contrast the better with the brown skin. For a negro, crimson lake and blue-black; the lights made with Chinese white and blue as before.

CHAPTER XX.

THE ESTIMATION OF DISTANCES AND HINTS ON FIELD OBSERVING.

ON MEASURING THE DISTANCE TRAVELLED BY WHEELED CARRIAGES.

WHEN no instrument for this purpose is obtainable, the best plan we know of is that adopted by the late Dr. Burchell, the eminent South African traveller, and after him by Captain Cornwallis Harris, the explorer and naturalist, in the more distant parts of the same country; and this is, to measure the large wheel carefully, to mark one of its spokes, and count its revolutions during any given time, say a minute, and then to convert the result into miles or parts of a mile per hour. Thus, if a wheel be 5yds. in circumference, and it makes six revolutions in a minute, the distance in that time will be 30yds., or 1800yds., i.e., 40yds. more than a mile per hour; twelve revolutions will of course be 80yds. over two miles; and, during former journeys, when our wheel was making eighteen revolutions, we used to reckon the waggon was going, allowing for occasional unavoidable stoppages, two and a half miles per hour. With a watch having a second hand it is easy to note any fraction of time, but with one not so provided less than a minute cannot easily be estimated. After a little practice we became so accustomed to this that we seldom used a watch; but when sitting on the waggon-box would just look over the side, and estimate the rate at which the wheel was going, just as a sailor would in like manner make a very fair estimate of the speed of his ship.

It will generally be found that an African ox-waggon, not over-loaded, and on tolerably fair ground, travels about two and a half miles an hour; and we have also found that with pack horses in Australia, if the same rate is assumed, the resulting measurement of the day's work will be very nearly correct.

We tried once to make a trocheameter, but at the time had never either see one or read a description of it, and therefore the principle cost us some thinking out. It was perfectly evident that, for motive power, an axle so weighted that it could not revolve in a revolving box would produce the same effect upon the works as an axle made to revolve, by weights or otherwise, in a fixed box would have on those of a clock. We therefore made a box of such a form as to fit between spokes of the hinder wheels of a waggon, and in it fitted an axle with a heavy plummet, so fixed to it as to prevent its turning when the box revolved; on this axle was one tooth fitting into the cogs of a sixty-toothed wheel, which therefore moved one tooth for every revolution, or once round for every sixty; the axle of this had also one tooth acting on another of sixty teeth, so the two were capable of registering sixty times sixty, or three thousand six hundred revolutions, which, supposing the wheel to be only 5yds. in circumference, would measure ten miles and a quarter, the number of revolutions being indicated by a hand fixed upon the axle of each wheel, each moving on its own dial-plate, like those of a patent log. We found that the machine answered quite well enough to convince us that we were right in principle, and to make us regret that we had not the tools and appliances at hand to fit it so perfectly as to insure smoothness and uniformity of action.

To all, however, who have the means, we would say do not fail to buy a trocheameter: it is a small, compact instrument, fitted in a copper case, capable of being strapped on any convenient part of the wheel; and one of fair quality need not cost above 2*l*. 10*s*. or 3*l*. The instrument is composed of two revolving toothed wheels, the upper wheel having 101 and the lower 100 teeth, suspended from and turned by an endless screw; there are two indices, that on the upper wheel pointing out every single revolution, and that on the lower every hundred. The whole circuit of the instrument is 10,100 revolutions, and the following is an example of its power:

"One complete circuit of 10,100 revolutions, with a carriage-wheel of 12ft. circumference, would indicate 23 miles, minus 80yds. Thus, 55 revolutions give 220yds., or 1 furlong; 110 give 440yds., or a quarter of a mile; 440 give 1760yds., or 1 mile; 7040 give 16 miles; 10,100 equal to 23 miles, minus 80yds.

"To set the instrument unscrew the milled nut from off the steel endless screw, and move the wheels round until both the indices coincide; screw the nut *firmly* in its place, shut up the instrument, and strap it securely to the off-wheel in the centre of the nave."

In Africa we cannot literally follow out these instructions, for the nave is not brass capped, as with carriage-wheels at home, but the end of the axle comes through, and the wheel is secured to it by a washer and a linch pin; therefore, we strap the trocheameter between the spokes as near to the nave as possible, and in our journey to the Zambesi Fall we secured a pint pannikin permanently between the spokes as a protection to the trocheameter, which just fitted nicely into it during this journey. We measured a distance of between 2000 and 3000 miles, and do not remember that this instrument failed, except once from being choked with fine dry sand, and once again from equally fine sand and water.

We subjoin a table, by which it will be seen that our waggon-wheel was 5yds. 2½in. circumference; this fraction gives some little trouble in the preliminary computation, and it looked very absurd to calculate the stages to half an inch, but if we had thrown it out a considerable error would have accumulated, and when the table was once formed the trouble was at an end.

TROCHEAMETER TABLE.

First Wheel.

No.	Fur.	Yds.	Ft.	In.	No.	Fur.	Yds.	Ft.	In.
1	—	5	0	2½	52	1	43	1	10
2	—	10	0	5	53	1	48	2	0½
3	—	15	0	7½	54	1	53	2	3
4	—	20	0	10	55	1	58	2	5½
5	—	25	1	0½	56	1	63	2	8
6	—	30	1	3	57	1	68	2	10½
7	—	35	1	5½	58	1	74	0	1
8	—	40	1	8	59	1	79	0	3½
9	—	45	1	10½	60	1	84	0	6
10	—	50	2	1	61	1	89	0	8½
11	—	55	2	3½	62	1	94	0	11
12	—	60	2	6	63	1	99	1	1½
13	—	65	2	8½	64	1	104	1	4
14	—	70	2	11	65	1	109	1	6½
15	—	76	0	1½	66	1	114	1	9
16	—	81	0	4	67	1	119	1	11½
17	—	86	0	6½	68	1	124	2	2
18	—	91	0	9	69	1	129	2	4½
19	—	96	0	11½	70	1	134	2	7
20	—	101	1	2	71	1	139	2	9½
21	—	106	1	4½	72	1	145	0	0
22	—	111	1	7	73	1	150	0	2½
23	—	116	1	9½	74	1	155	0	5
24	—	121	2	0	75	1	160	0	7½
25	—	126	2	2½	76	1	165	0	10
26	—	131	2	5	77	1	170	1	0½
27	—	136	2	7½	78	1	175	1	3
28	—	141	2	10	79	1	180	1	5½
29	—	147	0	0½	80	1	185	1	8
30	—	152	0	3	81	1	190	1	10½
31	—	157	0	5½	82	1	195	2	1
32	—	162	0	8	83	1	200	2	3½
33	—	167	0	10½	84	1	205	2	6
34	—	172	1	1	85	1	210	2	8½
35	—	177	1	3½	86	1	215	2	11
36	—	182	1	6	87	2	1	0	1½
37	—	187	1	8½	88	2	6	0	4
38	—	192	1	11	89	2	11	0	6
39	—	197	2	1½	90	2	16	0	9
40	—	202	2	4	91	2	21	0	11½
41	—	207	2	6½	92	2	26	1	2
42	—	212	2	9	93	2	31	1	4½
43	—	217	2	11½	94	2	36	1	7
44	1	3	0	2	95	2	41	1	9½
45	1	8	0	4½	96	2	46	2	0
46	1	13	0	7	97	2	51	2	2½
47	1	18	0	9½	98	2	56	2	5
48	1	23	1	0	99	2	61	2	7½
49	1	28	1	2½	100	2	66	2	10
50	1	33	1	5	101	2	72	0	0½
51	1	38	1	7½					

Second Wheel.

No.	Miles.	Fur.	Yds.	Ft.	In.	No.	Miles.	Fur.	Yds.	Ft.	In.
1	—	2	72	0	0½	20	5	6	120	0	10
2	—	4	144	0	1	30	8	5	180	1	3
3	—	6	216	0	1½	40	11	5	20	1	8
4	1	1	68	0	2	50	14	4	80	2	1
5	1	3	140	0	2½	60	17	3	140	2	6
6	1	5	212	0	3	70	20	2	200	2	11
7	2	0	64	0	3½	80	23	2	41	0	4
8	2	2	136	0	4	90	26	1	101	0	9
9	2	4	208	0	4½	100	29	0	161	1	2
10	2	7	60	0	5						

We give also an example of the work :—

December 27, 1861.—From Christmas Tree, south-west angle of Lake Ngami, two miles from Bolebeng—trocheameter at zero.

First halt south of the Lake :—

Trocheameter... 6 37

	m.	fur.	yds.	ft.	in.
6	1	5	212	0	3
37	0	0	187	1	8½
	1	6	179	1	11½

28th.—North of the Vlei Moslenyan :—

Trocheameter... 22 91
              6 37
           _____
             16 54

	m.	fur.	yds.	ft.	in.
10	2	7	60	0	5
6	1	5	212	0	3
54	0	1	53	2	3
	4	6	105	2	11

29th.—The Big Tree, or Baobab at Mamakahooie :—

Borrow 101
Trocheameter... 50 73
              22 91
           _____
             27 83

	m.	fur.	yds.	ft.	in.
20	5	6	120	0	10
7	2	0	64	0	3½
83	0	1	200	2	3½
	8	0	165	0	5

29th, p.m.—A hollow, with water :—

Borrow 101
Trocheameter ... 76   53
                 50   73
                 ─────
                 25   81

		m.		fur.		yds.		ft.		in.
20	....	5	......	6	......	120	......	0	.....	10
5	....	1	......	3	......	140	......	0	.....	2½
81	....	0	......	1	......	190	......	1	......	10½
		7	......	4	......	10	......	2	......	11

30th.—A small Vlei :—

Borrow 101
Trocheameter ... 93   44
                 76   53
                 ─────
                 16   92

		m.		fur.		yds.		ft.		in.
10	....	2	......	7	......	60	......	0	......	5
6	....	1	......	5	......	212	......	0	.....	3
92	....	0	......	2	......	26	......	1	......	2
		4	......	7	......	78	......	1	.....	10

31st.—Outspan in the Bush.

Trocheameter ... 12   89
Add.........100
                 ─────
                 112   89
                 93   44
                 ─────
                 19   45

		m.		fur.		yds.		ft.		in.
10	....	2	......	7	......	60	......	0	......	5
9	....	2	......	4	......	208	.....	0	......	4½
45	....	0	......	1	......	8	......	0	......	4½
		5	......	5	......	56	......	1	......	2

As a means of measuring a base line for triangulation of a country the trocheameter is invaluable. Suppose the course is north, and that a mountain bears 90°, or east; let the waggon travel till the mountain bears 45° more southerly, or 135°, *i.e.*, south-east; then stop the waggon, read the trocheameter, and the length of road travelled will be equal to the distance of the mountain from the starting place. Even if the course does not form a right angle with the bearing, the same method may be followed, involving only a little more calculation, or the trouble of laying down the angle upon paper. In places where a waggon cannot travel, it would be well to have a large wheel, on the principle of the old perambulator, and fix the trocheameter upon it; only let it be loaded, so as to bear the semblance of usefulness in the eyes of natives, or even of illiterate white men, or they will infallibly carry it over the bad places, as Captain Sturt's men did, to save themselves trouble. The trocheameter may be fitted to any piece of machinery, as the screw or paddles of a steamer, the sails of a windmill, a waterwheel, or anything capable of turning round.

To Ascertain the Variation of the Compass.

The rule for ascertaining this by the bearing of the rising or setting sun is given in all epitomes of navigation, and need not be repeated here; but this is only practicable in a level country, where the sun can be seen within at most a few minutes of the proper times, and cannot be carried out among mountains or thick forests. In such case we were in the habit of setting up two sticks (A A), stretching a thread (B) across them, and from the middle of this letting fall a

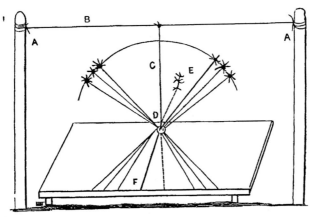

plumb line (C); then, taking a flat board, with a sheet of paper (D) stretched on it and projecting a little over the edge, make a hole in the projecting part to let the plumb line hang through, taking care not to vitiate its correctness; then select an object (E), the small upright stem of a tree, or set up a stick at a good distance, 100yds. or 200yds., or more, as nearly compass north of the plumb line as possible—if it is not exactly so, note its deviation on either side with the utmost correctness, and draw on the paper the line F D, which, if prolonged, would reach the tree at E. Then, between ten and eleven in the forenoon, set out the artificial horizon, and take an altitude of the sun; call "stop" sharply at the moment of observation, and let

T T

an assistant, with a straight-edged rule and pencil, draw the line of shadow cast by the plumb line at that moment; read off, and let your assistant record your observed altitude beside the line he has drawn; rest a minute or two at least; then take another observation, and so on, till three or five, or any odd number of lines have been drawn, forming a pencil of rays from the plumb line. Leave the sextant clamped at the last observation, and in the afternoon, before the sun comes down at that altitude, be ready with the horizon, and call "stop" at the moment, or even just before, the sun comes into contact, your assistant being ready, as before, to draw the shadow of the plumb line. You will now find that the short interval of rest taken between the morning observation will give you time to set your sextant to the next altitude, and to wait quietly till the sun comes down to it; do the same with the rest; and, when all are drawn, take the mean of each pencil of lines, and between them draw an exact central line, radiating like the rest from the plumb line; it will be evident that this must represent the shadow when the sun's centre was exactly on the meridian, and therefore it must be due north and south. Measure the angle between this and the magnetic north line already drawn, and the result in degrees and minutes will be the variation of your compass; or, take the bearing of the line by compass, and the result in points or in degrees will be the variation, which call east or west, as the compass north is to the east or west of the true meridian. Take the bearing again of the tree or mark set up in the morning to ascertain that your paper has not been shifted during the observations. If your magnetic line has not been drawn exactly north and south it is not of great importance; but remember that the exact error must be ascertained and allowed for by addition or subtraction in calculating the angle between it and the true north. An unknown error, however small, renders an observation useless; but a known error, however great, involves only the trouble of correction.

To obtain Levels or low Altitudes.

In mapping a country, it is desirable to give as nearly as possible the comparative heights of the hills; or it may be necessary to take the altitude of a low star, or the height of a tree or other object. For this purpose take a widemouthed jar or glass bottle, such as is used for the collection of specimens; round the neck of it splice or tie a cord or thong of leather to carry it by; then tie or fix by sealing-wax, gum, or resin, two hairs or threads crossing each other at right angles; and then, standing over the jar with the face towards the object to be measured, take a pocket, or full-sized sextant, and bring the top of the object to the spot where the threads cross each other, taking care to keep the eye so perpendicularly above their junction that the crossed lines and their reflected image may appear in one; then read off the observed angle—for instance 110° 42′ 30″. Apply the index error, which suppose to be 30″ subtracted, and subtract 90° from the corrected altitude, the remainder will be the true altitude; thus:

	°	′	″
Observed △	110	42	30
Index error	0	0	30
	110	42	0
	90	0	0
Altitude required	20	42	0

It will conduce very greatly to steadiness if a rest is used; the stand of a theodolite, with the instrument removed, or of a photographic camera, or three forked sticks set up so that the sight could be directed downwards through a central aperture, would answer the purpose. If the sextant is set to 90°, allowing for index error, and the horizon is swept round with it, the eye being kept steadily perpendicular to the cross lines, it will at once show what objects are above or below the level of the observer's eye. A looking-glass may be used in the same manner, but it must be very carefully tested in every direction with a spirit level; and 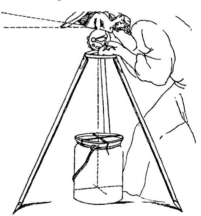 even then it is but an inefficient substitute for the mercury, which levels itself, and which *cannot* possibly give a false result, because nothing but agitation can destroy the perfect level of its surface, and unless it is at rest it cannot reflect an unbroken image, and no observation can be made.

A looking-glass may also be suspended vertically, its surface being tested by two plum lines, one on each side its centre. A horizontal line may be stretched at a foot or two from its front; then, if the observer, retiring a few paces, raises or lowers himself till the line and its reflection appear in one—his eye and the line must be in the same horizontal plane—and he may observe the altitude of the sun, or other celestial body, when in the zenith or too high to be observed in the mercurial artificial horizon; this plan, however, is only an approximation to correctness, and should only be used when the mercurial horizon is not available.

THE PLANE TABLE, AND ITS USE.

In making a plane table, discard all the complicated arrangements of sights, protractors, fixed compasses, spirit levels, and levelling

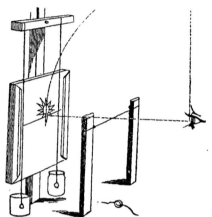

screws, each of which has an individual error, which must be found and allowed for before correctness can be attained; while the approximation to perfection gained by their most careful use is almost certain to be vitiated by the contraction of the paper when removed from the table on which it has been stretched.

Take any flat board—Fig. 1 (an artist's drawing-board) is as good as any—and stretch on it a sheet of drawing or stout cartridge paper: the best levelling apparatus is a wooden hemisphere (Fig. 2), screwed temporarily on its back, and working in a circular aperture (Fig. 3) in the top of such a stand as is used for the photographic camera or theo-

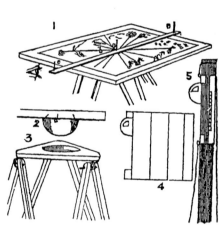

dolite; there is no necessity that the surface should be truly horizontal; indeed, it is much better that it should be capable of alteration of position, so that objects above or below its horizon may be sighted and mapped at pleasure. Set up a needle (a) in the centre of the drawing-paper, and lay against it a straight-edged rule (b) with two other needles (c c), set perfectly upright in each end as near as possible to the fiducial edge, as sights; then, choosing some principal object—say a well-marked conical peak, the bluff edge of a precipice, or a deep and narrow cleft in distant mountains—and keeping your ruler pressed against the central needle, bring the others, which serve as sights, in careful alignment with the object, and draw a pencil line along the fiducial edge right across the paper; then, with your prismatic compass (resting on the table for greater steadiness, if there is no iron in it to affect the magnet), take very carefully the bearing of the object, and note in it degrees from north, or zero, say 40°, on the line you have drawn; then lightly sketch the object on the line, estimating its distance from the centre, according to the scale on which you are working, say one or more inches to a mile. Direct the sights to any number of well-marked and recognisable objects, draw lines, and sketch them lightly at their estimated distances. Then have a mark set up as far off as possible, say a mile, or any carefully-measured distance, direct the sights, and draw a line towards it; mark its distance accurately on the paper, and insert the pivot needle there; remove the table to the marked spot, and, with your prismatic compass, set the first line again to 40°; then bring your sights to bear upon the object, draw another line along your straight edge, and the point at which this cuts the first will be the true position of your object; correct your first sketch still lightly, but do not efface anything; sight all the other objects, and sketch them where the second set of lines cut the first. Then choose another station, forming, if possible, an equilateral triangle with the other two; mark its position on the map, remove the proof needle there, carry the table to the spot, set the first line again to 40°, and sight the same objects a third time all round, and the third set of lines crossing the other two will give their true distance from the centre with sufficient accuracy for all ordinary purposes.

A ball and socket joint for adjusting the table to the necessary alterations of level may be made by nailing on beneath it a hemisphere of wood (Fig. 2), working in a circular hole (Fig. 3) in the top of the stand.

Extemporised Sight Vane for Levelling Staff.

Fig. 5. Suppose your staff 1½in. thick: take a piece of tin about 7in. wide, and of any convenient length, say nearly square; line it off as in Fig. 4, so that there shall be three divisions parallel to each other, as wide as the staff is thick, and on one side of them leave another division, about ¾in. wide, and on the other mark and cut out two projections ¾in. square, and a semicircular eyepiece, somewhat larger, with a quadrant-like aperture, as in the illustration (p. 644); bend the tin at the divisional lines, so as to clasp the staff loosely, with the sight vane projecting from it; let a cord be attached to the top of the tin, and pass through a hole in the top of the staff to draw it up by, and attach another cord to the bottom to draw it down again if required. Upon the edge of the narrowest divisions draw the subdivisions of the measures already marked upon your staff, letting them commence from the level of the bottom of the aperture in the sight vane, and read downwards; then, directing the telescope of your levelling instrument towards the staff, let an assistant lower or raise the sight vane according to your signals, and then read off the number of sub-

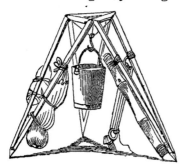

divisions on the vernier until you come down to a line, marking a division on the staff; read off this, and add the fractional parts, and the excess or deficiency over or below the height of the eye will be the difference of level in feet, inches, or whatever measurement may be used.

Movable stands for instruments must be light for the sake of portability, but steadiness cannot be obtained without weight; and for this purpose a bucket of water, a bamboo filled with water or sand, a bag of stones or sand, a large stone, or lashing to a tent peg driven into the ground, may be employed, as in our illustration.

Makeshift Clinometer.

Captain Lendy recommends a simple form of clinometer, which is constructed as follows: The clinometer consists of a quadrant of

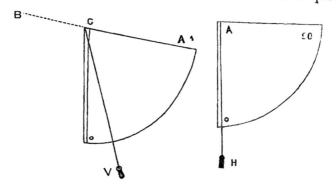

pasteboard or of brass, having a plummet, A H, suspended at its centre, and should be graduated, on both sides. When we require an angle of elevation, we look along the edge, A C, till B is in sight, when the plummet indicates the angle. For an angle of depression reverse the instrument. This instrument is an excellent substitute for the ordinary form of sextant in case of accident or breakage.

The same officer describes an ingenious substitute for an ordinary water level, which can always be replaced by a little ruler, A B, suspended by strings, C A, C B, having a little weight under it to prevent the wind from shaking it. When held by the string the line A B will give a horizontal direction. To make use of it for levelling along A B, start from A, hold the ruler up to the eye, and aiming

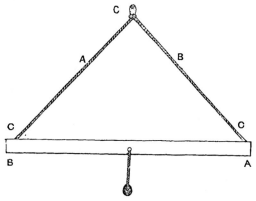

along its edge, notice to what point (B) of the ground the visual ray corresponds. Repair there, we shall have ascended a distance—the height of the eye above the ground. Start afresh from B, and in this manner the number of stations made between A and B, multiplied by the height of the eye above ground, will give the difference of level required.

The same author gives the following useful hints on the estimation of distance : " Pacing is generally resorted to while filling in the details of a survey. The trotting of a horse might also be made available. Distances can also be measured by time when we have previously ascertained over how many yards we walk or ride in a given time. This is not a rare occurrence in the field. When distances are measured by pacing or riding a correction is necessary, owing to the lengthening caused by acclivities and the turnings of roads. On slightly uneven ground we subtract 1-7th of the distance paced, and 1-5th when the inductions are more important."

When the atmosphere is even sound travels at the rate of 1118ft. per second ; therefore a musket fired may serve to measure a distance. A watch gives the number of seconds elapsed between the instant the light is seen and that when the report is heard ; that number, multiplied by 1118ft., gives very approximately the dis-

tance. If no watch is to be had the time is obtained by counting the
pulsations of an artery. A sound pulse averages from 75 to 80 in a
minute. Distances may even be guessed by observing that in clear
weather the windows of a house can be counted at 4000yds.
Horses and men appear as dots at 2200yds. A horse is clearly
seen at 1200yds. The movements of men are perceived at 800yds.;
and the head is distinctly visible at 400yds.

For the measurement of time, as we have said before, a thoroughly
well-made English lever watch is preferable to a chronometer, as it
will withstand the rough jolts and vibrations caused by being carried
on horseback, or in a waggon, far better. Sun-dials, properly so
called, are rarely of much use to the traveller; still the pocket compass
may be made to do duty as an indicator of time. There is a small and
very portable little instrument to be obtained of most opticians, in
the formation of which a silk cord is so attached to the border of the
compass case that on adjusting the compass, so that the needle shall
point to a black stud inserted for the purpose, a shadow is cast by the
silk on the figure indicating the hour of the day. A small equation
table is attached to the inside of the cover.

When no watch is at hand seconds can be indicated closely enough
for practical purposes by suspending a small bag of shot or bullets
from the end of a piece of fine fishing line or copper wire. Attach the
upper end to a cross bar, laid in the crutches of two forked sticks, let
the bag hang, and regulate the length of the string until you find that
it describes the proper arc in swinging; your own pulse, the number
of which has been already given, or that of a horse, which may be
roughly set down as thirty-six beats per minute, will be a sufficient
guide. If great accuracy is sought, recourse may be had to repeated
astronomical observations.

An excellent makeshift hour-glass can be made from two empty
soda-water bottles, and a little fine dry sand. A wooden plug of 3in.
long should be so cut as to fit the necks of the bottles tightly.
Through the centre of the plug, from end to end, burn with a red-
hot wire a fine even hole, then with your pocket-knife make a funnel-
shaped or flared-out mouth to each hole, cutting away until the
extreme edge of the plug is reached. See that your sand is free
from small stones or lumps, pour it into one of the bottles, insert
the plug half-way, and test the quantity by letting it run out at the
hole. When you have the proper charge to run for fifteen or thirty
minutes, place the bottles mouth to mouth in such a way that one-half
the plug shall be in the neck of each bottle. A bit of raw hide sewn
round the union of the bottle mouths makes all secure. The joined

bottles can then be mounted in a wooden frame for use. Two bits of flat square board, with holes in the centre for the bottoms of the bottles to come partly through, pinned at the corners by four bars of wood, is as good a form of frame as any.

The Malays make use of a very convenient and simple form of time indicator or water clock, which is made as follows :—A large-sized cocoa-nut shell is obtained ; this is first scraped perfectly smooth, and then at the bottom a very minute hole is bored. The nutshell is then set floating in a pail of sea water. As the shell fills it gradually settles deeper and deeper, and at last sinks to the bottom with a gurgle and a thud. The rapidity of filling, and consequent duration of time, is regulated by increasing or diminishing the size of the orifice. Thus a man may be set to keep a two-shell watch or a four shell watch, and so on. The instant the shell sinks to the bottom of the pail it attracts attention by the disturbance made. It is then immediately taken up, the water is poured out, and it is set afloat again. Excellent time can be kept by this primitive arrangement.

For ascertaining the altitude of high lands, ranges of hills or mountains, a thoroughly good "compensated" aneroid barometer should be taken. This will not only be valuable for measurements, but will be of considerable service in the observation of weather signs. We have one now in use made expressly for us by Mr. Cary, of 181, Strand. It is protected by a smooth wooden cover or case, enveloped in tightly-stretched leather. A sling is fitted to it by a swivel loop, which admits of its being carried over the shoulder or in the jacket pocket. The Table of Altitudes, given on the next page, will prove a useful guide when conducting observations with it.

TABLE OF ALTITUDES.

Aneroid or Corrected Barometer.	Height in feet.	Aneroid or Corrected Barometer.	Height in feet.	Aneroid or Corrected Barometer.	Height in feet.	Aneroid or Corrected Barometer.	Height in feet.	Aneroid or Corrected Barometer.	Height in feet.	Aneroid or Corrected Barometer	Height in feet.
in.	ft.	in.	ft.	in.	ft.	in.	ft.	in.	ft.	in.	ft.
31·00	0	28·80	2000	26·76	4000	24·87	6000	23·11	8000	21·47	10000
30·94	50	28·75	2050	26·72	4050	24·82	6050	23·07	8050	21·44	10050
30·88	100	28·70	2100	26·67	4100	24·78	6100	23·03	8100	21·40	10100
30·83	150	28·64	2150	26·62	4150	24·73	6150	22·98	8150	21·36	10150
30·77	200	28·59	2200	26·57	4200	24·69	6200	22·94	8200	21·32	10200
30·71	250	28·54	2250	26·52	4250	24·64	6250	22·90	8250	21·28	10250
30·66	300	28·49	2300	26·47	4300	24·60	6300	22·86	8300	21·24	10300
30·60	350	28·43	2350	26·42	4350	24·55	6350	22·82	8350	21·20	10350
30·54	400	28·38	2400	26·37	4400	24·51	6400	22·77	8400	21·16	10400
30·49	450	28·33	2450	26·33	4450	24·46	6450	22·73	8450	21·12	10450
30·43	500	28·28	2500	26·28	4500	24·42	6500	22·69	8500	21·08	10500
30·38	550	28·23	2550	26·23	4550	24·37	6550	22·65	8550	21·05	10550
30·32	600	28·18	2600	26·18	4600	24·33	6600	22·61	8600	21·01	10600
30·26	650	28·12	2650	26·13	4650	24·28	6650	22·57	8650	20·97	10650
30·21	700	28·07	2700	26·09	4700	24·24	6700	22·52	8700	20·93	10700
30·15	750	28·02	2750	26·04	4750	24·20	6750	22·48	8750	20·89	10750
30·10	800	27·97	2800	25·99	4800	24·15	6800	22·44	8800	20·85	10800
30·04	850	27·92	2850	25·94	4850	24·11	6850	22·40	8850	20·82	10850
29·99	900	27·87	2900	25·89	4900	24·06	6900	22·36	8900	20·78	10900
29·93	950	27·82	2950	25·85	4950	24·02	6950	22·32	8950	20·74	10950
29·88	1000	27·76	3000	25·80	5000	23·97	7000	22·28	9000	20·70	11000
29·82	1050	27·71	3050	25·75	5050	23·93	7050	22·24	9050	20·66	11050
29·77	1100	27·66	3100	25·71	5100	23·89	7100	22·20	9100	20·63	11100
29·71	1150	27·61	3150	25·66	5150	23·84	7150	22·16	9150	20·59	11150
29·66	1200	27·56	3200	25·61	5200	23·80	7200	22·11	9200	20·55	11200
29·61	1250	27·51	3250	25·56	5250	23·76	7250	22·07	9250	20·51	11250
29·55	1300	27·46	3300	25·52	5300	23·71	7300	22·03	9300	20·47	11300
29·50	1350	27·41	3350	25·47	5350	23·67	7350	21·99	9350	20·44	11350
29·44	1400	27·36	3400	25·42	5400	23·62	7400	21·95	9400	20·40	11400
29·39	1450	27·31	3450	25·38	5450	23·58	7450	21·91	9450	20·36	11450
29·34	1500	27·26	3500	25·33	5500	23·54	7500	21·87	9500	20·32	11500
29·28	1550	27·21	3550	25·28	5550	23·50	7550	21·83	9550	20·29	11550
29·23	1600	27·16	3600	25·24	5600	23·45	7600	21·79	9600	20·25	11600
29·17	1650	27·11	3650	25·19	5650	23·41	7650	21·75	9650	20·21	11650
29·12	1700	27·06	3700	25·15	5700	23·37	7700	21·71	9700	20·18	11700
29·07	1750	27·01	3750	25·10	5750	23·32	7750	21·67	9750	20·14	11750
29·01	1800	26·96	3800	25·05	5800	23·28	·7800	21·63	9800	20·10	11800
28·96	1850	26·91	3950	25·01	5850	23·24	7850	21·59	9850	20·07	11850
28·91	1900	26·86	3900	24.96	5900	23·20	7900	21·55	9900	20·03	11900
28·86	1950	26·81	3950	24·92	5950	23·15	7950	21·51	·9950	10·99	11950
28·80	2000	26·76	4000	24·87	6000	23·11	8000	21·47	10000	19·95	12000

This Table is intended more particularly for the graduation of aneroids with a circle of measures in feet concentric with the ordinary circle of barometric height measured in inches. The circle of feet is to be read off, at the upper and lower stations, by the index; and the rule for measuring the height will be : Subtract the reading at the lower station from the reading at the upper station; the difference is the height in feet.

EXAMPLE.

	In.	Ft.
Barometer at Upper Station, 23·50		7550
„ Lower „ 24·20		6750
Actual Height		800

There is no correction for temperature required with aneroids which are "compensated."

In using the instrument here described in the measurement of altitudes, the movable needle point which is turned by the mill-edged rim is set opposite the index hand. This is to be done at the foot of the mountain or hill. Then the difference between the index hand and the movable needle point will be the number of feet ascended (*vide* Table appended, and "Example"). Suppose the index hand stand when at the foot of the hill at 30in. $\frac{10}{100}$, and when you again look at the instrument you find the index hand has gone beck, or has fallen to 22in. $\frac{12}{100}$, then you would have ascended 900ft.

At page 22 of this work we referred to the hypsometrical or boiling-point apparatus used in taking altitudes. Since the remark there made was penned we have endeavoured, and we hope successfully, to so guard the improved form of aneroid barometer, referred to at p. 649, from the chance of accident, that it can be safely carried by the explorer of even the most rugged and inhospitable regions.

On the Use of the Sextant and Artificial Horizon.

We do not propose in this work to trespass on the province of books on nautical astronomy. We take it for granted that every traveller using a sextant will also provide himself with an Epitome—Norie's, Raper's, or Kerigan's (of course the latest possible edition of either), and with the "Nautical Almanac," which may be had for three years in advance, by persons contemplating a long journey.

The most important instrument is the sextant itself, and in the selection of this the greatest care should be used. Ebony or other wood may do for the frames of such as are to be used at sea in temperate climates, but for tropical use, even for sea service, we recommend a brass or gun-metal frame, and for observing on land no other should be used.

The quadrant, which is quite equal to the observation of altitude at sea, will take an angle of 90°, but should read up to 10° or 20° more; but the sextant, or sixth of a circle, is made to take in an angle of twice 60°, or 120°, and should also read 10° or 20° higher.

The sextant we generally use—and which we have tested by many years' constant use—is brass framed, reads to 126° 56', is of 8 inches radius, and has its arc and vernier on which the figures are engraved of gold, which has a soft lustre, exceedingly agreeable to the eye under a tropical sun, and is equally pleasant to read by lamp light; a screen of ground grass is placed before it to soften the light still more, and prevent annoying glitter and reflection; the degrees are divided into sixths of ten minutes each, and the minutes likewise into ten seconds; the microscope travels on a fixed frame, and a small milled-headed screw brings it to the figures to be read. A small lamp fixed on the axis of the index arm, with a reflector to shed the light upon the arc and vernier, is sometimes made use of.

For nearly all angular measurements that an explorer is likely to require, a really good sextant will be found sufficient, but some, for the sake of still greater power and accuracy, provide themselves with a repeating circle; but although this possesses many advantages, we doubt whether the expense of such an instrument will not place it beyond the reach of the generality of travellers, while the extra care required will constitute too great a claim upon the time of any who cannot devote themselves entirely to astronomical observations. The double sextant invented by Captain George, R.N., of the astronomical department of the Royal Geographical Society, described at page 23 of this work, will be found a portable and most convenient instrument for the use of explorers.

The theodolite has also many advantages, especially in taking a round of angles; but from what we have seen of it in practice we should be inclined to think that an explorer, with his sextant and compass, is more independent, and can do more than he could possibly effect with the theodolite.

The artificial horizon is, as its name imports, intended to obviate the difficulties caused by the fact that the real, or sea horizon, may be at times invisible, obscured by fog or clouds, or that the observer may be absent from it, and often far inland, where the unevenness of the earth's surface prevents anything like a reliable real horizon being found. Of the artificial horizons used at sea we have not much to say, the unsteadiness of the vessel forbidding the use of any instrument that can be disturbed by motion. The best we have seen is Captain Becher's pendulum horizon, a little frame swinging near the object-glass of the sextant, and carrying a couple of horizontal wires, so arranged that when they appear in one to the eye of the observer they ought to be on a level with the horizon and parallel with it; a small lamp is so fitted to the sextant as to render these wires visible at night if the altitude of the moon or a star is required; but we do not think the latitude deduced from such an observation can be more than approximately true.

It is on shore, and most of all in the far interior of the great continents of the world, that the artificial horizon is most needed, and that it renders the truest service to the explorer; and therefore it is of the greatest importance that the instrument should be at once simple in construction, easy of management, not easily put out of order, and, above all, perfectly reliable in the result obtain from it. The first requisite is a perfectly flat and horizontal reflecting surface, in which, when the observer looks down upon it, the image of the sun or star may be distinctly seen. Now, it is easy to find flatness: a disc of silvered glass, or polished metal, or even a bit of crown glass, painted black on the under side, or a common round shaving-glass would do if this only were required; but this flat surface must also be perfectly horizontal, and to attain this various arrangements of tangent screws and spirit levels have been invented, all of which require great care in levelling, and have the defect that the slightest accidental touch while they are in use may alter the level, and so vitiate the observation. By common consent, therefore, observers almost universally trust to fluid mirrors, which must be perfectly level if they are sufficiently quiescent to reflect a perfect image. Water, darkened with any colouring matter, as ink; water with a little treacle, to render it less liable to be agitated by the wind, or thin tar will do; but all these have disadvantages which render them only fit to be looked upon as substitutes when mercury cannot be obtained; in fact, long ago we were told by the late Captain Washington, Hydrographer to the Admiralty, to use nothing but mercury.

The horizon trough, as it is called, is simply a block of wood of oblong form, about 6in. long, 4in. wide, and 1in. thick; this is hollowed to the depth of about $\frac{3}{8}$in. or $\frac{1}{2}$in., leaving a sufficient rim to retain the mercury which is poured into it. Sometimes a hole is pierced in the rim, and is continued in the solid wood under the hollow, so that the mercury, being poured into a small funnel fitted in the rim, runs underneath and rises like a fountain in the centre of the trough. The various arrangements of this kind and others more complicated are called fountain horizons, but they are not really necessary, their principal object being to insure the perfect purity of the mercurial surface by forcing it to flow downward first through the funnel, and so to leave the scum behind; but this object may be just as well attained by inverting the bottle, so that all the impurities may float upon the surface, and allow the pure mercury to run through the perforated stopper into the trough. The bottle is generally of iron, and has the perforated stopper already mentioned, which, when the mercury has to be returned to it, serves also as a funnel. Wooden bottles are also made, but no traveller ought to depend upon them, as in hot climates they shrink and split; and we have found in Namaqualand all our mercury adrift in a tinned box, forming an amalgam which did not at all improve it. We have, therefore, for many years, kept it in a common stoneware ink bottle, with a bit of washleather tied over the cork, and have found this to answer admirably; in pouring out the mercury, having removed the cork, we stop the mouth of the bottle with the forefinger, completely invert it, and then, slightly moving the finger, leave an opening sufficient for a stream of pure mercury to flow into the horizon. Our trough is round, and about 4in. across, which is quite large enough. In perfectly calm weather we prefer to observe on the plain surface of the uncovered mercury; but if wind comes on, as it often does in Africa and Australia about noon, we cover it with a roof of the usual form, *i.e.*, two small panes of glass fixed in a frame so as to form an angle of 45° each with the horizon, or 90° with each other, and, standing like a roof over the mercury, allow the rays from the heavenly body to pass down to it, and be reflected to the eye of the observer. Various methods of rendering this roof as portable as possible have been tried; our own is figured in the first chapter of this work.

Captain George's new artificial horizon, however, bids fair to supersede all the old forms of arrangement, as its portability, strength, and simplicity of adjustment stand unrivalled. Captain George's horizon may be made sufficiently large to equal the surface of the one now used; but the portable or pocket form here alluded to is of the following dimensions :—

Self-replenishing, 6in. long, 2½in. broad, ¾in. thick, weighs 1¼lb., cubic measure 11¼in.

The wooden one of olden date, 9½in. long, 5½in. broad, 5½in. thick, weighs 5⅜lb., cubic measure 287⅓in.

Improved folding roof, &c., all iron, 8in. long, 4½in. broad, 2½in. thick, weighs 6¾lb., cubic measure 90in. .

The improvements herein specified are not only its reduced size and weight, but its mechanical arrangements, form, and moderate price.

It consists of two circular disc-like reservoirs, about 2½in. in diameter, and ¾in. in depth, made of iron, at the same casting; one contains the mercury, and the other is the trough, fitted with glass cover for observing.

The discs are connected at their circumference by a narrow neck, and in it is drilled a hole, through which the mercury passes from one reservoir to the other; and this communication is opened or shut off by a stop-cock, on the cone principle, such as is used for water or gas, so that the mercury can be passed from one disc to the other without removing the glass cover, or the risk of losing any mercury.

The mercurial disc, A, is fitted with a cylinder stopper, D, acting on a spiral spring, by which air can be admitted or allowed to escape.

The trough disc, B, is fitted with two glasses, G and E, which are ground mathematically parallel; one of the glasses is fitted to a frame, and screws on the disc, and is used while passing the mercury in or out of the trough; after which operation it is removed and replaced by the other glass, the edge of which next the stop-cock should be supported by the blade of a pocket-knife and then lowered on the mercury at the opposite side, and by a gentle pressure, force out the intervening air, leaving the glass to float on the surface of the mercury. Without this care, some of the mercury might be pressed over the edge of the disc.

The glass then presents a clear reflecting surface, which is not only protected from the effects of the wind, &c., but also maintains so great a steadiness as to mark a decided improvement over the old triangular glass roof which is placed over the mercury, instead of, as in this case, being on it.

It may be used afloat under favourable circumstances (the observer and artificial horizon being placed on a pendulum table). Another great advantage to this improved artificial horizon is the facility with which altitudes can be observed at 2° elevation, and consequently its adaptation for the measurement of very low stars, as well as the peaks of mountain ranges.

To return the mercury to its reservoir, remove the glass G that floats on the mercury, by lifting it up with the point of a knife, and then screw on the other glass cover, E. It is now only necessary to hold the instrument vertically, the trough end being uppermost (Fig. 4), turn the stop-cock, and press gently downward on the cylindrical stopper, and the mercury will rapidly return to its reservoir.

The following diagrams (half the actual size of the instrument), show the various parts of the instrument, and the method of filling and emptying the reservoir.

Fig. 1 is the instrument complete. A, the mercurial reservoir; B, the observing trough; C, the stop-cock; D, the cylindrical stop.

Fig. 2 is the instrument with the parts of the observing trough removed, which are shown above it. E, rim with glass shade; F, rim without glass shade; G, the glass that floats on the surface of the mercury.

Fig. 3. Position of the instrument while filling the observing trough.

Fig. 4. Position of the instrument while returning the mercury into its reservoir.

In moderate weather the glass G will be quite sufficient protection against the wind, but in gusty weather screw on the rim F, but it must not touch the glass G.

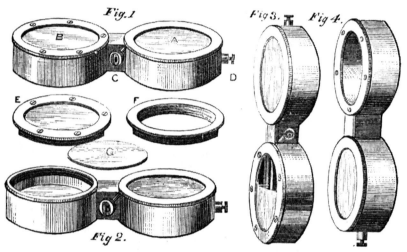

The glass E will protect it from any weather, taking care to level the ground on which the horizon stands.

In filling the observing trough, be careful that the glass cover, E, is screwed on tight; by pressing on the cylindrical stop D (Fig. 1) the mercury flows quickly: the trough half filled, as shown in Fig. 3, is sufficient for ordinary observations; but for very low altitudes the trough must be three-quarters filled or more as found necessary to raise glass G (Fig. 1).

Before returning the mercury into the reservoir, unscrew the short tube near the stop-cock, tapping it smartly at the same time, to shake down the globules of mercury that may remain in the tube; there is a small hole in the screw, which must be brought in sight, then turn the stop-cock, and the mercury will run rapidly into the reservoir. When about to use a sextant and artificial horizon of the common form of construction, our first care is to select a tolerably level, and, if there be wind, a sheltered spot of ground, with a clear view to the north or south, or, if the stars admit of a north and south observation, to see that the view is clear both ways. On this we place our artificial horizon, sometimes on our sextant case, sometimes on a stand (wash leather), but seldom, if we can avoid it, on the bare ground, because then the mercury if spilled, would be difficult to gather up. The horizon roof we keep near to cover the mercury, in case wind should arise, but we never use it unless in case of necessity; then, sitting either north or south of the horizon, according to the position of the celestial object, we look with the naked eye for its reflected image in the mercury, and so seat ourselves that we can conveniently keep it steadily in view. We set the sextant nearly to zero, and look up without the telescope to the sun or star, and then, gradually moving the index forward, we bring its image down to meet the reflection in the quicksilver; then, screwing

on the inverting telescope, which is the simplest and best for observation, we move the index by hand, till the contact is nearly perfect; then fasten the index by the clamping screw, and with the tangent screw complete the contact; and so long as the object is rising, by gradually turning the tangent screw we keep the images together; when they separate more slowly, and at length remain in contact for nearly half a minute, we know that the meridian altitude has been observed; we wait another minute to see them separate in the opposite direction as the body begins to descend, and then read off the observed altitude. Our illustration will sufficiently explain that the sextant is held in the left hand and the tangent screw worked with the thumb and forefinger of the right. Fig. 2 is the method recommended by Captain George: the arc is steadied by the forefinger, and the tangent screw turned by the middle finger and the thumb; a police or bull's-eye lantern is good to read off by, and the light, of whatever nature, should be placed behind the observer, so that it may not interfere with his work, and yet may be ready for him to use when he wishes to read his altitude.

Projection of Routes.

The following directions for the projections of routes by Captain George, R.N., are so thoroughly plain and practical that it will be well for the travelling observer to have recourse to them:—For out-door or field work the easiest method is by the plane projection, the data thus obtained being transferred to a Mercator's projection at the first halt or stopping station. In the plane projection one equal length is assigned to all the degrees of latitude and longitude. It was first adopted on the erroneous supposition that the earth's surface is a plane; it is still the best for the traveller to use in his early attempts to project his journey while the objects are still in sight. This projection is available as far as 20° on either side of the Equator; beyond the parallel of 20° and as far as 60° Mercator's projection is preferable. Between 60° and the pole the distortion of both the plane and Mercator's projection is so apparent, that a polar or circular projection must be adopted. Sheets of paper, ruled into squares by strong lines, and subdivided by finer ones, afford great assistance in map work. For out-door work the scale of 1in. to one mile is amply large enough to register every particular of one day's journey on a sheet of 12in. square. The in-door, or table plan, may be reduced ten miles to the inch, and plans for transmission home may be again reduced to 1in. to 1° when larger plans cannot be sent. The chief point aimed at in the following directions is to draw more attention than has hitherto been given to the true bearing of objects, for the following reasons : First. Any object whose true bearing is east or west must be in the same latitude as the place of the observer. Secondly. Any object whose true bearing is north or south must be in the same longitude as the place of the observer.

While travelling in a northerly or southerly direction, from a station whose latitude is known, and carefully noting the distance and direction travelled, it is only necessary to watch when objects come to the true east or west, and their latitude is obtained. When travelling in an easterly or westerly direction from a fixed station, noting distance and direction, it is only necessary to watch when objects come to the true north or south, and their difference of longitude can be obtained by using Table B, from the station left. Thus, suppose a traveller passes from A, whose latitude is known, towards some distant hill (B), his route making an angle of 25° with the meridian. He sets his sextant to 65° (65°+25°=90°), or to 115° (180°—65°); then as the objects 1, 2, 3, and 4 successively come into

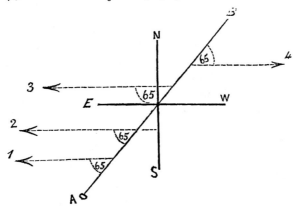

contact with B or A, as the case may be, he ascertains with precision the moment when they are truly east or west of him, and so, knowing the distance he has travelled from A, he can readily calculate or project their latitude.

When the traveller, as will frequently be the case, has to deviate from the line of route, his position can be determined by compass, or true bearing of any object, and an angle of a second object; or he may have recourse to transit observations; that is to say, wherever two fixed objects come in line, an angle to a third object will determine the position with great accuracy.

Observe that in travelling along X Y Z the hills A B C can be mapped for at X, or thereabouts; the bearing of B from C can be

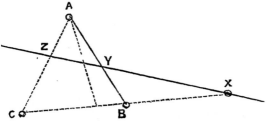

determined at Y; that of A from B; and at Z that of A from C, and so on, for any number of hills. And it is very important to recollect that it is not necessary to catch these lines of sight precisely, for by taking bearings twice, and the intermediate course approximately, there are sufficient data for protracting out upon paper the required bearing.

Thus, as soon as the peak of a distant hill is about to be occulted by the shoulder of a nearer one, a bearing should be taken, and again another as soon as it has reappeared on the other side, and the intermediate course noted.

The advantage of this method of filling up a field sketch will become more apparent as experience is gained. A third and accurate method of fixing the position is in general use among marine surveyors but has hitherto been but little resorted to by land travellers, viz., by the angles subtended between three known objects. The instrument called the station-pointer is generally used for this purpose, but the position may also be found with a pair of compasses and a protractor, or more simply as follows by means of a protractor and a sheet of tracing paper. Draw a line through the centre of the paper, place the protractor on it, near to the bottom of the sheet, lay off the right hand angle to the right, and the left hand angle to the left of the centre line; rule pencil lines, radiating from the point over which the centre of the protractor had been placed, to the points that had been laid off, then place the paper on the plan or map, and move it about until the three lines coincide with the objects taken, prick through the points that lay beneath the centre of the protractor, and the observer's position is transferred to the plan. When possible the centre object should be nearest.

To construct a Map on Mercator's Projection.

On a sheet of cartridge paper, 38in. by 20in., it is proposed to construct a map on Mercator's projection, on a scale of ten miles to an inch equatorial, *i.e.* 6in. to a degree of longitude.

Lat. 31° to 33° N.
Long. 34° to 36° E.

Draw a base line, find its centre, and erect a perpendicular to the top of the paper; the extremes of longitude 34° and 36°, added together and divided by 2°, give 35°, the central meridian, and which is represented by the perpendicular. On each side of it lay off 6in., and erect perpendiculars for the meridians 34° and 36°; divide the base line into ten mile divisions, and the part from 35° 50′ to 36° into miles for the latitude scale. From Table A take the following quantities :—

Lat. $3\overset{\circ}{1}$ to $3\overset{\circ}{2}$ = $\overset{\circ}{1}$ $1\overset{'}{0}$·4 = the distance between parallels $3\overset{\circ}{1}$ and $3\overset{\circ}{2}$
Lat. 32 to 33 = 1 11·1   ,,   ,,   32 and 33

2 21·5   31 to 33

Having thus obtained the distance between the required parallels, divide the map into squares of ten miles each way, and the map is ready for the projection of the route.

A.—Table to construct Maps on Mercator's Projection.

	0°	1°	2°	3°	4°	5°	6°	7°	8°	9°
0	° ′	1 00·0	1 00·1	1 00·1	1 00·1	1 00·2	1 00·3	1 00·4	1 00·5	1 00·6
10	1 00·9	1 01·0	1 01·2	1 01·5	1 00·7	1 02·0	1 02·2	1 02·6	1 02·9	1 03·3
20	1 03·6	1 04·1	1 04·5	1 04·9	1 05·5	1 05·9	1 06·5	1 07·0	1 07·7	2 08·2
30	1 09·0	1 09·6	1 10·4	1 11·1	1 12·0	1 12·8	1 13·7	1 14·6	1 15·7	1 16·7
40	1 17·6	1 19·0	1 20·1	1 21·4	1 22·7	1 24·2	1 25·6	1 27·1	1 28·8	1 30·6
50	1 32·4	1 34·3	1 36·4	1 38·6	1 40·8	1 43·4	1 45·9	1 49·0	1 51·4	1 54·8
60	1 58·3	2 01·8	2 05·8	2 09·9	2 14·5	2 19·14	2 24·7	2 30·5	2 36·8	2 43·8
70	2 51·3	2 59·8	3 09·1	3 19·6	3 31·3	3 44·6	3 59·8	4 17·1	4 37·4	5 01·1
80	5 29·5	6 03·0	6 46·4	7 40·3	8 51·1	10 27·7	12 47·9	16 29·6	32 14·3	39 42·2

Use of the table.—Find the required parallel; the tens at the side, and the units at the top. At their intersection will be found in degrees and minutes the distance of the required parallel from the next less degree, to be measured from the scale of longitude on the map in progress.

Given the parallel of 30°, required that of 31°. 30 at the side and 1 at the top intersects at 1° 09·6′, the required distance of the two parallels.

Given the parallel of 31°, required that of 33°.

$$32 = 1°\ 10·4′$$
$$33 = 1\ 11·1$$
$$\overline{}$$
$$2\ 21·5 \text{ the distance between the 31° and 33° parallels.}$$

B.—Given the Departure to find Difference of Longitude.

	0°	1°	2°	3°	4°	5°	6°	7°	8°	9°
0		1·0001	1·0006	1·0013	1·0026	1·0038	1·0055	1·0075	1·0098	1·0125
10	1·0154	1·0187	1·0224	1·0261	1·0306	1·0353	1·0403	1·0457	1·0514	1·0578
20	1·0642	1·0711	1·0785	1·0864	1·0946	1·1034	1·1126	1·1224	1·1326	1·1434
30	1·1547	1·1666	1·1792	1·1924	1·2062	1·2208	1·2361	1·2521	1·2690	1·2868
40	1·3054	1·3250	1.3456	1.3673	1·3902	1·4142	1·4395	1·4663	1·4945	1·5242
50	1·5557	1·5890	1·6242	1·6616	1·7013	1·7435	1·7883	1·8361	1·8871	1·9416
60	2·0000	2·0626	2·1301	2·2027	2·2812	2·3662	2·4586	2·5593	2·6695	2·7904
70	2·9238	3·0716	3·2361	3·4204	3·6280	3·8637	4·1337	4·4454	4·8097	5·2406
80	5·7587	6·3925	7·1856	8·2057	9·5664	11·475	14·334	19·108	28·653	57·307

Use of the table.—Find the required parallel, the tens at the side and the units at the top, at their intersection will be found a quantity, which, multiplied by the departure, gives the difference of longitude.

The departure from the meridian on the parallel of 34° was 25 miles, required the difference of longitude :

$25' \times 1\cdot20 = 30\cdot00'$ the difference of longitude.

In the parallel of 60° the departure was 30 miles.

$30' \times 2 = 60$ miles, or 1 degree.

In the parallel of 35° N. the route was N. 40° W. 37 miles distance.

By traverse table, 40° course, dist. 37° = dep. $23\cdot8' \times 1\cdot22 = 29\cdot03$ miles difference of longitude.

The following example will serve to show how the traveller's record of progress may be conveniently kept. It was framed by S. W. Norie expressly for the use of navigators ; but explorers and travellers will find it a simple and useful form for recording the day's work :

Corrected Courses.	Distance.	Difference of Latitude.		Departure.	
		N.	S.	E.	W.
N.E.	36	25·5		25·5	
N. by W.	14	13·7			2·7
N.E. by E. ½ E.	58	27·3		51·2	
N. by E.	42	41·2		8·2	
E.N.E.	29	11·1		26·8	
Difference of Lat...		118·8		111·7	2·7
				2·7	
			Dep....	109·0	

The difference of latitude 118·8 and departure 109·0 give the course N. 42° 32′ E., and distance 161·2.

Latitude left	52 36 N.	Merc. prjctns.	...3724...Longitude left.. 2i 45′ W.
Diff. lat.	1 59 N.		Diff. lon. 184 or 3 4 E.
Latitude in...	54 35 N.	Merc. prjctns.	...3925...Longitude in ...18 41 W.
Sum of lats. 2)107 11		Merc. diff. lat. 201	
Mid. lat.......	53 35		

TO MEASURE THE NUMBER OF CUBIC FEET OF WATER CONVEYED BY A RIVER IN EACH SECOND.

In traversing regions watered by rivers and running streams, it not unfrequently becomes important to ascertain the speed at which they flow in their downward course towards the sea, and the following directions given by Captain George, R.N., are so perfectly clear and practical that both time and trouble will be saved by the traveller who follows them out in conducting his investigations. The data required are—the area of the river, section, and the average velocity of the whole current. All that a traveller is likely to obtain without special equipment is the area of the river section, and the average velocity of the "surface" of the current which differs from that of its entire body, owing to fractional retardation at the bottom.

To make the necessary measurements, choose a piece where the river runs steadily in a straight and deep channel and where a boat can be had. Prepare half a dozen floats of dry bushes, with paper flags, and be assured they will act. Post an assistant on the river bank at a measured distance (of about 100 yards), down stream, in face of a well-marked object; row across stream, in a straight line, keeping two objects on a line in order to maintain your course. Sound at regular intervals from shore to shore, fixing your position on each occasion by a sextant angle between your starting place and your assistant's station, and throw the floats overboard, signalling to your assistant when you do so, that he may note the interval that elapses before they severally arrive opposite him. Take an angle from the opposite shore to give the breadth of the river. To make the calculation approximately, protract the section of the river on a paper, ruled to scale in square feet, and count the number of squares in the area of the section. Multiply this by the number of feet between you and the assistant, and divide by the number of seconds that the floats occupied on an average in reaching him.

Important rivers should always be measured above and below their confluence, for it settles the question of their relative sizes, and throws great light on the rainfall over their respective basins. The sectional area at the time of the highest water, as shown by marks on the banks and the slope of the bed, ought also to be ascertained.

ON OBTAINING GEOGRAPHICAL INFORMATION FROM NATIVES OR FRONTIER COLONISTS.

Many highly-accomplished travellers fail to obtain much reliable information beyond the actual limit of their own observation, because they do not sufficiently allow for the great difference in the manner of expressing a geographical idea between an educated European observer and an untutored savage; and yet it would not be too much to say that the latter has often enough a thoroughly practical idea of the district he actually knows.

The man who wants information must not talk latitude and longitude to a native or to an uneducated European, nor must he expect them to shape their answers to the form in which he expects to receive them; for if he does he may be told that "rivers run from the sea to the mountains," and other absurdities, which are related as proofs of native stupidity, when they are in reality no more than discrepancies between the form of question and that of the answer. At the same time he must estimate the mental calibre of his informant, and avoid wearying him too much; for sometimes the native mind, overburdened with a succession of ideas, becomes confused, and not unfrequently suspicious, and in this last case actual falsehoods will be told, in order to gain time to find out the intention of the questioner, before the truth is revealed.

In all dealings with natives the European must remember that they have no idea of the value we place upon time; there is no use in saying, "Let us come to the point at once." It is far better, indeed it is absolutely necessary, to delay judiciously, as there is always an implied contest between visitors; and the man who is in a hurry to speak loses dignity. Do not disturb your informant's train of thought, but try to accommodate your own to it. Let him tell as minutely and tediously as he pleases how he has travelled; how long he walked with the rising sun on his right or left; how much he turned either way; where he halted for rest or refreshment; whether he crossed rivers on foot or in canoes; induce him, if possible, to trace a map upon the ground, in doing which he will most probably begin by making the direction of all his lines coincide with the actual bearing of the country; for natives, though they may be brought to comprehend a map when its north point coincides with the real north, cannot believe that it is also right when it is placed in any other position. We have frequently tested Hottentots with regard to the direction of places a thousand miles distant, and have found them point as correctly as we could take the bearing with a pocket compass.

Sometimes it will be found that the same individual will give a river a dozen different names; and this is often because, in speaking of the different parts of it, he gives to each the name of the chief who has his village there, and who "drinks water" at the place which is called after him; therefore, endeavour to ascertain whether the river has a real name, and do not apply to it the first and, perhaps, the most inappropriate name that is given.

Europeans who have settled in the colonies, and have become traders or hunters, frequently push very far into the interior, and such men have generally very clear ideas of direction and locality, but are often very modest and diffident when asked to furnish information to be laid down on paper. In 1849, while staying at the Vaal River, we persuaded our friend Macabe, with some difficulty, to give us the length in " hours" and the direction of the various stages of his journey on the river Limpopo. These, with the rivers, mountains, villages, and other features of the country, we laid down, on a scale of one inch to a mile, on several sheets of cartridge paper, and tested the correctness of our work by laying it on the floor, with its north coinciding with the real north, and requesting our Dutch visitors to stand as if they were about commencing the same journey, and indicate how much they turned to the right or left as they proceeded.

The following facts relating to time should be impressed on the memory of every traveller :—The earth is divided in its circumference into $360°$; the day is divided into twenty-four hours. It therefore follows that $15°$ of longitude will represent one hour of time ; consequently, as you travel towards the east, when you have journeyed over $15°$, you will have gained one hour on the sun, which will rise just one hour earlier than it did at the starting point.

If natives accompany you on a journey, ask them to point in the direction of places at different times, and particularly to tell you when you are exactly abreast of them, as well as before, and after you have passed, and thus, by a kind of rough triangulation, you will gain their approximate position.

If cattle stray to great distances, ask the men who go after them the reason of their having taken any particular direction, and you will probably gain some information respecting the form of valleys or mountains, and perhaps of watering places.

In North Australia we were led by the tracks of horses, which had been lost about a fortnight, to a considerable stream.

CHAPTER XXI.

HINTS TO EXPLORERS ON COLLECTING AND PRESERVING OBJECTS OF NATURAL HISTORY.

By the courtesy of Mr. H. W. Bates, F.R.C.S. and Asst. Sec. R.G.S., we are enabled to furnish our readers with the following valuable and practical information regarding the gathering together and preserving such objects of natural history as he may be fortunate enough to discover:—

Travellers (says Mr. Bates) who intend devoting themselves especially to natural history will generally possess all the requisite information beforehand. It is to those whose objects or duties are of another nature, or who, whilst on a purely geographical land expedition, wish to know the readiest means of collecting, preserving, and safely transmitting specimens they collect, that the following hints are addressed.

Double barrel guns with spare nipples, and a few common guns to lend to native hunters, especially if going to the interior of tropical
Outfit.   America. Fine powder in canisters, and fine shot (Nos. 8 and 11), must be taken from England; coarse powder and shot can be had in any part; a good supply of the best caps. Arsenical soap, a few pounds in tin cases; brushes of different sizes; two or three scalpels; scissors (including a pair of short bladed ones); forceps of different sizes for inserting cotton into the necks of birds' skins; needles and thread. A few small traps with which to capture small (mostly nocturnal) animals; strong landing net for water mollusks, &c.; two stout insect sweeping nets; cylindrical tin box, with shoulder strap, for collecting plants: a few dozen of small and strong broad-mouthed bottles, and a couple of corked pocket boxes; insect pins, a few ounces each of Nos. 5, 14, and 11; stone jars, for reptiles and fishes in spirit, to fit four in a box, with wooden partitions. If animals in spirit are to be collected largely, a supply of sheet tin, or zinc, with a pair of soldering irons, and a supply of soft solder, must be taken instead of stone jars: cylindrical cases can be then made of any size required. By means of the soldering apparatus also empty powder canisters or other tin vessels can be easily converted into receptacles for specimens; a ream or two of botanical drying paper, with boards

of same size as the sheet, and leather straps ; a few gross of chip pill boxes in nests ; a dozen corked store boxes (about 14in. by 11in. and 2½in. deep) fitted perpendicularly in a tin chest ; a few yards of indiarubber waterproof sheeting, as temporary covering to collections in wet weather, or in crossing rivers ; a set of carpenter's tools.

An outfit may be much lightened by having all the provisions and other consumable articles packed in square tin cases, and in boxes and jars of such forms as may render them available for containing specimens. If the traveller is going to the humid regions of the Indian Archipelago, South-Eastern Asia, or tropical America, where excessive moisture, mildew, and ants are great enemies to the naturalist, he should add to his outfit two drying cages, for everything that is not put at once into spirits is liable to be destroyed before it is dry enough to be stowed away in boxes. They may be made of light wood, so arranged as to take to pieces and put together again readily ; one for birds should be about 2ft. 6in. long by 1ft. 6in. high, and 1ft. broad ; the other for insects and other small specimens may be about one-third less. They should have folding doors in front, having panels of perforated zinc, and the backs wholly of the latter material ; the sides fitted with racks to hold six or eight plain shelves, which in the smaller cage should be covered with cork or any soft wood that may be obtained in tropical countries. A strong fixed ring, fastened in the top of the cage, with a cord having a hook attached to the end, by which to hang it in an airy place ; it will keep the contained specimens out of harm's way until they are quite dry, when they may be stowed away in close fitting boxes. If this plan be not adopted, it will be almost impossible to preserve specimens in these countries.

The countries which are now the least known with regard to their natural history are New Guinea and the large islands to the east of it, Northern Australia, the island of Borneo, Tibet, and other parts of Central Asia, Equatorial Africa, and the eastern side of the Andes, from the east of Bogota to the south of Bolivia.

In most of the better-known countries botany has been better investigated than zoology; and in most countries there still remains much to be done in ascertaining the exact Collecting. station and the range both vertical and horizontal of known species. This leads us to one point which cannot be too strongly insisted on, namely, that some means should be adopted by the traveller to record the exact locality of the specimens he collects. In the larger-dried animals this may be done by written tickets attached to the specimens ;

in pinned insects a letter or number may be fixed on the pins of all specimens taken at one place and time, the mark to refer to a note book. The initial letter, or first two or three letters of the locality, is perhaps the readiest plan; and when all the specimens taken at one place can be put into a separate box, one memorandum upon the box itself will be sufficient. Reptiles and fishes can have small parchment tickets attached to them before placing them in spirits. A traveller may be puzzled in the midst of the profusion of animal and vegetable forms which he sees around him, to know what to secure and what to leave. Books can be of very little service to him on a journey, and he had better at once abandon all ideas of encumbering himself with them. A few days' study at the principal museums before he starts on his voyage may teach him a great deal, and the cultivation of a habit of close observation and minute comparison of the specimens he obtains will teach him a great deal more. As a general rule, all species which he may meet with for the first time far in the interior should be preferred to those common near the civilised parts. He should strive to obtain as much variety as possible, and not fill his boxes and jars with quantities of specimens of one or a few species. But as some of the rarest snd most interesting species have great resemblance to others which may be more common, he should avail himself of every opportunity of comparing the objects side by side. In most tropical countries the species found in open and semi-cultivated places are much less interesting than those inhabiting the interior of the forests; and it generally happens that the few handsome kinds which attract the attention of the natives are species well known in European museums.

In botany, a traveller, if obliged to restrict his collecting, might confine himself to those plants which are remarkable for their economical uses, always taking care to identify the flowers of the tree or shrub whose root, bark, leaves, wood, &c., are used by the natives, and preserving a few specimens of them. But if he is the first to ascend any high mountain, he should make as general a collection of the flowering plants as possible at the higher elevations. The same may be said of insects found on mountains, where they occur in very great diversity; on the shady and cold sides rather than on the sunny slopes; under stones and about the roots of herbage, especially near springs; on shrubs and low trees, and so forth; for upon a knowledge of the plants and insects of mountain ranges depend many curious questions in the geographical distribution of forms over the earth.

In reptiles, the smaller Batrachia (frogs, salamanders, &c.) should not be neglected, especially the extremely numerous family of tree frogs. Lizards may be caught generally with the insect-sweeping net; the arboreal species, seen out of reach, may be brought down with a charge of dust shot. Snakes should be taken without injuring the head, which is the most important part of the body. A cleft stick may be used in securing them by the neck, and on reaching camp they may be dropped into the jars of spirits. As large a collection as possible should be made of the smaller fishes of inland lakes and unexplored rivers. Dr. Günther, of the British Museum, has authorised me to say that a traveller cannot fail to make a large number of interesting discoveries if he collects a few specimens of the species he meets with in the lakes and rivers of the interior of any country. It can scarcely be expected that specimens of the larger animals can be brought away by a geographical expedition, although some species are still desiderata in the large museums of Europe. Additional specimens of all genera, of which there are numerous closely-allied species (*e.g.*, rhinoceros, antelopes, equus, &c.), would be very welcome for the better discrimination of the species. If only portions can be obtained, skulls are to be preferred. In humid tropical regions, entire skins cannot be dried in time to prevent decay, and it is necessary to place them, rolled up in a small compass, in spirits. The smaller mammals, of which there remain many to reward the explorer in almost all extra-European countries, may be skinned, dried, and packed in boxes in the same manner as birds. The smaller birds shot on an excursion should be carried to camp in the game bag, folded in paper, the wounds, mouth, and anus being first plugged with cotton. Powdered calcined gypsum will here be found very useful in absorbing blood from feathers, on account of the facility with which it can be afterwards cleared from the specimens. All plants, when gathered, are placed in the tin box which the traveller carries with him. Land and fresh water shells may be carried home in a bag. All hard-bodied insects, such as beetles, ants, and so forth, should be placed, in collecting, in small bottles, each bottle having a piece of slightly-moistened rag placed within it, to prevent the insects from crowding and injuring each other. The hint previously given, with regard to numbers of specimens, must be repeated here. Take as great a variety of species as possible, the sweeping-net should be freely used (except in very wet weather) in sweeping and beating the herbage and lower trees. In collecting ants, it is necessary to open nests and secure the winged individuals of each species, which must be afterwards kept together with the wingless ones, to secure the identification of the species. Bees and wasps may be caught in the net and then placed, by means of small forceps, in the collecting bottle, and afterwards killed in the same way as beetles and other hard-bodied insects. All soft-bodied insects should be killed on capture (by a slight pressure of the chest underneath the wings by thumb and finger), and then pinned in the pocket collecting box. If the traveller has leisure and inclination for the pursuit, he may readily make a large and varied collection of these, and will do good service to science if he notes carefully the exact localities of his captures, altitude above the sea, nature of country, the sexes of the species, if detected, and information on habits. The delicate species should be handled very carefully and put away into the drying cage immediately on return from an excursion. Spiders may be collected in bottles, and afterwards killed and pinned in the same way as other insects. Crustacea (shrimps, crawfish, &c.) in rivers and pools may be collected with the landing net, and afterwards well dried and pinned like hard-bodied insects, except when they are large in size, when their bodies must be opened and emptied of their contents.

Previous to skinning a small mammal or bird make a note of the colour of its eyes and soft parts, and, if time admits, of the dimensions of its trunk and limbs. It facilitates skinning Preserving and packing. of birds to break, before commencing, the first bone of the wings a short distance above the joint, which causes the members to lie open when the specimen is laid on its back on the skinning board. The animal should be laid with its tail towards the right hand of the operator, and the incision made from the breast bone nearly to the anus. A blunt wooden style is useful in commencing the operation of separating the skin from the flesh. When the leg is reached, cut through the knee joint, and then clear the flesh from the shank as far as can be done, afterwards washing the bone slightly with arsenical soap, winding a thin slip of cotton round it, and returning it to the skin. Repeat the process with the other leg, and then sever with the broad-bladed scissors the spine above the root of the tail. By carefully cutting into the flesh from above the spine is finally severed without injuring the skin of the back, and it is then easy to continue the skinning up to the wings, when the bones are cut through at the place where they had previously been broken, and the body finished as far as the commencement of the skull. A small piece of the skull is now cut away, together with the neck and body, and the brains and eyes are scooped out, the inside washed with soap, and clean cotton filled in, the eyes especially being made plump. In large headed parrots, woodpeckers, and some other birds, the head cannot thus be cleansed; an incision has therefore to be made either on one side or on the back of the neck, through which the back of the skull can be thrust a little way and then cleansed, the incision being afterwards closed by two or three stitches. The bones then remaining in each wing must be cleansed, but so as not to loosen the quill feathers. It is much better to take out the flesh by making an incision on the outside of the skin along the flesh on the inner side of the wing. The inside of the skin must now be washed with the soap, and a neck of cotton (not too thick) inserted by means of long narrow forceps, taking care to fix the end well inside the skull, and withdrawing the empty forceps without stretching the skin of the neck and thus distorting the shape of the bird. Skins need not be filled up with cotton or any other material, but laid with the feathers smoothed down on the boards of the drying cage until they are ready to be packed in boxes. In very humid climates, like that of Tropical America, oxide of arsenic in powder is preferable to arsenical soap, on account of the skins drying quicker, but it cannot be recommended to the general traveller, owing to the danger attending its use.

In mammals the tail offers some difficulty to a beginner. To skin it, the root (after severing it from the spine) should be secured by a piece of strong twine, which should then be attached to a nail or beam. With two pieces of flat wood (one placed on each side of the naked root) held firmly by the hand and pulled downwards, the skin is made rapidly to give way generally to the tip. The tails of some animals, however, can be skinned only by incisions made down the middle from the outside. The larger mammal skins may be inverted, and, after washing with soap, dried in the sun; and, as before remarked, it is often necessary to roll them up and preserve in spirits. The skins of small mammals and birds, after they are *quite* dry, may be packed in boxes, which must be previously well washed inside with arsenical soap, lined with paper, and again covered with a coating of the soap, and well dried in the sun. This is the very best means of securing the specimens from the attacks of noxious insects, which so often, to the great disgust of the traveller, destroy what he has taken so much pains to secure. Where wood is scarce, as in the interior of Africa, boxes may be made of the skins of antelopes, or other large animals, by stretching them, when newly stripped from the animal, over a square framework of sticks, and sewing up the edges after being dried in the sun; they make excellent packing-cases. With regard to reptiles and fishes, I cannot do better than quote the following remarks sent to me by Mr. Osbert Salvin, who collected these animals most successfully in Guatemala :—" Almost any spirit will answer for this purpose, its fitness consisting in the amount of alcohol contained in it. In all cases it is best to procure the strongest, being less bulky, and the water can always be obtained to reduce the strength to the requisite amount. When the spirit sold retail by natives is not sufficiently strong, by visiting the distillery the traveller can often obtain the first runnings (the strongest) of the still, which will be stronger than he requires undiluted. The spirit used should be reduced to about proof, and the traveller should always be provided with an alcoholometer. If this is not at hand, a little practice will enable him to ascertain the strength of the spirit from the rapidity with which the bubbles break when rising to the surface of a small quantity shaken in a bottle. When the spirit has been used, this test is of no value. When animals or fish are first immersed, it will be found that the spirit becomes rapidly weaker. Large specimens absorb the alcohol very speedily. The rapidity with which this absorption takes place should be carefully watched, and in warm climates the liquid tested at least every twelve hours, and fresh spirit added to restore it to its original strength. In colder climates it is not requisite to watch so closely, but practice will show what attention is necessary. It will be found that absorption of alcohol will be about proportionate to the rate of decomposition. Spirit should not be used too strong, as its effect is to contract the outer surface, and thus closing the pores prevent the alcohol from penetrating through to the inner parts of the specimen. The principal point, then, is to watch that the strength of the spirit does not get below a certain point while the specimen is absorbing alcohol when first put in. It will be found that after two or three days the spirit retains its strength; when this is the case, the specimen will be perfectly preserved. Spirit should not be thrown away, no matter how often used, so long as the traveller has a reserve sufficient to bring it back to its requisite strength. In selecting specimens for immersion, regard must be had to the means at the traveller's disposal. Fish up to 9in. long may be placed in spirit with simply a slit cut to allow the spirit to enter to the entrails. With larger specimens it is better to pass a long knife outside the ribs, so as to separate the muscles on each side of the vertebra. It is also as well to remove as much food from the entrails as possible, taking care to leave all these in. The larger specimens can be skinned, leaving, however, the intestines in, and simply removing the flesh; very large specimens preserved in this way absorb very little spirit. All half-digested food should be removed from snakes and animals. In spite of these precautions specimens will often appear to be decomposing, but by more constant attention to re-strengthening the spirit they will in most cases be preserved. A case (copper is best) with a top that can be unscrewed and refixed easily, should always be carried as a receptacle; the opening should be large enough to allow the hand to be inserted. This is to hold freshly caught specimens. When they have become preserved they can all be removed and soldered up in tin or zinc boxes; zinc is best, as it does not corrode so easily. The traveller will find it very convenient to take lessons in soldering, and so make his own boxes. (For directions for soldering, see p. 210 of this work.) If he takes boxes ready made they had best be arranged so as to fit one into another before they are filled. When moving about, all specimens should be wrapped in calico, linen, or other rags, to prevent their rubbing one against the other. This should also be done to the specimens in the copper case when a move is necessary, as well as to those finally packed for transportation to Europe. These last should have all their interstices between the specimens filled in with cotton wool or rags. If a leak should occur in a case, specimens thus packed will still be maintained moist, and will keep some time without much injury. Proof spirit should be used when the specimens are finally packed, but it is not necessary that it should be fresh. Land and fresh-water shells, on reaching camp, should be placed in a basin of cold water to entice the animals out, and then, after draining off, killed by pouring boiling water over them. They may be cleansed of flesh by means of a strong pin or penknife. The operculum or mouthpiece of all shells which possess it should be preserved and placed inside the empty shell. Each shell when dry should be wrapped in a piece of paper and the collection packed in a box well padded with cotton or other dry and elastic material.

"The insects collected on an excursion should be attended to immediately on arrival in camp. When leisure and space are limited all the hard-bodied ones may be put in bottles of spirit, and each bottle when nearly full should be filled up to the cork with a piece of rag, to prevent injury from shaking. Many species, however, become stained by spirit, and it is far better in dry countries, such as Africa, Australia, and Central Asia, to preserve all the hard bodied ones in a dry state in pill boxes. They are killed whilst in the collecting bottles by plunging for a few minutes the bottom half of the bottles in hot water. An hour afterwards the contents are shaken out over blotting paper and put into pill boxes, the bottoms of the boxes being padded with cotton, over which is placed a circular piece of blotting paper. The open pill boxes should then be placed in the drying cage for a day or two, and then filled up with more cotton, the layer of insects being first covered with a circular piece of paper.* The soft-bodied specimens which are brought home pinned, should be stuck in the drying cage until they are dry, and then pinned very close together in the store boxes. The store boxes, both bottom and sides, should each have inside a coating of arsenical soap before they are corked, and as they become filled one by one should be washed outside with the soap and pasted all over with paper. Camphor and other preservatives are of little or no use in tropical climates. In some countries where the traveller may wish to make a collection of the butterfly fauna, the best way is to preserve all the specimens in little paper envelopes. He should be careful not to press the insects too flat, simply killing them by pressure underneath the breast, folding their wings carefully backwards and slipping them each into its envelope. In very humid tropical countries, such as the river valleys of tropical America and the islands of the Eastern Archipelago, the plan of stowing away even hard-bodied insects in pill boxes does not answer, on account of the mould with which they soon become covered. There are, then, only two methods that can be adopted; one, preserving them at once in spirits, the other, pinning all those over a quarter of an inch long (running the pin through the right wing case, so as to come out beneath between the second and third pair of legs), and gumming those of smaller size on small sheets of card, cut of uniform size, so as to fit perpendicularly in racked boxes like those used to contain microscopical slides, but larger. The cards may be a few inches square, and each may hold several scores of specimens very lightly gummed down a short distance apart. After the cards are filled they should be well dried, and the box containing them washed outside with arsenical soap, and pasted over with paper. All the pinned specimens should be placed to dry for a few days in the drying cage, and afterwards pinned very close together in the cork store boxes.

"Plants are dried by pressure, by means of the boards and straps, between sheets of botanical drying paper, the paper requiring to be changed three or four times. When dry the specimens may be placed between sheets of old newspapers, together with notes the traveller may have made upon them, each placed upon the object to which it refers. Bundles of papers containing plants are not of difficult carriage. but they require to be guarded against wet, especially in fording rivers and in rainy weather, and should be wrapped in skins or India rubber

---

* The only preservative needed is a diluted wash of arsenical soap inside the pill boxes, which, as in all other cases when soap is used, must be well ¸ dried afterwards before the boxes are filled.

sheeting until they can be safely packed in wooden boxes and despatched to Europe.

" Seeds may be collected when quite ripe, and preserved in small packets of botanical paper, with numbers written on them, referring to preserved specimens of the flowers.

" Dry fruits and capsules should be collected when in countries not previously explored by botanists, if the traveller has means of identifying the species to which they belong.

" The collection of fossils and minerals, except in the case of the discovery of new localities for valuable metals, is not to be recommended to the traveller if he is not a geologist. Fossils from an unexplored country are of little use unless the nature and order of superposition of the strata in which they are found can be at the same time investigated. In the cases, however, of recent alluvial strata on the supposed beds of ancient lakes, or deposits in caves, or raised sea beaches containing shells or bones of vertebrate animals, the traveller will do well to bring away specimens if a good opportunity offers. If the plan of the expedition includes the collection of fossil remains, the traveller will of course provide himself with a proper geological outfit and obtain the necessary instructions before leaving Europe."

Whilst engaged in collecting the beautifully formed and delicate shells found adhering to the minute asperitis formed by the process of disintegration on the roofs of the crypts formed by the ancient Tauro-Scythian tribes, we proceeded as follows : After the discovery of an almost crystalline specimen we prepared a soft bed for its reception by arranging in nest form a very soft silk handkerchief in our well-worn forage cap, the gold band of which served as a sort of hoop of support. Thus arranged, the nest was held exactly under the fossil shell, which was in most cases freed from its attachments by a single sharp and well-directed blow from our pick head on the heel of a sharp well-tempered steel chisel (old files make the best). As the specimens were one by one taken from the cap-nest they were arranged carefully layer after layer in old preserved meat tins, bran being liberally sprinkled in over each distinct layer of shells. On the tin being nearly filled, more bran was added until the packing was firm and complete, the round tin cover was then forced in until about a quarter of an inch from the upper rim of the tin. A few cuts here and there in the tin with a pair of cutting nippers admitted of the turning in of a number of clip pieces by bending the cut tin in elbow form over the cover. These tins when duly numbered and noted were packed in a sixty-gallon barrel with fine soft hay made from steppe grass. The collections thus packed reached England in a perfect state of preservation.

In situations where old preserved meat tins cannot be obtained, large joints of bamboo, or the thin earthen pots used by natives, might be made available for depositing very fragile specimens in. Fine sawdust will answer nearly as well as bran for packing powder. Rotten wood from an old decaying log may be rubbed between the hands into fine dust, and made use of for the same purpose. "All collections made in tropical countries should be sent to Europe with the least possible delay, as they soon become deteriorated or spoilt, unless great care is bestowed on them. Dry skins of animals and birds may be packed in wooden cases, simply with sheets of paper to separate the skins. Shells and skulls should be provided with abundance of elastic padding, such as cotton. The boxes containing insects and crustacea should be placed in the middle of large boxes, surrounded by an ample bed of hay, or other light, dry, elastic material; if this last point be not carefully attended to, it will be doubtful whether such collections will sustain a voyage without much injury. Travellers have excellent opportunities of observing the habits of animals in a state of nature, and these hints would be very deficient were not a few words said upon the subject. To know what to observe in the economy of animals is in itself an accomplishment, which it would be unreasonable to expect the general traveller to possess, and without this he may bring home only insignificant details, contributing but little to our stock of knowledge. One general rule, however, may be kept always present to the mind, and this is that anything concerning animals which bears upon the relations of species to their conditions of life is well worth obtaining and recording. Thus, it is important to note the various enemies which each species has to contend with, not only at one epoch in its life, but at every stage from birth to death, and at different seasons and in different localities; the way in which the existence of enemies limits the range of a species should be also noticed. The inorganic influences which inimically affect species, especially intermittently (such as the occurrence of disastrous seasons), and which are likely to operate in limiting their ranges, are also important subjects of inquiry. The migrations of animals, and especially any parts where the irruption of species into districts previously uninhabited by them, are well worth recording. The food of each species should be noticed; and if any change of customary food is observed, owing to the failure of the supply, it should be carefully recorded. The use in nature of any peculiar physical conformation of animals, the object of ornamentation and so forth, should be also investigated wherever opportunity occurs. Any facts relating to the interbreeding in a state of nature of allied varieties or the converse—that is, the antipathy to intermingling of allied varieties—would be extremely interesting. In short, the traveller should bear in mind that facts having a philosophical bearing are much more important than mere anecdotes about animals. To observe the actions of the larger animals a telescope or opera-glass will be necessary, and the traveller should bear in mind, if a microscope is needed in his journey, that, by reversing the tubes of the telescope, in which all the small glasses are contained, a compound microscope of considerable power is produced."

The hunter of the fur-clad denizens of the forest and the field, who, for the love of sport and the obtainment of trophies of the chase, penetrates to little-known regions; and the hardy and keen trapper—who, with pack, traps, kit, and rifle, steers his own course to the most remote and untrodden solitudes— each require a somewhat different mode by which to fit their spoils when gathered for transport to either the cities of Europe or the trading port of the professional peltry dealers. It would be a hopeless task to attempt giving all the processes had recourse to by both classes of hunters, as many of them are kept scrupulously secret by their discoverers. Indians, too, profess to know more of skindressing than they care to divulge. We will, therefore, content ourselves by communicating to the reader such modes of skindressing as we have either practised ourselves, picked up from experienced and travelled comrades, or gleaned from the reports and experiences of practical explorers and slayers of large and small game in wild countries.

The character of the climate in which the hunter may be pursuing his vocation will determine the necessity for the immediate removal of the skins of the animals killed from the carcases, or the postponement of the operation until camp is reached and every assistance at hand. In dealing with the larger carnivora of tropical climates, too much expedition cannot be used in the performance of skinning operations. On no account, when by any possibility it can be avoided, should a dead and unskinned animal be exposed to the action of either wet or the sun's rays. Immediately on being found to be perfectly dead the animal should be conveyed to a cool shady situation, and the hide at once removed. The purpose for which the skin is ultimately intended will influence the method to be observed in removing it from the body. If to be preserved for stuffing, much greater care is required than is usually bestowed on hides merely intended for camp use, or sale to purchasers of roughly dried skins.

Great alertness and firmness are also required on the part of the

European hunter who is engaged in tiger shooting in India to prevent the native hunters and camp followers from burning off the whiskers of the slain beast, and stealing the claws. The whisker singeing ceremony arises from superstition, and the greatest anxiety exists to possess tiger claws, in order that they may be made use of as amulets. Keep, therefore, a very close watch on your tiger skins. When about to commence skinning a tiger, lion, leopard, or other of the large *Felidæ*, choose a level spot of ground, lay the animal on the flat of its back, with all four legs in the air. Prepare four stout sharp-pointed stakes and drive them into the ground at about six feet from the animal, placing a stake opposite each leg in a parallelogram. Now, with some pieces of spare rope, grass cord, raw hide thongs, or twisted creepers, fasten each paw to the head of a stake, and stretch the legs well out. With your skinning knife—which should be short in the blade, half round-pointed, and very long handled—commence your cut between the two centre lower teeth and carry it directly backwards along the centre of the belly to the vent, taking great care not to penetrate the abdominal cavity. A line down each leg from the paw joint to the centre line should now be cut; the hind legs should be first skinned by peeling off the hide completely round beneath the paw joints, which should be divided and the stumps thus formed fastened to the stake ropes; the skin can now be stripped and turned down over the thighs; a cut along the under side of the tail will enable the operator to skin that cleanly out, when it can be cut off at the root; the two fore legs may now be treated in the same manner as the hind, making the bare stumps fast and skinning down to the shoulder joints, and up the front of the neck and throat. The animal may now be turned on its belly and each leg stump hauled tightly out to the bottom of each stake; the skin is now turned up over the back, and stripped up as far as the attachment of the ears; great care must now be exercised in separating their roots from the head without cutting the skin; divide carefully round the eyes, lips, and corners of the mouth, and the skin will be free.

There are two ways of stretching out skins for the purpose of first freeing them from every particle of fat and adhering matter. One is to lay them on the ground, fur side downward, and then secure them by driving a number of sharp wooden pegs round the margins; the other is to cut one or two straight tough poles, lash their ends together, and make a hoop large enough to take in the skin, and allow of sufficient space to admit of its being tightly stretched out by being attached to the interior of the hoop by a rough system of lacing, as shown in the illustration on p. 679. A skin well secured in this way becomes as tense as a tambourine. The hoop can be set on its edge or inclined to facilitate the operation of fat trimming, which must be most strictly carried out, without cutting through the skin. A pair of strong broad pointed forceps much facilitates the operation. The point and edge of the skinning knife should be constantly touched up and renewed on a butcher's steel or bit of Norway stone. On no account allow your native followers to attempt the treatment of your stretched skins, as they will most certainly ruin them by the caustic nature of the ingredients they employ. Many mixtures of substances suitable for skin preservation are recommended, and we possess a considerable number of them. The following, communicated to the *Field* by a correspondent signing himself "I. F.," is a thoroughly good one, and easy of preparation in any part of India. After trimming off

all fatty matter, &c., apply the following mixture: powdered alum, one part; powdered turmeric (the *huldee* of the natives), four parts; powdered *kadukai* nuts, eight parts; to be well mixed, and diluted with water until just fluid. The *kadukai* nuts are the fruit of a tree (*Terminalia chebula*) common all over India. Its vernacular names are, in Hindostanee, "hurra;" in Tamil, "kadukai marum;" in Teloogoo, "karkai." The dried nuts are commonly sold in the native

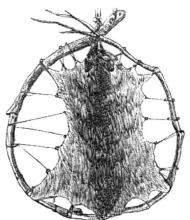

bazaars. When no preparation for skin dressing is at hand, firewood ashes may with advantage be sprinkled over the skins. The American trappers make use of no preparation whatever, but merely expose the perfectly cleaned and trimmed skin to the action of the air. Traps, when set for animals, should be visited frequently, in order that the game taken may be perfectly resh; tainted skins lose their hair, and become valueless for fur purposes. The smaller fur-bearing animals taken by the professional fur hunters of America, such as the fisher fox, raccoon, &c., are not skinned by being opened from end to end, but are treated in the following manner: incisions are made close to the hind paws; these are carried down to the borders of the vent; this is circled or cut round, and the tail opened and skinned out. An orifice will now exist large enough to admit of the skin being stripped from the animal, by turning it inside out, as the operation of skinning proceeds. Three modes are adopted for stretching skins so prepared : one is by what is called a board stretcher; this consists of three pieces of light tough wood, of the

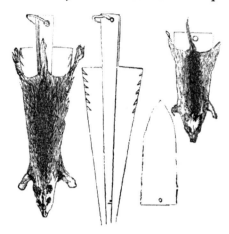

shape shown in the centre figure of the annexed illustration. The two flat side pieces are first placed in the pouch or pocket, formed by reversing the surfaces of the skin; the centre stick is then passed down between the two sides, which are nicely rounded off at the edges and point by scraping with glass or a sharp knife. When properly fitted to the stretcher like a glove on a wooden cleaning hand, a tack or two or a few cuts in the edges of the board will serve to hold the skin fast until dry enough to pack away. A strong flexible rod may be made use of as a skin stretcher, as shown in the annexed cut. The skins should be turned inside out before the bent twig is inserted; its own spring keeps the skin distended until dry, when it is removed and the skin packed ; or a long lancet-shaped board, with a hole in it, may be used for stretching the skins of marmots, musk rats, &c. One of these is represented in the illustration representing stretching boards, and

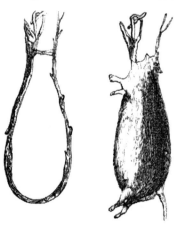

has a hole in it to be used for suspending the skins whilst drying. Stretching boards must be made of sizes proportioned to the skins they are intended for. Never dry skins either by the fire or in the sun.

A variety of methods are had recourse to for preparing the skins of animals useful to the traveller and explorer, by whom they can be employed either in a raw state, simply dried, or as leather. Raw hide, as it is called, is one of the most valuable and useful materials at the command of the traveller or hunter. It is to him a substitute for metal, rope, and twine, and with it breakages of the most extensive and apparently hopeless character can be effectually repaired. Lashings of raw hide for immediate use can be cut from the skin of an animal just killed. This, when tightly and evenly adjusted over a fractured object, contracts as it dries, and binds all firmly together. The hair may be removed from hides by soaking them in lime-water or placing them in the earth for a few days. Many of the African tribes prepare hides for use as garments, &c., by first pegging them out on the ground, trimming them clean, allowing them to dry slowly, and then braying their surfaces with a soft sand brick. Skins thus prepared wear well, so long as no water is allowed to reach them.

Skins may be "tawed," as it is called, by placing them to steep in a strong solution of alum and common salt. Hides collected in large numbers for transmission to the home market are usually salted or pickled. Settlers and colonists may find this mode of preserving skins of value, so we give Mr. Dana's account of the process, which will be found thoroughly practical, and can be relied on. Speaking of the treatment of hides brought to the sea side for shipment, he says: " The first thing is to put the hides to soak. This is done by carrying them down at low tide, and making them fast in small piles by ropes, and letting the tide come up and cover them. There they lie forty-eight hours, when they are taken out and rolled up in wheelbarrows, and thrown into vats. These vats contain brine, made very strong, being sea-water with great quantities of salt thrown in. This pickles the hides, and in this they lie forty-eight hours; the use of the sea-water into which they are first put being merely to soften and clean them. From these vats they are taken to lie on a platform twenty-four hours, and are then spread upon the ground and carefully stretched and staked out, so that they may dry smooth. After they were staked, and while yet wet and soft, we used to go upon them with our knives and carefully cut off all the bad parts, the pieces of meat and fat which would otherwise corrupt and affect the whole if stowed away in a vessel for months, the large flippers, the ears, and all other parts that prevent close stowage. This was the most difficult part of our duty, as it required much skill to take off everything necessary, and not to cut nor injure the hides." Skins of animals may be fitted for transport from the hunting grounds to a camp or depôt situated at a distance of several days' journey, by pegging them tightly out ; and then, when thoroughly freed from adhering fat, giving them a thorough sprinkling with wood ashes. Small quantities of leather may be made by sinking large native jars in the earth, partly filling them with tan, which is yielded by an almost endless number of trees and shrubs. Water, when added, extracts the tanning principle, and allows of its soaking freely into the pores of the skin under treatment. It is a good plan to make use of several jars arranged in a row; these should all contain strong bark or tan water, and as the skin becomes partly tanned in jar No. 1 it should, after being well squeezed and pressed, be passed to No. 2, and so on through the set.

Thus writes Sir Samuel Baker on the subject of skin dressing; " My antelope skins are just completed, and are thoroughly tanned, each skin required a double handful of the ' *garra* ' or fruit of the *Acacia arabica*. The process is simple. The skin being thoroughly wetted, the garra is pounded into a paste; this is rubbed into the hide with a rough piece of sandstone until it becomes perfectly clean and free from impurities; it is then wrapped up with a quantity of the paste, and is deposited in a trough, and kept in the shade twenty-four hours—it should undergo a similar rubbing daily, and be kept in the trough to soak in the garra for four or five days. After this process it should be well rubbed with fat, if required to keep soft and pliable when wetted. If soaked with milk after tanning, the leather will become waterproof. The large tanned ox hides used by the Arabs as coverlets are perfectly waterproof, and are simply prepared with milk. These are made in Abyssinia, and can be purchased from ten piastres to a dollar each. The Arabs thoroughly appreciate the value of leather, as they are entirely dependant upon such material for coverlets, water sacks, travelling bags, &c. The *sac de voyage* is a simple skin of either goat or sheep, drawn off the animal as a stocking is drawn from the leg. This is very neatly ornamented and arranged with loops which close the mouth, which is secured by a padlock. Very large sacks, capable of containing three hundred pounds of corn, are made in the same manner by drawing entire the skins of the larger antelopes; that of the *tetel* is considered the most valuable for this purpose. The hide of the wild ass is the finest of all leather, and is so close in the grain, that, before tanning, when dry and hardened in the sun, it resembles horn in transparency. I have made excellent mocassins with this skin, which are admirable if kept wetted." Most of the water sacks we used in Central India were prepared by withdrawing all the body of the animal—antelope or goat—piecemeal through the orifice left by cutting off the head. The legs were then removed to the hoof joint, and the tubes so formed so fitted with thongs, that they could be tied fast or left open at the will of the owner; burying the skin in the earth for a day or two caused the hair to become loose enough to rub off in water. A charge of pounded pomegranate rind mixed with water was then introduced to the interior of the skin sack, and well shaken about several times during the day.

This process was continued until the substance of the skin became converted into leather, and was perfectly free from the slightest tendency to taint. The neck orifice was then either sewn up with a thong, or left with a string round it, to be closed or left open as might be most convenient. Skins thus prepared we have found useful for an almost endless number of purposes.

The following directions for the manufacture of gazelle skin *girbas,* or water sacks, as practised by the Arabs, given by Sir Samuel Baker, will not fail to prove of interest and value to the reader : " The flaying process for this purpose is a delicate operation, as the knife must be so dexterously used that no false cut should injure the hide. The animal is hung up by the hind legs, an incision is then made along the inside of both thighs to the tail, and with some trouble the skin is drawn off the body towards the head, precisely as a stocking might be drawn from the leg ; by this operation the skin forms a seamless bag, open at both ends. To form a girba, the skin must be buried in the earth for about twenty-four hours ; it is then washed in water, and the hair is easily detached. Thus rendered clean, it is tanned by soaking for several days in a mixture of the bark of the mimosa and water, from this it is daily withdrawn and stretched out with pegs, upon the ground ; it is then well scrubbed with a rough stone, and fresh mimosa bark, well bruised, with water is rubbed in by friction. About four days are sufficient to tan the skin of a gazelle, which is much valued for its toughness and durability. The aperture at the hind quarters is sewn together, and the opening of the neck is closed when required by tying. A good water-skin should be porous, to allow the water to exude sufficiently to moisten the exterior ; thus the action of the air upon the exposed surface causes evaporation and imparts to the water within the skin a delicious coolness. The Arabs usually prepare their tanned skins with an empyreumatical oil, made from a variety of substances, the best of which is that from the sésamé grain. This has a powerful smell and renders the water so disagreeable that few Europeans could drink it. This oil is black and much resembles tar in appearance, it has the effect of preserving the leather and of rendering it perfectly water tight. In desert travelling, each person should have his own private water skin slung upon his dromedary ; for this purpose none is so good as a small sized gazelle skin that will contain about two gallons."

Snake skins can be converted into very useful and highly ornamental leather by tanning them. The Indians of North-west America add greatly to the value and durability of their prepared skins . by subjecting them to the smoking process. This is conducted by forming a miniature skin tent over a narrow deep hole dug in the earth; this, when filled with damp slow burning fuel, gives forth, when lighted, dense volumes of smoke, which, acting on the inner or flesh sides of the spread skins, imparts to them considerable power to resist damp and other deteriorating influences. Hides that are under the operation of dressing should never be allowed to become dry, as it is very difficult to restore perfect flexibility to them by the aid of water. Wet cow dung is the best material we know for preserving the moisture of the skins on which it is spread. Milk curds are made use of for the same purpose by the Tartar tribes. We have also seen ground oil seeds, converted into a paste with milk, used by some Indian hill tribes.

Parchment is a material which will be found useful for many purposes, such as labelling the species collected, &c.; almost any moderate-sized skin can be converted into this sub-stance. The first step is to remove the hair from its follicles. This may be done by burying the skin in moist earth for two or three days; it should, when found seasoned, be spread, hair side out, on a barrel or round log, and well scraped, until quite clean. Four long tough peeled rods or wands should now be passed through a train of small slits, like button-holes, in the edges of the skin, all four borders of the trimmed skin being furnished with its spreading wand. The ends of the wands are now to be cut off flush with the border of the skin. A pole hoop like that figured at page 679 should now be prepared, and the stretched skin laced to its centre by cords or thongs passed inside the wand until it is as tight as a tambourine. Every particle of adhering membrane should be carefully cut away, and the skin rubbed down to the required substance with a flat-surfaced sandstone; pumice-stone, when it can be obtained, is excellent for the purpose. When the parchment has undergone preparation, and is removed from the pole hoop, it may be fitted for writing on by first thoroughly rubbing its surface with a perfectly smooth water-worn pebble, and then touching its surface lightly over with ox-gall. Catgut can be made from the intestines of almost any animal, as follows: After carefully removing all impurities from the surfaces of the gut, place it in a pot of water for twenty-four hours, the outer sheath, or covering membrane, will more freely come away. Now double back a few inches of the end border of your gut tube, just as you would turn down the top border of a stocking, catching the bag thus formed between the finger and thumb; dip water up with it until the double fold is nearly full. The weight of this fluid will instantly cause the gut to become inverted,

Parchment and catgut. (margin note)

and bring its inner surface to the outside. This can now be easily freed from any adhering matter ; and if the gut is intended for twisting, set up two stiff stout stakes in the earth, a little wider apart than the length of the gut under treatment. Cut a saw cut in the head of each stake. Now firmly lash each end of your gut to the notched ends of two narrow flat pieces of wood, fashioned like stout knife blades, and thin enough to enter the saw cuts in the stake heads. By alternately twisting these and fixing them in the saw cuts, to prevent their running back, the gut may be evenly and neatly twisted after the manner of a single strand cord. The twisted material thus formed becomes, when dry and after it has been rubbed smooth with a woollen rag and a little grease, excellent catgut, fit for drill bows, bowstrings, lathe bands, thread for sewing strong leather work, &c. Bladders should always be saved. They only require inflation with air and drying to preserve them. Holes in hides, water-bags, or bladders, may be repaired by gathering up the lips of the orifice, pushing a sharp splinter or thorn through both lips, and then tying a string tightly behind the cross piece thus formed. The holes in large skins can be repaired by placing pebbles or stones, just too large to pass through, inside them. A few turns with a strip of raw hide behind the stone makes all secure and perfectly water-tight. A spherical bullet may be made use of in this manner to repair a thorn prick in a

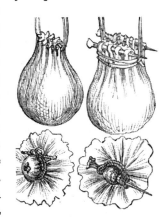

water-bag. A reference to the above illustration will serve to show how these repairs are effected. The horns of cattle can be made use of for a number of useful purposes. Soaking in boiling water softens them sufficiently to enable the ingenious operator to fashion them into almost any shape. Bones should never be heedlessly cast away ; sawn up they make excellent rings for dog harness or the head-lines of fishing-nets ; stilets for splicing cords, meshes for netting, &c. Tendons of animals make excellent glue, and can be easily split up into sewing thread. The swimming bladders of fish, when dried form excellent isinglass. Sole, shark, and dogfish skins, dried and mounted on handles, make very efficient rasps and files for woodwork. Eel-skins make most durable harness ties, and, twisted or plaited together, form very serviceable whips. Hides or skins can be cut into long strips for trail rope or lasso making by cutting them spirally with a sharp knife, just as a cobbler cuts out a leather boot-lace from a circular scrap of shoe leather. Hides and objects composed of either prepared hide or leather should be frequently treated with clean, well-softened grease, in order that they may retain their flexibility and toughness of texture. Hides used in covering the frames of "bull boats," as they are called by the traders and trappers of the north-west, who often use them, require to be frequently bleached, dried in the sun, and then greased, to render them sufficiently durable to encounter the deteriorating influences brought to bear on them during a long river or lake voyage.

In cutting up and trimming the carcases of large animals, considerable quantities of fat will be accumulated, provided that care is taken to prevent native fellows from appropriating it. Fat is valuable for an immense number of purposes. Its value as fuel has already been explained in that portion of our work devoted to a consideration of lamps. The bones of nearly all large animals may be made to yield a considerable quantity of fatty matter by crushing them to fragments between two heavy stones; boiling the mass thus obtained in any suitable vessel, and then skinning off the eyes of grease as they appear on the surface with a large shell fastened to the end of a stick, or an ox horn fashioned into a scoop. When fat is to be stored up for use it should be first melted, and, after all fragments of membrane, &c., have been separated by a rough system of straining, poured into hide bags to cool. All blubber-bearing cetaceans yield large quantities of oil, which is to be obtained by a process known amongst whalers as "trying out." Convenient sized pieces of the blubber are thrown into large cauldrons, which are mainly heated by the waste chip or used-up material left as a residue when the oil runs forth. The livers of sharks and other large fish also yield oil freely by treatment in the kettle. Besides being useful for wheel lubricating, leather-dressing, candle-making, and a variety of other useful purposes, fat can, by proper treatment, be made available as the principal ingredient in the manufacture of soap. Some care and management, however, are required to manufacture a really good and useful article. Sir Samuel Baker thus writes of his experiences in the matter: "Soap-boiling is not so easy as may be imagined. It requires not only much attention, but the quality is dependent upon the proper mixture of the alkalies. Sixty parts of potash and forty of lime are, I believe, the proportions for common soap. I had neither lime nor potash, but I shortly procured both. The *Hegleck tree (Balanites egyptiaca)* was extremely rich in potash; therefore I burned a large quantity, and made a strong ley with the ashes. This I concentrated by boiling. There was no lime-

Fat, to treat.

Soap, to prepare.

stone; but the river produced a plentiful supply of large oyster-shells, that, if burned, would yield excellent lime; accordingly, I constructed a kiln with the assistance of the white ants. The country was infested by these creatures, which erected their dwellings in all directions. There were cones from six to ten feet high, formed of clay, so thoroughly cemented by a glutinous preparation of the insects that it was harder than sun-baked brick. I selected an egg-shaped hill, and cut off the top exactly as we take off the slice from an egg. My Tookrooris then worked hard, and with a hoe and their lances they hollowed it out to the base, in spite of the attacks of the ants, which punished the legs of the intruders considerably. I made a draught hole from the outside base at right angles with the bottom of the hollow cone. My kiln was perfect. I loaded it with wood, upon which I piled about six bushels of oyster-shells, which I then covered with fuel, and kept it burning for twenty-four hours. This produced excellent lime, and I commenced my soap-boiling. We possessed an immense copper pot, of Egyptian manufacture, in addition to a large and deep copper basin, called a ' *teshti.*' These would contain about ten gallons. The ley having been boiled down to great strength, I added a quantity of lime and the necessary fat. It required ten hours' boiling, combined with careful management of the fire, as it would frequently ascend like foam, and overflow the edge of the utensils; however, at length having been constantly stirred, it turned to soap; before it became cold I formed it into cakes and balls with my hands, and the result of this manufacture was a weight of about forty pounds of most excellent soap of a very sporting description."

Fire and Waterproof Glue, to Make.—Take a handful of well burned quicklime and mix it with four ounces of linseed oil, rub the ingredients thoroughly together, and then boil the mixture until it is the consistence of ordinary paste. Throw it out on sheets of common tin to dry and harden. When required for use boil it as you would common glue.

If the traveller contemplates the prosecution of explorations in cold and inhospitable regions, it will be well for him to preserve a number of sheep or goats' skins, with the hair or wool on, Sleeping-which should be prepared for conversion into coverlets, bags. sleeping-bags, mats, overcoats, &c. A variety of forms of sleeping-bags are in use in various parts of the world; some, as in the case of those used by the frontier guard between France and Spain, are so constructed as to be doubled up, strapped together, and converted into a sort of knapsack. The down of waterfowl, especially that of the eider duck, when stitched between any suitable fabric and quilted, forms a most powerful non-conductor of heat. A very useful and cheap form of sleeping-bag can be made by pasting a number of old newspapers together, giving them a coat of boiled linseed oil, and then stitching them between two sheets of any tough durable fabric. The person about to be measured for a sleeping bag should have the extreme breadth of the shoulders, width across hips, and height taken, adding eighteen inches to the head of the bag to form a flap. Cut out your two main bag pieces, or top and bottom, to the shape of two large sleeve boards such as tailors use, now cut out two long narrow slips, about twenty inches wide, and long 'enough to go the whole length of both sides and round the tapered rounded bottom of the bag, and up to the end-borders of the mouth, these strips are sewn in exactly as the leather is attached to the upper and lower boards of a pair of common bellows. Sleeping-bags should be made very strong, in order that they may be used to carry a variety of odd articles in.

Capt. Butler thus writes:—"Before leaving Red River I had received from a gentleman well known in the Hudson's Bay Company, some most useful suggestions as to winter travel. His residence

Sleeping-bag.

for many years in the coldest parts of Labrador, and his long journey into the interior of that most wild and sterile land, had made him acquainted with all the vicissitudes of northern travel. Under his direction I had procured a number of the skins of the common (*cabri*) or small deer, had them made into a large sack of 7ft. in length, and 3ft. in diameter. The skin of this deer is very light,

but possesses for some reason with which I am unacquainted, a power of giving great warmth to the person it covers. The sack was made with the hair turned inside, and was covered on the outside with canvas. To make my bed therefore became a very simple operation—lay down a buffalo robe, unroll the sack, and the thing was done. To get into bed was simply to get into the sack, pull the hood over his head, and go to sleep."

Whilst on the subject of bags, it will be well to mention a most convenient description of sack used by the Tyrolese chamois hunters for

Ruck sacks.

carrying food, dead game, ammunition, &c. It is best made of light tanned canvas or flax cloth. A square bag of the required size is made from either of these materials, the mouth of the bag is made to draw in the usual way and tie, but to the loop of the neck string are attached two leather shoulder straps, to the ends of which wooden toggles and stout line loops have been sewn. Each lower corner of the bag should have a wooden or cork ball the size of a billiard ball, securely stitched into it. When the bag is placed on the back with its burden in it, the shoulder straps are passed over the shoulders, under the arms, and down to the ball-furnished corners, over which the slip-knots and loops of the toggle strings are now secured. The preceding illustration will serve to explain the nature of the arrangement, anything can be conveniently carried in this contrivance, from a single partridge to a full grown chamois or roebuck. A sack of this kind carefully fitted and made, is very superior to an ordinary knapsack.

CHAPTER XXII.

ROPES AND TWINE.

ROPES and twine of different sizes and lengths should always form part of the equipment of the traveller or explorer. These may be either home-made or manufactured from such suitable materials as may be obtainable in the regions travelled through. A great number of productions, vegetable and animal, are available for cord-making purposes; and not unfrequently it will be found in tropical regions that nature has herself formed the rope ready to the hand of him who will take the trouble to gather it. The rattan, which is a species of palm, although commonly and incorrectly called a cane, is a noteworthy example; it possesses extraordinary flexibility and toughness, is light, porous, covered with a waterproof glaze, and grows to a considerable length, often to the extent of 300ft. Rattans, when simply laid together, can be at once converted into ropes of almost any length and strength. Numbers of native suspension-bridges are supported by cables formed entirely from rattan. Warping ropes, used by the raftsmen of the Malay coast, are formed from this material; these curious ropes are not unfrequently the eighth of a mile in length, and possess immense strength. The "lianas," "monkey ropes," or parasitical creepers, too, which grow in such profusion in the tropical jungles, need little preparation to suit them for use as cordage. Willows and other tough flexible sticks or twigs are readily converted into rope by simply twisting them together; they should, however, be well soaked in water before twisting. An almost endless number of trees, shrubs, and plants yield fibre well calculated for cord or rope-making purposes. The bark of some of the mimosas is as tough as the finest hemp, and can be stripped from the trees in any quantity. Bast, or matting fibre, as it is called, is yielded by a number of trees, amongst which may be mentioned the linden or lime of our own country. For some purposes bast strips may be used without twisting by merely soaking them in water, and then dividing them into ribbons of the required strength. The inner bark of the elm, when well soaked, becomes extremely tough, and twists well. The long flag-like leaves of the *Phormium tenax,* or New Zealand hemp, can be used as ties or lashings without any treatment or preparation; separated from the juices and leaf-pulp by maceration and scraping with a muscle-shell, the fibre is found to be beautifully fine, and adapted for either spinning or weaving.

When gathering bark for rope or twine making purposes, it is always well to bear in mind that the outer or true bark, yielding little useful fibre, is, however, applicable to a variety of useful purposes, as

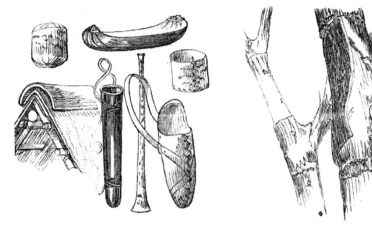

the above illustration, representing a number of articles, formed from outside bark will show. The method by which large sheets of bark are stripped from forest trees is shown in the annexed illustration.

Lap birch bark drinking and curve baling ladles.—A neat, strong, and most convenient form of ladle adapted for drinking from or use as a curve baler is in general use among the Laps. It is made by cutting and stripping off a sheet of smooth birch bark of suitable size. This is trimmed with a knife, cut to the shape shown in the annexed diagram A, folded as shown in B, and then fitted with a stout cleft stick for a handle as at C. It is worthy of remark that a ladle is a far more handy forest drinking vessel than a cup, as

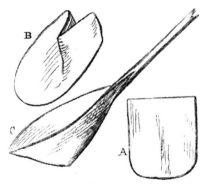

with it you can reach out some distance from the bank of a rivulet or pond, and by a few swims right and left, sweep away scum or floating water insects. We also found the Lap ladle a capital contrivance to hold the forest fruit and wild raspberries we gathered in, and to hold turpentine from the pine trees, for painting over the curve seams after caulking them with reindeer's fur.

The so-called Manilla hemp is not the product of the hemp plant, but is produced by a vegetable so closely resembling a Banana tree that it is difficult to distinguish one from the other. It is to be regretted that the names given by early travellers and others to productions of this kind, should be only calculated to mislead, instead of being guides to their origin; the so-called China grass is not a grass, but is obtained from a plant closely resembling a nettle (*Urtica tenacissima*). The common stinging nettle of this country contains a fibre out of which very good twine can be made; straw, hay, rushes, and swamp grass, make good tough bands, which are useful for many purposes. The Esparto grass, as it is called, is a dry ground rush, and was used in very early ages for the manufacture of ropes, but is now extensively applied to paper-making purposes. Cocoanut husks, and the leaves of all the agave tribes, the yuccas, and most of the aloe-shaped plants, yield an abundance of fibre, as does the pine apple plant by soaking or maceration in water. Cotton, wild or cultivated makes excellent cord. Smoked sea weed is used for lines by the British Columbian Indians. No one possessed of even ordinary powers of observation will fail in discovering a host of other fibre sources in travelling through tropical, or even temperate regions. A number of animal substances will also be found, which by the aid of ingenuity may be converted into thread and cordage. Fine strips of tendon scraped round and pointed make excellent sewing thread. Strips of raw hide, soaked, twisted or plaited, and greased, formed ropes or cords of immense strength and considerable durability : to form long strands for these, see the directions given at page 686. The hair or wool of animals, and the web spun by the wild silkworms are also available for twisting or working up into cord. Many methods more or less simple are had recourse to in different parts of the world, for so combining and intertwining fibres and other materials that, united, they may resist breaking, strains, and deteriorating influences. The untutored savage, as he is called, proceeds to gather his fibre, prepare it, and by the aid of his open palm and naked thigh only (as shown at page 531), twists it into an even, compact, and beautifully wrought line of any length, free from knots or irregularities, a task which the highly educated white man, unless tutored by savages, would vainly attempt to perform. "Laying up," as it is called, is another simple method by which a two or three strand cord or rope can be made. Each separate strand, when equally divided and secured at one end, is taken by the finger and thumb, or the hand, according to the size of the work, twisted on itself and passed over to the off side of the operator; the near side strand is now treated in the same way, and so on, fibre being carefully joined in with the fag end of each strand as it becomes too short for twisting: (*vide* pages 530, 531.) No two strands should be suffered to remain the same length, in order that no two unions of fresh fibres should take place at the same spot. A common three-plait is an expeditious mode by which three strips of sheeting, or other fabric, may be converted into a rope. Four strand round plait is formed by making each pair of strands cross each other from right to left alternately, until the

whole length required is completed; this form of plait is useful for whip thongs, and will run through the sheeve hole of a block. A single strand cord or twine may be twisted from loose fibre, by bending a winch handle in one end of a thick iron wire, and a hook in the other. Set up a stiff stake, waist high, in the earth, bore or burn a hole through it large enough to allow your wire to revolve freely in it, now split your post down to the hole, enter your wire and allow the cleft stake to retain the wire in the hole by its own spring; station some person to turn your winch handle, whilst you, with a good supply of fibre round your body, first hook on enough to form twine of the required size to the hook of the wire, and then walk backwards as the thread increases in length; a forked stick set up here and there serves to support the sag or belly of the twine as it is formed. A little thin glue or size rubbed on with a rag prevents the strands from opening too freely. Threads thus made may be either laid up by hand or spun into cordage by the regular ropemaker's wheel, a makeshift form of which may be easily extemporised by fitting a light flat hoop with a hub, a set of spokes, a wire handle, and a set of hook-axled cotton reels. With such a contrivance as this ropes and cords of small size may be twisted; but, for the manufacture of ropes of large dimensions, such an arrangement as that represented in the illustration (p. 693) must be made use of. An examination of it will show that an implement, called a *top*, is made use of in order to keep the strands in their proper relative positions. This top is merely a conical block of wood, with a set of deep grooves, according to the number of strands to be twisted, cut in it longitudinally. Tops may be made of almost any size, to suit the Straw-ropes, character of cord in the course of production. Grass or to spin. straw ropes may be conveniently and expeditiously spun to almost any length by the aid of an apparatus made as follows: Take four narrow flat pieces of board, say four inches wide, an inch thick, and three feet long, make two equal-sided crosses of them by nailing them together; take care, however, that no nails are used in the true centres of the crosses, as a two-inch augur hole will have to be bored in each. At one foot from the end of each arm of the crosses bore an inch hole, and into these fit a rounded stick, four feet long, in such away, that when pinned fast in the holes the whole arrangement may resemble a large-sized fishing reel without a handle. Now fashion a straight, smooth, one inch and a half stick in such a way as to leave a head like that of a large nail at one end and a point at the other. The pointed end must project about a foot beyond the hole in the inner cross when the stick is thrust through the centre hole in the crosses, and the head is brought in contact with the surface of the outer. To use this apparatus, bore a hole in a tree, insert the pointed end of the reel axle or stick; the reel formed by the crosses and bars will now, if properly made, revolve freely if struck with the hand. Gather up a long lock of grass, hay, or straw, and attach it to one of the cross-arms. Throw the arrangement round by giving a circular swing to your straw, keep up the revolving motion, and keep adding fresh material to the end of your rope until it becomes too long to be easily managed; wind the surplus length round the bars of the reel, or drum, and twist on until you have made as much rope as you require. Short hay or straw bands are made by catching a loop of the material over the turned-up thumb in such a way that it may form a loop; keep turning the hand, and gathering fresh material from below until the band is completed. "Thumb bands" is the name usually given to short grass ropes thus made.

Large ropes are very liable when new to give considerable trouble by their disposition to kink. It is therefore often necessary to Hard rove ropes, take the extra twist out of them by fastening one to treat. end high up in a conveniently grown tree, and suspending a spare waggon wheel from the other, as shown in the illustration (p. 693). The use of tar in the manufacture of rope tenders to impare its strength, but adds to its power to resist deteriorating influences.

It often becomes requisite, when loading waggons, packing animals, or loading boats, sledges, canoes or rafts, to Weight of rope, be enabled to form some estimate of the weight about to estimate. to be placed in them, and their are few aids to travel more difficult to weigh than rope, on account of its bulk and peculiar form of construction. It is well therefore to have recourse to a rough and ready system of calculation to arrive at the required information. The strength of ropes should also be approximately known before applying them.

Robinson gives the following simple rules for calculating the strength of ropes of the ordinary form of construction, and also their weights. Multiply the circumference of the rope in inches by itself, and the fifth part of the product will express the number of tons the rope will carry. For example, if the rope be six inches in circumference, $6 \times 6 = 36$, the fifth of which is $7\frac{1}{5}$, the number of tons which such a rope will sustain. To find the weight of shroud or hawser laid rope, multiply the circumference in inches by itself; then multiply the product by the length of the rope in fathoms, and divide by 420, the product will be the weight in cwts. Example—to find the weight] of a six-inch hawser laid rope 120 fathoms long; $6 \times 6 = 36 \times 120 = 4320$, which, divided by 420, gives the weight of the rope 10cwt. 1 qr. 4lb. To find the weight of cable-laid cordage, multiply its circumference in inches by itself, and divide by 4; the product will be the weight in cwts. of a cable 120 fathoms long, from which the weight of any other length may be readily reduced. Example—required the weight of a twelve-inch cable 120 fathoms long; $12 \times 12 = 144$, divide by 4, and the product, 36, is the weight in cwts.

To render ropes and cords available for the variety of purposes to which they are applied by the traveller, knots, hitches, splices, &c., must be had recourse to. These are so numerous in form Knots and mode of construction, that to describe half that are and Hitches. known to practical riggers and sailors would require a goodly volume. We shall, therefore, content ourselves by describing some of the most useful and generally available. It is impossible to teach the art of knot tying by written directions; we therefore give a sketch of each mentioned. It will be well for the student who wishes to acquire a knowledge of the manner in which they are formed to provide himself with a moderately stout piece of cord, and, by following out the lines

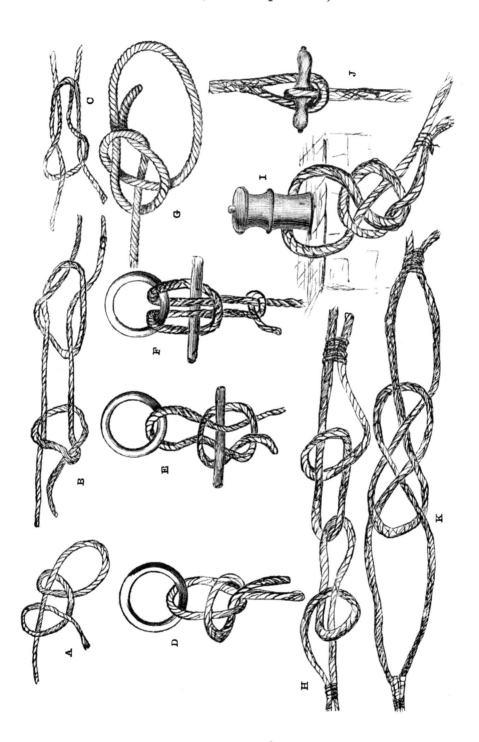

of turn, twist, and direction, given in the diagrams, and repeating the operation, he will soon acquire proficiency. A, in the accompanying full-page illustration, represents a pair of hitches, which can be caused to run firmly and freely home by hauling on the standing end, or converted into a useful loop by passing a few turns of stopping round both ends. B is a fisherman's bend, useful for an almost endless number of purposes. When the two knots in the short ends are pulled home, they run together by pulling the two main or free ends. C is a reef knot, used for knotting the reef points of sails or uniting the ends of ropes or cordage. D shows a mode by which the end of a rope may be quickly fastened to a ring. E and F are lark knots, used for fastening the painters of boats or canoes; it is only necessary, in case of sudden attack or alarm, to pull out the stop stick to instantly free the painter without untying. G is a bowline knot, which is applicable to any purpose where it is requisite to have a loop which will not run home. H is a hawser bend, which can be expeditiously made use of for joining the ends of large ropes. I is a knot commonly made use of for securing a hawser to a mooring post. J is an arrangement known as a toggle and loops, useful for a great number of purposes; the toggle, acting as a button, can be secured or released with great facility. K is a Carrick bend, useful for uniting tow ropes or large hawsers to each other. The "seizing" or stopping, represented as securing the short ends in some of these knots, may be composed of rope, yarn, or stout twine. A sheathing, or "parcelling," composed of old canvas, or some other stout material, should always be placed round ropes which are subjected to friction against quay walls or rocks, in order to protect them from chafe. The illustration on p. 698 also represents a number of useful knots, and modes of applying ropes and cords. Fig. 1 represents a timber hitch, which will be found most useful for taking a firm hold by cord on a round spar or pole. Fig. 2 is another method by which a rope can be secured round an upright post. Fig. 3 shows a sling, useful for raising or lowering packs, bales, or boxes. Fig. 4 is known as a harness loop; several of these can be tied in a drag rope, in order that men may make use of them as shoulder collars to draw by. Fig. 5 is a twisted or tail timber hitch, adapted for securing a log or piece of round timber for lowering or raising. Fig. 6 shows how to make a loop in the end of a pack or box lashing; the knot, running home, secures the loop, and prevents its drawing close. Fig. 7 is a sheepshank, used for shortening a long rope, and thus rendering cutting unnecessary. Fig. 8 is a loop-slip, used for uniting two looped ends securely. Fig. 9 is a weaver's or netter's knot, much used by those who repair or make nets for fishing.

Fig. 10 is a Tom Fool's knot, very useful for forming handles to jars and pots; the mouth of the vessel is placed in the centre of the knot, the two free ends tied fast, and the two loops left for the hand to grasp.   Fig. 11 is a brooch knot, used for forming the loop in rope for casting horses.   *(Vide* " Veterinary Surgery.")

The art of netting with the needle and mesh is so generally under-stood that it is not our intention to deal with the subject here further

Netting.   than to advise all those who may chance to be ignorant of the manner in which net making operations are conducted, to take a few lessons before quitting home to explore wild regions. The aborigines of every part of the known world can make nets, but it is well that the European traveller should be capable of manu-

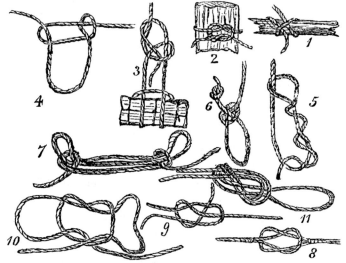

facturing his own.   Almost any piece of dry, tough wood, can, by the exercise of a little ingenuity, be fashioned into a needle and mesh, and twine, tendons, strips of hide, and a variety of other material, can be wrought into network, for hunting, fowling, fishing, &c.

Splicing is effected by opening the strands of the two ropes to be united, for some little distance down the cord.   The two sets of

Splicing.   diverging strands are then thrust between each other, so that they may be evenly reversed.   A sharp bone, metal, or hard wood stilet or pricker is now used to raise the strands one by one for the passage of the corresponding strand, until both sets have been worked far enough down the rope to render the union complete. A loop is spliced by opening the strands of the end, forming a loop in the rope of sufficient capacity, and then raising the strands, in the manner before described, one by one at the required point of union.

CHAPTER XXIII.

BUSH VETERINARY SURGERY AND MEDICINE.

BEFORE starting on an expedition in which the services of horses, mules, bullocks, and other animals are required it is well to be provided with such a store of veterinary requisites as are given at page 74 of this work; the nature of the work and the country in which it is intended to operate will mainly determine the necessity or otherwise for a portable forge and regular set of shoeing smith's appliances. When these are requisite it will be well to secure the services of one or more working farriers to take charge of and use them. A loose shoe, or even a set ready fitted, can be pretty successfully applied by an ingenious and handy amateur; but few, save those practically acquainted with the smith's art, could undertake the regular shoeing and fitting of an expedition train. Still we strongly recommend all those about to cast their fortunes in wild lands to attend frequently, before quitting England, at some good forge, in order that as many hints as possible may be gathered and stored up for future use. Horse shoeing like horse riding, cannot be taught by books. Every traveller should know how to take off and put on a shoe, and also how to use the drawing knife and searcher. In some countries horses are not shoed at all; in others, the fore feet only have shoes attached to them. And here we would offer a word of advice to travellers. Never attempt to alter the pattern of the shoe in which the horses of the country visited are in the habit of working, or disappointment and vexation are pretty sure to be the result. On our first visit to Turkey we regarded the round plates of iron with holes in their centres and hobnailed borders, called in that country by courtesy horse shoes, in the light of perfect abominations, and had our newly purchased animals shod in the English style. At the end of a week, however, we gladly gathered the cast off native shoes together and had them replaced by a native smith in order to avoid a broken neck. Should a horse or any other animal of burden, not excepting even an elephant, fall lame from any cause not absolutely patent and well known, look first to the foot of the affected limb and be sure that no stray nail, piece of broken iron, thorn, or other sharp substance, has found a lodgment. It is not our intention to enter on a consideration of the various diseases and ailments to which the animals of the traveller or settler are subject in different countries, as our space will not permit of our doing so. We must therefore content ourselves by giving such general hints and directions as may prove useful in the absence of a qualified veterinary surgeon. Many diseases to which pack and draught animals are subject are of such a character as to render it requisite that they should be either destroyed or left by the way in the hands of some responsible person for treatment.

It is never advisable to travel an animal suffering from lingering sickness. The first loss is generally the least in such cases. Severe cases of sore back should never occur in a well-regulated expedition; as pads or chambering should be had recourse to the very instant the slightest tendency to gall is perceived, and it is well, in many cases, to compel the rider of the animal to walk until the back is sound. Galls on the withers and poll of the head are more to be feared than any other injury of like kind, as matter is extremely liable to burrow in such situations, and lead to the formation of fistulous cavities and excessively troublesome wounds. Hot bathing and poultices formed from bran or ground oil seeds and warm water, should be first used, with a view to the palliation of the mischief; but when once matter is formed, freely opening the pouch formed from top to bottom is the only course. To make a horse-poultice bag sew two pieces of soft tough material together in the form of a common shot-bag, closing both ends and sides; fasten a wide soft string to each corner, cut a straight slit in one face of the bag, and through it thrust the mixed poultice material until it is nearly full, when it can be secured over the seat of injury. Animals obtained from natives not unfrequently suffer from a peculiar description of gall, known as a "sitfast." Examination shows an irregular piece of dry, hard, dead skin, surrounded by a border or channel of sore. The only way to effectually treat such a case as this is to first secure the animal, and then, with a sharp-pointed knife, cut the island of dead cuticle clean from the wound, which, if kept clean and properly treated with any simple dressing, will soon heal. A mixture consisting of common nitre, 1oz., to a pint of cold water, we have found very useful in such cases.

The frightful wounds on the backs of camels, too often caused by the carelessness of native camel-drivers, are particularly liable to take on an almost putrid condition. In the treatment of these we have found leather burned to a black, crisp mass, and then reduced to fine powder, a most valuable preparation. Simply strewed over and into the wound, it quickly causes healthy action to be set up. Any sproutings of new flesh which mount above the surface of the skin are known as " proud flesh," and should be reduced to the proper level by the use of nitrate of silver, blue stone (sulphate of copper), nitric acid, or even the red hot iron. In order

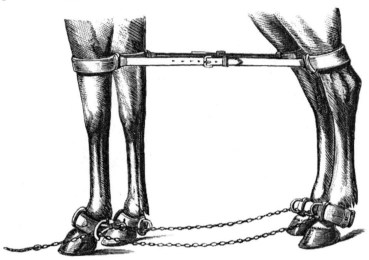

to perform many of the operations for the treatment of diseased or injured animals, it will be requisite to cast and properly secure them. The horse is best thrown by the aid of hobbles, a set of which, as adjusted for use, are represented in the above illustration. The leather strap attached from the fore to the hind-leg is put on after the animal has been thrown down by hauling on the rope-ended chain, shown at the front of the fore-foot. When the legs are drawn sufficiently close together, a spring clip is passed through a link of the chain; when the horse is to be released, a small screw-pin is drawn, which causes all the four hobbles to be set free, they then fall off as the animal rises. In the absence of regular hobbles, a very   Makeshift. good substitute may be formed by doubling a very long   casting ropes. pliant rope, knotting it securely far enough down the doubled end to form a collar for the head and neck of the animal to pass through (see Fig. 11, p. 698); the two free ends are now carried between the fore legs, under the body, inside the two hind legs, above the hocks; the ends are then brought forward on each side and passed from within outwards, through the collar rope. When all is adjusted, the hind-leg rope loops may be evenly and gently shaken down until they rest in the hollows of the fetlock joints. On the free ends being hauled on the horse will be thrown, when the ends of the rope are secured by half-hitches. The annexed illustration will serve to explain the nature of this contrivance. A soft spot should be chosen to cast on; a halter should always be securely placed on the head, and in cases of great timidity a folded rug as a blind over the eyes. The head of a cast horse should be firmly held down by a man

told off for the purpose, until the animal is freed from the ropes and about to rise. An ox is cast by catching his hind-leg, or both if possible, in a noose in the end of a reim held by means of a vangstock, or "catching stick;" another noose is thrown about his horns, one or two fellows catch his tail and pull against those who have the legs, while very likely, if he has tolerably large horns, another uses them as levers to throw him off his balance, and the spare hands assist by pushing with all their might at his broadside, when, as a matter of course, he must go down.

Large open gashes from horns, weapons, or tusks can be sewn up by separate stitches of either flexible wire or fine, smoothly-cut strips

Hints on camp medicine making. of raw hide. A very useful dressing for wounds of this character is made as follows : Common aloes, ½lb. ; gum myrrh, ¼lb.; spirits of almost any kind, 2 quarts; water, 1 quart; place the vessel containing this mixture in moderate sun heat for from twelve to fourteen days; strain and bottle for use; apply on lint, tow, or the plume of a large feather; myrrh can be obtained in the East from one of the Mimosa tribe, and aloes from the plant of that name.

In South Africa aloes juice is thus collected by the Hottentots : a hole is made in the earth, and a sheepskin forced into it. The leaves of the aloe are all cut off except two pairs of the youngest left in the form of a cross in the centre; the leaves are then ranged with their cut ends over the hollow in the sheepskin, and left to drain. If wind arises, however, it stops the drainage by coagulating the gum on the surface, and the labour is lost; the juice is thickened by boiling, and sold for exportation to England. The farmers use the fresh juice as a varnish for wood-work, to which it gives a good polish and a brown colour; it is said, also, to be an effectual vermifuge.

Wherever the aloe plant grows, the above rough and ready mode of obtaining its juices may be had recourse to. A very useful purgative for mules and horses is made by breaking a pound of aloes into rough pieces; throw these into seven pints of rain water, and then add a pint of spirit of some kind. The dose will vary with the size and condition of the animal from 4oz. to 6oz. Liquids are best given to animals from a small thin horn from which a long tapering slice has been cut, so as to form a sort of scoop.

The water and grain of some districts cause severe attacks of colic or gripes; these need immediate attention. A dose consisting of linseed oil, 1 pint; tincture of opium, 1oz.; nitric spirit of ether, 1oz.; mixed, should be given, and repeated in half an hour, if the pain is not subdued. Warm soapy water enemas should be frequently thrown up. An enema apparatus is easily extemporised from a large bladder or leather bag and hollow stick with its extreme end or mouth cut perfectly round and even. Soap suds are best formed by rubbing a piece of soap on a rough brush in a pail of warm water.

Opium is a most valuable pain-killer, either in its solid or liquid form. To prepare makeshift laudanum: Take of rough bazaar opium 3oz.; powder it roughly between two stones; throw the powder into an earthen pot, and add a quart of good, clear sound spirit; cover with a flat stone, and place in the shade for twelve days; strain through a double cotton cloth, and bottle for general use of man or beast.

Animals much fed on barley or other heating grain are very liable to become affected with mange. Separate all the diseased from the healthy, as the disease is exceedingly contagious. Dress all your diseased cases with the following mixture, which may be rubbed in with a brush or piece of hide with the hair on: Common oil of tar, 1 quart; common spirits of turpentine, 1 quart; fish oil of any kind, or, in the absence of that, native seed oil, 1 quart; powdered brimstone, ½lb.; mix thoroughly in a convenient vessel with a stick. Rub in the mixture every other day for three complete dressings, and on the day after the last, wash well with warm water and plenty of rough soap.

1oz. of gunpowder and ¼oz. of brimstone, rubbed into an ointment with 6oz. of fat, is a good makeshift remedy.

To prevent attacks of mange and other skin diseases in animals kept much on grain, it is well to give occasional doses of the following powder in the food: Common bazaar antimony (*the kohl* of the dealers) ½lb.; brimstone in powder, 1lb.; nitre, ½lb.; mix: dose ½oz. Strains or severe injuries to joints or tendons, are often benefited in their second stage, that is, after all the benefit arising from fomentations, poultices, &c., has been taken advantage of, by the action of counter-irritation, in the form of a blister. Cantharides, or Spanish flies are commonly used for blistering purposes, but the spotted fly of India (*Mylabris cichorii*) answers every purpose. Blistering oil, which is useful for sprains or to rub into sore throats, is made as follows: Dried flies, roughly crushed, 1oz.; good clear vegetable oil, 1 pint; spirits of turpentine, 4oz.; mix; place the whole in an earthen chatty pot or jar; put the vessel in warm camp fire ashes for three hours, and then strain for use. Blistering ointment is made by reducing the dry fly to powder, taking care to cover the nostrils during the operation, and mixing 1oz. of the dust to 6oz. of clear fat; stand the pot containing the mixture in the hot ashes for eight hours, and then strain whilst warm through a coarse cloth doubled. Horses when blistered should have cane joint necklaces, or cradles as they are called, fitted on their necks, in order to prevent them from biting the blistered surface. It is generally best to remove the hair before applying the blister. When the skin has been well acted on, the blister may be washed off with warm water and soap, and fat or palm-oil applied in order to allay irritation.

The flies of tropical countries are much to be dreaded when the wounds of animals are under treatment; ova deposited by them arrive at maturity in an incredibly short space of time, when Fly-invested animals, to treat. they burrow into the tissues, and cause much trouble to the attendant as well as pain to the animal. The "sheathes" of even healthy horses and mules not unfrequently become charged with a living mass of these carnivorous larvæ, which cause such irritation as to make the suffering animal kick violently up under its belly, and manifest other symptoms of uneasiness; a sharp watch should be kept for these symptoms, and when observed the animal at once cast, and the intruders routed out by manual manipulation; warm water and soap will cleanse the part, and a good dressing of oil will allay the irritation. Fly-infested wounds are best dressed with the following ointment: Common verdigris, ground to a very fine powder and sifted, 1oz.; common resin, 1oz.; fat or lard, 10oz.; first melt the fat in an earthen pot, and then stir in the powder; warm for one hour in the ashes, and stir till cold with a stick. There is an oil prepared from a species of Indian gum resin called " *diccimaulieh*," which is a valuable addition to the above ointment, as flies appear to entertain a rooted antipathy to it. Flies are not the only pests one has to guard against. Mules, especially those purchased   Mule leeches, in Spain, are not unfrequently found to have the insides   to destroy. of their mouths, as far back as the roots of their tongues, festooned with huge, bloated, black and green leeches. A number of our Andalusian mules were, on our voyage from Spain to the East, found by our chief muleteer to be so infested. We therefore brought the mules, one by one, to a stout post or stanchion, placed rope hobbles on their feet, and rope halters on their heads; when the head was well secured, a stout rope loop at the end of a stick was used to keep the mouth open, whilst a tow-ended stick, dipped in a strong solution of common salt in sea-water was used to thoroughly wash out the whole cavity of the mouth. The result was most satisfactory; the leeches tumbled helplessly out into the bucket of pickle held for their reception, and ultimately found their way into the sea. Our mules commenced to thrive from the day of our successful pickle hunt, and we never discovered another mule-leech during the expedition.

Both horses and mules will at times be found to "quid" their food as it is called, that is, to form during the process of mastication irregularly formed balls of partially crushed hay, straw,   Teeth, and their or grass. The discovery of these pellets should always   irregularities. be followed by an examination of the molar teeth, even should it be found necessary to cast the animal before the examination can be made, as loss of condition too frequently follows quidding. It will generally be found that irregularity of the edges of either the upper or lower rows of teeth have caused the infliction of wounds on the inside surfaces of the cheeks. In other cases, it will be found that from the decay of one or more teeth, those which should meet friction and consequent wear have, in the absence of it, grown to an inordinate and inconvenient length. These irregularities are best corrected by the aid of the tooth rasp, which is readily made by welding a worn out flat rasp to an iron rod about two feet in length. Bend your rasp, when united to the rod and still hot, into the form of a shallow gouge, and shorten it to about six inches; reset the teeth with a sharp punch, retemper, and insert in a common wooden handle for use.

When about to purchase either horses or mules, see that the upper row of incisor teeth do not overhang the lower, constituting what is called parrot mouth. Animals so malformed rarely thrive well, from Cautions regarding inability to crop their food. Always regard with glanders. extreme suspicion any animal suffering from a thin, glue-like discharge from either one or both nostrils: look well up the nose, and be perfectly certain that there are no ulcers on the membrane, or perchance you may introduce a glandered subject, which will endanger the lives of both men and animals. Should such appearances as those just described present themselves in an animal after purchase, order it to be instantly destroyed, together with all the woollen or leather equipment belonging to it. The metal can be rendered free from the glander poison by thoroughly heating it in the camp fire, and then throwing it whilst fizzing hot into water. Never attempt to treat a case of even suspected glanders whilst travelling: shooting is the only safe method of relieving the animal from its sufferings. Horses or mules can be readily shot dead with either ball or small shot. To do this instantly, stand on the off-side of the animal, about six feet from and in a line behind the shoulder; aim well below the ear, in a direction from behind forwards, and from below upwards. A charge thus delivered from a gun, rifle, or large heavy pistol—not an insignificant popgun revolver—will strike the creature dead on the spot, and thus save it unnecessary torture.

Before quitting the subject of "Veterinary Surgery," it may be well to caution the intending purchaser against laying out his money Hints on horse and in animals affected by cataract. In order to discover mule purchase. whether this defect exists, place the animal with its head just in a line with the two posts of a stable or shed doorway; screen the eye under examination from the direct rays of the sun with your cap or felt hat, look steadily and keenly down into the interior of the eye, and if a cataract is there it will be perceived in a pearl-tinted spot or patch on the crystalline lens of the eye, just as though the bull's-eye of a miniature lantern had received a mark from French chalk. Clouds on the outer surface of the ball of the eye or cornea are in no way to be confounded with cataract; clouds such as these are caused in a variety of ways—strokes from flexible branches, whip lashes, &c., and generally yield to treatment with as much calomel as will fill an ordinary percussion cap, rubbed up with half a tea-spoonful of honey. Place a piece as large as a No. 4 shot in the affected eye every other day, until the opacity passes away. Cataract, on the other hand, is beyond treatment, and greatly detracts from the value of the animal suffering from it.

Bony excrescences round the coronets, constituting ring bone, and slits in the wall of the hoof, called sand-cracks, also detract much from either a horse's or a mule's value for travelling, and should be carefully looked for. Do not, as a rule, purchase very young horses or mules, as they are far more likely to give trouble and fall sick than those of more matured age; those of from six to ten, or even eleven years old, if sound and in good condition, will do good service.

APPENDIX.

WEIGHT OF A SUPERFICIAL FOOT OF PLATE OR SHEET IRON.

No. of the wire gauge.	Thickness in inches.	Weight in pounds.	No. of the wire gauge.	Thickness in inches.	Weight in pounds.	No. of the wire gauge.	Thickness in inches.	Weight in pounds.
	1	40	5		8·74	18		1·86
	7/8	35	6		8·12	19		1·70
	3/4	30	7	3/16	7·5	20		1·54
	11/16	27·5	8		6·86	21		1·40
	5/8	25	9		6·24	22	1/32	1·25
	9/16	22·5	10		5·62	23		1·12
	1/2	20	11	1/8	5	24		1
	7/16	17·5	12		4·38	25		0·9
	3/8	15	13		3·75	26		0·8
1	5/16	12·5	14		3·12	27		0·72
2		12	15		2·82	28	1/64	0·64
3		11	16	1/16	2·50	29		0·65
4	1/4	10	17		2·18	30		0·50

WEIGHT OF ROD IRON ONE FOOT IN LENGTH OF THE FOLLOWING DIMENSIONS:

SQUARE IRON.		ROUND IRON.		FLAT IRON.	
Inch.	Pounds.	Inch.	Pounds.	Inch.	Pounds.
1/4	0·2	1/4	0·14	1/4 × 1	0·8
3/8	0·5	3/8	0·4	3/8 × 1	1·3
1/2	0·8	1/2	0·7	1/2 × 1	1·7
5/8	1·3	5/8	1·	5/8 × 1	2·1
3/4	1·9	3/4	1·5	3/4 × 1	2·5
7/8	2·6	7/8	2·	1/4 × 2	1·7
1	3·4	1	2·7	3/8 × 2	2·5
1 1/8	4·3	1 1/8	3·4	1/2 × 2	3·4
1 1/4	5·3	1 1/4	4·2	5/8 × 2	4·2
1 3/8	6·4	1 3/8	5·	3/4 × 2	5·1
1 1/2	7·6	1 1/2	6·	1/4 × 3	2·5
1 5/8	8·9	1 5/8	7·	3/8 × 3	3·8
1 3/4	10·4	1 3/4	8·1	1/2 × 3	5·1
1 7/8	11·9	1 7/8	9·3	5/8 × 3	6·3
2	13·5	2	10·6	3/4 × 3	7·6
2 1/4	17·1	2 1/4	13·5	1/4 × 4	3·4
2 1/2	21·1	2 1/2	16·7	3/8 × 4	5·1
2 3/4	21·6	2 3/4	20·1	1/2 × 4	6·8
3	30·4	3	23·9	5/8 × 4	8·4
3 1/2	41·4	3 1/2	32·5	3/4 × 4	10·1
4	54·1	4	42·5	1/4 × 5	4·2
5	84·5	5	66·8	3/8 × 5	6·3
6	121·7	6	95·6	1/2 × 5	8·4
7	165·6	7	130	5/8 × 5	10·6
8	216·3	8	169·9	3/4 × 5	12·7

Weight in Pounds of One Cubic Foot of the following Substances :

	lb.		lb.
Cast iron	450	Water	62·5
Wrought iron	486	Air	0·075
Steel	489	Steam	0·036
Pine wood	29·5		

Relative Heat-conducting Power of different Bodies.

Gold	1000	Fire brick	11
Platinum	981	Fire clay	11·4
Silver	973	*With Water as a Standard.*	
Copper	898	Water	10
Iron	574	Pine	39
Zinc	363	Lime	39
Tin	304	Oak	33
Lead	180	Ash	31
Marble	24	Apple	28
Porcelain	12·2	Ebony	22

Relative Conducting Power of different Substances compared with each other.

Hare's fur	1·315	Cotton	1·046
Eider down	1·305	Lint	1·032
Beaver's fur	1·296	Charcoal	·937
Raw silk	1·284	Ashes (wood)	·927
Wool	1·118	Sewing silk	·917
Lamp black	1·117	Air	·576

Relative Conducting Power of Fluids.

Mercury	1·000	Proof spirit	·312
Water	·357	Alcohol (pure)	·232

Radiating Power of different Bodies.

Water	100	Blackened tin	100
Lamp black	100	Clean tin	12
Writing paper	100	Scraped tin	16
Glass	90	Ice	85
Indian ink	88	Mercury	20
Bright lead	19	Polished iron	15
Silver	12	Copper	12

The Stone Weight.

The term "stone" is often used to indicate weight, but some confusion is apt to arise if the nature of the object or substance to be weighed is not clearly indicated; thus, in weighing men according to what is known as "horseman's weight," 14lb. avoirdupois are made use of; in weighing butcher's meat, 8lb.; iron, 14lb.; glass, 5lb.; hemp, 32lb.; cheese, 16lb.

To Ascertain the Contents of Casks.

If the diameter is equal everywhere, multiply the square of the diameter in inches by the depth, and divide the product by 359. Thus a barrel with a diameter of 36in. and 50in. deep, $36 \times 36 \times 50 = 64,800 \div 359 = 180\frac{1}{2}$ old measure $= 183\frac{1}{2}$ imperial gallons.

If the centre or bung diameter is larger than the ends, First square the centre diameter in inches, and then multiply it by 2, to which add the square of the diameter of the end. Then multiply this by the length of the cask, and divide by 1·077. Thus a barrel with a centre diameter of 28in., end 25in., and length 36in. $28 \times 28 \times 2 = 1568 \times 625$ $(25 \times 25) = 2193 \times 36 = 78,948 \div 1·077 = 73$ old measure, $74\frac{1}{4}$ imperial gallons.

Weight of Cattle, to Ascertain.

Measure the girth close behind the shoulder, and the length from the fore part of the shoulder blade along the back to the bone at the tail, which is in a vertical line with the buttock, measuring both in feet; multiply the square of the girth expressed in feet by five times the length, and divide the product by 21. The quotient is the weight nearly of the four quarters in imperial stones of 14lb. avoirdupois, for example, if the girth is $6\frac{1}{2}$ft. and the length $5\frac{1}{4}$ft., we shall have $6\frac{1}{2} \times 6\frac{1}{2} = 42\frac{1}{4}$ and $5\frac{1}{4} \times 5 = 26\frac{1}{4}$, then $42\frac{1}{4} \times 26\frac{1}{4} = 1109\frac{1}{16}$, and this divided by 21 gives $52\frac{4}{5}$ stones nearly, or 52 stones 11lb. It is to be observed, however, that in very fat cattle the four quarters will be about one-twentieth more, while in those in a very lean state they will be one-twentieth less than the weight obtained by the rule. The four quarters are a little more than half the weight of the living animal, the skin weighing about the eighteenth part and the tallow about the twelfth part of the whole.

Tanks, Pipes, Wells, &c., to Measure.

The following is a rough and ready way to ascertain the contents of circular tanks, wells, pipes, &c. Square the diameter in inches, and cut off the right hand figure as a decimal, and the result will be gallons in each 3ft. (yard) of depth, or length of a pipe, as :—

Pipes.

Diameter Inches.	Inches.			Square.		Gallons In 3 feet.
2	2	×	2	=	4	or	0·4
6	6	×	6	=	36	or	3·6
12	12	×	12	=	144	or	14·4

WELL OR TANK.

36	....	36 × 36	=	1296	or	129·6
100	....	100 × 100	=	10,000	or	1000·0

THE WEIGHT OF A HAYSTACK, TO ASCERTAIN.

Measure the length and breadth of the stack, then take its height from the ground to the eaves, and add to this last one-half of the weight from the eaves to the top, multiply the length by the breadth and the product by the height, all expressed in feet, divide the amount by twenty-seven to find the cubic yards, which multiply by the number of stones supposed to be in a cubic yard, viz., in a stack of new hay, 4 stones of 22lb. avoirdupois each, if the stack has stood some time 8 stones, and if old hay, 9 stones, and you have the weight in stones. For example, if a stack be 60ft. in length, 30ft. in breadth, 12ft. from the ground to the eaves and 9ft. (the half of which is $4\frac{1}{2}$) from the eaves to the top, then $60 \times 30 \times 16\frac{1}{2} = 29,700$, and $29,700 \div 27 = 1100$ and $1100 \times 9 = 9900$ stones of old hay.

THE QUALITIES OF GOLD.

Very few terms are more loosely used than that of gold, and it is therefore necessary that the traveller should make himself fully acquainted with the nature of the alloy made use of under the name of gold in the various countries he may chance to visit. Let him not suppose that, because the glittering chain or ring displayed in an English jeweller's window is marked in conspicuous letters, "Warranted fine gold," the ornament is as a matter of course composed of *pure gold*, or he will buy experience dearly. *Fine gold* means nothing further than that an alloy of some kind containing some gold is for sale. It is well, therefore, to insist on the exact quality of the article (in carats—18 carats, 22 carats, or whatever it is represented to be) being stated on the vendor's bill of charge.

The nature of gold alloy differs materially in various countries. We have, therefore, thought it well to provide the reader with the following useful tables compiled by Mr. E. W. Streeter, and used in his "Hints to Purchasers of Jewellery."

Qualities of Gold manufactured in different Parts of the World.

			£	s.	d.		£	s.	d.
England ....From	1 carat, worth	0	3	6	to 22 carats, worth	3	17	10½
France..................... ,,	18 carats ,,	3	3	8½	only common by special per-
Denmark................ ,,	18 ,, ,,	3	3	8½	[mission.
Baden .... ,,	14 ,, ;,	2	9	6½	
Germany (all States) ... ,,	12 ,, ,,	2	2	5½	to 15 carats, worth 2 13 1
Russia .... ,,	15 ,, ,,	2	13	1	to 22 ,, ... ,, 3 17 10½

			£	s.	d.		£	s.	d.
Austria	From 10 carats, worth		1	15	4¼	to 18 carats, worth	3	3	8½
Italy	,, 12 ,,	,,	2	2	5½	to 22 ,, ... ,,	3	17	10½
Holland	,, 4 ,,	,,	0	14	2	to 22 ,, ... ,,	3	17	10½
Africa	,, 23 ,,	,,	4	3	1½				
India	,, 22 ,,	,,	3	17	10½	to 23½ ,, ... ,,	4	3	1½
Rome	All 18 ,,	,,	3	3	8½				
U. States of America	From 1 ,,	,,	0	3	6	to 18 ,, ... ,,	3	3	8½
Norway and Sweden	All 18 ,,	,,	3	3	8½				
Belgium	From 18 ,,	,,	3	3	8½	to 22 ,, ... ,,	3	17	10½
Spain	All 18 ,,	,,	3	3	8½				
Switzerland	All 18 ,,	,,	3	3	8½				
Geneva	From 14 ,,	,,	2	9	6½	Watch cases only.			
China	From 16 ,,	,,	2	16	7½	to 23¾ carats, worth	4	4	0
Japan	From 18 ,,	,,	3	3	8½	to 23¾ ,, ... ,,	4	4	0
Brazil	All 18 ,,	,,	3	3	8½				
Hamburgh	From 13½ ,,	,,	2	11	3½	to 18 ,, ... ,,	3	3	8½
Turkey	,, 18 ,,	,,	3	3	8½				
Greece	,, 10 ,,	,,	1	15	4½	to 16 ,, ... ,,	2	16	7½
Persia	,, 3 ,,	,,	0	10	7½	to 23½ ,, ... ,,	4	3	1½
Egypt	,, 18 ,,	,,	3	3	8½				
Rio Janeiro	Imported from 1 carat		0	3	6	to 22 ,, ... ,,	3	17	10½
Chili	,,	,,	0	3	6	to 22 ,, ... ,,	3	17	10½
Peru	,,	,,	0	3	6	to 22 ,, ... ,,	3	17	10½

Siam nearly pure, fine work.

Australia ....Same as England, except that made up from the diggings.

Mexico ....Principal manufacture fine.

Any quality is allowed to be imported into these countries.

The following table by the same author will serve to show in a condensed form, the value of different gold alloys relatively, and also the extremely low standard at which so called "gold articles" are manufactured in this country.

Gold Value Table.

	£	s.	d.			£	s.	d.	
22-carat gold is worth	3	17	10½	per oz.	8-carat gold is worth	1	8	3¾	per oz.
18 ,, ,,	3	3	8½		6 ,, ,,	1	1	2½	
16 ,, ,,	2	16	7½		4 ,, ,,	0	14	2	
14 ,, ,,	2	9	6½		2 ,, ,,	0	7	1	
10 ,, ,,	1	15	4½		1 ,, ,,	0	3	6	
9 ,, ,,	1	11	10						

Since writing the early portion of this work, we have found it requisite, in order to supply a manifest want, to have manufactured a small leather case (on the exact model of our own) containing all the tests and appliances requisite for the identification of precious metals or precious stones.*

* This, together with its accompanying instruction book, can be obtained at the explorer's room, established by S. W. Silver & Co., 66 & 67, Cornhill.

We have also caused to be constructed, from our own pattern, a small triple branch of gold of different degrees of alloy. Each branch, when rubbed on the touchstone, and treated with nitric acid, will leave a characteristic streak, which may be compared with one formed by rubbing the article to be tested, and treating it with acid in the same manner; the nature of the alloy will thus be found by comparison.*

EMERSON'S TABLE OF STRENGTHS, SHOWING THE LOAD THAT CAN BE SAFELY BORNE BY A SQUARE INCH ROD OF EACH OF THE FOLLOWING SUBSTANCES:

	lb. avoir.		lb. avoir.
Iron rod, 1in. square, will bear	76,400	Walnut, red fir, holly, elder, plane crab	5,000
Brass	35,600	Cherry, hazel	4,760
Ivory	15,700	Alder, asp, birch, willow	5,000
Oak, box, yew, plum-tree	7,850	Lead	430
Elm, ash, beech	6,070	Freestone	914

Emerson's rule is, that a cylinder, the diameter of which is d inches loaded to one fourth of its absolute strength, will carry as follows:

	cwt.		cwt.
Iron	$135 \times d^2$	Oak	$14 \times d^2$
Good rope	$22 \times d^2$	Fir	$9 \times d^2$

Another of his rules is that a cylindrical rod of well seasoned clean-grown fir of an inch circumference drawn in length will bear at its extremity 400lb. and a spar of fir 2in. in diameter will bear about 7 tons, but not more. A well made and carefully kept hemp rope of one inch in circumference, will bear 1000lb. being at its extremity.

Mr. Barlow has formed the following table as a mean resulting from experiments on the strength of direct cohesion on a square inch of the following substances:

	lb.		lb.
Box	20,000	Beech	11,500
Ash	17,000	Oak	10,000
Teak	15,000	Pear	9,800
Fir	12,000	Mahogany	8,000

He also states as follows regarding the transverse strength of beams, &c. Mr. Weale thus quotes from Mr. Barlow's essay: "The transverse strength of rectangular beams, or the resistance which they offer to fracture, is as the breadth and square of the depth; therefore, if

* This test branch can be obtained either at the explorer's room, or from Mr. E. Streeter, Conduit-street, Bond-street.

two rectangular beams have the same depth, their strengths are to each other as their breadths, but if their breadths are the same, then their strengths are to each other as the square of their depths. The transverse strengths of square beams are as the cubes of the breadths or depths. Also in cylindrical beams the transverse strengths are as the cubes of the diameters. Thus, if a beam which is one foot broad and one foot deep support a given weight, then a beam of the same depth and two feet broad will support double the weight; but if a beam be one foot broad and two feet deep it will support four times as much as a beam one foot broad and one foot deep. If a beam one foot square support a given weight, then a beam two feet square will support eight times as much. Also a cylinder of two inches in diameter will support eight times as much as a cylinder one inch in diameter. The appended table gives data bearing on the subject.

Teak	2·462	Elm	1·013
English oak	1·672	Pitch pine	1·632
Canadian oak	1·766	Red pine	1·341
Dantzic oak	1·457	New England fir	1·102
Adriatic	1·383	Riga fir	1·108
Ash	2·026	Mar Forest fir	1·262
Beech	1·556	Larch	1·127

TIMBER TO MEASURE.

In order to find the centrals of unsquared timber, multiply the square of the quarter girth or of a quarter of the mean circumference by the length. In dealing with trees of tapering form the mean dimensions may be found by either girthing in the middle of the stick for mean girth, or girthing at both ends and then taking one half the measure produced. If this is not done, girth the tree in several places. These several girths when divided by this number will furnish a mean circumference, one fourth of which being squared and multiplied by the length will give the solid contents of the tree. The number of superficial feet in a board or plank is known by multiplying the length by the breadth. If the board is smaller at one end than the other add the breadth of the two ends together, and take half their sum for the mean breadth, with which multiply the length.

The solid contents of squared timber are ascertained by measuring the mean breadth by the mean thickness, and the product again by the length, or multiply the square of what is indeed the quarter girth in inches by the length in feet and divide by 144, when the contents in feet will be the result.

Branches of trees, the quarter girth of which is less than six inches, and portions of tree trunks less than two feet in circumference cannot be regarded as "timber" properly so called.

One and a half inches in every foot of quarter girth, or one eighth of the girth is allowed for bark, except in the case of elm trees, one inch in the circumference of the tree trunk or whole girth, or one-twelfth of the quarter girth is the general fair average allowed. The quarter girth is half the sum of the breadth and depth in the middle. The nearest approach to truth in measurement of timber is to multiply the square of one-fifth of the girth or circumference by double the length. The product will be the contents.

INDEX.

A

ABYSSINIAN mule platforms, 306
Accommodation of tents, to increase, 53
Adaptation of hames to collars, 411
Admiral Belcher's expedient for moving vessels during calms, 154
Adzes or axes, makeshift, 338
African boots, 369
Agricultural implements, 348
Aguardiente, to make, 513
Ague, remedy, 69
Ailments of natives, 73
Albatross, catching, 520
Alligators, catching, 523
    Securing snared fish from, 523
Aloe juice, extracting, 702
Altitudes, ascertaining, 649
    Low, or levels, to obtain, 642
    Table of, 650
Ambulances, &c., 601
American cordway, 287
    Indian lodges, 272
    Life raft, 147
    Portable boat, 136
    Wild fruits, 471
Ammunition, packing, 14
    Quantity to take, 14
    Taking abroad, 14, 16
Amphibious animals, trapping, 587
Anchors, 332
Angle at which to pitch a tent, 49
Animals, amphibious and fish, 518
    Calls of, 598
    Infested with fly, treatment of, 704
    Pack, 408, 413, 423
    Purgative for, 703
    Skin of, as food, 495
    Teeth and their irregularities, 705
    Wild, observation of the habits of, 676
Antidotes for poison, 71
    For poison from arrows, 549
Ants, locusts, and other insects and their larvæ as food, 498
Anvils, 169, 172
Aparejo, 413
Apparently drowned, treatment of, 164
Application of wind power to horizontal wheel, 455
Aps or chupatee, 483
Aquatic birds, traps for, 596
Arch, plank, 304
    Hints for the, 273
Arctic regions, camping, 356
    Travelling in, 358
Armament, hunter's, 576
Arobas waggon, 393

Arrest hemorrhage, 612
Arrow-fishing, 527
    Trap, 578
Arrows, harpoon, 527
    Poisoned, 548
    Rifling, 552
Artificial horizon, 25, 654
    And sextant, use of, 651
Artillery, charges for, 211
    Cartridges and wads for, 213
    Disabled, management of, 400
    Dromedary or Zamboureks, 215
    Field, 400
    Repairing, 213
    Shot for, 193, 216
    Sledges, 361
    Unspiking, 213
    Zemboureks, 215
Artist's materials, 18
Ascertaining altitudes, 649
    Contents of casks, 710
    Variations of the compass, 641
    Weight of cattle, 710
    Weight of haystack, 711
Ash cake, 487
Assegais, to render useless, 178
Attachment of straps, for sledges, 256
Auger, nave, 333
Australian bark canoe, 142
    Spears and spear throwing, 545
    Tent, 51
    Two-wheel drays, 405
Axes or adzes, makeshift, 338
Axles, to make and repair, 188

B

BAGGAGE derrick, extempore, 292
Bags, Ditty, 60
    Pack-saddle, 31
    Ships' water, 443
    Sleeping, 687
    Swedish throwing, 296
Baits, fish, hints on, 536
    For traps, 587
Baking bread, 488
    Cakes, 487
Baling and drinking ladles, Birch bark, 691
Ballast for boats, 155
Balsas canoe, 123
Bamboos, building with, 255
    Various uses for, 318
Bananas and plantains for food, 473
Bandages, surgical, 607
Bark, birch, drinking and baling ladles, Lap, 691
    Canoes, 93
    Canoes, Australian, 142

Bark (*continued*) :
　　Canoes, birch, 138
　　Canoes, Canadian, 138
　　Canoes, cedar, 140
　　Floats, 88
　　For canoes, mode of stripping, 137
　　Stripping from trees, 691
　　Uses of, 691
Barrow, hand, 346
Barrel rods, 16
Base metals, to detect, 231
Baskets, fire, 493
　　Fish traps, 527, 529
　　Waterproof, 444
Bayonets, 11
　　Sheath knives as, 176
Beams, masts, &c., for platform boats, 100
Bear trap, 583
Bechuana hut, 247
Beds, camp, 38
Beehive hut, Kafir, 246
Bees' nests, taking, 514
　　Wild, to smoke out, 477, 514
Bell mules, 416
Bellows, 61
　　And forge, extempore, 187
Bell-tent made to hold many people, 53
Belts, life, 83
Bent wood, 337
Birch bark drinking and baling ladles, Lap, 691
Billhooks, 36
Biltong, 509
Birch-bark canoes, 138
　　For canoes, 137
Birdlime, 598
Birds, aquatic, traps for, 595
　　Calls for, 598
　　Preserving, 509
　　Sea, cooking, 517
　　Snaring, 593
　　Traps for, 591
Bite of tsetse fly, 574
Bites of snakes, 72
Bits, 30
Blackcock trap, 592
Bladders and paunches for holding water, 444
　　And water-skins, repairing of, 685
　　Use of, 685
Blanket used for extemporising a tent, 51
Blindfolding pack animals, 415
Blockhouse, 262
Blocks and pulleys, 341
　　Double, 342
　　Signal, 342
　　Snatch, 342
Blue lights, matches from, 493
Board house, 245
　　Wigwam, 242
Boards, ice, 359
Boats, American portable, 136
　　Ballast for, 155
　　Balsas, 123
　　Bridges of, 311
　　Building, 112
　　Canvas or skin, 42, 89
　　Cape waggon, 114
　　Catamaran, 144
　　Cattle, Indian, 88
　　Clinker, 110, 113
　　Collapsible, 137
　　Connecting beams, masts, &c. for platform, 100

Boats (*continued*) :
　　Copper, 44, 104
　　Copper, materials used in, 47
　　Copper platform, 98
　　Coracle, 88
　　Corrugated iron, 44
　　Esquimaux, 92
　　Fitted with inflated tubes, 150
　　Inflated canvas, 42
　　Inflated, to make safe, 103
　　Iron, 44, 104, 109
　　Kite haul for, 353
　　Leaky, 80
　　Massoolah, 144
　　Metal life, 109
　　Metal platform, 95, 98
　　Metal, to connect odd sections of, 110
　　Mixture for painting metal, 100
　　Models of, 93, 105
　　Norwegian, 145
　　Leak stoppers, Norwegian, 81
　　Paddling, 118
　　Norwegian leak stoppers, 81
　　Outrigger, makeshift, 81
　　Platform, 93, 95, 98, 100, 101
　　Platform, models of, 93
　　Portable canvas, 42
　　Portable steel, 146
　　Proas, 118
　　Quagga hide, 91
　　Rafts, and makeshift floats, 80
　　Reed, 86
　　Rules for sailing, 155
　　Russian cargo, 91
　　Sailing, hints on, 154
　　Sculling, 116
　　Skin, 89
　　Things to be thought of when designing, 93
　　Torres Straits, 142
　　Wattled, 110
　　Whale, 540
　　Without nails, 145
　　Wooden platform, materials for, 100
　　(see also Canoes)
Boers' method of loading guns quickly, 199
Boiling meat, 490
　　Rice, 500
　　Water without pots, 490
Bolts, and gun barrel cutting, 173
　　And nuts, dies and taps for, 173
Bones, horns, tendons, fish skin, &c. use of, 685
　　Marrow, as food, 494
Books for travellers, 27
Boomerang, 546
Boot jack, German, 384
Boots, African, 369
　　And shoes, 6, 368
　　Clamps for, 375
　　Dog, 359
　　India rubber, to mend, 383
　　Laces, 7
　　Lapland, 366,
　　Lasts for, 371
　　Making, 371
　　Preparation of skin for, 370
　　Sledge dogs', 357
　　Snow shoe, 365
　　Stitching, 375
　　Thread for, 375
　　Wading among rocks, 383
Boring heavy logs, 333

Botanical specimens, collecting, 668
         Packing and preserving, 674
Boulders, to remove, 232
Bowls, wooden, 350
Bows, cross, Chinese, 551
        Pellet, Indian, 552
        Strings, tightening, 551
Boxes and trunks, 7
        As floats, 86
        Copper, 8
        For Cape waggon travelling, 8
        For rafts, 126
Box markings, 617
Braces, 5
Branch, peg, and log ladders, 309
Branding cattle, 433
Brands of camels, 435
        Cattle, making, 434
Brass for barter with natives, 183
        Guns and their charges, 211
        Softening and hardening, 183
Bread baking, 488
Breakers, rules for passing through, 155
Break for wheels, 397
Breech loaders, concentrating cartridges
   for, 206
Brick tea, 506
Bridge shears, to construct, 298
Bridges, boat, 311
        Cable and twig, 298
        Chain, 293
        Deodar beam, 302
        Fly, 294
        Gabion, 289
        Ice, 305
        Indian rope, 303
        Natural, 307
        One tree, 287
        Plank arch, 304
        Powder chambers for C.F., 9
        Rafter, plank, and slab, 304
        Rope, 303
        Shears, 298
        Swamp, 288
        Tartar, 291
Bridles, 29
Broken masts, 159
        Spars, scarfing, or fishing of, 158
Bruised gun barrels, to repair, 197
Buckets, bamboo, 318
        Canvas, 59
        Gutta percha, 64
        Leather, 63
        Palm, 465
Buck-shot moulds, 16, 194
Buik-waggon, 390
Building, bamboo for, 255
        Boats, clinker, 110, 113
        Boats, hints on, 112
        Boats of metal, 95, 110
        Boats of wood, 112
        Boats, things to be thought of when,
          93
        Crook and prong house, 251
        Fires, 478
        Jetty, 291
        Log house, 242
        Mission Churches, 266
        Portuguese, in Africa, 270
        Rafts, principles of, 129
        Walls, 258
        Wheels, 324, 329
Bullet moulds, 200

Bullets, cleft, 200
        Hardening, 200
Bullock trunks, 2
Bull's-eye lantern, 75
Buoys, life, 84
Burgs, waggon, to make, 263
Burning charcoal, 234
Bush knife, 11
        Veterinary surgery and medicine,
          699
Bushman's hut, 246
Bustard shooting, 590
Butter, preserving, 517
Buying horses, 511
        Mules, hints on, 416
        Second-hand guns, hints on, 11

C.

CABBAGE, palm, 464
Cable and twig bridge, 298
Cakes, baking, 487
        Meat, 502
        Sago, 493
Calabashes, float, 85
        For holding water, 444
Calls, bird and animal, 598
Calming troubled water by means of oil,
   154
Camels, 425
        Brands, 435
        Embarking, 430
        Feeding, 429
        Harnessing, 426
        Hints on, 429
        Journal or diary, 432
        Loads and distances for, 428
        On shipboard, fastening, 431
        Water in stomach, 430
        Wounds on backs of, 700
Camp beds, 38
        Cookery, 475
        Filters, 445
        Fires, caution as to, 481
        Furniture, 38, 346
        Medicine-making, hints on, 702
        Of ox waggons, to defend, 263
Camping, Arctic, 356
Canadian bark canoe, 138
Candles, 77
        Guttering, to prevent, 493
        Making, 77
        Malay, 78
        Packing, 78
        Screens for, 78
Cane and twig roadway, 297
Cannon, cartridges for, 213
        Charges, &c. 211
        Mounting, 208, 210
        Repairing, 213
        Shot for, 193, 246
        Unspiking, 213
        Wads, 213
        (See also artillery.)
Canoes, Australian bark, 142
        Balsas, 122
        Bark, 93, 138, 140, 142
        Birch for, 137
        Canadian bark, 138
        Carriage for, 139
        Cedar bark, 140
        Dug-out, 92, 143

Canoes (*continued*) :
    Fiji, 122
    Fuegian, 142
    Inflated canvas for one man, 44
    Long, 144
    Mode of stripping bark for, 137, 691
    Outriggers for, 87
    Queen Charlotte's Island, 139
    Shoe, 141
    Water transport, 442
Canteens, 61
Canvas boat, inflated, 42, 89
    Buckets, 59
    Canoe for one man, inflated, 44
    Or skin boat, 89
Cape waggon, 386
    Boats, 114, 131
    Chests as rafts, 123
    Load for, 404
    Tent, 52
    Tent or tilt, 114
    Wine, 392
Cap squares of a gun, makeshift for, 210
Caps for the head, 5
    Percussion, and their substitutes, 210
Capstan, gunner's, 332
Cargo boat, Russian, 91
Cariole, Swedish, 395
Carnivora, hunting of, 569
Carpenter's tools, 35
Carriages, canoe, 139
    Wheeled, measuring distances travelled by, 635
Carrier, kettle, Lapland, 346
Carrying deer, 581
    Rolling, and parbuckling heavy spars, 313
    Water, 441
Cartridges and wads for cannon, 213
    Concentrating for breech loaders, 206
    Extempore, 206
    Making, 203, 205
Case hardening, 179
Cases for saddles, 29
    Tin, utilisation of, 186
Casks, ascertaining contents of, 710
    Water, to embark, 336
Casting horses, 701
    Oxen, 702
    Ropes, for horses, 701
Catamaran float, 144
Catching albatrosses, 520
    Alligators, 523
    Cattle, 275
    Crayfish, lobsters, &c. 535
    Crows, 599
    Deer with thorn wreaths, 552
    Ducks, &c. 595
    Fish, 520
    Musk rats, 588
    Ostriches, emus, &c. 589
    Porpoises, 542
    Sea fish, 578
    Turkeys, 591
Catgut and parchment, 684
Cattle, ascertaining weight of, 710
    Boat, 88
    Brands, making, 434
    Catching, 575
    Drinking troughs for, 430
    Glanders, 706
    Hobbling, 418

Cattle (*continued*) :
    Marking, 433
    Watering. 430
Cautions regarding camp fires, 481
    Peas as projectiles, 217
Cedar bark canoe, 140
Cereals as food, 504
Chain and links, 413
    And rope ladders, 309
    Bridges, 293
    Pole, 297
Chalk lines, 258
Chambers, powder, for C.F. breech loaders, 9
Charcoal burning, 234
Charges, &c. for brass guns, 211
Chemical tests, for minerals and metals, 228
Chests as rafts. Cape waggon, 123
Chinese cross-bow, 552
    Slab and trestle bridge, 304
Chisels, cold, 178
    Making incisions in iron with, 170
"Chucknuck," or "strike-a-light," 477
Chupatee or aps, 483
Chupper screens. 260
Churches, fortifying, 266
    Mission, plans for building, 263
Cider, plantain, 473
Clamps for boot making, 375
Cleaning guns, 208
Clearing fine sand from gun-locks, 61
    Nut, 449
Cleft bullets, 200
Climb palms, to, 465
Clinker boat, 110, 113
Clinometer, makeshift, 646
Clip for holding post, &c. 241
Clock, water, 649
Cloths, saddle, 29
Coats, 5, 6
Cocoa nut palm, uses for, 319
    Shells, use of, 467
    Use of, 465
Cold chisel, making, 178
    Making incisions in iron with, 170
Colic or gripes, remedy for, 703
Collapsible boat, 137
Collars, horse, 409
Collecting botanical specimens, 668
    Dew, 460, 465
    Mineralogical and geological specimens. 675
    Natural history specimens, 667
    Water from rain-falls, 448
Colonists and natives, to obtain information from, 663
Common dog sledge, 360
Companions and servants, conduct to, 618
Compass, marking distances with, 26
    Pocket, 24
    Points of, 559
    Variation of, to ascertain, 641
Concentrating cartridges for breech loaders, 206
Conduct to companions and servants, 618
Connecting beams, masts, &c. for platform boats, 100
Contents of casks, ascertaining, 710
Contusions, remedy for, 70
Convenient tool hold-all, 37
Cooking, flesh, 489
    Pots, 62
    Sea birds, 517
    Stove, Norwegian, 495

Index.

721

Cooper's work, 335
Copper and iron, to tin, 184
    Boats, 44, 95, 98
    Boats, materials used in, 47
    Boxes, 8
    Skiff, 104
    Tinning, 184
    Water flasks, 441
Coracle, 88
Cordway, American, 287
Corrugated iron boat, 44
    Houses, 269
Cost and materials of metal platform boat, 99
Cotton torch, 78
Coverings, makeshift foot, 379
Covers for lamps, 76
Cravats, hog's, 349
Crayfish, lobsters, &c. to catch, 535
Creeper or grapnel, to trip, 535
Crimea, tent used in, 53
Crook and prong house, to build, 251
Crooks, pack saddle, 345
Cross-bow, Chinese, 552
Cross-tree saddles, 415
Crows, catching, 599
Cup lamp, 76
Cupping, 613
Cups, priming, to make, 214
Cure of wounds from poisoned arrows, 549
Cutlery, 35
Cutting bolts and gun-barrels, 173
    Sheet metal, snips for, 186
    Timber, season for, 238
    Up large game, 509

D.

D'Abri, Tente, 50
Damaras hut, 249
Damper, 487
Damp places, procuring water from, 438
Dams, strengthening, 292
    Weirs and spears, 528
Dead game, protecting, 581
Deep-water glass, 164
Deer catching with thorn wreaths, 552
    Enticing, 581
    Keeping and carrying, 581
    Traps, 580
Defensible camp with ox-waggons, 263
    Churches, 266
    Farm-house and village, 261, 264
Deodar beam bridge, 302
Deris, to make, 303
Derrick, baggage, 292
    Landing, 311
Destroy mule leeches, to, 705
Detection of base metal, 231
Dew, collecting, 461, 465
Diarrhœa and its remedy, 70
Diary, &c., in duplicate, 17
    Or journal, camel, 432
Dies and taps for bolts and nuts, 173
Dimensions of sledges, 351
Disabled artillery, management of, 400
Dishes and plates, to make, 186
Dislocated shoulder, reducing, 612
Distances, estimation of, 647
    For camels, 428
    Measurement, 26, 635
    Travelled by wheeled carriage, measuring, 635
Distil aguardiente, to, 513

Distil (continued):
    Water, to, 440
Ditty bag, 60
Dividing and packing venison, 582
Dogs, boots for, 359
    Free from the attacks of the tsetse fly, 573
    Packs for, 361
    Securing to sledges, 356
    Sledge and harness for, 353, 360
    Sledge, food for, 357
    Sledge, habits of, 357
Doors and gates, to make and hang, 255
Double boat of copper, 44
    Block, 342
    Canvas boat, inflated, 42
    Metal boats, 95
    Sextant, 24
Dough nuts, 488
Drags for wheels, 395
Draught oxen, yoking, 403
Drawing sledges, 352
Drays, Australian, 405
Dressing for wounds, 65
    Skins, 681
Dried flesh, 495
Drills and saws, 334
Drinking and baling ladles, birch bark, 691
    Troughs for cattle, 430
Driving a coracle, 88
    And leading horses, 422
Droge, the, 147
Dromedary brands, 435
    Points in the, 427
    (Zemboureks), artillery, 215
Drowned, treatment of the apparently, 164
Drugging fish, 537
Dubbin, to make, 383
Duck for ground sheet, &c. 5
Ducks, &c. catching, 595
Dug-out canoes, 92
Duplicates of correspondence, &c. 17

E.

Economy in food, 497
Edible frog, 500
Eggs, ostrich, 500
    Preserving, 517
    Shells of, horns and calabashes for holding water, 444
Elephant hunting, 566
Elg-Led, 579
Elk trap, 579
Embarking camels, 430
    Horses, 421
    Water casks, 336
Emus, ostriches, &c. catching, 589
England, outfit to take from, 3
Enticing deer, 581
Equipment, mule, hints on, 418
    North Australian expedition, 30
    Sledge, 356
    Waggon, 398
Erecting a perpendicular on a given point, 230
Escape, fire, 310
    Pole, Indian, 308
Esquimaux boat, 62
    Ice hut, 278
    Lamp, 76
    Sledges, 355
    Snow hut, &c. 274

A A A

Esquimaux (*continued*) :
 Summer tents, 278
Establishing communication with a lee shore by means of a kite, 162
Estimate distance, to, 647
 Strength of ropes, to, 695
 Time, 647
 Weight of rope, to, 695
Expedients for moving vessels during calms, Admiral Belcher's, 154
 For saving boats in rough water, 154
 For working ships' pumps, 154
Expedition by twenty-one men for eighteen months, stores, &c. required for, 40
Extracting gun nipple, 178
 Sap from timber, 315
Extricating waggons from quicksands, &c. 127

F.

FALL-TRAPS, 582
 Plank, 584
Farm house, defensible, 261, 264
 And village, to fortify, 264
Farrier's stores and horse medicines, 74
Fastening camels on shipboard, 431
 Horses, 421
 Makeshift, 297
 Shingles, 244
Fat, to treat, 686
Feathers, ostrich, packing, 551
Feeding of camels, 429
Feet, sore, 384
Felling timber, 236
Fences, 241, 269
Ferries and fly bridges, 294
Ferrying wheels over rivers, 126
Fever and its remedy, 67
Field artillery, 400
 Artillery sledges, 361
 Guns and their charges, 211
 Observing, hints on, 635
Figure of four traps, 583
Fiji canoes, 122
Filing up and trimming iron after forging, 170
Filters, camp, 445
 Extemporised, 445, 448, 450
 Grass, 448
 Patent, 501
Finding height of a tree or other object, whose base is accessible, without instruments, 284
 Points of the compass, 559
 River pearls, 225
 Water, 439
 Width of rivers or ravines without instruments, 281
Firearms, hints on, 207
 Makeshift, 214
 Testing, 12
Fire and waterproof glue, 687
 Baskets, 492
 Building, a, 478
 Caution as to camp, 481
 Escapes, 310
 Fuel for, 478, 493
 Making a, 475
 Maintaining, 481
 Places, makeshift, 491
 Producing, 476, 551

Fire (*continued*) :
 Signal, as a, 479
Fish and amphibious animals, 518
 Baits, hints on, 536
 Catching, 520
 Drugging, 537
 Haunts of, hints on, 536
 Hooks, makeshift. 519
 Roe, preserving. 516
 Sea, catching, 518
 Securing, from alligators, 523
 Skin, use of, 685
 Spearing, 538
 Spears, weirs, and dams, 528
 Torch, 78
 Traps, baskets, 527, 529
Fishing broken spars. 158
 Implements, 535
 Lines, to make, 529
 Nets, 532
 Tackle making, and hints on, 521
 Under ice, 533
Fitting-up of tents, 53
Flasks, water, copper, 441
Flat-bottomed steel boat, 146
Flesh cooking, 489
 Dried, 495
 Preserving, 507
 Transportation of, hints on, 510
Flint muskets, 10
Floating waggons, 127
Floats, bark, 88
 Boxes, 86
 Calabash, 85
 Catamaran, 165
 Inflated skin, 134
 Mangrove wood, 143
 Milk-bush, 143
 Skin, 88
 Skin for one man, 135
 Wood, 88, 143
Flour, preserving from weevils, 494
 From wrecks, 494
Fly bridge and ferries, 294
 Infested animals, treatment of, 704
 Tsetse, 572
Flying railway at Ichaboe, 300
Food, economy in, 497
 Gathering, hints on, 512
 Hints on, 494
 Insects and their larvæ as, 498. 515
 Reptiles as, 497, 500
 Roots, Lotus, 500
 Skins as, 495
 Sledge dogs', 357
 Various, 502
 Vegetable, 500, 503
Foot, coverings, makeshift, 379
Footways, tree, 293
Fording rivers, hints on, 305
Forecastle lamp, 76
Forge and bellows, extempore, 187
 Hints on the management of the. 168
Forked sticks, uses of, 345
Form of tent peg, 56
Fortifying camps, 263
 Churches, 266
 Farm and village, 264
Foundations for houses, 269
Fox trap, 584
 Wedge for tree nails, 240

Fracturing glass so as to obtain a sharp edge, 553
Fritters, 493
Frogs, edible, 500
Fruits, obnoxious juices, removing of, 462
Wild, 502
Wild, of America, 471
Fuegean pole house, 273
Canoe, 142
Fuel for fires, 478, 493
Furnace, makeshift, 491
Furniture, camp, 38, 346

G.

GABERDINE, 4
Gabion bridge, 289
Galls in horses, 700
Game, dead, protecting, 581
Pegs, &c. 349
Gates, latches for, 347
Making and hanging, 255
Gathering food, hints on, 572
Mushrooms, hints on, 516
General hints on boat building, 112
Geographical information, to obtain from natives and colonists, 663
Geological and mineralogical specimens, collecting, 675
Geology for travellers, 220
German boot jack, 384
Gharrie, Indian, 393
Gipsy tent, 49
Glanders, cautions regarding, 706
Glass bottles, lightning averted by, 255
Fracturing, so as to obtain a sharp edge, 553
Deep water, 164
Gloves, 5
Glue, fire and water proof, 687
Gold, identifying, 225
Qualities of, 711
Searchers, hints to, 220
Grapnel or creeper, to trip, 535
Grass filters, 448
Sedge, rafts, 132
Grease cartridge, making, 205
Grenades and rocket arrows, 216
Grindstones, mounting, 344
Gripes or colic, remedy for, 703
Ground for tent pitching, 58
Lines, and their management, 526
Sheets, 5
Guano stages at Ichaboe, 299
Gum-tree bark canoe, 142
Gun barrels, to cut, 173
Barrels, to repair when bruised, 197
Cleaning, 208
Locks, oil for, 207
Nipple, to extract a, 178
Repairing, 174
Rests, 177
Second-hand, hints on buying, 11
Sighting, 175
Sights, 175
Slings, 33
Spring, 577
Telling time by, 209
Gunner's capstan, 332
Gunpowder, to make, 217
Plan for securing, 32
Guns and rifles, 10
Gunyah, the, 246

Gut, silkworms, 531
Guttapercha buckets, 64
Guttering in candles, to prevent, 493, 409

H.

HABITS of sledge dogs, 357
Wild animals, observation of, 676
Halters, 32
Hames, adaptation to collars, 411
Makeshift, 409
Hammocks, 39
Handbarrow, makeshift, 346
Hand mill, 483
Hanging doors and gates, 255
Handles of stock whips and lead pencil 197
Hardening brass, 183
Case, 179
Bullets, 200
Wood, 317
Hard rove rope, treatment of, 694
Wood articles, 320
Harness and pack animals, 408
For dog sledge, 353
Hints on, 412
Mule, 410
Ox, 403
Tightening, 415
Harnessing and yoking draught oxen, 403
Camels, 426
Hints on, 412
Reindeer, 362
Harpooning hippopotami, 543
Seals under ice, 534
Harpoons, 539
Arrow, 527
Hartebeeste hut, 248
Hats and caps, 5
Haunts of fish, hints on, 536
Hay and straw ropes, spinning, 694
Haystack, ascertaining weight of, 711
Headstalls, 32
Heat-conducting bodies, 709
Heavy spars, to carry, roll, or parbuckle, 313
Height of a tree, or other object whose base is accessible, to find without instruments, 284
Hemorrhage, to arrest, 612
Hide boat, quagga, 91
Ropes, 685
Hints on boat building, 112
Boat sailing, 154
Buying second-hand guns, 11
Camels, 429
Camp medicine making, 702
Collecting and preserving objects of natural history, 666
Field observing, 635
Fire-arms, 207
Fish baits, 536
Fishing tackle, 521
Food, 494
Food gathering, 513
Fording rivers, 305
Gathering mushrooms, 516
Gold searching, 220
Harness and harnessing, 412
Haunts of fish, 536
Horse and mule purchase, 416, 511, 706
Hygeens, and camels, 429
Large game, 509

Hints on (*continued*) :
    Management of the forge, 168
    Matters connected with waggons, 398
    Mule equipment, 418
    Mule purchasing, 416, 706
    Pumping ships, 154
    Raft building, 129
    Sentries, 266
    Servants and slaves, 619
    Serving rations, 496
    Shoeing horses, 699
    Sledges, 357
    Springs, 446
    Transportation of flesh, 510
    Trapping, 587
    Travel, 623
    Travelling in the arctic regions, 273, 358
Hippopotami, use of, 545
    Harpooning, 543
Hitches and knots, 695
    On measuring lines, 324
Hobbles, 33
Hobbling cattle, 418
Hogs' cravats, 349
Hold-all for tools, 37
Holder for torches, 493
Honey, finding and taking, 514
Hook trap, 584
Hooks, fish, 183, 519
Hoop-iron, uses for, 169
Horizon, artificial, 25, 654
    Artificial, and sextant, use of, 651
Horizontal wheel, application of wind power to, 455
Horn lantern, 76
Horns for holding water, 444
    Use of, 685
Horse and mule waggons, 394
Horses, buying, 511, 705
    Casting ropes for, 701
    Collars, 409
    Embarking, 421
    Equipment, 28
    Fastening, 421
    Galls, 700
    Glanders, 706
    Leading and driving, 422
    Medicines and farrier's stores, 74
    Poultice, 700
    Purchase of, hints on, 511, 705
    Securing for an operation, 701
    Shoeing, hints on, 699
    Sledges, 361
    Sore backs, 700
    Teeth, and other irregularities, 705
    Throwing, 701
Hour glass, 648
Houses, African, Portuguese, 270
    Board, 245
    Block, 262
    Crook and prong, 251
    Corrugated iron for, 269
    Defensible farm, 261, 264
    Foundations for, 269
    Fuegean pole, 273
    Log, 242
    Logier hill, 253
    Plank, 245
    Reed, 260
    Thatches for, 252, 254
    (*See also Huts*)

Howitzers, and their charges, 212
Hunter's armaments, 576
Hunting elephants, 560
    Large carnivora, 569
    Lions, 566
Hurdle or wattle work, 340
Husks of cocoa nut, use of, 467
Huts, American Indian, 272
    Australian, 246
    Bechuana, 247
    Beehive, 246
    Bushman's, 246
    Damaras, 249
    Fuegean, 273
    Hartbeeste, 248
    Ice, 278
    Lining of, tents for, 53
    Namaqua Hottentot, 250
    Papuan tree, 272
    Peat, 273
    Rio Negro, 271
    Savages', 246
    Snow, 274
    Stone, 247
    Tartar, 260
    Thatches for, 252, 254
    Vaal River, 248
Hutting in the arctic regions, 273
Hygeens and camels, hints on, 479

I.

Ice boards, 359
    Bridging a river by means of, 305
    Fishing under, 533
    Harpooning seals under, 534
    Huts, 278
    Getting net under, 533
Ichaboe guano stages and flying railway, 299
Identification of gold, 225
    Of metals, 220
    Of precious stones, 223
Implements, fishing, 535
Impurities from water, removing, 449
Incisions in iron with cold chisels, to make, 170
Increase accommodation of tents, 53
    Size of bell-tent, 53
Indian (American) lodges, 272
    Cattle boat, 88
    Escape pole, 308
    Gharrie waggon, 393
    Lamp, 77
    Pellet bow, 552
    Rope bridge, 303
    Scaling ladder, 309
Indiarubber boots, to mend, 383
    Garments, 5
Inflated boats, to make safe, 103
    Canvas boat, 42
    Skin floats, 134
    Tubes, boats fitted with, 150
Information from natives and colonists, to obtain, 663
Insects and their larvæ as food, 498, 515
Inspanning, 404
Instruments for mapping, 26
    For mapping a route, 20
    Scientific, 20
    Stands for, 646
Intestines for holding water, 444
Introduction, 1
Iron articles, selection of, 398
    Boats, 44, 109

Iron (*continued*) :
    Corrugated, for houses, 269
    Making incisions with cold chisels in, 170
    Ore, to smelt, 226
    Platinising, 80
    Rod, weight of, 709
    Rusting, to prevent, 181
    Skiff, 104
    Test for wrought or malleable, 399
    Tinning, 184
    Trap, 586
    Uses for scrap and hoop, 169
    Welding of, 168
Irregularities of teeth in draught animals, 705
Irritated surfaces, remedy for, 70

J.

JACK BOOT, German, 384
Jackets, 4
    Making, 615
Jetty, to build an extempore, 291
Joiners' chisels, 170
Joining odd sections of metal boats, 110
    Sheet metal, 184
Journal in duplicate, 17
    Or diary, 17
    Or diary, camel, 432
Juices, obnoxious, removing from fruits, &c., 462

K.

KAFFIR beehive hut, 246
Keeping deer, 581
Kettle carrier, Lapland, 346
Key, watch, 178
Killing sheep, 496
Kites as auxiliaries to swimming, 160
    As sails, 159
    Establishing communication with a lee shore by means of, 162
    Hauls for sledges and boats, 353
    Scaling cliffs with, 162
    Signalling by means of, 161
    Tacking by means of, 161
Knives, 35
Knives, makeshift, 169
    Sheath and bayonets, 167

L.

LADDERS, 309
    Indian scaling, 309
    Makeshift, 308
    Miners', 307
    Peg, branch, and log, 309
    Rope and chain, 309
Ladles, spoons, and their substitutes, 199
Lamps, bull's-eye, 75
    Covers for, 76
    Cup, 75
    Esquimaux, 76
    Forecastle, 76
    Indian, 77
    Oils for, 75
    Portuguese, 74
    Railway, 76
    Reflecting, 76
    Wicks for, 75
Lancers' tent, 51

Landing derrick, 311
Lanterns, bull's-eye, 75
    Horn, 76
Lap birch bark drinking and curved baling ladles, 691
    Boot, 366
    Fish hook, 520
    Kettle carrier, 456
Lapmark grinding stones, 345
Larch trees, 317
Larvæ of insects as food, 498, 515
Lasts for boots, 371
Latches, 317, 347
Lathes, makeshift, 343
Laudanum, preparation of, 703
Leading and driving horses, 421
Lead ore smelting, 199
    Pencils and stock whip handles, 197
    Plates, to make, 197
    Uses of, 192
Leaf torch, 78
Leakage in water-skins, repairing of, 444
Leaky boats, to stop, 80
    Norwegian stopper for, 81
Leaping-poles, 307
Leather buckets, 63
Leaves, palm, use of, 465
Leeches, mule, to destroy, 705
Lee shore, establishing communication by kites with a, 152
Levelling, 301
    Staff, extemporised sight vane for, 645
Levels or low altitudes, to obtain, 642
    Water, substitute for, 647
Library, the traveller's, 25, 27
Life-belts, 83
    Boat, metal, 109
    Buoys, 84
    Line, 85
    Raft, American, 147
Liggers and trimmers, 523
Lighting a fire, 478, 479
Lightning, averted by glass bottle, 255
Line slings and lob sticks, 296
Lines, fishing, 529
    For measuring, 258, 323
    Ground, and their management, 526
    Measuring, 258, 323
Lining for old huts, tents as, 53
Links and chains, 413
Lion hunting, 566
Lizards, snakes, &c., as food, 497, 498, 500
Loads for camels, 428
    Cape waggon, 453, 404
Lobsters, crayfish, &c., to catch, 535
Lob sticks and line slings, 296
Locality for water, 437
Locusts, ants and other insects as food, 498
Lodges of the American Indian, 272
Log, boring a, 338
    Clip, 241
    For sledges, to make, 355
    House, to build, 242
    Peg and branch ladders, 309
    Splitting, 482
    Steaming, 317
Logging-up timber, 237
Logier hill house, 253
Long canoes, 144
Lotus roots and seeds as food, 500
Low altitude, or levels, to obtain, 642

M.

Maintaining a fire, 481
Maize preserving, 505
Malay torch, 78
Mallets for driving tent pegs, 56
Management of forges, hints on the, 168
    Disabled artillery, 400
    Ground line, 526
Mange, preventive and remedy, 703
Mangrove wood floats, 143
Manna and its preparation, 469
Maple sugar, 468
Mapping, 26
    Instruments for, 26
    On Mercator's projection, 660
    Routes, instruments for, 20
    Tables, 661
Marking boxes, 617
    Cattle, 433
Marrow bones, 494
Martin trap, 835
Massoolah boats, 144
Masts, broken, 159
    For platform boats, 101
Matches from blue lights, 493
Materials for artists, 18
    Copper boats, 47
    Metal platform boat, 99
    Ropes, 690, 692
    Sketching, &c. 18
    Wooden platform boat, 100
Mats, rush, 250
Measurement, extemporary, 322
    Of distances, 26, 635
    Of distances travelled by wheeled
      carriages, 635
    Of timber, 715
    Of time, 648
    Of waterflow of a river, 662
    Rough modes of, 322
Measuring lines, 258, 324
    Lines, hitches on, 324
    Tape, to make, 283
    Trees, 287
Meat, boiling, 490
    Cakes, 502
    Preserving, 507
    Roasting, 489
    Transportation of, hints on, 510
Medical stores, 65
Medicine and dressing for wounds, 65
    Surgery, bush veterinary, 699
Medicines, 65, 68, 702
    Hints on making, 702
    Horse, and farrier's stores, 74
Mercator's projection, mapping on, 660
Mescal, to make, 513
Metal (base), to detect, 231
    Boats, 44
    Boat, building a, 109
    Boat, double, 95, 98
    Boat, joining odd sections of, 110
    Boat life, 109
    Boat, mixture for painting, 100
    Boat platform, 95, 98
    Boat steel, 146
    Pannikin, making, 185
    Sheet, joining, 184
    Sheet, snips for cutting, 186
Metals, tests for, 220, 228
    Working in, 168

Milk-bush floats, 143
    Preserving, 515
    Spirit, 474
Mills, makeshift, 483
    Oil or sugar, 485
Mineralogical and geological specimens, collecting, 675
Minerals, chemical tests for, 228
Miner's pump, to make, 233
    Swing and ladder, 307
    Tools and mining, 221
Mining and miner's tools, 221
Mission churches, building, 266
Mixture for painting metal boats, 100
Mocassins, 378
Models of boats, 93, 105
Modes of securing tent ropes, 56
Mosquito nets, 59
Moulds, buck shot, 16, 194, 200
    Bullet, 8
    Shot, 193
Mounting cannon, 208, 210
    Grindstones, 344
Moving vessels during calms, Admiral Belcher's expedient for, 154
Mules, bell, 416
    Equipment, hints on, 418
    Harness for, 410
    Leeches, to destroy, 705
    Packing purposes, 416
    Platforms, Abyssinian, 306
    Purchase of, hints on, 416, 706
    Refractory, to secure, 410
    Teeth and their irregularities, 705
    Waggons for, 394
Mushrooms, hints on gathering, 516
Muskets, flints, 10
    Repairing, 182
Musk rats, catching, 588

N.

Namaqua Hottentot hut, 250
Nardoo for meal, 484
Natch block, 342
Native plough, 348
Natives, ailments of, 73
    And colonists, to obtain information from, 663
    Rewarding, 439
Natural bridges, 307
    History specimens, collecting, 667
    History specimens, preserving and packing, 670
Naturalists' outfit, 666
Nave auger, to work, 333
    Turning, 328
Necessaries for the table, 62
Necessary carpenter's tools, 35
Nets, fishing, 532, 534
    Mosquito, 59
Netting, 698
    Under ice, 533
Nipple of a gun, to extract, 178
North American wild fruits, 471
    Australian expedition, equipment of, 30
Norwegian boats, 145
    Cooking stove, 495
    Leak stoppers, 81
    Skidor, 366
Nuts and bolts, taps and dies for, 173
    Clearing, 449

O.

OARS for travellers, 101
Observation of the habits of wild animals, 676
Observatory, portable, 25
Obtain geographical information from natives and colonists, 663
    Levels or low altitudes, to, 642
Odds and ends for sledging, 358
    To take abroad, 64
Offal of animals, 494
Oil for gun locks, 207
    For lamps, 75
    On troubled waters, 154
    Or sugar cane mill, 485
    Palm, 467
Ointment for wounds, 702
Oneida trap, 586
One man, inflated canvas canoe for, 44
One-tree bridge, 287
Ore, iron, smelting, 226
    Lead, smelting, 199
Ostriches, catching, 589
    Eggs, 501
    Feathers, packing, 551
Otter, making and working, 525
Outfit for artists, 18
    Naturalist's, 666
Outfit to take abroad, 3
Outriggers for canoes, 87
    Makeshift, 81
Outspanning, 404
Ovens, makeshift, 488
Oxen, casting, 702
    Riding, 576
    Yoking and harnessing, 403

P.

PACK animals, 408, 413, 423
    Animals, blindfolding, 415
    Oxen, 575
    Ropes, 415
    Saddle, 30
    Saddle bags, 31
    Saddle crooks, 345
    Saddle, Spanish, 413
Packing ammunition, 14
    Botanical specimens, 674
    Candles, 78
    Natural history specimens, 670
    Ostrich feathers, 551
    Riding saddles, 32
    Venison, 582
Packs and pack animals, 408, 413, 423
    Dog, 361
Paddling, 118
Pail-yoke, 391
Pails, palm, 523
    Water, 441
Painting and sketching under difficulties of travel, 626
    Metal boats, mixture for, 100
Palanquins, stretchers, &c., 601
Palm, bucket of, 465
    Cabbage, 464
    Climbing, 465
    Cocoa nut, 319
    Leaves, use of, 465
    Oil, 467
    Range and uses of the, 465, 468

Palm (*continued*) :
    Sugar, 466
    Toddy, 466
    Vinegar, 466
Pannikin, to make, 185
Pans and pots, 62
Papuan tree hut, 272
Parbuckling, carrying, and rolling heavy spars, 313
Parchment and catgut, 634
Passing through breakers, rules for, 155
Patent filter, 450
Patrol tent, 48
Paunches and bladders for holding water, 444
Pearls, river, to find, 225
Peas as projectiles, 217
Peat hut, 273
Pegs and rests for guns, game, &c., 349
    Branch and log ladders, 309
    Tent, 56
Pellet bow, 552
Pemmican, 508
Pencils and stock whip handles, 197
Penetration of rifle balls, 14
Pen trap, 591
Perch bolts, to repair, 172
Percussion caps and their substitutes, 210
Perpendicular, on a given point, to erect, 282
Pipes, buckets, &c., of bamboo, 318
    Tanks, wells, &c., measuring, 711
Pistols, 15
Pitching tents, 48
    Selection of ground for, 58
Pitfall, 569
Plane table and its use, 644
Plank arch, 304
    Fall trap, 584
    House, 245
    Rafter, and slab bridges, 304
    Screens, to make, 258
Plans for building mission churches, 266
Plantains, cider, 473
    For food, 473
Plants holding water, 504, 448, 461
    Sap as substitute for water, 437, 459
Plates, lead, to make, 197
    Making, 186
Platform boats, connecting beams, masts, &c. for, 101
    Metal, 95, 98
    Models of, 93
    Wooden, 101
Platforms, Abyssinian mule, 306
Platinising iron, &c. 180
Ploughs, native, 348
    Settlers, 348
Pocket compass, 24
    Handkerchiefs, 4
Points in the dromedary, 427
    Of the compass, 559
Poisoned arrows, 548
    Cure of wounds from, 549
Poisons, 599
    And their antidotes, 71
Pole chains, 297
    House, Fuegean, 273
    Indian escape, 308
    Leaping, 307
    Repairing, 191
Porcupine trap, 578
Porpoises, catching, 542

Porpoises (*continued*) :
    Uses of, 542
Portable boat, American, 136
    Boat of inflated canvas, 42
    Boat, steel, 146
    Observatory, 25
    Tool chest, 38
Portuguese buildings in Africa, 270
    Lamp, 74
Potato whiskey, 473
Pots and pans, 62
    Raft of, 132
    Sugar making, 487
Poultice, horse, 700
Powder chambers for central fire breech loaders, 9
    Flasks, 16
Precious stones, to identify, 223
Preparation of American wild fruits, 471
    Laudanum, 703
    Manna, 469
    Skin for boots, 370
Preserved vegetables, 515
Preserving birds, 509
    Botanical specimens, 674
    Fish roe, eggs and butter, 516
    Flesh, 507
    Flour from weevils, 494
    Iron from rusting, 181
    Maize, 505
    Meat, 507
    Milk, 515
    Natural history specimens, 670
    Skins, 677
Preventing a candle from guttering, 493
    Iron rusting, 181
Preventive and remedy for mange, 703
    Of tsetse fly bite, 575
Priming cups, to make, 214
Principles of raft building, 129
Proas, 118
Procuring aloe juice, 702
    Fire, 476, 478, 551
    Water from damp places, 439
    Water from wells, 438
Producing fire, 476, 551
Projectiles, peas as, 217
Projection, Mercator's, mapping on, 660
    Of routes, 658
Prong and crook house, to build, 251
Protecting dead game, 581
Pulleys or blocks, 341
Pumping ships, 154
Pumps, extemporised, 458
    Miners', to make, 233
Punk, 477
Purchase of horses and mules, hints on, 416, 511, 706
Purgative for animals, 703
Purifying water, 451

Q.

Quadrant, 651
Quagga hide boat, 91
Qualities of gold, 711
Quantity and nature of stores required by 21 men for 18 months, 40
    Of ammunition to take abroad, 14
Quarrying stone, 231
Queen Charlotte's Island canoe, 139
Quern, the, 483
Quicksands, extricating waggons from, 127

R.

Radiating heat, power of various bodies, 710
Rafter, plank and slab bridges, 304
Rafts, American life, 147
    Balsas, 123
    Boats, and makeshift floats, 80
    Cape-waggon chests as, 123
    From wrecked ships, 82
    Inflated skin, 134
    Pot, 132
    Principles of building, 129
    Reed, 87
    Sedge grass, 132
    Trennelled, 129
Rail splitting, 240
Railway, flying, 300
    Lamp, 76
Rainfalls, collecting water from, 448
Raising a roof, 253
    Waggons, &c. from quicksands, &c. 127
    Water from wells, 451
Rakes, forks, &c. from sticks, 348
Rations for one man for six days, 502
    Hints on serving, 496
    Scale of, for rough travelling, 496
Ravines or rivers, to find the width of without instruments, 281
Reducing dislocated shoulder, 612
Reed boat, 86
    Houses, screens, and sheds, 260
    Raft, 87
Reefing of sails from the sides, 153
Reflecting lamp, 76
Reindeer, harnessing, 362
    Sledge, 362
Refractory mule, to secure, 410
Region of the tsetse fly, 572
Remedy for ague, 69
    Colic and gripes, 703
    Diarrhœa, 70
    Fever, 67
    Irritated surfaces, 70
    Mange, 703
    Snow blindness, 70
    Strains and contusions, 70
Removing boulders, 232
    Obnoxious juices from fruits, &c., 462
    Sand, &c. from gun locks, 61
Rendering boats safe, 81
Repairing axles, 188
    Bladders, water skins, &c. 635
    Bruised gun barrels, 197
    Cannon, 213
    Guns, 175
    Leakage in water skins, 444
    Muskets, 182
    Perch-bolts, 172
    Poles, 191
    Vessels, temporary, 148
    Wheels, 191
    Wheel-tires, 170
Reptiles as food, 497, 500
Rests for guns, &c. 178, 349
    Rifle shooting, 177
Revolvers, 15
Rewarding natives, 439
Rice, boiling, 501
Riders, roof, 245
Riding oxen, 576

Riding saddles, packing of, 32
Rifle balls, penetration of, 14
    For travellers, 202
    Rests, 178
    Selecting, 10
    Sights, 13, 177
    Shells, extempore, 198
    Sporting, 202
Rifles and guns, 10
Rifling arrows, 552
Rigs of vessels, 150
Rio Negro nuts, 271
Rivers, ferrying wheels over, 144
    Hints on fording, 305
    Or ravines, to find the width of without instruments, 281
    Pearls to find, 225
    Water flow, measurement of, 662
Rivets, 187
Roads, cane and twigs, 297
    Spong, 289
    Swamp, 280
Roadways, cable and twig, 298
Roasting meat, 409
Rocket arrows and grenades, 216
Rod iron, weight of, 709
Rolling, carrying, and parbuckling heavy spars, 313
Roof riders, 245
    To raise a, 253
Roots for food, 473
    Of lotus as food, 500
    Yielding sap as a substitute for water, 459, 460, 463
Rope bridge, Indian, 303
    Casting, for horses, 701
    Chain ladders, 309
    Hard rove, treatment of, 694
    Hay, 694
    Hide, 685
    Ladders, 309
    Making, 692
    Materials for, 690, 692
    Pack, 415
    Stone, 292
    Straw, 694
    Strength of, to estimate, 695
    Tent, modes of securing, 26
    Weight of, to estimate, 695
Routes, projection of, 658
Rucksacks, 688
Rudders, temporary, 156
Rue ruddy, 352
Rules for passing through breakers, 155
    For sailing boats, 144
    To be observed when sledging, 358
Rush mats, 250
Russian cargo boat, 91
Rusting, preserve iron from, 181

S.

SABOTS and socks, 382
Sacks, ruck, 687
    Water, skin, 682
Saddles, 28
    And gun rests, 349
    Cases, 29
    Cloths, 29
    Cross-tree, 415
    Pack, 30

Saddles (*continued*):
    Packing of, 32
    Spanish pack, 413
Sago cakes, 493
    Making, 472
Sailing boats, rules for, 155
Sails and their substitutes, 150, 159
    Kites used as, 159
    Substitutes for, 153
    To reef from the sides, 153
Samovar, 79
Sandals, 368, 380
Sand, &c. from gun locks, to remove, 61
Sap from timber, to extract, 315
    Of plants as substitute for water, 459, 460, 463
Savages' huts, 246
Saw-pit, substitute for, 241
Saws and drills, 334
Scale of rations for rough travelling, 496
Scaling cliffs, &c. kites for, 162
    Ladders, Indian, 309
Scarfing of broken spars, 158
Scientific instruments, 20
Scissors, 35
Scrap-iron, uses for, 169
Screens, Chuppar, 260
    For candles, 78
    Plank, 255
    Reed, 260
Sculling, 116
Sea birds, cooking, 517
Sea fish, catching, 578
Seals, harpooning under ice, 534
Season for cutting timber, 238
Seasoning wood, 315
Second-hand guns, hints on buying, 11
Sections, odd, of metal boats, to join, 110
Securing cattle, 418
    Fish from alligators, 522
    Gunpowder, mode of, 32
    Horse for an operation, 701
    Horses, 421
    Refractory mule, 410
    Tent ropes, modes of, 56
Seeds and roots of lotus as food, 500
Sedge grass raft, 132
Selection of bullet moulds, 8
    Ground for tent pitching, 58
    Guns, 8
    Iron articles, 398
    Rifles, 10
    Servants, 618
Sentries, hints for, 266
Servants and companions, conduct to, 618
    Slaves, hints on, 621
Serving rations, hints on, 496
Setting traps, 586
Settlers' plough, 348
Sextant and artificial horizon, use of, 651
Shears, to construct bridge, 298
Sheath knives or bayonets, 176
Sheds, reed, 260
Sheep killing, 496
Sheet-copper boat, 44
    Iron, weight of, 708
    Metal, snips for cutting, 186
    Metal, to join, 184
Shells for rifles, extempore, 198
    Of cocoa-nut, use of, 467
Shelves, makeshift, 259
Shingle spike and nail, 244
Shipboard, fastening camels on, 431

Ships, pumping, 154
    Rafts from, 82
    Water bags, 443
Shirts, 4
    Making, 613
Shoe canoe, 141
Shoeing horses, hints on, 699
Shoemaker's wax, 371
Shoes and boots, 368
    Snow, 364
Shooting bustards, 590
    Gear, 8
    Tortoises with arrows, 552
Shot belts, 16
    Cannon, 193
    Cannon, makeshift, 216
    Making, 195
    Moulds, 193
Shoulder, reducing dislocated, 612
Sighting guns, 175
Sights, gun, 175
    Rifle, 13, 175
Sight vane for levelling staff, extemporised, 645
Signal block, 342
    Fire as a, 497
Signalling by means of kites, 161
Signs of the weather, 162
Silkworm gut, 531
Sinking wells, 456
Skates and their substitutes, 367
Sketches and painting, under difficulties of travel, 626
Sketching materials, 18
Skidor, Norwegian, 366
Skiff of copper or iron, 104
Skin as food, 495
    Boat, 89
    Cattle boat, 88
    Dressing, 681
    Float for one man, 135
    Floats, 88
    Inflated rafts, 134
    Preparation of, for boots, 370
    Sleeping bags, 687
    Tanning, 681
    Treatment, 677
    Use of, 685
    Water, 441
    Water, and bladders, repairing, 685
    Water, repairing leakage in, 444
    Water sacks, 682
Slab plank and rafter bridges, 304
Slaughtering sheep, 496
Slaves and servants, hints on, 618, 621
Sledges, attachment of straps for, 356
    Dimensions, 351
    Dog, 353, 357, 360
    Drawing, 352
    Equipment of, 356
    Esquimaux, 355
    Field artillery, 361
    Harness for dog, 353
    Hints on, 357
    Horse, 361
    Ice board, 359
    Kite haul for, 353
    Log for, 355
    Reindeer, 362
    Runners of, to smooth, 355
    Speed of, to check, 356
    Stopping, 356
    Summer, 363

Sledges (*continued*):
    Tobogun, 359
    Travail, 360
    Whip, 354
Sleeping bags, 687
Slings for guns, 33
Slow match and tinder, 477
Slugs, making, 194
Smelting iron ore, 226
    Lead ore, 199
Smith's tools for travelling, 182
Smoking out wild bees, 477, 514
Smoothing roughened runners of sledges, 355
Snakes as food, 498
    Bites, &c. 72
Snares, 593
Snatch block, 342
Snips for cutting sheet metal, 186
Snow-blindness, and its remedy, 70
    Hut, 274
    Shoe boots, 365
    Shoes, 364
Soap making, 686
Socks and sabots, 382
    Stockings, 4
Softening brass, 183
Solids, weight of, 709
Sore backs, 700
    Feet, 384
Spanish pack saddle, 413
Spars, carrying, rolling, or parbuckling, 303
    Scarfing or fishing of broken, 158
Spawn, fish, preserving, 516
Spearing fish, 536
Spears, Australian, 545
    Fish, weirs and dams, 528
    Throwing, Australian, 545
    Turtle, 547
Specimens, botanical, collecting, 668
    Botanical, packing and preserving, 674
    Geological and mineralogical collecting, 675
    Natural history, collecting, 667
    Natural history, preserving and packing, 670
Speed of a sledge to check, 356
Spinning hay and straw ropes, 694
Spirit from milk, 474
Splicing, 698
Splints, surgical, 609
Splitting logs, 482
    Rails, 240
    Timber, 238
Spong roads, 289
Spoons, ladles, and their substitutes, 199
Spooring, 555
Sporting rifles, 202
Spring guns, 577
Springs, hints on, 446
Spurs, 29
Square, to make a, 283
Squirrel trap, 584
Stables, temporary, 260
Staff, levelling, sight vane for, 645
Stages at Ichaboe, guano, 299
Stands for instruments, 646
Stationary, 17
Steaming log, 316
Steel boat, portable, 146
    Making, 227
    Traps, 585

Steering wheel, to make, 330
Stern-posts, temporary, 158
Sticks, forked, uses of, 345
Still, makeshift, 440
Stirrups, 29, 334
Stitching boots, 375
Stockings and socks, 4
Stock-whip handles and lead pencils, 197
Stone hut, 247
    Quarry, 231.
    Ropes, 292
    Treatment of, 232
    Weapons, manufacture of, 553
    Weight of, 710
Stopping leaky boats, 80
Stores, &c. required by twenty-one men for
    an eighteen months' expedition, 40
    Farriers', and horse medicines, 74
    Medical, 65
Stoves, Norwegian, 495
Strains, remedy for, 70
Straps for sledges, attachment of, 356
Straw and hay ropes, spinning, 694
Strengthening dams, 292
Strength of ropes, to estimate, 695
    Various bodies, 713
Stretchers, palanquins, &c. 601
"Strike a light" or "Chucknuck," 477
Stripping bark for canoes, mode of, 137, 691
Substitutes for sails, 150
Sugar cane, or oil mill, 485
    Making, 485
    Maple, 468
    Palm, 466
    Pots, making, 487
Summer sledges, 363
    Tents, Esquimaux, 278
Supple jack, 349
Surgery and medicine, bush veterinary, 699
Surgical bandages, 607
    Splints, 609
Swamp bridge, to make, 288
    Roads, to make, 280
Swedish cariole, 395
    Throwing bag, 296
Swimming to a lee shore, kite as an assistance
    in, 162
Swing and ladder, miners', 307
Swinging derrick, 311
Swivels, wooden and other, 320
Symptoms of fever, 67
    Tsetse fly bite, 574

T.

Table necessaries, 62
    Plane, and its use, 644
Tables, altitudes, 650
    Heat conducting bodies, 709, 710
    Mapping, 661
    Quality of gold, 711
    Radiating heat power of bodies, 710
    Strength of various bodies, 713
    Trocheameter, 638
    Weight of rod iron, 709
    Weight of sheet iron, 708
    Weight of solids, 708
Tacking by means of kites, 161
Tackle, fishing, making, and hints on, 521
Tailor's work, 613
Taking bees' nests, 514
Tana trap, 584
Tanks, pipes, wells, &c. measuring, 711

Tanning skins, 681
Taps and dies for bolts and nuts, 173
Tartar bridges, 291
    Hut, 260
Tea, uses of, 505
Teeth of draught animals and their irregu-
    larities, 705
Tempering tools, 178
Temporary repairs of vessels, 118
    Rudders, 156
    Stables, 260
    Stern-posts, 158
    Wigwam, 245
Tendons, use of, 605
Tente d'abri, 50
Tents, Australian, 51
    Bell, to increase size of, 53
    Blanket, 51
    Cape-waggon, 52
    Crimean, 53
    D'abri, 50
    Esquimaux, 278
    Extemporary, 52
    Fitting up of, 53
    Gipsy, 49
    Lancers', 51
    Lining to old huts, 53
    Or tilt for Cape waggons, 114
    Patrol, 48
    Pegs, 56
    Pitching, 48
    Pitching, selection of ground for,
    58
    Ropes, modes of securing, 56
    Turkoman, 57
    Umbrella, 59
    Used in Crimea, 53
Testing firearms, 12
Tests for minerals and metals, 220, 228
    Wrought or malleable iron, 399
Thatches for houses and huts, 252, 254
Theodolite, 652
Thermometers, 22
Things to be thought of when designing a
    boat, 93
Thorn wreath, catching deer with, 552
Thread for boot making, 375
Throwing a horse, 701
    Bag, Swedish, 296
    Oil on troubled waters, 154
Tightening harness, 415
    String of bow, 551
Tilt or tent for Cape waggons, 114
Timber, extraction of sap, 315
    Felling, 236
    Hardening, 317
    Logging-up, 237
    Measuring, 715
    Seasoning, 315
    Splitting, 238
    Steaming, 316
    Vice for holding, 241
    When to cut, 238
Time, estimation of, 647
    Guns, 209
Tin cases, utilisation of, 186
Tinder and slow match, 477
Tinning copper and iron, 184
Tip-up, 534
Tires of wheels, to repair, 170
Tobogun sledge, 359
Toddy, palm, 466
Tool chest, portable, 38

Tools, carpenter's, 35
 For mining, 221
 Hold-all, convenient form of, 37
 Smith's, for travelling, 182
 Tempering, 178
 To take abroad, 37
Torches, 78
 Holder, 493
Torres Straits boats, 142
Tortillas, 483
Tortoises, shooting, with arrows, 552
Tourniquets, 612
Tracking, 555
Transportation of flesh, hints on, 510
Transport, canoe water, 442
Trapping amphibious animals, 587
Traps, aquatic bird, 595
 Arrow, 578
 Baits for, 587
 Bear, 583
 Bird, 593
 Blackcock, 592
 Deer, 580
 Elk, 579
 Fall, 582
 Figure of four, 583
 Fish, basket, 527, 529
 Fox, 534
 Hook, 584
 Iron, 586
 Martin, 583
 Oneida, 586
 Pen, 591
 Plank fall, 584
 Porcupine, 578
 Setting of, 586
 Squirrel, 584
 Tana, 584
 Turkey, 591
 Hints on, 587
Travail, sledge, 360
Travel, hints on, 623
 Painting and sketching during, 626
Traveller, making and working a, 526
Travellers, geology for, 230
 Library for, 25, 27
 Rifle for, 202
Treatment of apparently drowned persons, 164
 Fat, 684
 Fly infested animals, 704
 Hard rove rope, 694
 Skins, 677
 Stone, 232
 Tree footways, 293
Treenails, fox wedge for, 240
 Making, 289
Trees, larch, 317
 Measuring, 287
 Stripping bark from, 691
 Whose bases are accessible, to find the height of, without instruments, 284
 Yielding manna, 469
Trenneled, rafts, 129
Trestle bridge, Chinese, 304
Trimmers and liggers, 523
Trimming and filing up after forging, 170
Tripping a grapnel or creeper, 535
Trocheameter, 635
 Tables, 638
Troughs, cattle, for drinking, 430

Trousers, 4
 Making, 614
Trunks and boxes, 7
 Bullock, 7
Tsetse-fly, 572
 Preventive of bite, 575
 Region of the, 572
 Symptoms of bite, 574
Tubes of inflated canvas, boat fitted with, 150
Turkeys, catching, 591
 Traps, 591
Turkoman tent, 57
Turning wheel naves, 328
Turtle spears, 546
Twig and cable bridge, 298
 And cane roadway, 297
 Stirrup, 338
Twisting fishing lines, 529
 Ropes, 692
Two-wheeled drays, Australian, 405

U.

Umbrella tent, 59
Union links, 413
Unspiking cannon, 213
Useful roots for food, 473
Uses of bamboos, 318
 Bark, 691
 Bent wood, 337
 Bladders, 685
 Cocoa nut palms, 319
 Cold or joiner's chisels, 170
 Forked sticks, 345
 Horns, bones, tendons, fish skins, &c. 685
 Hippopotami, 545
 Lead, 192
 Plane table, 644
 Porpoises, 542
 Scrap and hook iron, 169
 Sextant and artificial horizon, 651
 Tea, 505
 Waggon wheels in tents, 55
Utilisation of tin cases, 186

V.

Vaal River hut, 248
Vane, sight, extemporised for levelling staff, 645
Variation of the compass, to ascertain, 641
Various foods, 502
Vegetables and fruit, 503
 Food, 500, 503
 Preserved, 515
Vehicles, wheeled, measuring distances travelled by, 635
Vessels during calms, Admiral Belcher's expedient for moving, 154
 Rigs of, 150
 Temporary repairs of, 148
Veterinary surgery and medicine, bush, 699
Vices and anvils, extempore, 172
 For holding timber, 146, 241
Village and farm, to fortify, 264
Vinegar, Palm, 466

W.

WADS and cartridges for cannon, 213
Waggons and other wheeled vehicles, 385
    Arobas, 393
    Australian two-wheeled, 405
    Buik, 390
    Burg, 263
    Cape, 386
    Cape, boats, 114
    Cape, chests as rafts, 123
    Cape tent, 52
    Cape wine, 392
    Equipment, 398
    Floating, 127
    From quicksands, &c. to extricate, 127
    Load for Cape, 404
    Indian gharrie, 393
    Hints on matters connected with, 398
    Horse and mule, 394
    Makeshift, 390
    Wilson (American), 394
Waistcoats, 4
Walls, to build, 258
Watch, 25
    Key, to make a, 178
Water and fire proof glue, 687
    And the sap of plants, 437
    Bags, ships', 443
    Baskets for holding, 444
    Bladders and paunches, for holding, 444
    Boiling without pots, 490
    Calabashes, horns, and egg shells for holding, 444
    Carrying, 441, 444
    Casks, to embark, 336
    Clock, 649
    Collecting from rainfalls, 448
    Dew collecting, 460, 465
    Distilling, 440
    Filters, 445, 448, 450
    Finding, 439
    Flasks, copper, 441
    Flow of river, measurement of, 662
    From damp places, procuring, 439
    From wells, procuring, 438
    Glass, the deep, 164
    In camel's stomach, 430
    Intestines for holding, 444
    Level, substitute for, 647
    Locality for, 437
    Pails and skins, 441
    Plants and roots yielding sap as a substitute, 459, 460, 463
    Plants holding, 448, 461
    Power wheels, 454
    Purifying, 451
    Raising from wells, 451
    Removing impurities, 449
    Sacks, skins, 682
    Skins and bladders, repairing, 685
    Skins and pails, 441
    Skins, repairing leakage in, 444
    Transport canoe, 442
Watering cattle, 430
Waterproofing, 163

Waterproof baskets, 444
Wattled boat, 110
Wattle on hurdle work, 340
Wax, shoemakers', 371
Weapons, stone, manufacture of, 553
Weather signs, 162
Wedges, fox, for tree nails, 240
Weevils, preserving flour from, 494
Weight of cattle, ascertaining, 710
    Haystack, ascertaining, 711
    Rod iron, 709
    Rope, to estimate, 695
    Sheet iron, 708
    Stone, the, 710
Weirs, dams, and fish spears, 528
Welding iron, 168
Wells, making extempore, 438
    Procuring water from, 492, 438
    Raising water from, 451
    Sinking, 456
    Tanks, pipes, &c. measuring, 711
Whale boat, 540
Whaling, 539
Wheeled carriages, measuring distances, travelled by, 635
    Vehicles, 385
Wheels, drags for, 395
    Horizontal, application of wind power to, 455
    In tents, use of, 55
    Making or building, 324, 329
    Over rivers, ferrying, 126
    Repairing, 191
    Steering, to make, 330
    Substitute for, 397
    Tires, to repair, 170
    Water power, 454
Whip handles and lead pencils, 197
    Sledge, 354
Whisky, potato, 473
White ants, locusts, and other insects, and their larvæ as food, 498
Wicks for lamps, 75
Width of rivers or ravines, to find without instruments, 281
Wigwam, board, 242
    Temporary, 245
Wild animals, observation of habits of, 676
    Bees, to smoke out, 477, 514
    Fruits of America, 471
Wind power to horizontal wheel, application of, 455
Windlasses, 331
Womera, 546
Wood, bent, 337
    Extraction of sap, 315
    Floats, 88, 143
    Hard, 317
    Hard, articles from, 320
    Hardening, 317
    Seasoning, 315
    Steaming, 316
Wooden bowls, 350
    Dingey, building a, 108
    Platform boat, 100
    Swivels, 320
Working a nave auger, 333
    In metals, 168
    Otter, 525
    Travellers, 526
    Trimmers and liggers, 523

Wounds, dressing for, 65
    From poisoned arrows, cure of, 549
    Ointment for, 702
    On camels' backs, 700
Wrappers as blankets, 40
Wreaths, thorn, catching deer with, 552
Wrecked ships, rafts from, 82
Wrecks, flour from, 494

Wrought or malleable iron, test for, 399

Y.

YOKE, pail, 349
Yoking and harnessing draught oxen, 403

Z.

ZEMBOUREKS or dromedary artillery, 215

———— ◆ • ◆ ————

London : Printed by HORACE COX, 346, Strand, W.C.

Printed in the United Kingdom
by Lightning Source UK Ltd.
129546UK00001B/1-6/A